The Quest for Full Assurance

The Legacy of Calvin and His Successors

Joel R. Beeke

THE BANNER OF TRUTH TRUST

THE BANNER OF TRUTH TRUST
3 Murrayfield Road, Edinburgh EH12 6EL
P.O.Box 621, Carlisle, Pennsylvania 17013, USA

*

© Banner of Truth Trust 1999
First published 1999
ISBN 0 85151 745 5

*

Typeset by
Gardner Graphics,
Grand Rapids, Michigan, USA
Printed in Finland
by WSOY

With heartfelt appreciation for

John Beeke (1919–93), my dear father
who taught me experiential theology,
often with tears

The Rev. J. C. Weststrate (1919–98)
who taught me systematic theology
as a father instructs his son

Dr Sinclair B. Ferguson
who taught me historical theology
with precision and warmth

Johanna Beeke, my dear mother
who is still teaching me practical theology
with her prayers and love

ACKNOWLEDGEMENTS

The present work is simplified and revised from a Ph.D. dissertation completed for Westminster Seminary in 1988, titled "Personal Assurance of Faith: English Puritanism and the Dutch 'Nadere Reformatie' from Westminster to Alexander Comrie (1640-1760)," and from *Assurance of Faith: Calvin, English Puritanism and the Dutch Second Reformation* (New York: Peter Lang, 1991; paperback edition, 1994). To serve busy pastors and laypeople, I have simplified complex sentences, reduced academic terminology, removed or translated foreign phrases, abridged both the footnotes and bibliography, and updated the work to incorporate recent scholarship.

I wish to thank scholars and friends who have contributed to this work over the years. I especially appreciated D. Clair Davis's insightful analyses and suggestions on my original dissertation. I also thank Sinclair Ferguson with whom I was privileged to team-teach for several years and who remains a close friend. He has provided valuable assistance and warm encouragement. Hearty thanks are also extended to Iain Murray for valuable suggestions made on the dissertation.

I appreciate as well the friendship of Richard A. Muller, whose reappraisal of Reformed scholastic orthodoxy served as a major incentive for this work. I trust that the pages that follow contribute to this reappraisal, particularly regarding the Dutch Second Reformation, about which little is written in English.

Biblical references are from the King James Version. Quotations from sixteenth- and seventeenth-century works are unchanged, with the exception of an occasional ambiguous spelling clarified in brackets. Responsibility for the translation of Dutch and Latin quotations is my own. I thank Bartel Elshout and Michael Bell for assistance in translating; Phyllis TenElshof for editing; Ray Lanning, Heidi Kortman, and Pauline Timmer for proofreading; Susan Freeland for typing; Gary and Linda den Hollander for typesetting. I also thank Willem Balke, Johan Mastenbroek, Cornelius Harinck, and Jonathan Gerstner, Jr., for assistance on the appendix.

I wish to acknowledge the help of librarians, too, at Westminster Seminary, Drew University, New Brunswick Theological Seminary,

Harvard Divinity School, Yale Divinity School, Union Theological Seminary, Calvin College/Seminary, Princeton Seminary, Gordon-Conwell Seminary, and New York Public Library.

I also owe hearty thanks to the loving flock I am privileged to serve as pastor, the Heritage Netherlands Reformed Congregation of Grand Rapids, Michigan. I am grateful to my children — Calvin, Esther, and Lydia — for their patience while this book was in progress. Finally, I especially thank my virtuous wife and true helpmeet, Mary, in whose tongue is "the law of kindness." "Her price is far above rubies."

Soli Deo Gloria!

— Joel R. Beeke
2917 Leonard NE
Grand Rapids, Michigan

October 1998

TABLE OF CONTENTS

Part Two
ASSURANCE FROM THE WESTMINSTER ASSEMBLY
TO ALEXANDER COMRIE

Part Three
COMPARISON OF ENGLISH PURITANISM AND THE DUTCH SECOND REFORMATION ON ASSURANCE

ABBREVIATIONS

Alle de wercken	*Alle de wercken van Mr. Willem Teellinck*
Brief	*Brief over de Rechtvaardigmakinge des Zondaars door de onmiddelyke Toereekening der Borggerechtigheit van Christus* (Comrie)
CO	*Opera quae supersunt omnia* (Calvin)
Commentary	*Calvin's Commentaries*
Decades	*The Decades of Henry Bullinger*
EZG	*Verhandeling van eenige Eigenschappen des Zaligmakenden Geloofs* (Comrie)
HC	*Stellige en Praktikale Verklaringe van den Heidelbergschen Catechismus* (Comrie)
Inst.	*Calvin's Institutes*
LC	*The Larger Catechism* (Westminster)
LR	*Verzameling van Leerredenen* (Comrie)
NPNF	*A Select Library of the Nicene and Post-Nicene Fathers of the Christian Church* (Schaff, ed.)
Reformers	*The Reformers and the Theology of the Reformation* (Cunningham)
SC	*The Shorter Catechism* (Westminster)
WA	*D. Martin Luthers Werke*
WCF	*Westminster Confession of Faith*
Works	*The Workes of . . . William Perkins*
Z	*Huldreich Zwinglis samtliche Werke*

PREFACE

It is a privilege to introduce Dr. Joel R. Beeke's fine work, *The Quest for Full Assurance: The Legacy of Calvin and His Successors*, to a wider public. It deals with a theme in historical theology which has created great interest in recent decades, namely the question of the continuity or discontinuity between the thought of the early Reformers and their seventeenth century descendants. In these pages this question has been narrowed down to that of the relation between the teaching of Calvin and that of the Puritans.

During recent decades the scholarly consensus has been that later Reformed theology deviated significantly from Calvin's thought under the influence of Theodore Beza in Geneva and William Perkins and others in England. This thesis has been developed and applied by various scholars. Its tendency is well encapsulated in the title of Basil Hall's 1966 essay "Calvin against the Calvinists."[1]

Reservations about this thesis have, on occasion, surfaced; but they have generally been ignored. However, more recent studies have emerged to question its integrity. Thus, in an incisive review of R.T. Kendall's version of the "deviation" thesis, no less a figure than the late Professor Gordon Rupp expressed his doubts whether this line of approach could stand the scrutiny of the most recent research.

The Quest for Full Assurance: The Legacy of Calvin and His Successors provides further confirmation of the suspicions which Professor Rupp entertained, and does so in an area of theology which was central in the thinking of both Calvin and the Puritans, namely faith and assurance. Here, Dr. Beeke displays an enviable breadth of familiarity with the relevant literature. Furthermore, drawing on his own ethnic roots, he traces the fascinating relationships between English and Dutch Reformed thought in this area in the period of the so-called "Second" or "Further" Reformation divines. The works of à Brakel and Comrie are as familiar to him as those of Calvin and Owen. He thus opens up an important aspect of international Calvinism.

Of great significance, in my own view, is Dr. Beeke's recognition that the development of classical Reformed thinking in the Puritan period was in fact an advance in its *Trinitarian* character. Rather than fall into a subjective imbalance, the later Reformed divines sought to honor and recognize the person and ministry of the Holy Spirit. In this sense they simply further developed B.B. Warfield's striking *bon mot* that Calvin was "the theologian of the Holy Spirit."

Dr. Beeke's study is a fine contribution to an ongoing scholarly debate. To it, however, he brings one further quality. He serves as pastor of a very large congregation in Grand Rapids, Michigan. Like all pastors, questions of assurance face him in a multitude of forms and guises every week. Thus his work is enriched by the perspective of pastoral ministry which he shares with both Calvin and the Puritans. An erudite treatise, *The Quest for Full Assurance: The Legacy of Calvin and His Successors* is also a valuable study in pastoral theology. It will therefore repay careful reading by scholar, pastor and lay people alike.

Sinclair B. Ferguson
St. George's-Tron
Glasgow, Scotland

[1] In G.E. Duffield, ed., *John Calvin* (Appleford: Abingdon, 1966).

I. INTRODUCTION

Theologians and pastors of post-Reformation churches struggled for theological precision in defining the relationship between personal assurance of faith and saving faith. Their labors produced a rich technical vocabulary that distinguished between assurance of faith and assurance of sense; direct (*actus directus*) and reflexive (*actus reflectus*) acts of faith; assurance of the uprightness of faith and of adoption; practical (*syllogismus practicus*) and mystical (*syllogismus mysticus*) syllogisms; the principle (*habitus*) and act (*actus*) of faith; objective and subjective assurance; assurance of faith, understanding, and hope; discursive and intuitive assurance; immediate and mediate witness in assurance; and the being and well-being of faith. They used such terms within the context of related issues, such as possibilities, kinds, degrees, foundations, experiences, means, times, obstacles, qualifications, and fruits of assurance — all within a scriptural, Christ-centered, and Trinitarian framework.

With such distinctions, most modern scholars have little patience. Such scholars no longer accept the view that this post-Reformation struggle was a faithful outworking of Reformation principles.[1] Rather, they regard post-Reformation efforts to develop a doctrine of assurance as antithetical to the early Reformers' insistence on the inseparability

---

[1] In the post-Reformation era, few noted the different emphases on faith and assurance provided by the early Reformers and the Reformed orthodox. Ludovico Le Blanc and John Owen were notable exceptions. Le Blanc viewed the Westminster Confession's exposition of assurance as firmly rooted in early Reformed theology, noting that some divines preferred to define faith in terms of its intrinsic nature, while others regarded faith more in terms of its distinctions from false forms of faith (*Theses theologicae variis temporibus in Academia Sedanense editae, et ad disputandam propositae*, editio tertia [Londini: Mosem Pitt, 1683], pp. 205-210).

Owen asserted that the differences among the Reformed on assurance were matters of terminology, not of substance. The early Reformers tended to define faith in terms of

THE QUEST FOR FULL ASSURANCE

of faith and assurance. Some argue that the Reformers, Calvin in particular, never used the practical syllogism and similar devices to help define subjective assurance. Rather, they say, we gain assurance exclusively by resting on the promises of God in Christ Jesus. With notable exceptions,[2] such scholars accuse post-Reformers for injecting a cold scholasticism into the warm biblicism of the Reformers.

Contemporary scholars, such as Basil Hall and R. T. Kendall,[3]

its "highest acting," whereas subsequent divines were more prone to discuss faith in a variety of "its other acts" and degrees ("The Doctrine of Justification by Faith through the Imputation of the Righteousness of Christ," in *The Works of John Owen*, vol. 5 [London: Banner of Truth Trust, 1967], pp. 84-85).

For nineteenth-century support of this traditional view, see William Cunningham, *The Reformers and the Theology of the Reformation* (London: Banner of Truth Trust, 1967), pp. 110-48.

[2]During the 1970s, several works offered a fresh evaluation of Protestant orthodoxy. These include Jill Raitt, *The Eucharistic Theology of Theodore Beza: Development of the Reformed Doctrine* (Chambersburg, Pa.: American Academy of Religion, 1972); John Patrick Donnelly, *Calvinism and Scholasticism in Vermigli's Doctrine of Man and Grace* (Leiden: E.J. Brill, 1976); John S. Bray, *Theodore Beza's Doctrine of Predestination* (Nieuwkoop: B. De Graaf, 1975); Olivier Fatio, *Méthode et théologie: Lambert Daneau et les débuts de la scholastique réformée* (Genève: Droz, 1976); Marvin W. Anderson, *Peter Martyr: A Reformer in Exile (1542-1562)* (Nieuwkoop: B. De Graaf, 1975); W. Robert Godfrey, "Tensions within International Calvinism: The Debate on the Atonement at the Synod of Dordt, 1618-1619" (Ph.D. dissertation, Stanford University, 1974).

In the 1980s, Richard A. Muller ably argued that late sixteenth- and seventeenth-century Reformed documents did not support the theory of a "predestinarian metaphysic" that smothered the biblicism of the first-generation Reformers. Muller said that although the theologians of the post-Reformation period used a scholastic methodology to clarify the Reformed theological system, they remained in essential agreement with the first generation of Reformed thought. According to Muller, post-Reformation orthodoxy often disagreed with the content of medieval scholasticism but advantageously used its organizational structure. Hence in post-Reformation scholastic orthodoxy, "scholastic" refers to the method of theology utilized, and "orthodoxy" to the content and doctrinal intention. Though Reformed scholastic orthodoxy was somewhat discontinuous with Calvin in methodology, it strongly affirmed Reformation teaching; indeed, the Reformation was incomplete without its confessional and theological codification (*Christ and the Decree: Christology and Predestination in Reformed Theology from Calvin to Perkins* [Grand Rapids: Baker, 1988]; *Post-Reformation Reformed Dogmatics*, vols. 1 and 2 [Grand Rapids: Baker, 1987-91]).

For support of Muller's basic reappraisal, but with unique emphases, see Donald W. Sinnema, "The Issue of Reprobation at the Synod of Dort (1618-19) in Light of the History of This Doctrine" (Ph.D. dissertation, University of St. Michael's College, 1985); Martin I. Klauber, "The Context and Development of the Views of Jean-Alphonse Turrettini (1671-1737) on Religious Authority" (Ph.D. dissertation, University of Wisconsin-Madison, 1987); Stephen R. Spencer, "Reformed Scholasticism in Medieval Perspective: Thomas Aquinas and Francis Turrettini on the Incarnation" (Ph.D. dissertation, Michigan State University, 1988).

[3]Basil Hall, "Calvin against the Calvinists," in *John Calvin*, ed. G.E. Duffield

regard Theodore Beza and William Perkins as the culprits who
pushed the post-Reformation doctrine of assurance down the slope
of experimental[4] subjectivity until it resulted in the Westminster
Assembly's betrayal of Calvinism through an "apparently un-
questioned acceptance of a distinction between faith and assurance,
for 'Faith' was one heading in the Confession, and 'Certainty of
Salvation' another."[5] According to Kendall, the Westminster
Assembly's theology represents a *qualitative* departure from Calvin
in a variety of doctrines related to assurance, such as the decrees of
God, the covenant of grace, sanctification, atonement, repentance,
and the role of the human will in soteriology.[6]

The following pages repudiate the sharp distinction many
contemporary scholars make between Calvin and Calvinism. I am
convinced that Calvinism's wrestlings with assurance were
quantitatively beyond, but not *qualitatively* contradictory to, that of

(Appleford: Sutton Courtenay Press, 1966), pp. 19-37; R.T. Kendall, "Living the
Christian Life in the Teaching of William Perkins and His Followers," *Living the
Christian Life* (London: The Westminster Conference, 1974), pp. 45-60; *Calvin and
English Calvinism to 1649* (New York: Oxford University Press, 1979); "The Puritan
Modification of Calvin's Theology," in *John Calvin*, ed. W. Stanford Reid (Grand Rapids:
Zondervan, 1982), pp. 199-214. Scholars with convictions similar to one or more of Hall's
and Kendall's theses include Brian Armstrong, Karl Barth, John Beardslee, M. Charles
Bell, Ernst Bizer, James Daane, Johannes Dantine, Edward Dowey, Otto Gründler,
Philip Holtrop, Walter Kickel, Donald McKim, Philip McNair, Jurgen Moltmann,
Charles Munson, Wilhelm Niesel, Norman Pettit, Pontien Polman, Jack Rogers, Holmes
Rolston III, and Hans Emil Weber (see bibliography).

[4]"Experimental" and "experiential" are used interchangeably. The latter is more
readily understood in contemporary thought but the former was more commonly used to
describe the inward life by post-Reformation divines. As Willem Balke points out, Calvin
also used *experientia* and *experimentum* interchangeably, since both words contain the
etymological implication of examining or testing (from *experiri*) experienced knowledge
by the touchstone of Scripture (Isaiah 8:20) ("The Word of God and *Experientia* according
to Calvin," in *Calvinus Ecclesiae Doctor* [Kampen: Kok, 1978], pp. 20-21).

[5]Kendall, "Puritan Modification," p. 214.

[6]*Calvin and English Calvinism to 1649.* In order to focus more narrowly on the
doctrine of assurance, I have minimized references to most ancillary doctrines, though
pertinent, related works are incorporated in the bibliography.

For review articles opposing Kendall's published dissertation, see William Young,
"Calvin and Westminster," *Bulwark* 2 (May-June 1980):15-18; A.N.S. Lane, *Themelios* 6.1
(September 1980): 29-31; Paul Helm, "Article Review: Calvin, English Calvinism and the
Logic of Doctrinal Development," *Scottish Journal of Theology* 34 (1981): 179-85; W.
Stanford Reid, *Westminster Theological Journal* 43 (1980): 155-64; George Harper, *Calvin
Theological Journal* 20 (1985): 255-62; Robert Letham, "Faith and Assurance in Early
Calvinism: A Model of Continuity and Diversity," in *Later Calvinism: International
Perspectives*, ed. W. Fred Graham (Kirksville, Mo.: Sixteenth Century Journal, 1994), pp.
355ff. Cf. Paul Helm, *Calvin and the Calvinists* (Edinburgh: Banner of Truth Trust, 1982).

Calvin.[7] Notwithstanding differences in matters of degree on the doctrine of assurance between Calvin and Calvinists, in substance there is little difference. By explaining assurance within a Trinitarian framework, post-Calvin Reformed scholars did not negate Calvin's Christology. Rather, they advanced Calvin's Christology and, thereby, his theology.

Their work on the quest for full assurance of faith merits a thorough multi-volume examination. At best, this study serves as an introduction to such a study by drawing on major doctrinal confessions, theological controversies, and English and Dutch divines. Many gaps remain. I have attempted to remedy this by including reference notes on significant theologians and movements.

My study takes a five-step historical approach. The first step is an overview of the doctrine of assurance in Christian thought prior to the 1640s, with particular emphasis on Calvin and the fathers of English Puritanism and the Dutch Second Reformation (*Nadere Reformatie*):[8] William Perkins and Willem Teellinck. The second examines in the context of English Puritanism the Reformation's definitive statement on assurance, contained in the Westminster Confession, chapter 18. The third singles out John Owen's augmentation of the Westminster standards on assurance. The fourth examines the impact of Dutch theologians on the faith-assurance discussion through one of the post-Reformation's most capable divines — the Scottish-turned-Dutch Alexander Comrie, who wrote extensively on the issues of faith and assurance. Comrie, who drew heavily from the Westminster standards, Owen, and the Scottish Marrow Men, reached several conclusions that continue to be relevant today. Finally, the fifth examines the work of Thomas Goodwin, whose work as a pastor in the Netherlands influenced his experiential thinking. I conclude with a comparison between the English Puritans and the Dutch Second Reformation divines on personal assurance of faith.

By limiting this study to the magisterial Reformers and subsequent English and Dutch influences, I do not intend to denigrate other significant contributions, such as German Pietism,[9] the Scottish

---

[7]For the terminology, "quantitative, not qualitative," I am indebted to John S. Bray (*Theodore Beza's Doctrine of Predestination*, p. 111), who reached a similar conclusion when comparing Calvin and Beza on assurance.

[8]See the appendix for a synopsis of the Dutch Second Reformation (*Nadere Reformatie*).

[9]For the views of Philip Spener and Friedrich Lampe on assurance, see Henry

"Marrow controversy" (1718-1723),[10] or New World theologians such as Thomas Hooker, Thomas Shepard, John Cotton, Jonathan Edwards, and Cotton Mather.[11] Finally, this study embraces only that kind of assurance that chapter 18 of the Westminster Confession describes as the undoubted certainty that a person belongs to Christ, possesses His saving grace, and will ultimately enjoy everlasting salvation. The

Burke Robins, *The Basis of Assurance in Recent Protestant Theologies* (Kansas City: Chas. E. Brown, 1912); F. Ernest Stoeffler, *German Pietism During the Eighteenth Century* (Leiden: E. J. Brill, 1973); Johannes Wallmann, *Philipp Jakob Spener und die Anfange des Piëtismus* (Tübingen: Mohr Siebeck, 1970); Carl Otto Thelemann, *Friedrich Adolf Lampe: sein Leben seine Theologie* (Bielefeld: Belhagen & Klasing, 1868); Gerrit Snijders, *Friedrich Adolph Lampe* (Hardewijk: Flevo v.h. Gebr. Mooij, 1954); C. Graafland, "Friedrich Adolph Lampe," in *De Nadere Reformatie in het Gereformeerd Piëtisme*, ed. W. van 't Spijker ('s-Gravenhage: Boekencentrum, 1989), pp. 243-74.

[10]Cf. David C. Lachman, *The Marrow Controversy*, Rutherford Studies Series One: Historical Theology (Edinburgh: Rutherford House, 1988); and his "The Marrow Controversy: An Historical Survey with special reference to the Free Offer of the Gospel, the Extent of the Atonement, and Assurance of Saving Faith" (Th.M. thesis, Westminster Theological Seminary, 1973); C. Harinck, *De Schotse Verbondsleer: Van Robert Rollock tot Thomas Boston* (Utrecht: De Banier, 1986).

[11]See the bibliography for primary sources.

For Thomas Hooker, see Norman Pettit, "Hooker's Doctrine of Assurance: A Critical Phase in New England's Spiritual Thought," *New England Quarterly* 47 (1974): 518-34; Everett H. Emerson, "Thomas Hooker and the Reformed Theology: The Relation of Hooker's Conversion Preaching to its Background" (Ph.D. dissertation, Louisiana State University, 1955). For additional works on Hooker, see Andrew Denholm, Hubert Pellman (includes a thorough listing of Hooker's writings), Norman Pettit, Frank Shuffleton, Keith Sprunger, and George Williams in the bibliography.

For Thomas Shepard, see R.A. Hasler, "Thomas Shepard: Pastor-Evangelist (1605-1649): A Study in New England Ministry" (Ph.D. dissertation, Hartford Seminary Foundation, 1964); Richard Alan Humphrey, "The Concept of Conversion in the Theology of Thomas Shepard (1605-1649)" (Ph.D. dissertation, Drew, 1967); Alexander Whyte, *Thomas Shepard, Pilgrim Father and Founder of Harvard. His Spiritual Experience and Experiential Preaching* (London: Oliphant, Anderson, & Ferrier, 1913).

For John Cotton, see Donald Come, Judith Welles, and Larzer Ziff in the bibliography. Cf. James Jones III, "The Beginnings of American Theology: John Cotton, Thomas Hooker, Thomas Shepard and Peter Bulkeley" (Ph.D. dissertation, Brown University, 1970).

For Jonathan Edwards, consult *The Religious Affections*, particularly his explanation that the fruits of a regenerated life are the most significant marks of assurance in the believer (New Haven: Yale University Press, 1959), p. 406. Cf. Conrad Cherry, *The Theology of Jonathan Edwards: A Reappraisal* (Gloucester, Mass.: Peter Smith, 1974), pp. 143-58; and works in the bibliography by Carl Bogue, John H. Gerstner, Walther Knoepp, David Laurence, Donald Rhoades, and Jan Ridderbos.

For Cotton Mather, see Richard Lovelace, *The American Pietism of Cotton Mather* (Grand Rapids: Eerdmans, 1979); Robert Middlekauff, *The Mathers* (New York: Oxford, 1971).

terms *assurance* and *full assurance* have the same meaning in this study as "assurance of faith" and "personal assurance of grace and salvation," unless specified otherwise.[12]

Such assurance is broad and full in scope. Donald Whitney summarizes: "Assurance of salvation is a God-given awareness that He has accepted the death of Christ on your behalf and forgiven you of your sins. It involves confidence that God loves you, that He has chosen you, and that you will go to heaven. Assurance includes a sense of freedom from the guilt of sin, relief from the fear of judgment, and joy in your relationship with God as your Father."[13] Assurance, wrote James W. Alexander, "carries with it the idea of fulness, such as of a tree laden with fruit, or of a vessel's sails when stretched by a favouring gale."[14] The quest for such assurance is a rich legacy of Calvin and his successors.

---

[12]The term "assurance of faith" frequently embraces bare assurance concerning the truth of the gospel itself or the fidelity of God as well as personal assurance of salvation. My use will only deal with the latter, presupposing the former. Assurance of faith in this sense necessarily includes the assurance of perseverance and final salvation. As such, assurance of election and of perseverance are viewed as aspects of the same reality, notwithstanding their different objects. Cf. Louis Berkhof, *The Assurance of Faith* (Grand Rapids: Smitter Book Co., 1928).

[13]*How Can I be Sure that I'm a Christian? What the Bible Says About Assurance of Salvation* (Colorado Springs: NavPress, 1994), p. 12.

[14]*Consolation in Discourses on Select Topics, Addressed to the Suffering People of God* (reprint ed., Ligonier, Pa.: Soli Deo Gloria Publications, 1992), p. 138.

PART I
Assurance Prior to the Westminster Assembly

II. THE EARLY AND MEDIEVAL CHURCH

Assurance of faith has been explained in various ways throughout the church's history. In the first few centuries it was described as direct apprehension; in the medieval era as a trust in the divinely established institution of the church; and in the scholastic centuries prior to the Reformation as reliance on the claims of reason and inference.[1]

In the early church the theology of the personal assurance of salvation, however, was seldom addressed for several reasons. First, as Robert Letham rightly states about the early church:

> It should be remembered that the absence of theological reflection on the matter [of assurance] was undoubtedly the result of pre-occupation with other issues. The emphasis in the early centuries was on the controverted areas of Christology and Trinitarianism. Questions concerning the application of redemption did not become a really major concern until the Reformation. Additionally, the lack of discussion of such matters was explained by the absence of controversy leaving no pressing need for close definitions to be made.[2]

This lack of discussion does not mean that personal assurance was a foreign concept to the early church; rather, assurance was verified by example and life.[3]

---

[1]F. Ernest Stoeffler, "Wesleyan Concept of Religious Certainty," *The London Quarterly and Holborn Review* 189 (April 1964):131-33. This chapter only serves as a generalized introduction to make a transition to the focus of our study in the Reformation and post-Reformation movements. For a more in-depth introduction of the patristic and medieval developments on faith and assurance, see Avery Dulles, *The Assurance of Things Hoped For* (Oxford: Oxford University Press, 1994), pp. 20-43.

[2]"The Relationship between Saving Faith and Assurance of Salvation" (Th.M. thesis, Westminster Theological Seminary, 1976), pp. 5-6.

[3]Jon Zens, "The Doctrine of Assurance: A History and an Application," *Baptist Reformation Review* 5 (Summer 1976): 35-37.

Second, the early church's failure to formulate a doctrine of assurance was connected to its misunderstanding that good works somehow contributed to salvation. Assurance through works became normative with time, though it assumed various forms. These included: an unwholesome attitude towards martyrdom; a Gnostic emphasis that knowledge which surpassed ordinary faith produced religious certainty; and Pelagianism or Semi-Pelagianism, which allowed for only a present-moment assurance based on the freedom and fickleness of the human will.[4]

A third obstacle hindering the church's doctrine of assurance surfaces in Augustine's theology. Despite his sweeping theological reflection and accent on grace as foundational for salvation, Augustine (354-430) was not able to formulate a doctrine of personal assurance. Augustinian theology may have implied assurance — which the Reformers and Puritans recognized and developed — but Augustine himself never formulated a doctrine of assurance. As Perry Miller noted:

> Puritans contended that regeneration was usually an ascertainable experience, that men could tell whether or not they were in a state of grace. With this conclusion they went beyond Augustine, for he would never have said point-blank that the presence of grace could be verified by external symptoms; he would never have claimed that a man himself could positively know whether he had it or not, much less that a set of impartial examiners could discover the true state of his soul. Yet Augustinian theology, in other hands than Augustine's, tends toward this deduction which the Reformation made explicit.[5]

In other words, something held Augustine back from asserting personal assurance. The tension between Augustine's attraction toward, yet withdrawal from, assurance extends beyond his insistence that faith includes assurance as to its objects, i.e., "certainty respecting the objective truths of revelation,"[6] for this never became an issue in Roman Catholic or Reformed theology. Augustine approved of basing one's certainty of faith in Christ on "the direct evidence of his own senses,"[7] and on at least one occasion seemed to

---

[4]Fred Klooster, "Assurance," in *Encyclopedia of Christianity*, vol. 1 (Wilmington, Del.: National Foundation for Christian Education, 1964), p. 447.

[5]*The New England Mind: The Seventeenth Century* (Cambridge: Harvard University Press, 1939; reprint ed., Boston: Beacon Press, 1961), p. 49. For Augustine's doctrine of faith, see Robert E. Cushman, "Faith and Reason in the Thought of Augustine," *Church History* 19 (1950): 271-94.

[6]Berkhof, *The Assurance of Faith*, p. 19.

[7]"On the Catechising of the Uninstructed," *A Select Library of the Nicene and*

connect God's promise of certainty to subjective assurance. He wrote, "To be assured of our salvation is no arrogant stoutness; it is our faith. It is no pride; it is devotion. It is no presumption; it is God's promise."[8]

Nevertheless, Augustine refused to go behond these implications. His refusal was the consequence of an exaggeration of the church's role in soteriology, and of a denial of the scriptural doctrine of the perseverance of the saints.[9] For Augustine could state that the grace given to the elect "begins a man's faith and . . . enables it to persevere unto the end." Yet he could also say that "some who have in good faith worshipped Him" did not receive from God the grace of perseverance to the end.[10]

In Augustine's view the perseverance of the saints depended on God's continuous grace exercised primarily through the church and its sacraments. God also has a purpose in mingling "some who would not persevere with a certain number of His saints"— namely, "that those for whom security from temptation in this life is not desirable may not be secure."[11]

Augustine concluded that, since God's predestinating will is hidden and an inward experience of grace could always be deceptive, active and continued participation in the church's worship and sacraments is the best sign that God's favor is enjoyed, though it is by no means a certain sign, for when faith is no longer exercised, perseverance also ceases. The believer could be relatively certain of present grace and embrace a reasonable hope for eternal life, but could never be absolutely certain of future salvation. Henry Robins summarized these Augustinian tensions:

> Augustine . . . is the true father of that Catholic mysticism which was at home within the Church until after the Council of Trent, but the assurance which such a mysticism expresses did not become doctrinally articulate with Augustine. Justification by faith as a subjective experience, is never complete in this life, for the simple

---

Post-Nicene Fathers of the Christian Church (hereafter, NPNF), First Series, ed. Philip Schaff, vol. 3 (Grand Rapids: Eerdmans, 1974), p. 239.

[8]Quoted by J. C. Ryle, *Holiness* (Grand Rapids: AP & A, 1971), p. 216.

[9]See pp. 167-73 below for John Owen's defense of perseverance.

[10]"De Dono Perseverantiae," NPNF 5:532, 538. Cf. Thomas Bradwardine's interpretation of Augustine on perseverance in Heiko Oberman, *Forerunners of the Reformation: The Shape of Late Medieval Thought Illustrated by Key Documents* (Philadelphia: Fortress Press, 1981), p. 159.

[11]NPNF 5:532.

reason that it contemplates the entire transformation of its subject. Grace, to be sure, is prevenient and irresistible; the external means of grace avail for the elect; but only perseverance to the end can reveal the real objects of irresistible grace. Even the called who do not possess this final grace of perseverance will be lost. In consequence, there is a wide range of contingency in this view. Yet for himself, Augustine was sure of communion with God; he really possessed the certainty of faith. Yet he held that no one can be certain that he is of the elect, and thus possess the *donum perseverantiae* [gift of perseverance].[12]

Fourth, by interweaving Semi-Pelagianism with the weaknesses of Augustinian theology in the areas of church authority and perseverance of the saints, the medieval church closed the door to developing a doctrine of assurance. Eventually that position led to *ecclesiastical* (rather than Christological) and *sacramental* (rather than pneumatological) concepts of certainty, which as Philip Hughes stressed, had devastating effects for a doctrine of personal assurance:

> It was not long [before] ... the doctrine was developed that at baptism all sins were washed away by the blood of Christ, but that this blood did not avail for sins committed after baptism, with the result that such sins could only be expiated by the endurance of such penalties and penances as the Church might impose on the offender. This led to the phase in church history when it became a common practice for persons to postpone their baptism, if possible, until the hour of death, in the hope that in this way they might be assured of passing into the next world free from sin. Such, indeed, was the spiritual insecurity and uncertainty engendered by this teaching that it led further to the doctrine of purgatory, according to which, no penances, however many and severe, being regarded as sufficient to purge away all the defilements of post-baptismal sin, the Christian man would ordinarily have to pass through a prolonged period of purgation by flames before he was fit to enter into the heavenly state. For ordinary-level Christians accordingly — and that meant the great mass of church members — the Christian way after baptism became one of self-effort and self-suffering, without that assured confidence in the redeeming work and suffering of Christ in which the New Testament encourages us to trust.[13]

---

[12]*Basis of Assurance*, pp. 13-14. Cf. Lynn Tipson, Jr., "The Development of a Puritan Understanding of Conversion" (Ph.D. dissertation, Yale University, 1972), pp. 30-36; Adolf Harnack, *History of Dogma*, trans. from third German edition by N. Buchanan, et al., vol. 5 (Boston: Roberts Brothers, 1897), pp. 20ff., 79ff., 125ff.; and compare Turretin's quotation of Augustine, *Reformed Dogmatics*, ed. John W. Beardslee III (Grand Rapids: Baker, 1977), p. 395 with NPNF, "On the Trinity," 3:167.

[13]*Theology of the English Reformers* (reprint ed., Grand Rapids: Baker, 1980), p. 62.

Consequently, Gregory the Great (d. 604), whom Philip Schaff said was the best representative of medieval Catholicism and Seeberg described as "consciously orthodox,"[14] could state both the impossibility and undesirability of obtaining assurance. Gregory wrote:

> The greater our sins the more we must do to make up for them. . . . Whether we have done enough to atone for them we cannot know until after death. . . . We can never be sure of success. . . . Assurance of salvation and the feeling of safety engendered by it are dangerous for anybody and would not be desirable even if possible.[15]

The theology of the Schoolmen only reinforced Pelagian and sacramental tendencies by molding the Christian life around the exercise of free will and participation in the sacraments. Thomas Aquinas (1225-1274) assumed a certainty of predestination (*certitudo praedestinationis*), but stated that God's predestinating grace lies "beyond the sphere of human perception." Hence Aquinas could not reach beyond a conjectural certainty (*certitudo coniecturae*) based on works.[16]

Thomas Bradwardine, a fourteenth-century Augustinian, opened the door of personal assurance no wider than Aquinas, though his motive for declining to do so was distinct. As Heiko Oberman explains:

> In a subjective sense assurance is impossible [for Bradwardine], not on account of the possibility of the free decision of man, but on account of the unknowableness of God's will, depending in its turn on the distance between Creator and creature. So Bradwardine does not teach a greater assurance of salvation than scholastic tradition before him; on the contrary, even the conjectural assurance, insofar as it is related to the observation of one's own good use of the will, has been made impossible by Bradwardine's limitation of merits to *meritum de condigno* [merit of congruity].[17]

[14]Reinhold Seeberg, *Text-book of the History of Doctrines*, trans. Charles Hay (Grand Rapids: Baker, 1966), 2:17 (cf. pp. 17-27 for Gregory's theology).

[15]Quoted by Arthur McGiffert, *A History of Christian Thought*, vol. 2 (New York: Scribner's, 1954), p. 153.

[16]Aquinas, *On Faith: Summa theologiae* 2-2: qu. 1-16, trans. Mark D. Jordan (Notre Dame, Ind.: University of Notre Dame, 1990). Cf. Seeberg, *History of Doctrines* 2:121, who also noted that the possibility of assurance on the basis of works was asserted by Duns Scotus (1265-1308), though rejected by Gabriel Biel (1420-1495), p. 202. Cf. Heiko Augustinus Oberman, "Archbishop Thomas Bradwardine: A Fourteenth Century Augustinian" (Th. D. dissertation, Utrecht University, 1957), pp. 153-55.

[17]"Bradwardine," pp. 154-55. In late medieval scholastic theology, a merit of congruity was a so-called half-merit or proportionate merit, which, in contrast to a

This tradition was crystallized in the Tridentine formulations of the Roman Catholic Church, which made formal dogma of what had long been piety and teaching. Thus, the Decree of the Council of Trent (Chapter XII) says about justification:

> No one, moreover, so long as he is in this mortal life, ought so far to presume as regards the secret mystery of divine predestination, as to determine for certain that he is assuredly in the number of the predestinate; as if it were true, that he that is justified, either cannot sin any more, or if he do sin, that he ought to promise himself an assured repentance; for except by special revelation, it can not be known whom God hath chosen unto everlasting life.[18]

In the following chapter on perseverance, the council adds: "Let no one herein promise himself any thing as certain with an absolute certainty; though all ought to place and repose a most firm hope in God's help."[19]

Contrary beliefs are anathematized in Canons XII-XVI.[20] Rome's presentation of subsequent commentary on Tridentine formulations supports the following generalizations:[21]

First, assurance was only possible in rare cases through a special revelation reserved largely for martyr-saints or eminent ascetics.

Second, for the ordinary believer, the maximum level of certainty obtainable was a moral probability or "a firm hope in God's help,"[22] since even a mature saint could not be certain of final perseverance. This is a natural outgrowth of Semi-Pelagianism and the penitential system of Rome.[23]

Third, even if assurance was possible for the ordinary believer, it

---

meritum de condigno (a merit of condignity or full merit), did not truly deserve grace though it often received grace based on divine generosity.

[18]Philip Schaff, ed., *The Creeds of Christendom, with a History and Critical Notes*, vol. 2 (New York: Harper and Brothers, 1878), p. 103. For differences between Roman Catholicism and Protestantism on justification by faith, see Joel R. Beeke, "Justification by Faith Alone: The Relation of Faith to Justification," in *Justification by Faith Alone*, ed. Don Kistler (Morgan, Pa.: Soli Deo Gloria, 1995), pp. 78-91.

[19]Schaff, *Creeds of Christendom*, p. 103.

[20]Ibid., pp. 113-14.

[21]That is not to say that there were not differences among Roman Catholic theologians both at Trent and post-Trent. E.g., William Cunningham noted significant distinctions between Catharinus and Bellarmine (*Reformers and the Theology of the Reformation*, pp. 143-45).

[22]Schaff, *Creeds* 2:103.

[23]Cf. *Dogmatic Constitution of the Church (Lumen Gentium)*, as quoted in "Faith," *The Catholic Encyclopedia, Revised and Updated Edition*, ed. Robert C. Broderick (Nashville: Thomas Nelson Publishers, 1986), p. 214.

would not be desirable. Louis Berkhof noted that Roman Catholicism considered it "wholesome and beneficial for the Christian to entertain honest doubts in the high matters of justification and salvation. Such doubts keep him from an overweening confidence in himself, minister to true humility of character, and serve as a more salutary restraint on the evil passions than joy and peace in believing could ever be."[24]

Fourth, the Council of Trent confirms that the doctrine of assurance cannot be sustained by a theology built on sacramental grace, such as that of Bellarmine who mentions twenty-two "ceremonies about baptism, exorcism, salt, spittle, cross, unction, wax-taper lighted, in token that the baptized person is translated from the power of darkness unto light."[25]

Finally, the effect of this lack of assurance made individuals feel dependent upon the church as God's peculiar channel of divine grace, so that the issue between Roman Catholicism and the Reformers was essentially one of ecclesiastical authority pitted against scriptural authority.[26] Thus the situation became ripe for a reaction on the part of the Protestant Reformers in support of a scriptural and personal quest for assurance of salvation.

[24]Berkhof, *Assurance of Faith*, p. 22.

[25]Thomas Doolittle, *Puritan Sermons, 1659-1689: Being the Morning Exercises at Cripplegate*, with notes and translations by James Nichols (reprint ed., Wheaton, Ill.: Richard Owen Roberts, 1981), 1:254. E.g., speaking of the wafer in the eucharist, Bellarmine said: "By this food the will is filled with the grace of most certain hope" (*Robert Bellarmine: Spiritual Writings*, trans. and ed. John P. Donnelly and R. J. Teske [Mahwah, N.J.: Paulist Press, 1989], p. 346).

[26]Letham, "Relationship between Saving Faith and Assurance," pp. 10-12. Cf. Adolf Stakemeier, *Das Konzil von Trent über die Heilsgewissheit* (Heidelberg: F.H. Kerle, 1947).

III. THE REFORMATION FROM LUTHER TO BULLINGER

In "The Reformers and the Doctrine of Assurance,"[1] William Cunningham said the Reformers embraced "exaggerated views and statements on personal assurance" as essential for believers for two reasons: "(1) their own personal experience as converted and believing men; and (2) the ground taken by the Romanists in arguing against them."[2] Cunningham explained that the Lord bestowed much assurance upon the Reformers to parallel their "difficult and arduous labours in the cause of Christ."[3] He also said that Rome's opposition to assurance, based on the need to retain ecclesiastical authority, stirred the Reformers to heighten their accent on assurance.

According to Cunningham, Romanists and Reformers were divided over *probable persuasion* versus *absolute certainty* on three counts: "1st, That the books [of Scripture] generally received, or any particular books specified, were possessed of divine authority; or 2d, That *this* and not *that* was the meaning of a scriptural passage, or the substance of what Scripture taught upon a particular topic; or 3d, That any particular individual was now in a state of grace, and would be finally saved."[4]

In harmony with Cunningham's position, John Macleod offered a third reason for the Reformers' emphasis on assurance as essential

---

[1] First published in the *British and Foreign Evangelical Review* (October, 1856). Pagination in subsequent notes adheres to its publication in *The Reformers and the Theology of the Reformation* as Essay III, pp. 110-48.

[2] Ibid., pp. 113, 116, 118.

[3] Ibid., p. 113.

[4] Ibid., p. 114. Cf. Joel R. Beeke, "William Cunningham," in *Historians of the Christian Tradition*, ed. Michael Bauman and Martin I. Klauber (Nashville: Broadman & Holman, 1995), pp. 209-226.

to salvation: *the newness of the Reformation movement as a whole* in being set free from the chains of Rome and ushered into the power of gospel truth. Macleod wrote: "In the Reformation age itself there was much of an assurance of personal salvation enjoyed by a generation of believers on which the Gospel of the free grace of God in Justification burst in all its wonder as something altogether new."[5]

Both Macleod and Cunningham faulted the Reformers for failing to develop a more thorough doctrine of assurance in its relationship to saving faith, particularly since they were familiar with the tensions involved in their high definitions of faith. For example, when Calvin tempered his definition of faith with statements about the conflict of doubt, Cunningham accused Calvin of inconsistency.[6] Macleod said that John Knox's relationships with people like his mother-in-law, Mrs. Bowes, who wrestled with spiritual darkness and doubt, should have halted all extreme statements that demanded assurance of faith.[7]

According to Cunningham and Macleod, the Reformers' inconsistent views on assurance were corrected by chapter 18 of the Westminster Confession, which distinguishes assurance from faith. Chapter 18 is an improvement on the doctrine of the early Reformers, though it does not depart from their more balanced statements. Hence the difference between Calvin and the Calvinists is substantial[8] but *not* antithetical, as Hall and Kendall advocate.[9]

Kendall asserted that the Reformers did not distinguish between faith and assurance in contrast to the Westminster Assembly's denial of a significant relationship between faith and assurance. But that approach is exaggerated and fallacious. It's exaggerated because the assembly's statement does not negate an organic relationship between faith and assurance. It's fallacious because the

---

[5]John Macleod, *Scottish Theology* (reprint ed., London: Banner of Truth Trust, 1974), p. 28.

[6]Cunningham, *Reformers*, p. 120.

[7]Macleod, *Scottish Theology*, p. 28. Macleod adds: "There was a call upon spiritual casuistry so that the presence of the true faith of the regenerate was recognised even when a certainty of one's own salvation was very much a matter of debate. And as the flood-tide of spiritual fullness and assurance ebbed, the teachers of the Reformed Church were increasingly called to minister to the questionings of many of their most godly and devoted hearers who could not, they felt, honestly claim that they had the possession of a full assurance of their good estate" (ibid).

[8]Ibid., pp. 28-29. Cf. Cunningham, *Reformers*, pp. 114ff.

[9]Cf. pp. 2-3 above.

Reformers were not as one-sided in their approach to faith and assurance as Kendall assumes. As Louis Berkhof noted:

> In their protest against Rome, [the Reformers] sometimes spoke as if one who lacks the assurance of salvation, the positive conviction that his sins are forgiven, did not possess true faith. The *fiducia* of faith was sometimes represented by them as the assured trust of the sinner that all his sins are pardoned for the sake of Christ. Yet it is quite evident from their writings, (a) that they did not mean to teach that this *fiducia* did not include other elements; and (b) that they did not intend to deny that true children of God must frequently struggle with all kinds of doubts and uncertainties.[10]

Though Cunningham was more historically accurate than Kendall, he also was not altogether correct. Neither reached the heart of the issue. Both exaggerated different emphases, Kendall in particular. Kendall's theory of fundamental deviation and Cunningham's less fundamental, yet substantial discrepancy in the matter of faith and assurance in Calvin and Calvinists were both erroneous.

The discrepancy between Calvin and Calvinism on faith and assurance was largely *quantitative* and *methodological*, i.e., a matter of emphasis and method, rather than *qualitative* or *substantial*. These quantitative differences stem largely from an emphasis that evolved in the wake of the Reformation. Second- and third-generation Protestants were compelled to clarify the Reformers' doctrine of assurance, largely because of peoples' tendency to take for granted God's saving grace. Many no longer regarded faith as a miracle but as something quite ordinary. This led to the fostering of dead orthodoxy, which regarded mere assent to the truths of Scripture as sufficient for salvation. It thus became essential to distinguish between assurance of personal grace and certainty based on mere assent to Bible truth. In this context, the English Puritans and Dutch Second Reformation divines labored to lead their flocks into a well-grounded assurance and urged them to avoid a false peace not "soundly bottomed."

The post-Reformation construction of a theology of assurance was a legitimate attempt to fill a gap in the understanding of assurance and doubt. Though Cunningham and Macleod recognized this, they failed to appreciate that the post-Reformation emphasis, which allowed for degrees in assurance, was embedded in the principles of the Reformers. Despite different emphases, both

---

[10]Louis Berkhof, *Systematic Theology* (reprint ed., London: Banner of Truth Trust, 1977), p. 507.

Calvin and Calvinism remained true to Scripture and to the believer's experience of assurance.

Prior to examining Calvin and several English Puritans and Dutch Second Reformation divines on the doctrine of assurance, I'll briefly explain the views of Martin Luther and Ulrich Zwingli, and their successors Philip Melanchthon and Heinrich Bullinger.

Martin Luther (1483-1546)

Martin Luther ushered in the Reformation, not by doctrinal criticism but by the imperative of religious experience. Overwhelmed by sin, Luther unsuccessfully tried to find assurance of faith through the church's agencies, sacraments, and penitential system. Ultimately, he found the grace of God in Christ, through whom forgiveness of sin is complete and not dependent on human merit.

Luther's Christ-centered approach to faith and assurance was rooted in personal experience.[11] Through his experience of God's graciousness in the incarnate, crucified, and risen Christ, Luther was empowered to lead Christianity out of the tyranny of an ecclesiastical hierarchy that determined what and how one could believe. Luther presented Christianity as believing assurance of the living God, who reveals Himself and opens His heart in Christ to sinners. Luther thus became instrumental in releasing the sixteenth-century church from a systematic denial of salvation's certainty and directed it toward the freedom of justification by gracious faith alone.

Subsequently Luther challenged the Semi-Pelagian system by asserting that assurance is the birthright of every Christian, since it

---

[11]The best edition of Luther's works is *D. Martin Luthers Werke*, ed. J. C. F. Knaake, et al. (Weimar: Herman Bohlaus, 1883-), denominated the Weimar Edition (hereafter: WA). The WA consists of four parts: Writings, 68 volumes (WA); Letters, 18 volumes (WA Br); Table Talk, 6 volumes (WA TR); and the German Bible, 12 volumes (WA DB). Only the first part containing the "writings" is not complete. For Luther in English, see *Luther's Works*, ed. J. Pelikan, et al., 55 vols. (St. Louis: Concordia [vols. 1-30]; Philadelphia: Fortress Press [vols. 31-55], 1955-79). Bernhard Lohse, *Martin Luther: An Introduction to His Life and Work*, trans. Robert C. Schultz (Philadelphia: Fortress Press, 1986), pp. 238-43, provides a handy overview of other editions of Luther's writings. For bibliographical guides to Luther studies, consult Roland Bainton and Eric W. Gritsch, eds., *Bibliography of the Continental Reformation: Materials Available in English*, 2nd ed. (Hamden, Conn.: Shoe String, 1973), pp. 57-106; Jack Bigame and Kenneth Hagen, *Annotated Bibliography of Luther Studies*, 1967-1976 (St. Louis: Center for Reformation Research, 1977); Mark U. Edwards, Jr., "Martin Luther," *Reformation Europe: A Guide to Research*, ed. Steven Ozment (St. Louis: Center for Reformation Research, 1982), pp. 59-83.

is the believer's privilege to know subjectively that God is gracious to him in His Son. Luther wrote:

> We must daily more and more endeavour to destroy at the root that pernicious error that man cannot know whether or not he is in a state of grace, by which the whole world is seduced. If we doubt God's grace and do not believe that God is well-pleased in us for Christ's sake, then we are denying that Christ has redeemed us — indeed, we question outright all his benefits.[12]

Luther had no patience for any view of assurance that returned the burden of salvation from God to man.[13] Hence he grounded his doctrine of assurance in Christ and His atoning work.[14] In expounding Psalm 90:17, Luther wrote:

> He who prays for remission of sins and hears the absolution of Christ should be certain that truly, just as the Word declares, his sins are forgiven; and he should be assured that this is in no sense man's work but God's work. Whatever, therefore, is done in the church must rest on certainty.[15]

Faith is thus nothing less than assurance of forgiveness. Understanding Scripture and agreeing with it from the heart are synonymous with trust in it, Luther said, for assent (*assensus*) and trust (*fiducia*) are one. Predestination,[16] faith, and assurance are inseparable from God's promises. Since God does not lie, anyone who trusts His promises "will be saved and chosen."[17] Faith lays hold of the promise of God, assents to it, and assures the believer that God is graciously inclined to him in Christ Jesus. All experiences of faith are bound both to God's promise and to Christ in the promise.[18] On Abraham's faith, Luther wrote:

---

[12]Cited in Stephan H. Pfürtner, *Luther and Aquinas, a Conversation: Our Salvation, Its Certainty and Peril*, trans. Edward Quinn (London: Darton, Longman, & Todd, 1964), p. 120.

[13]Mark Noll, "John Wesley and the Doctrine of Assurance," *Bibliotheca Sacra* 132 (1975):162.

[14]Lovelace, *American Pietism of Cotton Mather*, pp. 94, 101.

[15]"Selected Psalms II," *Luther's Works* 13:140.

[16]Luther found profit for believers even in reprobation. We draw comfort from reprobation: (1) by considering that God's distinguishing grace could justly have passed us by; (2) by remaining utterly humble in receiving grace as we are reminded of the "reprobation shadow," for otherwise faith would divorce itself from the humble fear of God and become swollen with pride; (3) by being moved to continually exercise faith in manifesting God's election rather than reprobation. Cf. Paul Althaus, *The Theology of Martin Luther*, trans. Robert Schultz (Philadelphia: Fortress Press), pp. 283-84.

[17]*Luther's Works* 54:387.

[18]W. van't Spijker, *Luther: belofte en ervaring* (Goes: Oosterbaan & Le Cointre, 1983), p. 198.

Abraham is righteous . . . because he believed God who gave a promise . . . . For faith is the firm and sure thought or trust that through Christ God is propitious and that through Christ His thoughts concerning us are thoughts of peace, not of affliction or wrath. God's thought or promise, and faith, by which I take hold of God's promise — these belong together. . . . The confident laying hold of the promise is called faith; and it justifies, not as our own work but as the work of God. . . . Faith alone lays hold of the promise, believes God when He gives the promise, stretches out its hand when God offers something, and accepts what He offers. . . . The only faith that justifies is the faith that deals with God in His promises and accepts them. . . . Furthermore, every promise of God includes Christ; for if it is separated from this Mediator, God is not dealing with us at all.[19]

For Luther, assurance was an integral part of saving faith. In a basic description of saving faith, Luther stated:

Faith is a living daring confidence in God's grace, so sure and certain that the believer would stake his life on it a thousand times. This knowledge and confidence in God's grace makes men glad and bold and happy in dealing with God.[20]

On occasion, Luther implied that lack of assurance is incompatible with being an authentic Christian. He wrote:

Should you...not believe that your sins are truly forgiven and removed, then you are a heathen, acting toward your Lord Christ like one who is an unbeliever and not a Christian; and this is the most serious sin of all against God. . . . By such disbelief you make God to be a liar. . . .[21]

These words should be written in letters of gold: Ours, Us, For Us. He who does not believe these words is not a Christian.[22]

Nevertheless, Luther usually refrained from stating outright that such a doubter *is* not a Christian; rather, he only *acts* like an unbeliever when he has no assurance. For, despite his accent on the righteousness of Christ *for* and *outside of* the believer,[23] Luther also viewed assurance as an internal phenomenon. This enabled him to balance his insistence on assurance with ongoing spiritual warfare

---

[19]"Lectures on Genesis," *Luther's Works* 3:18-26.

[20]*Luther's Works* 35:370-71.

[21]Ibid., p. 13.

[22]WA 31, II, 432, 17 (cited by Werner Elert, *The Structure of Lutheranism*, trans. Walter A. Hansen, vol. 1 [St. Louis: Concordia, 1962], p. 68n).

[23]Cf. Gottfried W. Locher, *Zwingli's Thought: New Perspectives* (Leiden: E.J. Brill, 1981), p. 183n.

within the believer. Indeed, Luther's concept of anxiety in the elect because of waning consciousness of faith, had a pervasive effect on how he regarded the practical outworkings of assurance.

Luther's doctrine of assurance, like much of his theology, includes paradox. For example, despite asserting the inseparability of faith and assurance, Luther also taught that the believer's continuing unrighteousness frequently weakens certainty of faith. He wrote: "Even though we are certain that we believe in Christ, we are not certain that we believe in all his words. Hence, also, 'the believing in him' is uncertain."[24] Moreover, Luther stated that security could be a sign of God's wrath, and that "it is fear and trembling that is the surest sign of grace."[25]

Luther distinguished security (securitas) from certainty (certitudo). He said that securitas brought him into the monastery. Securitas is derived from sine cura, that is, "being without care." For Luther, securitas seeks ease apart from the grace of God. Hence Luther could say that securitas in its deepest sense is a form of carelessness, since concern for divine righteousness and glory is secondary. By contrast, certitudo is a divine gift embraced by faith.[26]

Though assurance ought to be an abiding certainty for every believer on account of God's faithfulness, in practice, Luther said, it comes and goes because of human infirmity. Luther thus wrote: "When a man sins, the spiritual life in him does not die, but it is he who turns away from it that dies, while it remains in Christ forever."[27]

In Christ salvation is certain, but since the believer does not always remain consciously in Christ and must be continually called back to Christ by the Spirit, assurance may often be missing. Thus the believer has assurance when his pride is destroyed and he rests wholly on God's grace, but when pride reasserts itself, assurance vanishes.

In Treatise on Works, Luther went one step further in the matter of doubt. In an almost Perkinsian mode of casuistry,[28] Luther advised the believer of weak faith, "Begin with a weak spark of faith and daily strengthen it more and more by exercising it."[29]

---

[24]Luther, Lectures on Romans, ed. Wilhelm Pauck. Library of Christian Classics, vol. 15 (Philadelphia: Westminster Press, 1961), p. 105.

[25]Luther, Lectures on Romans, p. 392.

[26]Cf. van't Spijker, Luther: belofte en ervaring, p. 199.

[27]Luther, Lectures on Romans, p. 185.

[28]Cf. chapter 5 below on William Perkins, the father of Puritan casuistry.

[29]Works (Philadelphia: Muhlenberg Press, 1930) 1:228.

To console those with "weak sparks" of faith, Luther un-equivocally stated that infirmity of faith must be expected in all. He added: "There is no one on earth who does not have his share of it."[30] At best, assurance of salvation is never perfect in this life (hence Luther's expression, *fidei summus gradus* —"highest degree of faith");[31] at worst, a believer may have saving faith without being aware of it.[32] Luther could thus say that confidence and boldness must be regarded as the *fruit* of faith, leaving the impression that assurance may be a *result* rather than the *intrinsic property* of saving faith.[33] He could also explain assurance as an experiential transition from being justified by faith to a being raised to a higher level of full assurance.

Luther did avoid saying that lack of assurance could threaten, much less overthrow, saving grace.[34] In this, R.L. Dabney suggested that Luther added a scriptural balance that's lacking in Calvin. Dabney wrote, "Luther sometimes speaks more scripturally than Calvin, distinguishing between 'an assuring faith' (the fuller attainment) and 'a receiving faith,' which he regards as true faith, and justifying."[35]

We must thus understand both Luther's explanation of assurance as a constitutive element in the exercise of faith, and his writing against Agricola which does not discount sanctification as a prop to assurance.[36] Though such sanctification is secondary due to a believer's continuing inadequacy before God, Luther did not shrink from stating that the believer's assurance cannot be based solely on the testimony of Christ to him through Word and sacrament. Assurance must also be supported by the testimony of a good

---

[30]Ibid.

[31]WA 18, 633, 14.

[32]*Luther's Works* 35:101. Frederick Loetscher proposes that Luther himself underwent a development in personal, progressive certainty of his salvation, which found expression in his "post-Romans" works ("Luther and the Problem of Authority in Religion: Part II," *Princeton Theological Review* 16 [1918]:517).

[33]*Luther's Works* 35:374.

[34]Cf. Isaak A. Dorner, *History of Protestant Theology, Particularly in Germany*, trans. G. Robson and S. Taylor (Edinburgh: T. & T. Clark, 1871), vol. 1, p. 239.

[35]*Lectures in Systematic Theology* (reprint ed., Grand Rapids: Zondervan, 1972), p. 709. Dabney seems to ignore Calvin's similar, albeit more cautious view of faith-assurance questions, which strayed little from Luther's position despite several changes in terminology (see pp. 37ff. below).

[36]WA 31, II, 482, 34-37. Cf. Mark R. Shaw, "The Marrow of Practical Divinity: A Study in the Theology of William Perkins" (Th.D. dissertation, Westminster Theological Seminary, 1981), p. 161.

conscience based on works, said Luther. A good conscience testifies to the truth of a believer's faith, yet true faith trusts only in Christ and not in the testimony of conscience.[37]

In summary, Luther said that assurance is the birthright of every Christian, though such assurance may ebb and flow. To have assurance is a *normative state*, while to miss its security is a *common condition* which is not always unhealthy.[38] This paradoxical tension explains why Luther could state so strongly, that "It is not security *(securitas)*, but rather assurance *(certitudo)* that is promised to faith."[39]

Philip Melanchthon (1497-1560)

Under Luther's patronage, Philip Melanchthon rapidly acquired a reputation as an astute theologian.[40] His *Common Places (Loci communes)*, first published in 1521,[41] greatly influenced the infant German evangelical movement and served for decades as the major systematic text of Reformation doctrine in Europe.

In *Loci communes* and other early writings, Melanchthon echoed Luther's rejection of any synthesis between God and man in justification. After the 1520s, however, Melanchthon began to veer away from Luther's monergism. Though he continued to affirm that the Holy Spirit must help the believer bring an end to doubt,

---

[37]WA 20, 716, 24-28; 36, 365, 28-33; 36, 366, 12-15. Cf. Randall C. Zachman, *The Assurance of Faith: Conscience in the Theology of Martin Luther and John Calvin* (Minneapolis: Fortress Press, 1993), pp. 80-87.

[38]Luther taught that it is only right that the conscious security of assurance vacillates. Many Reformers and post-Reformers agreed. For example, Head V of the Canons of Dort says that when the believer backslides, he often loses a sense of God's assuring presence, which produces anxiety rather than security. The Holy Spirit uses this anxiety in making the believer aware of his backsliding and in leading him to return to God with repentance, thereby recovering assurance. If assurance did *not* vacillate, the doctrine of perseverance might be sorely misused by the believer when backsliding.

[39]Locher, *Zwingli's Thought*, p. 183n.

[40]For Melanchthon's works, see *Philippi Melancthonis opera quae supersunt omnia. Corpus Reformatorum*, vols. 1-28, ed. G. Bretschneider and H. E. Bindseil (Brunsvigae: C.A. Schwetschke et filium, 1834-60).

For an authoritative biography on Melanchthon with a postscript on research and bibliography, see Robert Stupperich, *Melanchthon*, trans. Robert H. Fischer (Philadelphia: Fortress Press, 1965). Cf. Clyde L. Manschreck, *Melanchthon: The Quiet Reformer* (New York: Abingdon Press, 1958) for a sympathetic treatment; Michael Rogness, *Philip Melanchthon. Reformer Without Honor* (Minneapolis: Augsburg Publishing House, 1969), for Melanchthon's relationship with Luther.

[41]Translated by Lowell J. Satre as "Loci communes theologici" in *Melanchthon and Bucer*, ed. Wilhelm Pauck (Philadelphia: Westminster Press, 1969), pp. 18ff.

Melanchthon was teaching by 1535 his infamous doctrine that the human will, in conjunction with the Word and Spirit, is the third cause of conversion.[42]

Melanchthon's later thought followed this trend.[43] Man is not passive in regeneration. Since God is no respecter of persons, something must be found in the individual to explain why one sinner believes and another does not. Melanchthon thus wrote, "The cause must be in man that Saul is cast away and David is accepted."[44] Though only the Holy Spirit can impart grace, free will at least includes a sinner's ability and responsibility to prepare himself for grace.[45]

Without intending to relinquish the sovereignty of God's grace, Melanchthon's increasing tendency towards synergism during his later years inevitably led him to adopt a *both/and* approach to the divine and human roles in justification. Also, by speaking of the human will as the third cause of salvation, Melanchthon could hardly escape a soteriology of cooperation and coordination throughout.[46] By 1555 his *Loci communes* included the following:

> Faith does not mean merely knowing the story of Christ, for even the devils confess that the Son of God appeared and arose from the dead, and in Judas there was a knowledge of Christ. *True faith* is truly to retain all the words which God has given to us, including the promise of grace; *it is a heartfelt reliance on the Savior Christ, a trust that God for his Son's sake* graciously forgives us our sin, receives us, and makes us heirs of eternal blessedness.[47]

With this definition, Melanchthon now treated faith as a prelude to grace. Moreover, by his final *Loci*, he was including faith along with contrition, which brought his doctrine of faith and assurance in line with his doctrine of the will. As Werner Elert wrote:

> In the final edition of the *Loci* he [Melanchthon] prefaces what he

---

[42]Melanchthon wrote, "The Holy Spirit and the word are first active in conversion, but the will of man is not wholly inactive; God draws, but draws him who is willing, for man is not a statue" (*Loci communes*, trans. and ed. Clyde L. Manschreck [reprint ed., Grand Rapids: Baker, 1982], p. xiii).

[43]Particularly his 1544-45, 1555, and final 1559 *Loci communes* editions explore the implications of the 1535 *causa concurrens* in detail and increasingly departed from Luther's absolute monergism.

[44]Cf. *Lutheran Church Review* 28 (1909):325ff.

[45]Cf. F. W. Walther, *The Proper Distinction between Law and Gospel* (St. Louis: Concordia, n.d.), p. 265.

[46]Cf. Gerhard Friedrich Bente, *Historical Introductions to the Book of Concord* (St. Louis: Concordia, 1965), p. 130.

[47]*Loci communes 1555*, p. 158.

taught about the "three reasons" (*tres causae*) —"the Word of God, the Holy Spirit, and the will of man that assents and does not resist the Word of God"— with a twofold reminder: that the promise of the Spirit is received "through faith" (*per fidem*) and that one dare not seek God without His Word. This means, then, that in the systematic classification of the emotions "faith" (*fides*) and "not resisting" (*non repugnare*) occupy exactly the same place. Yes, somewhat later "believing" (*credere*) is used almost as a synonym of "not resisting."[48]

According to Luther, the promise was the correlate of faith. While keeping many of Luther's terms, Melanchthon gradually promoted a more rationalistic, scholastic emphasis on assent (*assensus*) at some expense to trust (*fiducia*).[49]

In summary, though Melanchthon did not fundamentally reject Luther's understanding of evangelical assurance he did accent an objective presentation of "Christ for us" (*Christus pro nobis*) rather than a subjective experience of "Christ in us" (*Christus in nobis*). This difference wasn't fundamental, however, since both theologians embraced these truths in principle as noncontradictory.

Melanchthon retained assurance as an integral part of faith, though in later years he moved away from accenting personal assurance. Consequently, despite lifelong adherence to the Augsburg Confession statement on faith,[50] as well as agreement in principle with the forthcoming Formula of Concord statement[51]— both of which stress assurance as an element of faith, Melanchthon indirectly led Lutheranism away from the doctrine of personal assurance. That started with Melanchthon's denial of double predestination and monergistic salvation and was nourished by his incipient denial of perseverance.[52]

---

[48]*Structure of Lutheranism*, p. 100. Cf. *Philippi Melancthonis opera* 21:658.

[49]Robins, *Basis of Assurance*, pp. 21-22.

[50]Cf. esp. Article IV, which states that men are justified "when they believe that they are received into favor and that their sins are forgiven on account of Christ" (*The Book of Concord: The Confessions of the Evangelical Lutheran Church*, ed. and trans. Theodore Tappert [Philadelphia: Fortress Press, 1959], p. 30).

[51]Cf. esp. Article III, Affirmative VI, *The Book of Concord*, p. 540. For *Apology's* statements on assurance in a similar vein, see 138.224; 190.61; 191.64; 195.87; 213.20.

[52]This took scores of years to be realized, for of post-Melanchthon Lutheranism G.C. Berkouwer rightly notes: "The Lutherans *rejected* the doctrine of the perseverance of the saints, but they did not deny the assurance of salvation" (*Faith and Perseverance*, trans. Robert D. Knudsen [Grand Rapids: Eerdmans, 1958], p. 55). Cf. R. Preus, *The Theology of Post-Reformation Lutheranism: A Study of Theological Prolegomena*, 2 vols. (St. Louis: Concordia, 1970-72).

Huldrych Zwingli (1484-1531)

In German Switzerland, Huldrych Zwingli echoed and enlarged Luther's doctrine of personal assurance.[53] Like Luther, Zwingli stressed assurance as essential to faith. But for Zwingli, faith was more than an act of trust; faith embraced assurance of election and salvation in Christ. Faith was "peace and assurance through the merit of Christ."[54] Even more than Luther, Zwingli grounded faith and assurance in God's sovereign election and in Christ's work in fulfilling the covenant of grace. Thus, the object of faith is the triune God, who glorifies Himself by displaying His character in predestination — i.e., His mercy in graciously electing sinners to salvation in Christ and His power in justly reprobating the wicked to damnation.[55] Faith is assured by the gracious promises of God's Word for the sake of Christ's merits without any merit in the believer or in his faith.

Like Luther, Zwingli regarded assuring faith as "surrendering pride in one's supposed free will and bitterly renouncing the merit

[53]For Zwingli's writings, see *Huldreich Zwinglis sämtliche Werke* [hereafter: Z], ed. Emil Egli, George Finsler, et al., 14 vols. of the Corpus Reformatorum (Berlin: C.A. Schwetschke und Sohn; Leipzig: M. Heinsius; Zurich: Verlag Berichthaus, 1905-1968); *Opera*, ed. M. Chuler and J. Schulthess, 3 vols. (Zurich: F. Schulthessium, 1829-42); *The Latin Works and the Correspondence of Huldreich Zwingli*, ed. Samuel Macauley Jackson, et al., 3 vols. (Philadelphia: Heidelberg Press, 1912-29); *Zwingli and Bullinger: Selected Translations*, with intro. and notes by G. W. Bromiley (Philadelphia: Westminster Press, 1953).

For secondary sources on Zwingli, consult the bibliography for books and articles by Gottfried W. Locher. Also, see Paul Wernle, *Der evangelische glaube nach dem Hauptschriften der Reformatoren, Band II: Zwingli* (Tübingen, 1919); Walter Köhler, *Huldrych Zwingli* (Leipzig, 1943); Jacques Courvoisier, *Zwingli: A Reformed Theologian* (Richmond, Va.: John Knox Press, 1963); Jean H. Rilliet, *Zwingli: The Third Man of the Reformation*, trans. Harold Knight (London: Lutterworth Press, 1964); Jack W. Cottrell, "Covenant and Baptism in the Theology of H. Zwingli" (Th.D. dissertation, Princeton Theological Seminary, 1971); George R. Potter, *Zwingli* (Cambridge: Cambridge University Press, 1976); W. Balke, W. van't Spijker, C. A. Tukker, and K. M. *Witteveen, Zwingli in vierderlei perspectief* (Utrecht: De Banier, 1984); W. P. Stephens, *The Theology of Huldrych Zwingli* (New York: Oxford, 1986), Ulrich Gabler, *Huldrych Zwingli: His Life and Works*, trans. Ruth C. L. Gritsch (Philadelphia: Fortress Press, 1986). Gabler includes an excellent bibliographical survey.

For bibliography on Zwingli, cf. Bainton and Gritsch, *Bibliography of the Continental Reformation*, pp. 120-23; Wayne H. Pipkin, "A Zwingli Bibliography" (Ph.D. dissertation, Pittsburgh Theological Seminary, 1972), and the periodical, *Zwingliana*, in which an annual list of books and articles is published.

[54]Z 3:701; cf. Dorner, *Protestant Theology*, vol. 1, p. 292.

[55]Zwingli set the framework for later Bezan supralapsarianism by maintaining that God, for His own glory, elected and reprobated individuals as persons rather than as fallen sinners (cf. *Opera* 1: 365; 2:34; 4:431).

of personal action."[56] Unlike Luther, Zwingli consistently ended with this truth: Faith is assuring not because of personal fruits but because of God's electing grace. The doctrine of election governed Zwingli's teachings on faith and assurance, from an *a priori* and *a posteriori* perspective.[57] Since election in Christ is the sovereign work of God, assuring faith is the result of God's work;[58] it is a sure sign of election. On the other hand, from assuring faith the believer can assume his calling and election, thereby concluding with assurance that he is justified and possesses eternal salvation.[59]

Zwingli also emphasized the inseparability of election, the promises of God, Christ, faith, and assurance in the doctrine of God's providence. Faith in Christ's atonement — which lies at the heart of Zwingli's theology[60]— evidences itself as assuring trust in God throughout daily experiences. Zwingli wrote:

> Faith is nothing else than the certain assurance with which man relies on the merit of Christ. . . . That man himself contributes nothing, but believes all things are directed and ordered by God's providence, and this comes only from giving himself to God and trusting in him completely; that he understands in faith that God does everything, even though we cannot perceive it.[61]

For Zwingli, trust in God's providence never leads to indifference or fatalism. Rather, Gottfried Locher wrote, "Faith itself, being the work of the Spirit, is seen as *experientia* (experience) and as *fiducia* (trust) and must clearly be distinguished from *fides historica* (accepting as true) and *opinio* (personal opinion)."[62]

Consequently, historical faith, which merely accepts the outward truths of Scripture, is insufficient, for even the devils

---

[56]Locher, *Zwingli's Thought*, p. 166.

[57]Robert W. Letham, "Saving Faith and Assurance in Reformed Theology: Zwingli to the Synod of Dort" (Ph.D. dissertation, University of Aberdeen, 1979), 1:17ff.

[58]Specifically, the Holy Spirit arouses faith in the hearts of the elect by means of His Word (Zwingli, *Opera* 1:47, 182; 4:433, 549).

[59]Zwingli, *Opera* 2:34.

[60]In Zwingli's thought, Christology is never eclipsed by election (cf. Letham, "Saving Faith and Assurance in Reformed Theology," 1:19-20). In fact, Locher argued that Christology is the central motif of Zwingli's theology (*Die theologie H. Zwinglis im lichte seiner Christologie*, vol. 1 [Zürich: Zwingli-Verlag, 1952]). Cf. J. I. Good, *The Reformed Reformation* (Philadelphia: The Heidelberg Press, 1916), pp. 131-32, and *Famous Reformers of the Reformed and Presbyterian Churches* (Philadelphia: The Heidelberg Press, 1916), p. 28.

[61]Z 2:182.

[62]*Zwingli's Thought*, p. 185.

believe in this way (James 2:19). Historical faith is prompted by outward things, such as the Word and sacraments.[63] But saving faith receives such truths personally and by the direct testimony of the Spirit, who witnesses with our spirits through the Word that we are sons of God. This in turn strengthens assurance. Zwingli wrote:

> For the Spirit cannot deceive. If he tells us that God is our Father, and we with certainty and confidence call him Father, secure of eternal inheritance, it is certain that God's Spirit has been shed abroad in our hearts. It is therefore certain that he is elect who is so secure and safe, for they who believe are ordained to eternal life.[64]

According to Zwingli, since no one can pray "Our Father" who does not believe that God is his gracious Father in Christ, only the believer who has received the pledge and seal of the Holy Spirit in his heart, can pray with assurance, "Abba, Father!"[65] For Zwingli, this is a normative experience for the believer.

The Spirit strengthens assurance by means of sanctification and good works. This naturally led Zwingli to what subsequently will be called the practical syllogism (*syllogismus practicus*),[66] in which Zwingli's belief that sanctification gives evidence of assuring faith exceeds Luther's. For Zwingli, the law is to direct the believer's conduct without any danger of works-righteousness;[67] hence good works, while meriting nothing, are a necessary fruit of faith, an assuring sign of faith, and a valuable support for assurance.[68]

Good works necessarily flow out of faith as certainly as heat is diffused under a lit burner, said Zwingli.[69] So good works are a sign of faith just as faith is a sign of election. Zwingli wrote:

> Thus those who perform works of faith provide practical proof that they serve God, that is, that they have faith. They show this firstly

---

[63]"The sacraments do not give faith, but only historical faith.... For it is only those who have been taught inwardly by the Spirit to know the mystery of the divine goodness who can know and believe that Christ suffered for us" (Bromiley, *Zwingli and Bullinger*, pp. 260-61).

[64]Z 6 (2):800.

[65]Z 6 (1):348.

[66]See pp. 65-72 and 131-41 below for a discussion of the *syllogismus practicus*.

[67]For the difference between the Lutheran and the Reformed on the third use of the law (*tertius usus legis*), see Joel R. Beeke and Ray B. Lanning, "Glad Obedience: The Third Use of the Law," in *Trust and Obey*, ed. Don Kistler (Morgan, Pa.: Soli Deo Gloria, 1996), pp. 162-72.

[68]Z 3:257.

[69]Zwingli, Opera 1:371. Cf. Locher, *Zwingli's Thought*, p. 184n.

to themselves, and then to others, when they act with generosity and out of love to God and their neighbor, and not out of vainglory.[70]

Zwingli stressed that all such evidencing works are ultimately works of the *Holy Spirit* — for what assurance can there be without the Spirit?[71] Moreover, the Spirit moves the believer to more faith and love. He wrote: "The more faith grows, the more the doing of all good things grows, [for the believer is] moved to such action by God."[72]

By focusing on the Spirit's work — indeed, the triune God's work,[73] Zwingli safeguarded the utterly gracious character of assurance, while encouraging the believer in obedience by teaching that assurance and growth in good works are inseparable. For Zwingli, good works, faith, the atonement of Christ, the promises of God, and election were an unbreakable chain of grace which "provides the foundation and substance upon and within which faith can function as a *signum* [sign] and a *testimonium* [testimony] of our election."[74]

This does not mean that the believer is satisfied with his good works or that severe afflictions may not make him acutely aware of how weak he often is in faith. At those times, however, weakness of faith should move the afflicted believer to pray, "Lord, increase my faith," so that deep within he may still be certain that nothing shall keep him from the treasures he possesses in Christ Jesus.[75]

For Zwingli, the goal of sanctification is to be Christ-like — i.e., "not to blather about Christ, but to walk as he walked,"[76] and to be filled with the Spirit of Christ.[77]

In summary, for Zwingli sanctification plays a supportive, yet secondary, role in assurance. Sanctification confirms the assurance that is already inherent in faith. Hence the testimony of faith from good works must ultimately end in the promises of God that focus upon

---

[70]Cited by ibid., p. 186.

[71]For Zwingli, the Holy Spirit who alone works faith also gives assurance as an integral component of faith. Though the election of others may remain hidden, the Spirit normally gives assurance of salvation and election to the individual believer (*Opera* 2:557; 4:133); cf. Bromiley, *Zwingli and Bullinger*, p. 269.

[72]Z 2:183, 187.

[73]Stephens pointed out that at one juncture Zwingli wrote of "Christ, God, and the Spirit of God" as being the source of good works within seven lines! (Z 2:47; *The Theology of Huldrych Zwingli*, p. 158n).

[74]Letham, "Saving Faith and Assurance in Reformed Theology," 1:21.

[75]Zwingli, *Opera* 1:370.

[76]Z 3:705.

[77]Z 2:72-73.

Christ as the primary ground of assurance. "By faith, we are saved through Jesus Christ," Zwingli wrote.[78] Assurance is strengthened most when faith leans hard on God in Christ,[79] trusts in Him alone,[80] and lifts its eyes to Him,[81] all actions which are the fruit of divine grace. As Stephens wrote, "For Zwingli, in the end, whatever is ascribed to faith is quite simply to be ascribed to God."[82]

Heinrich Bullinger (1504-1575)

Like his predecessor Zwingli, Heinrich Bullinger[83] went directly from predestination and providence to personal assurance within a Christ-centered context. He wrote:

> The doctrine of the foreknowledge and predestination of God, which hath a certain likeness with his providence, doth no less comfort the godly worshippers of God. . . . If thou ask me whether thou art elected to life, or predestinate to death; . . . I answer simply: If thou hast communion or fellowship with Christ, howsoever otherwise thou seem to flourish in virtues, thou art predestinate to life . . . but if thou be a stranger from Christ, thou art predestinate unto death. . . . Faith therefore is a most assured sign that thou art elected; and whiles thou art called to the communion of Christ, and art taught faith, the most loving God declareth towards thee his election and good-will. . . .

---

[78]Zwingli, *Opera* 2:347.

[79]Ibid., 2:484.

[80]Ibid., 1:369-370; 2:123; 4:478.

[81]Ibid., 1:70.

[82]*The Theology of Huldrych Zwingli*, p. 164.

[83]Bullinger was a prolific writer: 150 treatises and manuscripts are credited to him. Some of his writings are confessional, resulting in significant statements of faith. Some are polemical, particularly those written against the Roman Catholics, Lutherans, and Anabaptists. But the majority are pastoral, taking the form of biblical commentaries and published lectures on theological doctrines. For this brief study, I have limited myself to an examination of Bullinger's writings found in the bibliography, and have focused in particular on three works. First, his most renowned work, *The Decades of Henry Bullinger*, trans. H. I., ed. for the Parker Society by Thomas Harding, 5 vols. in 4 (Cambridge: University Press, 1849-51) [hereafter: *Decades*], which contains fifty sermons. Second, *De gratia Dei iustificante nos propter Christum* (Tiguri: Froschoviana, 1554), Bullinger's major treatise on faith and justification. Third, *Confessio Helvetica posterior, A.D. 1566* (*The Second Helvetic Confession*), first composed as a private confession, subsequently approved by nearly all the Reformed churches, and ultimately one of the most influential of the Reformed confessional statements (see Schaff, *Creeds* 3:233-306 for a Latin text, and Joel R. Beeke and Sinclair Ferguson, *Reformed Confessions Harmonized* [Grand Rapids: Baker 1999] for an English text).

God's predestination is not stayed or stirred with any worthiness or unworthiness of ours; but of the mere grace and mercy of God the Father, it respecteth Christ alone. And because our salvation doth stay only upon him, it cannot but be most certain.[84]

In short, God's promises apply to all who believe in Christ; for them, assurance of salvation flows from predestination. Faith, in turn, is the gift of God bestowed only on the elect.[85] Salvation is certain because of God's work in Christ.[86] Bullinger wrote:

If thou believest, and art in Christ, thou mayest undoubtedly hold that thou art elected. For the Father has revealed unto us in Christ his eternal sentence of predestination.... Let Christ, therefore, be our mirror, in whom we may behold our predestination. We shall have a most evident and sure testimony that we are written in the Book of Life if we communicate with Christ, and he be ours, and we be his, by a true faith.[87]

Faith and assurance are grounded on the same foundations[88]— God's Word, God's Son, and God's promises[89]— all of which are inseparable. Faith is directed to God's promising Word and Son as "a most assured confidence of God's promises"[90] and adheres to these promises, all of which center in Christ. Thus faith receives an assuredness of conscience when it embraces Him.[91]

In his *Decades,* Bullinger confirmed assurance as an essential part of faith by quoting four divines, but subsequently he defined faith by deemphasizing a personal *consciousness* of assurance. He wrote:

Faith is a gift of God, poured into man from heaven, whereby he is taught with an undoubted persuasion wholly to lean to God and his word; in which word God doth freely promise life and all good things in Christ, and wherein all truth necessary to be believed is plainly declared.[92]

---

[84]*Decades* 4:185-88; cf. ibid., 3:187.

[85]*Second Helvetic Confession* 16:2 (Schaff, *Creeds* 3:268). Faith is "neither of our own nature, nor of our own merits, but it is by the grace of God poured into us through the Holy Spirit, which is given into our hearts" (*Decades* 3:251).

[86]*Second Helvetic Confession* 10:3 (Schaff, *Creeds* 3:252).

[87]*Second Helvetic Confession* 10:7-9 (Schaff, *Creeds* 3:253-54).

[88]Heinrich Bullinger, *A hundred sermons upon the Apocalipse of Iesu Christ, reveilled by the angell of the Lord: but seene or received and written by the holy apostle and evangelist S. Iohn* (London: Iohn Daye, 1561), pp. 257-58.

[89]*Second Helvetic Confession* 16:1 (Schaff, *Creeds* 3:268).

[90]*Decades* 1:82-84.

[91]Ibid., 1:83-90.

[92]Ibid., 1:84.

In later works Bullinger did not define faith as assurance of personal salvation, but viewed it as active trust from the heart. In the following definitions of faith, the element of assurance slips to the background:

> Faith is a certain knowledge of the truth, and a constant, firm and undoubted trust and assent of the human mind to the word of God, originating from the Holy Spirit, by which it believes all truth, principally the promises of God and in them Christ himself, in whom is set forth all fulness of life and salvation: which, since it receives all good things, has him indwelling and living. Or, faith is a certain knowledge, a firm trust and an undoubted assent to the word of God: which, inspired in our soul by the Spirit of God, believes piously all truth that is to be believed, receives Christ himself, and possesses in him life, righteousness and all good things.[93]

> Each and every one of the faithful in Christ ought to know that the faith by which we are justified is not only a knowledge of the mind but also a firm trust of the soul, by which we rest on God and his word and especially the divine promises made to us in Christ, and all those things that are comprehended in the symbol of the Christian faith.[94]

> Christian faith is not an opinion or human persuasion, but a sure trust, and an evident and stedfast assent of the mind; it is a most sure comprehension of the truth of God, set forth in the Scriptures and in the Apostles' Creed; yea, and of God himself, the chief blessedness; and especially of God's promise and of Christ, who is the consummation of all the promises. And this faith is the mere gift of God, because God alone of his power does give it to his elect . . . by his Holy Spirit, through the means of preaching the Gospel and of faithful prayer. This faith has also its measure of increase. . . .[95]

Bullinger further backed off from explicitly joining full assurance of salvation to faith when he dealt with pastoral concerns relative to believers' doubts.[96] Bullinger apparently had no problem in using the concept of a weak faith in contrast to what ought to be, a strong faith of firm assurance. He wrote:

[93]*De gratia Dei iustificante nos propter Christum*, p. 43 (trans. Letham, "Saving Faith and Assurance in Reformed Theology," p. 67). Speaking of this work, Letham concludes: "Bullinger carefully puts together all the ingredients necessary for an equation of faith and assurance, teaches as much and then proceeds to omit assurance from his definition of faith, stating that it is a fruit of faith rather than something which is of the essence of faith itself" (ibid., p. 65).

[94]Translated in ibid, p. 70 from *Compendium Christianae religionis decem librem comprehensum* (Tiguri: Frosch, 1556), p. 70.

[95]*Second Helvetic Confession* 16:1-2 (Schaff, *Creeds* 3:268).

[96]Cf. Tipson, "The Development of a Puritan Understanding of Conversion," p. 76.

> At the promise of God, this came into Abraham's mind: "What shall there a son be born to thee that art an hundred years old?" This was that infirmity, and stackering [staggering], or weakness of faith. But here the apostle, commending Abraham's faith, which overcame and yielded not, teaching us also of what sort faith ought to be, that is, a firm and most assured persuasion.[97]

In another volume of the *Decades*, under a most intriguing paragraph marginally summarized as "Faith hath her increasings," Bullinger wrote:

> If any therefore doth feel faith in his mind, let him not despair, although he know that it is weak enough, God wot, and feeble: let him cast himself wholly upon God's mercy; let him presume very little or nothing at all, of his own merits; let him pray incessantly for the increase of faith.[98]

In *De gratia Dei iustificante nos propter Christum*, Bullinger argued that although faith and hope are intertwined, they are still distinguishable. Faith is the fountain of all graces; it evidences itself by the practice of good works,[99] he said. Hope flows out of faith.[100] Hope is not faith so much as it is the perseverance of faith that waits upon the promises of God's Word.[101]

The implication is that as faith and hope are distinct from one another, so faith and assurance, though organically united, are also separate. When Bullinger taught that Christ *and faith itself* were grounds of assurance concerning the believer's election,[102] he anticipated what would later be called the reflex act of faith in which assurance is confirmed by looking at faith itself.

Is it possible that Perkins's later doctrine of assurance was merely a pastoral development of the framework presented by Bullinger? Was Bullinger himself aware of some excess in the Reformers in their stress on faith's assurance? Did he then find it necessary to quietly retreat from this position in an irenic, pastoral spirit so typical of the man himself?

Though the evidence is not conclusive, statements such as the following suggest that Bullinger may have served as a significant link between the Reformers and William Perkins, who, in turn,

---

[97]*Decades* 1:89.
[98]Ibid., 4:189-92.
[99]*De gratia Dei iustificante nos propter Christum*, pp. 66, 72-77.
[100]Ibid., pp. 87-90.
[101]Ibid., p. 87.
[102]*Decades* 3:186.

paved the way for the view of the Westminster Confession: "Faith doth bring an assured persuasion into the mind and heart of man."[103] At the very least, Bullinger's position on faith and assurance deserves a more impartial and thorough treatment than it has been given to date.[104]

---

[103]*Decades* 1:88.

[104]For the most thorough study of Bullinger on faith and assurance, see Letham, "Saving Faith and Assurance in Reformed Theology," 1:43-75. Though Letham's dissertation contains much original research and provides numerous insights, its weakness is a tendency to divide Reformed theologians into two parties according to their view of the covenant. Theologians with a unilateral view of the covenant are presented as exemplary and those with a bilateral view are judged severely. J. Wayne Baker's work suffers from the same flaw (*Heinrich Bullinger and the Covenant: The Other Reformed Tradition* [Athens: Ohio University Press, 1980]), prompting Christopher Burchill to comment that while the distinction bears some validity, it leads to "great confusion" ("On the Consolation of a Christian Scholar," *Journal of Ecclesiastical History* 37 [1986]:581n). Cf. Lyle D. Bierma, *German Calvinism in the Confessional Age: The Covenant Theology of Caspar Olevianus* (Grand Rapids: Baker, 1996), pp. 35-40, and Muller, *Christ and the Decree*, pp. 41, 197n, who more accurately argue that Bullinger consistently maintains a strong monergistic base to his system, even as he presents duopleuric language for the believer's life under the covenant. Also, see Paul R. Schaefer, Jr., "The Spiritual Brotherhood of the Heart: Cambridge Protestants and the Doctrine of Sanctification from William Perkins to Thomas Shepard" (Ph.D. dissertation, Keble College, Oxford University, 1994), pp. 184-85n.

IV. REFORMED DEVELOPMENT IN CALVIN AND BEZA

Under the leadership of John Calvin (1509-1564) and his successor, Theodore Beza (1519-1605), Geneva became a dominant theological, educational, and intellectual center for the Reformed faith. Notwithstanding Beza's longevity in Geneva and the underestimation of his influence, the major impetus of Geneva's reform was John Calvin. Though one of many great Reformers, Calvin certainly was *the* exegete and one of the most gifted theologians among his colleagues throughout Europe.[1] I'll examine his doctrine of assurance somewhat more closely than that of the other Reformers not only because of his commanding presence, but also to lay the groundwork for comparing his views with those of the Calvinist English Puritans and the Dutch Second Reformation divines.[2] Subsequently, Beza's contributions to the Reformed doctrine of assurance will be examined.

[1]Cf. Tony Lane, "The Quest for the Historical Calvin," *The Evangelical Quarterly* 55 (1983):96-97; Letham, "Faith and Assurance in Early Calvinism," pp. 358ff.

[2]For an annotated bibliographical guide to Calvin's vast corpus and material on his life and theology printed prior to 1964, see Lester de Koster, "Living Themes in the Thought of John Calvin: A Bibliographical Study" (Ph.D. dissertation, University of Michigan, 1964). For Calvin bibliography since the 1960s, see Peter De Klerk's annual articles in the *Calvin Theological Journal*. Cf. D. Kempff, *A Bibliography of Calviniana, 1959-1974* (Potchefstroom: I. A. C., 1975); Bainton and Gritsch, *Bibliography of the Continental Reformation*, pp. 161-84.

The best one-volume summary of Calvin's life and theology is François Wendel, *Calvin: The Origins and Development of His Religious Thought*, trans. Philip Mairet (New York: Harper & Row, 1963). The most exhaustive treatment of Calvin and his theology is Emile Doumergue, *Jean Calvin: Les hommes et les choses de son temps*, 7 vols. (vols. 1-5, Lausanne: Georges Bridel & Cie., 1899-1917; vols. 6-7, Neuilly sur Seine, editions de "La Cause," 1927-29). Significant works that deal exclusively with Calvin's doctrine of faith and assurance include Harry Booth Hazen, "Calvin's Doctrine of Faith" (Ph.D.

John Calvin (1509-1564)

Nature and Definition of Faith

Like Luther, John Calvin developed a scriptural doctrine of assurance as a confirmation of initial and ongoing experiences in the life of faith.[3] In a remarkable way, Calvin's doctrine of assurance reaffirmed the basic tenets of Luther and Zwingli and disclosed emphases of his own. Like Luther and Zwingli, Calvin said that faith is never merely assent (*assensus*), but involves both knowledge (*cognitio*) and trust (*fiducia*). He also taught that knowledge and trust are saving dimensions of the life of faith rather than notional matters. For Calvin, faith is not historical knowledge plus saving assent as Beza implied, but a saving and certain knowledge joined with a saving and assured trust.[4]

For Calvin, knowledge is foundational to faith. This knowledge rests upon *the Word of God,* which is essentially the Holy Scriptures, as well as the proclamation of the gospel.[5] Faith originates in the

---

dissertation, University of Chicago, 1903); S. P. Dee, *Het geloofsberijp van Calvijn* (Kampen: Kok, 1918); W. E. Stuermann, "A Critical Study of Calvin's Concept of Faith" (Ph.D. dissertation, University of Tulsa, 1952); Paul Sebestyén, "The Object of Faith in the Theology of Calvin" (Ph.D. dissertation, University of Chicago, 1963); K. Exalto, *De Zekerheid des Geloofs bij Calvijn* (Apeldoorn: Willem de Zwijgerstichting, 1978); Victor A. Shepherd, *The Nature and Function of Faith in the Theology of John Calvin* (Macon, Ga.: Mercer University Press, 1983); Zachman, *The Assurance of Faith: Conscience in the Theology of Martin Luther and John Calvin*; Jon Balsarek, "Toward an Understanding of Calvin's View of Faith" (Th.M. Thesis, Reformed Theological Seminary, 1996).

[3]Though Luther's struggles in attaining faith and assurance, documented copiously by himself and others, are well-known, J. H. Merle d'Aubigne provides evidence that Calvin's "chamber became the theatre of struggles as fierce as those in the cell at Erfurth" (*History of the Reformation in Europe in the Time of Calvin*, vol. 1 [London: Longman, Green, Longman, Roberts & Green, 1863], p. 522). Cf. ibid., pp. 521-38; C. Harinck, "Geloof en zekerheid bij Calvijn," *De Saambinder* 68 (1990) no. 38:5-6; H. J. Couvee, *Calvijn en Calvinisme: Een studie over Calvijn en ons geestelijk en kerkelijk leven* (Utrecht: Kemink en Zoon, 1936), pp. 70-95; and especially Calvin's preface to his commentary on the Psalms, where he confessed that he often identified with David's experiences (*Calvin's Commentaries* [reprint ed., Grand Rapids: Baker, 1979], vol. 4, p. xxxvii-xlix. [Hereafter: *Commentary*.])

[4]John Calvin, *Institutes of the Christian Religion,* [hereafter: Inst.], ed. John T. McNeill and trans. F. L. Battles (Philadelphia: Westminster Press, 1960), Book 3, chapter 2, section 14. (Hereafter the format, 3.2.14, will be used.) For Calvin's Latin works, see *Opera quae supersunt omnia,* ed. Guilielmus Baum, Eduardus Cunitz, and Eduardus Reuss, vols. 29-87 in Corpus Reformatorum (Brunsvigae: C. A. Schwetschke et filium, 1863-1900). Hereafter: *CO*.

[5]For Calvin, the "Word of the Lord" can also refer to the spoken word, especially to the "proclamation of the grace manifested in Christ" (Inst. 2.9.2; *Commentary* on 1 Peter 1:25). Hence Calvin's strong emphasis upon regarding the preaching of God's Word as

Word of God. Faith rests firmly upon God's Word;[6] hence assurance must be sought *in* the Word[7] and flows *out of* the Word.[8] Assurance is as inseparable from the Word as sunbeams are from the sun. Faith receives the entire Word of God.[9] Faith always says "amen" to the Scriptures.[10]

Faith is also inseparable from *Christ and the promise of Christ,* for the totality of the written Word is the living Word, Jesus Christ, in whom all God's promises are "yea and amen."[11] Faith rests on scriptural knowledge and on promises that are Christ-directed and Christ-centered. Faith receives Christ as He is clothed in the gospel and graciously offered by the Father.[12]

Thus, the knowledge of true faith focuses upon the Scriptures in general, and the promise of the grace of God in Christ in particular. Calvin makes much of the promises of God as the ground of assurance, for these are promises of the God who cannot lie. Since God promises mercy to sinners in their misery, faith relies upon such promises.[13] The promises focus upon and are fulfilled by Christ; hence Calvin directs sinners to Christ and to the promise as if they were synonymous.[14] Rightly understood, faith is scriptural by derived knowledge that rests on and appropriates the sure promises of God in Christ.[15]

Since faith takes its character from the promise on which it rests, faith takes on the infallible stamp of God's Word. Hence, it possesses assurance in its very nature. Assurance, certainty, trust — such is the essence of faith.

---

authoritative, as well as his accent upon the need for believers to know and study the Scriptures. Cf. David Foxgrover, "John Calvin's Understanding of Conscience" (Ph.D. dissertation, Claremont, 1978), pp. 407ff.

[6]*Commentary* (on John 3:33; Psalm 43:3).

[7]*Commentary* (on Matthew 8:13).

[8]*Commentary* (on John 4:22).

[9]*Commentary* (on Acts 10:33).

[10]Cf. Exalto, *De Zekerheid des Geloofs bij Calvijn,* p. 24. Edward Dowey mistakenly dichotomized the Scriptures and assurance when he asserted that the center of Calvin's doctrine of faith is assurance rather than the authority of the Scriptures. For Calvin, the separation of the Word of God from assurance is unthinkable (*The Knowledge of God in Calvin's Theology,* [New York: Columbia University Press, 1965], p. 182). Cf. Balsarek, "Toward an Understanding of Calvin's View of Faith," pp. 67-89.

[11]*Commentary* (on Genesis 15:6; Luke 2:21).

[12]Inst. 3.2.32.

[13]Inst. 3.2.29, 41; *Commentary* (on Acts 2:39).

[14]Inst. 3.2.32; *Commentary* (on Romans 4:3, 18; Hebrews 11:7, 11).

[15]Inst. 3.2.6, 15; *Commentary* (on 1 John 3:2).

This assuring faith is the *Holy Spirit's gift to the elect*. The Spirit persuades the elect sinner of the reliability of God's promise in Christ and grants faith to embrace that Word.[16]

Thus, for Calvin, assuring faith necessarily involves saving knowledge, the Scriptures, Jesus Christ, God's promises, the work of the Holy Spirit, and election. In a word, God Himself is the assurance of the elect.[17]

Consequently, Calvin's formal definition of faith, sandwiched between attacks on scholastic notions of faith,[18] reads like this: "Now we shall possess a right definition of faith if we call it a firm and certain knowledge of God's benevolence toward us, founded upon the truth of the freely given promise in Christ, both revealed to our minds and sealed upon our hearts through the Holy Spirit."[19]

In this definition, Calvin asserted that faith relies upon a Trinitarian framework. Faith is assurance of God's promise in Christ applied by the Spirit.[20] It involves the whole man in the use of the mind, the application to the heart, and the surrendering of the will.[21] Assurance is of the essence of faith.

Assurance of Essence of Faith

More specifically, Calvin argued that faith involves something more than objectively believing the promise of God. It involves personal, subjective assurance. In believing God's promise to sinners, the true believer recognizes and celebrates that God is gracious and benevolent to him in particular. Faith is an assured knowledge "of God's benevolence toward *us* . . . revealed to *our* minds . . . sealed

---

[16]Inst. 3.2.16.

[17]*Commentary* (on Romans 8:16; 1 Peter 1:4; Hebrews 4:10).

[18]For Calvin's opposition to scholastic notions of faith, see Exalto, *De Zekerheid des Geloofs bij Calvijn*, pp. 9, 27ff.; Foxgrover, "John Calvin's Understanding of Conscience," pp. 422-36.

[19]Inst. 3.2.7.

[20]This Trinitarian framework of faith is discussed in detail on pages 55-65 below.

[21]Calvin taught that the soul consists of two parts, the intellect and the will (Inst. 1.15.7). He was more ambiguous on the heart, sometimes referring it to the mind or intellect, but more commonly to the will. Lane points out that Kendall exaggerates by stating that the heart for Calvin simply means mind, and thereby reduces the heart to "a fully persuaded mind" ("Calvin's Doctrine of Assurance," p. 52n; cf. pp. 42-43). Calvin said that the sure knowledge of faith not only controls the understanding but also pierces the heart through the Spirit's application of the gospel. It is not sufficient for faith to merely illumine the mind; it must also strengthen the heart. Ultimately, the seat of true religion lies in the heart, not in the intellect. Faith is more heart than brain and cannot exist without a devout disposition of true piety (Inst. 3.2.8). Cf. *Commentary* (on Philippians 4:7).

upon *our* hearts."[22] Faith personally embraces the gospel promise and is inseparable from personal certainty. As Calvin wrote, "Here, indeed, is the hinge on which faith turns: that we do not regard the promises of mercy that God offers as true only outside ourselves, but not at all in us; rather that we make them ours by inwardly embracing them."[23]

Consequently, as Kendall notes, Calvin repeatedly described faith as "certainty, a firm conviction, assurance, firm assurance, and full assurance."[24] While faith consists of knowledge, it also is marked by heartfelt assurance rather than mere intellectual apprehension[25] and is therefore "a sure and secure possession of those things which God has promised us."[26]

Calvin emphasized also throughout his commentaries that assurance is integral to faith. For example, on Acts 2:39 he noted:

> This is required necessarily for the certainty of faith, that everyone be fully persuaded of this, that he is comprehended in the number of those unto whom God speaketh. This is the rule of a true faith, when I am thus persuaded that salvation is mine, because that promise appertaineth unto me which offereth the same.[27]

Typical is his comment on 1 Corinthians 2:12:

> The elect have the Spirit given them, by whose testimony they are assured that they have been adopted to the hope of eternal salvation.... Hence we may know the nature of faith to be this, that conscience has from the Holy Spirit a sure testimony of the good-will of God towards it, so that resting upon this, it does not hesitate to invoke God as a Father.... The word *know* is made use of to express more fully the assurance of confidence ... that being reconciled to God, and having obtained remission of sins, we know that we have been adopted to the hope of eternal life, and that, being sanctified by the Spirit of regeneration, we are made new creatures, that we may live to God.[28]

Calvin concluded that anyone who believes but lacks the conviction that he is saved by God is not a true believer after all:

> Briefly, he alone is a true believer, who convinced by a firm

---

[22]Inst. 3.2.7.

[23]Inst. 3.2.16; cf. 3.2.42.

[24]*Calvin and English Calvinism to 1649*, p. 19; cf. Inst. 3.2.6, 16, 22.

[25]Inst. 3.2.14.

[26]Inst. 3.2.41. Cf. Balsarek, "Toward an Understanding of Calvin's View of Faith," pp. 40-42, 70-77.

[27]*Commentary* 18:122.   [28]Ibid., 20:112.

conviction that God is a kindly and well-disposed Father toward him, promises himself all things on the basis of his generosity; who, relying upon the promises of divine benevolence toward him, lays hold on an undoubted expectation of salvation. . . . No man is a believer, I say, except him who, leaning upon the assurance of his salvation, confidently triumphs over the devil and death. . . . We cannot otherwise well comprehend the goodness of God unless we gather it from the fruit of great assurance.[29]

True believers must and do know themselves to be such, Calvin said. He wrote:

Let this truth then stand sure — that no one can be called a son of God, who does not know himself to be such. . . .

This so great an assurance, which dares to triumph over the devil, death, sin, and the gates of hell, ought to lodge deep in the hearts of all the godly; for our faith is nothing, except we feel assured that Christ is ours, and that the Father is in him propitious to us.[30]

In exegeting 2 Corinthians 13:5, Calvin even stated that those who doubt their union to Christ are reprobates:

[Paul] declares, that all are *reprobates,* who doubt whether they profess Christ and are a part of His body. Let us, therefore, reckon *that* alone to be right faith, which leads us to repose in safety in the favour of God, with no wavering opinion, but with a firm and steadfast assurance.[31]

That kind of statement prompted a charge of incautiousness against Calvin by William Cunningham and Robert Dabney.[32] A culling of Calvin's *Institutes,* commentaries, and sermons, however, presents a formidable number of equally intense, qualifying statements.

Qualifying Statements

Intermingled with his lofty view of faith, Calvin repeated these themes: unbelief dies hard; assurance is often contested by doubt; severe temptations, wrestlings, and strife are normative; Satan and the flesh assault faith; trust in God is hedged about with fear.[33] Freely Calvin acknowledged that assuring faith is not retained

[29]Inst. 3.2.16.

[30]*Commentary* (on Romans 8:16, 34); Inst. 3.2.2.

[31]*Commentary* 20:397.

[32]Cunningham, *Reformers,* pp. 119ff.; Dabney, *Discussions* 1:216ff., and *Systematic Theology,* pp. 702, 709.

[33]Inst. 3.2.7; *Commentary* (on Matthew 8:25; Luke 2:40).

without a severe struggle against unbelief, nor is it untinged by doubt and anxiety:

> Unbelief is, in all men, always mixed with faith. . . . For unbelief is so deeply rooted in our hearts, and we are so inclined to it, that not without hard struggle is each one able to persuade himself of what all confess with the mouth, namely, that God is faithful. Especially when it comes to reality itself, every man's wavering uncovers hidden weakness. . . .
>
> While we teach that faith ought to be certain and assured, we cannot imagine any certainty that is not tinged with doubt, or any assurance that is not assailed by some anxiety. On the other hand, we say that believers are in perpetual conflict with their own unbelief. . . .
>
> The greatest doubt and trepidation must be mixed up with such wrappings of ignorance, since our heart especially inclines by its own natural instinct toward unbelief. Besides this, there are innumerable and varied temptations that constantly assail us with great violence. But it is especially our conscience itself that, weighed down by a mass of sins, now complains and groans, now accuses itself, now murmurs secretly, now breaks out in open tumult. And so, whether adversities reveal God's wrath, or the conscience finds in itself the proof and ground thereof, thence unbelief obtains weapons and devices to overthrow faith.[34]

According to Calvin, faith ought to be assuring, but no *perfect* assurance exists in this life. Though faith as faith is not mingled with doubt since faith itself cannot doubt, faith is constantly harassed with the temptation of doubt.[35] The Christian strives for, but never wholly attains uninterrupted assurance in this life.

Calvin allowed varying degrees of faith and assurance. He utilized such concepts as "infancy of faith," "beginnings of faith," and "weak faith" more frequently even than Luther.[36] Calvin asserted that assurance is proportional to faith's development. More specifically, he taught that the Spirit is not only the initiator of faith, but also the cause and maintainer of its growth and advancement.[37] For Calvin, faith, repentance, sanctification, and assurance are all progressive.[38] Calvin wrote:

> Restoration does not take place in one moment or one day or one year; but through continual and sometimes slow advances God

[34]Inst. 3.2.4, 15, 17, 20.
[35]Inst. 3.2.18-20.
[36]Cf. Inst. 3.2.17-21; *Commentary* (on Galatians 4:6).
[37]Inst. 3.2.33ff.
[38]Inst. 3.2.14; *Commentary* (on John 2:11; 1 John 5:13).

wipes out in his elect the corruptions of the flesh, consecrates them to himself as temples renewing all their minds to true purity that they may practice repentance throughout their lives and know that this warfare will only end at death.[39]

Calvin claimed that all faith begins in infancy. Hence the cardinal issue at stake is not its degree, but the author of its implantation, for if the Spirit works faith it will be accepted of God. Commenting on John 7:31, Calvin noted: "When the Holy Spirit bestows so honourable a designation on a small spark of good disposition, it ought to encourage us, so as not to doubt that faith, however small it may be, is acceptable to God."[40]

Calvin's views at this juncture were summarized well by his comments on John 2:11:

> The forbearance of Christ is great in reckoning as disciples those whose faith is so small. And indeed this doctrine extends generally to us all; for the faith which is now full grown had at first its infancy, nor is it so perfect in any as not to make it necessary that all to a man should make progress in *believing*. Thus, they who now *believed* may be said to begin to *believe*, so far as they daily make progress towards the end of their faith. Let those who have obtained the first-fruits of faith labour always to make progress.[41]

In expounding John 20:3, Calvin seemed to contradict his former assertion that true believers know themselves to be such when he testified that the disciples had faith without awareness as they approached the empty tomb:

> There being so little faith, or rather almost no faith, both in the disciples and in the women, it is astonishing that they had so great zeal; and, indeed, it is not possible that religious feelings led them to seek Christ. Some seed of faith, therefore, remained in their hearts, but quenched for a time, so that they were not aware of having what they had. Thus the Spirit of God often works in the elect in a secret manner. In short, we must believe that there was some concealed root, from which we see fruit produced. Though this feeling of piety, which they possessed, was confused, and was accompanied by much superstition, still I give to it — though inaccurately — the name of *faith*, because it was only by the doctrine of the Gospel that it was produced, and it had no tendency

[39]Inst. 3.3.9. Stuermann noted that though Calvin was no perfectionist, the idea of growth and development is ubiquitous in his writings ("A Critical Study of Calvin's Concept of Faith," p. 117).
[40]*Commentary* 17:302.
[41]Ibid., pp. 89-90.

but towards Christ. From this seed there at length sprang a true and sincere *faith,* which, leaving the sepulchre, ascended to the heavenly glory of Christ.[42]

How do we make sense of these seeming contradictions in Calvin? How can he say in one breath of many Christians: "They are constrained with miserable anxiety at the same time as they are in doubt whether he will be merciful to them because they confine that very kindness of which they seem utterly persuaded within too narrow limits . . ."— and then promptly proceed to add: "but there is a far different feeling of full assurance that in the Scriptures is always attributed to faith. . ."?[43]

This prompts us to ask: How could Calvin say that assertions of faith are characterized by full assurance, yet still allow for the kind of faith that lacks assurance? The two statements appear antithetical. Assurance is free from doubt, yet not free. It does not hesitate, yet can hesitate; it contains security, but may be beset with anxiety; the faithful have assurance, yet waver and tremble.

Making Sense of Apparent Contradictions

How are these paradoxes resolved? Was Cunningham right in asserting that "Calvin never contradicted himself so plainly and palpably as this [when] in immediate connection with the definition given from him of saving faith, he had made statements, with respect to the condition of the mind that may exist in believers, which cannot well be reconciled with the formal definition"?[44]

Calvin used at least four principles to address this complex issue. Each helps make sense of his apparent contradictions.

Faith and Experience

First, consider Calvin's need to distinguish between *the definition of faith* and *the reality of the believer's experience.* Having explained faith as embracing "great assurance," Calvin addressed this tension as follows:

> Still, someone will say: "Believers *experience* something far different: In recognizing the grace of God toward themselves they are not only tried by disquiet, which often comes upon them, but they are repeatedly shaken by gravest terrors. For so violent are the

[42]Ibid., 18:250; cf. Inst. 3.2.12.
[43]Inst. 3.2.15.
[44]*Reformers,* p. 120.

temptations that trouble their minds as not to seem quite compatible with that certainty of faith." Accordingly, we shall have to solve this difficulty if we wish the above-stated doctrine to stand. Surely, while we teach that faith *ought* to be certain and assured, we cannot imagine any certainty that is not tinged with doubt, or any assurance that is not assailed [emphasis mine].[45]

Later, Calvin returned to this tension: "And I have not forgotten what I have previously said, the memory of which is repeatedly renewed by experience: faith is tossed about by various doubts, so that the minds of the godly are rarely at peace."[46]

Those quotations, and more of like nature (most notably when dealing with how faith is strengthened by the sacraments[47]), indicate that though Calvin was anxious to keep faith and assurance in close proximity by definition, he also recognized that in actual experience the Christian gradually grows into a more full faith in God's promises. This recognition is implicit in Calvin's use of expressions such as "full faith" in God's promises, as though he was distinguishing between the exercise of faith and what he calls "full faith." In short, Calvin distinguished between the "*ought to*" of faith in its essence, and the "*is*" of faith as wrestled out in daily life. Hence he felt free to use the terminology of "right faith" in such an "ought to" context, and also justified defining phenomena by notions of perfection without demeaning the essential concept of growth:

By these words Paul obviously shows that there is no *right faith* except when we dare with tranquil hearts to stand in God's sight. This boldness arises only out of a sure confidence in divine benevolence and salvation. This is so true that the word "faith" is very often used for confidence. . . .[48]

When anything is defined we should . . . seek its very integrity and perfection. Now this is not to deny a place for growth.[49]

Calvin's definition of faith served as a recommendation about how his readers ought "habitually and properly to think of faith."[50] Faith should always aim at full assurance, even though it cannot reach perfect assurance in actual experience. In *principle*, faith gains

[45]Cf. Inst. 3.2.16-17.
[46]Cf. Inst. 3.2.51.
[47]Cf. Inst. 4.14.7. Cf. pp. 50-51 below.
[48]Inst. 3.2.15.
[49]Inst. 3.3.8.
[50]Helm, *Calvin and the Calvinists*, p. 26.

the victory (1 John 5:4); in *practice*, it recognizes that it has not yet fully apprehended (Philippians 3:12-13).

Nevertheless, the practice and experience of faith — weak as it sometimes may be — validates that faith which trusts in the Word. Calvin was not as interested in experiences as he was in validating Word-grounded faith, which in turn affirms the testimony of the Holy Spirit in the believer's heart. Experience confirms faith, Calvin said. Faith "requires full and fixed certainty, such as men are wont to have from things experienced and proved."[51] Both the object of faith and the validation of faith by experience are gifts of God that confirm His graciousness in the fact and experience of the Word.

Thus, bare experience (*nuda experientia*) is not Calvin's goal, but experience grounded in the Word, flowing out of the fulfillment of the Word. Experimental knowledge of the Word is essential.[52] For Calvin, two kinds of knowledge are needed: the knowledge of faith (*scientia fidei*) that is received from the Word, "though it is not yet fully revealed," and the knowledge of experience (*scientia experentiae*) "springing from the fulfilling of the Word."[53]

The Word of God has precedence not only in the former kind of knowledge but also in the latter, for experience teaches us to know God as He declares Himself to be in His Word.[54] Experience not consonant with Scripture is never an experience of true faith. In short, though the believer's experience of true faith is far weaker than he desires, there is an organic unity in the Word between faith's perception (the *ought to* dimension of faith) and experience (the *is* dimension of faith).

Flesh versus Spirit

The second principle by which Calvin helps us comprehend his ought to/is tension in faith is the principle of *flesh versus spirit*. Calvin wrote:

> [Christians] sometimes become dumb as if their faith had been laid low.... In order to understand this, it is necessary to return to that division of flesh and spirit which we have mentioned

[51]Inst. 3.2.15.

[52]Inst. 1.7.5.

[53]Cf. Charles Partee, "Calvin and Experience," *Scottish Journal of Theology* 26 (1973):169-81 and W. Balke, "The Word of God and *Experientia* according to Calvin," in *Calvinus Ecclesiae Doctor* (Kampen: Kok, 1978), pp. 23ff., for Calvin's understanding of experience.

[54]Inst. 1.10.2.

elsewhere. It most clearly reveals itself at this point. Therefore the godly heart feels in itself a division because it is partly imbued with sweetness from its recognition of the divine goodness, partly grieves in bitterness from an awareness of its calamity; partly rests upon the promise of the gospel, partly trembles at the evidence of its own iniquity; partly rejoices at the expectation of life, partly shudders at death. This variation arises from imperfection of faith, since in the course of the present life it never goes so well with us that we are wholly cured of the disease of unbelief and entirely filled and possessed by faith. Hence arise those conflicts, when unbelief, which reposes in the remains of the flesh, rises up to attack the faith that has been inwardly conceived.[55]

Like Luther, Calvin set the ought to/is tension against the back-drop of spirit/flesh warfare.[56] Christians experience this spirit/flesh tension acutely because it is initiated and maintained by the Holy Spirit.[57] The paradoxes that permeate experiential faith (e.g., Romans 7:14-25 in the classical Reformed interpretation) find resolution in this tension: "So then with the mind [spirit] I myself serve the law of God; but with the flesh the law of sin" (v. 25). Hence Calvin wrote:

Nothing prevents believers from being afraid and at the same time possessing the surest consolation. . . . Fear and faith [can] dwell in the same mind. . . . Surely this is so: We ought not to separate Christ from ourselves or ourselves from him. Rather we ought to hold fast bravely with both hands to that fellowship by which he has bound himself to us.[58]

Calvin set the sure consolation of the spirit side-by-side with the imperfection of the flesh, for these are what the believer finds within himself. Since the final victory of the spirit over the flesh is an eschatological hope that will only be fulfilled at Christ's coming again, the Christian finds himself in a perpetual struggle in this life. His spirit fills him "with delight in recognizing the divine good-ness"[59] even as his flesh activates his natural proneness to unbelief.[60] He is beset with "daily struggles of conscience" as long as the

[55]Inst. 3.2.17-18.

[56]Cf. C. A. Hall, *With the Spirit's Sword: The Drama of Spiritual Warfare in the Theology of John Calvin* (Richmond, Va.: John Knox Press, 1970).

[57]Cf. Shepherd, *The Nature and Function of Faith in the Theology of John Calvin*, pp. 24-28.

[58]Inst. 3.2.24.

[59]Inst. 3.2.18.

[60]Inst. 3.2.20.

"vestiges of the flesh" remain.[61] The believer's "present state is far short of the glory of God's children," Calvin confessed. "Physically, we are dust and shadow, and death is always before our eyes. We are exposed to a thousand miseries. . . so that we always find a hell within us."[62] In the regenerate there remains a "disease of concupiscence so that they are tickled and incited either to lust or to avarice or to ambition."[63] While still in the flesh, the believer may even be tempted to doubt the whole gospel.[64]

The reprobate do not have these struggles for they neither love God nor hate sin. They indulge their own desires "without fear of God." But the more sincerely the believer "is devoted to God, he is just so much the more severely disquieted by the sense of his wrath."[65] For Calvin, assurance of God's favor and a sense of His wrath only appear to be contradictory, however. In reality, a reverential spirit of fear and trembling helps to establish faith and to prevent presumption, for fear stems from a proper sense of our unworthiness while confidence arises from God's faithfulness.[66] This spirit/flesh tension keeps the believer from indulging in the flesh and from yielding to despair.[67] The believer's spirit will never utterly despair; rather, faith grows on the very brink of despair. Strife strengthens faith. It makes the believer live circumspectly, not despondently.[68] Heavenly faith rises above all strife, trusting that God will be faithful to His own Word and promises.

Even as the believer is tormented with fleshly doubts, his spirit trusts God's mercy by invoking Him in prayer and by resting upon Him through the sacraments. Especially by prayer and the sacraments, which serve as assistants to assurance, faith gains the upper hand in its struggles with unbelief. "Faith ultimately triumphs over those difficulties which besiege and . . . imperil it."[69] Faith is like "a palm tree [that] strives against every burden and raises itself upward."[70] The hidden root of faith cannot die.[71] The

---

[61]*Commentary* (on John 13:9).
[62]*Commentary* (on 1 John 3:2).
[63]Inst. 3.3.10.
[64]See pp. 22-23 above for similarity to Luther.
[65]*Commentary* (on Psalm 6:6).
[66]Inst. 3.20.11.   [67]Inst. 3.2.17.
[68]Inst. 3.2.22-23.   [69]Inst. 3.2.17.
[70]Ibid.
[71]*Commentary* (on Jonah 2:7; 1 John 3:9).

reign of sin has been overthrown though sin has not been fully eradicated. The least drop of faith is more powerful than unbelief.[72]

Calvin addressed the reality of *prayer* to prove his point:

> When it seems that they will not at all be heard, they nonetheless call upon him. What point would there be in crying out to him if they hoped for no solace from him? Indeed, it would never enter their minds to call upon him if they did not believe that he had prepared help for them. Thus the disciples whom Christ rebuked for the smallness of their faith complained that they were perishing, and yet were imploring his help.[73]

For Calvin, the believer's checkered prayer-life testifies that assurance is anything but constant. When troubled by doubt, the believer calls upon God for deliverance. Though faith is strengthened, this renewed assurance will soon be attacked by doubts again.[74] Prayer is critical as a continual "lifting up of the spirit,"[75] for true prayer proceeds from faith in God's promises. In prayer God is set before the believer as a willing debtor who will act toward him in accord with His Word.[76]

Prayer is reassuring in many other respects. True prayer is a "true proof of their faith," Calvin wrote.[77] Through Spirit-given faith in prayer believers commune with God and feel they are united with Him — not in substance, but in will and purpose. True prayer approaches God with childlike repentance, gaining confidence from the "lovely and soothing" names of God delineated in Scripture.[78] In true prayer God's children are reassured of Christ's intercessions without which their prayers would be rejected.[79] In prayer the believer "beseeches God by the benefits which he has already experienced."[80] In a word, prayer is "the principal exercise of faith."[81]

---

[72]Inst. 3.2.17.

[73]Inst. 3.2.21.

[74]Ibid.

[75]Inst. 3.20.1, 5, 16, 28, 50.

[76]*Sermons of Master John Calvin upon the Fifthe Book of Moses called Deuteronomie*, trans. Arthur Golding (London, 1583), pp. 910ff.

[77]*Sermons of M. John Calvin, on the Epistles of S. Paule to Timothie and Titus*, trans. L. T. (London: G. Bishop and T. Woodcoke, 1579), pp. 135ff. (on 1 Timothy 1:1-2). Cf. Inst. 3.20.3-4; *Commentary* (on Psalm 119:58 and 145:18).

[78]Inst. 3.20.13.

[79]*Commentary* (on Hebrews 7:26).

[80]*Commentary* (on Numbers 14:19).

[81]For Calvin on prayer, see Ronald S. Wallace, *Calvin, Geneva and the Reformation* (Grand Rapids: Baker, 1988), pp. 211-14, and *Calvin's Doctrine of the Christian Life* (Edinburgh: Oliver and Boyd, 1959), pp. 271-95; R. D. Loggie, "Chief Exercise of Faith: An Exposition of Calvin's Doctrine of Prayer," *Hartford Quarterly* 5 (1965):65-81; H. W.

When discussing *the sacraments* as a means of strengthening faith and increasing assurance, Calvin unveiled his pastoral heart. Sacraments are given "to sustain the weakness of our faith."[82] He empathized with believers assaulted with doubts and stooped to the "little in faith." In this context he opposed those who teach that faith is not faith unless it confidently rests on God's mercy:

> We have determined therefore that sacraments are truly named the testimonies of God's grace and are like seals of the good will that he feels toward us, which by attesting that good will to us, sustain, nourish, confirm, and increase our faith.
>
> The reasons which some are accustomed to object against this opinion are too weak and trifling. They say that our faith cannot be made better if it is already good, for it is not faith unless it leans unshaken, firm, and steadfast upon God's mercy. It would have been better for them to pray with the apostles that the Lord increase their faith than confidently to pretend such perfection of faith as no one of the children of men ever attained or ever will attain in this life.
>
> Let them answer what sort of faith they think he had who said, "I believe, O Lord; help thou my unbelief." For that faith, although only begun, was good and could be made better after unbelief was taken away. But they are refuted by no surer argument than their own conscience. For if they confess themselves sinners . . . they must charge it to the imperfection of their own faith.[83]

Maurer, "An Examination of Form and Content in John Calvin's Prayers" (Ph.D. dissertation, Edinburgh, 1960).

[82]Inst. 4.14.1.

[83]Inst. 4.14.7; Calvin's opposition in Inst. 4.14.7 was directed primarily against Zwingli (cf. *Commentary on True and False Religion,* in *Zwingli and Bullinger,* ed. Geoffrey W. Bromiley) who did not allow as much room for the "imperfection" or "weakness" of faith in the believer as either Luther or Calvin. McNeill's notation (Inst., p. 1282n) is reinforced by van der Linde who sees Calvin differing on this from Zwingli "who only recognized the self-conscious, firm faith" (Cornelis Graafland, *De zekerheid van het geloof: Een onderzoek naar de geloofsbeschouwing van enige vertegenwoordigers van reformatie en nadere reformatie* [Wageningen: H. Veenman & Zonen, 1961], pp. 29-30n).

On the relationship of the sacraments to assurance in Calvin, see Inst. 4.14.14; 4.16.32; 4.17.1, 4; *Commentary* (on Genesis 9:12; Exodus 12:43, 48; 24:5; Deuteronomy 30:6; Psalm 42:1; Jeremiah 9:26; Ezekiel 11:24; Amos 5:25; John 20:22; 1 Corinthians 10:3, 16; 11:24, 28; Galatians 3:27, 5:3); *Tracts and Treatises,* trans. Henry Beveridge (Grand Rapids: Eerdmans, 1958), volume 2. Cf. Willem Frederik Dankbaar, *De sacramentsleer van Calvijn* (Leiden: H. J. Paris, 1941), pp. 75ff.; Ronald S. Wallace, *Calvin's Doctrine of Word and Sacrament* (Edinburgh: Oliver and Boyd, 1953), pp. 133ff.; Shepherd, *The Nature and Function of Faith in the Theology of John Calvin,* pp. 207-221; Alexander McNally, "Some Aspects of Thomas Goodwin's Doctrine of Assurance" (Th.M. thesis, Westminster Theological Seminary, 1972), pp. 102-104.

For Calvin the sacraments promote confidence in God's promises and the believer's assurance through Christ's "signified and sealed" redemptive death. Calvin wrote that since the sacraments "are covenants, they contain promises, by which consciences may be roused to an assurance of salvation. Hence it follows, that they are not merely outward signs of profession before men, but are inwardly, too, helps to faith."[84] Moreover, a sacrament "has not respect only to the external confession, but is an intervening pledge between God and the conscience of man."[85] The efficacy and use of baptism and the Lord's Supper are "peace of conscience"[86] and "a special assurance"[87] when the Holy Spirit confirms them to the believer by penetrating his heart and moving his affections to enable him to "see" the Word engraven upon the sacraments. Without the Spirit's action, the sacraments, even as seals, cannot confirm faith.

In short, Calvin teaches that from *the spirit* of the believer rise hope, joy, assurance; from *the flesh*, fear, doubt, disillusionment. Though spirit and flesh operate simultaneously, Calvin maintained that imperfection and doubt are integral only to the flesh, not to faith. The works of the flesh often *attend* faith, but do not *mix* with it. The true believer may lose spiritual battles along the pathway of life, but he will not lose the ultimate war against the flesh. Prayer and the sacraments assist the spirit of faith to gain the ultimate victory.

Germ of Faith versus Consciousness of Faith

Third, despite the tensions between definition and experience, spirit and flesh, Calvin maintained that faith and assurance are not so mixed with unbelief that the believer is left with probability rather than certainty.[88] Calvin escaped the Roman Catholic conclusion of mere probability by teaching that the smallest germ of faith contains assurance in its essence, even when the believer is not always able to grasp this assurance due to a weak consciousness of his faith. Calvin wrote:

> When first even the least drop of faith is instilled in our minds, we begin to contemplate God's face, peaceful and calm and gracious toward us. We see him afar off, but so clearly as to know we are not at

[84]*Commentary* (on 1 Corinthians 11:25).
[85]*Commentary* (on Genesis 17:9).
[86]*Commentary* (on Matthew 3:11; Acts 2:38; 1 Peter 3:21).
[87]*Sermons of M. John Calvin, on the Epistles of S. Paule to Timothie and Titus*, pp. 1061ff.
[88]Cf. Graafland, *Zekerheid van het geloof*, p. 31n.

all deceived.... What a sure and genuine taste of itself even a small drop of faith gives us when [Paul] declares that through the gospel, . . . we behold God's glory with such effect that we are transformed into his very likeness. . . .

Indeed, while [Christ] reproves them for their little faith, he does not cast them out from the ranks of his disciples or count them among unbelievers, but urges them to shake off that fault. Therefore we repeat what we have already stated: that the root of faith can never be torn from the godly breast, but clings so fast to the inmost parts that, however faith seems to be shaken or to bend this way or that, its light is never so extinguished or snuffed out that it does not at least lurk as it were beneath the ashes.[89]

Consequently, the Christian may be tossed about with doubt and perplexity when faith is not in practical exercise, but the seed of faith, implanted by the Spirit, cannot perish. Precisely because it is the Spirit's seed, faith contains and retains the element of assurance. The sense or feeling of assurance increases and decreases in proportion to the rise and decline of faith's exercises, but the seed of faith can never be destroyed. Calvin said, "In the meantime we ought to grasp this: however deficient or weak faith may be in the elect, still, because the Spirit of God is for them the sure guarantee and seal of their adoption (Eph. 1:14; 2 Cor. 1:22), the mark he has engraved can never be erased from their hearts."[90]

Calvin thus explained weak assurance in terms of weak faith without weakening the link between faith and assurance.[91] Assurance is normative, but varies in degree and constancy in the believer's consciousness of it. In responding to weak assurance, according to Calvin, a pastor should not deny the organic tie between faith and assurance but should urge the pursuit of stronger faith through the use of the means of grace and in dependence upon the Holy Spirit.

Taken together, these first three principles, operative in Calvin, allow us to draw several significant conclusions:

First, Calvin's concept of faith includes assurance in the essence and quintessence of faith without demanding that the believer feel assurance at all times. Many Calvin scholars, including William Cunningham, have overlooked that concept. Cunningham stated

---

[89]Inst. 3.2.19-21.

[90]Inst. 3.2.12. In his *Commentary* on Ephesians 3:12 and Colossians 2:2, Calvin used the analogy that as heat and light are related to the sun, so are confidence and assurance related to faith.

[91]Lane, "The Quest for the Historical Calvin," p. 103.

that the only way to remove contradiction from Calvin is to proceed "upon the assumption that the definition was intended not so much to state what was essential to true faith and always found in it, as to describe what true faith is, or includes, in its most perfect condition and its highest exercise."[92] But for Calvin, assurance is both essential for faith and contained in all its exercises, regardless of the believer's consciousness of his assurance.

Second, through this combination of principles, any radical discontinuity between Calvin and the Calvinists with regard to faith and assurance must be rejected. Despite varying emphases, Calvin and the Calvinists agreed that *assurance may be possessed without always being known*. As Peter Lewis explains:

> The difference [between the early Reformers and later Reformed and Puritan theology on assurance] was always one of emphasis rather than of principle. On the one hand, while Calvin maintained that saving faith had within itself confidence and certitude, he also recognized that Christians did often lack assurance [i.e., in personal consciousness] and might begin with various and varying degrees of it. On the other hand, those who differed from him in emphasis and expression — and this includes the English Puritans generally — were yet quite prepared to accept that faith had within itself an essential, germinal assurance that might simply pass unrecognized by the holder of it in his reflections upon his state; for, as they all held, at regeneration the Spirit communicates *himself* with all his powers and graces, and therefore the new-born Christian has within himself the root or seed or germ of all the graces — including, of course, assurance! Thus a bridge always existed uniting the two views. *A man may have assurance and not know that he has it.* . . . Thus the difference in emphasis is circumstantial . . . all sides agreed on the substance of the matter.[93]

Consequently, when Calvin defined faith as embracing assurance, he is not contradicting the Westminster Confession's distinction between faith and assurance, for Calvin and the Confession did not have the same concern in mind. Calvin was defining *faith in its assuring character*; the Confession was describing *what assurance is as a self-conscious, experimental phenomenon*.[94]

---

[92]*Reformers*, p. 120; cf. Gerrit H. Kersten, *Reformed Dogmatics*, vol. 2, trans. J. R. Beeke and J. C. Weststrate (Grand Rapids: Eerdmans, 1983), p. 404.

[93]Peter Lewis cited in Errol Hulse, *The Believer's Experience* (Haywards Heath, Sussex: Carey Pub., 1977), pp. 128-29. Cf. *Commentary* (on John 20:3).

[94]Cf. Sinclair Ferguson, "The Westminster Conference, 1976," *The Banner of Truth*, no. 168 (1977):20, and chapter 6 below.

Third, one area where Calvin and some Calvinists did differ was in how they distinguished degrees of assurance. Some Puritans distinguished "faith in exercise" from "full assurance of faith." Similarly, some Dutch Second Reformation divines distinguished "refuge-taking faith" from "assured faith." Calvin did not use such distinctions, though he was sympathetic to the idea of steps in the knowledge of faith. As Graafland comments:

> Now it is certainly very clear that Calvin did distinguish various steps in faith. The Holy Spirit is not only always the one who works faith in its origin, but He also increases it in its steps until He brings us by faith into the heavenly kingdom. . . . And this development also involves growing in assurance of faith. . . . But on the other hand Calvin also posits that assurance properly belongs to faith from its very origin. . . .
>
> Thus Calvin does not acknowledge a distinction between refuge-taking faith and assured faith. On the contrary, Calvin uses expressions which reject this distinction.[95]

Hence Calvin could assert that God assigns to each believer his "measure of faith"[96]— which obviously allows for degrees in faith — while he simultaneously merged refuge-taking and assuring faith in a statement such as this: Believers "with tranquil confidence nevertheless flee to God for refuge."[97]

Fourth, though Cunningham rightly asserted that Calvin did not work out all the details of the faith-assurance relation, he, Dabney, and Hodge exaggerated when they said Calvin's position is contradictory or ignorant of the issues that would surface in the century to come.[98]

Though the spiritual climate of the seventeenth century would vary considerably from the sixteenth, a thorough study of Calvin on the faith-assurance relationship reveals a tight-knit doctrine that is true to Scripture and experience. Calvin's stress on assurance throughout his *Institutes*, commentaries, and sermons proves that the issue of personal assurance was also very much alive in his generation. Phrases such as "this is how to come to assurance," "this is the kind of assurance we have," and "this is where our assurance

---

[95]*Zekerheid van het geloof*, pp. 40-41.

[96]Inst. 3.2.4.

[97]Inst. 3.2.12.

[98]Cunningham, *Reformers*, p. 120; Dabney, *Systematic Theology*, p. 702 and his *Discussions*, vol. 1, p. 216; Charles Hodge on 2 Corinthians 13:5, *Exposition of 1 and 2 Corinthians* (reprint ed., Wilmington, Del.: Sovereign Grace Pub., 1972), p. 367.

rests,"[99] show that Calvin was speaking to an audience that knew little assurance. Calvin addressed individuals newly delivered from the bondage of Rome, which had taught that assurance was heretical. By teaching that assurance ought to be normative, Calvin aimed to build assurance in the church on solid, biblical grounds. Consequently, he said unbelief is only a disease and an "interruption of faith" that will not have dominion over faith on a daily basis, nor shall it ever triumph ultimately.[100] Rather, God "wishes to cure the disease [of unbelief] so that among us he may obtain full faith in his promises."[101] Because it is of God, faith must triumph, for God will use even doubts and assaults to strengthen faith. Calvin said:

> Thus the godly mind, however strange the ways in which it is vexed and troubled, finally surmounts all difficulties and never allows itself to be deprived of assurance of divine mercy. Rather, all the contentions that try and weary it result in the certainty of this assurance. A proof of this is that while the saints seem to be very greatly pressed by God's vengeance, yet they lay their complaints before him. . . . Thus, if we may judge from the outcome, believers not only emerge safely from every battle, so that, having received fresh strength, they are shortly after ready to descend again into the arena. . . . And our faith will be victor not only in one battle, or a few, or against any particular assault; but, though it be assailed a thousand times, it will prevail over the entire world.[102]

Trinitarian Framework

Through a fourth sweeping principle, namely, *a Trinitarian framework* for the doctrines of faith and assurance, Calvin intended to spur forward believers who are prone to doubt. As surely as the *election* of the Father must prevail over the works of Satan; the *righteousness* of the Son over the sinfulness of the believer; the *assuring witness* of the Spirit over the soul's infirmities — so certainly assured faith shall and must conquer doubt and unbelief.

Calvin's arrangement of Book III reveals the "way" or movement of the grace of faith from God to man and man to God. The grace of faith is from the Father, in the Son, and through the Spirit, by which, in turn, the believer is brought into fellowship with the Son by the Spirit and consequently is reconciled to, and walks in fellowship with, the Father.

---

[99]Inst. 3.2.22. [100]Inst. 3.2.24.
[101]Inst. 3.2.15. [102]Inst. 3.2.21.

For Calvin, a complex set of factors establishes assurance, not the least of which is *the Father's election and preservation* in Christ. Hence Calvin wrote that "predestination duly considered does not shake faith, but rather affords the best confirmation of it,"[103] especially when viewed in the context of calling: "The firmness of our election is joined to our calling [and] is another means of establishing our assurance. For all whom [Christ] receives, the Father is said to have entrusted and committed to Him to keep to eternal life."[104]

The decree of election is a sure foundation for preservation, perseverance,[105] and assurance. This relationship is by no means coldly causal, as Gordon Keddie notes: "Election is never seen, in Calvin, in a purely deterministic light, in which God ... is viewed as 'a frightening idol' of 'mechanistic deterministic causality' and Christian experience is reduced to either cowering passivity or frantic activism, while waiting [for] some 'revelation' of God's hidden decree for one's self. For Calvin, as indeed in Scripture, election does not threaten, but rather undergirds, the certainty of salvation."[106]

The undergirding of the certainty of salvation by election is possible only in a Christ-centered context for Calvin; hence, his constant accent on Christ as the mirror of election "wherein we must, and without self-deception may, contemplate our own election."[107] Election turns the believer's eyes from the hopelessness of meeting

[103]Inst. 3.24.9.

[104]Inst. 3.24.6; cf. Wilhelm Niesel, *The Theology of Calvin*, trans. Harold Knight (reprint ed., Grand Rapids: Baker, 1980), p. 196, for Calvin's strong statement of affirmation in the first edition of his *Institutes*.

[105]Calvin confirmed the indispensable link of perseverance: "We are taught that ... calling and faith are of little account unless perseverance be added" (Inst. 3.24.6). Cf. Berkouwer, who concluded: "The doctrine of perseverance does not intend to be anything more than an expression of the mystery of preservation" (*Faith and Perseverance*, pp. 75-77, 80).

[106]"'Unfallible Certenty of the Pardon of Sinne and Life Everlasting': the Doctrine of Assurance in the Theology of William Perkins," *Evangelical Quarterly* 48 (1976):231; cf. Berkouwer, *Divine Election*, trans. Hugo Bekker (Grand Rapids: Eerdmans, 1960), pp. 10ff.

[107]Inst. 3.24.5; cf. John Calvin, *Sermons on the Epistle to the Ephesians* (reprint ed., Edinburgh: Banner of Truth Trust, 1973), p. 47. Also, see Calvin's sermon on "The Doctrine of Election" in *Sermons from Job* (Grand Rapids: Eerdmans, 1952), pp. 41ff. where he reminded his hearers, "When we inquire about our salvation, we must not begin to say, are we chosen? No, we can never climb so high; we shall be confounded a thousand times, and have our eyes dazzled, before we can come to God's counsel." This kind of question, Calvin asserted, separates what God has joined together, viz., the eternal counsel of God and the grace of Jesus Christ.

Barth (*Church Dogmatics*, vol. II/2, p. 111) and Barthians wrongly think that Calvin

any conditions of salvation to the comfort of Jesus Christ as God's pledge of undeserved love and mercy.[108] Thus, Calvin could proceed from the firmness of election as consolatory to the believer's union with Christ:

> Christ proclaims aloud that he has taken under his protection all whom the Father wishes to be saved. Therefore, if we desire to know whether God cares for our salvation, let us inquire whether he has entrusted us to Christ, whom he has established as the sole Savior of all his people. And if we are still in doubt whether we have been received by Christ into his care and protection, he meets that doubt willingly when he offers himself as shepherd, and declares that we shall be numbered among his flock if we hear his voice. Let us therefore embrace Christ, who is graciously offered to us, and comes to meet us. He will reckon us in his flock and enclose us within his fold.[109]

As Niesel noted, through union with Christ "the assurance of salvation becomes real and effective as the assurance of election" for Calvin.[110] Christ becomes ours in fulfilment of God's determination to redeem and resurrect us. Consequently, we ought not to think of Christ as "standing afar off, and not dwelling in us."[111] Since Christ is for us, to contemplate Him truly is to see Him forming in us what He desires to give us — *Himself* above all. God has made Himself "little in Christ," Calvin stated, so that we might comprehend and flee to Christ alone who can pacify our consciences.[112] Faith must begin, rest, and end in Christ. "True faith is so contained in Christ, that it neither knows, nor desires to know, anything beyond him," Calvin said.[113] Therefore, "we ought not to separate Christ from ourselves or ourselves from him," but ought to participate in Christ by faith, for only this participation "revives us from death to make us a new creature."[114]

---

failed to adequately center upon Christ in election (e.g., J. K. S. Reid, in his introduction to *Concerning the Eternal Predestination of God* [London: James Clarke, 1961], p. 40). But in ibid., p. 56 Calvin asserted that his goal in stressing election in Christ is directly related to assurance. Cf. *CO* 8:318-321; 9:757.

[108]As Chalker noted: "The fact that confidence rests on Christ and not on man is the inevitable corollary of Calvin's strictly Trinitarian understanding of faith" ("Calvin and Some Seventeenth Century English Calvinists," p. 66).

[109]Inst. 3.24.6.

[110]*The Theology of Calvin*, p. 196. Cf. Inst. 3.1.1.

[111]Inst. 3.2.24.

[112]*Commentary* (on 1 Peter 1:21).

[113]*Commentary* (on Ephesians 4:13).

[114]Inst. 3.2.24; *Commentary* (on 1 John 2:12). Cf. Inst. 2.9.3; 3.14.5; 4.17.11.

Union with Christ merges objective and subjective assurance; to look to Christ alone for assurance means also to look to ourselves in Christ as His body. As David Willis-Watkins notes, "It would be entirely hypothetical for faith to focus on ourselves apart from Christ — and it would be entirely hypothetical for faith to focus on Christ apart from his body. . . . Assurance of salvation is a derivative self-knowledge, whose focus remains on Christ as united to his body, the Church of which we are members."[115]

In this Christological manner, Calvin sought to reduce the distance between God's objective decree of election from the believer's subjective lack of assurance that he is elect. For Calvin, election answers, rather than raises the question of assurance. In Christ, the believer "sees" his election; in the gospel, he "hears" of his election.

Nevertheless, Calvin was acutely aware that a person may think that the Father has entrusted him to Christ when such is not the case. It is one thing to affirm Christ's task in salvation as the recipient and guardian of the elect; the center, author, and foundation of election; the guarantee, promise, and mirror of the believer's election and salvation.[116] But it is quite another to know how to inquire about whether a person has been joined to Christ by true faith. Many appear to be Christ's who are strangers to Him. Said Calvin: "It daily happens that those who seemed to be Christ's fall away from him again. . . . Such persons never cleaved to Christ with the heartfelt trust in which certainty of salvation has, I say, been established for us."[117]

Calvin never aimed to console his flock at the expense of discriminatory preaching.[118] Many scholars minimize Calvin's emphasis on the need for a subjective, experiential realization of faith and election by referring to Calvin's practice of approaching his congregation as saved hearers. They misunderstand. Though

[115]"The Third Part of Christian Freedom Misplaced, Being an inquiry into the Lectures of the Late Rev. Samuel Willard on the Assembly's Shorter Catechism," in *Later Calvinism: International Perspectives*, ed. W. Fred Graham (Kirksville, Mo.: Sixteenth Century Journal, 1994), pp. 484-85.

[116]For Calvin's emphasis on election in Christ, and bibliographical sources, see Niesel, *The Theology of Calvin*, p. 93.

[117]Inst. 3.24.7.

[118]Cf. Cornelis Graafland, "'Waarheid in het Binnenste': Geloofszekerheid bij Calvijn en de Nadere Reformatie," in *Een Vaste Burcht*, ed. by K. Exalto (Kampen: Kok, 1989), pp. 65-67.

Calvin exercised a "judgment of charity" with regard to the salvation of church members who maintain a commendable lifestyle,[119] he also frequently asserted that only a minority receive the preached Word with saving faith. He said, "For though all, without exception, to whom God's Word is preached, are taught, yet scarce one in ten so much as tastes it; yea, scarce one in a hundred profits to the extent of being enabled, thereby, to proceed in a right course to the end."[120]

Calvin believed that much which resembles faith lacks a saving character. He thus spoke of unformed faith, implicit faith, the preparation of faith, temporary faith, an illusion of faith, a false show of faith, shadow-types of faith, transitory faith, and faith under a cloak of hypocrisy.[121]

Self-deceit is a real possibility, Calvin said. The reprobate often feel something much like the faith of the elect: "There is a great likeness and affinity between God's elect and those who are given a transitory faith."[122] Consequently, self-examination is essential:

> The Holy Spirit admonishes us that it is not sufficient to suppose men members of the Church because the greater number seem to excel others, just as the chaff lies above the wheat and suffocates it: thus hypocrites bury the sons of God whose number is small. . . . Hence let us learn to examine ourselves, and to search whether those interior marks by which God distinguishes his children from strangers belong to us, viz., the living root of piety and faith.[123]

Happily, the truly saved will be preserved from self-deceit through proper examination directed by the Holy Spirit. Calvin wrote, "In the meantime, the faithful are taught to examine themselves with solicitude and humility, lest carnal security insinuate itself, instead of the assurance of faith."[124]

Foxgrover has shown with many quotations that Calvin saw the need for self-examination in a variety of topics, such as knowledge of

---

[119]Later embodied in the *Canons of Dort*, Head III-IV, Article 15.

[120]*Commentary* (on Psalm 119:101). Calvin referred to the fewness of those who possess vital faith more than thirty times in his *Commentary* (e.g., Acts 11:23 and Psalm 15:1) and nine times within the scope of the Inst. 3.21-3.24.

[121]Inst. 3.2.3, 5, 10-11. For Calvin on temporary faith, see David Foxgrover, "'Temporary Faith' and the Certainty of Salvation," *Calvin Theological Journal* 15 (1980):220-32; Lane, "Calvin's Doctrine of Assurance," pp. 45-46. On unformed faith, see Exalto, *De Zekerheid des Geloofs bij Calvijn*, pp. 15-20, 27-30. On preparation for faith, see Ferguson, "Westminster Conference, 1976," p. 21.

[122]Inst. 3.2.11.

[123]*Commentary* (on Ezekiel 13:9).

[124]Inst. 3.2.7.

God and ourselves, judgment, repentance, confession, affliction, the Lord's Supper, providence, duty, and the kingdom of God.[125]

Even in self-examination, Calvin emphasized Christ. He said we must examine ourselves to see if we are placing our trust in *Christ alone*, for this is the fruit of biblical experience. A. N. S. Lane says that for Calvin self-examination was not so much "Am I *trusting* in Christ?" as it is "Am I trusting in *Christ*?"[126] Self-examination must always direct us with our sins and unrighteousness to Christ and His promise. It must never be done apart from the aid of the Holy Spirit, who alone can shed light upon His own saving work by means of the Word. Apart from Christ, the Word, and the Spirit, said Calvin, "if you contemplate yourself, that is sure damnation."[127]

Thus, Calvin's line of reasoning proceeded like this: The purpose of election embraces salvation. The elect are not chosen for anything in themselves, but only in Christ. Since the elect are in Christ, the assurance of their election and salvation can never be found in themselves apart from Christ, or in the Father apart from Christ. Rather, assurance is found in Christ; hence vital communion with Him is the basis of assurance.[128]

The question remains however: How do the elect enjoy such communion, and how does that produce assurance? Calvin's answer was pneumatological: The *Holy Spirit* applies Christ and His benefits to the hearts and lives of guilty, elect sinners, through which they are assured by saving faith that Christ belongs to them and they to Him. The Holy Spirit confirms within them God's promises in Christ. Thus, personal assurance is never divorced from the election of the Father, the redemption of the Son, the application of the Spirit, and the instrumental means of saving faith.[129]

The Holy Spirit has an enormous role in the application of redemption, Calvin said. As personal comforter, seal, earnest, testimony, security, and anointing, the Holy Spirit bears witness of the believer's gracious adoption:

---

[125]"John Calvin's Understanding of Conscience," pp. 312ff., and "Self-Examination in John Calvin and William Ames," in *Later Calvinism*, ed. W. Fred Graham, pp. 451-69. Cf. J. P. Pelkonen, "The Teaching of John Calvin on the Nature and Function of the Conscience," *Lutheran Quarterly* 21 (1969):24-88.

[126]"Calvin's Doctrine of Assurance," p. 47.

[127]Inst. 3.2.24.

[128]See especially Inst. 3.24.5.

[129]This theme runs throughout Inst. 3.2.

God, by pouring down upon us the heavenly grace of the Spirit, does in this manner, *seal* upon our hearts the certainty of his own word.... For as the Spirit, in bearing witness of our adoption, is our security, and, by confirming the faith of the promises, is the *seal*, so it is on good grounds that he is called an *earnest*, because it is owing to him, that the covenant of God is ratified on both sides, which would, but for this, have hung in suspense.... Hence it is that he has those titles of distinction — the *Anointing*, the *Earnest*, the *Comforter*, and the *Seal*.[130]

Calvin affirmed that the testimony of the Spirit is absolutely essential for personal assurance and adoption: "The Spirit of God gives us such a testimony, that when he is our guide and teacher our spirit is made sure of the adoption of God; for our mind of itself, without the preceding testimony of the Spirit, could not convey to us this assurance."[131]

Calvin has rightly been called the theologian of the Holy Spirit. With respect to the doctrine of assurance, his pneumatological emphasis and balance were profound and ground-breaking. As Letham writes:

Calvin more than anyone else was responsible for the emergence of the doctrine of the internal testimony of the Holy Spirit and for stressing that it was this that was the root cause of all assurance that the Christian enjoyed, whether it be assurance concerning the divine nature and origin of Scripture or certainty in regard to his own adoption and sonship. Not that Calvin retreated into mysticism for at all times he preserved a close connection between the work of the Spirit and the objectivity of the Word. But it was he who brought the pneumatic nature of this assurance into focus.[132]

[130]*Commentary* (on 2 Corinthians 1:21-22). For Calvin, the "enlightening and sealing work of the Spirit in our heart and understanding also belongs to the essence of faith, hence also to the assurance of faith" (Graafland, "Waarheid in het Binnenste," p. 58). Accordingly, the Spirit seals in our hearts "those very promises the certainty of which it has previously impressed upon our minds, and takes the place of a guarantee to confirm and establish them" (*Commentary* on Ephesians 3:12).

Cf. John Calvin, Inst. 3.2.11, 34, 41; *Commentary* (on John 7:37-39; Acts 2:4; 3:8; 5:32; 13:48; 16:14; 23:11; Romans 8:15-17; 1 Corinthians 2:10-13; Galatians 3:2, 4:6; Ephesians 1:13-14, 4:30); *Tracts and Treatises*, vol. 3, pp. 253ff.; J. K. Parratt, "The Witness of the Holy Spirit: Calvin, the Puritans and St. Paul," *Evangelical Quarterly* 41 (1969):161-68; Theo Preiss, *Dass innere Zeugnis des heiligen Geistes* (Zurich, 1947); McNally, "Some Aspects of Thomas Goodwin's Doctrine of Assurance," pp. 16ff.

[131] *Commentary* (on Romans 8:16).

[132]"The Relationship between Saving Faith and Assurance of Salvation," pp. 20-21. For Calvin and the Reformers, the internal testimony of the Holy Spirit (*testimonium internum Spiritus Sancti*) seals to the believer the truth of Scripture. This *testimonium* is

For Calvin, the Holy Spirit's work underlies all assurance of salvation without detracting from the role of Christ, for the Spirit is the Spirit *of Christ* who assures the believer by leading him to Christ and His saving benefits.[133]

The unity of Christ and the Spirit has far-reaching implications for the doctrine of assurance. Most recent scholars minimize Calvin's emphasis on the necessity of the Spirit's work in assuring a believer by God's promises. The *ground* of assurance rests in God's promises, Christ Himself, and/or the Word of God, whereas the *cause* of assurance is said to be the Spirit, who works it in the heart. Cornelis Graafland argues, however, that this distinction is too simplistic, since the Spirit always works as the Spirit *of Christ*. Hence the objective and subjective elements in assurance cannot be so readily separated. They are unified, for the objective salvation in Christ is bound to the subjective sealing by the Spirit. Graafland concludes that "Christ in and through His Spirit is the ground of our faith."[134]

Moreover, for Calvin, a believer's objective reliance upon God's promises as the primary ground for assurance must be subjectively sealed by the Holy Spirit in order to distinguish the reprobate from the elect. For the reprobate may claim God's promises without experiencing the "feeling" (*sensus*) or consciousness of those promises. The Spirit often works in the reprobate, but in an inferior manner. Their minds may be momentarily illumined so that they may seem to have a "beginning of faith"; nevertheless, they "never receive anything but a confused awareness of grace."[135]

On the other hand, the elect are regenerated with incorruptible seed.[136] They receive subjective benefits that the reprobate never taste. They alone receive the promises of God through the Spirit as truth in the inward parts. They alone receive the testimony that can be called "the enlightening of the Spirit." They alone receive experiential, intuitive knowledge of God as He offers Himself to

---

self-authenticating (*Commentary* on 2 Peter 1:16), does not need to be justified by reason (Inst. 1.7.4, 5), and is necessary in order to subjectively receive the truth of Scripture unto salvation. It adds no new revelation or content to the Word; hence, the *testimonium* from the Word and the *testimonium* to personal salvation should not be severed from each other (Exalto, *De Zekerheid des Geloofs bij Calvijn*, p. 33).

[133]Inst. 3.2.34.

[134]"Waarheid in het Binnenste," pp. 58-60.

[135]Inst. 3.2.11.

[136]Inst. 3.2.41.

them in Christ.[137] Through the Spirit's application, the promises are felt in the heart. Spirit-worked faith in the promises of God effects union with Christ.[138] Calvin said the elect alone come to be "wholly kindled to love God"; they are "borne up to heaven itself" and "admitted to the most hidden treasures of God."[139] By the Spirit's internal witness, they alone receive a strong assurance that enables them to cry, "Abba Father!" (Galatians 4:6).[140] Moreover, "the Spirit, strictly speaking, seals forgiveness of sins in the elect alone, so that they apply it by special faith to their own use."[141] The elect alone come to know special faith and a special inward testimony.

According to Heribert Schutzeichel, a Roman Catholic theologian, Calvin's emphasis on *special* faith and a *special* testimony was reminiscent of the Council of Trent's insistence that assurance was always revealed in a special manner.[142] For the Council of Trent, however, assurance is special and rare; for Calvin, assurance is special and normative,[143] for it is part of the essence of faith. For Trent, assurance is separate from the Word; for Calvin, assurance is always bound to the Word. The Spirit's assuring testimony or seal does not add to the Word through some mystical vision or voice;[144] rather, it is accompanied by the Word. The Spirit's seal is a personal testimony, by means of the gospel, that God's promises are particularly for the believer. The promise of the Word becomes special for the elect when the Spirit confirms it within them. Calvin wrote, "Assurance . . . is a thing that is above the capacity of the human mind, it is the part of the Holy Spirit to confirm within us what God promises in his word."[145]

---

[137]Inst. 1.4.1; 2.6.4, 19.

[138]W. Balke, "The Word of God and *Experientia* according to Calvin," p. 26.

[139]Inst. 3.2.41.   [140]Inst. 3.2.11.

[141]Ibid.

[142]*Katholische Beiträge zur Calvinforschung* (Trier: Paulinus-Verlag, 1988).

[143]*Tracts and Treatises* 3:135ff. Eaton pointed out that statements by Calvin such as, "all who do not have the witness of the Holy Spirit ... have no right to be called Christians" (*Commentary* on 2 Corinthians 1:21-22) are in tension with scriptural passages that "point to an experiential sealing *after* faith." Such passages as Ephesians 1:13 and Galatians 3:2 Calvin expounded with some difficulty, even stating on occasion that the term "sealing" may refer to a post-regeneration "bestowal of the gifts of the Spirit" (*Baptism with the Spirit*, p. 49). The resolution of this tension for Calvin is that the sealing of the Spirit from God's side is always the cause of spiritual life, faith, and assurance, but from the believer's side this sealing is an inner work which he cannot always immediately ascertain. Nevertheless, as a general rule, the believer feels assured of the seal of the Spirit (ibid., pp. 44-55).

[144]*Commentary* (on Acts 7:31; 9:15; 23:11).

[145]*Commentary* (on 2 Corinthians 1:22).

The reprobate never experience such assurance, for they never taste the union of the objective truth of God's promise and the subjective sealing of the Spirit.

Ultimately, however, when he distinguished the elect from the reprobate, Calvin said more about what the Spirit does *in us* than what Christ does *for us*, for in the subjective the line of demarcation is sharper. He spoke much of inward experience,[146] of feeling, of enlightenment, of perception, even of "violent emotion." Though fully aware of the dangers of excessive subjectivity, Calvin recognized that the promises of God are sufficient for the believer only when they are brought by the Spirit within the scope, experience, and obedience of faith. That is the substance of Book 3 of the *Institutes*, aptly titled: "The Way in Which We Receive the Grace of Christ: What Benefits Come to Us from It, and what Effects Follow." Calvin wrote in the opening paragraph:

> We must understand that as long as Christ remains outside of us, and we are separated from him, all that he has suffered and done for the salvation of the human race remains useless and of no value for us. Therefore to share with us what he has received from the Father, he had to become ours and to dwell with us.... It is true that we obtain this by faith. Yet since we see that not all indiscriminately embrace that communion with Christ which is offered through the gospel, reason itself teaches us to climb higher and to examine into the secret energy of the Spirit, by which we come to enjoy Christ and all his benefits.[147]

In summary, for Calvin all three members of the Trinity are involved in the believer's assurance of faith. No member of the Trinity detracts from any other. The work of Christ and of the Holy Spirit are complementary. When Calvin replied to Pighius that "Christ is a thousand testimonies to me,"[148] he was saying that Christ is an overwhelming, foundational, and primary source of assurance for him precisely because of the Spirit's application of Christ and His benefits to and within him. Again, when Berkouwer says that Calvin's *Institutes* never tire "of repeating the warning against every attempt at gaining assurance apart from Christ and His cross,"[149] this must be

---

[146]"Too few scholars have been willing to recognize the intensely experiential nature of Calvin's doctrine of faith" (M. Charles Bell, *Calvin and Scottish Theology: The Doctrine of Assurance* [Edinburgh: The Handsel Press, 1985], p. 20).

[147]Inst. 3.1.1; cf Zachman, *Assurance of Faith*, pp. 198-203.

[148]Kendall, *Calvin and English Calvinism*, p. 28, and "Puritan Modification," p. 214.

[149]*Faith and Perseverance*, p. 61.

understood in terms of the work of the Spirit, since no one can ever be assured of Christ without the Spirit.[150] The Holy Spirit reveals to the believer that God is a propitious Father in the promises of His Word and enables him to look to Christ, and so embrace those promises by faith for himself.

By insisting that the Spirit's *primary method* of working assurance is to direct the believer to embrace the promises of God in Christ, Calvin rejected any confidence placed in the believer. Nevertheless, Calvin did not deny that a *subordinate means* to strengthen assurance is provided by the Spirit by His own work within the believer, which bears fruit in good works and various marks of grace. Specifically, the Holy Spirit may assure the believer that he is not reprobate or a temporary believer by revealing to him that he possesses "signs which are sure attestations"[151] of faith, such as "divine calling, illumination by Christ's Spirit, communion with Christ, receiving Christ by faith, the embracing of Christ, perseverance of the faith, the avoidance of self-confidence, and fear."[152] This leads us to consider the question of Calvin and the practical syllogism.

The Practical Syllogism *(syllogismus practicus)*

According to Wilhelm Niesel, Calvin rejected the practical syllogism[153] of later Calvinism, which appeared to abandon early Reformed thought by considering the signs of election apart from Christ. But Niesel was only partly correct. Calvin did not use the practical syllogism in a formal sense, as did later theologians. Rather, he used the principles of the syllogism in a practical sense. Niesel exaggerated the Calvin-Calvinist distinction on both sides. As Peter Lewis stated:

> The difference is not nearly so great as is sometimes supposed. First of all, Calvin said that while the promises and character of God is the first and main ground of assurance and has exclusive

---

[150]Inst. 3.2.35.

[151]Inst. 3.24.4.

[152]Helm, *Calvin and the Calvinists*, p. 28.

[153]Cf. *The Theology of Calvin*, pp. 170-81, and *"Syllogismus practicus?"* in *Aus Theologie und Geschichte der reformierten Kirche* (Neukirchen: K. Moers, 1933), pp. 158-79.

A "practical syllogism" *(syllogismus practicus)* is a conclusion drawn from an action. The basic form of the syllogism when it pertains to salvation is as follows:

Major premise: Those only who do 'x' are saved. Minor premise (practical): But I do 'x'. Conclusion: Therefore I am saved. (Cf. pp. 131-41 below.)

pride of place, yet general sanctification and godliness have a vital and supportive role (*Inst.* 3.14.18-20). On the other hand, the Puritans, while stressing the evidential value of sanctification and good works, roundly declared with Calvin that the prime place in assurance was to be given to the character and promises of God. Only after and under this was the evidential value of good works of value.[154]

Despite what Niesel and others said,[155] Calvin affirmed the type of assurance that flows out of the application of Christ's work and the hearing of the gospel.[156] Indeed, Calvin did not hesitate at times to explain assurance in a way that resembled the practical syllogism. He wrote:

> Therefore, as it is wrong to make the force of election contingent upon faith in the gospel, by which we feel that it appertains to us, so we shall be following the best order if, in seeking the certitude of our election, we cling to those latter signs which are sure attestation of it.[157]

Calvin went on to write:

> A conscience so founded, erected, and established is established also in the consideration of works, so far, that is, as these are testimonies of God dwelling and ruling in us. Inasmuch, therefore, as this reliance upon works has no place unless you first cast the whole confidence of your mind upon God's mercy, it ought not to seem contrary to that upon which it depends. Therefore, when we rule out reliance upon works, we mean only this: that the Christian

---

[154]Peter Lewis, cited in Errol Hulse, *The Believer's Experience*, p. 129, where Lewis lists Bridge, Sharpe, Sibbes, Goodwin, and Ames for support.

[155]For opinions on whether Calvin held to the *syllogismus practicus*, see Karl Barth, *Church Dogmatics*, ed. Geoffrey W. Bromiley and Thomas F. Torrance (Edinburgh: T. & T. Clark, 1942), vol. II/2, pp. 335ff.; Heinz Otten, *Calvins theologische anschauung von der prädestination* (München: Kaiser, 1938), pp. 54ff.; G. Oorthuys, "De beteekenis van het nieuwe leven voor de zekerheid des geloofs, volgens Calvijns Institutie," *Onder Eigen Vaandel* 13 (1938):264-65; Graafland, *De zekerheid van het geloof*, pp. 106-112, and "Van syllogismus practicus naar syllogismus mysticus," in *Wegen en Gestalten in het Gereformeerd Protestantisme*, ed. W. Balke, C. Graafland, and H. Harkema (Amsterdam: Ton Bolland, 1976), pp. 105-122; Berkouwer, *Divine Election*, pp. 287ff.; Ronald S. Wallace, *Calvin's Doctrine of the Christian Life* (Edinburgh: Oliver & Boyd, 1959), pp. 301-302; Fred Klooster, *Calvin's Doctrine of Predestination*, 2nd ed. (Grand Rapids: Baker, 1977), pp. 50-51; Marion W. Conditt, *More Acceptable than Sacrifice: Ethics and Election as Obedience to God's Will in the Theology of Calvin* (Basel: Friedrich Reinhardt Kommissionsverlag, 1973), pp. 106-113; David N. Wiley, "Calvin's Doctrine of Predestination: His Principal Soteriological and Polemical Doctrine" (Ph.D. dissertation, Duke University, 1971), pp. 3-4; Werner Krusche, *Das Wirken des Heiligen Geistes nach Calvin* (Göttingen: Vandenhoeck & Ruprecht, 1957), pp. 246ff; Schaefer, "The Spiritual Brotherhood of the Heart," pp. 120-124.

[156]Inst. 3.24.1-6.   [157]Inst. 3.24.4.

mind may not be turned back to the merit of works as to a help
toward salvation but should rely wholly on the free promise of
righteousness. But we do not forbid him from undergirding and
strengthening this faith by signs of the divine benevolence toward
him. For if, when all the gifts God has bestowed upon us are called
to mind, they are like rays of the divine countenance by which we
are illumined to contemplate that supreme light of goodness; much
more is this true of the grace of good works, which shows that the
Spirit of adoption has been given to us.[158]

Calvin further taught that the Spirit of adoption produced
evidences of grace. In commenting on Galatians 4:6, he wrote:

Adoption by God precedes the testimony of adoption given by the
Holy Spirit but the effect is the sign of the cause. And you dare to
call God your Father only by the instigation and incitement of the
Spirit of Christ. Therefore it is certain that you are the sons of God.
This means, as he often teaches elsewhere, that the Spirit is the
earnest and pledge of our adoption, so that we are surely convinced
of God's fatherly attitude towards us.[159]

Though Calvin was not as dependent on syllogistic reasoning as
most of his successors, he did, as William Bouwsma points out,[160] use
the Scholastic *quaestio* or direct syllogistic reasoning. Calvin wrote:

Let believers exercise themselves in constant meditation upon the
benefits of God, that they may encourage and confirm hope for the
future and always ponder in their mind this syllogism: God does
not forsake the work which His own hands have begun, as the
Prophet bears witness (Is. 64:8). We are the work of his hands.
Therefore he will complete what he has begun in us.[161]

Calvin implied that good works served an *a posteriori* role in the
cultivation of assurance of salvation by acknowledging that good
works strengthened faith and were evidence of election.[162] However,
he regarded the method of Spirit-worked reflection upon the

---

[158]Inst. 3.14.18; for more on the role of conscience, see Inst. 3.2.12 and 3.2.16, as
well as *Commentary* (on 2 Peter 1:10); Foxgrover, "John Calvin's Understanding of
Conscience," pp. 87-443; Zachman, *Assurance of Faith*, pp. 198-203.

[159]*Commentary* 21:120. Cf. Zachman, *Assurance of Faith*, pp. 204-223.

[160]*John Calvin: A Sixteenth Century Portrait* (New York: Oxford University Press,
1988), p. 102.

[161]*Commentary* (on Philippians 1:6). Cf. Calvin's subsequent comments on being
assured of the salvation of others "in so far as the grace of God shews itself in them so
that we come to know it." Calvin added, however, that for ourselves these evidences of
fruits must be coupled with the witnessing of the Spirit.

[162]Inst. 3.14.18; 3.24.4.

believer's graces an inferior sign of election. He wrote, "We do not deny that newness of life, as the effect of divine adoption, serves to confirm confidence, but as a secondary support."[163]

Kendall rightly assessed that position in stating: "To the degree that our obedience confirms our adoption, 'experimental knowledge' may give 'subsidiary aid to its confirmation.' But such fruits can only give comfort *a posteriori*. 'Love,' then, may serve as an 'inferior' aid, a 'prop to our faith.'"[164]

Furthermore, this "secondary support" is highly beneficial for the "further establishment" of assurance.[165] As Ronald Wallace noted:

> There is a state of assured "integrity of conscience" which we can be helped to attain by the signs of divine favour towards us that are manifested in our own good works. Our assurance . . . can be "further established" when we review ourselves before God and find evidence of God's dwelling and reigning within us in the works he has enabled us to do. Purity of life can be to us a true evidence and proof of election, for the righteousness which God gives us does not always remain buried in our hearts and our newness of life is testified by good works.[166]

In one sense, the secondary role of works can be regarded as essential, since Calvin taught that justification (the ground of assurance) and sanctification (the support of assurance) are inseparable. Though justification does not depend on works, the justified will do good works.[167] Gordon Rupp wrote:

> For if Calvin distinguishes theologically between justification and sanctification, they cannot be distinguished or separated in experience. "As Christ cannot be divided into two parts so the two things justification and sanctification which we perceive to be united together in Him cannot be separated. Whomsoever therefore God receives into His favour, He presents with the spirit of adoption, whose agency forms them anew into His image.[168]

For Calvin, the covenant included both an unconditional and

---

[163]*Commentary* (on 1 John 4:17).

[164]*Calvin and English Calvinism to 1649*, p. 28.

[165]*Commentary* (on 2 Peter 1:10). Cf. *CO* 55:450.

[166]*Calvin's Doctrine of the Christian Life*, p. 301. Cf. Inst. 3.14.18-19; *Commentary* (on 2 Peter 1:10; 1 John 3:7).

[167]Inst. 3.14.18; *Commentary* (on 1 John 3:22).

[168]"Patterns of Salvation in the First Age of the Reformation," *Archiv für Reformationsgeschichte* 57 (1966):63.

conditional aspect.[169] Recent scholars have failed to see that. But as James Veninga explained:

> The mutual nature of the covenant means that unless the covenant member lives a life of holiness his "malice shall cut off the course of God's goodness" (*Sermons on Deuteronomy* 1:34-40, pp. 42ff.). Likewise, Calvin states ". . . think not but that your God can drive you out of his heart and out of his church, if he find you unworthy of the benefit which he has offered to you" (*Sermons on Deuteronomy* 7:7-10, pp. 315ff.) . . . . Since fear remains in the life of the covenant member, the individual experience of faith cannot alone suffice in granting assurance of election. The believer is thrown back into the realm of morality in order to gain certainty of his election. If he fails in this realm, he must come to recognize that his original experience of faith, however real it may have seemed, was only a shadow of that which the elect experience. Calvin's emphasis on the necessity of morality does not deny the doctrine that one is justified by faith alone, since Calvin is convinced that good works in no way are involved in the process by which one obtains salvation. Obedience follows the experience of faith through the work of the Holy Spirit and the law. The point that is being made is that obedience becomes a criterion for determining whether one has obtained forgiveness of sins. Justification without sanctification is impossible; therefore the life that is lived obediently serves as a sign that justification has occurred, and that the individual is indeed a recipient of God's particular election.[170]

Veninga was largely correct, although he should have stressed that the goal of the believer is not to examine his works in themselves[171] but to observe the Spirit's works of grace in his life. The former offer no grounds of rest; the latter provide peace of conscience in Christ. For Christ fulfils the condition of sanctification through making the believer a partaker of His righteousness. Hence the promises and saving works of God in Christ remain primary for Calvin.

---

[169]See Anthony A. Hoekema, "The Covenant of Grace in Calvin's Teaching," *Calvin Theological Journal* 2 (1967):144ff.; Lane, "Calvin's Doctrine of Assurance," pp. 40-42, who argues that "it can be said Calvin likewise has a doctrine of 'double assurance' to accommodate the biblical teaching on assurance through works." Letham dissents from Hoekema ("Saving Faith and Assurance in Reformed Theology," 2:64). Everett H. Emerson, "Calvin and Covenant Theology," *Church History* 25 (1956):136-44, who argues for continuity between Calvin and later covenant theologians in contrast to Perry Miller, *Errand into the Wilderness* (Cambridge: Belknap Press, 1956), pp. 51ff. Cf. Peter Lillback, "The Binding of God: Calvin's Role in the Development of Covenant Theology" (Ph.D. dissertation, Westminster Theological Seminary, 1985).

[170]"Covenant Theology and Ethics in the Thought of John Calvin and John Preston" (Ph.D. dissertation, 1974), pp. 170-71.

[171]This will only produce reasons for condemnation (*Commentary* on Jeremiah 14:7).

Calvin did not deny the practical syllogism so much as warn against its misuse and misinterpretation.[172] The real issue, then, is what form the practical syllogism took within the systems of Calvin and the Calvinists and what that implied for both doctrine and life. In Calvin's theology, the occasional syllogism did not detract from Christ. The marks of grace in believers only proved that believers were joined to Christ, since no one could be obedient apart from Him. For Calvin, works pointed to all of Christ's work and led to "the confession that Christ, after He has redeemed us by his blood, also renews us after his own image by his Holy Spirit, that our whole life may show ourselves thankful for his benefits."[173] No reference can be made to the works of sanctification apart from faith in Christ because Christ, faith, and godly piety are inseparable.[174] As Calvin wrote: "Since Christ cannot be known apart from the sanctification of the Spirit, it follows that faith can in no wise be separated from a devout disposition."[175]

Calvin thus said that though works can never save us, they can help assure us if they are set in the context of the election of the Father, the redemption of Christ, the sanctification of the Spirit, and the exercise of saving faith.[176] Works then strengthen assurance, for we receive an inner conviction that we "look not so much on our works as upon [God's] grace in our works."[177]

In discussing Calvin's view of the practical syllogism, Karl Barth rightly stated that the Reformer made it dependent on the following conditions:

> First, the testimony of "works" must not take the first place and assume the role of a crown witness. . . . Secondly, the testimony of "works" must not be separated from faith. . . . And thirdly, the testimony of "works" must not be detached from the self-testimony of Christ, from the promise of the forgiveness of sins, or in general from the objective Word of God. . . .[178]

Barth said that Calvin's practical syllogism does not lead away from Christ; rather, when Calvin spoke of the role of works in assurance, he was preeminently concerned with the human "act and behavior

---

[172]Muller, *Christ and the Decree*, p. 25.
[173]Inst. 3.2.38-39.
[174]Inst. 3.2.38; 3.15.1-7; 3.14.9, 16.
[175]Inst. 3.2.8.
[176]*Commentary* (on 1 John 2:12).
[177]*Commentary* (on Hebrews 6:10).
[178]*Church Dogmatics*, vol. II/2, pp. 335ff.

in which man comes to rest in Christ as the only foundation."[179] In his *Commentary* on 1 John 2:3, Calvin presented a rather complicated instance of such syllogistic reasoning. He wrote:

> Obedience is so connected with knowledge, that the last is yet in order the first, as the cause is necessarily before its effect.... But we are not hence to conclude that faith recumbs on works; for though every one receives a testimony to his faith from his works, yet it does not follow that it is founded on them, since they are added as an evidence. Then the certainty of faith depends on the grace of Christ alone; but piety and holiness of life distinguish true faith from that knowledge of God which is fictitious and dead; for the truth is, that those who are in Christ, as Paul says, have put off the old man.[180]

In conclusion, if and when the practical syllogism (1) is treated as a primary ground of assurance, (2) is separated from the trinitarian framework of grace, or (3) is divorced from saving faith, its conclusions are far from assuring.[181] As Muller noted:

> It is in and through Christ that the connection may be drawn between election and calling, calling and faith, faith and sanctification, sanctification and assurance. The connection between sanctification and assurance, moreover, does not represent pridefulness or an overemphasis on works: "... on the contrary, those who prove that their calling is sure by their good works are in no danger of falling, because the grace of God by which they are supported is a sure foundation" [*Commentary* on II Pet. 1:12]. In calling, in faith, in sanctification, in the works of the regenerate life we see God's grace in Christ, Christ the mirror of election and the foundation of assurance. The works by which we gain assurance are ultimately the work of Christ in us, the proximate end of election [i. e., sanctification].[182]

Calvin thus implicitly and practically approved the practical syllogism within the context of *sola scriptura*,[183] *sola fide, sola gratia, solus Christus, soli Deo gloria*. Without all such principles, the concept becomes a curse instead of a blessing. That's because, at best, works serve as an adjunct to faith in Christ. They are the consequence, not

[179]Ibid., pp. 369-70; cf. Berkouwer, *Divine Election*, p. 290.

[180]*Commentary* 22:174-75.

[181]Inst. 3.2.23, 38; and much of Calvin's *Commentary* on 1 John (especially 2:12; 2:23; 3:19, and ch. 4).

[182]"Predestination and Christology in Sixteenth-Century Reformed Theology," pp. 93-94.

[183]Inst. 3.2.28-29; Graafland, *De zekerheid van het geloof*, pp. 31-39.

the precondition of salvation. The believer is not saved by works but demonstrates his salvation by works.

Good works are not the ground of *salvation*, but they do form a secondary ground of *assurance*. The practical syllogism may never push aside the ground of assurance in God's promises; it must always retain a supporting role. Otherwise, certainty will be replaced with uncertainty. In Calvin we thus find "the germs of future Puritanism."[184]

Theodore Beza (1519-1605)

Theodore Beza was only ten years younger than Calvin, but he outlived Calvin by forty-one years and can thus be classified as a third-generation Reformer.[185] Beza's background, personality, and experience differed significantly from Calvin's, but they shared the same pastoral concerns,[186] soteriological dynamics, and Christological emphases.[187] By the time Beza died in 1605 at the age of eighty-six, his influence had penetrated throughout Europe.[188] Having outlived by several decades all of the early Reformers, Beza represented a vital "link between the turbulent era of Calvin and Melanchthon and the

---

[184]Wendel, *Calvin*, p. 276.

[185]For brief summaries of Beza's life, theology, and influence, see Raitt, "Theodore Beza," *Shapers of Religious Traditions*, pp. 89-104; and Steinmetz, *Reformers in the Wings*, pp. 162-74. For larger works, see Friedrich Schlosser, *Leben des Theodor de Beza und des Peter Martyr Vermigli* (Heidelberg: Mohr und Zimmer, 1809); Johann Wilhelm Baum, *Theodor Beza*, 2 vols. (Leipzig: Weidmann'sche Buchhandlung, 1843-51); Heinrich Heppe, *Theodor Beza: Leben und ausgewahlte Schriften* (Elberfeld: R. L. Friedrichs, 1861); H. M. Baird, *Theodore Beza: the Counsellor of the French Reformation, 1519-1605* (New York: G. P. Putnam's Sons, 1899); Johannes Dantine, "Die prädestinationslehre bei Calvin und Beza" (Ph.D. dissertation, Göttingen University, 1965); Walter Kickel, *Vernunft und offenbarung bei Theodor Beza* (Neukirchen-Vluyn: Neukirchener Verlag des Erziehungsvereings, 1967); Raitt, *The Eucharistic Theology of Theodore Beza: Development of the Reformed Doctrine* (1972); Bray, *Theodore Beza's Doctrine of Predestination* (1975); Tadataka Maruyama, *The Ecclesiology of Theodore Beza* (Geneve: Librairie Droz, 1978); Ian McPhee, "Conserver or Transformer of Calvin's Theology? A Study of the Origins and Development of Theodore Beza's Thought, 1550-1570," 2 vols. (Ph.D. dissertation, University of Cambridge, 1979).

[186]Cf. repeated references in Baird, for the typical pastoral concern of Beza as illustrated in his last words: "Is the city in full safety and quiet?"

[187]Cf. Muller, *Christ and the Decree*, pp. 79-96, for Beza's soteriological and Christological emphases.

[188]For his influence in England, see O. T. Hargrave, "The Doctrine of Predestination in the English Reformation" (Ph.D. dissertation, Vanderbilt University, 1966), p. 204; in the Netherlands, see Graafland, *Zekerheid van het geloof*, p. 61.

new age of Protestant Orthodoxy."[189] After a brief summary of Beza's views on the doctrines of faith and assurance, I will explain how Beza and Calvin differ on the grounds of assurance.

Comparison with Calvin

Generally speaking, Beza was unconditionally supportive of Calvin's theology. But Beza went on to develop a more pervasive Trinitarian framework for Calvin's Christocentricity.[190]

Beza was willing to go beyond Calvin in theological issues, such as supralapsarianism and secondary evidences in assurance, partly because he was more of a rationalist than Calvin. But much of Beza's innovation was also due to his historical context, which demanded explanations of predestination and assurance beyond those given by Calvin. Beza said that his primary concern in dealing with predestination was to foster assurance in the believer.[191]

On the doctrine of faith, Beza and Calvin substantially agree, with the major exception being Beza's presentation of the elements in faith: knowledge (*notitia*), assent (*assensus*), and trust (*fiducia*). In his *Quaestionum et responsionum christianarum libellus*, Beza defined faith as follows:

> The faith by which the sons of light are distinguished from the sons of darkness is not simply that which we call knowledge which is

[189]Steinmetz, *Reformers in the Wings*, p. 170.

[190]Beza's one slip in minimizing Christ-centeredness is to be found in his *Tabula* chart of the order of causes of salvation and damnation. The accompanying commentary, however, corrects this lack. The commentary was first translated into English by William Whittingham as *A Brief Declaration of the Chief Points of Religion* (London: David Moptid and Iohn Mather, 1575), but is more readily available in a subsequent translation of John Stockwood as *The Treasure of Trueth, Touching the grounde works of man his salvation, and Chiefest Points of Christian Religion* (London: Thomas Woodcocke, 1576). Unfortunately, most contemporary scholars do not go beyond the *Tabula* chart in research nor acknowledge that Calvin gave approval for the publication of the chart.

William Perkins's chart, attached to his *The Golden Chain* and based on Beza's *Tabula*, includes a center Christological column which bears direct relationship to every step of grace in the life of the believer. Cf. Ian Breward, ed., *The Work of William Perkins*, vol. 3 in The Courtenay Library of Reformation Classics (Abingdon: Sutton Courtenay Press, 1970), p. 168.

[191]Historians such as Bizer blame Beza (particularly in his *Tabula praedestinationis*, 1555) for introducing a rationalistic spirit into the Reformed faith as well as for moving the doctrine of predestination out of soteriology where Calvin had placed it and into the doctrine of God where it became a necessary corollary of divine sovereignty. Muller defends Beza on both issues, showing that Beza did not formulate a "necessitarian system" based exclusively on predestination, but remained true to the essential nature of Calvin's theology (*Christ and the Decree*, pp. 82, 95, 96).

common even to the demons, by which one might know to be true whatever is contained in the writings of the prophets and the apostles, but besides that a firm assent of the soul accompanies this knowledge by which the person is able to apply to himself as his own the promise of eternal life in Christ, just as if it was now fully his and he possessed the thing itself.[192]

That statement, along with subsequent descriptions by Beza,[193] show that Calvin and Beza differed somewhat on the understanding of each element of faith.

For Calvin, faith *is* knowledge — saving, supernatural knowledge; for Beza, the element of knowledge is not enough because some knowledge is only historical knowledge, which even devils possess. Beza stressed the danger of possessing only historical knowledge, which is the shell, not the kernel, of faith. But Beza also said that certain and assuring knowledge is organically related to saving faith. Through "certain knowledge" applied to the heart by the Holy Spirit, the believer may be assured of his election.[194] Compared to Calvin, Beza downgraded knowledge as an element of faith. That was reflected in Beza's increased tendency to examine the authenticity of faith by looking within one's own heart and life rather than only toward the promise and Word of God. Still, Calvin and Beza differed only in emphasis, for like Calvin, Beza also taught that God's Word and promises in Jesus Christ are central to faith and assurance.[195]

As for assent (*assensus*), Calvin incorporated that into knowledge and trust, whereas Beza explained it as the essence of faith. For Beza, faith was knowledge plus saving assent. In assent, therefore, the believer is persuaded that the promises of salvation belong particularly to him. Through Spirit-worked assent, the believer applies Christ to himself and is certain of his election.[196] For Beza,

---

[192]*Theodori Bezae Vezelii Volumen primum (-tertium) Tractationum Theologicarum*, 2nd ed. (Genevae: apud Eustathium Vignon, 1582), 1:678. [Hereafter, *Tractationes Theologicae*.]

[193]Ibid., and 3:405.

[194]*A briefe and pithie summe of Christian faith made in forme of a Confession*, trans. R(obert) F(yll) (London: Roger Ward, 1639), p. 19.

[195]*Tractationes Theologicae* 1:175.

[196]*Jesu Christi domini nostri novum testamentum, sive novum foedus; cuius graeco contextui respondent interpretationes duae Theodori Bezae*, accessit etiam Joachimi Camerarii in Novum foedus commentarius (Cantabrigiae: Roger Daniel, 1642), on Romans 1:17. [Hereafter, *Novum Testamentum*]. Cf. *Tractationes Theologicae* 1:186, 678; *Theses Theologicae* (London: Mosem Pitt, 1683), p. 250.

the believer's appropriation of the promises of God results from the assent that these promises are true.[197]

While Calvin's view of trust included assent, Beza's view enclosed trust within assent so that through trusting assent the believer comes to own the promise of eternal life. Ludovico LeBlanc said Beza did not regard trust as a necessary element of saving faith but as an effect of faith inseparably joined to it.[198] At times Beza did write as if trust were not intrinsic to faith, but at other times he clearly included it under the umbrella of assent. For Beza believed that assent properly belongs to the heart of faith. That coincided with his view that faith is properly an act of the *will*,[199] for ultimately the will must surrender to the promise of God in Jesus Christ.

Calvin's emphasis on faith as knowledge led him to accent faith as trustful *understanding*. That, in turn, allowed Calvin to regard the object of faith as the entire Word of God. By contrast, Beza's accent on assent and the will confined faith's object largely to the promise of eternal life in Christ.[200] Practically speaking, Beza appeared to lean toward the voluntarism Calvin was careful to avoid; nevertheless, Beza defused this danger by stressing that only God's grace can prompt the initial and renewed surrendering of the will.[201]

The Grounds of Assurance[202]

Like Calvin and the Westminster Assembly, Beza addressed three means of assurance: the promise of the gospel in Jesus Christ, the

---

[197]*Tractationes Theologicae* 3:405.

[198]*Theses Theologicae*, p. 220. Cf. Kendall's quotation of Beza, *Calvin and English Calvinism*, p. 34n.

[199]Graafland, *Zekerheid van het geloof*, pp. 64ff. Beza also writes of faith as located in the heart (*cor*), the mind (*mens*), and the soul (*animus*) (*Confessio*, p. 19; *Tractationes Theologicae* 1:185-86; *Novum Testamentum* on Romans 1:17).

[200]Letham points out that though Beza did speak of the Word of God as the object of faith (cf. *Tractationes Theologicae* 1:200; *Novum Testamentum* on John 16:20 and Romans 1:17), he usually stressed Christ as the object of faith (cf. *Tractationes Theologicae* 1:186, 684; *Theses Theologicae*, pp. 55-56, 144, 250; *Novum Testamentum* on John 16:20, Acts 6:8, and Romans 4:25) ("Saving Faith and Assurance in Reformed Theology," 1:153, 2:84n).

[201]Contra Kendall who admits that Beza taught "if a man believes at all — indeed, that his will is moved to seek after God — is only to be explained in terms of God's enabling grace," but then concludes that Beza plants the "seed of voluntarism" in the following: "Q. And they which have this fayth, are they saved? Yea of necessitie, for God hath given his sonne to the ende that every one which believeth in him, should have life everlasting: and he is not a lyer" (*Calvin and English Calvinism*, p. 34).

[202]For the distinction between grounds of *assurance* and grounds of *salvation*, see Helm, *Calvin and the Calvinists*, p. 28.

internal witness of the Holy Spirit, and sanctification. In his *Tabula*, Beza explained that the believer gains assurance by heeding the call of God "to Christ the only mediator," by obeying "the Spirit of adoption" within, and by feeling the inward working of the Spirit which produces sanctification and good works.[203]

On the primary ground of assurance, the promise of the gospel in Jesus Christ, Beza differed little from Calvin. "Faith in Jesus Christ is a sure witness of our election," Beza wrote.[204] He added for the sake of believers not beset with overwhelming trials: "We receive assurance of election from Christ himself rather than from the secondary causes of salvation."[205] Beza did insist more strongly than Calvin that the promise of Christ must be appropriated by the believer to realize its comfort, for the believer must "apply Christ" to himself.[206] Beza also considered it insufficient to believe with the mind that Jesus Christ came to save sinners. Therefore, when Beza spoke of "a certain knowledge," he was referring to a particular application of Christ to the believer's soul.[207] Beza defined true faith as a "stedfast assent of the mind" whereby "eche man applieth particularly to himself, the promise of everlasting life in Christ."[208] In *Summa totius Christianismi*, Beza said this personal application of Christ by faith prompts personal assurance of salvation and election: "[That] which is proper and peculiar to the elect, in which he rests, is such that when Christ is universally and freely offered, we apply this to ourselves just as if it were ours, and thereby we are rendered more certain of our election each time we do so."[209]

Nevertheless, Beza said believers of weak faith do not reap assurance of salvation, because they are unable to answer the question, "How may I know that I have been elected?" In this Beza differed from Calvin by upgrading the external testimony of sanctification and the internal testimony of the Spirit as two pillars upon which assurance rests as firmly as on the applied promise of God in Christ. Graafland explained Beza's position this way:

---

[203]*Treasure of Trueth*, p. 2.

[204]*Novum Testamentum* on John 6:37.

[205]*Tractationes Theologicae* 1:175.

[206]*A briefe and pithie summe*, p. 15.

[207]*A booke of Christian Questions and answers. Wherein are set foorth the cheef points of the Christian religion*, trans. Arthur Golding (London: William Horn, for Abraham Veale, 1574), pp. 23-24.

[208]Ibid.

[209]*Tractationes Theologicae* 1:186.

To these acts Beza reckons, in the very first place, sanctification, which is begun in us and consists of a hatred of sin and a love for righteousness. Secondly, Beza speaks of the witness of the Holy Spirit, which encourages my conscience. It appears that these two acts of the Spirit are so clearly recognizable that they can form a ground which enables us to ascertain and be assured of our faith and election. For election, which from eternity lay in the secret of God, is subsequently explained to us, partly by the internal witness of the Holy Spirit within us, which witness is bound to the external preaching, and partly by the power and work of the same Spirit who, having freed the elect from the slavery of sin, leads them to begin to will and to perform those things which are of God.[210]

Beza so accented this first testimony of sanctification that one might conclude that the first testimony was more important than the second, namely the witness of the Spirit. As he wrote in *A briefe and pithie summe*:

When Satan putteth us in doubt of our election, we may not search first the resolution in the eternal counsel of God, whose majesty we cannot comprehend, but on the contrary we must begin at the sanctification which we feel in ourselves to ascend up more higher, for as much as our sanctification, from whence proceedeth good works, is a certain effect of the faith, or rather of Jesus Christ dwelling in us by faith. . . . Sanctification, with the fruits thereof, is the first step or degree whereby we begin to ascend up to the first and true cause of our salvation, to wit, of our free eternal election.[211]

Or, in *A booke of Christian Questions and answers*:

But whither may I flee for succor in the perilous temptations of particular election? Ans. Unto the effects whereby the spiritual life is certainly discerned, and so consequently our election, like as the life of the body is perceived by feeling and moving . . . that I am chosen, I shall perceive first by that holiness or sanctification begun in me, that is to say my hating of sin and by my loving of righteousness. Hereunto I shall add the witness of the Holy Ghost comforting my conscience. Upon this sanctification and comfort of the Holy Ghost, we gather faith. And thereby we rise up unto Christ, to whom whosoever is given, is of necessity chosen in Him from afore all worlds.[212]

---

[210]*De zekerheid van het geloof,* p. 69. Consequently, Beza advised the pastor in a case where a person was in doubt of his salvation to examine his conscience to see whether he loved God and hated sin.

[211]Pp. 71-72.

[212]P. 16.

In this Beza has been misunderstood, however. Contrary to what Barth said, Beza did not say that works of sanctification are the primary witness, nor did he separate his practical syllogism from saving faith, much less from Jesus Christ and a Trinitarian framework rooted in the promise and Word of God. Beza and Calvin did not differ as much as others assume, for Calvin also said that a believer's election may be fortified in works that flow out of faith. The difference between Calvin and Beza wasn't in a pastoral approach to believers who were secure in their faith. In that context, both Calvin and Beza pointed to the primary grounds of God's promise in Christ, with secondary support in sanctification and the Spirit's witness. The real difference between Calvin and Beza was in assisting the believer who was anxious over his lack of assurance about his election, who could not call upon God as his "Father" with freedom, and who could not be certain of the Spirit's internal testimony that he was a child of God. While Calvin seldom discussed such cases, Beza felt obliged to do so. But though Beza taught that the elect received assurance at least once before they died, he also recognized "that sometimes faith [may] lie buried in the chosen for a season, insomuch that it may seem to be wholly extinguished or quenched."[213]

For such souls, Beza emphasized the practical syllogism, reasoning like this: Though the elect sinner may not be able to attain to an assurance of God's promise and the Spirit's testimony, neither does true sanctification completely disappear. Specifically, faith "never goeth so far away that the love of God and their neighbor is utterly plucked out of their minds."[214] Consequently, the doubting believer who cannot deny that he loves God and his neighbor and who hates sin and desires righteousness, may be assured of his election because of God's continuing work in him, even when he feels no recourse by faith to God's promise or to the Spirit's direct testimony. To this doubting child of God who believes he had exercises of faith in the past but feels those exercises are so remote at present that he despairs that his former experience only represents the "taste" of faith frequently shared by the reprobate, the minister may answer that such temptations are not uncommon among true Christians. He may tell such persons that they may still be assured

---

[213]*Treasure of Trueth*, p. 80.
[214]Ibid.

that they possess faith by recognizing the fruits of faith within them, namely, love for God and hatred for sin. Rather than sinking in despair, the doubter may turn to the evidence of sanctification to verify his salvation and dispense with unwarranted fears.

Calvin maintained a secondary status at best for assurance by works, but Beza nearly equalized the three grounds of assurance by using the practical syllogism more freely than Calvin.[215] He wrote in *A briefe and pithie summe*, "Good works be certain testimonies of our faith, and also do assure us of our eternal election."[216] The question at stake here is whether Beza's reductionistic approach connecting election, through God's promise and the Spirit's testimony, to sanctification and works is justifiable.[217]

Combining a pastoral concern with a more rationalistic theology than Calvin, Beza justified this approach on the basis of what William Perkins would later call the "golden chain" of the *ordo salutis*.[218] Beza used that approach to encourage the weak believer by arguing that if he could grasp any link in the chain of salvation, he might feel with certainty the tug of all the rest. For Beza, the inseparableness of election, Christ, the Spirit of Christ, faith, justification, sanctification, and good works both assures and reassures the true believer. Beza wove all of that together in the following pastoral encouragement:

Seeing that good works are for us the certain evidences of our faith, they also bring to us afterwards the certainty of our eternal election. Faith lays hold of Christ, by which, being justified and sanctified, we have the enjoyment of the glory to which we have been destined before the foundation of the world (Rom. 8:39; Eph. 1:3-4). This is so much the more important because the world holds it in less esteem, as if the doctrine of particular election were a curious and incomprehensible thing. On the contrary, faith is nothing other than that by which we have the certainty that we possess life eternal; by it we know that before the foundation of the world God has destined that we should possess, through Christ, a very great salvation and a most excellent glory. This is why all that we have said of faith and of its effects would be useless if we would not add this point of eternal election as the sole foundation and support of all the assurance of Christians.[219]

---

[215]Cf. Muller, "Predestination and Christology," pp. 197-98.

[216]P. 71. Cf. Peter White, *Predestination, policy and polemic* (Cambridge: Cambridge University Press, 1992), pp. 20-21.

[217]Berkouwer, *Divine Election*, p. 287.

[218]Like Beza, Perkins also combined a supralapsarian approach with warm pastoral concern. See chapter 5 below.

[219]*A briefe and pithie summe*, p. 19.

Beza's transition from the subordinated practical syllogism of Calvin to a practical syllogism of prominence was thus made in support of both *sola fide* and *solus Christus*. When Beza pointed first to sanctification for assurance, he never intended a dominant significance — despite the claims of Barth, Bray, and Kendall.[220] Rather, Beza started with the "lowest order" in order to reach the higher plane of Christ, God's promise, and election. Bray admitted as much when he wrote:

> The logic that undergirded Beza's argument was simple enough. One should begin with the quest for assurance at the "lowest order" [i. e., *only* if one could not grasp its higher aspects]. That is, the fact that one responded to the Gospel positively and exercised faith is a mark of the redeemed. True, saving faith — in contrast to faith for a season — is known by justification and sanctification. The testimony that one has been justified and sanctified is two-fold: good works and the witness of the Holy Spirit.[221]

Bray should have concluded with a threefold testimony, for he failed to mention Beza's stress on relying on God's promises for obtaining assurance. Beza did not stress sanctification and the Spirit's witness because these are primary, but because this twofold testimony helps the believer receive God's promises. Through sanctification and the Spirit's testimony, the promises of God become more real, lose their impersonal character, and help the believer to rise Christward and Godward. In *Tractationes Theologicae* Beza wrote:

> What if these witnesses [i.e., sanctification and the Spirit] become weak? Then we know how it is again to be demonstrated that these things may help in corroborating the otherwise indefinite promises to us, despite our accusing listlessness or at least our fainting heart.[222]

Beza included no "inferior signs" of assurance, since all God does is part of the sure chain of salvation. Nor does that threaten Christ-centeredness since every part of sanctification and faith leads back to Christ: "Thereby we rise up unto Christ."[223]

The differences between Calvin and Beza have been exaggerated

---

[220]Barth, *Dogmatics*, II/2, p. 336; John S. Bray, "The Value of Works in the Theology of Calvin and Beza," *Sixteenth Century Journal* 4 (1973):77-86; Kendall, *Calvin and English Calvinism*, p. 33, and "Puritan Modification," p. 206.

[221]Bray, "Works in Calvin and Beza," p. 82.

[222]1:702.

[223]*A briefe and pithie summe*, p. 72.

by recent scholarship.[224] For Beza and Calvin, what's crucial is *faith in Christ*. They did not essentially differ in their views on assurance, though their emphases and methods varied considerably — probably partly because of their different milieus. For believers who lacked assurance, Beza opened doors that Calvin kept shut. We don't know whether Calvin would have followed Beza's approach to questions about assurance had he lived until the seventeenth century.[225] Would he also have presented three anchors of assurance to the faltering believer so he could grasp at least one to strengthen his faith? And in the event that all three anchors became weak, would Calvin have agreed that participation in Christ does not demand a "full faith," but only the "root" of faith?[226] One thing is certain: If Beza overemphasized subjective assurance,[227] he did so within the Trinitarian and Christological context of saving faith as well as out of authentic pastoral concern.[228] For Beza, as for Calvin, Christ functioned as the ultimate basis of assurance of election. From sanctification, Beza wrote, "We rise up to Christ who has been given to whoever from eternity was elect in him."[229] As Letham concluded, "Beza's formulations on faith and assurance in connection with election, Christ, sanctification and the Spirit all undermine the idea of a deep-seated departure from his predecessor."[230]

---

[224]"Saving Faith and Assurance in Reformed Theology," 1:154; see also 1:142ff. for Letham's defense of this conclusion. Cf. Letham's "Theodore Beza: A Reassessment," *Scottish Journal of Theology* 40 (1987): 25-40.

[225]Kendall's conclusions are too radical (*Calvin and English Calvinism*, p. 29).

[226]Bray, "Works in Calvin and Beza," p. 84.

[227]Cf. Graafland, *Zekerheid van het geloof*, p. 70. Subjective is used here in the sense of Muller's comments on Beza's doctrine: "Assurance of election is felt in *the heart*: it is not to be judged of others. The number and identity of the elect and the reprobate can be known only to God. Assurance is personal, not corporate. It is inwardly discerned not outwardly visible" ("Predestination and Christology," p. 204).

[228]Bray, *Predestination*, p. 111.

[229]*Tractationes Theologicae* 1:687-88.

[230]*Scottish Journal of Theology* 40 (1987): 39-40.

V. THE FATHERS OF ENGLISH PURITANISM AND THE DUTCH SECOND REFORMATION

The transition from the magisterial Reformers and their successors to full-blown Puritanism[1] in England and the Second Reformation

[1]The term *Puritan* is difficult to define. "Throughout the sixteenth century it was used more often as a scornful adjective than as a substantive noun, and was rejected as slanderous in whatever quarter it was applied" (Leonard J. Trinterud, *Elizabethan Puritanism* [New York: Oxford, 1971], pp. 3ff.). For Perkins it was "a vile term" that described people with perfectionist tendencies (William Perkins, *The Workes of That Famovs and VVorthy Minister of Christ in the Vniuersitie of Cambridge, Mr. William Perkins* [London: John Legatt, 1612-13] [hereafter: *Works*], 1:342, 3:15).

The essence of Puritanism has been variously defined. William Haller saw the "central dogma of Puritanism [as] an all-embracing determinism, theologically formulated as the doctrine of predestination" (*The Rise of Puritanism* [New York: Columbia, 1938], p. 83). Perry Miller found the "marrow of Puritan divinity" in the idea of the covenant (*Errand into the Wilderness*, pp. 48-89); Alan Simpson, in the concept of conversion (*Puritanism in Old and New England* [Chicago: University of Chicago Press, 1955], p. 2). Christopher Hill emphasized the importance of new social and political ideas in Puritanism (*Society and Puritanism* [New York: Schocken, 1967]). John Coolidge tied the distinctive Puritan emphasis to a rejection of the Anglican doctrine of *adiaphora* or things indifferent (*The Pauline Renaissance in England: Puritanism and the Bible* [Oxford: Oxford University Press, 1970]). R. M. Hawkes summarizes: "Was [English Puritanism] essentially a theological movement, emphasizing covenant theology, predestination, and a reformed church service? Or was the heart of the matter political, asserting the inalienable rights of conscience before God, the rule of natural law over arbitrary prerogative courts, the dependency of the king in parliament, the foundation of state authority in the people? Some modern research has pointed to a third possibility, that the essence of Puritanism was its piety, a stress on conversion, on existential, heartfelt religion" ("The Logic of Assurance in English Puritan Theology," *Westminster Theological Journal* 52 [1990]:247).

I use "Puritan" as a combination of the first and third alternatives presented by Hawkes, i. e., of those who desired to reform and purify the Church of England and were concerned about living a godly life consonant with the Reformed doctrines of grace. Puritanism "grew out of three great areas: the New Testament pattern of personal piety,

in the Netherlands[2] was significantly influenced by two divines, William Perkins of Cambridge and Willem Teellinck of Zeeland. A discussion of these popular theologians will lead us to the era of the Westminster Assembly.

William Perkins (1558-1602)

Structuring Principles

William Perkins provided a major link in Reformed thought between Beza and the Westminster Confession. Born in Warwickshire in 1558, Perkins entered Christ's College in Cambridge (1577), where he earned a bachelor's degree in 1581 and a master's degree in 1584. While a student, Perkins experienced a powerful conversion. Soon after that he joined Laurence Chaderton, Richard Greenham, Richard Rogers, and others in espousing Puritan convictions.

Perkins served as lecturer, or preacher, at St. Andrew's church parish, Cambridge from 1584 until his death in 1602, and as a Fellow of Christ's College from 1584 to 1595. He was endowed with unusual preaching gifts and an uncanny ability to reach the common man with plain theology. In time he became the principle architect of the young Puritan movement. Certainly Perkins was the best known and most widely read divine of the Elizabethan church. By the time of his death from kidney stones at the age of forty-four,

---

sound doctrine and a properly ordered Church-life" (Peter Lewis, *The Genius of Puritanism* [Haywards Heath, Sussex: Carey, 1975], pp. 11ff.).

For the difficulties in and attempts at defining Puritanism, see Ralph Bronkema, *The Essence of Puritanism* (Goes: Oosterbaan and LeCointre, 1929); Leonard J. Trinterud, "The Origins of Puritanism," *Church History* 20 (1951):37-57; Jerald C. Brauer, "Reflections on the Nature of English Puritanism," *Church History* 23 (1954):98-109; Basil Hall, "Puritanism: The Problem of Definition," in G. J. Cumming, ed., *Studies in Church History*, vol. 2 (London: Nelson, 1965), pp. 283-96; Charles H. George, "Puritanism as History and Historiography," *Past and Present* 41 (1968):77-104; William Lamont, "Puritanism as History and Historiography: Some Further Thoughts," *Past and Present* 42 (1969):133-46; Lionel Greve, "Freedom and Discipline in the Theology of John Calvin, William Perkins, and John Wesley: An Examination of the Origin and Nature of Pietism" (Ph.D. dissertation, Hartford Seminary Foundation, 1976), pp. 151ff.; Richard Greaves, "The Nature of the Puritan Tradition," in R. Buick Knox, ed., *Reformation, Conformity and Dissent: Essays in Honour of Geoffrey Nuttall* (London: Epworth Press, 1977), pp. 255-73; D. M. Lloyd-Jones, "Puritanism and Its Origins," *The Puritans: Their Origins and Successors* (Edinburgh: Banner of Truth Trust, 1987), pp. 237-59; J. I. Packer, "Why We Need the Puritans," in *A Quest for Godliness: The Puritan Vision of the Christian Life* (Wheaton, Ill.: Crossway Books, 1990), pp. 21ff.

[2]For the Dutch Second Reformation, see the appendix below.

Perkins had produced writings which, in England, were outselling those of Calvin, Beza, and Bullinger combined.[3]

Perkins's influence continued through such theologians as William Ames, John Cotton, and Gisbertus Voetius. Thomas Goodwin wrote that when he entered Cambridge, six of his instructors who had sat under the tutelage of Perkins were still passing on his teaching. Ten years after Perkins's death, Cambridge was still "filled with the discourse of the power of Mr. William Perkins' ministry," Goodwin said.[4]

Perkins's legacy was a highly refined experiential predestinarianism, which fleshed out the practical theology of Beza and Zanchius and was subsequently validated by the Westminster Assembly. Perkins used Beza's method for comforting people who lacked assurance, but he also provided a more schematic, experiential *ordo salutis* with which to examine faith and doubt. He organized insights from Puritan preachers like Richard Greenham, who explained conversion "as a progression of inner states."[5]

As the premier Puritan preacher of Elizabethan England, Perkins taught and published supralapsarian, decretal theology interwoven with experimental soul-examination. He did all of that

[3]Ian Breward, "The Significance of William Perkins," *Journal of Religious History* 4 (1966):116. Moreover, as Breward points out, through the translation of Perkins's writings a genuine "two-way traffic in theology between England and the Continent" commenced (ibid, p. 116). J. van der Haar has recorded 185 printings in seventeenth-century Netherlands of Perkins's individual or collected works translated into Dutch (*From Abbadie to Young. A Bibliography of English, mostly Puritan Works, Translated i/t Dutch Language* [Veenendaal: Kool, 1980], 1:96-108). Cf. Cornelis W. Schoneveld, *Intertraffic of the Mind: Studies in Seventeenth-Century Anglo-Dutch Translation with a Checklist of Books Translated from English into Dutch, 1600-1700* (Leiden: Brill, 1983), pp. 220-26, which affirms that Perkins was printed in seventeenth-century Netherlands more than twice as much as any other Puritan.

[4]"Memoir of Thomas Goodwin," *The Works of Thomas Goodwin, D. D.*, ed. John C. Miller (Edinburgh: James Nichol, 1862), vol. 2, pp. xiii-xiv. Thomas Fuller provided the basics of the little that is known about Perkins's life (*Abel Redevivus; or, The Dead Yet Speaking*, volume 2 [London: William Tegg, 1867], pp. 145-56). See Ian Breward, "The Life and Theology of William Perkins" (Ph.D. dissertation, University of Manchester, 1963), his introduction in *The Work of William Perkins*, and Charles Robert Munson, "William Perkins: Theologian of Transition" (Ph.D. dissertation, Case Western Reserve, 1971), pp. 5-62, for the best accounts to date.

[5]Charles Cohen, *God's Caress: The Psychology of Puritan Religious Experience* (New York: Oxford, 1986), p. 11. Cf. Ian Breward, "William Perkins and the Origins of Reformed Casuistry," *Evangelical Quarterly* 40 (1968):3-20; Richard Greenham, *The Works of the Reverend and faithfull servant of Iesus Christ M. Richard Greenham* (reprint ed., New York: De Capo Press, 1973).

in layman's terms. Throughout his prolific writings, Perkins taught the regenerate and unregenerate how to search their consciences for even the least evidence of predestination based on the foundation of Christ's work. Perkins viewed such efforts as part of the pastor's fundamental task to keep "balance in the sanctuary"[6] between divine sovereignty and human responsibility. He did not consider sovereignty and responsibility as antagonistic but treated them as friends who need no reconciliation. His ability to wed decretal and practical theology into a happy, biblical marriage is remarkable and worthy of investigation.[7]

The principal means God uses to execute His decree is the covenant, Perkins said. In stressing sovereign predestination along with the covenant,[8] Perkins knew that his hearers might ask such questions as: "Am I one of the elect — one of the true children of God united with Jesus Christ? How can I have salvation in Christ? How may I be sure that I have true faith? If reprobates appear to be

---

[6]Cf. chapter 2 of Irvonwy Morgan, *Puritan Spirituality: Illustrated from the Life and Times of the Rev. Dr. John Preston* (London: Epworth Press, 1973).

[7]For this study I used Perkins's *Works* (3 vols.); Thomas F. Merrill, ed., *William Perkins, 1558-1602, English Puritanist. His Pioneer Works on Casuistry: "A Discourse of Conscience" and "The Whole Treatise of Cases of Conscience"* (Nieuwkoop: B. DeGraaf, 1966); Ian Breward, ed., *The Work of William Perkins.*

Several dissertations (in addition to those of Breward, Munson, and Greve) are valuable contributions to an understanding of Perkins's theology: Donald Keith McKim, *Ramism in William Perkins's Theology* (New York: Peter Lang, 1987) — see pp. 245-46 for articles on Perkins; C. C. Markham, "William Perkins' Understanding of the Function of Conscience" (Ph.D., Vanderbilt University, 1967); Willem Jan op 't Hof, *Engelse piëtistische geschriften in het Nederlands, 1598-1622* (Rotterdam: Lindenberg, 1987), pp. 280-387; Joseph A. Pipa, Jr., "William Perkins and the Development of Puritan Preaching" (Ph.D., Westminster Seminary, 1985); Victor L. Priebe, "The Covenant Theology of William Perkins" (Ph.D., Drew University, 1967); Mark Shaw, "The Marrow of Practical Divinity: A Study in the Theology of William Perkins"; Rosemary A. Sisson, "William Perkins" (M. Litt., Cambridge, 1952); Lynn Baird Tipson, Jr., "The Development of a Puritan Understanding of Conversion"; J. R. Tufft, "William Perkins, 1558-1602" (Ph.D., Edinburgh, 1952); Jan Jacobus van Baarsel, *William Perkins: Eene bijdrage tot de Kennis der religieuse ontwikkeling in Engeland ten tijde, van Koningin Elisabeth* ('s-Gravenhage: H. P. De Swart & Zoon, 1912); William G. Wilcox, "New England Covenant Theology: Its English Precursors and Early American Exponents" (Ph.D., Duke, 1959).

For a listing of other works that include some extended treatment of Perkins, see William Perkins, *A Commentary on Galatians*, ed. Gerald T. Sheppard (reprint ed., New York: The Pilgrim Press, 1989), pp. xlii-xliii.

[8]This is Munson's key theme in "William Perkins: Theologian of Transition," which is ably supported by Perkins's writings.

motivated by grace, how may I know whether I am a child of God? How can I be assured that Christ has died for *me*?"[9]

Perkins earnestly worked to address such questions, for preaching predestination decretally necessitated experimental preaching. Sinners had to be shown how God's immovable will moved the will of man. They had to be shown how to look for evidence of predestination and inclusion in the covenant. They also had to be taught how to make their election sure by living a life consonant with God's choice. For those prone to doubt, Perkins carefully explained how to examine conscience for the smallest measure of faith required for salvation.

Perkins wrote several works in the late 1580s and 1590s that explained how one may know he is saved: *A Golden Chaine: Or, The Description of Theologie: Containing the Order of the Causes of Salvation and Damnation;*[10] *A Treatise Tending unto a Declaration, Whether a Man be in the Estate of Damnation or in the Estate of Grace;*[11] *A Case of Conscience, the Greatest that ever was: how a man may know whether he be the childe of God or no;*[12] *A Discourse of Conscience: Wherein is set down the nature, properties, and differences thereof: as also the way to get and keepe a good Conscience;*[13] *A graine of Musterd-seede: Or, the Least Measure of Grace that is or can be effectuall to salvation.*[14]

Such writings show Perkins's conviction that experimental preaching was the "instrument of transition"[15] from decretal predestination to Christian living and assurance. The golden chain of the causes of salvation (effectual calling, justification, sanctification, and glorification) was linked to the elect through the instrument of preaching God's gracious covenant. Consequently, while Perkins preached about God's sovereign grace toward His elect from eternity and God's covenant acts of salvation by which election is realized, he was particularly concerned in his practical theology with how this redemptive process became evident in the experience of the elect. He wanted to explain how the elect responded to God's overtures and acts, and how the second side of

---

[9]Cf. William H. Chalker, "Calvin and Some Seventeenth Century English Calvinists" (Ph.D. dissertation, Duke University, 1961), p. 91.

[10]*Works* 1:9-116.

[11]*Works* 1:353-420.

[12]*Works* 1:421-28.

[13]*Works* 1:515-54.

[14]*Works* 1:627-34.

[15]Munson, "William Perkins: Theologian of Transition," pp. 183ff.

the covenant of grace — the will of man — developed experimentally from early faith to full assurance.

The Grounds of Assurance

In his commentary on Galatians, Perkins explained the grounds of assurance as follows: first, the general *promise of the gospel*, which by faith becomes a personal promise; second, *the testimony of the Holy Spirit* witnessing with our spirit that we are the children of God; and third, *the syllogism,* which rests partly on the gospel and partly on experience.[16] His work on assurance is patterned on that of Beza and Zanchius, and only implicitly on the work of Calvin. Calvin planted the seeds for this threefold division, which would later be established by the Westminster Assembly.

While these grounds of assurance are not new, Perkins does provide a new twist by offering a series of distinctions.[17] These vary from one composition to another and at times appear to contradict each other. For example, he wrote: "Whereas some are of the opinion, that faith is assiance [assurance] or confidence, that seems to be otherwise; for it is a fruite of faith."[18] At the same time he wrote elsewhere: "True faith is both an unfallible assurance, and a particular assurance of the remission of sins, and of life everlasting."[19]

Such apparent contradictions have led some scholars to assert that either Perkins was not a first-rate theologian[20] or that he simply wrote from his limited context. When opposing Roman Catholicism, scholars say, Perkins confirmed the certainty of faith. But when he spoke against the extreme assertions of the early Reformers on assurance, Perkins tended to divorce faith and assurance.[21] Such

---

[16]In addition to Perkins's *Works* 1:124, cf. Graafland, *Zekerheid van het geloof,* p. 136.

[17]Breward argues that this is Perkins's unique gift. "[Perkins's] gift for . . . clarity of thought and expression, felicity with his pen and influence in Cambridge enabled him both to reach a wide audience and fill some of the yawning gaps in the theological equipment of the Elizabethan Church. Ability to extract ideas from others, to combine them with his own insights and to relate the result to the needs of laity, ministers and scholars over a wide range of subjects helped embed Puritan piety and Reformed theology in the Church of England" ("The Significance of William Perkins," p. 116).

[18]*Works* 1:125.   [19]Ibid., p. 564.

[20]See Breward, *Work,* throughout introduction; Marshall Knappen, *Tudor Puritanism: A Chapter in the History of Idealism* (Chicago: University of Chicago Press, 1939), p. 219. For a more sympathetic treatment, see Richard A. Muller, "Perkins' *A Golden Chaine*: Predestinarian System or Schematized *Ordo Salutis?*," *Sixteenth Century Journal* 9 (1978):69-81, and *Christ and the Decree,* pp. 160-73.

[21]E.g., Letham, "Relationship between Faith and Assurance," pp. 29-30.

scholars cannot seriously entertain these distinctions in light of Perkins's own thought, however. Perkins knew very well what he was saying; he intended to teach that assurance is and is not part of the essence of faith, depending on which assurance is discussed.

To understand Perkins on faith and assurance, we must understand the two ways he used the term *assurance*. The first kind of assurance, *objective assurance*, enables the sinner to view his sins as pardonable apart from the personal realization of such forgiveness. The second kind, *subjective assurance*, is the full assurance that enables the sinner to believe that God, for Christ's sake, personally forgives all his sins. This two-part definition of assurance foreshadows what Ebenezer Erskine would later call *assurance of faith* and *assurance of sense*,[22] which, in turn, would influence Dutch theologians, such as Alexander Comrie.[23]

Perkins also distinguished between a general, moral, and special certainty, but did not always define the kind of certainty he was talking about. For such reasons, some critics called him a "sub-intellectual theologian" or "theologian of partiality."[24]

A more balanced look at how Perkins defined assurance involves, first, a realization that Perkins (as well as many later Puritans) divided faith "into a succession of recognizable stages,"[25] substantially beyond what Calvin did; and second, an examination of these precise stages to understand how the process of conversion and assurance was woven into Perkins's thought and preaching. While Perkins divided conversion into steps or degrees, his primary list of ten stages may be summarized under four headings: humiliation, faith, repentance, and new obedience.[26] Here is a basic description of those steps, with a focus on faith.

Conversion's Steps
Step #1: Humiliation
According to Perkins, the first step of conversion includes four

[22]See especially Erskine's sermons on Hebrews 10:22, "The Assurance of Faith, Opened and Applied," *The Whole Works of Ebenezer Erskine* (London: W. Baynes, 1810), 1:234ff.

[23]*Stellige en Praktikale Verklaaringe van den Heidelbergschen Catechismus* (Amsterdam: N. Byl, 1753), p. 456. See chapter 8 below.

[24]Cf. Lachman, "Marrow Controversy: An Historical Survey," p. 12.

[25]Edmund Morgan, *Visible Saints* (New York: University Press, 1963), pp. 68-69.

[26]Shaw, "A Study in the Theology of William Perkins," p. 127; cf. V. L. Priebe, "The Covenant Theology of William Perkins," pp. 151ff.

stages or "actions of grace" that flow out of experimental predestinarianism: attentive hearing of the Word; awareness of God's commanding and prohibiting law; conviction of sin; and despair of salvation. Perkins defined these stages as follows:

[Action of grace #1:] The ministrie of the word [and with it] some outward or inward crosse, to breake and subdue the stubborness of our nature, that it may be plyable to the will of God.

[Action of grace #2:] God brings the minde of man to a consideration of the Law, and therein generally to see what is good and what is euill. . . .

[Action of grace #3:] God makes a man particularly to see and know his owne peculiar and proper sinnes, whereby he offends God.

[Action of grace #4:] God smites the heart with a legall feare, whereby when man seeth his sinnes, he makes him to feare punishment and hell, and to despaire of saluation, in regard to any thing in himself.[27]

These four "workes of preparation" precede the work of grace. Since these are not fruits of grace per se (though they *may* be), and since the reprobate may travel this far in the garb of temporary faith,[28] several interpreters have labeled Perkins as an undiluted preparationist. For Perkins, however, these actions were preparatory not so much *in the elect*, but because one would not know if these steps were saving until they led to further steps of grace.[29] In Perkins's theology, the needy sinner must be driven onward to find rest exclusively in Christ.

Step #2: Faith in Christ

The second step of conversion, Perkins said, includes four stages of grace. These stages separate the elect from the reprobate:

[Action of grace #5:] . . . to stirre vp the minde to a serious consideration of the promise of saluation, propounded and published in the Gospell.

---

[27]*Works* 2:13.

[28]For how far the reprobate may proceed with temporary faith, see *Works* 1:107ff., 244ff., 356ff.; cf. Tipson, "The Development of a Puritan Understanding of Conversion," pp. 252-57, and Kendall, *Calvin and English Calvinism to 1649*, pp. 67-76.

[29]Cf. Shaw, "A Study in the Theology of William Perkins," p. 128 with Pettit, *Heart Prepared*, pp. 44ff., and Herman Witsius, *The Oeconomy of the Covenants between God and Man, Comprehending a Complete Body of Divinity*, trans. William Crookshank (London: Edward Dilly, 1762), III, vi., 11.

[Action of grace #6:] . . . to kindle in the heart some seedes or sparkes of faith, that is, a will and desire to beleeue, and grace to striue against doubting and despaire.

[Action of grace #7:] . . . as soone as faith is put into the heart, there is presently a combate: for it fighteth with doubting, despaire, and distrust [evidenced by] feruent, constant, and earnest inuocation for pardon: and . . . a prevailing of this desire.

[Action of grace #8:] God in mercy quiets and settles the Conscience, as touching the saluation of the soule, and the promise of life, whereupon it resteth and staieth it selfe.[30]

The "objective assurance of the sinner's 'forgivableness'" lies in actions #5-7, whereas the "subjective assurance of being forgiven" is in action #8, which, for Perkins, is a further step in grace. Nevertheless, in neither case is the object of faith in the sinner or in his experience of faith, but solely in Jesus Christ. As Mark Shaw notes:

Christ is ever the object of a growing faith which after initially seeing him as a sacrifice on the cross for the remission of sins, continues to see Christ as the strength to win in the warfare with temptation, as the comfort which alone soothes in the storm of affliction and ultimately grows to see in Christ all things needful in this life and in the life to come.[31]

For Perkins, faith has no meaning outside of Christ, who is the substance of election and the covenant, and therefore of all gospel preaching. He wrote, "Faith is . . . a principall grace of God, whereby man is ingrafted into Christ and thereby becomes one with Christ, and Christ one with him."[32]

Consequently, full assurance of faith is the *personal* receiving of Christ, when "euery seuerall person doth particularly applie vnto himself, Christ with his merits, by an inward persuasion of the heart which cometh none other way, but by the effectuall certificate of the holy Ghost concerning the mercie of God in Christ Iesus."[33]

The receiving of Christ involves five steps, only the fifth of which represents this full assurance of strong faith. As Perkins explained:

The first, is knowledge of the Gospell, by the illumination of Gods Spirit. . . .

The second, is hope of pardon, whereby a sinner, albeit he yet

---

[30]*Works* 2:13.
[31]"A Study in the Theology of William Perkins," p. 138.
[32]*Works* 2:18.
[33]*Works* 1:79.

feeleth not that his sinnes are certenly pardoned, yet he beleeueth that they are pardonable. . . .

The third, is an hungring and thirsting after that grace which is offered to him in Christ Iesus, as a man hungreth and thirsteth after meate and drinke. . . .

The fourth, is the approaching to the throne of grace, that there flying from the terrour of the Law, he may take holde of Christ, and finde fauour with God. . . . This approaching hath two parts. The first, is an humble confession of our sinnes before God particularly, if they be knowne sins, and generally, if unknowne: this donne, the Lord forthwith remitteth all our sinnes. . . . The second, is for crauing pardon of some sins, with vnspeakable sighes, and in perseuerance. . . .

The fifth arising of the former, is an especiall perswasion imprinted in the heart by the holy Ghost, whereby euery faithfull man doth particularly applie vnto himself those promises which are made in the Gospel. . . .[34]

Such steps of awareness in saving faith are subjective, but they lead the Christian to a fuller realization of Christ through a growing assurance of His promises. Perkins's goal was not endless introspection. Rather, it was to bring the believer to full assurance of salvation, which occurs when a "Christian much more firmly taking hold of Christ Jesus, maketh full and resolute account that God loveth him, and that he will give to him by name, Christ and all his graces pertaining to eternal life."[35]

In this context, Perkins developed his major contribution to the discussion of assurance by making a distinction between *weak faith* and *strong faith*. For Perkins, even weak faith is a *certain* persuasion, since there can be no doubt in faith, and assurance is also part of the essence of faith in its weakest actions. But strong faith is *full* persuasion, which claims the assurance of God's promise as a personal possession.

Hence, two truths converge in Perkins. First, assurance is intrinsic to the nature of saving faith, but in weak faith such assurance is only seen in God's promises and is not yet appropriated by the co-witness of Spirit and conscience within the Christian. Second, in strong faith, full assurance arises not as intrinsic to faith, but as a benefit or fruit of faith, ascertained by a personal, Spirit-worked apprehension of the benefits of faith.

By establishing two degrees of saving faith, Perkins maintained

[34]Ibid., pp. 79-80.
[35]Ibid., p. 80.

that assurance is of the *essence* of faith (i.e., inherent even in weak faith), and is the *fruit* of faith above and beyond its essence (i.e., in strong faith).[36] All Christians possess the former, but only a minority enjoy the latter, and then by means of the above steps experienced over a period of time.[37] Nevertheless, all believers must seek strong faith. According to Perkins, a believer ought to be brought to such full consciousness of faith, not "at the first, but in some continuance of time, after that for a long space he hath kept a good conscience before God, and before men, and hath had divers experiences of God's love and favor towards him in Christ."[38] Perkins was dismayed that most believers he knew had some degree of weak faith rather than strong faith: "Indeede this testimonie [of full assurance of forgiveness] is weak in most men and can scarce bee perceived because most Christians, even though they be old in respect of yeres; yet generally they are babes in Christ."[39]

Pastorally, the distinction between weak and strong faith allowed Perkins to encourage weak believers and to keep them from despair by stressing that weak faith was still authentic faith. Quality, not quantity, of faith was the definitive factor, he said. Moreover, Perkins could encourage weak believers to press forward in faith and obedience for the full assurance of having been "grasped" by divine grace. Perkins encouraged believers to seek the witness of the Spirit which seals forgiveness to the soul and moves the conscience through the practical syllogism to the certainty of salvation and to the confession: "Christ is *my* Sauiour . . . I am elected, iustified, sanctified, and shall be glorified."[40]

Thus, Perkins moved from God's assurance of salvation to the elect's assurance. The golden chain of divine sovereignty, covenant-establishment, mediatorial satisfaction, and Spirit-worked faith in

---

[36]Kendall fails to see that in Perkins strong faith does not add assurance to weak faith, but only develops what is inherently within faith. He misconstrues Perkins further by asserting that Perkins is at heart a voluntarist since he distinguishes faith into two separate acts of apprehending and applying Christ. Both Kendall and Chalker wrongly conclude that Perkins has made faith into a new work (Kendall, *Calvin and English Calvinism to 1649*, pp. 61-62; Chalker, "Calvin and Some Seventeenth Century English Calvinists," pp. 55ff.).

[37]Cf. Tipson, "Puritan Conversion," pp. 243-46 for a synopsis of Perkins's concepts of weak and strong faith.

[38]*Works* 1:367 (and cf., ibid., 1:606); also, Keddie, "Assurance in William Perkins," pp. 232, 237; Cunningham, *Reformers*, p. 125n; and John von Rohr, "Covenant and Assurance in Early English Puritanism," *Church History* 34 (1965):195.

[39]*Works* 1:369.   [40]Ibid., p. 523.

Christ, with its accompanying seal of witness, cannot help but lead to full, personal assurance. The human spirit witnesses in response to the inward, saving work of the triune God. The believer is assured of salvation by "the testimonie of the Spirit, and . . . the testimonie of the heart and conscience purified and sanctified in the blood of Christ."[41] This "assurance of conscience" may never be divorced from the work of the Spirit in prompting faith, for "the principal agent and beginner thereof, is the Holy Ghost, enlightening the mind and conscience with spiritual, divine light, and the instrument is the ministry of the gospel received by faith."[42] Perkins thus wrote, "[Assurance is] by litle and litle conceived in a form of reasoning or practical syllogism framed in the mind by the Holy Ghost."[43]

For Perkins, the practical syllogism, and what was later called the reflex act of faith, never pointed away from Christ, the Spirit, or saving faith. Rather, Spirit-worked faith was chained to Christ. Perkins advised those who doubted they were elect to defend themselves against doubt by remembering "not to behold faith, but the object of faith which is Christ."[44] Because all of salvation was Christ-centered and part of an unbreakable divine chain rooted in eternity past, Perkins could speak of the practical syllogism as an "infallible certainty." Like Calvin, he viewed the syllogistic witness of the Spirit in full harmony with "naked reliance upon Christ."[45] Hence, though Perkins placed more emphasis than Calvin on the secondary grounds of assurance, these grounds were only valid because they were evidence of the primary grounds: the sovereign work of the Father, the redeeming work of the Son, and the applying work of the Spirit. Like Calvin, Perkins said that works would never succeed in saving the elect. Nonetheless, they ought to provide some kind of assurance. The smoke of sanctification must flow from the fire of grace, he said. Therefore works, when evidenced as the fruits of grace, "certify election and salvation."[46] These works include

---

[41]Ibid., pp. 284-86.

[42]Merrill, ed., *William Perkins*, p. 61.

[43]*Works* 1:547.

[44]*Works* 1:87.

[45]Shaw, "A study in the Theology of William Perkins," p. 161n. Perkins wrote, "I speak this [practical syllogism] not to make men secure and to content themselves with these small beginnings in grace, but only to show how any may assure themselves that they are at least babes in Christ" (*Works* 1:286-87).

[46]Breward, "The Significance of William Perkins," p. 123.

"outward actions" as well as "inward motives." A list of such works of sanctification might include:

> I. To feel our wants, and in the bitterness of heart to bewail the offence of God in every sin. II. To strive against the flesh, that is, to resist, and to hate the ungodly motions thereof, and with grief to think them burdernous and troublesome. III. To desire earnestly and vehemently the grace of God, and merit of Christ to obtain eternal life. IV. When it is obtained, to account it a most precious jewel . . . . V. To love the minister of God's word, in that he is a minister, and a Christian. . . . VI. To call upon God earnestly, and with tears. VII. To desire and love Christ's coming, and the day of judgment, that an end may be made of the days of sin. VIII. To fly all occasions of sin, and seriously to endeavor to come to newness of life. IX. To persevere in these things to the last gasp of life.[47]

Such fruits of sanctification are not the cause of salvation, of course. They only show evidence of salvation — even if the conscience can only claim one of these fruits. As Perkins explained in answer to the question

> *How a man may be in conscience assured of his owne election?*
>
> Before I come to the Question it selfe, this conclusion is to be laid down as a maine Ground: That Election, vocation, faith, adoption, justification, sanctification, and eternal glorification, are never separated in the salvation of any man, but like inseparable companions, goe hand in hand; so as he that can be assured of one of them, may infallibly conclude in his owne heart, that he hath, and shall have interest in all the other in his due time. . . . In a chaine, the two extreames, are knit together, by the middle linkes; and in the order of causes of happinesse and salvation, faith hath a middle place, and by it hath the child of God assured hold of his election, and effectuall vocation, and consequently of his glorification in the kingdome of heaven.[48]

In short, as Shaw notes:

> The child of God can grab that link [e.g., sanctification, good works, faith] in the golden chain and feel with certainty the tug of all the rest. . . . [Perkins's] general principle is clear: "Grab any part of the *ordo salutis* within reach and you have the whole chain. Anyone clutching the middle links (the covenant of grace, justification by faith, and sanctification by the Spirit) can be assured of possessing the end links (election and glorification)."[49]

---

[47]*Works* 1:115.
[48]Merrill, ed., *William Perkins*, pp. 111-12.
[49]"A Study in the Theology of William Perkins," p. 166.

But what if the believer cannot grasp any link in that golden chain, or if self-examination fails to produce significant marks of sanctification? Perkins would say that such a believer must examine himself for the least measure of saving grace, such as a dislike for sin, a desire for reconciliation with God,[50] and "the desire to beleeve ... and repent" which in itself *is* faith and repentance.[51] "One apple is sufficient to manifest the life of the tree, and one good and constant motion of grace is sufficient to manifest sanctification," Perkins would say.[52] If a Christian cannot claim even the smallest measure of grace, he should not despair but recognize that "though he want assurance now, yet he may obtaine the same hereafter."[53] He must also persevere in a diligent use of the means of grace.[54]

It is normal for the elect to gain some sense of assurance, however, not from "the first causes of election, but rather from the last effects thereof ... the testimonie of Gods Spirit and the works of Sanctification."[55] The Holy Spirit seals adoption by moving the believer to embrace the promises as his own and to observe the works of grace in his life. This sealing, communicated through the Word, moves and transforms the human faculties.[56]

The movement of the divine will upon the human will and the impossibility of the human will to foil the divine decree and the Spirit's testimony, produces certainty — not uncertainty — even in the weakest of saints through predestinarian preaching. Assurance is assurance because of election. Divine sovereignty is comforting; it is the sinner's only hope. What Dewey Wallace said about predestinarian Puritans was already true of Perkins:

> The piety of predestinarian grace as an experience was particularly focused on providing assurance and certainty, as anxieties dissolved in the experience of being seized, in spite of one's unworthiness, as one of the chosen of that awesome yet gracious number upon which one was totally dependent. It must be remembered that the powerful religious experience was always that of being chosen, not of being left out, and thus certainty and reassurance, not despair, were derived from the unique logic of this way-of-being-religious.[57]

[50]*Works* 1:286.   [51]Ibid., p. 629.
[52]Ibid., p. 18.   [53]Ibid., p. 287.
[54]Ibid., pp. 113-14, 287. Cf. *Canons of Dort* I, 16.
[55]*Works* 1:112.   [56]Ibid., pp. 104-105.
[57]*Puritans and Predestination: Grace in English Protestant Theology, 1515-1695* (Chapel Hill: University of North Carolina Press, 1982), pp. 195-96. Thus, the ultimate

Steps #3-4: Repentance and New Obedience

By placing *repentance* subsequent to faith as action of grace #9, Perkins emphasized that evangelical repentance refines the soul and persuades the elect to live wholly to God and to hate sin more than death. True gospel sorrow must thus flow from the inward conviction of having "offended so merciful a God and loving Father" and must yield a wholehearted Godward change "of the mind and whole man in affection, life, and conversation."[58]

The sequel to this is action of grace #10: *new obedience,* "when the believer obeys the commands of God and begins to walk in newness of life."[59] The whole man then endeavors "to keep the whole Law in his mind, will, affections, and all the faculties of soul and body."[60] Here Perkins linked divine election and Reformed piety. The elect will walk in godly piety as a fruit of divine decree and personal assurance, he said. They will perform good works, often parallel to their degree of assurance, always in the strength of Christ who must cleanse all their works from corruption. In this manner, the golden chain is partly consummated on earth in a daily walk in the assurance "of sense" by means of "inward tokens" and "outward fruites,"[61] and will finally be realized in heaven to the glory of an electing God.[62]

Repentance and obedience augment the believer's assurance, strengthened by the means of grace, such as prayer and the sacraments. True prayer and a right use of the sacraments repeatedly remind the believer that he is elect.

Prayer indicates piety. For Perkins, to pray is to put up our request to God with assurance, according to his Word, from a contrite heart in the name of Christ.[63] He thus wrote: "Prayer is to be made with faith, whereby a man must have certaine assurance to be

---

question for Perkins and the Puritans was not "Am I elect?" but "Am I manifesting the marks and fruits of electing grace?" (David Sceats, *The Experience of Grace: Aspects of the Faith and Spirituality of the Puritans* [Cambridge: Grove, 1997], pp. 7-8).

[58]Merrill, ed., *William Perkins,* p. 106.

[59]Ibid., p. 107.   [60]*Works* 2:16.

[61]*Works* 1:291.

[62]Consequently, predestination in Perkins, as in Calvinism, promoted activism, not fatalism. As Alister McGrath notes: "At the theoretical level, predestination might seem to encourage quietism: if one is elected, why bother doing anything active? In fact, however, its effect was quite the reverse: to ensure that one is elected, one must throw oneself wholeheartedly into appropriate action" (*A Life of John Calvin: A Study in the Shaping of Western Culture* [Oxford: Basil Blackwell, 1990], pp. 242-43).

[63]*Works* 1:329.

heard. For he that praieth, must steadfastly beleeve, that God in Christ wil grant his petition."[64]

Conscience plays a key role in praying with assurance. Perkins wrote, "For unless a man be in conscience in some measure pereswaded that all his sins are pardoned, & that he stands reconciled to God in Christ, he cannot beleeve any other promises revealed in the word, nor that any of his praiers shall be heard."[65]

Perkins taught that a sacrament is "a proppe and stay for faith to leane upon. For it cannot entitle us into the inheritance of the sonnes of God, as the covenant doth, but onely by reason of faith going before, it doth seale that which before was bestowed upon us."[66] Through the sacraments, the Holy Spirit confirms faith, restores piety, and works a new willingness in the heart to practice cross-bearing and self-denial for Christ's sake, Perkins said. Moreover, the elements in the sacraments can strengthen assurance in God's promises. Perkins's syllogism for that is: "He which uses the elements aright shall receive the promise: But I do, or have, used the elements aright. Therefore I shall receive the promises."[67]

Finally, Perkins taught that even full assurance might vanish in the midst of strong temptation. As long as believers are "in this world according to their own feeling, there is an access and recess of the Spirit,"[68] Perkins said. This lack of feeling could be due to a weak conscience, strong doubts, failure to grasp any part of the *ordo salutis,* or simply the sovereignty of the Spirit. The testimony of the Spirit, which could be temporarily lost at any moment, emphasizes the need for continual self-examination, repentance, and a godly walk.

In summary, William Perkins differed from the Reformers by emphasizing the covenant, secondary grounds of assurance, active pursuit of assurance,[69] subjective feeling,[70] and steps of faith. He also stressed the role of conscience in relationship to covenantal obedience, particularly in his practical syllogism.[71] Growth in grace

---

[64]Ibid., p. 330. [65]Ibid., p. 331.
[66]Ibid., p. 73. [67]Ibid., p. 541.
[68]Ibid., p. 413.

[69]Perkins's emphasis was not on the passive reception of initial grace, but on the believer's active nourishment of the first seeds of faith. By fanning the smoking flax into flame the believer may know that his weak faith is more than "flittering and fleeting motions" (ibid., p. 629).

[70]"But the knowledge of the elect is pure, certain, sure, distinct & particular: for it is joyned with a feeling & inward experience of the thing known" (ibid., p. 363).

[71]As Markham noted: "Searching of conscience becomes invaluable as a means by

as a sign of assurance was inseparable from intense examination of the conscience, he said.

Perkins, however, did not abandon the Reformers' teachings on faith and assurance. Rather, his emphases rose out of pastoral concerns. Though at times Perkins's emphases were more on salvation than on the primacy of God and His grace, Perkins did not shift the ground of assurance from Christ, nor did he abandon *sola gratia*.

Perkins was no voluntarist. He said the conditions of the covenant must be fulfilled, but God enables the believer to fulfil them. "He that turnes to God must first of all be turned of God, and after that we are turned, then we repent,"[72] he wrote. Perkins continued to maintain that the object of saving faith is Jesus Christ and the primary ground of assurance rests in the Christological promises of a triune God as they are apprehended by faith. He wrote:

> Faith is a supernatural gift of God, apprehending the saving promise with all the promises that depend on it. . . .[73]
>
> This apprehending of Christ is not done by any corporall touching of him, but spiritually by *assurance* which is, when the elect, are perswaded in their hearts by the holy Ghost, of the forgivenesse of their own sinnes, and of Gods infinite mercie towards them in Jesus Christ.[74]

Perkins's emphases were not foreign to the Reformers. They differed in emphases but not in substance.

Willem Teellinck (1579-1629)

What William Perkins was to English Puritanism, Willem Teellinck was to the Dutch Second Reformation.[75]

Teellinck was converted while residing in a model Puritan home in England. He studied under Lucas Trelcatius, Franciscus Gomarus,

---

which one can be assured that salvation is his in particular, thereby removing the threat of rejection at the last judgment. Conscience, therefore, becomes the focal point for ascertaining a knowledge of the presence of faith through the testimony of works" ("William Perkins' Understanding of the Function of Conscience," p. 26). Cf. Greve, "Freedom and Discipline in the Theology of John Calvin, William Perkins, and John Wesley," pp. 189ff.

[72]*Works* 1:453.　　　　　　　　　[73]Ibid., p. 124.

[74]Ibid., p. 363.

[75]For biographical and theological material on Teellinck, see Heinrich Heppe, *Geschichte des Pietismus und der Mystik in der Reformierten Kirche, namentlich der Niederlande* (Leiden: E.J. Brill, 1879), pp. 106-40; Willem Jodocus Matthias Engelberts, *Willem*

and James Arminius at Leiden and earned a doctorate in theology during the tense period when Gomarus and Arminius were in conflict. In the meantime, Teellinck married a young Puritan woman from England. In 1606 he accepted a pastoral call to Haamstede, and in 1613 to Middelburg, where he remained until his death in 1629.

Teellinck's lifelong goal was to bring English-style, pietistic Puritanism to the Dutch. He succeeded in doing that. More than any other divine of his day, he contributed to the Dutch Second Reformation. That movement was so like English Puritanism that it is often called Dutch Puritanism.[76] Teellinck's *Noodwendigh Vertoogh aangaende de tegenwoordige bedroefde staet van Gods volck* (Urgent Discourse concerning the Lamentable Condition of God's People at the Present Time) set the agenda for the Dutch Second Reformation for several generations.

Teellinck unceasingly called church members to repentance, encouraged them in the faith, and labored to move the Reformed church beyond reformation in doctrine and polity to reformation in life and practice. At times, Teellinck was criticized for being legalistic (*wettisch*) for his sermons against luxury in dress, amorous literature, excessive drinking, dancing, traveling on the Sabbath, overindulgence in feasting, and neglect of fasting.[77] However, that

Teellinck (Amsterdam: Scheffer & Co., 1898); R. Hamming, "Willem Teellinck," *Gereformeerd Theologisch Tijdschrift* 27 (1926-27):97-115; H. Bouwman, *Willem Teellinck en de practijk der godzaligheid* (Kampen: Kok, 1928); Graafland, *Zekerheid van het Geloof*, pp. 171-80; W. van't Spijker, "Teellinck's opvatting van de menselijke wil," *Theologia Reformata* 7 (1964):125-42; Johannes De Boer, *De Verzegeling met de Heilige Geest, volgens de opvatting van de Nadere Reformatie* (Rotterdam: Bronder, 1968), pp. 77-99; F. Ernest Stoeffler, *The Rise of Evangelical Pietism*, Studies in the History of Religion, no. 9 (Leiden: E. J. Brill, 1971), pp. 127-31; S. van der Linde, "De Godservaring bij W. Teellinck, D. G. à Brakel en A. Comrie," *Theologia Reformata* 16 (1973):193-205; W. Goeters, *Die Vorbereitung des Pietismus in der Reformierten Kirche der Niederlande* (reprint ed., Amsterdam: Ton Bolland, 1974), pp. 84-92; M. Eugene Osterhaven, "The Experiential Theology of Early Dutch Calvinism," *Reformed Review* 27 (1974): 180-89; G. M. Alexander, *Changes for the Better*, vol. 2 (Ossett, W. Yorks: Zoar, 1978), pp. 65-68; K. Exalto, "Willem Teellinck (1579-1629)," in *De Nadere Reformatie: Beschrijving van haar voornaamste vertegenwoordigers*, ('s-Gravenhage: Boekencentrum, 1986), pp. 17-47; op 't Hof, *Engelse piëtistische geschriften in het Nederlands, 1598-1622*, pp. 494-508; M. Golverdingen, *Avonden met Teellinck: Actuele thema's uit zijn werk* (Houten: Den Hertog, 1993); W.J. op 't Hof, *Bibliografische lijst van de geschriften van Willem Teellinck* (Rotterdam, 1993), and an ongoing series of articles by op 't Hof on Teellinck in *Documentatieblad Nadere Reformatie* (see bibliography).

[76]See the appendix, for further details on the Dutch Second Reformation.

[77]Even Gomarus felt obliged to write against Teellinck in defending Jacob Burs

was only one strand in a complex web of practical godliness that Teellinck sought to weave in the hearts and lives of his parishioners.

Teellinck was a "repentance preacher" (*boeteprediker*) who lived what he preached. He was a simple and godly man. All three of his sons followed his example of piety and became pastors. However, none became as renowned as the father.[78]

Teellinck was most influenced in his early days by William Perkins.[79] Like Perkins, Teellinck was a popular preacher and pastor who used the Puritan "plain method" approach. Teellinck was also deeply concerned for the spiritual welfare of sinners, evidenced by his compassion and seemingly unending stream of writings.[80]

Teellinck was not a duplicate of Perkins, however. In some senses he outdid the father of Puritanism by his emphasis on godly living, fruits of love, marks of grace, and primacy of the will.[81]

The Netherlands was not as ready for Teellinck as England had been for Perkins, though. Teellinck's insistence on connecting the fruits of love with the acts of justifying faith did not win the full acceptance of his peers. Many found his call for renewal in church, school, family, government, and society simply too intense. On the one hand, the Reformed orthodox were uncomfortable with Teellinck's repetitive rebuttals of "dead orthodoxy" and his countless rules on nearly every detail of life.[82] On the other hand, the

---

who had opposed Teellinck's legalism (G. P. Itterzon, *Franciscus Gomarus* [Groningen: Martinus Nijhoff, 1930], ch. 6).

[78]K. Exalto, "Willem Teellinck (1579-1629)," in *De Nadere Reformatie*, pp. 17-21.

[79]Cf. Engelberts, *Willem Teellinck*, pp. 96ff.

[80]Teellinck penned 127 manuscripts, half of which have never been printed. The bulk of his printed works were collected in three folios, *Alle de wercken van Mr. Willem Teellinck* (Utrecht: Johannes van Someren, 1659-64) [hereafter: *Alle de wercken*]. Four of Teellinck's writings have been translated into English: *Pauls Complaint against his Naturall Corruption: With the Means how to bee Delivered from the power of the same* (London: John Dawson for I. Bellamie, 1621); *The Ballance of the Sanctuarie, shewing how we must Behave our selves when wee see and behold the People of God in Miserie and Oppression under the Tyranny of their Enemies*, trans. C. Harmar, ed. T. Gataker (London: I. D. for William Sheffard, 1621); *The Christian Conflict and Conquest* (London: John Dawson for I. Bellamie, 1622); *The Resting Place of the Minde, That is, a Propounding of the Wonderfull Providence of God whereupon a Christian man ought to Rest and Repose Himselfe when Outward Means Fail Them*, ed. T. Gataker (London: Iohn Haviland for Edward Brewster, 1622).

[81]Cf. the discussion of Engelberts, *Willem Teellinck*, pp. 109-112; also, de Boer, *De Verzegeling met de Heilige Geest, volgens de opvatting van de Nadere Reformatie*, pp. 97-98, who unjustly charges Teellinck with voluntarism. Teellinck did embrace the doctrines of total depravity and human inability, but they received little accent in his writings due to a heavy stress on repentance and godly living.

[82]Some Reformed orthodox feared Teellinck was leaving no room for Christian

Arminians rejected him outright as a pillar of Reformed orthodoxy and resented his popularity with lay people.[83]

That didn't stop Teellinck. His goal was too earnest and life too short for that. Believing that the Reformers fell short in emphasizing works of holiness, Teellinck's goal was to preserve the doctrinal basis of the first Reformation, while moving it beyond that into the practice of daily piety.[84]

Teellinck stressed the need for an individual and collective call to new life in Christ. For Teellinck, that meant the stripping away of self-righteousness, a life of self-denial, submission under adversity, ethical ordering of daily life, scrupulous Sabbath-keeping — in short, daily devotion (*devotie*).

Teellinck's most extensive work, *Sleutel der Devotie Ons opende de Deure des Hemels* (The Key of Devotion which Opens to Us the Door of Heaven) is nearly 800 pages of fine print. It is divided into six sections, which develop Teellinck's concept of devotion. Teellinck's preface explains "devotion" as commitment to God in Christ, which is man's highest calling. The first section covers communion with and love for Christ. The Christian "must receive, keep, and increase in the communion and love of Christ."[85] His "regard and great desire for the Lord Jesus" will mortify all other lusts and desires.[86] Such a believer will be humble and volunteer "to suffer the Christian life";[87] he will serve the Lord alone, meditate on eternity, and practice the presence (*gemeynschap*) of Christ. The second section details self-denial, chapter 8 bearing this heading, "How important it is, that the Christian must deny himself."[88] The third section shows "how we must use all spiritual means, and especially heed well the movements of the Spirit, in order really to deny ourselves, and to be one with (*aenkleven*) Christ."[89] The fourth section treats of the "modesty and lowliness, which one must observe in the use of the means to receive the gracious gifts of God."[90] The fifth section shows how faith discerns the many errors of the day. The sixth section speaks about divine grace, without which the Christian life is impossible.[91]

---

liberty and the *adiaphora* (cf. K. Exalto, "Willem Teellinck [1579-1629]," in *De Nadere Reformatie*, pp. 24ff.).

[83]Ibid., p. 23.   [84]Ibid., p. 32.
[85]*Alle de Wercken* 3:19.   [86]Ibid., p. 14.
[87]Ibid., p. 27.   [88]Ibid., p. 72.
[89]Ibid., p. 80.   [90]Ibid., p. 243.
[91]Stoeffler, *The Rise of Evangelical Pietism*, pp. 132-33.

Teellinck's emphasis on devotion has been misinterpreted by some scholars, who say Teellinck either supported the notion that faith is a sort of voluntaristic effort that contains no assurance[92] or advocated devotional repentance as conditional for salvation. De Boer argues:

> Another deficiency is much more serious, namely, that Teellinck uses such a legalistic approach in his exhortations. Teellinck repeatedly says that you must first acknowledge your sins and humble yourself — only subsequent to this you may give heed to what the Lord promises in the gospel. The promises of God are for those who mourn, i.e., for repentant sinners. Teellinck fears that men will rashly set themselves at ease with the notion that God is gracious. In order to prevent this he places all emphasis on the *condition*: you must first repent. Perkins states in *A Treatise of the Nature and Exercise of Repentance* that "in working repentance only the administration of the gospel is the instrument of the Holy Spirit and not the law" (*Works* 3:288). Teellinck, on the contrary, writes in *Nieuwe historie van de oude mensche* (New History of the Old Man), "that the Lord first causes His law to be preached in order that man may perceive his condemnable state and humble himself. However, subsequent to this He reveals His grace in Christ Jesus to all who repent."[93]

De Boer then quotes C. N. Impeta, who writes: "This position of Teellinck is still adhered to in our time by C. Steenblok who was opposed to a general, well-meant, and unconditional offer of grace to all."[94]

Teellinck may have exaggerated the need for personally prescribed, detailed Christian living, but he never intended to teach what De Boer, Hamming, and Impeta said he did. Teellinck's fear of a shallow Christian profession devoid of cross-bearing led him to some imbalance but never at the expense of Reformed orthodoxy. De Boer and others have ignored several aspects of Teellinck's presentation.

First, Teellinck affirmed the Heidelberg Catechism's definition of saving faith as a "certain knowledge" (Question 21). In *De Toets-steen des Geloofs* (The Touchstone of Faith), Teellinck defined faith as "a supernatural gift of God by which man is fully qualified

---

[92]Hamming, "Willem Teellinck," pp. 97-115.

[93]*De Verzegeling met de Heilige Geest, volgens de opvatting van de Nadere Reformatie*, pp. 79-80.

[94]Cited by ibid., p. 81 from *Kaart van kerkelijk Nederland* (Ecclesiastical Map of the Netherlands), p. 144.

by God to receive the Lord Christ, the Savior of the world as his Savior."[95] Like Perkins, Teellinck taught that assurance was part of the essence of faith and that faith was a gift of God, not a condition for the sinner to fill on his own. De Boer and others failed to consider that *quantitatively* Teellinck's writings dealt with the practice of godliness, as well as with the fruits of faith and repentance.

Second, though Teellinck was not as free in proclaiming the offer of grace as the "Marrow Men,"[96] his gospel presentation was not essentially different from that of Perkins. Both emphasized steps in grace, and both earnestly called people to repentance and faith in Jesus Christ. Thus, to separate Teellinck from Perkins and ally him with Steenblok is unfair.[97] Teellinck did believe in the unconditional offer of grace to all hearers, but, like Perkins, he also carefully explained how God brought sinners to Christ in true repentance and saving faith.

C. Steenblok (1894-1966) taught that the offer of grace comes to "sensible sinners." Since he viewed sensible sinners as regenerate, the invitations of the gospel are basically reserved for the elect. Steenblok taught that since the natural man is unable to respond to the gospel, he may not be invited to respond to it. By contrast, Teellinck said that the offer of grace comes to all men, while the promises of God do not.[98] He thus wrote: "The man who receives

---

[95]*De Toets-steen des Geloofs waerin de gelegentheyt des waren Saligmakende geloofs nader ontdekt wordt, zoodat een yder sich selven daer aen kan Toetsen, of hij oock het ware salighmakende geloove heeft* (Utrecht: Johannes van Someren, 1662), pp. 446-47. Hereafter, *Toets-steen des Geloofs.*

[96]Reference is here made to the Marrow Controversy which agitated the Church of Scotland from 1718 to 1723. The Marrow Men (of whom the most prominent were Thomas Boston and Ralph and Ebenezer Erskine) believed that not only the invitation to grace but also the promises of God were for all men. This raised opposition among the controlling party of the church, who affirmed that the gospel could only be offered upon the conditions of faith and repentance having been met. For the anti-Marrow party the offer of grace should be extended only to "sensible sinners," whereas Boston and the Erskines insisted that it be proclaimed to all who hear the gospel. (See Lachman, *The Marrow Controversy.*)

[97]For C. Steenblok's life see J. H. R. Verboom and L. M. P. Scholten, *Leven en leer van Dr. C. Steenblok* (Barneveld: Van Horssen, 1967). For his writings (all of which are published by Gereformeerde Pers at Gouda), see his studies on Voetius: *Voetius en de sabbat* (1975); *Gisbertus Voetius: zijn leven en werken* (1976). Also *Om de Oude Waarheid* (1978) and *Rondom Verbond, Roeping en Doop* (1979) address issues related to the offer of grace. *Nabij God te zijn* (2 vols., 1974-75) is a collection of 165 meditations. *Het Pleiten van een Wees* (1976) and *De Roepstem tot Bekering* (1978) contain sermons.

[98]Thus taking a mediating position between the Marrow Men on the one hand and the anti-Marrow party and Steenblok on the other.

Christ as He is offered to him by God in His Word receives true faith from God; those who thus engage themselves — and they only — are true believers."[99]

Third, when Teellinck affirmed that the law produced knowledge of sin and experiential room for Christ in the heart, he taught nothing different from what's said in Question 3 of the Heidelberg Catechism: "Whence knowest thou thy misery? Out of the law of God." Like the catechism, Teellinck insisted that the law was embedded in the gospel, both historically and theologically. Hence the catechism's follow-up question, "What doth the law require of us?" begins with Christ as teacher. That is to say, the convicting law is inseparable from the gracious operation of the Holy Spirit and the teachings of Christ.[100] Like the catechism, Teellinck had the same view of the law as the Puritans, seeing it as the means by which sinners were brought to Christ, and obedience to it as the fruit of having been saved by Christ.[101] Both convicting by the law and living in obedience to the law are the work of Christ and His Spirit, for faith in all its acts rests upon the righteousness of Christ.[102] Both are personal, experimental, and practical but not voluntaristic.

Fourth, because conviction of sin by the law is inseparable from the gospel, Teellinck's call to repent is no more voluntaristic than Scripture's mandates to humble ourselves before God. Teellinck taught that genuine conviction was the gracious work of the Holy Spirit. Though he probably should have linked that more often with Christ, Teellinck's basic thrust was Christological, either by implication or direct assertion.

Assurance by Faith Working Through Love

Teellinck's approach to assurance of faith must be set in context. For example, is it surprising that he strongly emphasized the practical syllogism, when the core of his thinking was that faith in Christ cannot be separated from a holy life? For Teellinck, faith is not only a hand that receives the grace of Christ; it is also a hand that performs the commands of Christ. Consequently, he wrote: "The

[99]*Toets-steen des Geloofs*, pp. 448-52.

[100]Cf. G. C. Berkouwer's in-depth discussion of "The Knowledge of Sin" in chapters 6 and 7 of *Sin*, trans. Philip C. Holtrop (Grand Rapids: Eerdmans, 1971), pp. 149-234.

[101]Ernest Kevan, *The Grace of Law: A Study in Puritan Theology* (London: Carey Kingsgate Press, 1964; reprint ed., Ligonier, Pa.: Soli Deo Gloria, 1993).

[102]*De Toets-steen des Geloofs*, pp. 414, 418.

entire work of our salvation boils down to this, that we receive Him and thus become partakers of Him.... True faith seeks everything in Christ, relies upon Him, and begins to hear the voice of Christ and follow His commandments."[103]

Teellinck taught that assurance may be promoted by marks of grace such as experiencing true gratitude; doing good works that show the uprightness of faith, for "good works are the good children of a good faith"; and true love, for "faith always works by love."[104] This assurance may be strong at times, but it can also weaken rapidly, for when good works diminish, the comfort of assuring faith also diminishes. Moreover, sin weakens assurance. When faith and works are active and focus upon Christ, though, they comfort the Christian by assuring him that he is a partaker of Christ, for works of faith are not to be found in the natural man.[105] Since only the child of God has such exercises of faith as well as works of love, it follows that he must be a Christian, that is, a partaker of Christ and His salvation.

Self-examination is necessary for assurance that focuses on our love to God and our being in Christ, Teellinck said. We may know such assurance if we live Christ-like lives as children of the King, if we feel comfort and joy in the presence of Christ, and if we grieve when we do not feel this presence. The ways to gain this kind of assurance include receiving God's ordinances; exercising faith, hope, and love; and following Christ's commandments.[106]

Teellinck saw sanctification, which is marked by love, communion with Christ, and avoidance of evil, as an important route to assurance. The Christian who lives piously may thus reflect on the marks of grace God has worked in his life and draw assurance from them.

Assurance by the Promises of God

True faith, which evidences itself in Christ-centered obedience and a sanctified life of devotion, is not the only way to assurance, however. Indeed, Teellinck believed that only one in ten believers receives assurance in such a way. Rather, many believers falter when

---

[103]Ibid., pp. 452-55.

[104]*Huys-boeck, of te een Voudighe Verklaringhe en toe-eygheninghe, van de Voor-naemste Vraeghstrucke des Nederlandschen Christelijcken catechismi* (Middelburgh: voor Gillis Horthemels, 1650), pp. 6, 614-15, 620, 689. Hereafter, *Huys-boeck.*

[105]Ibid., pp. 97, 106, 279, 450.

[106]*De Mensche Godts*, in *Alle de wercken* 1:985-987.

reflecting upon their uprightness of faith. They have doubts about marks of grace in their lives. Even the saintliest of God's children find such assurance difficult to grasp.

Happily, there is another way to find assurance. That is through the promises of God which rest in faith's ultimate object, Jesus Christ. As Teellinck wrote, "True faith is such a knowledge of heavenly things which God the Lord has promised us in His Word and which we through hope anticipate."[107]

Faith is not only knowledge and assent to what God has revealed in Scripture, but is also "a depending upon the promises," "a receiving of the promises," and "a trusting in the Savior."[108] Out of such faith assurance flows.

Assurance is thus attainable. Like Perkins, Teellinck said the believer could gain assurance by reasoning such as: "I hear the gospel that promises Christ is for sinners. I know myself to be such a sinner for whom the promised Christ has come. Consequently, by a special appropriating act of faith, I take Christ at His own Word and receive Him upon the ground of the gospel-promise."[109]

For Teellinck, divine promises and a godly walk were inherently inseparable. He wrote, "God in His holy Word, gives no promises, however small or great they may be, except to those who repent from their transgressions."[110]

Teellinck also used this approach of ascertaining the assurance of faith in order to distinguish saving faith from temporary faith. In chapter 8 of *Toets-steen des Geloofs* he wrote, "In order for anyone to receive the Lord Christ by faith, he must prior to this, being allured by the precious promises of God made in Christ Jesus our Lord, be inclined to separate himself from the world, come to Christ, and henceforth live according to the doctrine of Christ; for such only, and no others, who have thus engaged themselves have become partakers of the Lord."[111]

In summary, a person who has saving faith receives the promises of God and seeks to live according to the will of God (Acts 4:12; 1 Peter 4:2). If a person lacks either of these elements, he can have no assurance of salvation for any length of time.

---

[107] *Toets-steen des Geloofs*, p. 444.

[108] Ibid., pp. 447, 465-66.

[109] *Huys-boeck*, p. 102.

[110] Ibid.

[111] *Toets-steen des Geloofs*, p. 460.

Assurance by the Immediate Witness of the Holy Spirit

Finally, though Teellinck made much of the promises of God and sanctification in his teaching on assurance, he did not neglect the witness of the Holy Spirit. While exegeting Romans 8:16, in book 5 of *Sleutel der Devotie*, Teellinck wrote:

> The apostle here presupposes, in addition to the witness of our spirit, the witness of the Holy Spirit. Therefore, a true child of God upon being assured of his salvation has, in addition to the witness of his own spirit, also the witness of the Holy Spirit, and this witness is such that the two can be distinguished from each other. Therefore, even if we have valid reason to suspect the witness of our own spirit when we have nothing more than that, we neither can nor may doubt the witness of the Holy Spirit, for it is beyond all dispute that His witness is true (1 John 5:6). He bears witness with our spirit and we can know this.[112]

Teellinck appeared to move beyond Perkins with regard to the testimony of the Spirit in assurance. By viewing this testimony as distinct from that of the believer's own spirit, Teellinck paved the way for some Dutch Second Reformation theologians, who viewed the Spirit's testimony as an experience above and beyond assurance from the promises of God and sanctification.[113]

Teellinck also said that this special form of assurance from the Spirit could be experienced apart from the Word, though it is usually accompanied by the Word.[114] He viewed this assurance as the "most extraordinary" (*allerzonderlingste*) work of the Spirit.[115]

Like Perkins, Teellinck taught there are steps in grace. The Holy Spirit's convincings are the best forms of assurance, for then the redeemed sinner has "refuge-taking trust" (*toevluchtnemend vertrouwen*), as when he flees to the promises of God. But he also has a "possessing trust" (*bezittend vertrouwen*). He has an "unconscious trust" (*onbewust vertrouwen*), which he experiences when he relies on the uprightness of faith, as well as a "conscious trust" (*bewust vertrouwen*), which flows out of the Spirit's direct testimony. Unlike Calvin, Teellinck offered a twofold mode of thinking on assurance, which would be further developed by some Dutch Second

---

[112]*Alle de wercken* 1:141-43.

[113]One year before *Sleutel der Devotie* appeared, Gisbertus Voetius had provided a similar exegesis of Romans 8:16 in *Proeve van de Kracht der Godzaligheid* (Utrecht: Simon de Vries, 1656), pp. 263-64.

[114]*Alle de Wercken* 2:37; *Huys-boeck*, p. 340.

[115]Ibid., p. 338.

Reformation divines and be brought into English Puritan thinking by Thomas Goodwin.[116]

Teellinck maintained that the Spirit often works gradually toward His immediate witness of assurance. In *Huys-boeck* he listed six such steps: (1) receiving an eye to see that salvation is possible by Jesus Christ, (2) longing for Christ, (3) providing all necessary means to receive Christ, (4) seeing that Christ has satisfied all the conditions of satisfaction for the sinner, so that God's promises may be freely given, (5) applying Christ to the soul, and (6) sealing the assurance of the forgiveness of sins.[117]

In summary, Teellinck's doctrine of assurance showed certain elements of Calvin[118] and Perkins. Both of those influences would continue in the Dutch Second Reformation as well as in German Pietism[119] and English Puritanism. Both also would be further refined by the Westminster Assembly.

---

[116]Cf. chapter 9 below. Graafland thinks that Teellinck teaches a twofold trust and a twofold assurance (*Zekerheid van het geloof*, pp. 176-77).

[117]*Huys-boeck*, pp. 598ff.

[118]This is not to deny a considerable difference in emphasis between Calvin and Teellinck with regard to faith. "Calvin views faith primarily as the knowledge of God's benevolence towards us. Although Teellinck will not deny this, he lays more emphasis on feeling spiritual communion with God" (Hamming, "Willem Teellinck," p. 111).

[119]F. A. Lampe often cited Teellinck (ibid., p. 114).

PART II
Assurance from the Westminster
Assembly to Alexander Comrie

VI.   ENGLISH PURITANISM AND THE
WESTMINSTER CONFESSION, CHAPTER 18

William Perkins's influence on the Puritan doctrine of assurance
was substantial.[1] As Gordon Keddie wrote: "A cursory examination
of the Westminster Confession must show the close approximation
of its statement of the doctrine of assurance to that — in much less
concise terms — of Perkins a half-century before. All that is in the
Confession is already in Perkins — it is in him that we see perhaps
the first formulation in English theology of what was to become
Presbyterian orthodoxy in centuries to come."[2]

By the time the Westminster Confession of Faith, the Larger
Catechism, and the Shorter Catechism[3] were written by the
Westminster Assembly[4] in the 1640s, Puritanism had reached its

---

[1]McNally, "Some Aspects of Thomas Goodwin's Doctrine of Assurance," p. 42;
Letham, "The Relationship between Saving Faith and Assurance," pp. 27-29; Lachman,
The Marrow Controversy, pp. 9-12; Kendall, "The Puritan Modification of Calvin's
Theology," pp. 197-98.

[2]"The Doctrine of Assurance in William Perkins," p. 244.

[3]The Shorter Catechism does not add to the teaching of the Westminster Confession
of Faith on assurance or its ancillary doctrines. The Larger Catechism, usually regarded as
the assembly's most definitive statement since it was completed last, provides a few minor
clarifications in questions 80-81 which deal with assurance. First, it ties assurance more
tightly to perseverance: "be infallibly assured that they are in the estate of grace, and shall
persevere therein unto salvation" (Q. 80). But this is hardly substantial since the
Westminster Confession of Faith has assurance (chapter 18) flow naturally out of
perseverance (chapter 17). Second, it drops the *"so belong"* of 18.3, causing some to claim
that the Larger Catechism proceeded a step further in separating assurance from faith so
as to conclude that assurance is in *no* sense of the essence of faith. But that is a
misconception (see pp. 147-48 below). Cf. James Benjamin Green, *A Harmony of the
Westminster Presbyterian Standards* (New York: Wm. Collins and World, 1976), pp. 107-109.

[4]The most important literature on the Puritan Westminster Assembly is Robert
Baillie, *The Letters and Journals of Robert Baillie*, 3 vols., ed. David Laing (Edinburgh:

apex. The doctrine of assurance was codified by the Westminster Assembly in chapter 18 of the Confession. Though that chapter did not deviate in essence from the teaching of the Reformers, it did include emphases that were minimized by Calvin.

These emphases were well-established in Puritan writings prior to the assembly. Consequently, no significant debate accompanied the writing of the chapter on assurance.[5] Despite what Robert Kendall and Holmes Rolston wrote, such unanimity would hardly have been possible if the assembly had departed substantially from the doctrine of Calvin.[6] J.I. Packer has rightly noted the paradox of Kendall's contention "that Puritan theology, setting out to be

Robert Ogle, 1841-42); S. W. Carruthers, *The Westminster Confession of Faith* (Manchester: R. Aikman & Son, 1937), and *The Everyday Work of the Westminster Assembly* (Philadelphia: Presbyterian Historical Society, 1943); George Gillespie, "Notes of Debates and Proceedings of the Assembly of Divines and Other Commissioners at Westminster, February 1644 to January 1645," *The Presbyterian Armoury*, vol. 2 (Edinburgh: Robert Ogle, Oliver and Boyd, 1846); W. M. Hetherington, *History of the Westminster Assembly of Divines* (New York: Robert Carter & Brothers, 1859); Larry Holley, "The Divines of the Westminster Assembly: A Study of Puritanism and Parliament" (Ph.D. dissertation, Yale, 1979); John Leith, *Assembly at Westminster: Reformed Theology in the Making* (Richmond, Va.: John Knox Press, 1973); John Lightfoot, "The Journal of the Proceedings of the Assembly of Divines from January 1, 1643, to December 31, 1644; and Letters to and from Dr. Lightfoot," vol. 13 in *The Whole Works of the Rev. John Lightfoot*, ed. John Rogers Pitman (London: J. F. Dove, 1844); "Minutes of the Sessions of the Assembly of Divines, from August 4th, 1643, to March 25th, 1652," transcripts by E. Maunde Thompson and John Struthers, 3 vols. (original manuscripts in Dr. Williams' Library, London; transcripts in Advocates' Library, Edinburgh); *Minutes of the Sessions of the Westminster Divines*, ed. Alexander F. Mitchell and John Struthers (Edinburgh: William Blackwood, 1874); Alexander F. Mitchell, *The Westminster Assembly: Its History and Standards* (Philadelphia: Presbyterian Board of Publications, 1884); James Reid, *Memoirs of the Lives and Writings of those Eminent Divines who convened in the famous Assembly at Westminster in the Seventeenth Century*, 2 vols. (Paisley: Stephen and Andrew Young, 1811); Wayne Spear, "Covenantal Uniformity in Religion: The Influence of the Scottish Commissioners Upon the Ecclesiology of the Westminster Assembly" (Ph.D. dissertation, University of Pittsburgh, 1976); Benjamin B. Warfield, *The Westminster Assembly and Its Work* (reprint ed., Cherry Hill: Mack Publishing Co., 1972); John Richard de Witt, *Jus Divinum: The Westminster Assembly and the Divine Right of Church Government* (Kampen: Kok, 1969).

Scores of expositions have been written on the assembly's doctrinal writings. See especially A. A. Hodge, John MacPherson, Robert Shaw, and G. I. Williamson on the Confession of Faith; Thomas Ridgley on the Larger Catechism; Thomas Boston, John Brown, Ebenezer Erskine and James Fisher, John Flavel, Ashbel Green, Thomas Vincent, Thomas Watson, and Alexander Whyte on the Shorter Catechism; Francis Beattie and Edward Morris on all three documents.

[5]*Minutes of the Sessions of the Westminster Divines*, ed. Alexander F. Mitchell and John Struthers, p. 282.

[6]*John Calvin versus the Westminster Confession* (Richmond, Va.: John Knox Press, 1972).

Calvinistic, turned within half a century into Arminian legalism without anyone noticing."[7]

The assembly's divines were well-versed on the subject of assurance. At least twenty-five members of the assembly wrote treatises on the doctrines of faith and assurance. They included John Arrowsmith, William Bridge, Anthony Burgess, Cornelius Burgess, Jeremiah Burroughs, Richard Byfield, Joseph Caryl, Daniel Cawdrey, Thomas Gataker, George Gillespie, Thomas Goodwin, William Gouge, William Greenhill, Robert Harris, John Ley, John Lightfoot, Philip Nye, Edward Reynolds, Samuel Rutherford, Henry Scudder, Obadiah Sedgwick, William Spurstowe, William Twisse, Richard Vines, and Jeremiah Whitaker.[8] By the 1640s, English Puritan thought was nearly unanimous on the following distinctives of assurance.[9]

Puritan Thought on Assurance by the 1640s

First, the Puritans taught that *saving faith* must be distinguished from *assurance*. Though saving faith includes assurance by definition, full assurance of salvation must be regarded as a *fruit* of faith rather than of faith's *essence*.[10] As Samuel Rutherford wrote, "That faith is essentially a perswasion and assurance of the love of God to me in Christ, its more then I could ever learne to bee the nature of Faith, a consequent separable I believe it is."[11]

---

[7] *A Quest for Godliness: The Puritan Vision of the Christian Life*, p. 338n.

[8] See notes below and bibliography for details. Almost all of these authors' treatises have been consulted. Deviations between them on assurance are minor, with the exception noted below on the witness of the Spirit (pp. 142-46).

[9] The most reliable secondary sources on the Puritan doctrine of assurance are Richard M. Hawkes, "The Logic of Assurance in English Puritan Theology," *Westminster Theological Journal* 52 (1990):247-61, and "The Logic of Grace in John Owen, D.D.: An Analysis, Exposition, and Defense of John Owen's Puritan Theology of Grace" (Ph.D. dissertation, Westminster Theological Seminary, 1987), pp. 344-67; Geoffrey F. Nuttall, *The Holy Spirit in Puritan Faith and Experience* (Oxford: Basil Blackwell, 1946), pp. 34-61, 138-41; John von Rohr, "Covenant and Assurance in Early English Puritanism," *Church History* 34 (1965):195-203 and *The Covenant of Grace in Puritan Thought* (Atlanta: Scholars Press, 1986), pp. 155-91; C. J. Sommerville, "Conversion, Sacrament and Assurance in the Puritan Covenant of Grace to 1650" (M.A. thesis, University of Kansas, 1963); William K. B. Stoever, '*A Fair and Easie Way to Heaven': Covenant Theology and Antinomianism in Early Massachusetts* (Middletown: Wesleyan University Press, 1978), pp. 119-60.

[10] J.C. Ryle, *Assurance* (reprint ed., Houston: Christian Focus, 1989), pp. 125-50.

[11] *Christ Dying and Drawing Sinners to Himselfe* (London: J. D. for Andrew Cooke, 1647), p. 85.

The Puritans did not deny that there was some assurance in every exercise of faith, so they could speak of all believers possessing assurance at times. "There be Christians of all ages and of all sizes in Gods family," wrote Robert Harris; hence "all Gods children have some assurance, though all have not alike."[12] According to Rutherford, faith and assurance are organically related. He wrote, "Faith is ane assurance of knowledge that Christ cam into the world to die for sinners, and a resting and a hanging upon Christ with all the heart for salvation."[13] The assurance such divines most commonly wrote about, however, accompanied mature, self-conscious faith. In that sense, assurance is not of the essence of faith but of the "cream of faith."

This dual use of the term explains why the Puritans could state that "assurance is not of the essence of a Christian," yet is organically of the essence of faith. Richard Hawkes rightly notes, "While the Puritans distinguish full assurance from the initial trust of faith, they will not allow a division between the two, for full assurance grows out of an assurance implicit in the first act of faith."[14] Hence Puritan divines could speak of assurance growing out of faith as well as of faith growing into assurance. For example, Thomas Brooks wrote, "Faith, in time, will of its own accord raise and advance itself to assurance."[15]

This distinction between faith and assurance had profound doctrinal and pastoral implications. To make justification dependent upon assurance compelled the believer to rely upon his own condition rather than on the sufficiency of a triune God in redemption. Such reliance is not only unsound doctrine but also bears adverse pastoral effects. God does not require full and perfect faith, but sincere and unfeigned faith. Fulfilment of God's promises depends on receiving Christ's righteousness, not upon the degree of assurance in that act.[16] If salvation depended on full assurance of

---

[12]*The VVay to True Happinesse. Deliuered in xxiv. sermons vpon the beatitudes* (London: I. Bartlett, 1632), 2:51.

[13]*Catechisms of the Second Reformation*, ed. Alexander F. Mitchell (London: James Nisbet & Co., 1886), p. 203.

[14]"The Logic of Assurance in English Puritan Theology," p. 250.

[15]*Heaven on Earth* (reprint ed., London: Banner of Truth Trust, 1961), pp. 15, 21. John Dod distinguished between "moon-shine" assurance given upon assenting to and trusting in the promise and "sun-shine" assurance attained with "full assurance" (*The Ten Commandments*, p. 10).

[16]John Ball, *A Treatise of Faith* (London: Edward Brewster, 1657), pp. 84-87.

faith, many would despair, for then "the palsied hand of faith should not receive Christ," John Downame wrote.[17]

Happily, the certainty of salvation does not depend on the believer, for "believers do not have the same assurance of grace and favor of God, nor do the same ones have it at all times."[18] Pastorally, it is critical to maintain that doubt can accompany even justifying faith.

Consequently, the Puritans differentiated between the faith of *adherency* to Christ and the faith of *assurance* (or *evidence*) in Christ, whereby the believer *knows* that Christ has died particularly for him.[19] According to Anthony Burgess, one of the Westminster divines: "Faith of adherence is many times where this faith of evidence is not.... [By sin we often] chase away our assurance; many times the people of God may walk without this comfortable perswasion" of the faith of evidence.[20] Spiritual life and participation in the covenant are not dependent upon experimental certainty. True faith may be planted in the heart even when assurance is missing. "It is one thing for me to believe, and another thing for me to believe that I believe," wrote Thomas Brooks.[21]

Second, the Puritans taught that a believer comes to personal assurance through the *work of the Holy Spirit,* in particular: (1) through an application of God's promises in Christ which the believer appropriates by faith, (2) through an act of faith inseparable from the practical and mystical syllogisms, and (3) through the Spirit's direct witness by the Word to the believer that Christ is *his* Savior and has forgiven *his* sins.[22]

Thus, the Spirit helps the believer to reach assurance in varying degrees through a variety of means.[23] "The Spirit doth withal

[17]*A Treatise of the True Nature and Definition of Justifying Faith* (Oxford: I. Lichfield for E. Forrest, 1635), pp. 12-13.

[18]William Ames, *Medvlla SS. Theologiae, ex sacris literis, earumque interpretibus, extracts & methodice disposita* (Amstelodami: Joannem Janssonium, 1627), 1.27.19.

[19]Ames, *Medvlla,* 1.27.16; Ball, *A Treatise of Faith,* pp. 90ff.; Robert Bolton, *Some General Directions for a Comfortable Walking with God* (London: Felix Kyngston, 1625), pp. 321-22; John Preston, *The Breast-Plate of Faith and Love,* 5th ed. (London: W. I. for Nicholas Bourne, 1632), part 1, pp. 63-64.

[20]*Spiritual Refining or a Treatise of Grace and Assurance. Wherein are handled, the doctrine of assurance. The use of signs in self-examination.* (reprint ed., Ames, Ia.: International Outreach, 1990), p. 672. (Hereafter, *Spiritual Refining*).

[21]Brooks, *Heaven on Earth,* p. 14.

[22]Cf. Burgess, *Spiritual Refining,* pp. 51, 54, 59, 671.

[23]Paul Baynes, *A Helpe to trve Happinesse. Or, a briefe and learned exposition of the*

immediately assist the mind of man," wrote Richard Fairclough.[24] Without the Holy Spirit, there can be no real assurance.[25]

Third, the Puritan writers said this assuring work of the Spirit is based upon the sure *covenant of grace* and the *saving work of Christ*, which in turn is grounded in God's sovereign good pleasure and love in eternal *election*.[26] Assurance flows out of the certainty that God will not disinherit His adopted children. His covenant cannot be broken, for it is fixed in His eternal decree and promises.

Consequently, the believer may plead for the fulfilment of the covenant on the ground that God promised to do so. Many Puritans gave the same rationale for claiming forgiveness of sins, sanctification, deliverance from afflictions, and virtually every spiritual need. John Preston said, "Plead the covenant hard with God . . . . Goe to God now, and tell him it is a part of his Covenant to deliver thee, and . . . take no denyall, though the Lord may deferre long, yet he will doe it, he cannot chuse; for it is part of his Covenant. . . and he cannot be a Covenant-breaker."[27] On occasion, they even spoke of "suing God for grace." For example, Robert Harris wrote, "The more we urge him with his covenant and hold him to it, the better he likes it and the sooner he inclines to us."[28]

Perry Miller said this about that Puritan approach: "The end of the Covenant of Grace is to give security to the transactions between God and men, for by binding God to the terms, it binds Him to save those who make good the terms."[29]

As von Rohr points out, however, Miller overlooked the Puritan teaching that the ultimate security of the covenant rests in the one-sided action of God's sovereign grace. Von Rohr explains:

maine and fundamental points of Christian religion (London: I. H. for W. Bladen, 1622), pp. 191-92.

[24]"The Nature of a True Believer's Attaining to a Certain Knowledge," in *Puritan Sermons 1659-1689: Being the Morning Exercises at Cripplegate, St. Giles in the Fields, and in Southwark by Seventy-five Ministers of the Gospel in or near London*, 6 vols. (reprint ed., Wheaton, Ill.: Richard Owen Roberts, 1981), 6:404.

[25]See pp. 146-47 below.

[26]Jeremiah Burroughs, *An Exposition of the Prophecy of Hosea* (reprint ed., Morgan, Pa.: Soli Deo Gloria, 1988), p. 590. Cf. Peter Lake, *Moderate Puritans and the Elizabethan Church* (Cambridge: University of Cambridge Press, 1982), pp. 99-104.

[27]*The New Covenant or the Saints Portion: A Treatise Unfolding the all-sufficiencie of God, Man's uprightness, and the Covenant of Grace*, 10th ed. (London: I. D. for Nicholas Bourne, 1639), pp. 224ff.

[28]*A Treatise of the New Covenant* (London: for Nicholas Bourne, 1632), part 2, p. 163.

[29]*The New England Mind: The Seventeenth Century*, p. 389.

The Covenant of Grace is both conditional and absolute. Faith is required as a condition within it antecedent to salvation, but that very faith is already granted by it as a gift consequent of election. As Ames put it, "the condition of the Covenant is also promised in the Covenant".... For Ames the promise of fulfillment of covenant conditions was itself covenant promise. And Preston designated it a "double covenant" in which "God doth not onely promise for his part, but makes a covenant to inable us to performe the conditions on our part".... In the Covenant, in this final sense, grace does all, and reliance must be upon this promise.... The doctrines of total depravity and of total divine sovereignty could not be relinquished. Thus as God's Covenant was also his divine gift of faith to his elect, assurance must likewise look to the absolute character of his promises and to that immutable good pleasure of his will upon which all things depend.[30]

Miller exaggerated the Puritan concept of covenant, saying it weakened or even usurped divine predestination. But in reality, the Puritans taught that election and covenant reinforce each other. As William Stoever noted: "Puritan covenant theology offered troubled saints a double source of assurance. It allowed them to plead the covenant with God, importuning him to fulfill his part of the bargain by performing what he had promised; and it encouraged them to seek comfort in the sufficiency of prevenient grace and in the immutability of God's will in election, which underlay the covenant itself and their own participation in it."[31]

God's *absolute promises* in election and covenant convince the believer that even if he lacks the acts of faith at a given moment, he cannot utterly lose the principle of faith, for faith is rooted in the electing, covenantal God.[32] Not even sin can break that covenant.[33]

Nevertheless, assurance is affected by the *conditional* dimension of the covenant. As Peter Bulkeley said, "The absolute promises are laid before us as the foundation of our salvation ... and the conditionall as the foundation of our assurance."[34] The conditional promises are inseparable from the believer's daily renewal of the covenant by

---

[30]"Covenant and Assurance in Early English Puritanism," pp. 199-202.

[31]*'A Faire and Easie Way to Heaven,'* pp. 147-48. Cf. Lachman, *Marrow Controversy*, pp. 53-54.

[32]Peter Bulkeley, *The Gospel-Covenant; or the Covenant of Grace Opened*, 2nd ed. (London: Matthew Simmons, 1651), p. 276.

[33]Richard Sibbes, *The Complete Works of Richard Sibbes*, ed. with memoir by A. B. Grosart (Edinburgh: James Nichol, 1862), 1:220.

[34]Peter Bulkeley, *The Gospel-Covenant*, pp. 323-24.

means of prayer, meditation, and worship. The sacraments also offer important seasonal reminders of covenant-renewal.[35] "To gather up assurance from the conditions of the covenant is the highest pitch of Christianity," wrote Thomas Blake.[36]

Ultimately, however, even a believer at the "highest pitch" must return to God's absolute promises, for, as William Perkins said, "the anker of hope must be fixed in that truth and stability of the immutable good pleasure of God."[37] This "good pleasure" is not arbitrary, but testifies of God's faithfulness in the covenant. The God of election, of covenant, and of absolute promises also grants grace to perform the conditional promises. As von Rohr concluded: "Though grounds for assurance are in the conditional covenant, they are not removed from the covenant as absolute. Reliance must somehow be upon the promises of the latter in order that it may also be on the conditions of the former."[38]

Fourth, though assurance is not complete in this life, being subject to doubt and trial, it must be diligently sought after through the means of grace.[39] With the exception of salvation, full assurance is life's supreme goal. "The being in a state of grace will yield a man heaven hereafter, but the seeing of himself in this state will yield him both a heaven here and a heaven hereafter," wrote Thomas Brooks.[40]

Such assurance is well-grounded only when regarded as a sovereign gift of God and when it accompanies evidences of a new heart and life. Those evidences include humiliation, self-denial, "reuerent feare" of God's will, eagerness to serve and please the Lord, a sincere love for God and the saints, an intense cleaving to Christ, peace and joy in receiving the Spirit's benefits, and good works.[41]

For the Puritans, having the principle or "habit" of faith is not sufficient because inactive faith is false faith. As John Preston wrote:

---

[35]Von Rohr, *The Covenant of Grace in Puritan Thought*, p. 186. See E. Brooks Holifield, *The Covenant Sealed: The Development of Puritan Sacramental Theology in Old and New England, 1570-1720* (New Haven: Yale University Press, 1974), pp. 38-61 for how the Puritans viewed the sacraments as fostering assurance.

[36]*Vindiciae Foederis, or a Treatise of the Covenant of God entered with man-kinde, in the several Kindes and Degrees of it* (London: A. Roper, 1653).

[37]Perkins, *Works* 1:114.

[38]Von Rohr, *The Covenant of Grace in Puritan Thought*, p. 190.

[39]William Gouge, *A Learned and very useful Commentary on the whole Epistle to the Hebrews, being the substance of thirty years Wednesdayes lectures at Black-fryers* (reprint ed., Grand Rapids: Kregel, 1980), p. 426.

[40]Brooks, *Heaven on Earth*, p. 14.

[41]Cf. Cohen, *God's Caress*, p. 101; pp. 155-56 below.

A woman many times thinkes she is with childe, but if she finde no motion or stirring, it is an arguement she was deceived: So, when a man thinkes he hath faith in his heart, but yet he finds no life, no motion, no stirring, there is no work proceeding from his faith, it is an argument he was mistaken, hee was deceived in it: for if it be a right faith, it will worke, there will be life and motion in it.[42]

The Puritans denounced works-righteousness as legalism, but they also rejected assurance that rests on mere doctrine. Works cannot merit salvation, but they are fruits of salvation that flow out of grateful obedience to God.

The Puritans aimed to explain how faith is rightly strengthened by activity. "Working by faith is the shortest way to know God's will," Goodwin noted.[43] True faith is active, warm, and real. Faith has eyes and ears that behold Christ, feet that run to Him, and hands that appropriate His benefits.[44] Faith rests on Christ's faithfulness; it comes with the whole soul to Christ. By faith the believer "doth wholly leane upon Christ as his Saviour."[45] As Hawkes summarizes: "The Puritan offered an assurance founded in a lively, progressive, and personal encounter with a covenanting God. Faith and works were not in tension, for they were the coordinates around which the Christian's life cycled. . . . The Puritans conceive of works as one part of the spiraling growth in a knowledge of God, working, evaluating in faith, endeavoring anew out of sincere gratitude. Works are contained within the spiral of the life of faith."[46]

Chapter 18 of the Westminster Confession affirms this most succinctly. Its four brief paragraphs include the following themes: the *possibility* of assurance (18.1), the *foundation* of assurance (18.2), the *cultivation* of assurance (18.3), and the *renewal* of assurance (18.4).

18.1: Threefold Possibility

Although hypocrites, and other unregenerate men, may vainly deceive themselves with false hopes and carnal presumptions of being in the favour of God, and estate of salvation (which hope of theirs shall perish): yet such as truly believe in the Lord Jesus and love Him in sincerity,

---

[42]*The New Covenant* 2:145.

[43]*The Works of Thomas Goodwin* 7:144.

[44]John Preston, *The Saints Qualification; or, a Treatise of Humiliation and Sanctification*, 3rd ed. (London: I. D. for Nicholas Bourne, 1639), p. 332.

[45]Ames, *Medvlla*, 1.26.26.

[46]"The Logic of Assurance in English Puritan Theology," pp. 249, 253.

endeavouring to walk in all good conscience before Him, may, in this life, be certainly assured that they are in the state of grace, and may rejoice in the hope of the glory of God, which hope shall never make them ashamed.

Chapter 18.1 of the Confession presents three possibilities in relation to assurance: the possibility of false assurance, the possibility of true assurance, and the possibility of a lack of true assurance.

False Assurance

The Puritans were deeply convinced of the significance of the Confession's expression, "false hopes and carnal presumptions." That is shown in their detailing of religious exercises that fall under the umbrella of historical or temporary faith. They took Jeremiah 17:9 seriously: "The heart is deceitful above all things, and desperately wicked: who can know it?" The Puritans took to heart Christ's warning that some who professed to serve Him would be told in the final judgment, "I never knew you: depart from me" (Matthew 7:23).

In the sixth sermon of *Spiritual Refining*, "Shewing the Difference between true Assurance and Presumption," Anthony Burgess provided a typical, Puritan example of discriminating preaching. He first warned that false assurance is common among those who claim to be Christians: "The greatest part of Christians are delivered up to such a carnal confidence [that they] are like that mad *Athenian* who thought all the Ships on the Sea were his. How many are there, who when they hear the exact Discoveries that are made of Grace, whereby they may evidently conclude, that they are for the present shut out of this Kingdom, do yet blesse themselves, as if all were well with them!" True assurance and false assurance are vastly different, Burgess said. First, they differ in their "efficient cause or principle." False assurance is motivated by self-love and an outward belief in the gospel without any "apprehension of the depth of sinne." Second, the grounds of false assurance arise from "a meer naturall light and judgement about the state of regeneration," and from "outward comforts and plenty" enjoyed. Third, false assurance cannot identify with "the Manner and Method [by which] the Spirit of God doth usually work Assurance," which involves "serious Humiliation for sin, and feeling the burden of it . . . conflicts and doubts, and opposition of unbelief . . . [and] vehement and fiery assaults of Satan." Fourth, false assurance is exposed by lack of effects, such as little "diligent use of the means," no real inflaming of "the heart with love to God," and an inability to "keep up the heart under all discouragements and desolations." Fifth, false assurance is not accompanied by "the Companions of Concomitants" of true assurance, namely, "holy fear and trembling" as well as "Humility and lowlinesse of minde." Finally, false assurance will be shaken by some outward troubles rather than by sin, whereas true assurance remains strong in trials.[47]

After identifying false assurance, Burgess commented on remedies that the Holy Spirit can use to overthrow false assurance, even though "carnal presumers are seldom debased and humbled." Those remedies include a powerful and searching ministry that pierces the soul, a strong and particular application of the law, a discovery of the fullness and necessity of Christ, a profound affliction, an experience of the dreadful deathbed of a carnal professor of Christianity, and a serious consideration of how mistaken we can be in other areas of our lives.[48]

The Puritan concern about false assurance is summarized well by Sinclair Ferguson:

> It is . . . terribly possible for someone to have a kind of faith and assurance that is little more than self-confidence, born out of an intellectual conviction (what our fathers called historical faith) rather than out of a helpless casting of one's sinful self upon a willing Saviour. But so long as there is a vestige of reliance on *my* righteousness, *my* service, *my* knowledge of Scripture — so long as I rely on *my* faith rather than on Christ's work alone — so long am I the possessor of a false and temporal assurance. The sands of time are littered with the strewn wreckage of men and women who have made shipwreck of their souls because they went forward with a false assurance, not having really laid the foundation of Jesus Christ and him crucified. That is a tremendous danger.[49]

True Assurance

Chapter 18.1 of the Confession clearly says that assurance is possible for Christians, but it also stresses that assurance cannot be obtained apart from faith in Christ. Every part of section 18.1 is connected with Him: believe in *Him*; love *Him*; walk before *Him*. Assurance is a Christ-centered phenomenon, interwoven with

---

[47]*Spiritual Refining*, pp. 27-32.

[48]Ibid., pp. 33-34.

[49]*Taking the Christian Life Seriously* (Grand Rapids: Zondervan, 1982), p. 47. Cf. Samuel Rutherford, *The Trial and Triumph of Faith* (Edinburgh: William Collins, 1845), pp. 297-306; Whitney, *How Can I be Sure I'm a Christian?*, pp. 14-17, 115-33.

Christian believing, Christian loving, and fruits of faith in Christ. The essence of assurance is living in Christ.

Westminster and post-Westminster divines affirmed the possibility of assurance in a variety of ways: (1) biblical saints whose lives evidenced assurance; (2) many scriptures, that show how Christians may attain assurance; (3) commands in Scripture, such as 2 Peter 1:10, that Christians seriously search for assurance; (4) God's covenant promises that a Christian might get assurance; (5) "the Institution of Sacraments, as Signs and Seals particularly to Witnesse Gods love to us"; (6) the exercises of divine graces, including "the joy and thankfulness" of God's people; (7) "signs of grace, whereby a man may discern what he is"; and, most importantly, (8) "the peculiar office and work attributed to Gods Spirit . . . to witness with our spirit, to seal unto us" our salvation.[50]

Lacking the Consciousness of Assurance

Finally, section 18.1 and the writings of the assembly's theologians underscored a third option: Believers may possess saving faith without the assurance that they possess it. Assurance augments the joy of faith, but it is not essential to salvation. Faith *alone* justifies through Christ *alone*; assurance is the conscious enjoyment of that justifying salvation. For the Westminster divines, full assurance belonged more properly to the *well-being* (i.e., the healthy condition and robust prosperity) of faith, than to the *being* (i.e., the essence or state) of faith. Though there is some degree of assurance in every exercise of saving faith, the Christian may continue long without embracing full assurance, progressing no further than "the child of light walking in darkness" (Isaiah 50).[51] Every Christian, however, must seek to reach such a "comfortable assurance," for chapter 18 of the Confession is clearly written in the spirit of 1 John 5:13, "These things have I written unto you that believe on the name of the Son of God; that ye may know that ye have eternal life."

Assurance is necessary for spiritual health but not absolutely necessary for salvation. Burgess devoted the first two sermons of *Spiritual Refining* to "How necessary and advantageous the Assurance

---

[50]Anthony Burgess, *Spiritual Refining*, pp. 23-24, 676-77; Andrew Gray, *The Works of the Reverend and Pious Andrew Gray* (Glasgow: D. M'Kenzie, 1813), p. 205. Cf. John Brown, *A Compendious View of Natural and Revealed Religion*, 2nd ed. (Edinburgh: Murray and Cochrane, 1796), p. 423.

[51]Thomas Goodwin, *The Works of Thomas Goodwin, D.D.* 3:231-352.

of our being in the state of Grace is."[52] The advantages of assurance are so great that Burgess called assurance "Necessary": (1) "from the nature of faith," (2) "from God's glory," (3) to "have more Joy and Peace in our hearts," and (4) "in the usefulnesse of it, [for] hereby we shall be enlarged and quickened up to all holy Duties."[53] Nevertheless, assurance is "not of absolute necessity to salvation: Its not a necessary effect of our calling and election at all times."[54]

Another Westminster divine, William Bridge, typically summarized a variety of possibilities for the believer with regard to assurance:

> 1. Though it be possible for a man to attain to full assurance of God's love, yet he may have saving faith that hath no assurance. . . . 2. As a man may have true saving faith, and yet no assurance, so a man may have strong faith and assurance, yet many doubts, fears, and mistrustings may be left in his soul. . . . 3. A man may have strong faith and assurance, yet for a long time may be deprived of the feeling of it. . . . 4. It is possible a man may be a godly, gracious man, yet may continue and go on doubting for a long time, yea possibly, he may die doubting also.[55]

18.2: The Foundations of Personal Assurance

This certainty is not a bare conjectural and probable persuasion grounded upon a fallible hope; but an infallible assurance of faith founded upon the divine truth of the promises of salvation, the inward evidence of those graces unto which these promises are made, the testimony of the Spirit of adoption witnessing with our spirits that we are the children of God, which Spirit is the earnest of our inheritance, whereby we are sealed to the day of redemption.

The essential core of the Westminster Confession's doctrine of assurance lies in section 18.2. The heart of the Calvin versus Calvinist debate centers here. The rest of chapter 18 is a practical, appended commentary.

The Confession addresses the foundations of assurance in section 18.2. It is important here not to confuse the foundations or

---

[52]*Spiritual Refining*, pp. 1-11.

[53]Ibid., pp. 24-25.

[54]Ibid., pp. 24-25, 672.

[55]*The Works of William Bridge* (reprint ed., Beaver Falls, Pa.: Soli Deo Gloria Publications, 1989), 2:139-40.

grounds of *assurance*[56] with the foundations or grounds of *salvation*.[57] As John Murray clarified: "When we speak of the grounds of assurance, we are thinking of the ways in which a believer comes to entertain this assurance, not of the grounds on which his salvation rests. The grounds of salvation are as secure for the person who does not have full assurance as for the person who has."[58]

In this sense, section 18.2 presents a complex ground of assurance,[59] which includes a *primary, objective ground* ("divine truth of the promises of salvation," 18.2) and one or two *secondary, subjective grounds* ("the inward evidence of those graces unto which these promises are made," and "the testimony of the Spirit of adoption witnessing with our spirits"). When combined, *full* assurance of salvation[60] is affirmed by those grounds. As Louis Berkhof wrote: "It should be noted that the Confession speaks of a complex assurance.... It calls this the 'infallible (full) assurance of faith,' and asserts that this is not necessarily enjoyed by believers from the very moment that they accept Christ by faith."[61]

Divine Promises in Christ

In the first place, section 18.2 points to "the divine truth of the promises of salvation" as a ground for assurance. That emphasis implies several things for a believer's experience of assurance:

[56]Helm, *Calvin and the Calvinists*, p. 75.

[57]Ibid., p. 28, contra Kendall, *Calvin and English Calvinism to 1649*, p. 204. Kendall argues that section 18.2 "makes the inward evidences virtually the ground not merely of assurance but of salvation," but neglects to see that the promises are said to be made to the graces, not to the inward evidences of the graces. Moreover, Kendall fails to note that the assembly's divines believed that only the Holy Spirit can grant the syllogism.

[58]*Collected Writings* (Edinburgh: Banner of Truth Trust, 1980) 2:270. Cf. *The Works of Thomas Brooks* 3:249; G. Wisse, *Uit het Zieleleven over Geloofs-verzekerheid* (Kampen: Kok, 1920), p. 58, who preferred to use "fruit" over "ground," but was speaking of "the life of grace."

[59]James Buchanan, *The Doctrine of Justification: An Outline of Its History in the Church and of Its Exposition from Scripture* (Edinburgh: T. & T. Clark, 1867), p. 184.

[60]For the degree of infallibility, see Keddie, "The Doctrine of Assurance in William Perkins," pp. 232ff., and Bray, "The Value of Works in the Theology of Calvin and Beza," p. 80, where Beza is cited as moving beyond most Reformed writers by stating that this certainty is so infallible that it is as if the believer "had heard from God's own mouth His eternal decree and purpose" (*Tractationes Theologicae* 1:200). Cf. Francis Turretin, *Institutes of Elenctic Theology*, trans. George M. Giger (Phillipsburg, N.J.: P&R Publishers, 1994), 2:617-20; Thomas Ridgley, *A Body of Divinity on the Assembly's Larger Catechism* (Philadelphia: William W. Woodward, 1815), 3:244-45.

[61]Berkhof, *Assurance of Faith*, p. 28.

First, the believer does not gain assurance by looking at himself or anything he has produced apart from God's promises but primarily by looking to God's faithfulness in Christ as revealed in the promises of the gospel. John Owen wrote: "This assurance did not arise nor was taken from any thing that was peculiar unto [the believer,] but merely from the consideration of the faithfulness of God himself."[62] Unworthy believers find assurance through Spirit-worked faith which believes the gospel that God has given His Son to the death of the cross, so that forgiveness, righteousness, and eternal life are all free gifts. The same promises of the gospel that lead to salvation are sufficient to lead the believer to assurance, even when faith is viewed as conditional to the promise.[63] For when the believer exercises faith, said Rutherford, it is God "who of grace gives the condition of beleeving, and of grace the reward conditioned, so that faith binds all the weight upon God only, even in conditionall Gospel promises."[64] Ultimately, all hope and salvation rest upon God's gracious promises because those promises are propositions of divine and absolute truth spoken by the God who cannot lie. The believer finds his anchor-ground of assurance in the divine character of God's promises in Christ. As Edward Reynolds wrote: "To hope without a promise . . . is but to let an Anchor hang in the water, or catch in a Wave, and thereby to expect safety to the Vessell. . . . Promises are the efficient causes of our purification, as they are the objects of our Faith: For wee dare not beleeve without Promises."[65]

Second, as assurance grows, God's promises become increasingly real to the believer personally and experimentally. Burgess wrote, "Where there is this experimental knowledge, that mans heart is as it were the Bible's counterpane. The Scripture is the

---

[62] *The Works of John Owen* 3:367.

[63] Hence the gospel is ultimately unconditional, though many of its promises appear conditional. William Bridge quipped: "What if the condition of one promise, be the thing promised in another promise? . . . Now so it is, that the condition of one, is the thing promised in another promise. For example: in one promise, repentance is the condition of the promise, 2 Chron. vi. 37, 38; Joel ii. 15-19. But in another promise, repentance is the thing promised, Ezek. xxxvi. 26. . . . The Lord Jesus Christ hath performed the condition of the promise for you, better than you can perform it" (*The Works of William Bridge* 2:132-33).

[64] *The Covenant of Life Opened, or a Treatise of the Covenant of Grace* (Edinburgh: Andro Anderson for Robert Broun, 1655), p. 17.

[65] *Three Treatises of The Vanity of the Creature. The Sinfulnesse of Sinne. The Life of Christ* (London: B. B. for Rob Bastocke and George Badger, 1642), part 1, pp. 340, 342. Hereafter, *Three Treatises*.

original, and his heart is the copy of it, he can read over the Promises,... and can say, *Probatum est"* [It is proven].[66] Counterpane here is an archaic variant of counterpart, used in its technical, legal sense of being a duplicate or copy of the original. In this case, comparing scriptural promises with what has been experienced in the heart, the believer may conclude, "My salvation is proven!"

Third, by speaking of assurance resting upon God's promises as its primary ground, section 18.2 effectively ties the knot between *divine perseverance* (for God's promises are inseparable from His immutable character, His eternal election, and His gracious covenant) and the *believer's perseverance* already made explicit in chapter 3.8 of the Confession.[67] William Twisse, the chairman of the assembly, wrote that the best way to confirm the "golden chain" of William Perkins was to view experimental assurance in light of God's eternal commitment.[68]

Fourth, the Christ-centeredness of personal assurance is accented in God's promises, for Jesus Christ Himself is the "summe, fountaine, seal, treasury of all the promises."[69] In Him, the promises of God are "yea and amen" (2 Corinthians 1:20). Though the Savoy Declaration would be more poignant, stating that assurance is "founded on the blood and righteousness of Christ revealed in the gospel,"[70] yet the Confession's divines saw that Christ is inseparable from a promising God. As Rutherford states in his *Catechism*: "The new covenant is a masse of promises laying the weight of our salvatione upon a stronger

---

[66]*Spiritual Refining*, pp. 5-6.

[67]Cf. Graafland, *Zekerheid van het geloof*, p. 118; von Rohr, "Covenant and Assurance in Early English Puritanism," pp. 195ff., and *The Covenant of Grace in Puritan Thought*, pp. 3, 12-13, 46-54, 83-85, 102-105, 119-23, 179-91; Chalker, "Calvin and Some Seventeenth Century Calvinists," pp. 66-77; Wallace, *Puritans and Predestination*, pp. 45-52, 196; Berkouwer, *Faith and Perseverance*, pp. 57-60, 69; Stoever, *'A Faire and Easie Way to Heaven,'* pp. 109-118.

[68]*The Doctrine of the Synod of Dort and Arles, reduced to the practise* (Amsterdam: G. Thorp, 1631), pp. 146-48, and *A treatise of Mr. Cottons, Clearing certaine Doubts Concerning Predestination, Together with an Examination Thereof* (London: Printed by J. D. for Andrew Crook, 1646), pp. 63, 94-95, 104-113.

[69]Reynolds, *Three Treatises*, part 1, p. 365.

[70]Cf. pp. 187-89 below. Cf., "The promises are instrumental in the coming of Christ and the soul together; they are the warrant by which faith is emboldened to come to him, and take hold of him; but the union which faith makes, is not between a believer and the promise, but between a believer and Christ" (William Spurstowe, *The Wells of Salvation Opened: or, A Treatise discerning the nature, preciousness, and usefulness of the Gospel Promises and Rules for the Right Application of Them* [London: T.R. & E.M. for Ralph Smith, 1655], pp. 44-45).

than wee ar, to witt upon Christ, and faith grippeth [i.e., grasps or seizes hold of] promises and maketh us to goe out of ourselves to Christ as being homelie [i.e., familiar] with Christ."[71]

Thomas Goodwin said: "For if one promise do belong to thee, then all do; for every one conveys [the] whole Christ in whom all the promises are made and who is the matter of them."[72] And Edward Reynolds explained: "All the promises are made *in Christ* being purchased by his merits, and they are all perform'd *in Christ*, being administred by his power and office. . . . Promises . . . are *the Raies and Beames of Christ the Sonne of Righteousnesse*, in whom they are all founded and established. . . . *Every promise by Faith apprehended carries a man to Christ*, and to the consideration of our unity with him, in the right whereof we have claime to the *Promises*."[73]

The practical conclusion of such Christ-centeredness in assurance is forthright: "Let thy eye and heart, first, most, and last, be fixed upon Christ, then will assurance bed and board with thee," said Brooks.[74]

Finally, giving the divine promises priority coincides with an experimental order as well, for though full assurance in its complex grounds does not accompany all true faith, this lack does not lie in the object of faith, which is the triune God in Jesus Christ, nor in the salvation accomplished by Christ. All of Westminster's divines would undoubtedly have concurred with what John Murray wrote three centuries later: "Faith is not compatible with uncertainty as to its object, though it may consist with uncertainty as to the possession of the salvation which is the result of faith. Neither does it mean that there is any insecurity in the salvation of those who believe. The security does not rest upon the stability of the assurance the believer entertains of that security; the security resides in the faithfulness of the Saviour."[75]

Thus, the promises of God must always retain the first place because they are the believer's first, ultimate, and primary ground of assurance through a living faith. "The promises of God are a Christian's *magna charta*, his chiefest evidences for heaven," wrote Brooks, and then offered nine ways "a person may know whether he

---

[71]*Catechisms of the Second Reformation*, ed. Alex. Mitchell, p. 176.

[72]*The Works of Thomas Goodwin* 3:321.

[73]*Three Treatises*, part 1, pp. 356-57, 345.

[74]*Heaven on Earth*, p. 307.

[75]*Collected Writings* 2:266-67.

has a real and saving interest in the promises or no."[76] William Bridge said, "A promise once given unto a soul, shall never be reversed or repealed, and have ye not the whole gospel before you [as] a bag of golden promises?"[77]

The Westminster divines emphasized that though subjective phenomena may sometimes *feel* more sure than faith in God's promises, such experiences give less glory to God than divine promises apprehended directly by faith. William Spurstowe explained how faith revels in direct meditation on the promises:

> I have sometimes thought that a believer's looking on a promise, is not unlike a man's beholding of the heavens in a still and serene evening, who, when he first casts up his eye, sees haply a star or two only to peep, and with difficulty to put forth a feeble and disappearing light. By and by, he looks up again, and both their number and lustre are increased. A while after, he views the heavens again, and then the whole firmament, from every quarter, with a numberless multitude of stars, is richly enammelled as with so many golden studs.
>
> So when a Christian first turns his thoughts toward the promises, the appearances of light and comfort which shine from them, do oft times seem to be as weak and imperfect rays, which neither scatter fears nor darkness. When again he sets himself to ripen and improve his thoughts upon them, then the evidence and comfort which they yield to the soul is both clear and distinct: but when the heart and the affections are fully fixed in the meditation of a promise, oh ... what legions of beauties do then appear from every part of it which both ravish and fill the soul of the believer with delight![78]

Moreover, William Bridge advised: "If the promise does not come to you, go you to it. Sometimes the promise comes to us, sometimes we go to it. When the promise comes to you, you have joy; when you go to it, you have peace, and this peace may last longer than the joy. But remember this as an everlasting rule, that your very relying upon the promise makes it yours."[79]

The Confession's divines consistently reminded believers that the objective promise embraced by faith (never apart from faith)[80] is

---

[76]*The Works of Thomas Brooks* 3:254-59.

[77]*The Works of William Bridge* 2:130, 135.

[78]*A Treatise of Gospel*, pp. 78-79.

[79]*The Works of William Bridge* 2:40.

[80]Bridge portrayed God as saying to believers, "Here take the key of faith, for faith is the key, and hath a power to unlock all the promises. I give thee faith, and by this faith, I give thee a power to go unto all my promises" (ibid., 2:130).

infallible because it is God's all-comprehensive and faithful covenant promise. Spurstowe wrote, "Eye God in the promises, for the promises seal heaven to believers in the other life and begin it in this life."[81] Consequently, subjective evidence, though necessary, must always be based upon the promise and be regarded as secondary, for it is often mixed with human convictions and feelings even when it gazes upon the work of God. Rutherford rebuked those who place human feeling above divine promise. He wrote: "If any should buy a ship, and think it no bargain at all, except he might carry away the ship on his back, should not this make him a ridiculous merchant? God's law of faith, Christ's concluding atonement, is better and surer than your feeling. All that sense and comfort saith, is not canonic Scripture; it is adultery to seek a sign because we cannot rest on our husband's word."[82]

All exercises of saving faith apprehend to some degree the primary ground of divine promise in Christ.[83] Subjective experience must always be rooted in the objective promise.[84] Secondary grounds of assurance have validity only when subjective experience relies on the objective promise, for the subjective is nothing more than the application to the believer's consciousness of the objective. Consequently, like the objective ground, subjective grounds must never be separated from faith, the blood of Christ, the Holy Spirit, the covenant of grace, and the Word of God. When that is the case, God's promises purify the believer and conform him to the image of Christ.[85]

Those were the convictions of the Westminster Assembly's divines. By placing a heavier emphasis than did Calvin and the early Reformers on the secondary, subjective grounds of assurance, they did not contradict the Reformers. Their varying emphases related to the questions raised in the early and later Reformation era. Calvin was concerned largely with assurance of God's benevolence; the Puritans, with assurance of personal faith.[86] Calvin focused on the certainty of salvation in Christ; the Puritans dwelt on how the believer could be assured of his own salvation in Christ.[87] Questions raised with

[81]*A Treatise of Gospel Promises*, pp. 30ff. Cf. Charles Hodge, *Systematic Theology* (New York: Scribner, Armstrong, & Co., 1877), 3:107.

[82]*The Trial and Triumph of Faith*, pp. 33-34.

[83]Cf. Thomas Doolittle, *Puritan Sermons 1659-1689* 1:253.

[84]Berkhof, *Assurance of Faith*, pp. 51, 54.

[85]*Three Treatises*, part 1, pp. 344-45.

[86]Ferguson, "The Westminster Conference," p. 20.

[87]Hawkes, "The Logic of Assurance in English Puritan Theology," p. 251.

different emphases understandably received answers with different emphases. Calvin's teaching prompted fresh pastoral questions for subsequent generations. When the birth pangs of the Reformation subsided, a pressing need arose for detailed pastoral guidance on how objective truth is certified in the conscience of the believer.

Consequently, the Puritans used the Spirit's work of salvation to help believers toward assurance by directing them, in the tradition of Beza and Perkins, to grasp any link of the order of salvation in order to "press toward the mark for the prize of the high calling of God in Christ Jesus" (Philippians 3:14). As Burgess typically noted: "[Since] it is more difficult to finde some [signs of grace] in our selves then others, yet we are to proceed from those that are more facile, to those that are more difficult."[88] And John Downame concluded: "When we are to gather assurance of our election, we are to begin where the Lord endeth, and so ascend from the lowest degree [of sanctification] till wee come to the highest."[89]

Inward Evidences of Saving Grace

The Seat of Assurance: Christ's Internal Presence

The Puritans coveted a life that evidenced Christ's internal presence. Nevertheless, "Christ within" the believer became their seat of *assurance* (not seat of *faith*) only on the basis of Christ's meritorious work outside of the believer. They eschewed two kinds of religion, one that separated subjective experience from the objective Word which reaps man-centered mysticism, and one that presumed salvation on the fallacious grounds of historical or temporary faith. The possibility of falling into those errors lent earnestness to their call to procure subjective verification of the objective gospel: "What certainty can there be of election, remission of sin, justification, or glorification, if there be not a certainty of your sanctification and renovation? If that persuasion that is in you about your grace or sanctification be false, then that persuasion that is in you concerning remission of sin, predestination, justification, and eternal salvation is false. This highly concerns all to consider, that would not be miserable in both worlds," wrote Brooks.[90]

---

[88]*Spiritual Refining*, p. 53.

[89]*The Christian Warfare aginst the Deuill, World, and Flesh* (London: William Stansby, 1634), p. 231. Cf. von Rohr, "Covenant and Assurance in Early English Puritanism," p. 198.

[90]*The Works of Thomas Brooks* 3:469. Cf. Lake, *Moderate Puritans and the Elizabethan Church*, pp. 102, 156ff.

The Puritans believed that all Christ did outside of the Christian had its counterpart within him. The Christ who chiselled out everlasting salvation for His elect must also put them in possession of it; He who purchased for them a heavenly kingdom makes them "fit for the enjoyment of it."[91] This He does by means of what John Forbes called His "experienced word": God "speakes the word of trueth to the heart," causes the heart "to beleeve that which it hath heard and receyved," and adds "his spirit: and by the testimonie thereof . . . makes Adoption and eternall life, most certaine and sure to the soule."[92] An unspeakable interchange then transpires between the objective and the subjective, between the Christ and the Christian with respect to the promises of God. As Rutherford explained:

> The promise acteth upon the believer to quicken him, and he again putteth forth an act of life to embrace the promise, and putteth forth on it some act of vital heat to adhere and cleave to, and with warmness of heart to love it. And here the case is, as when the living hand layeth hold on the living hand; they warm one another mutually, according to that which Paul saith, "But I follow after, if that I may apprehend that for which also I am apprehended of Christ Jesus." (Phil. 3:12.) Here be two living things, Christ, and believing Paul, acting mutually upon another; there is a heart and a life upon each side.[93]

When the theologians of the Westminster Assembly regarded Christ's internal presence as the seat of assurance, they did not imply that the believer is justified by Christ within him; rather, Christ's internal presence represents the seat of assurance as the fruit of justification, as the evidence of vital union with Christ. Assurance embraces Christ's internal presence through enjoying the benefits of His justifying death and resurrection.

The Method of Assurance: The Practical and Mystical Syllogisms

The Puritans were convinced that the grace of God within believers confirms the reality of faith. William Ames wrote: "Hee that doth rightly understand the promise of the covenant, cannot be

---

[91]John Mason, *The Writings of the late John M. Mason* (New York: Ebenezer Mason, 1832), 1:330.

[92]*A Letter for resolving this Question: How a Christian man may discerne the testimonie of Gods spirit, from the testimonie of his owne spirit, in witnessing his Adoption* (Middelbvrgh: Richard Schilders, 1616), p. 37.

[93]*The Trial and Triumph of Faith*, pp. 297-98.

sure of his salvation, unlesse he perceive in himselfe true Faith and repentance."[94] They often viewed that grace of God within believers in terms of syllogisms which use the so-called reflex or reflective act of faith. John Flavel said, "The soul hath not only a power to *project*, but a power also to *reflect* upon its own actions; not only to put forth a *direct act* of faith on Jesus Christ, but to judge and discern that act also, 2 Tim. 1. 12. *I know in whom I have believed*. And this is the way in which believers attain their certainty and knowledge of their union with Christ."[95]

By the reflective act of faith, the Holy Spirit sheds light upon His own work in the believer, enabling him to conclude that his faith is saving because its exercises have a saving character. As Burgess wrote: "There are first the *direct acts* of the soul, whereby it is carried out immediately to some object. And there are secondly *reflex acts*, whereby the soul considers and takes notice of what acts it doth. It's as if the eye were turned inward to see itself. The Apostle John expresseth it fully, *We know that we know*, 1 John 2:3. So that when we believe in God, that is a direct act of the soul; when we repent of sin, because God is dishonoured, that is a direct act; but when we know that we do believe, and that we do repent, this is a reflex act."[96]

The Puritans talked about two closely related, yet distinct, syllogisms that fortify assurance — the practical syllogism and the mystical syllogism.[97] The practical syllogism was based on the believer's sanctification and good works in daily life. It emphasized the believer's life of obedience that confirmed his experience of grace. It went something like this: *Major premise*: According to Scripture, only those who possess saving faith will receive the Spirit's testimony that their lives manifest fruits of sanctification and good works. *Minor premise*: I cannot deny that by the grace of God I have received the Spirit's testimony that I manifest fruits of sanctification and good works. *Conclusion*: I am a partaker of saving faith.

The mystical syllogism was based on the believer's internal exercises and progress in the steps of grace. It focused on the inward man and went something like this: *Major premise*: According to Scripture, only those who possess saving faith will so experience the

---

[94]*Medvlla*, 1.3.22.

[95]John Flavel, *The Works of John Flavel* (reprint ed., London: Banner of Truth Trust, 1968), 2:330.

[96]*Spiritual Refining*, p. 672.

[97]Cf. pp. 65-72 above.

Spirit's confirmation of inward grace and godliness that self will decrease and Christ will increase. *Minor premise*: I cannot deny that by the grace of God I experience the Spirit's testimony confirming inward grace and godliness such that self decreases and Christ increases. *Conclusion*: I am a partaker of saving faith.

By the 1640s, Puritans were accepting the mystical syllogism on a par with the practical syllogism.[98] This balance appears in the Westminster Confession of Faith as well. The inclination of section 18.2 to lean to the mystical syllogism is counterbalanced with section 16.2: "These good works, done in obedience to God's commandments, are the fruits and evidences of a true and lively faith: and by them believers manifest their thankfulness, strengthen their assurance, edify their brethren, adorn the profession of the gospel, stop the mouths of the adversaries, and glorify God, whose workmanship they are, created in Christ Jesus thereunto, that, having their fruit unto holiness, they may have the end, eternal life."[99]

Consequently, mid-seventeenth century Puritan preachers often answered the great case of conscience, "How do I know whether or not I am a believer?" by offering a combination of signs that contained the good works of the practical syllogism as well as the steps of grace of the mystical syllogism. For example, after preaching eleven sermons on assurance, Burgess delivered eight messages on the true signs of grace and fifteen on the false signs of grace. True signs include obedience, sincerity, opposition against and abstinence from sin, openness to divine examination, growth in grace, spiritual performance of duties, and love to the godly. Signs that could fall short of saving grace include outward church privileges; spiritual gifts; affections of the heart in holy things; judgments and opinions about spiritual truth; great sufferings for Christ; strictness in religion; zeal in false worship; external obedience to the law of God; a belief of the truths of religion; a peaceable frame of heart and persuasion of God's love; outward success; prosperity and greatness in the world; and an abandonment of gross sins. The section on false signs concludes with a sermon on

---

[98]Graafland asserts that in the Netherlands the mystical syllogism came to the fore after the Synod of Dort. By the 18th century, it had superseded the practical syllogism in the Dutch Second Reformation ("Van *syllogismus practicus* naar *syllogismus mysticus*," p. 105).

[99]Cf. sections 18.3 and 18.4, as well as the emphasis on a "good conscience" in section 18.1 and the LC, Q. 80. Also, the appended "Sum of Saving Knowledge" should be consulted (*The Confession of Faith, the Larger and Shorter Catechisms together with The Sum of Saving Knowledge* [Inverness: Eccleslitho, 1970], pp. [322], 332-43).

"the difficulty, and in some sense, impossibility of salvation, notwithstanding the easinesse which men fancy to themselves thereof."[100] Thomas Brooks listed knowledge, faith, repentance, obedience, love, prayer, perseverance, and hope as marks of grace that accompany salvation.[101]

The practical syllogism was based on such texts as 2 Peter 1:5-10, which stresses virtue, knowledge, temperance, patience, godliness, brotherly love,[102] as well as a variety of texts from 1 John stressing the Christian walk. For example, "hereby we do know that we know him, if we keep his commandments" (1 John 2:3). "Whoso keepeth his word, in him verily is the love of God perfected: hereby know we that we are in him" (2:5). "We know that we have passed from death unto life, because we love the brethren" (3:14). "By this we know that we love the children of God, when we love God" (5:2).

The mystical syllogism evidenced itself in a variety of ways.[103] Burgess wrote: "Sometimes *Fear of God* is a signe, sometimes *Poverty of Spirit*, sometimes *Hungring and thirsting after Righteousnesse*, sometimes *Repentance*, sometimes *Love*, and sometimes *Patience*, So that if a godly man can finde any one of these in himself, he may conclude of his Salvation and Justification."[104]

A formal mystical syllogism was presented by Petrus Immens:

> The believer looking into the word of God, discovers therein what is declared with respect to the heirs of salvation, to wit, that they have fled for refuge to lay hold on the hope set before them; — that they hunger and thirst after the righteousness of Christ; — that God gives to them a new heart, by taking away the stony heart out of their flesh, and giving them a heart of flesh; — that they love God with all their strength, and are inclined to follow after holiness, without which no man can see the Lord. He then examines with the strictest scrutiny his heart upon all these points; and the result is, that he finds that all these things, in a greater or

---

[100]*Spiritual Refining*, pp. 61-200.

[101]*Heaven on Earth*, pp. 173-80.

[102]One of the assembly's two assessors, Cornelius Burgess, said on 2 Peter 1:5-7 that good works are "the way to heaven, not the cause of obtaining it, nor of reigning there; as fruits of faith, proving that it is lively; as effects and evidences of our justification by the righteousness of Christ, not contributing to it in the least degree; as testimonies of real gratitude unto God, and of conformity to the image of Christ" (*A Chain of Graces drawn out at length for a Reformation of Manners* [London, 1622], chapter 3).

[103]William Twisse, *The Doctrine of the Synod of Dort and Arles*, p. 158.

[104]*Spiritual Refining*, p. 41.

less degree, his soul has experienced — and directly draws the delightful conclusion, "I am an heir of salvation."[105]

In relation to section 18.2 of the Confession, those divines who regarded the "inward evidences" and "the testimony of the Spirit" as one phenomenon, were likely to emphasize the practical syllogism and sanctification. Others who were inclined to regard these as distinct phenomena were likely to focus on the mystical syllogism and steps in grace. Some of these divines, such as Thomas Goodwin, tended to view the inward evidences as ordinary and the testimony of the Spirit as extraordinary.[106]

In either case, however, the reflex act of faith is the key to both syllogisms. As Gerrit C. Berkouwer rightly concluded: "In both instances we are confronted with the same question, namely, the *syllogismus,* the 'conclusion' which is drawn from what is actually present in the believers."[107] The spirit of the reflex act of faith is expressed well by Francis Turretin. He wrote:

> By the direct act man believes the promises of the gospel: while by the reflex he looking upon his faith knows that he believes. The direct act precedes, the reflex follows, and such a subordination exists between them, that just as the direct draws the reflex after it, so the reflex necessarily supposes the first, nor has it a place unless the direct has gone before, for example, a person cannot know that he believes, unless he really believes, he cannot know Christ as his own, unless he believes Christ was given for all believers and penitents.[108]

To this it must be added that the reflective process can also be at times a spontaneous conviction that need not follow a conscious process.[109]

Anthony Burgess raised and answered six objections against the use of syllogisms and the reflex act of faith. In the fifth objection he came to the heart of the matter: "A fifth doubt *may be from the difficulty, if not impossibility of any certanty by signes:* for take we any signe, suppose love of the brethren, that must be explained of such

---

[105]*The Pious Communicant Encouraged*, trans. John Bassett (New York: Isaac Collins, 1801), 1:95.

[106]See chapter 9 below. This may help account for the difference between Richard Lovelace's definition of the mystical syllogism as "direct assurance by the Spirit" (*The American Pietism of Cotton Mather*, p. 96), and Letham's definition which focuses on assurance being derived from subjective inner attitudes ("Saving Faith and Assurance in Reformed Theology," 1:14).

[107]*Divine Election*, p. 286.

[108]*Institutes of Elenctic Theology*, 2:616-32.

[109]Berkhof, *Assurance of Faith*, pp. 59, 64. Cf. J. van Genderen, *Het practisch syllogisme: De sluitrede des geloofs* (Alphen a/d Rijn: Buijs, 1954), pp. 10ff.

love as is because they are brethren, and of such a love as proceedeth from upright principles, and pure motives, and with many other qualifications, which will be as hard to know, as the inward root of grace it self." Burgess answered that objection by stating: First, if only a few, yes, even one sign of grace is affirmed by the reflex act of faith, the believer "may assuredly gather all the rest are there, for the whole harmony and connexion of grace is compared to the image of God, which doth consist of all its due lineaments."

Second, the reflex act of faith is the easiest way to reach assurance, for our natures are more prone to proceed from the effect to the cause — i.e. from signs of grace to God as the author of grace — than from cause to effect.

Third, *although a man may doubt of some Signes, yet it doth not follow he will doubt of all, because his temptation may be stronger about one Sign then another, and one Sign may be more easily perceived than another; And so a godly man may argue from that which is lesse known, to the other that is more known.*"[110]

George Gillespie, a highly influential Scottish delegate to the assembly, said that even though Satan deceives many "syllogistically by false reasonings," the "way of marks is a sure and safe way in itself" when the syllogism is directed by the Spirit, for the Spirit cannot err. On the other hand, Gillespie warned that all seriously err who use the syllogisms to contribute to justification or to be led away from Christ and the Spirit.[111]

The Puritans were aware of possible "free-will" overtones in the "reflex act" and took pains to keep it within the confines of the doctrines of grace by further analysis of the syllogism:

First, the syllogism itself was regarded as rooted in God. All believers were forbidden to trust in their *own* trusting or the conclusions they drew from it. Richard Sibbes said, "God hath prescribed trust as the way to carry our souls to himself, in whom we should only rely, and not in our imperfect trust, which hath its ebbing and flowing."[112] All assurance, including both forms of syllogism, remains just as much a divine work as justification, sanctification, and perseverance. In the syllogism sanctification is

---

[110]*Spiritual Refining*, pp. 52-54.

[111]*A Treatise of Miscellany Questions* (Edinburgh: Gideon Lithgovv, 1649), pp. 104ff. Cf. Bell, *Calvin and Scottish Theology: The Doctrine of Assurance*, p. 114.

[112]*The Complete Works of Richard Sibbes* 1:220.

confirmed, which in turn is the test of justification, both of which are ultimately of God in Christ (1 Corinthians 1:30).

Second, the Puritans taught that the syllogism flowed out of the living Word, Jesus Christ,[113] and was based on the written Word for its very framework.[114] The syllogism must always be subordinated to Christ. Thomas Brooks wrote: "We may and ought to make a sober use of characters and evidences of our gracious estates, to support, comfort, and encourage us on our way to heaven, but still in subordination to Christ, and to the fresh and frequent exercises of faith upon the person, blood, and righteousness of Jesus."[115]

The reflex act of faith arises from the believer seeing in himself Christ's "special, peculiar, and distinguishing graces"[116] as they conform to the Word of God. John Ball said, "Ordinary assurance is concluded by joining the light of their conscience kindled by the Holy Ghost, and ruled by the scriptures, to the immediate light of the conditions revealed in the scriptures. . . . The rule by which a man discerns himself to believe, is the doctrine of God's word, declaring the quality of faith."[117]

Third, the syllogism must be considered as the work of the Spirit. "Assurance consists of a practical syllogism, in which the Word of God is the major, conscience the minor, and the Spirit of God the conclusion," said Thomas Watson.[118] Though some Westminster divines assumed their readers knew that the syllogism can never be a mere human conclusion separated from the Spirit and the gracious faith He works, others emphasized precisely that point.[119] The Spirit "writes first all graces in us, and then teaches us to read his handwriting," wrote Thomas Goodwin.[120] "Only so far as

---

[113]*The Works of Thomas Goodwin* 3:321.

[114]Pronk, "Assurance of Faith," *The Messenger* 24 (May 1977), pp. 5-6.

[115]*The Works of Thomas Brooks* 3:237.

[116]Ibid., 2:316.

[117]John Ball, *A Treatise of Faith*, p. 95. Cf. the meeting of Christian and Ignorance in Bunyan's *Pilgrim Progress*, which concludes with Christian saying to Ignorance: "Your heart tells you so? . . . Except the Word of God bears witness in this matter, other testimony is of no value" (*The Complete Works of John Bunyan*, vol. 2 [reprint ed., Marshalltown: National Foundation for Christian Education, 1968], pp. 67-68).

[118]*A Body of Divinity* (reprint ed., Grand Rapids: Sovereign Grace Publishers, n.d.), p. 250.

[119]E.g., Burgess, *Spiritual Refining*, p. 671; Henry Scudder, *The Christian's Daily Walk in Holy Security and Peace* (reprint ed., Harrisonburg, Va.: Sprinkle Publications, 1984), pp. 335ff.; *The Works of Thomas Goodwin* 7:65.

[120]Ibid., 6:27.

the Spirit of God does witness to your spirits that it is so, are you indeed his children," Henry Scudder said.[121] And Anthony Burgess stressed that the Spirit may not be separated from the reflex act of faith: "We say not the Graces of Gods Spirit, can or do witnesse of themselves, The sealing and witnessing is efficiently from the Spirit of God, they are only the means by which Gods Spirit makes known it self. And therefore as colours, though they be the object of sight, yet they cannot actually be seen without light shining upon them: so neither are we able to behold the good things God hath wrought for us without the Spirit of God." Burgess concluded, "In Philosophy, reason makes the major and minor in any Syllogism; [but] in spiritual things, the Spirit of God enableth a man to make a whole Syllogism for a believers comfort and establishment."[122]

For the Puritans, reason, though helpless without the Spirit, is a ready instrument by which the Spirit may in due time establish faith.[123] Consequently, if we desire to attempt to increase assurance by syllogism we must "above all pray to God for his Spirit, so to enlighten our eyes. . . . For the Spirit of God is the efficient cause of all this Certainty," Burgess said.[124] As Jon Zens concludes: "The three pillars of the Westminster Confession are all directly related to the work of the Spirit. He produces the inward graces and reveals this transformation to the mind of the believer. He makes the promises of the Word real to the believer and He bears direct witness with the spirit of the saint that he is a child of God."[125]

The syllogism leaves no room for any human merit based on sanctification, faith, experience, or works. Hawkes rightly notes, "In Puritan theology, assurance has nothing to do with meritorious works. It is rather the way by which the Christian discovers the unmerited grace of Christ working in him and is to be desired not as a subjective good, but for the knowledge of the glory of Christ it bears with it."[126] Both forms of syllogism are essentially anti-voluntaristic at root according to the minds of Westminster divines, notwithstanding the interpretation R. T. Kendall imposes on

---

[121]*The Christian's Daily Walk in Holy Security and Peace*, p. 335.

[122]*Spiritual Refining*, pp. 51, 54.

[123]Hawkes, "The Logic of Assurance in English Puritan Theology," p. 255; Brooks, *Heaven on Earth*, p. 109.

[124]*Spiritual Refining*, p. 59.

[125]"The Doctrine of Assurance," p. 45.

[126]"The Logic of Assurance in English Puritan Theology," p. 251.

them.[127] Paul Helm's argument is conclusive here: "It is necessary to emphasize that not only did the Westminster divines fail to teach that good works merit salvation, they quite deliberately repudiated the position. They were alert to the danger of substituting works for Christ or Christian graces for Christ. To do so would be to dishonor Christ by undermining the sufficiency of his work." Helm then quotes Burgess, who wrote of this danger: "*A man may as lawfully join Saints or Angels in his mediation with Christ, as graces.* Why is that doctrine of making Angels and Saints mediators and intercessors so odious, but because it joineth Christ and others together in that great work? Dost not thou the like when thou joinest thy love and grace with Christ's obedience?"[128]

Finally, the Westminster divines qualified the syllogism and reflex act by allowing it only a secondary status. Burgess wrote: "Though the sight of thy graces be comfortable, yet that of Christ ought to be much more. These graces are but the handmaids and servants that wait upon Christ, they are but tokens from him, they are not himself: A man is not only to go out of his sins, but also out of his graces unto Christ.... Let not therefore the desire after inherent righteousnesse make thee forget imputed righteousnesse: This is to take the friend of the Bridegroom for the Bridegroom it self."[129]

If introspective probing of the realm of private experience takes precedence over seeking communion with God in Christ, the resulting imbalance will bring more darkness than light. Divorced from God's promises, the reflex act would be more disheartening than assuring, for the Christian often discovers in self-examination that he is either missing many of the marks of grace or else finds them so defective that he would despair if faith did not rest on God's Word.[130] Thomas Goodwin warned of inviting desertion or engendering false assurance if the syllogism was inflated in importance: "We [can] put too much of our confidence upon signs, though true, and trust too much to our comforts and former revelations, and witnesses of God's Spirit, and to

---

[127]Contrast Burgess, *Spiritual Refining*, pp. 51-52 with Kendall, *Calvin and English Calvinism to 1649*, pp. 8-9, 28n, 29, 33-34, 40-41, 56-57, 63, 69-74, 125, 148, 150, 163n, 168n, 179-81, 211.

[128]*Calvin and the Calvinists*, p. 76; cf. Anthony Burgess, *Vindiciae Legis: or, A Vindication of the Moral Law, and the Covenants, from the Errors of Papists, Arminians, Socinians, and more especially, Antinomians*, 2nd ed. (London: James Young, 1647), pp. 25-26; *Spiritual Refining*, p. 41.

[129]Ibid., pp. 57, 53.

[130]*The Works of William Bridge* 2:131.

our graces, which are all but creatures [created things], acts of God upon us and in us. When, therefore, we let the weight of our support to hang on these, God, in this case, often leaves us, 'that no flesh should glory in his presence.'"[131]

And William Bridge wrote:

> When a man draws his comfort only from something that he finds within himself; from grace that he finds within, and not from grace without, then his comfort will not hold. . . . Grace without is perpetual, that is to say, Christ's own personal obedience, in the merit of it, is perpetual. But the actings of grace within us are not perpetual, or not perpetually obvious to sight, and therefore cannot perpetually comfort. . . . When therefore, you see the streams of a man's comfort run in this channel, when he draws all his comfort *only or principally* from . . . the actings of grace within, then you may say: Though the stream be now full, stay but a little, and ere long you will see it dried, and this man will be much discouraged.[132]

Consequently, Richard Baxter advised his parishioners to "be sure that the first, and far greater part of your time, pains, and care, and inquiries, be for the getting and increasing of your grace, than for the discerning it. . . . See that you ask ten times at least, How should I get or increase my faith, my love to Christ, and to his people? for once that you ask, How shall I know that I believe or love?"[133]

Thus, when properly undertaken, self-examination is valuable on three counts: First, it is essential for assuring the believer that his salvation is based on the right foundation, Jesus Christ and Him crucified. George Gillespie stated that "we cannot distinguish between a well-grounded and an ill-grounded assurance, . . . between the consolation of the Spirit of God and a delusion" without Spirit-enlightened self-examination.[134] Second, by means of the reflex act, self-examination reinforces the direct act of faith. Walter Marshall wrote, "We must have some assurance of our salvation in the direct act of faith before we can, upon any good ground, assure ourselves, that we are already in a state of grace, by that which we call the reflex act."[135]

---

[131]*The Works of Thomas Goodwin* 3:293.

[132]*The Works of William Bridge* 2:32. Cf. Owen who calls this a "temptation" (*The Works of John Owen* 6:600).

[133]*Catholic Theologie* 9:138-39, cited in J. I. Packer, "The Redemption and Restoration of Man in the Thought of Richard Baxter" (D.Phil. dissertation, Oxford, 1954), p. 401.

[134]*A Treatise of Miscellany Questions*, p. 105.

[135]*The Gospel Mystery of Sanctification Open'd in Sundry Practical Directions*, 2nd ed. (London: for J. L., J. N., and B. S. and N. Cliff and D. Jackson, 1714), p. 130.

Hence, far from dichotomizing the two,[136] the reflex act is rightly fenced in by the direct act of faith so as to retain divine roots, Christ-centeredness, and Spirit-worked faith based on God's promising Word. Third, when performed rightly, self-examination is a positive, growth-producing phenomenon. As R.L. Dabney wrote: "A faithful self-inspection usually reveals so much that is defective, that its first result is rather the discouragement than the encouragement of hope. But this leads the humbled Christian to look away from himself to the Redeemer; and thus assurance, which is the reflex act of faith, is strengthened by strengthening the direct actings of faith itself."[137]

The syllogisms and the reflex act of faith prompt the important question: Can anything other than Christ be the object of faith? The Puritans said no. They believed that there is a reciprocal relationship between God's promise in Christ and "the inward evidence of those graces unto which these promises are made." Just as the divine promises must be inwardly experienced, so the inward evidence of divine graces points directly back to Christ, ending in Him as the object of faith. Therefore the very foundation of the syllogisms and the reflex act, when properly exercised, are Christ-centered. The believer learns to count but loss and dung all that is not Christ in order to increasingly know Him and the power of His resurrection (Philippians 3:10).

Consequently, in proper self-examination believers' recognized strengths (by the grace of God) and weaknesses (due to remaining infirmities arising from the old corrupt nature) drive them to Christ, as Perkins said, "that they might be *all in all* out of themselves in Christ."[138] There could be no better defusing of the objective-subjective tension in assurance than this! In Christ, the objective and subjective need not be dichotomized, for they owe their all to Him, receive their all from Him, and end with all in Him. In Christ, objective promises and subjective experience are complementary.

The Puritan emphasis on self-examination and piety did not divert their gaze from Christ. J.I. Packer said, "The Puritans ripped

[136]Cf. Shaw, "A Study in the Theology of William Perkins," p. 157 in opposition to Chalker, "Calvin and Some Seventeenth Century English Calvinists," pp. 76-77.

[137]*Systematic Theology*, p. 708. Cf. Murray, *Collected Writings* 2:264-65 on the relation between the direct and reflex acts, and 2:271 for a defense of the necessity of self-examination. See Ridgley, *Body of Divinity* 3:255-59, for a scriptural method of self-examination.

[138]*Works* 2:44.

up consciences in the pulpit and urged self-trial in the closet only in order to drive sinners to Christ and to teach them to live by faith in him.... A study of Puritan sermons will show that the preachers' constant concern, in all their detailed detecting of sins, was to lead their hearers into the life of faith and a good conscience; which, they said, is the most joyous life that man can know in this world."[139]

The Witnessing Testimony of the Spirit

Concerning the last ground of assurance in section 18.2 (i.e., "the testimony of the Spirit of adoption witnessing with our spirits that we are the children of God . . ."), Kendall was correct in saying that it was not explained, but he was not accurate in implying that none of the Confession's divines affirmed the kind of direct witness of the Spirit John Cotton meant.[140] The writers of the Westminster Confession knew that the most difficult ground of assurance to comprehend was the witnessing of the Holy Spirit. They confessed that vast mysteries surrounded them when they spoke of that subject.[141] One reason the assembly did not detail the Spirit's testimony in assurance more specifically was to allow for the freedom of the Spirit. A second, related reason was that the assembly wanted to allow freedom of conscience to those who differed among themselves about the details of the Spirit's testimony. Most of the members of the assembly had one of two emphases.

Some of the assembly, such as Jeremiah Burroughs, Anthony Burgess, and George Gillespie, emphasized that the witnessing testimony of the Holy Spirit coincides with assurance gleaned from inward evidences of grace.[142] They believed that the Spirit's witness referred exclusively to His activity in connection with the syllogisms, whereby He brings conscience to unite with His witness that the Christian is a child of God. According to that view, the witness of the Holy Spirit conjoins *with* the witness of the believer's spirit. Romans 8:15 and 8:16 are thus synonymous.[143] Burgess argued that if this

---

[139]*A Quest for Godliness: The Puritan Vision of the Christian Life*, pp. 117-18; cf. Burgess, *Spiritual Refining*, p. 57.

[140]*Calvin and English Calvinism to 1649*, p. 205.

[141]Cf. *The Works of the Rev. John Newton* (reprint ed., Edinburgh: Banner of Truth Trust, 1985), 1:185.

[142]Burroughs, *The Saints' Happiness, together with the several steps leading thereunto. Delivered in Divers Lectures on the Beatitudes* (reprint ed., Beaver Falls, Pa.: Soli Deo Gloria, 1988), p. 196; *Spiritual Refining*, p. 44; Gillespie, *A Treatise of Miscellany Questions*, pp. 105-109.

[143]Cf. Burgess's exegesis of Romans 8:15-16, Ephesians 1:13, and 1 John 5:8 in *Spiritual Refining*, pp. 49-50.

were not so and the believer received assurance through the direct testimony of the Spirit, then there would be no need to pursue assurance through inward graces, for such a pursuit would be "to light a candle when the Sunne shineth; but the testimony of the Spirit and the evidence of graces make up one compleat witnesse, and therefore are not to be disjoyned, much lesse opposed."[144]

These divines believed the secondary grounds of assurance did not break down because the inward evidences of grace and the testimony of the Spirit are essentially one. The syllogisms meant full assurance. These divines felt this perspective was important to maintain in opposition to mysticism and antinomianism, which tend to emphasize a direct testimony of the Spirit disjoined from the need to produce practical fruits of faith and repentance.[145]

Other divines of the assembly, such as Samuel Rutherford, William Twisse, Henry Scudder, and Thomas Goodwin, presented another emphasis. They said the witness of the Spirit described in Romans 8:15 contains something distinct from that of verse 16.[146] They distinguished the Spirit witnessing *with* the believer's spirit by syllogism from His witnessing *to* the believer's spirit by direct applications of the Word. As the New Testament commentator Heinrich Meyer pointed out, the former, the Spirit witnessing *with* the believer's spirit, leaves in its wake the self-conscious conviction "*I* am a child of God" and, on the basis of such Spirit-worked syllogisms, finds freedom to approach God as Father. The latter, the Spirit witnessing *to* the believer's spirit, speaks of the Spirit's pronouncement on behalf of the Father, "*You* are a child of God," and, on the basis of hearing of its sonship from God's own Word by the Spirit, approaches Him with the familiarity of a child.[147] Henry Scudder's teaching of the Spirit's witness is typical of this second emphasis: "This Spirit does witness to a man, that he is the child of God, two ways: First, By immediate witness and suggestion. Secondly, By necessary inferences, by signs from the infallible fruits of the said Spirit."[148]

---

[144]Ibid., pp. 47-48.   [145]Ibid., p. 52.

[146]Rutherford, *The Covenant of Life Opened*, pp. 65ff.; Twisse, *The Doctrine of the Synod of Dort and Arles, reduced to the practise*, pp. 147ff.; Scudder, *The Christian's Daily Walk*, pp. 338-42; *The Works of Thomas Goodwin* 6:27; 7:66; 8:351, 363.

[147]*Critical and Exegetical Hand-book to The Epistle of the Romans* (New York: Funk & Wagnalls, Publishers, 1889), p. 316. Cf. R. Bolton, *Some General Directions for a Comfortable Walking with God*, p. 326.

[148]*The Christian's Daily Walk*, p. 338.

Those who accepted two secondary grounds of assurance differed as to whether the Spirit's testimony should be regarded as more powerful than His syllogistic testimony and hence be placed practically on a higher level. The most common approach was that of Rutherford. He allowed for the direct testimony, but then said the reflex act of faith is as a rule "more spiritual and helpful" than direct acts.[149] Consequently, all believers should be regularly praying for the Spirit's illumination to guide them into syllogistic conclusions. Twisse and Scudder distinguished the Spirit's testifying with our spirit from His direct witnessing of personal adoption without determining which is more valuable.[150] Goodwin however, said that the direct witness of the Spirit supersedes the co-witnessing of the Spirit and the believer through the syllogisms.[151] Generally speaking, however, these divines did not view the direct testimony of the Spirit as superior to or independent of the syllogisms but as added to them. Burgess summarized the view of those who differed in emphasis when he stated, "Some Divines do not indeed deny the

---

[149]*Catechisms of the Second Reformation*, ed. Alex. Mitchell, p. 207; *The Trial and Triumph of Faith*, pp. 88ff.; *Christ Dying and Drawing Sinners to Himselfe*, p. 71; also, ibid., pp. 94ff. for Rutherford's fear of antinomianism. See D.R. Strickland, "Union with Christ in the Theology of Samuel Rutherford: an examination of his doctrine of the Holy Spirit" (Ph.D. dissertation, Edinburgh, 1972). Burgess agreed with Rutherford, stating that if the direct testimony be "allowed" it is "more subject to dangerous delusions," for the reflex act "goeth upon a [more] sure ground, the fruits of mortification, and vivification" (*Spiritual Refining*, p. 672). Thomas Brooks said, "Immediate revelations are fleeting and inconstant; and therefore men had need be careful how they build upon them" (*The Works of Thomas Brooks* 2:318n; cf. ibid., 3:251-52 and 2:519-23, where Brooks supplied nine marks to differentiate the direct testimony of the Spirit from the whisperings of Satan).

New England Puritanism also agreed: "Against the antinomian high estimation of the inward testimony of the Spirit to the exclusion of holy works as signs of faith, the orthodox Puritans turned more and more to holy practice as the principal means used by the Holy Spirit to testify to a man of his salvation.... Edwards... praised his friend David Brainerd for finding assurance of saving faith in its 'evidences' in his sanctified life rather than in immediate whisperings of the Holy Spirit. Edwards had no patience with those enthusiasts who limited the testimony of the Spirit to inward, invisible, 'impractical' flashes of assurance: such testimony is too ephemeral and too often deluding" (Cherry, *The Theology of Jonathan Edwards*, pp. 144ff.). See also *The Complete Works of Thomas Shepard*, ed. John A. Albro (Boston: Doctrinal Tract & Book Society, 1853) 1:258-59.

[150]"That there is a Spirit of adoption, whereby we cry Abba Father, is as true as the word of God is true; as *also*, that his Spirit doth testifie together with our Spirit, that we are the Sonnes of God" (*The Doctrine of the Synod of Dort and Arles, reduced to the practise*, p. 156; cf. ibid., p. 147). Scudder's emphasis, however, is clearly on the reflex act of faith (*The Christian's Daily Walk*, pp. 338-42).

[151]*The Works of Thomas Goodwin* 1:233; 8:366.

possibilty of such an immediate Testimony, but yet they conclude the ordinary and safe way, is, to look for the Testimony, which is by the effects, and fruits of Gods Spirit."[152] Most of the assembly's divines agreed that regardless of what you believe about the direct witness of the Spirit, it is hard to see that it is the most important kind of assurance, for Christians are called to live daily in the joy of assurance, and such assurance cannot be maintained on the basis of occasional experiences.[153] Some Westminster divines, such as William Bridge and Samuel Rutherford, believed that assurance by the Spirit's direct witness becomes the portion of many but not all Christians before they die.[154] A few, however, such as Thomas Goodwin,[155] influenced by the Dutch Second Reformation and the Cotton-Preston tradition in Puritanism,[156] placed this experience far above the pale of the ordinary believer. In fact, Goodwin said that experiencing full assurance pronounced by the Spirit "immediately" is comparable to "a new conversion."[157] For Goodwin, full assurance is the zenith of experimental life. Such assurance is separate from the syllogisms. Goodwin wrote, "This witness is immediate, that is, it builds not his testimony on anything in us; it is

---

[152]Burgess, *Spiritual Refining*, p. 52.

[153]Cf. Iain Murray, *D. Martyn Lloyd-Jones: The Fight of Faith* (Edinburgh: The Banner of Truth Trust, 1990), 2:483-92; Eaton, *Baptism with the Spirit: The Teaching of Dr Martyn Lloyd-Jones*, pp. 161ff.

[154]*The Works of William Bridge* 2:140. The Westminster Confession does not address the question if the believer may die without attaining any degree of conscious assurance. R. T. Kendall assumes that such may be the case (*Calvin and English Calvinism to 1649*, p. 203). This question should be approached more cautiously, however, as contrary opinions were held by the divines. Those who do retain the possibility usually appear to be talking about *full* assurance. For example, Rutherford taught that some believers retain "weak faith" throughout their lives, such that they reside "in the borders of hell, and never have fair sayling, nor fulness of assurance, until they be upon the shoar" (*Influences of the Life of Grace* [London: for Andrew Crook, 1659], p. 150). Most Puritans believed that it was normative for believers to reach varying *degrees* of assurance though few reached *full* assurance (*The Works of Thomas Brooks* 2:132-36). For typically Puritan reasons why many don't "attain to a distinct knowledge of their interest in Christ," see Guthrie, *Christian's Great Interest* (reprint ed., Edinburgh: Banner of Truth Trust, 1982), pp. 26-36.

[155]Cf. chapter 9 below.

[156]In Puritan theology, assurance by means of the direct and immediate witness of the Holy Spirit is intimately associated with the theological development of the sealing of the Spirit (see pp. 201-208 below). Cf. *The Works of Richard Sibbes* 5:409ff., 440; Preston, *The New Covenant* 2:144ff., 172, 400ff., and *The Breast-Plate of Faith and Love* 2:84ff.; William Guthrie, *The Christian's Great Interest* (reprint ed., Edinburgh: Banner of Truth Trust, 1982), pp. 108-109.

[157]*The Works of Thomas Goodwin* 1:251.

not a testimony fetched out of a man's self, or the work of the Spirit in man, as the others were; for the Spirit speaks not by his effects, but speaks from himself."[158]

Goodwin repeatedly used terminology such as immediate light, joy unspeakable, transcendent, glorious, and intuitive in describing the experience of full assurance. Indeed, it is beyond human description: "Those who have attained it cannot demonstrate it to others, especially not to those who have not experience of it, for it is a white stone which no one knows but he that receives it."[159]

English and Dutch divines have frequently described such a transcendent experience as "justification in the court of conscience," which emphasized that the believer, in his conscience, is pronounced forgiven by the Father and sealed by the Spirit to full restoration with God.[160] For descriptive purposes, it also was common to speak in terms of a mutual experiential embrace between God as Father and the believer as the grateful, overwhelmed child.[161]

The assembly's divines, however, unitedly asserted that the Spirit's testimony is always tied to, and may never contradict, the Word of God. Only then can antinomianism be avoided, they said, and the freedom of the Spirit be protected.

For the Westminster divines, all the grounds of faith in God's promises, inward evidences of grace, and the witness of the Spirit, must be pursued to obtain as full a measure of assurance as possible by the grace of God. If any of these grounds are emphasized at the expense of others, the teaching of assurance loses balance and becomes dangerous. No Puritan of the stature of Westminster's Assembly of divines would teach that assurance is obtainable from trusting only in the promises, in inward evidences, or in the witness of the Holy Spirit. Rather, they taught that the believer cannot truly trust the promises without the aid of the Holy Spirit, and that he cannot with any degree of safety examine himself without the illumination of the Spirit. Although the Confession's divines gave

---

[158]Ibid., 8:366.

[159]Ibid., 8:351.

[160]For Dutch divines, see chapter 8 on Comrie below. Examples of English Puritans who have spoken of justification in the court of conscience include Twisse, *The Doctrine of the Synod of Dort and Arles, reduced to the practise*, p. 163; *The Works of Richard Sibbes* 3:210ff.; Guthrie, *The Christian's Great Interest*, pp. 110-111; Samuel Bolton, *The True Bounds of Christian Freedom* (reprint ed., London: Banner of Truth Trust, 1964), p. 188; *The Works of Thomas Brooks* 5:228ff. Cf. Packer, *A Quest for Godliness*, pp. 110-111.

[161]Immens, *The Pious Communicant Encouraged*, pp. 95-96, 104-105.

the syllogisms a more intrinsic role in assurance and placed greater emphasis upon them than did Calvin,[162] the promises of God continued to be regarded as the primary ground for assurance.[163]

The activity of the Spirit is essential in every part of assurance.[164] Without the application of the Spirit, the promises of God lead to self-deceit and carnal presumption. Without the illumination of the Spirit, self-examination tends to introspection, bondage, and legalism. The witness of the Spirit, divorced from the promises of God and from scriptural inward evidences, can degenerate into unbiblical mysticism and excessive emotionalism. These great strands cannot be separated from each other.

18.3: The Cultivation of Assurance

This infallible assurance doth not so belong to the essence of faith, but that a true believer may wait long, and conflict with many difficulties, before he be partaker of it: yet, being enabled by the Spirit to know the things which are freely given him of God, he may, without extraordinary revelation, in the right use of ordinary means, attain thereunto. And therefore it is the duty of every one to give all diligence to make his calling and election sure, that thereby his heart may be enlarged in peace and joy in the Holy Ghost, in love and thankfulness to God, and in strength and cheerfulness in the duties of obedience, the proper fruits of this assurance; so far is it from inclining men to looseness.

Several practical issues on assurance are covered in section 18.3 of the Westminster Confession: the organic relation of faith to assurance, the means of attaining assurance, the duty of seeking assurance, and the fruit of experimental assurance.

The Organic Relation of Faith to Assurance

English, Scottish, and Dutch theologians have written much about the meaning of the Confession's words "doth not *so* belong to the essence of faith." Typical of the Reformed interpretation of the phrase was Thomas Boston's assertion that, while the Confession emphasizes the goal of mature assurance, the germ of assurance is implicit in the reference to faith "growing in many to the attainment of a full assurance." Boston quipped, "How Faith can grow in any to a full Assurance, if there be no Assurance in the Nature of it, I

---

[162]Graafland, "Van *syllogismus practicus* naar *syllogismus mysticus*," pp. 108.

[163]Burgess, *Spiritual Refining*, p. 51.

[164]Burgess, *The True Doctrine of Iustification*, 273.

cannot comprehend."[165] Some critics argued against that, saying the Westminster Assembly denied an organic relationship between faith and assurance. As evidence, they cited question 81 of the Larger Catechism, which includes the phrase "Assurance of grace and salvation not being of the essence of faith."[166] What those critics failed to recognize was that in this context the Confession uses assurance in the sense of faith's *well-being* (*bene-esse*), not of its essence or *being* (*esse*), which must necessarily include assurance.[167]

The relationship between the being and well-being of faith, between saving faith and developed assurance, was critical for the Puritans from a pastoral perspective.[168] First, it enabled the Puritan pastor to encourage the weak believer by teaching that the smallest spark of faith is as valid as mature assurance in terms of salvation. "Neyther are we saved by the worth or quantitie of our Faith, but by Christ, which is laid hold of by a weake Faith, as well as a strong," wrote John Rogers.[169] "A little faith is enough to put a man within the Covenant," John Preston said.[170] Robert Bolton added, "Christ doth not say, Blessed are the strong in Faith, the fully assured ... but, Blessed are they which doe hunger and thirst after righteousnesse."[171] If mature assurance is required, Rutherford warned, "none should be justified and saved but the strong beleever, whereas Christ died for the weak in the faith."[172] Indeed, true faith could be so weak that it could be called mere *desire* for God, grace, salvation, forgiveness, and assurance. As Robert Bolton wrote, "Our desire of grace, faith and repentance, are the graces themselves which we desire."[173]

Second, to encourage growth in the believer, the Puritan pastor emphasized that though weak faith is true faith, a believer should

[165]E[dward] F[isher], *The Marrow of Modern Divinity. Touching both the Covenant of Works and the Covenant of Grace: with their use and end*, 5th ed. (London: R. Ibbitson for G. Calvert, 1647; reprint ed., with notes by Thomas Boston, London: T. Tegg, 1837), p. 167. Cf. Lachman, "The Marrow Controversy: An Historical Survey," pp. 12ff.

[166]*Confession of Faith*, p. 171.

[167]*The Works of Thomas Brooks* 2:371. Cf. Berkhof, *Assurance of Faith*, pp. 27-29, 43-44; Buchanan, *The Doctrine of Justification*, pp. 185, 378; Alexander M'Leod, *The Life and Power of True Godliness* (New York: Eastburn, 1816), pp. 246-47.

[168]See pp. 114-15 above.

[169]*The Doctrine of Faith: wherein are particularly handled twelve Principall Points, which explaine the Nature and Vse of it* (London: N. Newbery and H. Overton, 1629), p. 201.

[170]*The Breast-Plate of Faith and Love* 1:131.

[171]*Some General Directions for a Comfortable Walking with God*, p. 380.

[172]*The Covenant of Life Opened*, p. 155.

[173]*Instructions for a Right Comforting of Afflicted Consciences, with speciall Antidotes against some grievous temptations* (London: Felix Kyngston for Thomas Weaver, 1631), p. 375.

never be content with weak faith. Those who are satisfied with desiring God rather than embracing Him by faith deceive themselves. As Perkins wrote, "He which thinkes hee hath a desire to beleeve, and contents himself therewith; hath indeede no true desire to beleeve."[174]

Third, pastors could talk about the seed of assurance in faith to encourage believers to pursue greater degrees of assurance. "The least grace, if true, is sufficient to salvation, and therefore the sense of the least grace, or of the least measure of grace, should be sufficient to assurance of salvation," wrote Thomas Brooks.[175] And John Rogers said, "The greatest Giant was in swaddling clothes, the tallest Oake was a twigge, and Faith groweth from a graine of mustard-seede to a tall tree."[176]

Two subsequent distinctions have made the organic faith-assurance relationship in the Confession more clear: the implicit assurance in faith and explicit assurance in the conscience;[177] and assurance of faith and assurance of hope or sense.[178] In time, Reformed thinkers became convinced that the Westminster Assembly's intent was to steer between saving faith apart from all assurance *and* the unbearable pastoral burden that no one could claim saving faith without full assurance. As Dabney stated: "No supporter of the Westminster view denies that even the weakest true faith is attended with an element of hope, more or less consciously felt; all we assert is that there may be saving faith, and yet not a πληροφορία ελπιδος [full assurance of hope]."[179]

From the Dutch perspective, Louis Berkhof said it this way: "There are two extremes that should be avoided: on the one hand the position that it is possible to have a true living faith without any degree of subjective assurance; and on the other hand the standpoint

---

[174]Perkins, *Works* 1:605-606.

[175]*The Works of Thomas Brooks* 1:464.

[176]*The Doctrine of Faith*, p. 200.

[177]Berkhof, *Assurance of Faith*, p. 71; Murray, *Collected Writings* 2:265.

[178]Ebenezer Erskine, *The Whole Works* 1:254; A. A. Hodge, *The Confession of Faith* (reprint ed., London: Banner of Truth Trust, 1961), p. 244; Brown, *A Compendious View of Natural and Revealed Religion*, p. 423; Ebenezer Erskine and James Fisher, *The Westminster's Shorter Catechism Explained*, 14th ed. (Edinburgh: D. Schaw, 1800), pp. 224-25, Q. 8. Cf. William Gouge, who frequently wrote on the "assurance of hope": *The Works in Two Volumes: the First, Domesticall Duties. The Second, The Whole Armour of God* (London: John Beale, 1627), vol. 2, part 7, sections 3-4 on Ephesians 6:17; *Exposition of Hebrews*, pp. 230, 426.

[179]*Systematic Theology*, p. 699.

of Jean de Labadie that no one is in a state of grace who does not have absolute assurance."[180]

G. H. Kersten elaborated on this: "There is a difference, not in essence, but in the exercise of it, between refuge-taking faith and assured confidence; between the being of faith and the well-being of faith; but this difference does not mean that in the essence of faith confidence would ever be lacking. However many troubles and doubts may beset the believer, sometimes even for long periods of time, faith itself is not only a knowledge, but also a sincere confidence; according to its nature it includes an absolute certainty, as even one of little faith experiences in each exercise of faith."[181]

The Time Element in Faith's Maturation

According to the Westminster Confession, the relationship between faith and assurance strengthens over time: "growing up in many to the attainment of a full assurance" (14.3). The acorn of faith will often evolve into the oak of full assurance. Temporarily, faith may bring forth only thirtyfold, but with proper nourishment will frequently produce a hundredfold (Matthew 13:8).

God is sovereign over how long this takes. He is able to plant faith and full assurance simultaneously,[182] but more typically He works it by degrees[183] so that the believer's doubts about his salvation decrease as he grows in grace.

Grace usually grows with age, and as faith increases, other graces increase. Young believers normally display much zeal, but elderly saints "grow more in strength and stableness, and are more refined," said Richard Sibbes.[184] And Thomas Brooks wrote, "Assurance is meat for strong men; few babes, if any, are able to bear it, and digest it."[185] Faith therefore usually reaches full maturity in old age, so that "the time of death is one of the most usual seasons wherein God gives his children the sweetest and fullest assurance of his love, of their interest in him, and of their right to glory."[186]

---

[180]*Assurance of Faith*, p. 71.

[181]*Reformed Dogmatics* 2:405.

[182]Murray, *Collected Writings* 2:265.

[183]Anthony Burgess, *The True Doctrine of Iustification Asserted and Vindicated, From the Errors of Papists, Arminians, Socinians, and more especially Antinomians* (London: Robert White for Thomas Vnderhil, 1648), 1:152.

[184]*The Works of Richard Sibbes* 7:222-23.

[185]*The Works of Thomas Brooks* 2:371; cf. 2:316, 335, 359.

[186]Ibid., 1:464.

God uses conflicts, doubts, and trials to mature the believer in faith. "Assurance comes not at first when we believe, but little by little as God seeth it requisite, according to the triall he hath appointed to make of us," John Ball wrote.[187] Such assurance provides peace after intense spiritual warfare; it wears battle scars.[188] As Thomas Goodwin wrote: "A man's faith must fight first, and have a conquest, and then assurance is the crown, the triumph of faith; but faith must be tried first; and what tries faith more than temptations, and fears, and doubts, and reasonings against a man's estate?"[189]

Assurance is the fruit of faith that has been seasoned and strengthened. The newborn soul should not expect full assurance immediately, for, according to the Westminster divine, Obadiah Sedgwick, this would be like "the Sun at his first peeping were in the height of heaven; or that a Schollar must be placed in the upper forme as soone as he enters the Schoole."[190]

But age and experience do not guarantee assurance, either. As in conversion, God remains sovereign in the dispensing of assurance. As Thomas Ridgley said, "The sovereignty of God discovers itself herein, as much as it does when he makes the ordinances effectual to salvation, in giving converting grace unto those who attend upon them. Some are called early to be made partakers of that salvation that is in Christ, others late. The same may be said with respect to God's giving assurance. Some are favoured with this privilege soon after, or when first they believe; others are like those whom the apostle speaks of, who, through fear of death are all their life-time subject to bondage."[191]

Finally, as George Downame noted, even the most assured believers may grow in assurance: "Some are incipients, some proficients, some perfect or growne men in Christ . . . [nevertheless,] none are so perfect, but that their assurance may be increased."[192] The believer has a lifelong call to make diligent use of the means of grace in pursuit of ever greater degrees of assurance.

[187]*A Treatise of Faith*, p. 96.

[188]Preston, *The Breast-Plate of Faith and Love* 2:109.

[189]*The Works of Thomas Goodwin* 8:346.

[190]*The Doubting Beleever: or, A Treatise Containing 1. The Nature 2. The Kinds 3. The Springs 4. The Remedies of Dovbtings, incident to weak Beleevers* (London: M. F. for Thomas Nicols, 1641), p. 60.

[191]*Body of Divinity* 3:272.

[192]*The Covenant of Grace* (Dublin: Society of Stationers, 1631), p. 109.

The Means of Attaining Assurance

In bequeathing assurance, God uses means. Consequently, the Westminster Assembly recommends "the right use of ordinary means" as a method of fostering assurance. William Gouge thus wrote: "If we think assurance of hope worth the having, let us do to the utmost what God enableth us to do for attaining thereunto. Let us acquaint ourselves with the grounds of hope, God's promises and properties, and frequently and seriously meditate thereon. Let us conscionably attend God's ordinances, and earnestly pray that God would add his blessing to our endeavour."[193]

Meditation on God's Word, participation in the sacraments, and perseverance in prayer are the means God ordinarily uses to increase assurance. In this, the Confession returns to the primacy of the *Word*.

Consequently, Robert Harris advised, "Thou must deny thine owne sense and feeling; rest upon the word, if thou would'st be on sure ground."[194] Obadiah Sedgwick likewise responded to a seeker: "Experiences are good encouragements to the future acts of faith, but the Word of God is still the ground of faith."[195]

The Lord also increases assurance through the *sacraments*. As Richard Rogers wrote: "The Sacraments are meanes and helpes to set [the believer] forward in a godly life (as too few doe finde to be)... [so that he is] assured that his soul may be comforted by Christ."[196] They are "a principall meanes that God hath ordained for the reviving, strengthening, and increasing of our faith," said Arthur Hildersham.[197] Furthermore, the sacraments are divine seals that confirm God's eternal commitments to believers, thereby multiplying assurance.[198] "Although God has given us his Promise, and nothing can be surer than that," Burgess wrote, "yet he addeth Sacraments to seal and confirm his Promise unto us."[199] When the

---

[193]*Exposition of Hebrews*, pp. 230, 426.

[194]*The VVay to Trve Happinesse* 2:50ff.

[195]*The Dovbting Beleever*, pp. 125-27.

[196]*Seven Treatises Containing Such Direction as Is Gathered out of the Holy Scriptures, Leading and Guiding to True Happiness, Both in This Life, and in the Life to Come* (London: Felix Kyngston for Thomas Man, 1610), pp. 233-34.

[197]*The Doctrine of Communicating Worthily* (London: Iohn Hauiland, 1630), p. 21; cf. John Downame, *A Guide to Godlynesse, or a treatise of Christian Life. Shewing the duties, helpes & Impediments* (London: Felix Kyngston, for Ed. Weuer & W. Bladen, 1622), pp. 492-97.

[198]Perkins, *Works* 1:71ff.; 3:520.

[199]*Spiritual Refining*, p. 53.

believer participates in the sacraments by faith, he receives certification of that which is promised by God and renews covenant with God. Covenant assurance and obligation then unite.[200] The promises of God are made visible and personal in the sacraments. "Sacraments are as seales annexed to the letters patent of Gods evangelicall promises," wrote George Downame.[201] Sibbes added: "The sacraments seal unto us all the comforts we have by the death of Christ."[202] Even as in secular life "the sight of his evidences confirmes a man in the hope of the quiet possession of his Land," Francis Taylor wrote, so "the right use of the Sacraments assures us of Gods favour."[203]

Finally, Word and sacrament must be accompanied by *prayer.* "We must give all diligence and heed to the obtaining of this priviledge [of assurance]," Burgess wrote. "We must make it our businesse; it must be importunately begged for in praier."[204] "The more we seek Gods favour by fervent prayer, the more will he assure us," Francis Taylor added.[205] Reynolds wrote this: "God will not performe promises, till by prayer they be sought for from him. . . . As promises are the Rule of what wee may pray for in faith; so prayer is the ground of what we may expect with comfort."[206]

Though God uses means to bestow assurance, ultimately assurance remains God's sovereign gift. Ferguson writes like a Puritan when he says: "Some discover assurance after long battles; others never know what it is to be without it; for some it comes through sorrows, for others through joys. It is as individual as it is sovereign, and necessarily so, because it leads us to say, 'The Son of God, who *loved me* and gave himself *for me.*'"[207]

The believer must not look for extraordinary revelation as a way of obtaining assurance, however. Rather, he must be constant in

---

[200]Von Rohr, *The Covenant of Grace in Puritan Thought,* pp. 178-79; Holifield, *The Covenant Sealed,* pp. 38-61; Sommerville, "Conversion, Sacrament, and Assurance in the Puritan Covenant of Grace to 1650," pp. 50ff.

[201]*A Treatise of the Certainty of Perseverance* (Dublin: Society of Stationers), p. 395.

[202]*The Works of Richard Sibbes* 1:122.

[203]*Gods Choise and Mans Diligence: in which is explained the Doctrine of free Election, and Vocation answerable to it* (London: E.C. for G. and H. Eversden, 1654), p. 199.

[204]*Spiritual Refining,* p. 673.

[205]*Gods Choise and Mans Diligence,* p. 199.

[206]*Three Treatises,* pp. 364-66.

[207]*Taking the Christian Life Seriously,* p. 58.

using the ordinary means, walking with good conscience before God. Assurance so sought ordinarily will be granted by God in varying degrees.[208]

The Duty of Seeking Assurance

Furthermore, the Westminster Confession says that it is the believer's duty to seek assurance.[209] As Jeremiah Burroughs wrote: "Our duty . . . is . . . to labour for the assurance of [God's] free love. It will assist us in all duties; it will arm us against all temptations; it will answer all objections that can be made against the soul's peace; it will sustain us in all conditions, into which the saddest of times may bring us."[210]

God commands the believer to pursue assurance prayerfully and fervently, promising that He will bless it. "A good improvement of what we have of the grace of God at present, pleases God, and ingages him to give us more," John Bunyan wrote. "Therefore, get more grace."[211] William Guthrie explained how that works: "Learn to lay your weight upon the blood of Christ, and study purity and holiness in all manner of conversation: and pray for the witness of God's Spirit to join with the blood and the water; and His testimony added unto these will establish you in the faith of an interest in Christ."[212] Sibbes advised that we should "never rest therefore till we can prove ourselves to be in the covenant of grace, till we can say, God is my God."[213]

The Puritan stress on duty reinforced the conviction that assurance must never be regarded as only the privilege of exceptional saints.[214] The Puritans agreed that the failure to recognize that at least some degree of assurance is normal for the believer tends to leave people in a barren spiritual condition. As Cunningham warned in the nineteenth century: "We believe that the prevailing practical disregard of the privilege and the duty of having assurance, is, to no inconsiderable extent, at once the cause

---

[208]Brown, *A Compendious View of Natural and Revealed Religion*, p. 424; Watson, *A Body of Divinity*, p. 179.

[209]*The Works of William Bridge* 1:145ff. See Gray, *Works*, pp. 213-14, and Murray, *Collected Writings* 2:268, for a list of proof texts.

[210]*An Exposition of the Prophecy of Hosea*, p. 654. Cf. Gillespie, *A Treatise of Miscellany Questions*, p. 57.

[211]Cited in Richard L. Greaves, *John Bunyan* (Grand Rapids: Eerdmans, 1969), p. 149.

[212]*The Christian's Great Interest*, p. 196.

[213]*The Works of Richard Sibbes* 6:15.

[214]Lake, *Moderate Puritans and the Elizabethan Church*, p. 159; cf. ibid., pp. 157-68.

and the effect of the low state of vital religion amongst us — one mean reason why there is so little of real communion with God as our reconciled Father, and so little of real, hearty devotedness to His cause and service."[215]

The Fruit of Assurance

Finally, assurance bears fruit. It produces a life marked by peace and joy, love and thankfulness to God, strength and obedience in duty. It also distances the believer from loose living and moral indifference.[216]

According to Thomas Brooks, assurance makes "heavy afflictions light, long afflictions short, bitter afflictions sweet." It "makes the soul sing care away." It also makes the believer "more motion than notion, more work than word, more life than lip, more hand than tongue."[217]

Anthony Burgess wrote in detail how assurance produces fruit:

[Assurance] keeps up excellent Fellowship and Acquaintance with God. . . . It will work a Filial and an Evangelical frame of heart. . . . [It] makes us also have the humble disposition of Sons; Hereby we are carried out to do him service for pure intentions and motives. . . . It will support, although there be nothing but outward misery and trouble. . . . It will much enflame in Prayer. . . . It makes a man walk with much tendernesse against sinne. . . . [The] heart will be impatient and earnest till the coming of Christ. . . . The soul is more inflamed and inlarged to love God. . . . [It] will breed much spirituall strength and heavenly ability to all graces and duties, to go through all relations with much holinesse and lively vigor. . . . [It] is a strong and mighty buckler against all those violent assaults and temptations, that the devil useth to exercise the godly with. . . . [It] is a speciall means to breed contentation [i.e., contentment] of minde, and a thankfull, cheerfull heart in every condition. . . . [It] is a sure and speciall antidote against death in all the fears of it.[218]

Instead of making the believer proud, secure and "presumptuous in sinning,"[219] assurance makes the believer love the Lord

---

[215]*Reformers*, pp. 147-48.

[216]*The Works of William Bridge* 1:145ff.

[217]Cited in *The Golden Treasury of Puritan Quotations*, compiled by I. D. E. Thomas (Chicago: Moody Press, 1975), p. 26; *Gathered Gold*, compiled by John Blanchard (Hertfordshire, England: Evangelical Press, 1984), p. 7.

[218]*Spiritual Refining*, pp. 26, 681-83. Cf. Thomas Boston, *The Complete Works of the Late Rev. Thomas Boston, Ettrick* (reprint ed., Wheaton, Ill.: Richard Owen Roberts, Publishers, 1980), 2:17-18.

[219]*The Works of Thomas Goodwin* 3:417.

fervently and obey Him carefully.[220] John Ball wrote, "He who is best
assured hath most power of Gods Spirit, and the stronger the Spirit
of God is within, the more holinesse and fruits and grace without."[221]
The very nature of assurance, Burgess said, cannot "breed any arro-
gance, or neglect of God and godliness," since "its onely maintained
and kept up by humility and holy fear: So that when a man ceaseth to
be humble, to have an holy fear of God, his certainty likewise
ceaseth, even as the lamp goeth out when the oyl is taken away."[222]

Humility is a special fruit of assurance. Through assurance, self
decreases and Christ increases (John 3:30). As Robert Harris wrote,
"The more one growes in grace, the more hee growes out of himselfe. . . . We become more humble and low in our owne eyes."[223]

18.4 Assurance Lost and Renewed

*True believers may have the assurance of their salvation divers ways
shaken, diminished, and intermitted; as, by negligence in preserving of it,
by falling into some special sin which woundeth the conscience and
grieveth the Spirit; by some sudden or vehement temptation, by God's
withdrawing the light of His countenance, and suffering even such as fear
Him to walk in darkness and have no light: yet are they never utterly
destitute of that seed of God, and life of faith, that love of Christ and the
brethren, that sincerity of heart, and conscience of duty, out of which, by
the operation of the Spirit, this assurance may, in due time, be revived;
and by the which, in the mean time, they are supported from utter despair.*

The Causes of an "Unreachable" Assurance
Causes in the Believer: Sin and Backsliding

This section of the Westminster Confession offers a magnificent
link between Reformed theology and Puritan piety. It says that the
reasons for a lack of assurance are found primarily in the believer.
They include negligence in preserving assurance by exercise, falling
into a special sin, and yielding to sudden temptation. Burgess wrote,
"It is true the most tender and exact godly ones, as *Job* and *David* are
sometimes in desertions, and cry out God hath forsaken them, but
ordinarily the more formal and carelesse we are in our approaches to
God, the more are our doubts and fears."[224]

---

[220]G. Downame, *A Treatise of the Certainty of Perseverance*, p. 410.

[221]*A Treatise of Faith*, p. 278.

[222]*Spiritual Refining*, pp. 679-80.

[223]*The VVay to True Happinesse* 2:91.

[224]Anthony Burgess, *CXLV Expository Sermons upon the whole 17ᵗʰ Chapter of the Gospel*

Burgess said that assurance may be hindered, even lost, for several reasons: (1) Assurance can be diminished when we deeply feel the guilt of sin, for then we tend to look upon God as one who will take vengeance rather than forgive. (2) Satan hates assurance, and will do everything he can to keep doubts and fears alive within us. (3) Most commonly, the hypocrisy of our hearts and the carelessness of our living hinders assurance.[225]

Such causes are explained in the preceding chapter of the Confession on perseverance, which says: "Nevertheless, [the saints] may, through the temptations of Satan and of the world, the prevalency of corruption remaining in them, and the neglect of the means of their preservation, fall into grievous sins; and, for a time, continue therein: whereby they incur God's displeasure, and grieve His Holy Spirit, come to be deprived of some measure of their graces and comforts, have their hearts hardened, and their consciences wounded; hurt and scandalize others, and bring temporal judgments upon themselves" (17.3).

Assurance that weakens is also suggested in the chapter on saving faith: "This faith is different in degrees, weak or strong; may be often and many ways assailed, and weakened, but gets the victory: growing up in many to the attainment of a full assurance, through Christ, who is both the author and finisher of our faith" (14.3).

The Westminster Confession is clear: *The Christian cannot enjoy high levels of assurance while he persists in low levels of obedience.*[226] Then "we chase away our assurance," Burgess explained. "Nothing will darken thy soul more than dull, lazy and negligent walking."[227] For the Puritan, that was only right. If assurance remained high while obedience faltered, the believer might take for granted the great privilege of adopted sonship and grow spiritually lazy.[228] Knowing that backsliding diminishes assurance keeps the saints active in searching their souls. When assurance degenerates into presumption, it is good that doubts and fears prompt fresh desire for assurance. This urges repentance and acts of faith that may renew

According to St. John: or Christ's Prayer Before his Passion Explication, and both Practically and Polemically Improved (London: Abraham Miller for Thomas Underhill, 1656), p. 356.

[225]*Spiritual Refining*, pp. 25-26.

[226]This is typically Reformed as well, as the German and Dutch family of Reformed standards make clear. Cf. Belgic Confession, art. 24; Heidelberg Catechism, Lord's Day 24; Canons of Dort, Head V.

[227]*Spiritual Refining*, pp. 672-73.

[228]J. Rogers, *The Doctrine of Faith*, p. 388.

assurance. "Fear to fall and assurance to stand are two sisters," wrote Thomas Fuller.[229]

The Puritan refusal to link assurance with disobedience refutes Pelagian and antinomian tendencies.[230] It refutes Pelagianism, since assurance that can be lost or is unattainable shows that salvation is all of grace. The human will, stripped of divine grace, has no strength to reach or retain assurance. To the antinomian, "unreachable" or "losable" assurance implies that sin has serious consequences for the child of God. God's saints cannot sin without great cost. Sin grievously interrupts a close walk with the Lord (Isaiah 59:2). "Sin can never quite bereave a saint of his jewel, his grace, but it may steal away the key of the cabinet, his assurance," wrote William Jenkyn.[231]

Chapter 17 of the Confession thus offers a balanced view of perseverance: true believers can "neither totally nor finally fall away from the state of grace, but shall certainly persevere therein to the end, and be eternally saved" (17.1). Nevertheless, sin will have serious consequences, such as (1) incurring God's displeasure, (2) grieving the Holy Spirit, (3) depriving a measure of grace and comfort, (4) hardening the heart, (5) wounding the conscience, (6) hurting others, and (7) bringing temporal judgments (17.3).[232]

The conclusion is clear: Despite the great injury that ensues from backsliding, God's people shall persevere. Their perseverance is secured by their persevering God. Divine perseverance is Trinitarian in its outworking, consisting of the perseverance of the Father's eternal good pleasure toward them, the perseverance of

---

[229]Cited in *More Gathered Gold*, compiled by John Blanchard (Hertfordshire, England: Evangelical Press, 1986), pp. 12-13.

[230]According to Pelagius, there are three features in human action: power (*posse*), will (*velle*), and the realization (*esse*). The first is granted exclusively by God; the others belong to man. Cf. R. F. Evans, *Pelagius: Inquiries and Reappraisals* (London, 1968), and *Four Letters of Pelagius* (London, 1968). Semi-Pelagian tendencies later surfaced in Roman Catholicism, as well as in Arminianism's voluntaristic view of faith.

Antinomianism (*anti* [against], *nomos* [law]) teaches that it is not essential for Christians to use the Ten Commandments as a rule of conduct for daily living. The term was coined by Luther in his struggle with a former student, Johann Agricola. Agricola believed that repentance should not be prompted by the law but by the preaching of the gospel through faith in Christ.

[231]Cited in *Gathered Gold*, p. 8.

[232]Cf. Canons of Dort, Head V, article 5a: "By such enormous sins, however, they very highly offend God, incur a deadly guilt, grieve the Holy Spirit, interrupt the exercise of faith, very grievously wound their consciences, and sometimes lose the sense of God's favor, for a time."

Christ in His sufferings and intercession for them, and the perseverance of the Spirit working within them. Election, covenant, providence, satisfaction, and perseverance are inseparable from each other and from assurance. Thus, when the believer lacks assurance, the responsibility is his. No enemy shall keep him out of heaven, but he may well keep heaven out of his heart by sinning against God. Burgess concluded, "It is therefore an unworthy thing to speak of doubting, and complain of the losse of Gods favour, and that thou hast no Assurance, when all thy Duties and Performances are careless and withered."[233]

Causes in God: Withdrawing and "Tempting"

The Confession does not stop here. Surprisingly, it also offers the possibility of God's involvement in the believer's lack of assurance. Unreachable or lost assurance may be the result of God's "withdrawing of the light of His countenance" or of "some sudden and vehement temptation."

Does the Westminster Confession go beyond Scripture in saying that God has reasons to withhold assurance from some believers? Burgess said not. He first acknowledged, however, that it seemed senseless at first sight for God to withhold assurance from a believer, for assurance is "wings and legs in a mans service to God. It would enflame him more to promote Gods glory." Burgess went on to ask, "How frequently doth God keep his own people in darkness?" He then offered five reasons God would withhold assurance from His people:

> First, *That hereby we may taste and see how bitter sinne is.* Second, *Hereby God would keep us low and humble in ourselves.* Third, *God may therefore keep Assurance from our knowledge, that so when we have it, we may the more esteem it, and the more prize it, taking the greater heed how we lose it.* Fourth, *God doth it that thou mayest demonstrate thy obedience unto him, and give the greater honour to him.* Fifth, *God withholdeth the sense of pardon, that thou mayest be an experienced Christian able to comfort others in their distresse.* [234]

We may be inclined to look askance at some of Burgess's reasons for the "withdrawment" of God. But bear in mind two things: First, to understand Burgess, we need to recognize that the Puritans

---

[233]*Spiritual Refining*, pp. 34-35.

[234]Ibid., pp. 35-36. See *The Works of Thomas Brooks* 2:330-334, for a similar list. Cf. Rutherford, *Christ Dying and Drawing Sinners to Himselfe*, pp. 49-50; *Influences of the Life of Grace*, p. 265; *The Covenant of Life Opened*, p. 219.

believed that "withdrawment" on God's part was usually for holy reasons beyond the comprehension of the believer, who by faith simply has to trust God's intentions. Second, those reasons were as so many pieces of a jigsaw puzzle, possible and partial explanations which were experienced. Neither Burgess nor the Puritans offered a complete list of reasons. Rather, they grappled with the experimental and pastoral reality of times when they or their parishioners might *not* be backsliding, *yet* might lack assurance and feel distant from God. Burgess was trying to deal compassionately with those who earnestly sought greater assurance but had not obtained it.

To understand this better, we should observe the connection between assurance and several doctrines taught in the Confession. These include the eternal decree (ch. 3), providence (ch. 5), and sin (ch. 6). In the Confession, God's decree and providence cover everything, including sin, desertion, and "withdrawment." The Confession prompts these questions: May not God, who decrees everything for His glory, also get glory through withdrawing from the consciousness of His children in order to lead them in sanctified ways above their comprehension? (3.3) May not God who "doth uphold, direct, dispose, and govern all creatures, actions, and things, from the greatest even to the least, by His most wise and holy providence" (5.1) — a providence in which He is free to "work without, above, and against [means], at his pleasure" (5.3) — also direct His apparent withdrawings to their benefit? May not God who hates but forgives sin, chastise His children by withdrawing His felt presence in order to preserve within them a holy hatred for sin? (6.5)

In each chapter on decree, providence, and sin, the Puritan divines of the Confession affirm a lofty, holy God, who rises above understanding in complex reasons for being both a deserting God and a withholding God in the matter of assurance. God's holiness is paramount in this regard. The decree is described as the *holy* counsel of His own will (3.1). Sin is permitted according to God's *holy* counsel (6.1). Providence is denominated most wise and *holy* (5.1), and ordered in all things for *holy* ends (5.4). The climax of this holiness relative to God's "withdrawment" is in section 5.4:

> The most wise, righteous, and gracious God doth oftentimes leave, for a season, His own children to manifold temptations, and the corruption of their own hearts, to chastise them for their former sins, or to discover unto them the hidden strength of corruption and deceitfulness of their hearts, that they may be humbled; and, to raise them to a more close and constant dependence for their

support upon Himself, and to make them more watchful against all future occasions of sin, and for sundry other just and holy ends.

The key here is that *God is above us.* In desertion, in withdrawal, in vehement temptation, even in delayed assurance, God has His *holy* reasons. According to the Westminster divines, what God does now, we often know not, but shall know "hereafter" (John 13:7) — perhaps tomorrow, perhaps not until eternity. But hereafter shall come. It is enough for us to know that God always carries Himself — both His "comings and goings" — with twin goals in mind: His glory and the true benefit of His elect. Hence, as William Gurnall wrote, "The Christian must trust in a withdrawing God."[235]

In the matter of "vehement temptations" (18.4), that is, trials or afflictions external in providence or internal in the soul's condition,[236] the Westminster divines advised the following. First, when the afflicted believer receives no light for his soul, and the evidences of God's saving work in his life appear as "muddied waters, the proper duty of a godly man is to throw himself boldly upon the promise, to go unto God and relie upon him, in which sense Job said, Though he kill me, yet will I trust in him."[237] Second, even when God leaves believers "to manifold temptations" (1 Peter 1:6), He has His glory and their good in view. He will draw men to Himself and minister to them through affliction. William Twisse thus noted that afflictions can be "as pangs of child birth, to deliver souls into the world of the sons of God."[238]

Third, believers should appreciate rather than reject afflictions, for afflictions work medicinally to increase assurance. Afflictions wean the believer from this world, stimulate his spiritual growth, open new vistas of faith, increase his intimacy with God and submission to His attributes, and act overall as healing tonic for his soul. Still, Robert Harris said that this healing process may be so slow in coming that the believer may only realize it when he is healed: "A man seeth himselfe cured, but how and when [affliction] healeth, he sees not."[239] But by means of the Spirit's sanctifying

---

[235]*The Christian in Complete Armour* (reprint ed., Edinburgh: Banner of Truth Trust, 1974), 2:145.

[236]Burgess, *Spiritual Refining*, p. 58.

[237]Ibid., pp. 43-44; cf. *The Works of Richard Sibbes* 1:124.

[238]*The Riches of Gods Love Unto the Vessells of Mercy*, p. 287.

[239]*A Treatise of the New Covenant* 1:44.

grace, the believer reaches heights of spiritual maturation that cannot be reached without affliction.

Many of the Puritans, including the Westminster divines, gave advice on how to cope with affliction. For example, Rutherford's renowned *Letters* are filled with gems on profiting from trials:

> However ye may be ducked, yet ye cannot drown, being in his company; and ye may, all the way to glory, see the way bedewed with His blood, who is the Forerunner.... When he is striking you in love, beware to strike again; that is dangerous, for those who strike again shall get the last blow.... Your Lord will make joy and gladness out of your afflictions; for all his roses have a fragrant smell.... When I am in the cellar of affliction, I look for the Lord's choicest wines. . . . There is no cross or misery that befalls the church of God or any of His children, but it is related to God....[240]

In sum, God's withdrawal and placing of trials in the path of the believer are motivated by His *fatherly discipline*, which teaches "right walking"; by His *fatherly sovereignty*, which teaches dependence; and by His *fatherly wisdom*, which teaches that He knows and does what is best for His own.[241]

The Revival of Assurance

According to the Westminster Confession, the "unreachableness" of assurance does not negate the germ of faith in the Christian; the believer is never destitute of God's saving work despite the failure to see it. Indeed, the child of God may be losing assurance even while he advances in grace. As Rutherford wrote: "Deserted souls not conscious of the reflex acts of believing and longing for Christ, think themselves apostates, when they are advancing in their way."[242]

The *grace* and *essence* of faith abides with the believer even though he is blind to the *acts* and *practice* of faith. Faith cannot die, though its actions may wither to such a degree that the believer is unable to enjoy much assurance. As John Murray wrote:

> The germ of assurance is surely implicit in the salvation which the believer comes to possess by faith, it is implicit in the change that has been wrought in his state and condition. However weak may be the faith of a true believer, however severe may be his temptations,

---

[240]*Letters of the Rev. Samuel Rutherford* (New York: Robert Carter & Brothers, 1881), pp. 52ff.

[241]Rutherford, *The Trial and Triumph of Faith*, pp. 326-29; Goodwin, *The Works of Thomas Goodwin* 3:231ff.

[242]*The Trial and Triumph of Faith*, pp. 139-40.

however perturbed his heart may be respecting his own condition, he is never, as regards consciousness, in the condition that preceded the exercise of faith. The consciousness of the believer differs by a whole diameter from that of the unbeliever. At the lowest ebb of faith and hope and love his consciousness never drops to the level of the unbeliever at its highest pitch of confidence and assurance.[243]

The essence and implicity of faith offers hope for the revival of assurance. The Holy Spirit does more than save the believer from utter despair in this condition; He does more than retain the germs of faith and assurance within the believer. The Spirit's operations promise the revival of assurance "in due time."

Though the Confession urges regaining assurance by means of what Richard Sibbes called "exact walking,"[244] its final accent is on the operations of the Spirit. To say of the Confession's theology, as Kendall did, that "the *only* way to recover assurance is to till the ground — conscience — by measuring up to the law,"[245] is irresponsible, for it ignores the Confession's recognition of rooting assurance and its revival in the Holy Spirit's irresistible operations.

Assurance is revived the same way it was obtained the first time. Burgess told how this should be done. Believers should review their lives, confess their backsliding, and humbly cast themselves upon their covenant-keeping God and His gracious promises in Christ. They should use the means of grace diligently, pursue holiness, exercise tender watchfulness, and take heed of grieving or quenching the Spirit. In other words, they are to be converted afresh, which results in more assurance, godliness, and evangelistic zeal.[246] Spirit-worked conversion is a lifelong process of losing one's life and reviving assurance through nearness to Christ. "Be always converting and always converted . . . more humble, more sensible of sin, more near to Christ Jesus; and then you that are sure may be more sure," said Thomas Shepard.[247] As Hawkes concludes:

> The work of assurance is a continuing exercise, a cycle, but an ascending cycle because it is God working to raise the believer up

---

[243]Murray, *Collected Writings* 2:265.

[244]*The Works of Richard Sibbes* 5:393; cited by Kendall, *Calvin and English Calvinism to 1649*, pp. 109, 205.

[245]Ibid., p. 208.

[246]A. Burgess, *Spiritual Refining*, pp. 673-75; cf. ibid., pp. 34-35; Joel R. Beeke, *A Tocha Dos Puritanos: Evangelização Bíblica São Paulo: Evangélicas Selecionadas*, 1996), pp. 42-68.

[247]*The Complete Works of Thomas Shepard* 2:632.

to himself. . . . By a helical process of trust, obedience, evaluation, and learning, God draws the believer from an initial approbation of the way of salvation in Christ to a full restful assurance that encompasses all aspects of the believer's life and consciousness. . . . This is the very hopeful message of the Puritans' doctrine of assurance. It is by no means the heavy burden of self-justification or even self-assurance, but rather the light yoke of faith in the work of another.[248]

Conclusion

All of the Westminster Confession's statements on assurance have the goal of leading the church to make her calling and election sure by finding everything necessary for time and eternity in the Spirit-applied grace of God in Jesus Christ. Its other goals include: (1) meeting God's children in their concrete, daily life, by explaining the Spirit's work; (2) motivating the believer to grow in grace; (3) resolving contemporary Reformed debate, as well as defeating Roman Catholic and Arminian arguments relative to assurance. As such, chapter 18 of the Confession is highly successful. Thus, R. L. Dabney could affirm in the late nineteenth century: "The Calvinistic world has now generally settled down upon the doctrine of the Westminster Assembly, that assurance of hope is not of the essence of saving faith; so that many believers may be justified though not having the former: and may remain long without it; but yet an infallible assurance, founded on a comparison of their hearts and lives with Scripture, and the teaching and light of the Holy Ghost, through and in the Word, is the privilege, and should be the aim of every true believer."[249]

---

[248]"The Logic of Assurance in English Puritan Theology," pp. 259-61.
[249]*Systematic Theology*, p. 702.

VII. JOHN OWEN

The Calvinistic English theologian John Owen (1616-1683) was a clear advocate of the Westminster Assembly's doctrine of assurance.[1] Owen didn't merely parrot the Westminster standards, however. Rather, using the Confession's foundation, he added his own biblically based thoughts on assurance of salvation.

Owen seldom quoted the Confession directly on assurance, however.[2] Furthermore, in the eighty works he wrote, Owen never produced a full-length treatise on assurance. He explained his doctrine of assurance most fully in *A Practical Exposition Upon Psalm*

---

[1]For biographical accounts of Owen, consult Robert Asty, "Memoirs of the Life of Dr. Owen," in *A Complete Collection of the Sermons of the Reverend and Learned John Owen, D.D.* (London: John Clark, 1721); William Orme, *Life of the Rev. John Owen, D.D.* (reprint ed., Choteau, Mont.: Gospel Mission Press, 1981); Andrew Thomson, "Life of Dr. Owen," in *The Works of John Owen, D.D.*, vol. 1 (reprint ed., Edinburgh: Banner of Truth Trust, 1976); Dewey D. Wallace, Jr., "The Life and Thought of John Owen to 1660: A Study of the Significance of Calvinist Theology in English Puritanism" (Ph.D. dissertation, Princeton University, 1965); *The Correspondence of John Owen*, ed. Peter Toon (London: James Clarke, 1970); Peter Toon, *God's Statesman: The Life and Work of John Owen* (Exeter: Paternoster, 1971); Sinclair Ferguson, *John Owen on the Christian Life* (Edinburgh: Banner of Truth Trust, 1987), pp. 1-19. For dissertations on Owen's theology, see Bass, Davis, Everson, Pytches, Stover, and Vose in the bibliography.

[2]*The Works of John Owen*, ed. William H. Goold (reprint ed., Edinburgh: Banner of Truth Trust, 1967), 16:616. (Hereafter in chapter 7 only the volume and page number is noted.) The Goold edition was originally printed in 24 vols. by Johnstone & Hunter, 1850-53 (including 17 vols. of works plus 7 vols. containing his *Commentary on Hebrews*). In the 16-volume reprint by Banner of Truth, the Hebrews exposition is lacking, the English material from vol. 17 is transferred to vol. 16, and Owen's Latin writings in vols. 16 and 17 have been omitted. (Most of those were translated into English by Stephen Westcott and published by Soli Deo Gloria as *Biblical Theology* in 1994). I used the Goold reprint as it is more reliable than Russell's 21-vol. edition (London: for Richard Baynes, 1826). Goold's edition is also used for *An Exposition of the Epistle to the Hebrews*, 7 vols. (reprint ed., Grand Rapids: Baker, 1980).

CXXX. A half-dozen of his other works address the issue as well. We'll examine these works in chronological order.[3]

Two Short Catechisms (1645)[4]

Owen produced a Lesser and Greater Catechism to help with home instruction.[5] The Lesser Catechism, which contains thirty-two questions, was intended for children; the Greater Catechism, 145 questions for adults. In The Lesser Catechism Owen included this question and answer:

> *Q. What is a lively faith?*
> A. An assured resting of the soul upon God's promises of mercy in Jesus Christ, for pardon of sins here and glory hereafter.[6]

This connection of assurance with saving faith is even stronger in The Greater Catechism:

> *Q. 2. What is a justifying faith?*
> A. A gracious resting upon the free promises of God in Jesus Christ for mercy, with a firm persuasion of heart that God is a reconciled Father unto us in the Son of his love.[7]

Those statements on faith and assurance are important because, first, they reveal Owen's early conviction that assurance is an integral part of faith. Second, Owen's later modification of this position in response to the Westminster Confession makes us wonder: Did the assembly influence Owen's new direction? Or was this shift caused more by his theological maturation, personal experience, and contacts with parishioners who seemed to have faith, yet lacked full assurance? Later development in Owen's thought, commencing with *Doctrine of the Saints' Perseverance* in 1654, offers some insights.

---

[3]With the exception of Owen's teaching on the sealing of the Spirit (see pp. 201-208 below).

[4]Full title: *Two Short Catechisms: wherein the Principles of the Doctrine of Christ are Unfolded and Explained* 1:463-94.

[5]"Dr Owen had at that time the charge of the parish of Fordham in Essex, and laboured diligently for the instruction and benefit of his flock, by catechising from house to house. The Catechisms were prepared in order that he might accomplish these parochial duties with greater efficiency and success" (1:[464]).

[6]1:468.

[7]1:486.

The Doctrine of the Saints' Perseverance (1654)[8]

Section 17.1 of the Westminster Confession defines the doctrine of the perseverance of the saints this way: "They whom God hath accepted in his Beloved, effectually called and sanctified by his Spirit, can neither totally nor finally fall away from the state of grace; but shall certainly persevere therein to the end and be eternally saved." Like most Reformed theology, the Confession places the doctrine of perseverance before that of assurance. Perseverance is foundational to assurance, and is practically inseparable from it.[9] As G. C. Berkouwer noted: "The perseverance of the saints is unbreakably connected with the assurance of faith, in which the believer faces the future with confidence — not with the idea that all dangers and threats have been removed, but rather with the assurance that they shall be conquered indeed."[10] For the believer, this knowledge offers the assurance that nothing will ever separate him from God's love in Christ (Romans 8:38-39).

Polemical Response to John Goodwin

No Reformed writer has matched Owen's profound thinking, thorough exposition, and rigorous application in the matter of perseverance and assurance. Owen's defense of perseverance was a response to a treatise by John Goodwin, titled *Redemption Redeemed*, in which Goodwin denied that God secures the continuance of faith in a believer.[11] Because Goodwin's work was rambling and repetitious and lacked logical progression, Owen's rebuttal suffered the same asymmetry. However, Owen essentially responded to the four major objections Goodwin repeatedly raised against the doctrine of perseverance. Two of those objections were theological, and two, practical. Owen clearly felt that leaving those four objections unanswered would also undermine the doctrine of personal assurance.[12]

---

[8]11:1-666.

[9]For Owen, predestination compels covenant; covenant, perseverance; perseverance, assurance (11:78).

[10]*Faith and Perseverance*, p. 11.

[11]Owen's running commentary contra John Goodwin (not to be confused with Thomas Goodwin), grew into an extended book review of nearly 700 pages! Owen concluded that Goodwin borrowed the unsuccessful arguments of the Remonstrants. Although the Remonstrants initially deferred judgment on whether they held to the doctrine of perseverance, by the mid-1600s logic compelled most of them to deny it, for they increasingly realized that Calvinism could only be accepted or rejected as an organic whole. For John Goodwin, see Wallace, "Life and Thought of John Owen," pp. 242-47.

[12]11:82ff.

In *The Doctrine of the Saints' Perseverance Explained and Confirmed* (1654) Owen addressed Goodwin's objection to perseverance due to *the reality of apostasy*. Goodwin insisted that such passages as Hebrews 6:1-8 and 10:26-39, taught the possibility of the believer's defection from a state of grace. Goodwin said that was confirmed by the large numbers of churchgoers who had been zealous but were now indifferent.

Owen made no attempt to deny the existence of backsliders and apostates. Rather, he suggested that Goodwin's error, like that of all Arminians, was assuming that all professors of religion were true believers. In exhaustive detail, Owen examined scriptural passages describing those who fell away from faith and concluded that every one of those apostates had never been true believers. Owen said such apostates had experienced only a "temporary holiness" that did not change their natures.[13] Each time Scripture mentioned a Hymenaeus or a Philetus, for example, it then made a declaration, such as, "nevertheless, the firm foundation of God standeth sure, having this seal, The Lord knoweth them that are his."[14] Thus hypocrites in Scripture, who were like tares among the Lord's wheat, are not convincing arguments against perseverance.

Before stating his own position on perseverance, Owen established a biblical basis for perseverance by exegeting Philippians 1:6, 1 Peter 1:5, and John 10:27-29. He then offered the following syllogism to respond to Goodwin's objection:

1. The elect cannot fall away (John 10:27-29, etc.).
2. Some professors do fall away.
3. Hence, those professors are not elect believers.[15]

Next, Owen explained the doctrine of perseverance in relationship to:

(1) *The immutable nature of God as well as His promises and eternal purposes*, which extend to His elective love and covenant. The gifts and calling of God are irrevocable (Romans 11:29).[16] Those gifts include perseverance, for God is bonded to His people through His promises, which form the heart of the covenant of grace.[17] The

[13] 11:90.

[14] 2 Timothy 2:17-19; cf. Hebrews 6:1-9; 10:26-39.

[15] 11:113ff.

[16] Owen similarly treated the everlasting covenant of God, the irrevocable promises and oath of God, and the irresistible grace of God (11: chps. 4-8).

[17] 11:227.

covenant then becomes an unconditional *promise* of grace and perseverance for the believer through the mediatorial work of Christ.[18] God's foreknowledge, power, promises, covenant, and immutability are all part of His sovereign, eternal love. And perseverance is part of the unbreakable chain of salvation granted to the elect.

(2) *The nature of grace itself,* which always triumphs in Scripture. Since grace perseveres, God Himself perseveres with the believer, making grace a conquering thing and Christ a conquering King.[19] Christ has also granted the Spirit to Christians. This Spirit secures their perseverance, for in fulfilling the covenant of grace, the Comforter shall dwell with the elect forever (John 14:16).[20]

(3) *The integral unity of the plan of salvation.* If the outcome of God's salvation activity in the believer is questionable, the entire enterprise of salvation must fail. If the Holy Spirit does not keep believers in grace, neither can He call, regenerate, sanctify, and assure them, for all these are indissolubly linked.[21] Christ must also then be an impotent intercessor.[22]

Goodwin's second argument against perseverance was based on Scriptures that urge Christians to maintain themselves in a state of grace. Goodwin said such texts prove that *perseverance is the sole responsibility of the believer.*

Owen's reply was that Goodwin failed to see that *obligation does not entail ability.* In other words, even though sinners are obligated to repent and believe, this doesn't prove they have the power to do so. Similarly, just because God commands his saints to use the means of grace and to persevere in faith doesn't mean they can do that in their own strength. Granted, they must strive to enter the narrow gate (Luke 13:24), must hold fast the Word preached (1 Corinthians 15:2), and must be diligent to make their calling and election sure (2 Peter 1:10), but it is only through God, who will perform this in His elect. Believers work out their salvation with fear and trembling, not of doubt and uncertainty but of holy awe, for it is God Himself who is at work in them both to will and do (Philippians 2:12-13). As Owen wrote: "It is utterly denied, that men, the best of men, have in themselves, and of themselves, arising upon the account of any considerations whatsoever, a power, ability, or strength, vigorously

---

[18]11:289ff.   [19]11:172-73.
[20]11:308-315.   [21]6:145-46.
[22]11:499.

or at all acceptably to God, to incline their hearts to the performance of anything that is spiritually good, or in a gospel tendency to walking with God."[23]

To believe, like the Arminians, that the saints maintain their own faith is to minimize the doctrine of total depravity, for even after regeneration the believer does not have perfect knowledge of the good, much less the desire or ability to carry it out.[24] The believer works at salvation, but only through God's eternal power, which works mightily in him (Colossians 1:29). In short, Owen taught that assurance is to perseverance what perseverance is to divine election and faithfulness. Election therefore must be a motive for perseverance, holiness, and assurance. He wrote:

> [Election] hath the same tendency and effect in the *assurance* we have from thence, that notwithstanding all the oppositions we meet withal, we shall not utterly and finally miscarry. God's "election" will at last "obtain," Rom. xi. 7; and "his foundation standeth sure," 2 Tim. ii. 19. His purpose, which is "according unto election," is unchangeable; and, therefore, the final perseverance and salvation of those concerned in it are everlastingly secured.... And there is no greater encouragement to grow and persist in holiness than what is administered by this assurance of a blessed end and issue of it.[25]

Goodwin offered two more objections to perseverance. The first was *the danger of antinomianism.* He said widespread teaching of the doctrine of perseverance would give rise to lawlessness and disregard for the moral code of Scripture. The second objection was that perseverance minimizes *the importance of God's exhortations and commands.* Goodwin wrote, "If it is absolutely certain that God will preserve his people from apostasy, and he intends so to do, why then does he appeal to them to strive and to use the means of grace? This doctrine empties God's every command of all meaning."[26]

The essence of Owen's reply to Goodwin concerning antinomianism was simple: God preserves His saints *in holiness.* Christ saves His people *from*, not *in*, their sins. Justification is inseparable from sanctification; new birth necessarily results in new life. Far from promoting loose living, perseverance promises the

---

[23]6:165.
[24]Owen based this on Romans 7:17-21 and John 15:5 (6:153-56).
[25]3:601-602. Cf. *Hebrews* 4:155-57.
[26]11:243.

assurance of eternal salvation by the only path that will get the believer to heaven: the King's highway of holiness.[27] The doctrine of perseverance stimulates love, which can only yield obedience, for "it is the Spirit of Christ in the gospel that cuts [sin's] throat and destroys it," Owen wrote.[28] Though the Christian may fall into occasional sin, Christ effectually prays that his faith may not fail.[29] Consequently, perseverance guarantees the believer's continued sanctification and eventual glorification.[30]

Owen responded to Goodwin's concern that perseverance minimizes God's exhortations by stating that it is the moral duty of everyone to obey God's commands, and when believers do so, that signifies God's work within them. Hence, the sovereign activity of God neither negates the means of grace nor their efficacy. God has created the universe to work through the medium of cause and effect. Consequently, no one has an excuse to disobey God's moral imperatives. As Owen wrote: "As well might we argue that it is unnecessary for us to breathe because God gives us breath, or that Hezekiah need no longer to eat and drink because God had promised he should live another fifteen years. . . . Grace does not annul our responsibility but fits us to discharge it; it relieves from no duties, but equips for the performance of them."[31]

Setting the Stage for Elaboration on Assurance

In his defense of perseverance, Owen offered three particulars on assurance, which he later developed more fully:

First, unlike what he stated in his early catechisms, Owen now seemed to allow some distinction between faith and assurance by describing several *degrees* of, and *foundations* in, assurance. With degrees of assurance, he distinguished the weakest witness, "one of the lowest voices of all [the believer's] store" from stronger forms of witness.[32] In addition, he said that the foundation of assurance must not be limited to "the testimony of [the believer's] own conscience concerning his own regular walking in ways of righteousness."[33] Rather, it was evident, "and the saints acknowledge it," that Scripture

---

[27]11:254ff.   [28]11:393.
[29]11:495.
[30]Cf. 2 Thessalonians 1:3-5, 2:13; Hebrews 12:14; 1 Peter 1:2; 1 Corinthians 6:9-11; Ephesians 5:3-6.
[31]11:280.   [32]11:85.
[33]11:86.

built assurance on other foundations.[34] The reflex act of faith, which forms an essential role in the practical syllogism, is therefore not an integral part of every kind of assurance. Owen's space here between faith and assurance was not as great as it would later become. He wrote: "Yea, in the very graces themselves of faith and uprightness of heart, there is such a seal and stamp, impressing the image of God upon the soul, as, without any reflex act or actual contemplation of those graces themselves, have an influence into the establishment of the souls of men in whom they are unto a quiet, comfortable, assured repose of themselves upon the love and faithfulness of God."[35]

Second, Owen stated for the first time his conviction that doubts and fears are possible in the believer without a substantial loss of assurance. He wrote: "Neither is the spiritual confidence of the saints shaken, much less cast to the ground, by their conflicting with fears, scruples, and doubtful apprehensions, seeing in all these conflicts they have the pledge of the faithfulness of God that they shall be more than conquerors. Though they are exercised by them, they are not dejected with them, nor deprived of that comforting assurance and joy which they have in believing."[36]

Owen stated God Himself is glorified by such "trials and exercises of their graces whereunto he calls them." He may even use these fears to establish His saints. "It is no singular thing for the saints of God to be exercised with a thousand fears and jealousies, and through them to grow to great establishment," he wrote.[37]

Finally, Owen acknowledged that some degree of assurance was normal in the believer. In response to Goodwin's comment, "There is not one true believer of a hundred, yea, of many thousands, who hath any such assurance of his faith as is built upon solid and pregnant foundations," Owen stated:

> I no way doubt but many thousands of believers, whose apprehensions of the nature, properties, and conditions of things, as they are in themselves, are low, weak, and confused, yet, having received the Spirit of adoption, bearing witness with their spirits that they are the children of God, and having the testimony in themselves, have been taken up into as high a degree of comforting and cheering assurance, and that upon the most infallible foundation imaginable (for "the Spirit beareth witness, because the

[34]11:84.   [35]11:83.
[36]11:83-84.   [37]11:85.

Spirit is truth," 1 John v.6), as ever the most seraphically illuminated person in the world attained unto.[38]

Owen later modified this remarkable statement, though he maintained its principle throughout his career.

Communion with God the Father, Son, and Holy Ghost (1657)

In addition to providing a foundation for assurance of salvation through the doctrine of divine preservation rooted in eternal election, Owen offered a subjective approach to assurance by describing the communion between the Christian and the three Persons of the Trinity. In *Of Communion with God the Father, Son, and Holy Ghost, Each Person Distinctly, in Love, Grace, and Consolation,* Owen said that the believer communes with God, not in general, but with God's three Persons. The believer communes with each Person distinctly,[39] which, in turn, promotes assurance.

Owen found scriptural support for "distinct communion" in such texts as John 14:23; 1 Corinthians 1:9, 12:4-6; 2 Corinthians 3:14; 1 John 1:3, 5:7; and Revelation 3:20. Sinclair Ferguson writes of Owen's use of such passages: "Owen adds the axiom that all the activity of faith has reference to one distinct person of the Trinity, as do all receptions of grace. This is what he means by fellowship or communion. Thus the Father communicates by original authority, the Son from a purchased treasury and the Spirit in immediate efficacy. This is the classical doctrine of *Appropriations*."[40]

Before examining this treatise, here are some comments about the context in which it was written. First, the theme of communion with God was critically important to Owen's generation of Puritan divines. Their preoccupation with the subject of communion between God and His elect was not an attempt to humanize God or to deify man, however.[41] Rather, Owen and his colleagues wanted to explain, from within a Trinitarian framework, how God deals with needy sinners. The divines were not so much concerned with

[38]11:83.

[39]2:9ff.

[40]*John Owen on the Christian Life*, pp. 75-76.

[41]E.g., see Dale Arden Stover, "The Pneumatology of John Owen: A Study of the Role of the Holy Spirit in Relation to the Shape of a Theology" (Ph.D. dissertation, McGill University, 1967), pp. 304-305.

religious experience as an end in itself (which often is today's concern in a kind of *negative pietism*), as they were with religious experience as a revelation of God and His astonishing grace (or *positive pietism*). J. I. Packer rightly stated: "In modern spiritual autobiography [for example], the hero and chief actor is usually the writer himself; he is the centre of interest, and God comes in only as a part of his story. His theme is in effect '*I* — and God.' But in Puritan autobiography, God is at the centre throughout. He, not the writer, is the focus of interest; the subject of the book is in effect '*God* — and me.'"[42]

Second, Owen's theme of having communion with distinct divine Persons was a familiar one in Puritan literature.[43] In *The Object and Acts of Justifying Faith*, for example, Thomas Goodwin wrote of an intimate connection between assurance of faith and distinct communion:

> In assurance. . . a man's communion and converse is . . . sometimes with the Father, then with the Son, and then with the Holy Ghost; sometimes his heart is drawn out to consider the Father's love in choosing, and then the love of Christ in redeeming, and so again the love of the Holy Ghost, that searcheth the deep things of God, and revealeth them to us, and taketh all the pains with us; and so a man goes from one witness to another distinctly. . . . We should never be satisfied till all three persons lie level in us, and all make their abode with us, and we sit as it were in the midst of them, while they all manifest their love unto us.[44]

Third, Owen's *Communion with God* was unique in how it worked the idea of communion with distinct Persons of the Trinity into a systematic treatise. That is what prompted Daniel Burgess to write, "This treatise . . . is the only one extant upon its great and necessary subject."[45]

Fourth, *Communion with God* was favorably received from the time of its 1657 printing until its 1674 reprinting, after which it drew

---

[42]"The Puritan Idea of Communion with God," in *Press Toward the Mark* (London: n.p., 1962), p. 7.

[43]E.g., consult any Puritan commentary on the Song of Solomon (Richard Sibbes, John Dove, Nathaniel Homes, James Durham, and John Collinges). Collinges wrote 909 pages on chapter 1 and 530 on chapter 2 (*The Intercourses of Divine Love betwixt Christ and the Church* [London: A. Maxwell for Tho. Parkhurst, 1676]) on the communion of Christ and His church as represented by the communion of the Bridegroom and his bride.

[44]*The Works of Thomas Goodwin* 8:379.

[45]2:[4].

a rather inept attack from William Sherlock. Owen responded with *A Vindication*[46] but seemed genuinely surprised that this work should be subject to criticism, since it was "wholly practical, designed for popular edification, without a direct engagement into things controversial." He added, "I do know that multitudes of persons fearing God, and desiring to walk before him in sincerity, are ready, if occasion require to give testimony unto the benefit which they received thereby."[47]

Communion with God was popular among Dutch Calvinists as well. It was translated into Dutch by J. H. Hofman and published in 1717.[48] For many of English and Dutch descent, the work merited Daniel Burgess's commendation: "The very highest of angel's food is here set before thee."[49] No doubt this book was also angelic food for Owen, who was at the time of its writing, extremely busy serving as Vice-Chancellor at Oxford University.[50]

Andrew Thomson's criticism that Owen carried the idea of distinct communion between the believer and each of the Persons of the Godhead beyond Scripture,[51] did not do justice to Owen's careful, biblical scholarship. Reginald Kirby's assessment was more accurate: "Owen is but setting forth what is the experience of those who do enter into communion with God, and shows that the doctrine of the Trinity has its basis in human experience as well as Divine revelation."[52]

Owen's concept of communion with "distinct Persons" was innocent of Dale Stover's charge that "when God is known in this philosophical way, then epistemology is inevitably detached from soteriology."[53] As we shall see, Owen's *Communion with God* actually merged epistemology and soteriology spiritually and biblically. His treatise was more like a sermon than a philosophy lecture.

For Owen, communion between a believer and any Person of the Trinity represented a living relationship of mutual exchange. This mutual communication must be in and through Christ, for without

---

[46]2:275-365. [47]2:277.

[48]Cf. J. van der Haar, *Van Abbadie tot Young: Een Bibliografie van Engelse, veelal Puritaanse, in het Nederlands vertaalde Werken* (Veenendaal: Uitgeverij Kool, 1980), p. 89.

[49]2:[4].

[50]Cf. A. Thomson's synopsis, 1:lxxii-lxxiii, and Reginald Kirby, *The Threefold Bond* (London: Marshall, Morgan, and Scott, n.d.), p. 25.

[51]1:lxxii.

[52]*Threefold Bond*, p. 25.

[53]"The Pneumatology of John Owen," p. 304.

Christ no communion between God and man can exist.[54] From the outset Owen established a Christological focus for his Trinitarian framework. He said fellowship, or communion with God, "consisteth in his *communication of himself unto us, with our return unto him* of that which he requireth and accepteth, flowing from that *union* which in Jesus Christ we have with him."[55] Owen did not stress Christ at the expense of the Father and the Spirit, however, for that would have been false Christomonism. For Owen, theocentricity and Christocentricity walk together as friends, not as rivals. As F.R. Entwistle noted: "It is sometimes suggested that modern, Christological theology is more honouring to Christ than the older Trinitarianism, and in such a suggestion lies its appeal to the Christian. But this is not so. Owen's full Trinitarianism is not less honouring to Christ: to give glory to the Father and the Spirit does not detract from the glory of the Son."[56]

Within that framework, Owen taught distinct roles or economies for the Father, Son, and Spirit. He said the first Person, the Father, is *initiator*, who chooses whom and how He will save. The second Person is the Son and Word of God, who images the Father and does His will as Mediator to *redeem* sinners. The third Person proceeds from the first two as their *executive*, conveying to God's elect their sure salvation.

Since all three Persons are active in salvation, bestowing distinct gifts according to their roles, the believer should distinctly acknowledge each Person. Owen explained the biblical, experiential basis for that through two principles: First, "there is no grace whereby our souls go forth unto God, no act of divine worship yielded to Him, no duty or obedience performed, but they are distinctly directed unto Father, Son and Spirit"; and second, "by what act soever we hold communion with any Person there is an influence from every Person to the putting forth of that act."[57]

---

[54]For Owen, all such "communion is entered only through the 'door' of 'grace and pardoning mercy,' purchased for the elect by the merit of Christ" (Wallace, "Life and Thought of John Owen," p. 265).

[55]2:8. Consequently, for Owen "both the union with Christ which gives the Christian his *status* before God, and the communion with God which is the fruit of that status, are thus subsumed under the notion of communion, and this is the sense in which Owen generally employs the expression" (Ferguson, *John Owen on the Christian Life*, p. 75).

[56]"Some Aspects of John Owen's Doctrine of the Person and Work of Christ," *Faith and a Good Conscience* (papers read at Puritan and Reformed Studies Conference, 1962), p. 51.

[57]2:15, 18.

Communion with the Father: Love

Owen described the distinctive relationship saints have with the Father as preeminently a *communion of love*. Though careful not to present Christ's love as "winning over" a reluctant Father's love, Owen insisted that divine love has its deepest roots in the bosom of the Father. The Father delights to bestow divine love on the elect (Philippians 1:28), Owen said. And Scripture's references to the love of God most frequently mean the love of the Father. Christ's words "The Father himself loveth you" (John 16:27) assure the believer of God the Father's role in his salvation.[58]

The way to exercise communion with the Father is to *receive* His love by faith, and to *return* this love to Him by faith.[59] This twofold act of faith always takes place through the Son. As Owen wrote: "Jesus Christ in respect of the love of the Father, is but the beam, the stream, wherein though actually all our light, our refreshment lies, yet by him we are led to the fountain, the sun of eternal love itself [i.e., the Father]. The soul being thus by faith through Christ . . . brought unto the bosom of God, into a comfortable persuasion, and spiritual perception and sense of his love, there reposes and rests itself."[60]

In resting in the bosom of the Father through Christ, the believer returns the Father's love in his heart to the heart of the Father, from whom it originated. This returned love consists of rest, delight, reverence, and obedience.

When the Christian encounters obstacles in loving God, he must contemplate the nature of the Father's love, Owen said. First, the believer must remember not to invert God's order of love, thinking that the believer's love comes first. Second, he should meditate on the eternal quality and unchangeableness of the Father's love. Third, he should remember that the cross of Christ is the sign and seal of God's love, assuring him that the Father's *antecedent* love wins his *consequent* love through the Mediator.[61] He who returns to the Father with such meditations will find assurance of the Father's love. As Owen wrote: "Never any one from the foundation of the world, who believed such love in the Father, and made returns of love to him again, was deceived. . . . If thou believest and receivest the Father as love, he will infallibly be so to thee."[62]

[58]2:20.   [59]2:26-40.
[60]2:22-23.   [61]2:29.
[62]2:36-37.

Communion with the Son: Grace

The special gift of the second Person of the Trinity is *communion of grace*. According to Owen, Christ is the Mediator of the new covenant, and the new covenant is of grace. Grace is in Him and everywhere ascribed to Him (John 1:14). The believer receives grace by receiving Christ. As John 1:16 says, "Of his fulness have all we received, and grace for grace." Christ's very Person is the essence of grace.[63] What's more, Christ is pleased to manifest His gracious Person to sinners out of the free favor of His merits despite their demerits.

Christ's grace is the same as mediatorial, "purchased" grace,[64] for the distinct communion believers have with Him involves Christ *as Mediator*. As Mediator, Christ lays His hand on God (Zechariah 13:7) and on man (Hebrews 2:14-16), thereby becoming the "daysman" or "umpire" for His elect. Christ is eminently suited to accomplish this, for He has the true likeness of both natures in one Person (Acts 3:21).

Conjugal Relationship

In explaining how the Christian comes to know this fellowship of Christ's mediatorial grace, Owen emphasized the *conjugal relationship* between Christ and His people in terms of Song of Solomon 2:1-7 and chapter 5.[65] Christ woos and wins His bride, drawing His elect "to receive, embrace and submit unto the Lord Jesus as their husband, Lord, and Saviour, — to abide with him, subject their souls unto him, and to be ruled by him for ever,"[66] Owen said. The inevitable result of receiving Christ is communion with Him. Owen explained:

> When the soul consents to take Christ on his own terms, to save him in his own way, and says, "Lord, I would have had thee and salvation in my way, that it might have been partly of mine endeavours, and as it were by the works of the law; I am now willing to receive thee and to be saved in thy way, — merely by grace: and though I would have

---

[63]2:47; 3:414.

[64]For Owen's usage of and safeguards on the expression "purchased grace," see Ferguson, *John Owen on the Christian Life*, pp. 86-88.

[65]Cf. note 43 above. This is not to say that Owen developed his Christology or its experimental aspects from the Song of Solomon. Rather, he illustrated the believer's experience of communion with Christ through its poetry. Ferguson notes, "He does not subjectivize Christ to the point of mysticism, but rather tries to describe the subjective experience of the objective Christ to whom the rest of Scripture bears witness" (*John Owen on the Christian Life*, pp. 78ff.).

[66]2:58.

walked according to my own mind, yet now I wholly give up myself to be ruled by thy Spirit; for in thee have I righteousness and strength, in thee am I justified and do glory;"— then doth it carry on communion with Christ as to the grace of his person. This it is to receive the Lord Jesus in his comeliness and eminency.[67]

In short, the same faith that responds to the Father, responds to Christ. That response is brought to fruition by faith acting in *marital chastity* towards Christ. Such chastity trusts in Christ alone for acceptance with God. It cherishes the Spirit of Christ and relishes pure worship of Christ.

Mutual resignation is intrinsic to that relationship. "Christ having given himself to the soul, loves the soul, and the soul having given itself to Christ loveth Him also," Owen wrote.[68] A sweet mystical knowledge and communion flows into this reciprocal relationship, which Christ initiates by giving Himself to the soul. All of Christ's excellencies, preciousness, and everything that grace entails are poured into the believer when Christ becomes Savior, Head, Husband, and Indweller.

In return, the believer receives grace to *receive* Christ, not only in initial trust, but also in intimate communion, in a continued loving of Him with his will and all his affections. In communing with Christ, the believer's will becomes subordinate to Christ's, and his love uplifted by Christ's. And increasingly, the believer's experiences with Christ make him more conscious of the love of the Father.

This communion results in deliberate, daily submission to Christ as gracious Lord. In resigning himself to Christ, the believer brings each day's sins to Christ for forgiveness, each day's mercies to Christ for praise, each day's needs to Christ for the sanctifying and purifying supply of His Spirit.[69] It is this daily returning that brings peace and fellowship and such intimacy that Owen could write: "There is not anything in the heart of Christ wherein those friends of his are concerned that he doth not reveal to them."[70]

Through fellowship with Christ the believer comes to know both Christ and himself. Christ becomes the mirror of the believer's soul, the unveiler of the secret intuitions of the believer's heart. In revealing Himself, Christ also reveals the believer's self. In making his mind known to Christ in confession and praise, the child of God may enjoy constantly renewed forgiveness and friendship. As Owen wrote: "This

[67]2:58-59.   [68]2:56ff.
[69]2:197-207.   [70]2:59.

does he who hath communion with Christ: he watcheth daily and diligently over his own heart that nothing creep into its affections to give it any peace or establishment before God, but Christ only."[71]

The result of this mutual giving — Christ to the believer, and the believer in gratitude to Christ — is deep, constant assurance of faith.

Adoption

The most direct result of communion with Christ that enhances assurance is *adoption*.[72] Adoption is what makes sanctification possible and becomes the crowning work of grace in the final analysis. Thus, adoption is both the means by which we enter the family of God and the result of it. As Owen wrote: "Adoption is the authoritative translation of a believer, by Jesus Christ, from the family of the world and Satan into the family of God, with his investiture in all the privileges and advantages of that family."[73]

In the matter of adoption, Owen stressed that communion with Christ is central. Our standing in God is made possible by our adoption through Christ. Through fellowship with Him, we share the benefits of God's family. In the process of adoption and the assurance that follows, Christ is essential as the Person who carries out the Father's will.

Adoption involved five things for Owen, which Sinclair Ferguson summarized as follows: "(1) that the person first belongs to another family; (2) that there is a family to which he has no right to belong; (3) that there is an authoritative legal translation from one family to another; (4) that the adopted person is freed from all the legal obligations of the family from which he came; (5) and that by virtue of his translation he is invested with all the rights, privileges, and advantages of the new family."[74]

Through Christ the Christian experiences the annulment of sin's penalty, victory over sin, and new family privileges such as liberty, a title to all adoptive blessings, boldness with God, and correction through fatherly dealings.[75] The child of God gains

---

[71]2:146.

[72]Other benefits believers gain from communing with Christ include: approving of the divine way of salvation, maintaining a sense of continuing sinfulness, and yielding to holiness as a response to the holiness of Christ (2:187-207).

[73]2:207; cf. 2:173.

[74]*John Owen on the Christian Life*, pp. 90-91; cf. 2:207-208.

[75]2:211ff.

acquaintance with God as Father[76] and Christ as Elder Brother, which is accompanied by a deepening conviction that Christ belongs to him and he to Christ.[77]

The bond between communion with Christ and assurance of salvation is inseparable,[78] though Owen didn't make much of that link here. Thomas Goodwin stressed assurance that flows out of communion with Christ, but Owen preferred to focus on the believer's duty to grow in communion with Christ and His grace.[79]

Owen would have agreed with Goodwin's view of certain steps in grace being more advanced than others and that advancement in assurance roughly parallels advancement in grace, but Owen did not dwell on the steps in grace. Rather, he branched out of his experimental theology often covering nearly the entire order of salvation as he did under his consideration of adoption. Ultimately Owen wanted to stress that "the Spirit of Christ testifies to the heart and conscience of a believer that he is freed from all engagement unto the family of Satan, and is become the son of God, which enables him to cry, 'Abba, Father.'" He thus wrote of adoption applied to the conscience, but also in a broader sense as being brought by Christ from Satan's family into the family of God, with all the privileges of that family.[80] Within that framework, Owen stressed that every mark of grace is possessed in principle by each Christian from regeneration onward, despite the fact that its consciousness may not be yet realized. For example, in *A Discourse of the Work of the Holy Spirit in Prayer*, he wrote: "But believers have it [i.e., assurance or boldness] always in the root and principle, even all that have received the Spirit of adoption, and are ordinarily assisted in the use of it."[81]

Communion with the Spirit: Comfort

Finally, the third Person of the Trinity communes with the believer as *Comforter*. Though he acknowledged that the Spirit as Paraclete acts as both Advocate and Comforter, Owen chose to stress the role

---

[76]Sinclair Ferguson, "Doctrine of the Christian Life in the Teaching of Dr John Owen [1616-83]," [Ph.D. dissertation, University of Aberdeen, 1979], pp. 175-76.

[77]2:187.

[78]2:218.

[79]Cf. J. I. Packer, "Puritan Idea of Communion with God," p. 12.

[80]2:207ff. *Contra* Stover, the Spirit *of Christ* was emphasized by Owen (2:207, 210). Owen also used the terminology, Spirit *of the Father* (2:241), particularly with regard to adoption. Cf. 4:265-69; 292-94.

[81]4:294.

of Comforter.[82] Later, in *A Discourse on the Holy Spirit as Comforter,* Owen wrote about the Spirit's role of Advocate, unction, and seal in assurance. We'll examine that later.[83]

At this point, Owen stressed how the Spirit as Consoler communes with the believer in these ways: (1) the Spirit helps the believer remember the words of Christ and teaches him what they mean; (2) the Spirit glorifies Christ; (3) He spreads the love of God in the Christian's heart; (4) He convinces the believer that he is a child of God; (5) He seals faith in the Christian, (6) assures him of that as his earnest, (7) anoints him, (8) adopts him, and (9) grants him the Spirit of supplication.[84]

Five of those comforting forms of communion directly contribute to personal assurance, and two of those here represent Owen's most definitive treatment. The two are the Spirit's witness to the believer's conscience that he is a justified child of God, and the Spirit sealing that promise as an earnest to the Christian.[85]

Witnessing in the Court of Conscience

Owen said the witness of the Spirit, adoption into the divine family, and personal justification in the court of one's own conscience were some of the strongest promoters of assurance. Concerning the Spirit's witness in the believer's court of conscience, Owen wrote:

> The soul, by the power of its own conscience, is brought before the law of God. There a man puts in his plea,— that he is a child of God, that he belongs to God's family; and for this end produceth all his evidences, every thing whereby faith gives him an interest in God. Satan, in the meantime, opposeth with all his might; sin and law assist him; many flaws are found in his evidences; the truth of them all is questioned; and the soul hangs in suspense as to the issue. In the midst of the plea and contest the Comforter comes, and, by a word of promise or otherwise, overpowers the heart with a comfortable persuasion (and bears down all objections) that his plea is good, and that he is a child of God. . . . When our spirits are pleading their right and title, he comes in and bears witness on our side; at the same time enabling us to put forth acts of filial obedience, kind and child-like; which is called "crying, Abba, Father," Gal. iv. 6.

---

[82]2:225.

[83]See pp. 200-208 below. For Holy Spirit as advocate, see 4:361-68; as unction, 4:389ff.; as seal, 4:399-406.

[84]2:236-49.

[85]For the other three, see pp. 180-81 above for adoption and pp. 201-208 below for sealing and anointing.

Owen explained that the believer's court case may last long before it is settled:

> Sometimes the dispute hangs long,— the cause is pleading many years. The law seems sometimes to prevail, sin and Satan to rejoice; and the poor soul is filled with dread about its inheritance. Perhaps its own witness, from its faith, sanctification, former experience, keeps up the plea with some life and comfort; but the work is not done, the conquest is not fully obtained, until the Spirit, who worketh freely and effectually, when and how he will, comes in with his testimony also; clothing his power with a word of promise, he makes all parties concerned to attend unto him, and puts an end to the controversy. . . . When the Holy Ghost by one word stills the tumults and storms that are raised in the soul, giving it an immediate claim and security, it knows his divine power, and rejoices in his presence.[86]

Several comments are in order here:

First, Owen's concept of a "courtroom-conscience," complete with judge, plaintiff, prosecuting witnesses, and defense attorney, is not a unique illustration used by Reformed theologians to describe how justification is experienced.[87] Though English Puritan divines made only passing references to this, Dutch theologians more frequently explained justification in the court of conscience as an advanced step of grace that illustrated reaching an established state of assurance.[88]

Nevertheless, for Owen (as well as anyone else who used that example), assurance that came from justification in the court of conscience represented a high certainty of divine acceptance applied to the believer's conscience. Owen later made a distinction in *An Exposition Upon Psalm CXXX* between the *state of adherence* (i.e., a saving "persuasion or discovery of forgiveness in God, where there is no assurance of any particular interest therein . . . that our own sins in particular are pardoned"),[89] and the *state of assurance* (i.e., a saving application that this discovery of God's forgiveness belongs to one's self through its being "testified unto the conscience in a word of promise mixed by faith").[90] That distinction won whole-

---

[86]2:241-42.

[87]See p. 146 above.

[88]See chapter 8 on Alexander Comrie's view of assurance. Cf. Joel R. Beeke, *Jehovah Shepherding His Sheep* (Grand Rapids: Eerdmans, 1982), pp. 90-98.

[89]6:415, 426.

[90]Ibid.

hearted acceptance among the Dutch divines. Owen's elaboration of how deeply one may be encouraged through personal discovery of forgiveness while remaining outside of the personal application of that forgiveness likewise received their approval.[91] But some Dutch theologians' explanation of conversion went beyond Owen to a more detailed analysis of the steps in grace. Consequently, it is understandable that for Owen and others the higher step of grace in courtroom justification was more accessible to the average believer than for some Dutch divines, who viewed it as a scarce, sovereign gift that must nevertheless be sought by the conscientious believer.

Second, Owen offered several thoughts on justification in the court of conscience that differed in emphasis from the Dutch divines:

(1) Whereas justification in the court of conscience is sometimes regarded as an instantaneous divine act and an unforgettable, once-for-all experience by Dutch theologians, Owen viewed it as a longer process that can be held in the balance for years before the plaintiff's case is settled. He wrote, "Hence sometimes the dispute hangs long,— the cause is pleading many years."[92] Owen later reinforced that in his remarks on Hebrews 2:2-4: "The promise of the gospel, conveyed unto the soul by the Holy Spirit, and entertained by faith, completes the justification of a believer in his own conscience, and gives him *assured peace* with God."[93]

(2) Owen regarded the role of the plaintiff as *self-defense* based on God's saving work, whereas most Dutch theologians said the plaintiff comes before God the Judge as a *self-condemned* sinner. True, Owen's plaintiff becomes self-condemning after the testimonies of witnesses, yet there is a tendency here that leads to another intriguing difference.

(3) For Owen, the plaintiff is justified in his conscience by *the Holy Spirit's* affirming God's saving work within him by applying one or more scriptural promises. For some Dutch Second Reformation divines, the plaintiff's attorney is not the Holy Spirit at all, but Jesus Christ as Mediator who demands the justification of the plaintiff by His Father as Judge on the basis of Christ's payment of the penalty of sin. *The Father* thus acquits the sinner on the basis

[91] 6:416-27.

[92] 2:241. Cf. Alexander Comrie, *The ABC of Faith*, trans. J. M. Banfield (Ossett, W. Yorks: Zoar, 1978), p. 74. See chapter 8 below.

[93] *Hebrews* 3:300.

of His Son's mediation and advocacy. The Spirit then seals that pronouncement in the sinner's heart.

Owen stressed the role of the Spirit, whereas the Dutch divines stressed the role of God the Father as Judge. In addition, the Dutch distinguished between justification and adoption, saying justification is a *judicial* act of the Father as Judge, which results in reconciliation, whereas adoption is a *paternal* act of the Father as Father, which results in full restoration.[94] To be fair, Owen further developed his position on the Father's role. Eleven years later, in *An Exposition Upon Psalm CXXX*, Owen stated that acquittal ultimately flows from the first Person. He wrote, "The true nature of gospel forgiveness . . . flows from the gracious heart of the Father through the blood of the Son."[95]

The Believer's "Earnest"

Owen offered a concise description of how the Holy Spirit serves as *earnest*, or pledge, to the believer. He noted that in 2 Corinthians 1:22 and 5:5 believers are said to have the earnest of the Spirit, whereas in Ephesians 1:13-14 the Spirit Himself is said to be the believer's earnest.[96] Owen wrote that the Spirit is the believer's earnest as the Spirit of *promise*, while distinguishing between the Spirit's role as earnest "on the part of God" and "on the part of believers."[97]

Describing the earnest as "part of that which is to come and but a part of it,"[98] Owen argued that "the Spirit given us for the fitting of us for enjoyment of God in some measure, whilst we are here, is the earnest of the whole" inheritance to come.[99] Thus, the Lord looks upon His elect and views their inheritance as integral with His grace. The Spirit is also an earnest within the Christian, teaching him about the inheritance that shall be his. All of this enhances assurance. As Owen wrote, "So is he in all respects completely an earnest,— given of God, received by us, as the beginning of our inheritance, and the assurance of it."[100]

Thus, Owen saw the earnest of the Spirit not as an act, but as an office of the Spirit Himself,[101] particularly as a pledge of the

---

[94]Cf. Beeke, *Jehovah Shepherding His Sheep*, p. 95.

[95]6:420; cf. 6:510, 538, 540.

[96]2:243-44.   [97]2:244-45.

[98]2:244; cf. 4:407.   [99]2:245.

[100]2:246.

[101]4:407; cf. 4:384 and 11:329ff. Also, Thomas Goodwin, *Works* 6:63-67, and John Preston, *Sinnes Overthrow*, 3rd ed., (London: F. Kingston for A. Crooke, 1635), p. 39, both

believer's inheritance that was lost by the first Adam and regained by the last Adam. Through union with Christ, the Spirit becomes an earnest, thereby stabilizing the Christian, for his hope shall not be disappointed.[102] As earnest, the Spirit assures the believer that though his experience of salvation is yet imperfect and will be until Judgment Day[103]— perfection will surely come. The Spirit is Christ's own earnest (ἀρραβών) of this perfect inheritance.

In *A Discourse on the Holy Spirit as a Comforter* (written, according to Owen, to augment *Communion with God* and *Perseverance of the Saints*[104]), Owen reaffirmed his early convictions on how the Spirit's earnest leads to assurance. He wrote: "The meaning therefore . . . is that God gives unto us his Holy Spirit to dwell in us, and to abide with us, as an earnest of our future inheritance . . . wherein God intends our assurance only, and not his own."[105]

Owen also clarified his earlier suggestion about the role of the Father in giving the Spirit to show the believer that he is a co-heir with Christ. He wrote that the Spirit represents "the first-fruits of our spiritual and eternal redemption [because] He is the Spirit of adoption and the Spirit of the Son, [so that] in the giving of his Spirit unto us, God the Father making of us co-heirs with Christ, we have the greatest and most assured earnest and pledge of our future inheritance."[106]

In sum, Owen showed how the earnest, sealing, and anointing of the Spirit fortify the Christian's assurance of eternal salvation:

> No one way, or thing, or similitude, can express or represent the greatness of this privilege, for in this one privilege of receiving the Spirit are all others inwrapped. It is *anointing*, it is *sealing*, it is an *earnest* and *first-fruit*,— every thing whereby the love of God and the blessed security of our condition may be expressed or intimated unto us; for what greater pledge can we have of the love and favour of God, what greater dignities can we be made partakers of, what greater assurance of a future blessed condition, than that God hath given us of his Holy Spirit?[107]

---

of whom maintain the personal indwelling of the Holy Spirit in opposition to R. Hollingworth, *The Holy Ghost on the Bench, other spirits at the bar; or the judgment of the Holy Spirit of God upon the spirits of the times* (London: J. M. for Luke Fawn, 1656), pp. 8, 10.

[102]2:253.

[103]4:411.

[104]4:352.

[105]4:408.

[106]Cf. 4:407-412.

[107]4:412.

Owen also taught that, in response to the work of the Spirit, the believer must avoid grieving the Spirit by negligence or sin (Ephesians 4:30), quenching Him by opposing or hindering His work (1 Thessalonians 5:19), and resisting Him by refusing His word (Acts 7:51). The Spirit deserves constant thanks and continual petitioning for ongoing peace, Owen said.[108]

Packer aptly summarized Owen's emphasis by writing: "This, then, according to Owen, should be the pattern of our regular communion with the three Persons of the Godhead, in meditation, prayer, and a duly ordered life. We should dwell on the special mercy and ministry of each Person towards us, and make our proper response of love and communion distinctly to each. Thus we are to maintain a full-orbed communion with God."[109]

The Savoy Declaration of Faith and Order (1658)

The Savoy Declaration of Faith and Order, which was written in 1658 to consolidate conservative independents, was strongly influenced by Owen.[110] In addition to writing the Declaration's lengthy introduction, Owen made his theological mark throughout the Declaration proper, particularly in what it incorporated and changed from the Westminster Confession of Faith. Three of the changes it made were in reference to section 18.2 of the Confession. The Declaration said:

> This certainty is not a bare conjectural and probable persuasion, grounded upon a fallible hope, but an infallible assurance of faith, founded *on the blood and righteousness of Christ, revealed in the Gospel, and also upon* the inward evidence of those graces unto which

[108]2:264-74; Packer, "Puritan Idea of Communion with God," p. 12.

[109]Ibid.

[110]For general information, consult *The Savoy Declaration of Faith and Order*, ed. A. G. Matthews (London: Independent Press Ltd., 1959), which includes a helpful historical introduction and an accurate Savoy text highlighting each departure from or addition to the Confession. The working committee of the Savoy Declaration consisted of Thomas Goodwin, Philip Nye, William Bridge, William Greenhil, Joseph Caryl (all of whom were members of the Westminster Assembly), and John Owen, who, since the Westminster Standards, had attained the reputation of being one of the most influential theologians in England. For Owen's particular influence and leadership at Savoy, shared to a degree with Nye, see Wallace, "Life and Thought of John Owen," pp. 298-308. (See Williston Walker, ed., *The Creeds and Platforms of Congregationalism* [New York: Charles Scribner's Sons, 1893], pp. 340ff. for general information and bibliographical material on The Savoy Declaration.)

> promises are made, *and on the immediate witness* of the Spirit, *testifying our* Adoption, and *as a fruit thereof, leaving the heart more humble and holy.*[111]

Though these changes did not depart from the doctrine of the Confession, they did add Owen's particular emphases. For example, the first change linked the foundation of assurance to "the blood and righteousness of *Christ* revealed in the Gospel," rather than to the more general wording, "the truth of the promises of salvation." Obviously this isn't an essential change, as all the promises of God are "amen" only in and through Christ Jesus (2 Corinthians 1:20); nonetheless, The Savoy Declaration's wording (later adopted by the Second London Confession), like Owen's, was more pointed.

In *The Doctrine of Justification by Faith*, Owen made a point of discussing where Reformed thought fixed assurance and trust. He said that was: (1) "principally on the grace, love, and mercy of God"; (2) "principally on the Lord Christ, his mediation, and the benefits thereof"; (3) "in believing on the promises"; and (4) on "the pardon of sin and eternal life." His conclusion was:

> Allowing therefore their proper place unto the promises, and unto the effect of all in the pardon of sins and eternal life, that which I shall further confirm is, *that the Lord Christ, in the work of his mediation, as the ordinance of God for the recovery and salvation of lost sinners, is the proper adequate object of justifying faith.*[112]

Owen was concerned here with more than Socinianism, which he later refuted. He also was trying to hold back the winds of Quakerism, which taught that Christ formed within us justifies. Owen wanted to stress that *Christ's blood* secures salvation, and *His righteousness* covers sin. Hence, assurance does not come from anything we accomplish. Neither does it come primarily through Christ formed within us, for Christ only dwells in those who have learned by grace to trust in His saving death. Christ within does not justify — only His death does that. Christ within, together with its fruits, is the result of justification.

The second change, which substituted "and on the immediate witness of the Spirit" for "the testimony of the Spirit," filled in the silence of the Confession on whether this testimony is synonymous

---

[111]Matthews, *The Savoy Declaration*, p. 98. I have italicized the changes from the Confession. Sections 18.3 and 18.4 of the Confession were left unchanged. In Section 18.1 "hypocrites" was changed to "temporary believers."

[112]5:88-89.

with or different from the practical syllogism. Both the "and," as well as the "immediate," were consistent with Owen's view. However, it may be that Thomas Goodwin should be credited with this change because of his insistence on separating the syllogisms from the immediate witness of the Spirit.[113]

The third change, which put "testify our adoption" in place of "whereby we are sealed," appeared to concede to Owen's view that the sealing of the Spirit is common to every believer. "Testifying" is harmonious with Owen's conviction that in full assurance the Spirit testifies to the believer what he already possesses from God's side.

The multiple authorship of The Savoy Declaration makes Owen's direct influence difficult to prove, however. So let us simply agree here that The Savoy Declaration retains and explains in its own way what's written in the Westminster Confession.[114]

An Exposition Upon Psalm CXXX (1668)

Personal Crises

Two crises in the life of Owen contributed to his most exhaustive treatment of assurance. Owen included that treatment of assurance in *An Exposition upon Psalm CXXX*, 75 per cent of which is devoted to the verse: "But there is forgiveness with thee, that thou mayest be feared." Hence Owen's treatment of assurance is expository, not systematic.

One crisis that led to this exposition of Psalm 130 was Owen's five-year struggle for personal assurance of salvation. That struggle was not resolved until the winter of 1642-43, when Owen was helped by a preacher, whose name we do not know. Owen's struggle had already intensified in 1637 when he left Oxford to become chaplain to Sir Robert Dormar of Ascot. Owen's early biographer described the chaplain's spiritual state during this period as follows: "About this time he was also exercised with many perplexing thoughts about his spiritual state, which joined with outward discouragements, threw him into a deep melancholy, that continued in its extremity for a quarter of a year; during which time he avoided almost all manner of converse, and very hardly could be induced to speak a word, and when he did speak, it was with such disorder as rendered him a wonder to many."[115]

---

[113]Cf. *The Works of Thomas Goodwin*, 1:227-67. See pp. 259-65 below.
[114]See Matthews, *The Savoy Declaration*, pp. 39ff. for the aftermath of Savoy.
[115]Asty, "Memoirs," p. iv.; cf. Orme, *Life of the Rev. John Owen*, pp. 11-12.

Though some historians suggested that Owen's agony lessened substantially between 1638 and 1642, we know that "solid comfort"[116] came quite suddenly to him through a sermon he heard in 1643 at Aldermanbury Chapel.

Owen had gone with a cousin to hear the famous Presbyterian minister, Edmund Calamy. Calamy was unexpectedly absent, and Owen was disappointed to see a stranger ascend the pulpit. The stranger, who preached from Matthew 8:26, "Why are ye fearful, O ye of little faith," answered all the objections Owen had raised against his own salvation. Wallace wrote, "This sermon . . . was blest for the removing of all his doubts, and laid the foundation of that solid peace, and comfort which he enjoyed as long as he lived."[117]

This experience of grace at the end of a long period of spiritual depression set the tone for writings of the 26-year-old Owen that would span the next four decades. Owen's stress on conviction of sin as a necessary prelude to experimental grace never diminished. More than a quarter of a century later, Owen's experience of personal assurance was still coloring his exposition of Psalm 130. Indeed, some writers have suggested that the entire exposition was largely an account of Owen's spiritual development.[118]

Another crisis in Owen's life prompted his exposition of *Psalm CXXX*. Owen said to a friend who visited him:

> I myself preached Christ some years, when I had but very little, if any, experimental acquaintance with access to God through Christ; until the Lord was pleased to visit me with sore affliction, whereby I was brought to the mouth of the grave and under which my soul was oppressed with horror and darkness; but God graciously relieved my spirit by a powerful application of Psalm cxxx.4, 'But there is forgiveness with thee, that thou mayest be feared;' from whence I received special instruction, peace, and comfort, in drawing near to God through the Mediator, and preached thereupon immediately after my recovery.[119]

William Goold wrote, "The incident to which he refers had occurred at an early period in his public life; and it is probable this Exposition

---

[116]Ibid., p. 17.

[117]Wallace, "Life and Thought of John Owen," p. 115. See Orme, *Life of the Rev. John Owen*, pp. 12ff.; Godfrey Noel Vose, "Profile of a Puritan: John Owen, 1616-1683" (Ph.D. dissertation, State University of Iowa, 1963), p. 34.

[118]Kirby, *Threefold Bond*, p. 19; cf. Orme, *Life of the Rev. John Owen*, pp. 17-18. For the popularity of this work in the Netherlands, see van der Haar, *From Abbadie to Young*, p. 92.

[119]6:324. Cf. Middleton, *Biographia Evangelica* 3:473.

is the substance of the discourses which he preached on his recovery from affliction, under the influence of enlivened faith in the mediation of Christ."[120]

Enlargement Upon the Westminster Confession

Owen's exposition on assurance in *Psalm CXXX* can best be understood within the framework of the Westminster Confession's teachings on assurance.

The Attainability of Assurance

Owen plainly asserted the attainability of assurance. He wrote: "There may be a gracious persuasion and assurance of faith in a man concerning his own *particular interest* in forgiveness. A man may, many do, believe it for themselves, so as not only to have the benefit of it but the comfort also."[121]

The attainability of assurance must be understood in relationship to faith, however. Owen unreservedly supported an organic relationship between faith and assurance but no confusion between the two. He believed faith included persuasion of the availability of divine forgiveness, but said that did not necessarily include the personal application of forgiveness — which alone gives rise to full assurance. He wrote, "There is or may be a saving persuasion or discovery of forgiveness in God, where there is no assurance of any particular interest therein."[122]

Of the element of trust in faith that cleaves to God, Owen wrote: "This a soul *cannot* do, without a discovery of forgiveness in God; but this a soul *may* do, without a special assurance of his own interest therein."[123] For Owen, personal knowledge of inclusion in God's grace usually happens sometime after initial belief, according to God's sovereign timing. Consequently, Owen could write that regarding assurance of salvation and its accompanying phenomena of joy and glorying in the Lord as of the essence of faith, would result in soul deception:

> It is this peace, this joy, this glorying in the Lord, that you would always be in the possession of. I say, you do well to desire them, to seek and labour after them,— they are purchased by Christ for believers; but you will do well to consider under what notion you do desire them. If you look on these things as belonging to the *essence*

120 6:324.   121 6:413.
122 6:415.   123 Ibid.

of faith, without which you can have no real interest in forgiveness or acceptance with God, you greatly deceive your own souls, and put yourselves out of the way of obtaining of them. These things are not believing, nor adequate effects of it, so as immediately to be produced wherever faith is; but they are such consequents of it as may or may not ensue upon it, according to the will of God. Faith is a seed that contains them *virtually,* and out of which they may be in due time educed by the working of the word and Spirit; and the way for any soul to be made partaker of them is to wait on the sovereignty of God's grace, who createth peace in the exercise of faith upon the promises.[124]

Assurance Normative but not Common

Like the Westminster Confession, Owen regarded assurance as normative though not necessarily common. That was consistent with the Confession's teaching that there are degrees and various kinds of assurance. All true believers possess some assurance, but few can claim the blessing of "full assurance." Owen wrote, *"This discovery of forgiveness in God is great, holy, and mysterious, and which very few on gospel grounds do attain unto.* . . . Even one experimental embracement of it [i.e., the full assurance of personal interest in divine forgiveness], even at the hour of death, doth well deserve the waiting and obedience of the whole course of a man's life. . . . It is a great and rare thing to have forgiveness in God discovered unto a sinful soul. . . ."[125]

Believers who gain full assurance of forgiveness by God don't find it quickly or easily. Those who don't understand that can substitute a notion of forgiveness in God for personal forgiveness from God. Owen wrote of such people:

> To convince such poor creatures of the folly of their presumption, I would but desire them to go to some real believers that are or may be known unto them. Let them be asked whether they came so easily by their faith and apprehensions of forgiveness or no. "Alas!" saith one, "these twenty years have I been following after God, and yet I have not arrived unto an abiding cheering persuasion of it." "I know what it cost me, what trials, difficulties, temptations I wrestled with, and went through withal, before I obtained it," saith another.[126]

Owen also believed that believers with full assurance were never

[124]6:563.
[125]6:386, 431, 598. (Cf. 6:414, 423, 425, 505-511.)
[126]6:508-509.

safe from attacks on their faith. Still, even when a believer is spiritually "cast down," assurance is not altogether lost (Psalm 42); rather, assurance may continue even under a deep sense of indwelling sin and infirmity. Owen wrote:

> This life is not a season to be always taking wages in; our work is not yet done; we are not always to abide in this mount; we must down again into the battle,— fight again, cry again, complain again. Shall the soul be thought now to have lost its assurance? Not at all. It had before assurance with joy, triumph, and exaltation; it hath it now, or may have, with wrestling, cries, tears, and supplications. And a man's assurance may be as good, as true, when he lies on the earth with a sense of sin, as when he is carried up to the third heaven with a sense of love and foretaste of glory.[127]

Here Owen not only confirmed but went beyond section 18.4 of the Westminster Confession. For Owen, conviction of sin and assurance of salvation were not antagonistic. Rather, both should be sought, and both are given and retained by God's grace. Though full assurance is difficult to obtain, true believers must strive for it. As Owen wrote: "*It is the duty of every believer to labour after an assurance of a personal interest in forgiveness,* and to be diligent in the cherishing and preservation of it when it is attained. . . . It is no small evil in believers not to be pressing after perfection in believing and obedience."[128]

The Christian need not despair if he comes short of reaching such assurance, for God may have wise reasons for withholding it from him. Owen wrote: "Some servants that are ill husbands must have their wages kept for them to the year's end, or it will do them no good. It may be, some would be such spendthrifts of satisfying peace and joy, and be so diverted by them from attending unto some necessary duties,— as of humiliation, mortification, and self-abasement, without which their souls cannot live,— that it would not be much to their advantage to be intrusted with assurance. It is from the same care and love that peace and joy are detained from some believers, and granted unto others."[129]

Despite God's wisdom and sovereignty, however, lack of assurance is ordinarily due to the believer's shortcomings. As Owen

[127]6:551; cf. 6:548-51.

[128]6:413; cf. 6:414 where Owen implied that the Christian's striving after full assurance is a mark of grace.

[129]6:563; cf. 6:554. The notion that God "gives us such assurance as is appropriate for us" is common to later writers as well (cf. John Colquhoun, *A Treatise on Spiritual Comfort* [London: for J. Ogle, 1814], p. 20).

wrote: "In *ordinary dispensations of God* towards us, and dealings with us, *it is mostly our own negligence and sloth* that we come short of this assurance. . . . Considering what promises are made unto us, what encouragments are given us, what love and tenderness there is in God to receive us, I cannot but conclude that ordinarily the cause of our coming short of this assurance is where I have fixed it."[130]

Owen went on to show how lack of assurance is primarily the believer's fault by citing saints of Scripture, who possessed full assurance. He wrote: "Generally, all the saints mentioned in Scripture had this [full] assurance, unless it were in the case of depths, distresses, and desertions, such as that in this psalm [i.e., Psalm 130]. David expresseth his confidence of the love and favour of God unto his own soul hundreds of times; Paul doth the same for himself: Gal. ii., 20, 'Christ loved me, and gave himself for me.'"[131]

Although Owen did not specifically say so, those examples helped him keep a balance between the supposed normality of full assurance and the lack of assurance he saw in most of the believers of his day. Hence, Owen believed that many believers were living below their privileges, not sufficiently relishing the comfort of full assurance, either out of ignorance or because of sin. In either case, the contemporary church was backsliding compared to scriptural saints.

Finally, Owen tried to lessen the gap between the normative assurance of the biblical saints and the predominant lack of assurance in his generation. He did that by distinguishing between full assurance applied on a regular basis for daily living and full assurance received for fleeting moments particularly in times of heavy trial. Though Christians of his day did not commonly experience full assurance on a daily basis as scriptural saints did, they did receive full assurance in times of heavy trial. As Owen wrote:

> I am persuaded that there are but few believers, but that God doth, at one time or other, in one duty or other, entering into or coming out of one temptation or another, give some singular testimony unto their own soul and consciences concerning their sincerity and his acceptance of them. Sometimes he doth this in a duty, wherein he hath enabled the soul to make so near an approach unto him as that it hath been warmed, enlivened, sweetened, satisfied with the presence, the gracious presence of God;— sometimes, when a man is entering into any great temptation, trial, difficult or dangerous

[130]6:413-15.
[131]6:413.

duty, that death itself is feared in it, God comes in, by one means or other ... and thereby testifies to him his sincerity ...;— sometimes he is pleased to shine immediately into the soul in the midst of its darkness and sorrow; wherewith it is ... thereby relieved against its own pressing self-condemnation. ... But now these are all wrought by a transient operation of the Spirit. ... These things abide not in their sense and in their power which they have upon our affections, but immediately pass away.[132]

Owen's approach to assurance may be summarized in the following chart:

Normativity of Assurance

Degrees of assurance	Biblical saints	Owen's contemporaries
1. Is there a regular degree of assurance for believers who trust in God's forgiveness of sinners?	Yes, for this degree of assurance is part of faith itself.	Same as for biblical saints.
2. Is there a full degree of assurance for believers that comes for brief moments, particularly in times of trial, i.e., that God's forgiveness is also personally for them?	Yes, generally speaking.	Yes, generally speaking, though such experiences may be rare and fleeting, and in some lacking altogether.
3. Is there a full degree of assurance for believers that comes in a more regular, abiding, strengthening manner, and which reaps a comfortable sense of daily favor except in uncommon periods of divine desertion?	Yes, generally speaking, though such believers remained subject to many assaults and much variation with regards to their full assurance.	Usually not, for few come up to this gospel assurance. Those who experience this have found it difficult to retain; they remain subject to assaults and variations on full assurance.

Owen's approach to full assurance was in harmony with that of

[132]6:593.

the Westminster Confession, though he moved beyond it by distinguishing full assurance in an abiding sense from a more fleeting sense; and by distinguishing the state of adherence from the state of assurance.[133]

How Assurance is Obtained

Owen's theology on *how assurance is obtained* is very much like that of the Westminster Confession, section 18.2, which says assurance is obtained through the promises of salvation in Jesus Christ, as well as through inward evidences of saving grace and the testimony of the Spirit of adoption. Specifically, Owen taught the following:

(1) The primary ground of assurance is the promises of God, specifically the satisfying blood and righteousness of Jesus Christ, embraced by faith. Owen wrote: "The soul, by a direct act of faith, believes its own forgiveness, without making inferences or gathering conclusions; and may do so upon the proposition of it to be believed in the promise."[134]

Aside from stressing the Christ-centered focus of these promises as previously discussed,[135] Owen had nothing new to add to this ground of assurance.

(2) The primary ground of assurance leads the believer to the secondary ground, for he who trusts in the objective promises of God in Jesus Christ will yearn to have those promises to be subjectively "testified unto his conscience in a word of promise mixed by faith."[136] According to Owen, that testimony is one of two secondary grounds of assurance and is based on inward evidences of saving grace realized syllogistically. Here Owen's view varied slightly from the Westminster Confession, which left open the possibility that the secondary grounds of assurance could be treated as a single unity. Along with his recognition of the immediate witness of the Spirit, Owen validated the practical syllogism as God's ordinary way of bestowing assurance. He wrote, "A due spiritual consideration of the causes and effects of regeneration is the ordinary way and means whereby the souls of believers come to be satisfied concerning that work of God in them and upon them."[137]

Owen then added three warnings about the practical syllogism.

---

[133]6:426-27. Cf. 6:413-25, 593-95, and 3:388.
[134]6:413; cf. 6:407.   [135]See pp. 187-88 above.
[136]6:424.   [137]6:5; cf. 6:8, 455-60.

He said, first, direct acts of faith do not excuse the individual from seeking the certainty of the Spirit's work.[138] Second, Owen emphasized that the Holy Spirit sheds light upon His own work in the soul by the Word, thereby giving the believer liberty to embrace the "evidence of those graces unto which these promises are made" (Westminster Confession, 18.2). Owen wrote:

> The Spirit of Christ acquaints the soul that this and that grace is from him, that this or that duty was performed in his strength. He brings to mind what at such and such times was wrought in men by himself, to give them supportment and relief in the times of depths and darkness. And when it hath been clearly discovered unto the soul at any time by the Holy Ghost, that any thing wrought in it or done by it hath been truly saving, the comfort of it will abide in the midst of many shakings and temptations.[139]

Third, Owen insisted that this form of assurance may be consciously absent from the believer, regardless of whether the Spirit's graces are presently active within him. He explained:

> A man may have grace, and yet not have it at sometimes much acting; he may have grace for life, when he hath it not for fruitfulness and comfort, though it be his duty so to have it, Rev. iii. 2; 2 Tim. i. 6. And a man may have *grace acting* in him, and yet *not know*, not be sensible, that he hath acting grace. We see persons frequently under great temptations of apprehension that they have no grace at all, and yet at the same time, to the clearest conviction of all who are able to discern spiritual things, sweetly and genuinely to act faith, love, submission unto God, and that in a high and eminent manner.[140]

(3) In advocating an immediate witness of the Spirit, Owen prevented this experience from becoming too mystical in the following ways. First, he said the Holy Spirit applies His immediate witness through the Word, not beyond the Word. Thus this witness, which is the direct, miraculous, and powerful application of the Word in God's sovereign time and way, is both Spirit-applied *and* Word-centered.[141]

Second, Owen said the immediate witness wasn't always separated from the practical syllogism; consequently, they often supported each other. Owen illustrated that in his dialogue with a

---

[138]6:413.

[139]6:546; cf. 6:407.

[140]6:564.

[141]Cf. Nuttall, *The Holy Spirit in Puritan Faith and Practice*, pp. 41, 43 and John Murray's review of Nuttall, *Collected Writings* 3:328.

"poor soul that now walks comfortably under the light of God's countenance." In answer to the question "But how are you confirmed in this persuasion?" he wrote:

> That *sense* of it which I have in my heart; that *sweetness* and rest which I have experience of; that *influence* it hath upon my soul; that *obligation* I find laid upon me by it unto all thankful obedience; that relief, supportment, and consolation that it hath afforded me in trials and troubles, in the mouth of the grave and entrances of eternity,— all answering what is declared concerning these things in the word,— will not suffer me to be deceived. I could not, indeed, receive it until God was pleased to speak it unto me; but now let Satan do his utmost, I shall never cease to bear this testimony, that there is mercy and forgiveness with him.[142]

Third, Owen said that the immediate testimony of the Spirit should not be expected or depended upon because of its extraordinary role as a sovereign gift. Moreover, because the Spirit's immediate testimony is sovereign, no one can say exactly how full assurance should be experienced. Owen thus wrote:

> *If you are doubtful concerning your state and condition, do not expect an extraordinary determination of it by an immediate testimony of the Spirit of God.* I do grant that God doth sometimes, by this means, bring in peace and satisfaction unto the soul. He gives his own Spirit immediately "to bear witness with ours that we are the children of God," both upon the account of regeneration and adoption. He doth so; but, as far as we can observe, in a way of sovereignty, when and to whom he pleaseth.... No one man's experience is a rule unto others, and an undue apprehension of it is a matter of great danger. Yet it is certain that humble souls in extraordinary cases may have recourse unto it with benefit and relief thereby. This, then, you may desire, you may pray for, but not with such a frame of spirit as to refuse that other satisfaction which in the ways of truth and peace you may find. This is the putting of the hand into the side of Christ; but "blessed are they that have not seen, and yet have believed."[143]

Retaining, Renewing, and Improving Assurance

Finally, in *Psalm CXXX*, Owen showed how a believer may retain, renew, and improve personal assurance of grace. He said that can be done through three activities of faith: "recalling" grace, "waiting on" grace, and fruitful obedience.[144]

---

[142]6:460.   [143]6:594.

[144]Owen also gave guidelines for richer discoveries of assurance. He advised: allow

The Christian must first seek grace to recall the Spirit's past, assuring work in order to improve upon his present degree of assurance. Owen indicated in the following passage that he knew the typical believer seeks such grace far too seldom:

> The true use of [past assurances of divine favor] is, to lay them up and ponder them in our hearts, that they may be supportments and testimonies unto us in a time of need. Have you, then, who are now in the dark as to your state or conditions, whether you are regenerate or no, ever received any such refreshing and cheering testimony from God given unto your integrity, and your acceptance with him thereupon? Call it over again, and make use of it against those discouragements which arise from your present darkness in this matter, and which keep you off from sharing in the consolation tendered unto you in this word of grace.[145]

Recalling grace may also reveal defects in the believer that thwart assurance. As Owen said:

> Call to mind whether you have broken off the treaty with God, and refused his terms. What is the reason, since God hath graciously begun to deal thus with you, that you are not yet come to a thorough close with him in the work and design of his grace? The defect must of necessity lie on your parts. God doth nothing in vain. Had he not been willing to receive you, he would not have dealt with you so far as he hath done. There is nothing, then, remains to firm your condition but a resolved act of your own wills in answering the mind and will of God. And by this search may the soul come to satisfaction in this matter, or at least find out and discover where the stick is whence their uncertainty doth arise, and what is wanting to complete their desire.[146]

Next, the Christian must wait for grace in order to renew and improve assurance. As Owen wrote: "*Whatever your condition be, and your apprehension of it, yet continue waiting for a better issue,* and give not over through weariness or impatience. . . . Waiting is the only way to establishment and assurance; we cannot speed by haste; yea,

Christ to be the judge of your spiritual condition; remember that "self-condemnation and abhorrency do very well consist with gospel justification and peace"; consider that patient waiting will reap a fuller sense of forgiveness in due season; engage in self-examination, "even to the sins of youth"; learn to distinguish between unbelief and jealousy, as well as between faith and spiritual sense; do not mix "foundation [Christ alone] and building work [holiness and obedience] too much together"; "take heed of spending time in complaints when vigorous actings of grace are your duty"; beware of hard thoughts against God; make use of every appearance of God (2:542-74).
[145]6:595.
[146]6:596.

nothing puts the end so far away as making too much haste.... Doth not the nature of [assurance] require humble waiting? . . . No disappointment, then, no tediousness or weariness, should make the soul leave waiting on God, if it intend to attain consolation and establishment."[147]

Finally, while recalling and waiting for grace, the Christian must strive for obedience. Indeed, faith and obedience are ultimately inseparable. Said Owen, "The more faith that is true and of the right kind, the more obedience; for all our obedience is the obedience of faith."[148]

According to Owen, such obedience manifests itself in "the choicest actings of our souls towards God,— as love, delight, rejoicing in the Lord, peace, joy, and consolation in ourselves, readiness to do or suffer, cheerfulness in so doing. If they grow not from this root, yet their flourishing wholly depends upon it; so that surely it is the duty of every believer to break through all difficulties in pressing after this particular assurance."[149] In short, the way to retain and improve assurance is through obedience, which is also the fruit of assurance.

Pneumatologia:
A Discourse on the Holy Spirit (1674ff.)

In the preface of his most influential work, *Pneumatologia*, Owen admitted he was doing pioneer work. He wrote: "Whereas I know not any who ever went before me in this design of representing the whole economy of the Holy Spirit, with all his adjuncts, operations, and effects, whereof this is the first part, . . . as the difficulty of my work was increased thereby so it may plead my excuse if anything be found not to answer so regular a projection or just a method as the nature of the subject requireth and as was aimed at."[150]

Later theologians weren't so modest about Owen's 1,200-page treatise on the Holy Spirit. George Smeaton called it "the most important work on the Spirit in any literature."[151] Abraham Kuyper said the work was incomparable and unsurpassed.[152] Geoffrey

[147]6:553-55; cf. 6:563.
[148]6:414.
[149]Ibid.; cf. 6:551-53 where hope, casting out fear, and dying for Christ are also expounded as marks of the obedience of faith.
[150]3:7.
[151]*Work of the Holy Spirit* (reprint ed., Edinburgh: Banner of Truth Trust, 1974), p. 329.
[152]*Work of the Holy Spirit*, trans. Henri de Vries (New York: Funk & Wagnalls, 1900), p. x.

Nuttall affirmed Owen's pioneer attempt, particularly in the domain of experimental theology;[153] while Jerry Brauer acknowledged that Owen wrote "the most comprehensive treatise on the Spirit since the days of the Church fathers."[154] Though Puritan writers produced many works on the Spirit, Owen was unquestionably the leader in this field.

Most of *Pneumatologia* was published in 1674.[155] Other parts were published piecemeal. Owen himself was never certain that he would complete the project, which would include "The Reason of Faith" (1677), "The Causes, Ways, and Means of Understanding the Mind of God" (1678), "The Work of the Holy Spirit in Prayer" (1682), "On the Work of the Spirit as a Comforter," and "Spiritual Gifts" (both published in 1693 after Owen's death). That completed, according to Owen's notes, his entire schema on the Holy Spirit.

In his section on the Spirit as Comforter, Owen addressed the question of assurance by dealing with two aspects of the Spirit's work not yet examined: sealing and unction.

The Sealing of the Spirit

The sealing of the Spirit was a common theme in the seventeenth century. Most Puritan writers believed that sealing came with assurance,[156] even though early Reformers had clearly maintained a one-to-one correlation between those regenerated by the Spirit and those sealed by the Spirit. Calvin, for example, would have refuted the Puritan notion that it was possible to believe without being sealed with the Spirit by declaring that the seal is the Holy Spirit Himself[157] and that the sealing work of the Spirit belongs to the essence of faith.[158] Beza also appeared to have that belief. He wrote: "Now he maketh the Ephesians (or rather all the Gentiles) equall to the Jewes, because that

---

[153]*The Holy Spirit in Puritan Faith and Experience*, p. 7.

[154]"Reflections on the Nature of English Puritanism," *Church History* 23 (1954):102.

[155]Volume 3 of the Goold edition, which may be subsumed under doctrinal and experimental theology. Under doctrinal theology, Owen considered the deity of the Spirit and His relation to creation and the Person of Christ; under experimental theology, he examined regeneration and sanctification. Little of this volume relates directly to assurance, however, with the exception of two passages on sanctification.

[156]Cf. Ferguson, *John Owen on the Christian Life*, pp. 116-24; Robert Martin Boyle, "The Doctrine of the Witness of the Holy Spirit in John Calvin's Theology against an Historical Background" (M.A. thesis, Abilene Christian College, 1967).

[157]E.g., *Commentary* (on Ephesians 1:13-14, 3:12); Inst. 3.2.11, 34, 41. Cf. Parratt, "The Witness of the Holy Spirit: Calvin, the Puritans and St. Paul," pp. 161ff.

[158]Graafland, "Waarheid in het Binnenste," p. 58.

notwithstanding they came last, yet being called by the same Gospel, they embraced it by faith and were sealed up with the same Spirit, which is the pledge of election until the inheritance it selfe be seene."[159]

By the time of Perkins, however, theologians were devoting less time to the Spirit as sealer and more to the Spirit's activity in sealing the promise to the believer. As Perkins noted: "Things that passe too and fro among men, though they be in question, yet when the seale is put too, they are made out of doubt: and therefore when God by his spirit is said to seale the promise in the heart of every particular beleever, it signifieth that hee gives unto them evident assurance that the promise of life belongs unto them."[160] Thus, in sealing, Perkins taught that the Spirit begets an assured "trust and confidence" in the promises so that the believer is moved to experimentally embrace the promises as his own.[161]

Paul Baynes, who succeeded Perkins at Cambridge University,[162] attempted to unite the Spirit's roles as indweller and seal in an attempt to bring harmony between the Reformed and Puritan views.[163] "The Holy Spirit, and the graces of the Spirit are the seale assuring our redemption," he wrote.[164] For Baynes, the Spirit was thus both "the seale and the sealer."[165] He wrote: "We are confirmed touching salvation, both by the Spirit of God, who is as it were the seale sealing, and by the graces of the Spirit, which is as it were the seal sealed and printed upon us; yea, these two, both of them, are together as a seal."[166]

Baynes distinguished being sealed by the Spirit (which all believers possess) and being made conscious of such sealing (which only those who are conscious of the graces of the Spirit possess). Baynes thus could speak of an immediate witness in the sealing of the Holy Spirit, while linking such a witness to the practical syllogism, since only a sanctified conscience could echo the Spirit's testimony. He wrote: "This certainty is no other thing than the

---

[159]Beza, *Novum Testamentum* (on Ephesians 1:13).

[160]Merrill, *William Perkins, 1558-1602*, on *Discourse on Conscience*, pp. 50-51.

[161]Perkins, *Works* 1:104-105. Cf. Preston, *The Breast-Plate of Faith and Love* 2:53-55.

[162]As Baynes published no writings himself, we are indebted to William Ames and others for seeing his writings to press posthumously (cf. bibliography). See Kendall, *Calvin and English Calvinism to 1649*, pp. 94-102, for a brief biography and synopsis of Baynes's doctrine of faith and assurance.

[163]Paul Baynes, *An Entire Commentary vpon the whole Epistle of the Apostle Paul to the Ephesians* (London: M. F. for Milbourne and I. Bartlet, 1643), pp. 80-81.

[164]Ibid., eighth unnumbered prefatory page.

[165]Ibid., p. 137.   [166]Ibid., p. 143.

testimony of a renewed conscience, which doth witnesse through the spirit, that we are in a state of grace. . . . I call it a testimony of the conscience . . . for the conscience doth but speake it as an echo; that it testifieth to us both our present state of Grace."[167]

Though the Spirit's sealing grants the believer infallible assurance,[168] many years may pass before the believer experiences it. Baynes pictured the Christian's growth in assurance as stages. "Childhoode or infancie" lacks full assurance, "middle age" has some measure of assurance, and "olde age, or the experienced estate hath assurance accompanying it for the most part usually."[169]

Richard Sibbes (1577-1635),[170] agreed with his predecessor Baynes, though he emphasized the sealing of the Spirit as a "superadded work and confirmation" of the believer's faith.[171] In so doing, Sibbes turned the doctrine of the sealing of the Spirit in a direction that would gain prominence among the Puritans for several decades.[172]

Sibbes thought of the Spirit's sealing in two ways: (1) a one-time sealing, and (2) a sealing that came later as one matured in the Christian life. The once-and-for-all sealing of salvation is granted when a person first believes in Christ and God's promises. Sibbes taught that as a king's image is stamped upon wax, so the Spirit stamps believers' souls with the image of Christ from the very moment of believing. Such sealing produces in every believer a lifelong desire to be transformed fully into the image of Christ.[173]

The second aspect of Sibbes's doctrine of sealing is more elusive. Owen argued that Sibbes said sealing had to occur twice in the life of

---

[167]Ibid., p. 146.   [168]Ibid., p. 143.

[169]*Briefe Directions unto a Godly Life: wherein every Christian is furnished with most Necessary Helps for the Furthering of him in a godly Course here upon Earth, so that He may Attaine Eternall Happiness in Heaven* (London: A. Griffins for J. Norton, 1637), pp. 44-46, 92-94.

[170]See *The Complete Works of Richard Sibbes* 1:xix-cxxi for a biographical sketch of Sibbes. (Hereafter, *Complete Works*.) Cf. Mark Dever, "Richard Sibbes and the 'Truly Evangelicall Church of England': A Study in Reformed Divinity and Early Stuart Conformity" (Ph.D. dissertation, Cambridge University, 1992)."

[171]Sibbes preached often on the Spirit's sealing. First, a series of sermons transcribed by a noblewoman, Lady Elizabeth Brooke, was published in 1637 as *A Fountain Sealed* (*Complete Works* 5:409-456). Second, sermons on 2 Corinthians 1:21-22 in the *Exposition of Second Corinthians Chapter 1*, were published in 1655 (*Complete Works* 3:420-84). Third, a sermon on Romans 8:15-16, *The Witness of the Spirit*, was first published in 1692 (*Complete Works* 7:367-85). Cf. ibid., 2:453-64, 4:132ff., 6:374-79, 428-30.

[172]Ferguson, *John Owen on the Christian Life*, p. 118. Cf. Eaton, *Baptism with the Spirit*, pp. 67-75.

[173]*Complete Works* 3:453.

the believer. But Sibbes was not arguing for a second measure of *positional assurance*, as if to imply that God was not altogether sure of our stance with Him or His stance towards us upon conversion. Sibbes plainly stated: "Sealing of us by the Spirit is not in regard of God but ourselves. God knoweth who are His, but we know not that we are His but by sealing. The sealing then is *for our benefit exclusively*, and not for God."[174]

So the second kind of sealing Sibbes wrote about was a process. It was the kind of assurance that could increase gradually throughout believers' lives by means of singular experiences and by daily, spiritual growth. This sealing had degrees; it could grow with spiritual maturity. Sibbes wrote: "The Spirit sealeth by degrees. As our care of pleasing the Spirit increaseth so our comfort increaseth. Our light will increase as the morning light unto the perfect day. Yielding to the Spirit in one holy motion will cause him to lead us to another, and so on forwards, until we be more deeply acquainted with the whole counsel of God concerning our salvation."[175]

Sibbes learned through pastoral experience that many believers are content with the measure of faith and assurance they receive upon their conversion and do not labor for further growth. That prompted Sibbes to suggest that there are three kinds of Christians: First, those who have the seed of saving faith but live under a spirit of bondage;[176] those who are sealed with "sanctifying grace" by means of Spirit-worked evidences of faith but are often beset with doubt; and established believers, "who are carried with large spirits to obey their Father"[177] as the fruit of the direct seal of the Spirit which provides a conscious persuasion of their sonship to God.[178] "Large spirits" receive a "privy seal," or the unmistakable, conclusive, inward witness of the Spirit[179] that is a "stablishing, confirming grace."[180] That seal grants believers freedom to appropriate full assurance through the work of each Person in the Trinity. The emphasis here is on the Spirit in His saving activity. Sibbes thus wrote:

> Every person in the blessed Trinity hath their several work. The Father chooseth us and passeth a decree upon the whole groundwork of our salvation. The Son executeth it to the full. The Spirit applieth it, and witnesseth our interest in it by leading our

---

[174]*Complete Works* 3:453ff.
[175]Ibid.
[176]*Complete Works* 5:437.
[177]Ibid., 3:110ff.; 5:488.
[178]Ibid., 7:382-83.
[179]Ibid., 4:138-39, 5:433.
[180]Ibid., 3:422.

souls to lay hold upon him, and by raising up our souls in the assurance of it, and by breeding and cherishing sweet communion with Father and Son, who both of them seal us likewise by the Spirit. This joy and comfort is so appropriated to the Spirit, as it carrieth the very name of the Spirit.[181]

Sibbes sounds mystical at times in describing this special sealing, particularly in statements such as "the Holy Ghost slides and insinuates and infuseth himself into our souls."[182] But Sibbes warded off mysticism in two ways. First, he maintained that this special sealing must never be divorced from the Word of God. By speaking of sealing in degrees, Sibbes linked all advancement in grace to the Spirit and Word, for any consciousness of sealing by the Spirit is always through the applied Word.[183]

Second, Sibbes said that the genuineness of such sealing may be readily examined. One may know the voice of the Spirit of God by inquiring what went before, what went with, and what followed "this ravishing joy" of experimental sealing, Sibbes wrote.[184] Fruits of sanctification, such as peace of conscience, the spirit of adoption, prayers of fervent supplication, conformity with the heavenly image of Christ,[185] and applying ourselves to holy duties rather than old lusts inevitably result from such "a secret whispering and intimation to the soul.[186] Sibbes thus emphasized both the intuitive testimony of the Spirit and the sanctifying fruits of the Spirit.[187] The Spirit's sealing is inward in its essence and outward in its fruit.

Owen understood why Sibbes and other Puritans in his era proposed what he considered a second kind of sealing. He recognized that Sibbes and others were attempting to call believers

---

[181]Ibid., 5:439.   [182]Ibid., 1:24; cf. 4:215, 295.

[183]Cary Weisiger III neglected Sibbes's connection between Word and Spirit when he concluded that "the sealing of the Spirit in Sibbes is as close as Puritanism came to the Pentecostal emphasis on the baptism of the Spirit" ("The Doctrine of the Holy Spirit in the Preaching of Richard Sibbes" [Ph.D. dissertation, Fuller Theological Seminary, 1984], pp. i, 327ff.). Cf. Bert Affleck, Jr., "The Theology of Richard Sibbes, 1577-1635" (Ph.D. dissertation, Drew University, 1968), pp. 166-203; Frank E. Farrell, "Richard Sibbes: A Study in Early Seventeenth Century English Puritanism" (Ph.D. dissertation, Edinburgh, 1955).

[184]*Complete Works* 5:441-44.

[185]The sealing Spirit "makes them every way like Christ in their proportion" (ibid., 3:453-54; 4:132-33).

[186]Ibid., 4:134-36, 5:409. Cf. Weisiger, "The Doctrine of the Holy Spirit in the Preaching of Richard Sibbes," pp. 290-95.

[187]For Sibbes on assurance of sanctification, see Affleck, "The Theology of Richard Sibbes," pp. 323-27.

to a life of *assuredness*. Owen affirmed the call for this kind of assurance, yet he argued against equating full assurance with the sealing of the Spirit. He felt that the exegesis of Ephesians 1:13 didn't support such a view.

Moving a step beyond Sibbes, John Preston (1587-1628)[188] taught that the sealing of the Spirit was a second work given to those who overcome.[189] The seal was so "high" in the Christian's experience that when pressed for a definition, Preston could only write: "It is a thing that we cannot expresse, it is a certain divine expression of light, a certain unexpressable assurance that we are the sonnes of God; a certaine secret manifestation, that God hath received us and put away our sinnes; I say, it is such a thing, that no man knowes, but they that have it."[190]

Thomas Goodwin[191] developed the thinking of Sibbes and Preston on the sealing of the Spirit even more, defining it as a "light beyond the light of ordinary faith."[192] Goodwin wrote: "There is an immediate assurance of the Holy Ghost, by a heavenly and divine light, of a divine authority, which the Holy Ghost sheddeth in a man's heart, (not having relation to grace wrought or anything in a man's self,) whereby he sealeth him up to the day of redemption."[193] He added, "It is the next thing to heaven . . . you can have no more until you come thither."[194] Furthermore, the "whispering" of the Holy Spirit tells the believer that he is elect of God, has his sins forgiven, and belongs to Him forever — both intuitively and directly.[195]

Richard Baxter, David Clarkson (formerly Owen's assistant), and several Puritan writers followed in varying degrees Goodwin's teaching, making a direct tie between the sealing of the Spirit and full assurance of faith.

As late as 1657, Owen had not resolved the matter of the Spirit's sealing. "I am not very clear in the certain peculiar intendment of

---

[188]For the life and times of Preston, see Irvonwy Morgan, *Puritan Spirituality* (London: Epworth Press, 1973). Preston was Cotton's most renowned "Old England" convert. Due in part to the antinomian controversy in conjunction with Anne Hutchinson, Cotton would not commit himself definitively on whether the sealing of the Spirit should be regarded as including all believers or only those who received full assurance of faith (Ferguson, *John Owen on the Christian Life*, p. 119).

[189]*The New Covenant, or the Saint's Portion* 2:416-17.

[190]Ibid., 2:416; cf. 2:400-421.

[191]See chapter 9 below.

[192]*The Works of Thomas Goodwin* 1:236.

[193]Ibid., p. 233.　　　　　　　　　　[194]Ibid., p. 236.

[195]Ibid., pp. 236-37.

this metaphor," he wrote.[196] Ultimately, however, Owen did resolve the matter. In *Pneumatologia*, he explained how:

First, unlike Calvin, Owen said that the sealing of the Spirit applies to persons, not promises.[197] Moreover, he added, "When we seal a deed or grant to any one, we do not say the man is sealed, but the deed or grant."[198]

Second, like Calvin, Owen said the Spirit's sealing, representing the presence of the Spirit in His Person rather than an act of the Spirit within a believer, serves as the ground of assurance. He explained: "It is not said that the Holy Spirit seals us, but that we are sealed with him. He is God's seal unto us. . . . The effects of this sealing are gracious operations of the Holy Spirit in and upon believers; but the sealing itself is the communication of the Spirit unto them."[199]

Third, because Owen took issue with the idea that the seal of the Spirit was a particular act instead of the gift of the Spirit Himself, it was exegetically impossible to say that sealing was restricted to some believers rather than to all, for sealing accompanies regeneration.[200]

Finally, the sealing of the Christian points directly to the sealing of Christ by the Father, Owen said. As Christ was sealed with the Spirit without measure, so each believer is sealed with the Spirit in proper measure sufficient to salvation.[201]

Owen clearly recognized a difference between "full assurance by the immediate witness of the Spirit" and "the sealing of the Spirit," despite the opinions of some of his closest friends.[202] The former is related to the latter as effect to cause, i.e., the sealing of the Spirit is not assurance in itself, but produces assurance. As Owen wrote:

> It hath been generally conceived that this sealing with the Spirit is that which gives assurance unto believers — and so indeed, it doth, although the way whereby it doth it hath not been rightly apprehended; and, therefore, none have been able to declare the especial nature of that act of the Spirit whereby he seals us, whence such assurance should ensue. . . . That God abideth in us and we in him is the subject-matter of our assurance. . . . The Spirit himself . . . is the great evidence, the great ground of assurance, which we have that God hath taken us into a near and dear relation unto himself, "because he hath given us of his Spirit" (1 John 4:13).[203]

[196]2:242.
[198]1:243.
[200]4:400.
[202]4:400-401.
[203]4:405. Cf. Eaton, *Baptism with the Spirit*, pp. 104ff.

[197]1:400; cf. 2:242-43.
[199]4:401, 404.
[201]4:403-406.

In short, Spirit-sealing is no special *act* of assurance, but reaps the special *effect* of assurance, which, by grace, grows in degrees of consciousness to a full and firm persuasion within the believer.[204] Hence, assurance is not the same as the gift of the Spirit (the seal), even though it may accompany the gift. Though he would not deny the joy resulting from the Spirit's immediate witness of full assurance,[205] Owen downplayed the unusual manifestations of the Spirit in favor of a more normal recognition of the presence of the Spirit.

The Unction of the Spirit

In Book VIII, chapter 4 of *Pneumatologia*, Owen also explained the Spirit's unction. He said the Spirit anoints all believers;[206] such anointing happens by Christ's own anointing with the Spirit without measure and by believers receiving their unction "immediately from Christ" as efficient cause;[207] and it is the Spirit of Christ Himself who is the anointing.[208] All of this takes place within a Trinitarian framework: the "supreme donation" of the Spirit as unction is from the Father; the "immediate collation" from the Son; and the "actual anointing" from the Spirit.[209]

Nevertheless, the Spirit's unction has special effects: "Spiritual instruction, by saving illumination in the mind of God and the mysteries of the gospel; and a special dedication unto God, in the way of a spiritual privilege."[210] These effects serve as assistants to assurance, particularly when the soul is attacked by seducers of faith. As Owen wrote: "It is hereon that our stability in believing doth depend; for it is pleaded unto this purpose in a peculiar manner by the apostle, I John ii. 20, 27. It was the 'unction from the Holy One' which then kept believers from being carried from the faith by the craft of seducers. Hereby he makes men, according unto their measure, 'of quick understanding in the fear of the Lord.'"[211]

In sum, the Spirit in His divine Person is the believer's seal and his unction, resulting in the solidifying of assurance.

---

[204]This merges well with Owen's conviction that the case may hang "for years" in justification in the court of conscience (2:241).

[205]J. I. Packer, "The Witness of the Spirit: The Puritan Teaching," *The Wisdom of Our Fathers* (Puritan Conference, 1956), p. 25.

[206]4:391.   [207]4:391-93.

[208]4:396.

[209]4:393, 396.   [210]4:395.

[211]Ibid.

The Doctrine of Justification by Faith (1677)

In his work on justifying faith, Owen presented his theologically mature definition of faith. He wrote, "It is the heart's approbation of the way of justification and salvation of sinners by Jesus Christ, proposed in the gospel, as proceeding from the grace, wisdom, and love of God, with its acquiescency therein as unto its own concernment and condition."[212]

Here Owen lessened his earlier emphasis on "resting" assurance as essential to faith, while he was simultaneously cautious not to exclude a trust of acquiescency. Without trust, the soul must despair, he said. Nevertheless, such trust is not *necessarily* persuasion of one's own salvation, for that is not of the essence of faith. What is essential to faith is that the soul recognizes that the only way of salvation is in Jesus Christ and acquiesces to being included in that redemption. Hence, the soul is not bound to believe the pardon of its *own* sins antecedent to justification.[213] Here Owen parted ways with the early Reformers, as David Lachman noted:

> [Owen] objects to the doctrine of the first Reformers not on the grounds that an assurance was included in justifying faith, but on the grounds that they made the pardon of our own sins in particular the object of justifying faith, making faith itself to be a fiduciary trust. But, denying that any of them affirmed that every true believer always had a full assurance and commending their objective of directing men to seek for peace with God by placing their trust and confidence in his mercy by Christ alone, he refuses to oppose or reject their judgments, and leaves them as he finds them, "unto the use of the church."[214]

Indeed, Owen had concluded: "For I shall not contend with any about the way and manner of expressing the truth, where the *substance* of it is retained. That which in these things is aimed at, is the advancement and glory of the grace of God in Christ, with the conduct of the souls of men unto rest and peace with him. Where this is attained or aimed at, and that in the way of truth for the substance of it, variety of apprehensions and expressions concerning the same things may tend unto the useful exercise of faith and the edification of the church."[215]

[212]5:93.
[213]5:75, 76, 102.
[214]*The Marrow Controversy*, p. 18; cf. 5:85.
[215]5:85.

Robert Letham took issue with Lachman's position, citing Owen's assertion that assurance is a fruit of faith, not of its essence. He concluded that Owen fundamentally differed from the Reformers. Letham, however, failed to notice two things: first, that Owen's assertion —"All these things are rather fruits or effects of faith, as under exercise and improvement, than of the essence of it, as it is the instrument in our justification"[216]— dealt with *full* assurance of faith that one's own sins are forgiven, not with all degrees of assurance. Second, concerning "lower degrees" of assurance, Owen did not think it necessary to determine whether such trust or confidence is of the essence of faith or the first fruits of it, but he did describe it as "that which belongs to justifying faith, and is inseparable from it."[217] Owen refused to repudiate the position of the Reformers but accepted it as a variation of his own.

In *Gospel Grounds and Evidences of the Faith of God's Elect* (published in 1695), Owen defined full assurance as a step forward *in* faith. He wrote: "Faith is not an especial assurance of a man's own justification and salvation by Christ; that it will produce, but not until another step or two in its progress be over; but faith is a satisfactory persuasion that the way of God proposed in the gospel is fitted, suited, and able to save the soul in particular that doth believe,— not only that it is a blessed way to save sinners in general, but that it is such a way to save him in particular."[218]

This distinction between trusting that Christ is perfectly *suited to save* the individual and being assured that *he has forgiven* the individual allowed Owen to accommodate the Reformers somewhat. It allowed him to accept a measure of assurance in saving faith, while enabling him to remain faithful to the Westminster Confession's statement "This infallible assurance doth not *so* belong to the essence of faith." Second, it freed him to teach advancement in the steps of grace, while avoiding a two-tier approach to the experience of salvation. Finally, this distinction allowed Owen to retain Christological centrality in the notion of faith without quenching the smoking flax or breaking bruised reeds.[219]

---

[216]5:102, and Letham, "The Relationship Between Saving Faith and Assurance," pp. 49ff.

[217]5:101.

[218]5:419.

[219]For Owen, not breaking "bruised reeds" did not intend to promote carelessness in self-examination. In fact, Keith Sprunger states that Owen's meetings held to examine consciences were referred to by the students as "the scruple shop" (*The Learned Doctor*

An Exposition of the Epistle to the Hebrews (1668-1684)[220]

Owen's comments on assurance in his seven-volume work on Hebrews reaffirmed earlier writings.[221] Two quotations are particularly enlightening.

First, Owen's notes on Hebrews 6:11 offered one of his clearest statements on full assurance as a high degree of faith that yields strength for the holy warfare of daily life. Owen wrote:

> This "full assurance" is not of the nature or essence of [hope], but an *especial degree* of it in its own improvement. A weak, imperfect hope, will give but weak and imperfect relief under trouble; but that which riseth up unto the full assurance will complete our relief. Wherefore, as hope itself is necessary, so is this degree of it, especially where trials do abound. Yet neither is hope in this degree absolute, or absolutely perfect. Our minds in this world are not capable of such a degree of assurance in spiritual things as to free us from assaults to the contrary, and impressions of fear sometimes from those assaults: but there is such a degree attainable as is always victorious; which will give the soul peace at all times, and sometimes fill it with joy.[222]

Second, in his comments on Hebrews 3:12-14, Owen provided a striking conclusion on sacramental assurance. He wrote:

> [Salvation] is also confirmed unto us from the nature and *use of the sacraments.* . . . In the one of them God sets his seal unto our initiation into Christ: for it is, as circumcision was of old, the "seal of the righteousness of faith," Rom. iv. 11. . . . The other expressly confirms our participation of Christ, and our interest in the pardon of sins through his blood; being appointed of God as the way whereby mutually is testified his grace unto us and our faith in him. . . . And if we may not, if we ought not, to rest assured of what God testifies unto us and sets his seal unto, it cannot but be our duty sometimes to make God a liar; for so we do when we believe not his testimony.[223]

William Ames: Dutch Backgrounds of English and American Puritanism [Chicago: University of Illinois Press, 1972], p. 163).

[220]Owen's four volume work in original folios was dated 1668, 1674, 1680, and 1684 respectively (Toon, *Correspondence of John Owen, 1616-1683*, pp. 176-77).

[221]E.g., cf. *Hebrews* 4:152-55 and 5:192, 198-202, 270-75.

[222]Ibid., 5:200.

[223]Ibid., 4:155. For a summary of Owen on the Lord's Supper as a "covenant seal," see Ferguson, *John Owen on the Christian Life*, pp. 220-24.

Conclusion: Owen's Influence and Pneumatological Emphasis

Owen's writings on faith and assurance have been incalculably influential. Thomas Halyburton defended Owen's final definition of faith.[224] John Wesley appealed to Owen to support his own emphasis on the Holy Spirit's testimony in assurance.[225] Theologians supportive of the "Marrow theology," such as James Hog and Thomas Boston, confessed their debt to Owen's views on assurance.[226] Dutch theologians translated all of Owen's pertinent treatises related to faith.[227]

In short, scores of Reformed theologians from Owen's day to ours, have honored him as a theologian among theologians. His doctrine of assurance is but one more proof of his pervasive probing of Christian experience. The beauty of Owen's theology is his accent on the Spirit's work without a loss of biblical and theological grounding. Far from reducing experimental theology to anthropological notes, Owen retained a rich God-centeredness by stressing that Christian experience is always the fruit of the Spirit's efficacious work. As Godfrey Vose noted:

> Where doctrine and life meet and fuse in human experience, and the elements of that experience are properly delineated, the result is *"experimental"* theology. In Owen's eyes, no man was a Christian unless he had "the root of the matter" within him; that is, unless he had inwardly appropriated the doctrinal truths he professed. But this did not mean that such theology was merely an elevated form of psychology. The puritan theologian certainly had psychological insights, but in studying the experiential side of doctrine, his emphasis was always Godward: Christian experience was *the experience of God the Holy Spirit* within the arena of the human soul.[228]

Throughout his writings, Owen's concern for a vital spirituality, without which "Christianity is plucked up by the roots,"[229] enabled him to present a vital "treatment of the objective-subjective tensions in revelational theology,"[230] particularly in his doctrine of assurance.

---

[224]*The Works of Thomas Halyburton*, ed. Robert Burns (Glasgow: Blackie & Son, 1837), p. 567.
[225]Zens, "The Doctrine of Assurance," pp. 41-42.
[226]Lachman, "The Marrow Controversy: An Historical Survey," pp. 126-27.
[227]Van der Haar, *From Abbadie to Young*, pp. 89-94.
[228]Vose, "Profile of a Puritan: John Owen," p. 153.
[229]3:8.
[230]Stover, "The Pneumatology of John Owen," p. 27.

For Owen, those tensions could only be resolved by preserving both a Christological and a pneumatological emphasis.

Owen's pneumatological concern was also polemical, for he defended a biblical and truly spiritual pneumatology against the polarizing extremes of Socinianism (which rejected experimental pneumatology) and Quakerism (which viewed such pneumatology as a rapturous end in itself). Furthermore, as Andrew Thomson stated:

> There was a third class of writers at that time, from whom Owen apprehended more danger than either,— men who, in their preaching, dwelt much upon the credentials of the Bible, but little upon its truths,— who would have defended even the doctrine of the Holy Spirit as an article of their creed, and at the same time would have derided all reference to the actual work of divine grace upon a human heart as the "weak imagination of distempered minds." Much of Owen's writing has reference to these accommodating and courtly divines, and is, in fact, a vindication of the reality of the spiritual life.[231]

Within the context of these concerns, it is understandable that Owen's most important contribution to the doctrine of assurance was the primacy of the Holy Spirit. He viewed the Spirit as intimately involved with each of the three foundations of assurance stipulated by *The Savoy Declaration*: "the blood and righteousness of Christ"; "the inward evidence of . . . graces"; and "the immediate witness of the Spirit."[232] Although his stress on the Spirit was within an experimental, doctrinal, and Trinitarian framework (witness *Communion with God*), Owen accented the variety of Spirit workings that reinforced the believer's assurance — whether in sealing, anointing, comforting, pronouncement of justification, earnest of inheritance, confirmation of adoption, persevering grace, gift of recalling and waiting on grace, direct or reflex acts of faith initiated within the believer, or immediate Word-applied testimony of full assurance of faith. In every case, Owen shed light on the Spirit's internal activities. Hence, if Puritanism has been defined as "the feeling of which Protestantism was the argument,"[233] then in Owen's theology — particularly so in assurance —"Protestant Puritanism" and "Puritan Protestantism" are permanently interwoven.

---

[231]Thomson, "Life of Dr. Owen," l:cxi.
[232]*Savoy* 18.2.
[233]Thomson, "Life of Dr. Owen," 1:cxi.

VIII. ALEXANDER COMRIE

Historical and Biographical Context

Alexander Comrie was born in 1706 during the twilight of the Dutch Second Reformation.[1] He defended the basic tenets of that Second Reformation, believing they were thoroughly Reformed. Like Voetius, Comrie attempted to merge various streams of thought. His attempts to blend Reformed theology with scholasticism and pietism[2] were most productive. Despite his inability to revive the Dutch Second Reformation, Comrie left behind a legacy of writings that are still widely read in the Netherlands.

In regard to the Dutch Second Reformation, Comrie took on three major tasks: (1) helping church members progress in experiential truth by means of scriptural, Christ-centered sermons; (2) clarifying the doctrine of faith and its relationship to justification and assurance;[3] and (3) attacking various forms of

---

[1]The Second Reformation in the Netherlands aimed to apply Reformed truth to daily life and experience in reaction to a cold rationalism that had evolved in some circles of orthodoxy. See the appendix below.

[2]Whereas some Second Reformation divines, like Voetius and Comrie, attempted to coalesce scholastic thinking and godly living on the foundation of the sixteenth-century Reformation, others, such as the Teellincks and Brakels, placed prime emphasis on piety.

[3]Kersten summarized the internal Reformed dispute as follows: "In the middle of the eighteenth century a difference arose among the Dutch theologians concerning the essence of faith, especially about the question whether assurance belongs to the essence of faith. Brakel denied it. He considered assurance as a fruit of faith, and counted hungering and thirsting after Christ as belonging to refuge-taking faith, which belongs to the essence of faith. Theodore VanderGroe taught that assurance is an essential element of faith, and for this statement was severely criticized by Jacob Groenewegen, who was often rash in his attacks. Theodore VanThuynen, with whom Ph. Themmen

heresy in Romanism, Arminianism, neonomianism, and Rationalism.[4]

Alexander Comrie was eminently qualified for those tasks. Born in Perth, Scotland, Comrie grew under the godly training of parents who wanted him to follow his great-grandfather, Andrew Gray, and, his mother's step-father, George Hutcheson, into the ministry. As a young boy, Comrie was catechized by Ebenezer (1680-1754) and Ralph Erskine (1685-1752). Comrie later referred to Ralph Erskine as "my faithful old friend, whom God used as the guide of my youth."[5] Comrie was probably converted as a boy under the Erskines' teaching. The greatest theological influence on him during those early years, however, was the work of Thomas Boston (1677-1732).[6]

Comrie had an excellent education, but relinquished his studies at the age of twenty because of economic hardship. He went to the Low Countries, where he got a job from a God-fearing man, Adriaan

agreed, opposed Brakel; according to him, faith consists in an assured confidence. Driessen and Lampe took the side of Brakel. In the essence of faith which reveals itself in hungering and thirsting after the righteousness of Christ, A. Driessen saw a refuge-taking confidence, out of which the assured confidence grows. Comrie was grieved about these disputes. He explained that confidence and assurance certainly belong to the essence of faith, but that not all, indeed, only few come to the conscious confirmation of their state in Christ (*Reformed Dogmatics* 2:404).

For further information on this dispute, and the theologians involved, see Klaas Schilder, *Heidelbergse Catechismus* (Kampen: Kok, 1940), 2:571-78; Herman Bavinck, *Gereformeerde Dogmatiek*, 4th ed. (Kampen: Kok, 1930), 4:92-95; and Graafland, *Zekerheid van het Geloof*, pp. 200-244.

[4]I.e., particularly in connection with the spirit of the Enlightenment as represented by Antonious van den Os and others, whom Comrie opposed in a variety of pamphlets and books.

[5]*The ABC of Faith*, trans. and introduced by J. Marcus Banfield (Ossett, W. Yorks: Zoar Publications, 1978), p. 1. In addition to Banfield's biographical introduction on Comrie, see C. Graafland, "Alexander Comrie," in *De Nadere Reformatie: Beschrijving van haar voornaamste vertegenwoordigers*, ed. T. Brienen, et al., pp. 315-48; Abraham Kuyper, "Alexander Comrie: His Life and Work in Holland," *Catholic Presbyterian* 7 (1882):20-29, 192-201, 278-84; Geoffrey Thomas, "Alexander Comrie: Contender for the Faith," *Banner of Truth*, nos. 65-66 (Feb-Mar 1969):4-8, 29-35; W. Van Gorsel, *De IJver Zijn Huis: De Nadere Reformatie en haar belangrijkste vertegenwoordigers* (N.p.: Pieters-Groede, 1981), pp. 108-115; A. Vergunst, "Dr. Alexander Comrie," *De Saambinder* 51 (1973): no. 25, p. 2; no. 27, p. 2; no. 29, p. 1; no. 31, p. 3; no. 32, p. 2, and "Comrie on Faith," *Insight Into* (June 1983), pp. 3-7. Two dissertations have been published on Comrie: Anthonia Gerrit Honig, *Alexander Comrie* (Utrecht: H. Honig, 1892), which includes an extensive account of his life, pp. 1-182, and J. H. R. Verboom, *Dr. Alexander Comrie, predikant van Woubrugge* (Utrecht: De Banier, 1964), which includes a history of his congregation as well.

[6]Graafland, "Alexander Comrie (1706-1774)," in *De Nadere Reformatie*, p. 316; Macleod, *Scottish Theology*, p. 130.

van der Willigen, who was a merchant in Rotterdam.[7] Two years later, Comrie enrolled at Groningen University as a student of divinity. There he studied under two champions of Reformed theology, Anthonias Driessen and Cornelius van Velsen. In 1733, Comrie transferred to Leiden University to study philosophy under W. J. 's-Gravesande. Comrie said that teacher had the greatest single influence over him of any of his teachers.[8] Comrie earned a doctorate in philosophy in 1734, with a critical study of René Descartes's thought, titled *De Moralitatis Fundamento et Natura Virtutis*.

Comrie then applied to the Classis of Leiden and Neder-Rhynland to be examined for the ministry. On November 2, 1734, he gave a required sermon to classis on 2 Timothy 2:20-21, answered questions on biblical languages and theology, and explained his calling to the ministry. After classis approved him, Comrie accepted a call to the Dutch church of Woubrugge. He was installed there by his lifelong friend and occasional coauthor, Nicolaus Holtius, who preached from John 3:14-15. Comrie's inaugural sermon on Zechariah 6:15, which stressed divine sovereignty and human responsibility, was typical of his thirty-eight years of preaching at Woubrugge.

Through Comrie, the church at Woubrugge became the center of a spiritual movement that spread through a large portion of the Netherlands. Comrie was instrumental in strengthening the faith of so many God-fearing people that when he retired from the pastorate on April 4, 1773, due to illness, many people felt that one of God's choicest gifts to His church in the Netherlands had been taken away. Comrie had been an effective pastor and preacher of the Word. He balanced those gifts well throughout his long ministry. He visited everyone in his congregation of 125 families two or three times per year, and those visits notably strengthened the church. They were pastoral, practical, and generally at least one hour long.[9] Comrie served as pastoral supply the last two years of his life. He died in December 1774.[10]

During his years in Woubrugge, Comrie wrote extensively on the doctrine of saving faith and its relationship to justification.[11] His

[7]Verboom, *Dr. Alexander Comrie, predikant van Woubrugge*, p. 74.

[8]For Comrie's philosophical teachers and the methods of teaching they employed, see Honig, *Alexander Comrie*, pp. 33-53; Verboom, *Dr. Alexander Comrie, predikant van Woubrugge*, pp. 86-96.

[9]Verboom, *Dr. Alexander Comrie, predikant van Woubrugge*, pp. 123-50.

[10]Ibid., pp. 176-80.

[11]The major works of Comrie are abbreviated in the footnotes below as follows:

work on faith earned recognition among his peers and pious believers throughout the Netherlands. Hence we'll focus on Comrie rather than on other Dutch theologians, such as Wilhelmus à Brakel or Petrus van Mastricht, who were better known practical theologians but did not probe the doctrines of faith and assurance as deeply as Comrie.

Saving Faith

In the mid-eighteenth century in Holland, theological debate centered on justification by faith alone. In an age that was falling prey to Rationalism and Arminianism, Comrie wrestled with three truths: the doctrine of saving faith, the doctrine of gratuitous justification, and the relationship between saving faith and gratuitous justification. For Comrie, the least taint of Rationalism or Arminianism on these cardinal issues had to be condemned as an attack upon the heart of soteriological grace and the glory of God.

What drove Comrie's prolific writing on the doctrine of faith was his concern for the triumph of grace in every part of salvation. He was not motivated by pride or contentiousness but by grief over divisions among Reformed believers on the definition, essence, activities, and assurance of faith, as well as its role in justification.[12] Throughout his writings, Comrie attempted to mediate the disputes,[13] while upholding the views of Calvin, Reformed orthodoxy, the Canons of Dort, and the Puritans, all of whom he viewed as harmonious.[14] When

---

HC=Stellige en Praktikale Verklaringe van den Heidelbergschen Catechismus (Amsterdam: N. Byl, 1753; reprint ed., Barneveld: G. J. van Horssen, 1976); *LR=Verzameling van Leerredenen* (Leiden: Johannes Hasebroek, 1749); *EZG=Verhandeling van eenige Eigenschappen des Zaligmakenden Geloofs* (Leiden: Johannes Hasebroek, 1744)—his *magnum opus*, which has only been partially translated into English; *Brief=Brief over de Rechtvaardigmakinge des Zondaars door de onmiddelyke Toereekening der Borggerechtigheit van Christus* (Amsterdam: N. Byl, 1761). Two major works not abbreviated are *A.B.C. dess Geloofs* (Sneek: F. Holtkamp, 1860), and *Examen van het Ontwerp van Tolerantie* (Amsterdam: N. Byl, 1753-59). Cf. bibliography for full titles and minor works as well.

[12]Kersten, *Reformed Dogmatics* 2:404.

[13]For example, Comrie appeased the van der Groe, van Thuynen, and Themmen group by maintaining that confidence and assurance belong to the essence of faith, while he simultaneously leaned toward à Brakel, Driessen, and Lampe when he held that few believers reached the level of full assurance of faith in this life.

[14]*Examen van het Ontwerp van Tolerantie*, pp. 20ff.; cf. Graafland, "Alexander Comrie (1706-1774)," in *De Nadere Reformatie*, pp. 326ff., who asserts that Comrie gave supremacy to the Canons of Dort: "He read 'Dort' into Calvin, specifically in respect to faith, as he also read 'Dort' into the Belgic Confession and the Heidelberg Catechism" (p. 330).

the doctrines of grace were at stake, however, he pointed out the errors of friend and foe alike.[15]

The center of the faith debate, it became apparent, was not distinguishing false faith from true[16] as much as making distinctions within saving faith itself. Comrie stressed that failing to acknowledge and properly balance a certain distinction within the doctrine of saving faith would play havoc with the gratuitous nature of the entire order of salvation. That distinction, *habitus* (habit) and *actus* (act) of faith, which served as the foundation of Comrie's doctrine of faith, was not new,[17] but he did treat it in a new manner.

The Habit and Act of Faith

Comrie believed that a primary cause of disharmony on the matter of faith throughout the Second Reformation in the Netherlands was the failure to distinguish between faith as an implanted habit coinciding with regeneration and faith in its various activities, which the Holy Spirit helps the believer to do when the habit of faith is exercised. By *habitus*, Comrie meant the principle, capacity, ability (*potentia*), faculty, "increated" (*ingeschapen*), and inherent (*inklevende*) habit of faith. He said such faith was "wrought in the elect by the Holy Ghost with re-creating and irresistible power, when they are incorporated into Christ; by which they receive all the impressions which God the Holy Ghost imparts unto them through the Word . . . and by which they are active according to the nature and the contents of the Word, the objects of which are revealed to their souls."[18]

By *actus*, Comrie meant activities, such as saving knowledge,

---

[15]Comrie feared especially the influences of the Enlightenment which he thought were rooted in Amyraldianism. Comrie viewed the theological system developed by Moise Amyraut (1596-1664), a French Reformed theologian associated with the theological school at Saumur, as a dangerous attempt to "mix works and grace" by which grace is no longer "supernatural" and total depravity is denied. (ibid., pp. 331-32).

[16]Comrie followed the traditional fourfold division of faith: historical, miraculous, temporary, and saving (cf. Wilhelmus à Brakel, *The Christian's Reasonable Service*, trans. Bartel Elshout [Ligonier, Pa.: Soli Deo Gloria, 1993], 2:263-64).

[17]Originally a Thomistic notion, several Reformers with scholastic tendencies found it helpful for distinguishing "faith as an infused habit" and "faith as an act arising out of the infused habit" (Zacharias Ursinus, *Opera theologica* [Heidelbergae: Impensis Iona Rosae, 1612], 3:210; Hieronymus Zanchius, *Clariss. Viri D. Hier Zanchii Omnium operum theologicorum* [Genevae: Samuelis Crispini, 1619], 4:241-42). The Puritans used the *habitus-actus* distinction pastorally. See Reynolds *Three Treatises*, p. 508; Cohen, *God's Caress: The Psychology of Puritan Religious Experience*, pp. 97-98.

[18]Trans. by Henri de Vries in Abraham Kuyper, *The Work of the Holy Spirit*, p. 393. (Cf. *HC*, Questions 20-21).

saving assent, and saving confidence, which flow out of the habit or principle of faith.[19] Thus, the habit of faith is infused into the soul by God, whereas the acts of faith make faith a practical reality. With this distinction, Comrie stressed that faith (*geloof*) must be distinguished from believing (*gelooven*). He said *habitus* refers to the implanting of the Holy Spirit,[20] whereas *actus* refers to the activity of the soul. To illustrate, Comrie said that faith is to sight (*habitus*) as believing is to seeing (*actus*). Anyone who lacks *habitus* will never be able to exercise *actus*. *Habitus* is foundational, and *actus* is dependent upon it. As Comrie wrote: "Hence the reality or sincerity of the imparted faith does not depend upon the acts of faith, but the sincerity of these acts depends upon the reality and sincerity of the faculty or habit from which they spring."[21]

Comrie found support for his distinction between *habitus* and *actus* in the Belgic Confession,[22] the Heidelberg Catechism,[23] the Canons of Dort,[24] and the Westminster Confession of Faith.[25] He said that theologians who ignore this distinction tend to lose themselves in prioritizing the acts of faith, overestimating some functions and underestimating others. Consequently, Comrie refused to take sides in the debate between van Thuynen and Driessen over which act of faith is primary because he was convinced that both theologians had succumbed to a faulty premise. Comrie said they were being influenced by à Brakel's accent on faith as an act (*daad*) at the expense of the principle (*habitus*) of faith.[26]

Comrie regarded the *habitus* of faith as the focus of historic Protestantism. Here is his definition of faith:

> By faith we understand the habit or principle, which God the Holy Spirit has poured into the hearts of the elect, together with the new nature as its first and most important element, by which they attain out of Christ and passing into them from Christ, the ability to receive all the impressions which the Divine Word makes upon

[19]*HC*, p. 429.
[20]Ibid., pp. 447-48.
[21]Kuyper, *Holy Spirit*, pp. 393-94.
[22]*HC*, p. 425.
[23]Ibid., pp. 447-49 (cf. Q. 21 of the *Heidelberg Catechism*).
[24]Ibid., p. 424 (cf. *Canons*, Head III-IV, arts. 11-14).
[25]Ibid., pp. 428-29 (cf. WCF, 14.2).
[26]Honig, *Alexander Comrie*, p. 209; J. W. Verschoor, "Het geloof bij Brakel en Comrie," *Onder Eigen Vaandel* 3 (1928): 282ff.; Woelderink, "Geloof en bevinding," in *Onder Eigen Vaandel* 3 (1928):18; *EZG*, p. 242.

this faculty, and according to the impressions of the Word to be active, agreeable to the nature of the faculty and the contents of those texts that are brought to the soul with supernatural light, and are received with more or less conviction, instruction, admonition, and comfort.[27]

Along with that definition, Comrie included the following emphases:

(1) By emphasizing the Spirit's implanting of faith, Comrie avoided regarding a particular act of faith so highly (such as accepting or closing with Christ) that the act itself might seem to have some degree of justifying power. When faith *as an act* justifies us, Comrie argued, then justification is of works and of man rather than of grace and of God.[28] For Comrie, this danger was sufficient to reject à Brakel's emphasis on the *actus* and to regard the *habitus* as foundational.

(2) By accenting the *habitus* of faith, Comrie promoted divine grace as the *sole cause* of faith. He said that it is the sole prerogative of the Holy Spirit to implant this *habitus* in the elect who are spiritually dead.[29] *In* this implanting of faith, the sinner is utterly *passive; with* this implanting, he is engrafted into Jesus Christ; and *from* this implanting, the elect will become *active* in exercising faith.[30] Thus, Comrie's stress on implantation (synonymous with regeneration) was never separate from the living out of conversion. Ultimately, Comrie's definition of regeneration included the initial moment of new life as well as the entire process of sanctification.[31] Nevertheless, his accent was first on the impartation of new life; then, second, on the *actus* of faith — though both must still be attributed to divine grace.[32]

(3) Along with this emphasis on faith as *habitus* and *actus*, Comrie stressed faith's *union with Christ*. Specifically, engrafting into Christ is primary, for it is through this engrafting that the believer receives Christ's benefits.[33] Christ as Benefactor takes priority over His benefits; His Person is greater than His gifts. Indeed, faith's union with Christ in *Himself* is what validates the benefits in *themselves*.

---

[27]*HC*, pp. 428-29; Kersten, *Reformed Dogmatics* 2:404.

[28]*HC*, pp. 429-30.

[29]Ibid., p. 381.

[30]Ibid., p. 383.

[31]Creedally, this distinction is borne out in the Belgic Confession's view of regeneration in its wider sense (art. 24) as compared to the Canons of Dort's presentation of its narrower sense (i.e., only the initial implantation of new life, III-IV, art. 12).

[32]*HC*, p. 414.

[33]Ibid., p. 377.

Graafland faults Comrie for saying that the *habitus* of faith precedes the elect's engrafting into Christ *or* directly follows it, charging him with inconsistency. But Comrie saw no inconsistency in maintaining that, from *God's side*, union with Christ is necessarily first because such union is the *source* of faith via decretal justification, while from the perspective of the *believer*, faith is the vital link between Christ and the soul.[34] Chronologically, both occur together, as Comrie stated in his definition of faith. Theologically, however, it was essential for him to maintain "that God imputes the righteousness and satisfaction of Christ to the elect sinner in the time of love by an immediate, direct imputation, an imputation *preceding all acts of faith*,"[35] in order to ward off the Roman Catholic error that the righteousness of Christ is imputed *upon* the act of faith. According to Comrie, this would necessitate an internal change in the elect sinner before God justified him.[36]

Comrie acknowledged that the believer's union with Christ in faith was a mystery. It was out of a sense of failure to comprehend this mystery — not out of weak theology, as Graafland asserted[37]— that Comrie asked for help from anyone who had clearer light on this vital union than he presently possessed.

While faith is the source of the spiritual life, it is not the root of spiritual life *itself*. Accordingly, Comrie recognized various degrees of union between Christ and the elect sinner, even when the sinner is dead in sin. In discussing Question 20 of the Heidelberg Catechism, Comrie named three such degrees:

> 1. A natural union due to partaking of the same human nature. 2. A lawful union whereby Christ and the elect are one under the law's exacting requirements and claims. 3. A covenantal union whereby Christ, as Surety, assumes their state so fully that He permits their sins to become His by imputation.[38]

This covenantal union, however, can only be made vital in the time of love (*tijd der minne*). As Comrie said, "Then Christ, through the Holy Spirit, unites Himself to them and works faith in their

---

[34]Only from this perspective of the believer is Banfield correct in saying that Comrie taught: "It is not faith as *our act* that unites savingly to Jesus Christ, but faith, that *in-wrought spiritual capacity which is of God*" (*The ABC of Faith*, p. xiii).

[35]*Brief*, pp. 124ff.

[36]Ibid., p. 127.

[37]*Zekerheid van het geloof*, pp. 221-22.

[38]*HC*, pp. 381-82.

hearts whereby they are united to Him in their effectual calling."[39] Thus, Christ unites the dead, *godless* sinner to Himself,[40] cementing this union with the Spirit-wrought gift of saving faith (*habitus*), thereby exchanging the state of death ("under the wrath and curse of God, even as all others") for the state of life and grace ("in which he shall partake of all the benefits which Christ has merited").[41]

(4) By accenting the *habitus*, Comrie retained dependence on the grace of God in the *actus* of faith. Though the grace of faith (*habitus*) is perfect and abides in the soul in which it is planted, the activity of faith (*actus*) is not always strong, for it has no power to act in and of itself, but must be acted upon by the Spirit who implants the *habitus*. Kuyper aptly summarized Comrie's emphasis on the Spirit's role: "That the Holy Ghost, in order to incline the will of the sinner, and to give him the capability of accepting this Gospel as a certain and undoubtable personal grant of pardon and eternal happiness to himself, infuses into his soul a potential faith, develops this faith from *potentia* into *actum* by the preaching of the Word, and qualifies him by the means of this acting faith to embrace Christ, and to accept all His treasures."[42]

Comrie said that true spiritual exercises flow from Christ, are activated by the Spirit of Christ, and are inseparable from the Word of God.[43] Contrary to Kromigst's objection that Comrie separated the Spirit from the Word, Comrie worked hard to maintain an intimate Word-Spirit connection.[44] One of Comrie's strongest passages on the Spirit's work was in his sermon on Jeremiah 2:13. He wrote:

---

[39]Ibid., p. 381. Cf. *Brief*, p. 131.

[40]Though the differences between the à Brakels and Comrie should not be exaggerated, Comrie's emphasis on the habit of faith did influence him to stress the experience of justification as an *ungodly* sinner more than Brakel. Predictably, W. à Brakel emphasized the act of faith, the need for a daily renewal of justification, and sanctification more than Comrie. Cf. C. Graafland, "De Gereformeerde Orthodoxie en het Pietisme in Nederland," *Nederlands Theologisch Tijdschrift* 19 (1965): 472; S. van der Linde, "De Godservaring bij W. Teellinck, D. G. à Brakel en A. Comrie," *Theologia Reformata* 16 (1973):198 (reprinted with revisions in *Opgang en voortgang der reformatie* [Amsterdam: Ton Bolland, 1976], pp. 159-70).

[41]*Brief*, p. 136.

[42]"Alexander Comrie," *Catholic Presbyterian* 7 (1882):200.

[43]*HC*, pp. 433-34.

[44]De Boer rejected Kromigst's thesis: "[In Comrie] the Holy Spirit is the Spirit of the Word. He speaks in, with, and by the Word" (*De Verzegeling met de Heilige Geest volgens de opvatting van de Nadere Reformatie*, pp. 194-99). Cf. P. J. Kromigst, "Het geloof," *Troffel en Zwaard* 1 (1903):104.

This faith, being an infused propensity in the soul or an inwrought faith by the Holy Spirit, always retains its nature and manner of operation. In the course of time it always maintains the same propensity and functions in identical fashion as it did at the very outset. This is as much as to say that the infused propensity of faith can never be exercised except that — by the immediate operation of the Holy Spirit in and by means of the promise — it first receives the gift of divine grace passively, and then becomes active subsequent to and by means of this.[45]

The Spirit accomplishes this *habitus* and *actus* of faith through the Word of God and Word-centered activities. As Comrie wrote, "Faith gradually attains to its perfection — from being less to being more, from being weaker to being stronger. And thus all the means of grace — the Word, prayer, the preaching of the Word, the sacraments, and the gatherings of the saints — function as means, by the cooperation of the Holy Spirit, to build us up in the faith."[46]

Comrie never stressed the Spirit at the expense of the Word,[47] not even to accommodate Zanchius's assertion that the *habitus* of faith may be separate from the Word so that even heathen subjects may be saved without coming into contact with this Word.[48] Rather, Comrie maintained the inseparability of the decree of the Father, union with the Son through His righteousness, application of the Spirit, *and* the means of the Word. It pleases God to work through the channel of His Word.[49] He said that in conjunction with the Word, the Holy Spirit plants the *habitus* of faith, and through law and gospel He causes the activities of faith to spring forth. In short, if the principle of faith is implanted by the Spirit, the acts of faith must come to fruition through the Word, though growth in grace is frequently a slow and gradual process.[50]

(5) By distinguishing between the faculty and the act of faith, Comrie helped protect Calvinism from being infected with neonomianism. Comrie knew that Calvinism could lapse into

[45]*LR* 2:72.

[46]*HC*, pp. 429-30.

[47]De Boer, *De Verzegeling met de Heilige Geest*, p. 199.

[48]Cf. W. G. T. Shedd, *Dogmatic Theology* (reprint ed., Grand Rapids: Zondervan, 1971), 1:436ff., who supported Zanchius.

[49]*HC*, p. 438.

[50]The pastoral overtones implicit here are evident in Comrie's correspondence with his brother. G. H. Leurdijk shows how Comrie used his *habitus-actus* distinction to comfort his brother who had been in spiritual darkness for eleven years ("Alexander Comrie: 'Een vaderlijke vriend,'" *De Saambinder* 61 [1983]: 3-4 [3 Feb], 2-3 [10 Feb]).

neonomianism, thereby jeopardizing the concept of justification by faith alone. That is what happened with Richard Baxter (1615-1691), who regarded himself as a staunch Calvinist despite his rejection of limited atonement, his sympathies with Amyraldianism, and his practical implementation of neonomianism in steering sinners to salvation.[51] This also happened at the close of the seventeenth century, when one group of English Dissenters (represented by Isaac Chauncy) was charged with antinomianism, and the other (represented by Daniel Williams) was accused of neonomianism.[52] Since these issues were never resolved, it was hardly surprising that neonomianism reared its head again in Scotland in the Marrow controversy (1717-1722).[53]

As a disciple of the Marrow Men, Comrie was particularly sensitive to neonomian tendencies. When some of his con-

---

[51]In *Reliquae* 1:110, Baxter said he approved "of Camero and Amiraldus's way about universal redemption and grace." Edward Dowden rightly asserted that Baxter's middle way of individualism makes him "too Arminian for the high Calvinists and too Calvinistic for the Arminians"(*Puritan and Anglican: Studies in Literature* [New York: Holt, 1901], p. 216). Cf. Richard Baxter, *The Life of Faith, as it is the Evidence of Things Unseen* (London: Printed by R. W. and A. M. for Francis Tyton and Jane Underhill, 1660); *The Practical Works of Richard Baxter,* 23 vols. (London: James Duncan, 1830); Hugh Martin, *Puritanism and Richard Baxter* (London: SCM Press Ltd., 1954); Irvonwy Morgan, *The Nonconformity of Richard Baxter* (London: Epworth Press, 1946); William Orme, *The Life and Times of Richard Baxter, with a critical examination of his writings,* 2 vols. (New York: J. Leavitt, 1831).

[52]Williams defended his beliefs in *Gospel Truth Stated* (London, 1691). After distancing himself from Socinians, Roman Catholics, and Arminians, he focused on the real differences between himself and the followers of Chauncy (many of whom leaned toward the writings of Tobias Crisp just as many of Williams's adherents supported Baxter). Cf. Isaac Chauncy, *Neonomianism Unmask'd: or, The Ancient Gospel Pleaded, against the other, called, the new law* (London: H. Barnard, 1693), which was translated into Dutch by Comrie. Chauncy was John Owen's successor in London for seventeen years; Owen had already claimed to find Arminian tendencies in Baxter.

Comrie's *habitus* functions as a safeguard against making acts of faith "a subordinate righteousness," for when the *habitus* is the infusion of the Holy Spirit, and all his acts of faith proceed from it, none of those acts form a subordinate human righteousness, but ultimately flow out of the righteousness of Christ alone. On the other hand, by insisting upon the acts of faith, Comrie safeguarded himself from some of the antinomian tendencies of Crisp, for the habit of faith will be active in works of love, repentance, faith, and obedience.

[53]For the best source on the Marrow Controversy, see Lachman, *The Marrow Controversy.* The controversy is summarized by Douglas Kelly: "Between approximately 1717 and 1722 the Church of Scotland was agitated by a controversy between evangelicals, known as 'Marrow Men,' and moderates, or 'neonomians,' over the relationship between law and gospel in salvation. Prominent evangelical ministers such as Thomas Boston and Ralph and Ebenezer Erskine had reprinted *The Marrow of Modern*

temporaries stressed the acts of faith, while neglecting the *habitus,* implying that man must *first* repent and believe, then God will reward those acts with acquittal, Comrie viewed this as a new kind of nomism. By emphasizing *habitus* as the Spirit's infusion, Comrie aimed to affirm the Westminster Confession as well as help prevent justification from collapsing into neonomianism.[54] For both the Westminster standards and Comrie, *all* acts of faith flow out of the Spirit's implantation; hence, the acts themselves (contrary to what Kendall said) cannot be voluntaristic, i.e., exercised by "free will." William Young pointed that out in his review of Kendall's *Calvin and English Calvinism to 1649.* He wrote:

> "Assenting" is listed among voluntaristic words [by Kendall], although *The Larger Catechism* Q. 72 clearly distinguishes assenting to the truth of the promise of the gospel from the volitional acts of receiving and resting upon Christ and his righteousness. It is represented as involving the whole soul, including intellect and will. A deeper insight may disclose, as Alexander Comrie had occasion to point out, that the definition of faith in Christ as a saving grace implies that saving faith is essentially not an act of the soul, but an infused habit that comes to expression in its acts. . . . Dr. Kendall's lack of sensitivity to the precise scholastic distinctions underlying the simple expressions of the Westminster Standards is to be deplored.[55]

Divinity (ascribed by some to Edward Fisher of London in 1645), which maintained an immediate free offer of salvation by looking to Christ in faith. This raised the opposition of the controlling party of the church, who as neonomians held that the gospel is a 'new law' (*neonomos*), replacing the OT law with the legal conditions of faith and repentance needing to be met before salvation can be offered. They maintained the necessity of forsaking sin before Christ can be received, whereas the Marrow Men replied that only union to Christ can give us power to be holy. Hence the neonomians considered the call to immediate trust in Christ and to full assurance to be dangerously antinomian. Led by Principal Haddow of St. Andrews, the church condemned *The Marrow of Modern Divinity* in 1720. The evangelicals protested this action without avail. They were formally rebuked by the church's General Assembly in 1722 but not removed from their ministries" (*Evangelical Dictionary of Theology,* ed. Walter A. Elwell, p. 695).

[54]Arie Vergunst, *Neem de Wacht des Heeren Waar* (Utrecht: Den Hertog, 1983), pp. 108-109.

[55]"Calvin and Westminster," *Bulwark* 2 (May-June, 1980):15-16. Both the Westminster Confession of Faith and Comrie were summarized by John Murray on this point. He wrote: "Faith is of God, but faith itself is the whole-souled movement of the person in entrustment to Christ" (*Collective Writings* 2:235ff.) — i.e., understanding and will inclusive. It is true that some Second Reformation divines leaned toward emphasizing the understanding (especially the more scholastically oriented, such as Voetius) while others underscored the will (especially the more pietistically oriented, such as Wilhelmus à Brakel), but Comrie, like Calvin (1.15.7) and the Westminster

Finally, Comrie's emphasis on the habit of faith has its weaknesses. Graafland feels Comrie's fears were excessive in this area and motivated by philosophical influences. He says that Comrie's emphasis upon the habit of faith engendered a passivity that "proved to be disastrous, for the exhortation to grow and increase in faith loses its effect if the least act which issues forth from 'inwrought' faith does not differ in its essential nature from the greatest act."[56] Moreover, as Herman Bavinck pointed out, Comrie's *habitus-actus* distinction is not supported by the Heidelberg Catechism's definition of faith.[57]

Unity and Oneness (*eenheid*) of Faith

Despite Comrie's emphasis on the *habitus* and *actus* of faith, he did not approve of a split concept of faith. Rather, his *habitus-actus* distinction emphasized the unity and oneness (*eenheid*[58]) of faith. He wrote:

> Thus you see that as the Word being one and the same in itself, but sending its rays into the soul in three respects, so also faith, which is wrought in the soul, although being in itself a single *faculty*, when it becomes actual, made active by the Word and Spirit, shows itself active. This should be noticed so that we would never say that *faith in its nature*, as it is an inwrought faculty, *gains something that it did not have*, but receives everything at once in its working, so that everything that comes forth from this inwrought faith is a sign and evidence that it is created in its own nature by the operation of the supernatural and re-creating power of the Holy Spirit.[59]

This view of faith did two important things. First, it allowed Comrie to ground the facult*ies* or acts of faith in *the* faculty or habit of faith, so as to maintain that the essence of faith is always one, constant, perfect seed *in itself*, as a result of Spirit-implantation and

standards, aimed at the whole-soul, whole-man concept (cf. de Boer, *Verzegeling met de Heilige Geest*, pp. 97-98).

Hence, Kendall's attempt to limit the Confession's doctrine of faith and assurance primarily to the will lacks historical awareness of the Reformed scholastic tendencies out of which these divines operated. Comrie made no apologies for such scholastic terminology as *habitus* and *actus*, despite the fact that this was used heavily in late medieval scholasticism (e.g., it predominates in Duns Scotus) and resurfaced in the early 1600s in Reformed scholasticism. Comrie, like Voetius, was trained to use scholastic terminology and philosophical concepts as handmaidens to theology.

[56]*Zekerheid van het Geloof*, p. 234.

[57]*Gereformeerde Dogmatiek* 4:103ff.; cf. Heidelberg Catechism, Q. 21.

[58]This Dutch noun expresses both the English ideas of "oneness" and "unity."

[59]*HC*, p. 428.

maintenance. Second, it allowed him to cut off debate about the location of the essence of faith as well as the value of acts of faith.[60] For Comrie, the value of the acts of faith was irrelevant since all true acts of faith had the same quality in the genus or essence of faith (*habitus*), for every act of faith flows out of the Spirit applying the Word to the habit of faith.

In analyzing the *eenheid* of faith, Comrie taught that its essence was inseparable from conviction or persuasion, for faith cannot exist without the conviction that the heart of the matter believed is true. Saving faith, therefore, is advanced by persuasion of the truth of divine testimony.[61] Comrie added: "The clearer the testimonies of the God of truth concerning the things of our lost state and the way of redemption persuasively penetrate this inwrought faith, the more the conviction of truth — or the contents of those testimonies — shall be certain and persuasive."[62]

Comrie taught that the most important seal of this conviction by divine testimony lies in the understanding, though he also emphasized that it was in the entire man — soul, understanding, will, judgment, and knowledge — for Scripture viewed faith as a matter of the heart.[63]

Like Calvin, Comrie emphasized the *eenheid* of faith as well as a distinction between various acts of faith in this *eenheid*. To avoid Semi-Pelagianism, Comrie stated that he preferred to call these acts "essentialities" (*wezenlijkheden*) rather than acts (*daden*), to show the acts are not parts that together form the habit of faith, but are drawn from the central *eenheid* of the habit of faith. Hence, they are faculties of the faculty.[64]

Three Faculties of Faith

Unlike Witsius, Lampe, Turretin, and others who named numerous acts of faith, Comrie concentrated on the three most commonly accepted faculties or elements: knowledge (*kennis*), assent (*toestemming*), and trust or confidence (*vertrouwen*).[65] Comrie said that while the

---

[60]Because Comrie did not place one act of faith above another, he was able to follow the alphabet randomly when dealing with the various acts of faith (cf. *A.B.C. dess Geloofs*).

[61]*HC*, p. 411.

[62]Ibid., p. 451.

[63]*EZG*, p. 319; *A.B.C. dess Geloofs*, p. 140.

[64]*HC*, p. 445.

[65]Comrie believed that every act of faith could be subsumed under one of these three elements.

faculty of faith is passive in receiving Christ, it becomes active in knowing, assenting, and trusting. Faith becomes mature (Philippians 3:15) by acting on what is inherent in implantation.[66]

When the believer is spiritually healthy he gradually grows in spiritual knowledge, assent, and confidence. Thus, Comrie allowed for growth in faith, and stressed the supernatural character of each element.

Spiritual Knowledge

Comrie defined spiritual knowledge as follows: "It is a supernatural knowledge which the Holy Spirit, by means of the Word, works in the hearts of the elect when effectually calling them. The objects of faith, in their very essence, are unveiled by divine light and discovered to this inwrought faith. By means of those revelations He quickens and qualifies this faith to know and understand those things savingly which must be known unto salvation."[67]

For Comrie, spiritual knowledge was an inward persuasion from the Holy Spirit, through which the sinner receives subjective light and insight into the Word of God. The elect increase in knowledge through gradual degrees. "This knowledge gradually arrives at its fulness by means of the active deeds of knowing — slowly but surely, from the one act or step to the other," Comrie wrote.[68]

For Comrie, spiritual knowledge is totally different from natural knowledge or historical faith that knows Christ only by "the letter."[69] The regenerate who has enlightened understanding possesses the kind of knowledge lacking in the natural man.[70] Consequently, Comrie rejected the definition of saving faith as historical knowledge *plus* assent and trust.[71] Rather, spiritual knowledge is experimentally applied by Word and Spirit to the believer. Comrie said that through spiritual knowledge the believer stands guilty before God's law. He

---

[66]By maintaining that "no act or acts can give faith its form or being," Comrie avoided the debate concerning the proper or formal act of faith (*actus formalis fidei*), which in his day included possibilities such as assent, coming to Christ, receiving Christ, and trusting in Christ. Cf. Kuyper, *Holy Spirit*, p. 395.

[67]*HC*, p. 454.

[68]Ibid., p. 480.

[69]Ibid., pp. 415, 424.

[70]Ibid., pp. 416, 438-40.

[71]Comrie followed the Classis of Welcheren (1693), which deemed it necessary to compose five articles, to refute the errors of Roell and others who ascribed to man's reason the ability to know God. Cf. J. J. Brahe, *Aanmerkingen over de Vijf Walchersche Artikelen* (reprint ed., Rotterdam: De Banier, 1937).

is guilty on account of heart corruption, guilty by virtue of divine justice, and guilty through the imputation of Adam's representative sin which manifests itself in inability and unwillingness.[72] This clear knowledge causes the soul to die to self and to fall prostrate or "sink away" before God.[73] Furthermore, this knowledge directs the lost and needy soul to the necessity, sufficiency, suitableness, and willingness of Christ as Savior.[74]

Spiritual knowledge performs two tasks in deliverance: the literal (*woordelijke*) and the essential (*wezenlijke*), which Comrie identified as the gospel and Jesus Christ in the gospel.[75] The gospel is the mirror, but if Christ does not appear before the mirror, He will not be seen. Here Comrie seemed to allow a wider distinction between the Word and Christ than Calvin did. Comrie said that the Word is the mediate (*middellijke*) object of faith, whereas Christ is the immediate (*onmiddellijke*) object.[76] Jesus Christ is the ultimate object of faith on whom saving knowledge relies and terminates.[77]

Spiritual Assent

Comrie called assent the twin sister of knowledge, since assent accompanies and follows knowledge.[78] Assent is faith's "amen" as it embraces spiritual knowledge.[79] It is the echo of the soul to the truth of God's Word and to Christ revealed in it.[80] It is the soul's wholehearted surrender to the divine way of salvation — the way of *sola gratia* and negation of human merit.

By spiritual assent, the believer "takes refuge" (*toevlucht-nemend*) in Christ to embrace Him and to find rest only in Him.[81] Though Comrie would not say that any act of faith was the essence of faith, he did imply that assent was the most prominent act of faith.[82]

Spiritual assent differs from temporary faith as spiritual knowledge differs from historical faith, Comrie said. Temporary faith only cares about the benefits of Christ, but saving assent receives Christ first, and thus receives His benefits.[83] Like spiritual knowledge, spiritual assent regards Christ as the sole object of faith. According to Comrie, this is how the Holy Spirit works spiritual

---

[72]*HC*, pp. 419-21.
[74]Ibid., pp. 433-35.
[76]Ibid.
[78]*HC*, p. 440.
[80]*HC*, p. 442.
[82]Ibid., p. 399.

[73]Ibid., pp. 425-28.
[75]Ibid., p. 436.
[77]*Brief*, p. 148.
[79]*A.B.C. dess Geloofs*, p. 55.
[81]Ibid., pp. 405, 443.
[83]*A.B.C. dess Geloofs*, p. 132.

assent: "The second matter or the second aspect which belongs to the nature of inwrought faith is the ability to receive and assent — by divine persuasion — to the divine testimony by the light of the Holy Spirit shining forth in the soul. In doing so I not only embrace it as very truth, but also as a truth which is of the greatest importance for me and of which I am a partaker."[84]

Like spiritual knowledge, spiritual assent involves the understanding and the will.[85] Spiritual trust, however, only involves the will.[86]

Spiritual Trust

Comrie defined spiritual trust, the third element of faith, as follows: "Now we must speak of confidence, for faith is not only the possession of divine light in the intellect, but also the exercise of divine power upon the will. It is an assured confidence which the Holy Ghost works by the gospel, in my heart; that not only to others, but to me also, remission of sin, everlasting righteousness and salvation are freely given by God merely of grace, only for the sake of Christ's merits."[87]

Comrie dealt with spiritual trust more extensively than with other elements of faith because of the debate among Reformed theologians about whether assurance belonged to faith.[88] Comrie distinguished faith in *abstracto* from faith in *concreto*. He said that in *abstracto*, faith cannot doubt. But "abstract faith" is found in the lives of elect *sinners* who are prone to doubt. Thus, though faith in *abstracto* knows no doubt, there is no such thing as doubt-free believers in concrete, daily life, for faith belongs to sinners who wrestle with unbelieving and corrupt hearts. Even when faith is exercised, it remains in an imperfect state. Consequently, even when assurance is strong, it can never be complete during this life. *Essentially*, then, assurance belongs to faith, but *concretely* the soul in which that faith is planted often robs it of the sweetness of assurance. Hence, Scripture speaks of weak and strong faith as well as of growth in faith and grace. All such terms refer to faith in its concrete, existential environment, and must not be applied to faith itself, which is inseparable from assurance when considered in *abstracto*.[89]

---

[84]*HC*, p. 484.

[85]*HC*, pp. 440-43.

[86]Ibid., p. 444.

[87]Ibid., p. 488. Cf. Question 21 of the Heidelberg Catechism.

[88]Kersten, *Reformed Dogmatics* 2:404; Honig, *Alexander Comrie*, pp. 217-18.

[89]Cf. *EZG*, pp. 238-55.

With that distinction, Comrie protected himself from two errors: (1) the error of à Brakel, who said that assurance does not belong to the essence of faith, but is only a fruit of faith;[90] and (2) the error of van Thuynen, who taught that assurance is essential to partake of saving faith.[91] Between these schools of thought, Comrie, like Calvin, maintained that assurance belongs to the essence of faith but is not always grasped by Christians.

In sum, Comrie's position was this: The seed of assurance is in refuge-taking faith, albeit largely dormant, but the goal of the believer is to grow in the consciousness of what he already possesses in principle, in order to arrive in due season at the sovereign gift of full assurance in Christ. The dilemma of assurance being the essence of faith, yet distinguishable from it, could best be resolved by making four theological distinctions, Comrie believed. Those distinctions are as follows.

Assurance of Faith

The Direct and Reflex Acts of Faith
Comrie explained how the elect are gradually brought to full assurance of faith by making use of the direct and reflex acts of faith (*directe en reflexive geloofsdaden*).[92]

---

[90]À Brakel viewed hungering and thirsting after Christ as belonging to refuge-taking faith, and regarded this as the essence of faith. For à Brakel, desiring and seeking constituted the *being* of faith, and assurance the *well-being* of faith (*The Christian's Reasonable Service*, 2:391ff). He was supported in these views by Jacob Groenewegen and Friedrich Lampe. À Brakel, Groenewegen, and Lampe were convinced that the attachment of assurance to faith was pastorally injurious by discouraging "beginners in grace." The dangers Comrie saw in this viewpoint were primarily pastoral. He felt that this doctrine would be prone to influence seeking souls to rest in their seeking, i. e., short of Christ Himself, and it would remove the weight of Peter's injunction to the believer to make his calling and election sure (2 Peter 1:10).

[91]Van der Groe and Themmen supported van Thuynen. They said that Calvin maintained that one who lacks assurance lacks saving faith. They felt that the views of à Brakel and Lampe left open a danger that convicted sinners hungering for Christ might be encouraged to build faith on hunger without ever receiving Christ by assured faith. Van der Groe in particular was criticized by Groenewegen for this view, and subsequently came to adopt Comrie's mediating position as the only tenable one.

[92]In this distinction Comrie followed theologians such as William Ames (*Marrow of Theology*, trans. from the 3rd Latin edition and ed. John E. Eusden [Boston: Pilgrim Press, 1968], XXVII, 16); Johannes Maccovius (*Loci communes theologici*, editio postrema, Opera & Studio Nicolai Arnoldi [Amstelodami: apud Ludovicum & Danielem Elzevirios, 1658], p. 765); Petrus Van Mastricht (*Beschouwende en praktikale Godgeleerdheit* [Rotterdam: Van Pelt, 1749], I, 1, 25); à Brakel (*The Christian's Reasonable*

Using section 18.2 of the Westminster Confession as a definition of assurance, Comrie affirmed that "the divine truth of the promises" illustrates the *direct* act of faith, while the "inward evidences of graces" and the "testimony of the Spirit" are *reflex* acts of faith.[93]

Comrie defined *direct act of faith* as follows: "One is fully convinced of these divine truths in general as well as of the free offer of grace not only to others but also specifically to me. This is not only due to being convicted of the doctrine of truth, but also because the Holy Spirit assures and seals these things to the heart of the undone sinner, so that his obstacles are overcome due to divine light arising in his soul."[94]

In this, Comrie echoed Calvin and Reformation doctrine, and showed the influence of Ralph and Ebenezer Erskine. Consequently, he advocated an assurance of faith that derives its liberty directly from gospel promises.[95]

Comrie said this direct act of faith included an immediate apprehension of God's revelation as truth, most specifically those gospel promises that encouraged sinners they would not be cast out if they came to Christ. The certainty resulting from this direct belief in God's promises introduces an array of activities by which the needy hunger and thirst after the righteousness of Christ.[96] The Holy Spirit grants such acts by an increasing realization of need until the elect embrace Christ in His fullness.[97] When that happens, the promises of God are applied to the believer as his own through the sealing work of the Spirit. As Comrie explained: "In the promise of the gospel, God the Holy Spirit attests to the divine childhood of the soul, assuring and convincing her of the same. He does so by His own divine and immediate voice, announcing to, speaking within, and impressing upon the soul that she is a child of God by His immediate operation upon the promise of the gospel. He simultaneously gives her so much liberty and assurance in her heart by faith, that she — with full trust and being assured within her soul — can and may call God 'my Father.'"[98]

Service, 2:356-57); and Turretin (*Institutes of Elenctic Theology,* 2:560-62). Comrie stressed more strongly than these writers the Spirit's role in the reflex act of faith.

[93]*LR,* on Heb. 10:22; *EZG,* pp. 345-46.

[94]Ibid., p. 246.

[95]De Boer, *De Verzegeling van de Heilige Geest,* p. 188.

[96]*EZG,* p. 214 where Comrie listed seven activities.

[97]Ibid., pp. 247-48.

[98]*LR,* pp. 78-79.

Thus, the direct act of faith is occupied with the promises of the gospel in Christ, while the reflexive act looks back on the direct act "which assures the soul of personally being a partaker of Christ."[99] Comrie listed five such reflexive acts:

1) Faith, as being *the eye of the soul*, is confirmed, regulated, and arrested by previous and present experiences of God's manifestations towards her and by her exercises concerning this. This makes the soul receptive and qualified for the following matters — and without this the soul will always remain a troubled sea. 2) Faith observes in its activity the *essential deeds* whereby the soul has taken or presently still takes hold of *Christ*, and perceives the *deeds and fruits* of them in her own soul. 3) Faith sees *God's own mark and stamp* upon everything, for when grace is observed by divine light, then the soul perceives that it is indeed a work of God and that it does not issue forth out of her own heart. 4) Faith, not being impeded by accusations or strong insinuations, perceives this as God's work *with a conscience void of offense towards God.* 5) Faith consequently fills the heart with inward *joy and peace in believing*. It is thus evident from everything that this assurance consists in the Spirit convicting the soul by the *reflexive acts of faith* of truly being a child of God who shall safely arrive in eternal glory. This gives liberty to the soul and fills her with joy, as she now knows in whom she has believed.[100]

Comrie added that the believer cannot exercise any of these reflexive acts of faith in his own strength. Such acts are always the gift of the Holy Spirit and must be ratified by His inward testimony.[101] Comrie emphasized more strongly than à Brakel and many Second Reformation divines that the reflex act of faith is only valid when sealed by the Spirit.[102] This relationship of the Spirit to the reflex act was clarified further in the next distinction Comrie made.

Assurance of the Uprightness of Faith and of Adoption

For Comrie, the difference between assurance of the uprightness of faith (*zekerheid van de oprechtheid van het geloof*) and assurance of adoption (*zekerheid van het kindschap Gods*) was critical. That distinction helped fill the gap between the direct and reflex acts of faith. By assurance of the uprightness of faith, Comrie meant the Spirit-wrought freedom granted to the elect to reflect on how God

---

[99]Ibid., p. 249.

[100]*EZG*, pp. 251-52.

[101]*EZG*, p. 251; *LR*, pp. 78ff. Cf. de Boer, *De Verzegeling van de Heilege Geest*, p. 185.

[102]*The Christian's Reasonable Service*, 2:287-88.

has led them, as well as the conviction that what happened was the fruit of saving faith. The result is the conviction that their faith is uprightly grounded in God Triune. Consequently, in the "uprightness of faith," the marks of grace do not play a creative but a confirming role.[103]

Assurance of adoption goes deeper. In this kind of assurance faith is not merely reassured momentarily, but salvation itself is permanently sealed.[104] The route to the assurance of adoption or sonship is through the direct, immediate sealing of the Spirit, whereas assurance of the uprightness of faith is through the Spirit-wrought conclusion derived from reason.[105] Assurance of adoption brings conscious acquittal from sin by God the Father and a guarantee of belonging to the divine family forever. Assurance of adoption is the gift through which God provides a degree of steadfastness in faith that's reserved only for a minority of believers. Comrie wrote: "You must know that the possession of a steadfast assurance…is a jewel which God grants to few, or else they must be very exercised and tender Christians and be subject to many trials and tribulations. For faith, when brought into exercise, trusts that Christ, His righteousness, and the forgiveness of sin has been granted or given her of God, and that the Holy Spirit seals this to the soul."[106]

Assurance of adoption offers strength to the believer in times of light and darkness. It is deeper and stronger than what those who lack this internal testimony experience. Still, assurance of the uprightness of faith gives strength as long as faith is exercised, even if such assurance is more prone to succumb to temptation, persecution, and darkness than the assurance of adoption. Nevertheless, even believers assured of their adoption continue to wrestle with unbelief and temptation, and infirmities of flesh and blood, for trials often come on the heels of grace. As Comrie wrote: "As soon as the old, atheistic, unbelieving flesh surfaces, doubts likewise surface which no believer can overcome until God by renewal reveals His Son in his soul."[107]

Assurance of Faith and Assurance of Sense

Comrie clarified his first two distinctions by adding a third: the assurance of faith (*geloofszekerheid*) and the assurance of sense

---

[103]*LR*, pp. 29-31.
[104]*A.B.C. dess Geloofs*, p. 238.
[105]Cf. Graafland, *Zekerheid van het geloof*, p. 230.
[106]*LR*, p. 125.   [107]Ibid.

(*gevoelszekerheid*). Here he picked up on the distinction made by Perkins and expanded by Ebenezer Erskine. Erskine wrote:

> There is a great difference betwixt the assurance of *faith*, and the assurance of *sense*, which follows upon faith. The assurance of faith is a *direct*, but the assurance of sense is a *reflex* act of the soul. The assurance of faith hath its object and foundation from *without*, but that of sense has them *within*. The object of the assurance of faith is *a Christ revealed, promised, and offered in the word*; the object of the assurance of sense is *a Christ formed within us by the Holy Spirit*. The assurance of faith is the *cause*, that of sense is the *effect*; the first is the *root*, and the other is the *fruit*. The assurance of faith eyes the promise in its *stability*, flowing from the *veracity* of the promiser; the assurance of sense, it eyes the promise in its *actual accomplishment*. By the assurance of faith, Abraham believed that he should have a son in his old age, because God who cannot lie had promised; but by the assurance of sense, he believed it when he got Isaac in his arms.[108]

In essence, Comrie echoed Erskine's distinction, though Comrie went further in explaining the role of the promise. With this distinction, Comrie defined assurance of faith as follows: "The assurance of faith rests in God's truth alone, having been pledged to us in the divine promise. Even though we do not have the matter of the promise in actual possession and a thousand difficulties and apparent impossibilities rise up against this, we thereby rely steadfastly upon the word of the promising God, so that we view this matter as ours and with a quiet heart receive it as being ours prior to having the matter in actual possession."[109]

Whereas assurance of faith reckons with God's truth by viewing the divine promise as a pledge, assurance of sense experiences the divine promise in fulfilment to the soul's great joy. Comrie wrote: "The assurance of sense consists in a joyous affection which arises in the heart from a conviction which the Holy Spirit works in the heart that we possess and enjoy in actuality (i.e., in very deed) all that has been promised. This is comforting to the soul, but is enjoyed neither by all nor at all times. Rather, it is very frequently assaulted by Satan and under attack by unbelief, so that a person is as one ready to die (Psalm 88). In the meantime, the assurance of faith is and can frequently be very strong without the assurance of sense."[110]

Comrie offered three distinctions between *geloofszekerheid* and

---

[108]"The Assurance of Faith, opened and applied," *The Whole Works of Ebenezer Erskine* 1:254.

[109]*HC*, p. 446. [110]Ibid., p. 447.

gevoelszekerheid, which have evoked charges of mystical tendencies.[111] He said:

> First of all, faith and sense are distinguished from each other as far as object is concerned, for the object of faith is Christ in the word of the promise, but the object of sense is Christ as He manifests Himself immediately in the soul in a soul-ravishing manner, so that the soul, with the old Simeon, has the child in its arms and is able to praise God. Second, faith and sense are also distinguished in their activity; for faith reaches out to a full Jesus for everything and rejoices that everything is in Jesus. However, sense does not focus upon that which is to be found in Jesus to comfort itself with this, but rather upon that which it derives from Jesus and rejoices to the degree that it beholds much within itself. Third, faith and sense are distinguished in the steadfastness of their assurance, for the assurance of faith, leaning upon the Lord's promises, is not moved by improbability, darkness, etc. However, the assurance of sense rests upon the spiritual frame and sensible exercise, endures no longer than the spiritual frame, and not being able to look beyond the improbabilities is ready to say: there shall be no deliverance.[112]

This last distinction offered a parallel between Comrie's *geloofszekerheid-gevoelszekerheid* distinction and that of "the promise and the promised matter" (*de belofte en de beloofde zaak*).[113] For Comrie, the *promise* can only be believed by faith, whereas the *promised matter* can be enjoyed and possessed.[114]

Conditional and Unconditional Promises

Comrie said the promises are either conditional (*voorwaardelijke*) and absolute (*volstrekte*) or unconditional (*onvoorwaardelijke*). Conditional promises are suggested by such texts as, "Look unto me and be ye saved" (Isaiah 45:22), and are used by God to comfort His afflicted children when they believe that they possess the stipulation laid down in the promise. Such promises offer only a relative degree of assurance, for when the true believer walks in darkness, he loses

---

[111]Particularly by A. A. van Ruler, "De bevinding en de prediking," in *Theologisch Werk* (Nijkerk, 1971), 3:61-81, and K. Schilder, *Heidelbergse Catechismus* 1:34. Schilder did not accept Comrie's distinction that assurance of faith refers to faith's being, and assurance of sense to its well-being. Schilder believed that this further distinction led Comrie to view assurance of faith as a common experience, and assurance of sense as uncommon or extraordinary. Schilder concluded: "In this way Comrie returns again to mystical thinking." Cf. de Boer, *De Verzegeling van de Heilige Geest*, pp. 194ff. for an acquittal of Comrie on the charge of mysticism.

[112]*EZG*, pp. 418-19.   [113]Ibid., p. 366.
[114]Ibid., pp. 372-77.

the ability to believe he is meeting the required condition. Such an experience leads the elect to God's absolute promises, however, where they cast themselves unconditionally upon the faithfulness of God in Christ. The bottom line of God's promises is the unconditionality of divine grace in Christ and the necessity of being driven to Christ through the Word, not through feelings divorced from the Word. Our frames, tears, and feelings, Comrie noted, "can neither be the foundation nor the fulfillment of any condition to come to Christ."[115] He added: "For even though a believer may be fond of feelings, the foundation of his assurance may nevertheless not be his feelings and Christ together, for otherwise he shall continually stagger. Rather, it must be Christ alone, and then he shall be able to remain standing."[116]

In sum, Comrie introduced distinctions about assurance primarily to help believers make their calling and election sure through the unconditional grace of God in Jesus Christ. In doing so, Comrie also helped resolve differences in Reformed thinking about assurance, taught believers how the Holy Spirit works in their lives, and encouraged struggling believers to press forward for greater degrees of assurance.

Faith and Justification

Comrie's doctrine of saving faith influenced all of his theology, particularly the doctrine of gratuitous justification. Comrie did not merely parrot his predecessors in saying that saving faith was the instrumental cause of justification. Nor did he confine himself to saying that justification is not *because of*, but *by*, faith. Rather, to safeguard justification from any possible human merit (including à Brakel's inclination to grant faith a creative function[117]), Comrie affirmed that justification is *to* faith. In other words, justification goes both *before* and *by* faith. Faith is the organizing principle of justification. Comrie explained this doctrine of justification in five steps:

---

[115]*A.B.C. dess Geloofs*, p. 160.

[116]*EZG*, p. 419.

[117]Comrie feared that ascribing to faith an active or creative role in justification would lead to Remonstrant thinking. Against à Brakel, Comrie noted that "they who speak so broadly of the acts of faith to justification, by which we are justified in the tribunal of God, secretly bring us back to the Remonstrants' doctrine" (*HC*, p. xvi). Cf. Honig, *Alexander Comrie*, pp. 232-38.

Justification *before* faith:

> Step #1 — *Eternal justification* in the decree of God.
>
> Step #2 — *Collective justification* in the resurrection of Christ.

Justification *by* faith:

> Step #3 — *Actual* (and *active*, i.e., from God's side) *justification,* which takes place by the direct imputation of the righteousness and satisfaction of Christ to the elect, and results in regeneration, by means of which the elect are reckoned fully justified on the side of God, are placed in a state of reconciliation with Him, and receive *saving faith* in their souls by the implantation of the Holy Spirit.
>
> Step #4 — *Passive justification* in the tribunal of conscience, when the Holy Spirit is pleased to seal to the elect sinner the assurance of justification as the Father's judicial pronouncement for Christ's sake.

Justification *following* faith:

> Step #5 — *Public justification* at the second coming of Christ when the elect shall be declared righteous, shall inherit the kingdom prepared for them from before the foundation of the world, and shall experience faith swallowed up in eternal love.[118]

Through these steps, Comrie tried to mediate between differences of Reformed thinkers on the doctrine of justification. He refused to join the antinomians, for they taught *full* justification from eternity. Comrie wrote: "I have never taught that justification, as it is an immanent act of God, is justification in its full scope. On the contrary, I have taught that to place justification [in its full scope] in eternity, would be antinomian."[119]

But Comrie also distanced himself from à Brakel and others who denied justification from eternity in every respect.[120] Rather, Comrie maintained that justification must be worked out in time to be validated in the elect, who are *ungodly* in themselves and need to be transferred from the state of death to the state of life.[121] This divine working-out (*uitwerking*) cannot be fully subsumed under God's decretal justification nor under His eternal foreknowledge *from man's side*, though from God's perspective there is no distance between His

---

[118]*Brief,* p. 142. Some of the Puritans presented a similar doctrine of fivefold justification, e.g., Samuel Bolton (*True Bounds of Christian Freedom,* p. 188).

[119]*Brief,* p. 147.

[120]Brakel, *The Christian's Reasonable Service,* 2:376-78.

[121]Graafland asserts that for Comrie time and history are no more than "a ripple in the stream of eternity" ("Alexander Comrie [1706-1774]," in *De Nadere Reformatie,* p. 336).

foreknowledge and *uitwerking*. For God, justification *is* from eternity. From God's side decreed justification precedes the implantation of saving faith, for faith is comprehended in election.[122]

That compelled Comrie to view election and justification from eternity as nearly indistinguishable. Both are immanent acts of God from eternity. Their similarity is because of God's simplicity. Nevertheless, there is an important difference. In predestination God views the elect without any moral qualities of good or evil. In eternal justification, God views the elect as fallen, lying under His wrath and curse. Comrie said that for them, God "by an eternal immanent act of His will within Himself, on grounds consistent with His attributes and perfections, justifies, forgives their sins, and grants a right to eternal life."[123]

Graafland concludes that Comrie's emphasis downplayed the need for active faith. Comrie did try to deal with that dilemma. He explained that if there is no justification *before* faith, then justification *by* faith implies a change in God, as if God moves from wrath to grace *within Himself*; but if justification *by* faith does not transfer a sinner from wrath to grace and is merely an assertion of justification from eternity, then all historical relevance of justification by faith alone is swept away.[124] If Comrie erred in emphasizing justification from eternity too strongly, he did so within the boundaries of historic Reformed faith.

Collective justification doesn't bring in *full* justification, either. Comrie explained: "Although, then, I place justification as an immanent act of God, in eternity, and also assert that we are justified in and with Christ through His resurrection, I nevertheless maintain that we notwithstanding, are not fully justified, or, in other words, that justification is not complete until this benefit is actually and personally applied to us."[125]

By maintaining that only actual justification brings full justification, Comrie stuck to his mediating position. He said: "I teach then: 1. That God imputes the righteousness and satisfaction of Christ to the elect sinner in the time of love by an immediate, direct imputation, an imputation preceding all acts of faith. 2. That this imputation in the time of love has two immediate effects: (a) At

---

[122]Cf. Gravemeijer, *Gereformeerde Geloofsleer* 2:690ff.

[123]"Alexander Comrie (1706-1774)," in *De Nadere Reformatie*, p. 338.

[124]According to Honig, Comrie is thus not willing to go as far as the Kuypers (cf. *Holy Spirit*, pp. 354-77.) Cf. Kersten *Reformed Dogmatics* 2:417.

[125]*Brief*, p. 151.

this imputation the sins of the elect sinner are forgiven and a right to eternal life is granted to him. . . . (b) A new life is imparted, that is, the dead sinner is made alive."[126]

In working out passive justification, Comrie talked about the whole life of conversion. He said that God sets up a tribunal, "*not* in heaven, but in the heart of the chosen, quickened sinner,"[127] which follows a series of three divine acts:

> God's *first* act in this tribunal is conviction of sin by the Holy Ghost, by means of God's holy law. God's *second* act in the court of conscience is the enlightenment of the understanding in the knowledge of Christ, wrought by the Holy Spirit by means of the gospel. . . bringing them to embrace Christ Jesus Himself from faith to faith. The *third* act in the court of conscience is the assurance in our own mind of our actual and personal participation in this benefit of the covenant.[128]

In a sermon on Romans 5:1, Comrie said that justification in the court of conscience usually happens gradually and follows these basic steps, most of which are normative for believers. Many believers fail to realize the final act, which may be called "full assurance." Like Owen, Comrie said this act could take place "mediately" or "immediately." It is not a second justification, but a personal sealing of actual justification. He said when the sinner is brought to acknowledge his condemnableness before God, Christ intervenes to plead his case as Advocate. The Father then pronounces forgiveness on the basis of Christ's merits, and the Spirit seals this pardon to the believer's soul. The sinner is led to embrace forgiveness by faith and is assured of his right to eternal life for Christ's sake. He is assured that he has been transferred from the state of wrath to the state of grace on the basis of divine acquittal. Comrie urged believers to pray for the consciousness of this acquittal to enlarge their assurance, joy, and peace.[129]

Finally, Comrie concluded his discussion of justification with four causes:

1. The grace of God as the *moving* cause, from which this benefit flows.

2. Christ's active and passive obedience as the *meritorious* cause.

---

[126]Ibid., p. 152. [127]Ibid., pp. 154-55.
[128]Ibid., pp. 157-58.
[129]*EZG*, pp. 28-56. See pp. 182-85 above for more on justification in the court of conscience.

3. The immediate, direct, and antecedent imputation of this obedience, as the *formal* cause, as the sole foundation upon which rests the forgiveness of our sin and the allocation of the right to eternal life, as well as the inward change which is wrought in us in effectual calling as an immediate result thereof.

4. Faith is the *instrumental* cause, whereby alone we receive the benefit, appropriate it, and rely upon it to salvation.[130]

Comrie's doctrine of faith and justification was the heart of his theology. It represented his life-long effort to help the church return to the knowledge and experience of Reformation truth. At a 1923 gathering of the Reformed Alliance (*Gereformeerde Bond*), J. G. Woelderink aptly summarized Comrie's attempt to preserve the Reformed heritage of the essence of faith: "It must be stated as a compliment to Comrie that, in the eighteenth century and in a dwindling generation of Reformed theologians, he was one of the few — if not the only one — who has been deeply conscious of the breach, and who, in order to get on the right track again as far as the essence of faith and other doctrines are concerned, has returned to the writings of the Reformers as well as to the confessions of the various Protestant churches."[131]

---

[130]Comrie and other Reformed scholastics are often charged excessively with a radical departure from Calvin. Though Calvin never developed a philosophical set of assumptions with regard to the Aristotelian division into efficient, material, formal (or instrumental), and final causes in dealing with salvation, his repeated use of this classification reveals a more significant role than a rhetorical device (John Weeks, "A Comparison of Calvin and Edwards on the Doctrine of Election" [Ph.D. dissertation, University of Chicago, 1963], p. 117). The fact that Calvin was not concerned with solving the problems of philosophical determinism, nor about producing a philosophical theology (Dowey, *The Knowledge of God in Calvin's Theology*, pp. 218-19; Bray, *Theodore Beza's Doctrine of Predestination*, p. 52), did not make him a thoroughgoing anti-scholastic (cf. Wendel, *Calvin*, pp. 123ff.). For further usage of Aristotelian fourfold causation in a scriptural framework, see Calvin's *Commentary* on Romans 3:24, as well as Inst. 3.14.17 and 3.14.21.

Calvin's use of metaphysical categories, however, showed that he was of an anti-metaphysical bent in *structural* terms. Due to his fear of transgressing scriptural boundaries through philosophical speculation and on account of his background in Renaissance humanism (cf. Quirinus Breen, *John Calvin: A Study in French Humanism* [Grand Rapids: Eerdmans, 1931]), Calvin used Aristotelian categories cautiously and exclusively for theological concerns, not for the promulgation of a metaphysical structure. Comrie and Reformed orthodox theologians went a step further than Calvin by viewing metaphysical structuring in a favorable light; nevertheless, they were ultimately concerned with theological, not philosophical truth. Philosophy served as an assistant to theology, not vice versa.

[131]Cited by Verschoor, "Het geloof bij Brakel en Comrie," *Onder Eigen Vaandel* 3 (1928):281.

PART III
Comparison of English Puritanism and the
Dutch Second Reformation on Assurance

IX. THOMAS GOODWIN: THE MERGING OF ENGLISH AND DUTCH THINKING ON ASSURANCE

Thomas Goodwin (1600-1679) is the ideal theologian to help us understand the relationship between English Puritanism and the Dutch Second Reformation on assurance of faith. Goodwin spent several years in the Netherlands, where he interacted with Dutch divines.[1] He seems to have added a number of their emphases to his own on assurance of faith. For example, the Dutch divines were fond

[1] Thomas Goodwin entered Christ's College, Cambridge at the age of twelve. He earned his B.A. in 1616, his M.A. in 1620, and his B.D. in 1630. At the age of twenty, he aligned himself with the theological tradition of Perkins, Baynes, Sibbes, and Preston. He served as preacher at Cambridge University and lecturer at Trinity Church (1625-1634). Several who became Puritan pastors were converted under his ministry during those years. On account of preaching restrictions, Goodwin fled to the Netherlands and served an independent church at Arnhem from 1639-1641. In 1641, Goodwin returned to England and formed a prominent Independent church in London. In the mid-1640s he was an influential figure at the Westminster Assembly. In 1650, he was appointed president of Magdalene College, Oxford, and established it as a reputable Calvinistic institution. In 1653, Goodwin had a doctorate of divinity conferred. After 1660, he returned to the pastoral ministry and organized another London church. He spent most of his last years writing. Goodwin gained preeminence as a writer, a leader of Independency, and a principal architect of the Cromwellian domestic settlement. For biographical material on Goodwin, see "Memoir of Thomas Goodwin, D.D.," by Robert Halley, and "Memoir of Thomas Goodwin, D.D., Composed out of his own papers and memoirs, by his son," *The Works of Thomas Goodwin*, vol. 2, pp. ix-lxxv; Alexander Whyte, *Thirteen Appreciations* (Edinburgh: Oliphant, Anderson and Ferrier, 1913), pp. 157-76; Reid, "Life of Thomas Goodwin," in *Memoirs of the Westminster Divines*, pp. 319-43; Stanley Fienberg, "Thomas Goodwin, Puritan Pastor and Independent Divine" (Ph.D. dissertation, University of Chicago, 1974), pp. 2-79; Brian Freer, "Thomas Goodwin, the Peaceable Puritan," Graham Harrison, "Thomas Goodwin and Independency," and Paul Cook, "Thomas Goodwin — Mystic?", in *Diversities of Gifts*, Westminster Conference Reports, 1980 (London: The Westminster Conference, 1981), pp. 7-56; Joel R. Beeke, "Introduction," in the *Works of Thomas Goodwin* (reprint, Eureka, Calif.: Tanski Publications, 1996), pp. 1-23;

of stressing the *steps* of experiential grace, while the English Puritans wrote profusely on the *marks* of grace.[2] Goodwin emphasized both marks and steps of grace in his writing.[3]

Goodwin's works brought together the spiritual vigor of the earlier Puritans (William Perkins, Richard Sibbes, John Rogers, etc.) with the mature thought of later Puritans, such as John Owen.[4] Goodwin said most about assurance of faith in his *Exposition of the Epistle to the Ephesians*, and *Of the Object and Acts of Justifying Faith*.[5] Additional thoughts on assurance are woven into several other works, most notably *A Child of Light Walking in Darkness*, *The Return of Prayers*, and *The Trial of a Christian's Growth*.[6]

Gordon Douglas Crompton, "The Life and Theology of Thomas Goodwin" (Th.M. thesis, Greenville Presbyterian Theological Seminary, 1997), pp. 10-30.

[2]These emphases varied among individual preachers and writers, but in general Dutch Second Reformation divines were more intent on ascertaining Christian experience *within* themselves, while the Puritans focused on Christian living *outside of* themselves. Both groups, however, appreciated Christian experience and practice.

[3]Major studies on Goodwin's theology are few. The best are Michael Horton, "Christ Set Forth: Thomas Goodwin and the Puritan Doctrine of Assurance" (Ph.D. dissertation, Wycliffe Hall, Oxford and Coventry University, 1996), and Crompton, "The Life and Theology of Thomas Goodwin." For Goodwin on assurance, see McNally, "Some Aspects of Thomas Goodwin's Doctrine of Assurance," pp. 66-117. For Goodwin on the covenant of grace, see Paul Edward Brown, "The Principle of the Covenant in the Theology of Thomas Goodwin" (Ph.D. dissertation, Drew University, 1950).

[4]John Cotton, Jonathan Edwards, George Whitefield, and John Gill have noted their indebtedness to Goodwin's writings. Alexander Whyte confessed: "I have read no other author so much and so often. And I continue to read him to this day, as if I had never read him before" (*Thirteen Appreciations*, pp. 158ff.). And J. I. Packer wrote: "Whyte called Goodwin 'the greatest pulpit exegete of Paul that has ever lived,' and perhaps justly; Goodwin's Biblical expositions are quite unique, even among the Puritans, in the degree to which they combine theological breadth with experimental depth. John Owen saw into the mind of Paul as clearly as Goodwin — sometimes, on points of detail, more clearly — but not even Owen ever saw so deep into Paul's heart" ("The Witness of the Spirit: The Puritan Teaching," p. 14). Cf. J. C. Philpot, *Reviews by the late Mr. J. C. Philpot* (London: Frederick Kirby, 1901), 2:479ff.

[5]*Works of Goodwin* 1:206-252 and 8:338-419.

[6]E.g., in *A Child of Light Walking in Darkness*, Goodwin affirmed that the lack of assurance is compatible with faith (*Works of Goodwin* 3:238). In *The Return of Prayers*, Goodwin distinguished assurance from "recumbency" (3:368), indicated that the doctrine of assurance will not make believers presumptuous unless it is abused (3:417), and stressed that assurance may be lost (3:422). In *The Trial of a Christian's Growth*, Goodwin said that God purges out corruption by assuring the believer of His love (3:480). In 4:207 Goodwin defined assurance as a persuasion that God and Christ "are prepared to save a man's own self in particular." In volume 5 he wrote that perseverance does not make the Christian less resolute in resisting temptation (p. 325), but acknowledged that many believers lack full assurance (p. 394). Moreover, assurance always presupposes a first act of faith's recumbency (5:403).

Goodwin's views on assurance have already been introduced.[7] Now we'll explain how his emphases compare with those of Owen and Comrie as representatives of English Puritanism and the Second Dutch Reformation. And we will show how Goodwin acted as a mediator in English and Dutch thinking.

Goodwin and Owen

The similarities between Goodwin and Owen in theology far outweigh their dissimilarities. In experimental assurance, however, they differ practically in several matters.

Goodwin and Owen knew each other well.[8] In the 1650s they alternated preaching on Sunday afternoons to Oxford University students.[9] They reportedly met together often,[10] and their names were linked as "the two great Atlases and patriarchs of Independency."[11] Nevertheless, as Dewey Wallace pointed out, Owen's rapid rise to influence among the staunchly Calvinistic Independents soon eclipsed Goodwin's leadership.[12]

Spiritual Experience and Dutch Influence

Like Owen,[13] Goodwin's views on personal assurance were affected by his spiritual experience. Neither Owen nor Goodwin found assurance of faith quickly or easily. Of his pre-conversion days, Goodwin wrote:

> I received the sacrament at Easter, when I was fourteen years old, and for that prepared myself as I was able. I set myself to examine

---

[7]See pp. 145-46, 174, 181, 206 above.

[8]Although Goodwin was sixteen years older than Owen, they were close friends and respected each other deeply. Owen referred to Goodwin as "one among ourselves, my very learned colleague, and a very eminent man" (*Works of John Owen* 3:80; 10:494).

[9]Freer, "Thomas Goodwin, the Peaceable Puritan," p. 14.

[10]G. Lyon Turner, "Williamson's Spy Book," *Congregational Historical Society Transactions* 5 (1912):249, 253.

[11]Anthony Wood, in his *Athanae Oxonienses*, quoted in M'Clintock and Strong, *Cyclopaedia of Biblical, Theological, and Ecclesiastical Literature* 3:926.

[12]*Puritans and Predestination*, p. 149. Robert Halley made the following comparisons between Owen and Goodwin: "Goodwin was more of a Puritan than Owen, Owen more of a Biblical scholar than Goodwin. If Owen had more profound critical learning, Goodwin was not inferior to him in general scholarship. Goodwin had his favourite authors, and he loved them fondly; Owen indiscriminately read whatever of theology he could lay his hand upon. Goodwin concentrated his thoughts upon a given subject; Owen spread his widely over it and around it" (*Works of Goodwin* 2:xlvii).

[13]See pp. 189-91 above.

whether I had grace or not; and by all the signs in Ursin's Catechism, which was in use among the Puritans in the College, I found them all, as I thought, in me. The love of God to such a sinner, and Christ's dying for me, did greatly affect me; and at that first sacrament I received, with what inward joy and comfort did I sing with the rest the 103d Psalm, which was usually sung during the administration! After having received it, I felt my heart cheered after a wonderful manner, thinking myself sure of heaven, and judging all these workings to be infallible tokens of God's love to me, and of grace in me: all this while not considering that these were but more strong fits of nature's working. God hereby made way to advance the power of his grace the more in me, by shewing me how far I might go and yet deceive myself, and making me know that grace is a thing surpassing the power of nature; and therefore he suffered me to fall away, not from these good motions, for I could raise them when I would, but from the practice of them; insomuch as then my heart began to suspect them as counterfeit.[14]

Young Goodwin was seriously unsettled when his tutor prevented him from receiving the Lord's Supper because he was so young. Goodwin had to leave the communion table in the presence of "all the College, which I did." The bitter disappointment that followed dampened his spiritual desires. He stopped reading Reformed and Puritan literature and no longer went to hear Richard Sibbes preach.[15]

Secretly Goodwin began listening to "flaunting" discourses and the Arminianism that was coming from the Netherlands. The godliness of several young Puritans eventually persuaded Goodwin that such things were neither edifying or true. His interest in true religion became spasmodic, particularly in relation to the Lord's Supper. He was finally brought to full conviction of sin on October 2, 1620, just after his twentieth birthday. He wrote:

Dr. Bainbridge preached a sermon which I had heard once before, on that text in Luke xix. 41, 42. . . . I thought myself to be as one struck down by a mighty power. . . . The sinfulness of my sin was exceedingly enlarged . . . but still God continued his hand over me, and held me, intent to consider and pierce into what should be the first causes of so much actual sinfulness; and he presented to me, as in answer thereunto, — for it was transacted as a conference by God with me, — the original corruption of my nature, and evil

---

[14]*Works of Goodwin* 2:lii.

[15]Goodwin would later edit numerous sermons of Sibbes for print (Haller, *Rise of Puritanism*, pp. 66-67).

constitution and depravation of all my faculties; the inclinations and disposednesses of heart unto all evil, and averseness from all spiritual good and acceptableness unto God.

My sight of my heart was, to my sense, that it was utterly without Christ.... I was surrounded and shut up, and saw no way to escape: but together with the sight of all this sinfulness, hell opened his mouth upon me, threatening to devour and destroy me.[16]

Hours later "before God, who after we are regenerate is so faithful and mindful of his word,"[17] he found a "speedy word" of deliverance in Ezekiel 16. Goodwin wrote:

So God was pleased on the sudden, and as it were in an instant, to alter the whole of his former dispensation towards me, and said of and to my soul, Yea, live; yea, live, I say, said God: and as he created the world and the matter of all things by a word, so he created and put a new life and spirit into my soul, and so great an alteration was strange to me.

The word of promise which he let fall into my heart, and which was but as it were softly whispered to my soul; and as when a man speaks afar off, he gives a still, yet a certain sound, or as one hath expressed the preachings of the gospel by the apostles, that God whispered the gospel out of Zion, but the sound thereof went forth over the whole earth: so this speaking of God to my soul, although it was but a gentle sound, yet it made a noise over my whole heart, and filled and possessed all the faculties of my whole soul.[18]

Goodwin offered four reasons why he could believe these promises of deliverance and pardon were from God: (1) the condition of his heart prior to receiving this scripture of God's willingness to pardon; (2) the appropriateness of this divine word when it did come; (3) the source of this word as "not an ungrounded fancy, but the pure word of God, which is the ground of faith and hope"; and (4) the consequences of this word, including an altered disposition of soul; a dissolution of the works of Satan; an enlightened understanding; a melted will disposed to turn to God; a new nature "inclining me to good"; the Spirit of God as "a new indweller"; and "an actual turning from all known sins, and my entertaining the truth of all godliness."[19]

Several years after that experience, Goodwin appears to have experienced a sweet assurance sealed to his heart by the Holy Spirit, which was far beyond anything he had previously experienced. Prior

---

[16]*Works of Goodwin* 2:lii-lx.
[18]Ibid., pp. lxi-lxii.

[17]Ibid., p. lxi.
[19]Ibid., pp. lxii-lxiv.

to that assurance, however, Goodwin was largely "intent on the conviction God had wrought in him, of the heinousness of sin, and of his own sinful and miserable state by nature; of the difference between the workings of natural conscience, though enlightened, and the motions of a holy soul, changed and acted by the Spirit, in an effectual work of peculiar saving grace."[20]

Through correspondence with a godly minister, Mr. Price, who Goodwin said was the greatest man for experimental acquaintance with Christ that he had ever met, Goodwin was gradually led to "live by faith in Christ, and to derive from him life and strength for sanctification, and all comfort and joy through believing."[21] Goodwin found assurance in Christ after he learned that he could not live from syllogisms *alone*. In a letter to Price, Goodwin admitted: "I am come to this pass now, that signs will do me no good alone; I have trusted too much to habitual grace for assurance of justification; I tell you Christ is worth all." Goodwin's son later wrote of his father: "Thus coming unto Christ, his weary soul found rest, when in all its unquiet motions it could not find it anywhere else."[22]

Goodwin's preaching immediately became more Christ-centered. Wholeheartedly he could now agree with Sibbes's advice: "Young man, if you ever would do good, you must preach the gospel and the free grace of God in Christ Jesus."[23]

Along with assurance through Christ, Goodwin began to experience communion with each member of the Trinity. This relationship so strengthened with time that he clung to it on his death bed. As Goodwin's son wrote: "He rejoiced in the thoughts that he was dying, and going to have a full and uninterrupted communion with God. 'I am going,' said he, 'to the three Persons, with whom I have had communion: they have taken me; I did not take them. . . . I could not have imagined I should ever have had such a measure of faith in this hour. . . . Christ cannot love me better than he doth; I think I cannot love Christ better than I do; I am swallowed up in God. . . . With this assurance of faith, and fulness of joy, his soul left this world."[24]

Goodwin's experiences were significant for several reasons:

First, according to Goodwin's son, his father left autobiographical notes "to give from his own experience a testimony of the difference between common grace, which by some is thought

---

[20]Ibid., lxviii.   [21]Ibid.
[22]Ibid., p. lxx.   [23]Ibid., p. lxxi.
[24]Ibid., pp. lxxiv-lxxv.

sufficient, and that special saving grace, which indeed is alone sufficient" unto everlasting salvation.[25]

Second, Goodwin left notes of his experiences to serve as a pattern for others. "His sermons being the result of these [spiritual meditations and experiences], had a great deal of spiritual heat in them, and were blessed by God to the conviction and conversion of many young scholars, who flocked to his ministry," Goodwin's son said.[26] Robert Halley noted that Goodwin reasoned from his own experience,[27] and Alan Simpson commented: "We can easily imagine how many sermons were based on it."[28] Indeed, Goodwin admitted that he could hardly count the number of times he had related his experience. He added: "I remember that I, preaching at Ely two years after, urged to the people the example of Paul as an example to win others, in having in my eye and thoughts the said experience of God's dealing with me in the same kind; and that the examples of such are to be held forth by God as flags of mercy before a company of rebels to win them in."[29]

Third, Goodwin's experiences helped develop a Puritan morphology of conversion.[30] In telling his conversion, Goodwin suggested that was the way God normally worked in salvation. For example, his own sense of the wrath of God lasted only a few hours. He thus regarded that time as normative, saying, "God does not often suffer a destroying apprehension to continue long upon us. . . . I do not speak now of temptations, but of the just conviction which many such souls have, previous to their believing."[31]

---

[25]Ibid., p. lxvii. [26]Ibid., p. lxviii.

[27]Ibid., p. xlvii.

[28]*Puritanism in Old and New England* (Chicago: University of Chicago Press, 1955), p. 2.

[29]*Works of Goodwin* 2:lxii. "As flags of mercy . . . to win them in," shows Goodwin's evangelistic thrust even in communicating personal experiences. No doubt this thrust, as Irvonwy Morgan pointed out, assisted him (and Puritanism as a whole) in avoiding the pitfalls of introversion: "This urge to evangelism applies also to Puritan preaching for every sermon had to have its 'use' in bringing men to decision. Every sermon was a personal testimony in that the dynamic of the Preacher's appeal was grounded in his own experience, though the actual experience is very rarely mentioned" (*Puritan Spirituality*, pp. 123-24). Cf. Owen C. Watkins, *The Puritan Experience* (London: Routledge & Kegan Paul, 1972), pp. 85-88; William Haller, *The Rise of Puritanism* (New York: Columbia University Press, 1938), pp. 75-79, 94-96.

[30]Cf. Edmund Morgan, *The Puritan Dilemma: The Story of John Winthrop* (Boston: Little, Brown and Co., 1958), pp. 68ff.; Perry Miller, *The New England Mind: The Seventeenth Century* (Cambridge: Harvard University Press, 1953; reprint ed., Boston: Beacon Press, 1961), pp. 365ff.

[31]*Works of Goodwin* 2:xlvii.

Fourth, the distinctions on assurance that Owen and Goodwin developed were inseparable from their individual spiritual pilgrimages. For example, Goodwin's emphasis on the immediate witness of the Spirit was more dramatic than Owen's, who had a similar but somewhat less dramatic experience. Owen made less of his experience as a pattern for others than he did of the experiences of others.[32] We should remember those tendencies when studying the distinctions these theologians made in assurance of faith.

To illustrate, consider the difference in *Pilgrim's Progress* between John Bunyan's "Christian," patterned after his own experiences, and his "Christiana," patterned after the experiences of his wife and numerous parishioners. Christian's tortuous way through the Slough of Despond was markedly different from Christiana's simple passing through "on steps." Much like that, Owen would have preached about God's dealings with his *parishioners*, whereas Goodwin would have preached on God's dealings with *himself.*[33] In addition, because the Puritans taught that God's messengers usually have deeper experiences than ordinary believers so they can help others through great trials, Goodwin tended to stress the advanced steps of grace more than Owen did. This may explain why Owen regarded the sealing of the Spirit as normative, while Goodwin saw it as extraordinary.

Another experience that influenced Goodwin's theology was his three-year pastorate in Arnhem, the Netherlands. In Arnhem, the capital city of Gelderland, Goodwin served a small but active English-speaking church that existed from 1638 to approximately 1650.

The congregation started with about twelve families, or one hundred people, who had left England because of their objections to the ceremonies of the Church of England.[34] Three ministers served the church: John Archer, Goodwin, and Philip Nye. All three were influenced by Congregationalism.[35] They thus organized the church

---

[32]*Works of Goodwin* 2:xlvi.

[33]Cf. Haller, *The Rise of Puritanism*, pp. 143ff.

[34]Keith Sprunger, *Dutch Puritanism: A History of English and Scottish Churches of the Netherlands in the Sixteenth and Seventeenth Centuries* (Leiden: E. J. Brill, 1982), p. 236.

[35]Goodwin and Nye were major spokesmen for the five Dissenting Brethren at the Westminster Assembly. For Goodwin's role in the Presbyterian-Independent controversy, see Fienberg, "Thomas Goodwin: Puritan Pastor and Independent Divine," pp. 80-360; Berndt Gustafsson, *The Five Dissenting Brethren: A Study of the Dutch Background of Their Independentism* (London: C. W. K. Gloerup, 1955); R. B. Carter, "The Presbyterian-Independent Controversy with Special Reference to Dr. Thomas Goodwin and the Years

according to an independent covenant, which Goodwin defined as "an assent and resolution professed (by them to be admitted by us) with promise to walk in all those ways pertaining to this fellowship, so far as they shall be revealed to them in the gospel."[36] One could become a member of the church only if "truly godly."

By "truly godly," Goodwin meant being able to give an account of how the Lord had convicted a person of sin and led him to trust in Christ alone for salvation. As Patricia Caldwell pointed out, Goodwin "sharply distinguished between the saint's duty to be judged by a conversion story upon admission and his additional duty to continue communicating his experiences for the good of others in these meetings."[37] Goodwin expected the applicant for membership to provide for church leaders a "Set Narration," that is, an account of how God converted him. Church leaders ought not expect to hear advanced steps of grace in the Set Narration. An account of the beginning of spiritual life was sufficient. Growth in grace subsequent to membership was expected, but the initial requirement for church membership was minimal with regard to Christian experience.[38]

As Thomas Hooker said in *The Application of Redemption*, the grace a new believer received would cause the "first impressions of the Lord upon the soul . . . to renew and act over dayly these first Editions."[39] In introducing this series of Hooker's sermons, Goodwin and Nye said this growth was expected, for, as with the disciples, the Holy Spirit will "go over the whole of that Work again and again in the hearts of Christians," causing them to progress towards assurance and holiness. They wrote: "And the *coming of the Holy Ghost* upon them, at and after *Pentecost*, was as a New Conversion unto them, making them to differ as much *from themselves*, in *what* they were *afore*, as well-nigh they themselves (though afore truly wrought on) did then differe from other men. The Spirit of

---

1640 to 1660" (Ph.D. dissertation, Edinburgh, 1961); David R. Ehalt, "The Development of Early Congregational Theory of the Church with Special Reference to the Five 'Dissenting Brethren' at the Westminster Assembly" (Ph.D. dissertation, Claremont, 1969).

[36]*Works of Goodwin* 11:536.

[37]*The Puritan conversion narrative* (New York: Cambridge University Press, 1985), p. 77. Cf. *Works of Goodwin* 4:302.

[38]Caldwell, *The Puritan conversion narrative*, p. 77.

[39]*The Application of Redemption by the Effectual Work of the Word and Spirit of Christ, for the Bringing Home of Lost Sinners to God* (London: Peter Cole, 1657-59; reprint ed., New York: Arno Press, 1972), p. 377.

God himself goes over this Work afresh in all the parts of it: As to *humble* anew, to *draw to Christ*, to *change* and raise *the heart* to higher strains of *Holiness*."[40]

After Goodwin and Nye returned to England and Archer died, the pastorless congregation took on Anabaptist tendencies, rejected the Westminster standards, and eventually refused to listen to orthodox Puritan preachers. The church dwindled rapidly until about 1650 when the remaining members, who could now speak Dutch, began listening to Dutch preachers.[41]

Several Dutch Second Reformation divines began emphasizing advanced steps in grace, as Goodwin had, but it is difficult to know what influence that had on Goodwin's interpretation of assurance of faith. Goodwin's stay in the Netherlands did have considerable impact, not so much in forging new experiences within him as in providing him with a fresh experimental interpretation. Goodwin found a close link between the teaching of Dutch divines on assurance and his own experience.

It is only natural that the Dutch and Goodwin influenced each other. The writings of Dutch Second Reformation divines were rapidly being translated into English, but the English Puritan writings were being translated into Dutch at nearly twice the rate. J. Van der Haar lists more than 2,000 Dutch translations of English Puritan works that were printed in the seventeenth century alone.[42] A collection of Goodwin's writings translated by Second Reformation divines J. Koelman, J. Grindal, and J. Sanderus was printed already in 1664 and reprinted three times in the 1700s.[43] Individual works of Goodwin translated into Dutch within twenty years of the *original* English date of publication (the second date behind each volume) include: *De Ware Vrucht des Gebedts* (1639;

---

[40]Ibid., p. "sig. Dr."

[41]Steven, *The History of the Scottish Church, Rotterdam*, p. 284. Cf. *Works of Goodwin* 2:xxiv-xxvii.

[42]Van der Haar concludes: "It is generally assumed that Puritanism in England and Scotland . . . found in the 'Second Reformation' in our country [i.e., the Netherlands] a kind of parallel movement. But the relation was much closer, far deeper. In spite of many wars fought between England and Holland there existed a kind of kinship, a bond of friendship, of brotherly love between the two nations, a bond not weakened by the Channel, nor severed by wars" (*From Abbadie to Young* p. [iii]). Cf. also Sprunger, *Dutch Puritanism*, p. 359.

[43]*Opera, Ofte alle de Theol. Werken, Meest betreffende de Praktijke der Godtsaligheydt* (Amsterdam: Jan Hz. Boom, 1664). This set included only about half of Nichol's English set of Goodwin.

1636), *De Wederkeeringh van de Gebeden* (1639; 1636), *De IJdelheit der Gedachten* (1646; 1637), *Een Kindt des Lichts, wandelende in duysternisse* (1655; 1636), *Moedt-gevingen om te Gelooven* (1657; 1642), *De Toets-steen van des Wasdoms v.e. Christen: 3 pts* (1658; 1641), *Verswaring van de Sonde in 't Gemeen* (1659; 1637), *Het Hert Christi in den Hemel, 3 pts* (1659; 1642), and *Christus het exempel des Geloofs, in 5 pts* (1660; 1642).[44]

Still, the question remains whether the Dutch had as great an impact on Goodwin as he had on them. Theologically, they appear to have had a comparable influence. It is interesting to note, for example, that Goodwin's emphasis on the sealing of the Spirit as a direct testimony to the believer subsequent to regeneneration and distinct from the syllogisms (more like the emphasis of the Second Reformation divines on the steps of grace than the Puritan emphasis on the marks of grace) first appeared in his lectures on Ephesians 1, which he preached upon his return from the Netherlands.[45]

Goodwin's daily interaction with Dutch divines, however, may have been quite limited. Sprunger claimed that the Arnhem church had little interaction with Dutch Reformed or English Reformed churches nearby.[46]

At any rate, personal experience and the Dutch influence should be factored into the following discussion on Goodwin and Owen's explanations of assurance of faith. We'll consider three areas in which to compare them in greater detail.[47]

Faith's Relation to Assurance

First, Goodwin and Owen have the same basic understanding of *faith and its relationship to assurance.* Like most Puritans, they taught

---

[44]Cf. van der Haar, *From Abbadie to Young,* pp. 60-62; Schoneveld, *Intertraffic of the Mind,* pp. 200-201. For Goodwin's influence on Herman Witsius, cf. J. van Genderen, *Herman Witsius: Bijdrage tot de Kennis der Gereformeerde Theologie* ('s-Gravenhage: Guido de Bres, 1953), pp. 73, 124, 250.

[45]I.e., 1641, but not printed until 1681 (*Works of Goodwin* 1:xxxi). Notwithstanding John Owen's contrary view, Goodwin never retracted his belief that the sealing of the Spirit is an immediate assurance. For Goodwin full assurance and the sealing of the Spirit were synonymous. Of the Spirit's sealing, he wrote: "There is a light that cometh and overpowereth a man's soul and assureth him that God is his and he is God's, and that God loveth him from everlasting" (*Works of Goodwin* 1:233). Cf. pp. 206-207 above and 262-65 below.

[46]*Dutch Puritanism,* p. 228; cf. pp. 226-32.

[47]See pp. 174, 181, 206 above, where we have already noted that Owen, more than Goodwin, emphasized the believer's duty to obtain assurance and to grow in communion with Christ, though Goodwin, in turn, stressed this duty more than Comrie (*Works of Goodwin* 8:371-74). Conversely, Comrie accented the sovereign nature of the gift of

that faith includes saving knowledge, saving assent, and saving trust. When writing of faith, Goodwin included knowledge with assent, defining assent as "a spiritual knowledge . . . a sight beyond that of reason," which embraces assurance of the truth, the Word, and the promises of God and Christ. Assent is a "fixedness, an assuredness, a persuasion . . . of the things that I do believe," Goodwin said. It is the saving knowledge of "a real sight of Christ and of spiritual things."[48]

Saving trust is the "faith of recumbency," or the believer's reliance on Christ. It is "an act of application. . . to cast myself upon him," Goodwin said.[49] What "recumbency" is to Goodwin, "refuge-taking" faith is to the Second Reformation divines. For Goodwin, Owen, and most Dutch divines, however, such trust falls short of the "settled, well-grounded assurance" that comes as a special, sovereign blessing to those who have long struggled for it.[50]

In the faith of recumbency, the believer has not yet personally embraced the promise of salvation as his own. The believer only trusts that he *may be* justified by Christ. In times of temptation, his will "steadfastly cleaves unto Christ,"[51] but he does not know for certain that he is elect. The recumbent believer is neither in complete doubt nor in full assurance. Goodwin wrote: "There is stamped upon the heart of a Christian some secret hint or whisper of mercy to him; I do not say it riseth to assurance, for then it would quell all doubtings; but in every one that God takes to himself, as he lets him see the readiness that is in Christ to receive sinners indefinitely, so there is some secret kind of whisper of mercy and grace to him."[52]

Though assurance is part of the essence of faith in the sense that faith cannot doubt, there is a vast difference between persuasion of the truth of God's promises *and* a Spirit-sealed consciousness that all my sins are forgiven for Christ's sake.[53] Goodwin and Owen would agree that this kind of assurance belongs to faith's "well-being," not its "being."[54]

Goodwin defined *this* assurance as both "a branch and appendix

---

assurance more than Goodwin, who, in turn, stressed this sovereignty more than Owen. Moreover, Goodwin schematized the advanced steps of grace more than Owen, but not as much as Comrie (see pp. 265-68 below).

[48]*Works of Goodwin* 8:265-67.
[49]Ibid., p. 273.
[50]Ibid., p. 346.
[51]Ibid., pp. 223-24.
[52]Ibid., p. 271.
[53]Cf. *Works of Owen* 6:431.
[54]This is typical of the Puritan view (e.g., see *The Works of Thomas Brooks* 2:317).

of faith, an addition or complement to faith" and "faith elevated and raised up above its ordinary rate."[55] He wrote, "The Scripture speaks of it as a thing distinct from faith (though it doth coalesce with it, and they both make one.)"[56] In all of this, Goodwin's views were consistent with those of most Puritans, including Owen,[57] as well as those of Second Reformation divines.

Assurance and Knowledge of the Divine Persons

Second, Goodwin, like Owen, believed that full assurance of faith is intimately tied to a Trinitarian analysis of communion with God actualized in intimate, experimental acquaintance with the three divine Persons.[58] Goodwin's brief exposition of that in *Object and Acts of Justifying Faith*[59] preceded Owen's *Communion with God* (1657) by fifteen years. Goodwin sounded much like Owen when he introduced this subject: "There is communion and fellowship with all the persons, Father, Son, and Holy Ghost, and their love, severally and distinctly."[60]

In explaining the concept, Goodwin offered these distinctions:

(1) A believer may have *implicit* communion with the three Persons of the Trinity without realizing it (John 14:7, 9), much like Philip who "spake he knew not what." Only *realized* communion, apprehended by faith, brings abiding assurance of faith.

(2) When the believer has fellowship with one member of the Trinity, he implicitly enjoys fellowship with the others, whether he is conscious of that or not. That point is important because it saved Goodwin from unbiblical mysticism and separation of the divine Trinity.[61]

(3) The believer may know the three Persons of the Trinity in their *saving work* without knowing them specifically in their *divine Persons*. As Goodwin wrote: "There is an implicit knowledge of the Holy Ghost: 'You know him,' saith Christ to his disciples, John xiv.17; that is, they knew him in his work, but they knew him not in his love distinctly, and they had not acquaintance with his person, and they had not the love of the Holy Ghost brought home to them."[62]

[55]*Works of Goodwin* 8:346, 352.
[56]Ibid., 1:236.
[57]Cf. J. I. Packer, "The Witness of the Spirit: The Puritan Teaching," pp. 15ff.
[58]See pp. 173-76 above.
[59]*Works of Goodwin* 8:376-79.
[60]Ibid., p. 376.
[61]Cf. Cook, "Thomas Goodwin — Mystic?", pp. 45-56.
[62]*Works of Goodwin* 8:377.

Owen did not make such a clear-cut distinction between an experimental knowledge of the work of the three divine Persons and an experimental knowledge of the Persons themselves, even if that was implied in his *Communion with God.* Goodwin was more like Comrie and several Second Reformation divines in this regard.[63]

(4) Like Owen, Goodwin maintained that all distinct communion with the Persons of the Trinity must be in and through Christ,[64] based on a Trinitarian model. Hence Goodwin argued that as each divine Person distinctly witnessed Christ's baptism (i.e., the Father by speaking, "This is my beloved Son"; the Son, by submitting to baptism; the Spirit, by descending upon Him "like a dove"), so a believer also is capable of receiving such a witness. He wrote: "For the three persons, as they loved us distinctly, so they bring home their love distinctly and apart to the soul, and the communion that John would raise us up unto is with all three persons distinctly, to view their love severally, and have it all severally brought home to our hearts, all of them manifesting their love unto the soul. . . . Get the love of the Son brought home to thee too, and then rest not until all three persons manifest their love to thee."[65]

Goodwin spoke of love as the essence of this communion, but Owen went further, relating the Father's communion to love, the Son's to grace, and the Spirit's to comfort.[66] In this respect, Owen appeared to add to what Goodwin taught, since Goodwin never attempted to designate a special gift of communion to each Person of the Trinity.

(5) To a greater degree than Owen, however, Goodwin linked assurance to distinct communion with the Persons of the Trinity. He wrote: "So it is in assurance: sometimes a man's communion and converse is with the one, sometimes with the other; sometimes with the Father, then with the Son, and then with the Holy Ghost; sometimes his heart is drawn out to consider the Father's love in choosing, and then the love of Christ in redeeming, and so the love of the Holy Ghost, that searcheth the deep things of God, and revealeth them to us, and taketh all the pains with us; and so a man goes from one witness to another distinctly."[67]

---

[63]See the comparison of Goodwin with Comrie (pp. 265-68 below).

[64]Goodwin wrote: "To talk of such a communion, wherein men betake themselves to the Father, and go to him immediately, this is not the communion which John had; and he that denies the Son, and communion with him, denies the Father also" (*Works of Goodwin* 8:379).

[65]Ibid., p. 378.   [66]Ibid., p. 377; see pp. 177-85 above.

[67]*Works of Goodwin* 8:378-79.

For Goodwin, such assurance was above all syllogisms; indeed, it was the pinnacle of spiritual experience. He wrote: "This assurance it is not a knowledge by way of argument or deduction, whereby we infer that if one loveth me then the other loveth me, but it is intuitively, as I may so express it, and we should never be satisfied till we have attained it, and till all three persons lie level in us, and all make their abode with us, and we sit as it were in the midst of them, while they all manifest their love unto us; this is John's communion, and this is the highest that ever Christ promises in this life."[68]

(6) Finally, in explaining the believer's "several and distinct" communion with the divine Persons, Goodwin provided more scriptural proof than Owen. Nearly all his assertions included scriptural support. For example, four pages on distinct communion cite these texts: John 8:13-14; 14:1, 7, 9, 17, 20, 21, 23; 1 Corinthians 12:7; 1 John 1:3; 4:13; 5:7-8;[69] and Revelation 1:4-5.[70]

Discursive and Intuitive Assurance

Third, though Goodwin's writings as a whole did not reveal different levels to Christian experience, his doctrine of assurance seemed to suggest that direction.[71] More than other Puritan divines, Goodwin used the *discursive* and *intuitive* distinction in experiencing assurance.[72] He stated that explicitly when explaining Ephesians 1:13-14:

> There is, first, an assurance by sense, by conditional promises, whereby a man, seeing the image of God upon his heart, to which promises are made, cometh comfortably to believe that he is in the estate of grace. But then, secondly, there is an immediate assurance of the Holy Ghost, by a heavenly and divine light, of a divine authority, which the Holy Ghost sheddeth in a man's heart . . . whereby he sealeth him up to the day of redemption . . . . The one way is discursive; a man gathereth that God loveth him from the

---

[68]Ibid., p. 379.

[69]See McNally, "Some Aspects of Thomas Goodwin's Doctrine of Assurance," p. 96, for Goodwin's use of 1 John 5:7.

[70]*Works of Goodwin* 8:376-79.

[71]In exegeting 1 John 5:8, Goodwin implied three levels of assurance. "Blood" refers to assurance of faith in Christ's death; "water" alludes to assurance through observing the marks of grace in oneself; "the Spirit" insinuates direct testimony through the sealing of personal forgiveness (ibid., 1:234-35; cf. Sibbes's view of degrees of sealing, *Works of Richard Sibbes* 5:437ff.; Eaton, *Baptism with the Spirit*, pp. 71-73, 85). Normally, however, Goodwin viewed assurance as consisting of two levels: deductive assurance through the syllogisms, and intuitive assurance through the Spirit's direct testimony.

[72]See pp. 142-44 above.

effects, as we gather there is fire because there is smoke. But the other is intuitive, as the angels are said to know things. ... There is light that cometh and overpowereth a man's soul, and assureth him that God is his, and he is God's.[73]

For Goodwin, discursive assurance may be inferior to intuitive assurance, but it is nonetheless legitimate and normative in believers. It can be realized only through Spirit-given faith, not merely by human reasoning, for "even in these arguings and deductions, there accompanies a light that faith strikes in with, a light beyond the force in the reason."[74] A believer can receive no comfort from signs unless the Spirit grants revelation to "cast the balance," and to witness "with our spirits as Romans 8.16 [says], beyond the power of the sign."[75]

Goodwin emphasized the Spirit's work in discursive assurance to ground the syllogisms in divine initiation as well as to preserve the objective promises of God as the ultimate ground of assurance.[76] His emphasis on the Spirit's activity in discursive assurance also allowed him to mediate between some of the Dutch divines who refrained from using the syllogisms and some of the English Puritans who scarcely mentioned the Spirit's role in the syllogisms.

According to Goodwin, in discursive assurance the Holy Spirit uses various marks of sanctification to witness with believers that they are children of God. Those marks included a "new spring of gracious dispositions," which yields love to God and Christ (John 4:14); walking in the light (1 John 1:5-7); confession of sins (1 John 1:9); observance of God's precepts from the heart (1 John 2:3, 5); love for fellow-believers (1 John 2:10). Moreover, the stronger hope becomes through deductive assurance, the more it will purify the believer (1 John 3:3), which purity in itself becomes a mark of grace.[77] Said Goodwin: "All these signs of salvation which the Spirit hath inserted in the Scriptures, he hath written in the hearts of believers, and hath taught them to read them in themselves as well as in this Epistle, so that there is no need that any man should teach us" (1 John 2:27).[78]

---

[73]*Works of Goodwin* 1:233. Goodwin said that assurance of God's love is "either from signs only, or from an immediate light of the Spirit revealing God's heart and mind towards us" (ibid., 7:66).

[74]Ibid., p. 64.

[75]Ibid., p. 65.

[76]Cf. McNally, "Some Aspects of Thomas Goodwin's Doctrine of Assurance," p. 90.

[77]*Works of Goodwin* 8:364-65.

[78]Ibid., p. 395.

The believer need not despair if he cannot see all these marks of grace within himself, either, for if the Spirit does not help him see one sign, He may show another. Goodwin offered many signs that may console a believer.[79] Like Perkins, he implied that if the believer can grasp but one sign, he may be assured, for will he not then also tug at the entire golden chain of salvation? This distinction allowed Goodwin to encourage believers of weak faith to aim for higher degrees of assurance.

Goodwin said doubting believers should identify the promises of God and the marks of grace and seek comfort and assurance from God by asking Him to apply those to their hearts. Nevertheless, those forms of assurance are not the same as the direct, intuitive witness of the Holy Spirit. The syllogisms are useful at times even for the advanced believer who cannot always lay hold of intuitive assurance. At such times, Goodwin said, "the believer's grace and duties are the 'daughters of faith,' who 'may in time of need indeed nourish their mother.'"[80]

As Alexander McNally points out, however, "Goodwin exhibits a remarkable distrust of the use of the syllogism, even though the premises of the syllogism are dependent upon the Spirit's witness for authentication."[81] The believer's problem is that often the power and guilt of sin prevail over the syllogism. Then the testimony of sanctification may be "worn out and obliterated by the power of sin, which also strengthens guilt," Goodwin said. So if assurance were dependent on the "prevalency of the fruits of grace" alone, it would certainly fluctuate often. Consequently, said Goodwin, the "soul lingers after and waits for a further discovery" and is taught by the Spirit to wait for His immediate witness, which raises "the heart up to see its adoption and sonship by an immediate discovery of God's mind to it, and what love he hath borne to it."[82]

For Goodwin, the Holy Spirit has a distinct witness apart from that given through the promises of God and the work of the Spirit-applied syllogism. The Spirit witnesses to the believer in a distinct, immediate, intuitive manner, which is not to be confused with the joint testimony of his spirit with the Holy Spirit. Indeed, the difference between the Spirit's witnessing *with* the believer's spirit (i.e., discursive) from witnessing *to* the believer's spirit by a personal, immediate (i.e., intuitive) application of the Word of God

---

[79]Ibid., pp. 364-65. [80]Ibid., 4:13.
[81]"Some Aspects of Thomas Goodwin's Doctrine of Assurance," p. 116.
[82]*Works of Goodwin* 8:366.

is essentially incommunicable.[83] As Goodwin said, this assurance is "fetched out of the records in God's own breast, and quoteth not, nor referreth us not to any dealing of God with us, or work in us, but is an immediate voice of God's Spirit."[84] It is "'hidden manna, a white stone which none knows but he that receives it,' Rev. 2:17."[85] Discursive assurance is the Spirit's regular work in the regenerate;[86] intuitive assurance is His rare work as seal and sealer. Intuitive assurance is "superadded" to discursive; it is beyond the pale of the typical Christian. Intuitive assurance produces almost as great a change in the believer's feelings as his initial conversion. Goodwin was even prepared to call it a "new conversion." He wrote: "There is a new edition of all a man's graces, when the Holy Ghost cometh as a sealer."[87]

For Goodwin, assurance by syllogism was legitimate, but it was not *full* assurance. Full assurance was reserved for the immediate, intuitive, Spirit-sealing pronouncement. In addition to assurance by the promises of God and by syllogism, Goodwin wrote:

> There is a third testimony, and that is of the Holy Ghost himself, which is immediate; that is, though it backs and confirms what the other two said, yet quotes them not, builds not his testimony on them, but raiseth the heart up to see its adoption and sonship, by an immediate discovery of God's mind to it, and what love he hath borne to it; which is not argued from what is wrought in itself, but God says unto a man's soul (as David desires), 'I am thy salvation,' Ps. xxxv. 3, and as Christ said upon earth to some few, 'Thy sins are forgiven thee,' so from heaven it is spoken by his Spirit (which yet dwells in the heart afore), that a man's sins are forgiven, and he is owned by the whole Trinity to be God's child. . . . And this witness, though it is placed first, yet comes in as the last of the three, as being the greatest, and that which puts all out of question, which the other did not so fully.[88]

For Goodwin, intuitive assurance, though rare, ought to be the believer's goal. When believers couldn't embrace full assurance, however, they could fall back for comfort on discursive assurance, provided they did not remain content with that.

Repeatedly Goodwin urged believers to seek full assurance. To initiate holy jealousy for such great blessings, and to attempt some description of this intuitive experience, Goodwin resorted to the

---

[83]Ibid., 6:27-28.
[85]Ibid., 8:351.
[87]Ibid., 1:251.

[84]Ibid., p. 363.
[86]Ibid., 6:27.
[88]Ibid., 8:366-67.

language of *sense perception*.[89] He used words such as immediate light, spring thaw, transcendent and glorious vision. He said full assurance will produce a "light beyond the ordinary light of faith,"[90] and "all three persons will be enjoyed and possessed by vision."[91]

Using such sense perception to describe spiritual experience was not unique. Scripture is filled with it (e.g., Malachi 4:2). Goodwin's peers, including Owen, used it frequently. For example, in *Divine Original,* Owen stated: "He gives a spiritual sense, a taste of the things themselves upon the mind, heart, and conscience; when we have 'senses exercised' to discern such things."[92]

Geoffrey Nuttall claimed that Sibbes introduced such language among the Puritans.[93] He said Goodwin made the most of the simile of light, and acknowledged that it worked well in his discursive-intuitive distinction. "It was possible to avoid the charge of dependence upon something irrational by pointing out that reason has an intuitive aspect as well as a discursive," Nuttall said.[94]

Goodwin's heavier use of sense-perception and discursive-intuitive terminology, along with emphasizing full assurance experientially, provided a slightly different flavor to his view of assurance from that of Owen. In addition, his view of the sealing of the Spirit in full assurance had a lasting influence on several Second Reformation divines and English Puritans.[95] Here is a summary of Goodwin's view:

> The difference [between the discursive and intuitive methods of obtaining knowledge] may be expressed by way of similitude, by the several ways of assurance of God's love. Look what difference there is between that way, when we know God's love to us but by signs only: this is knowing and gathering his love *ex alio,* by effect, collecting it from another thing, and so is but discursive; as when

[89]Cf. Haller, *The Rise of Puritanism,* pp. 143-46, for how Goodwin used sense perception to comfort those who suffer from lacking assurance of their justification.

[90]*Works of Goodwin* 1:236.

[91]Ibid., 8:379.

[92]*Works of John Owen* 16:327.

[93]*Works of Richard Sibbes* 3:434; 4:334f., 363; 2:495; 4:412. See *The Holy Spirit in Puritan Faith and Experience,* pp. 38-41, for a discussion of sense-perception among the Puritans.

[94]Ibid., pp. 38, 40-41. The major difference between Goodwin and the radical Puritans in sense-perception lay in Goodwin's linking intuitive assurance to the Word of God at all times (e.g., *Works of Goodwin* 1:250). Cf. Louis Bouyer, *A History of Christian Spirituality* (London: Burns & Oates, 1963), pp. 140-42, and Edward Ingram Watkin, *Poets and Mystics* (Freeport, NY: Books for Librarie Press, 1968), pp. 56ff.

[95]See pp. 206-207 above.

the cause is known by the effects, though the Spirit secretly joins a testimony in the conclusion; and that other which comes from an immediate light of the Spirit's sealing up that light, and the taste of it, and revealing God's heart and mind in itself towards us. This is so transcendant, as it works joy unspeakable and glorious; it is intuitive; not so the other.[96]

Owen, who also used sense-perception and discursive-intuitive terminology, sidestepped viewing intuitive assurance as higher than deductive assurance by rejecting the sealing of the Spirit as a post-conversion experience.[97] Thus, for Goodwin, unlike Owen, intuitive assurance was synonymous with the sealing of the Holy Spirit.[98] Intuitive assurance provided both certainty of personal interest in Christ *and* fruits of personal holiness from Christ. As Goodwin wrote: "A seal hath two ends and uses, the first is to assure and certify, and the other is to stamp an image; for so always a seal doth. Now they are both here [in Ephesians 1:13-14]. He is called the Spirit of promise, because he bringeth home the promise to a man's heart and assureth him of an interest. He is called the Holy Spirit of promise in sealing because he stampeth the image of holiness upon you, and makes you more holy than before."[99]

Owen also expected fruit from assurance, but Goodwin expected double fruit from intuitive assurance because of the power that accompanies this experience. Happily, Goodwin did not value intuitive assurance simply for its own sake. He said its authenticity will be marked by greater God-glorifying fruit in daily life. This emphasis on fruits of godliness flowing from intuitive assurance allowed Goodwin to distance himself from false mysticism or radical Puritanism that showed Quaker tendencies. Goodwin explained this in his discussion of Ephesians 1:13-14:

[Intuitive assurance] makes a man work for God ten times more than before, or else at least more kindly. . . . My brethren, [intuitive assurance] is the next thing to heaven, therefore it must needs make

---

[96]*Works of Goodwin* 7:66; cf. 4:305-306; 6:256; 7:143-144, for examples of sense-perception of spiritual matters.

[97]Goodwin argued for his interpretation on the basis that since Paul used the aorist participle in Ephesians 1:13, sealing must be a work subsequent to regeneration. For the grammar of the aorist participle, see E. W. Burton, *Syntax of the Moods and Tenses in New Testament Greek* (Edinburgh: T. & T. Clark, 1966), pp. 59-70.

[98]Cf. McNally, "Some Aspects of Thomas Goodwin's Doctrine of Assurance," pp. 102-112, 117.

[99]*Works of Goodwin* 1:252.

a man heavenly. If there were nothing but self-love in a man, it is true he would abuse it when he hath assurance; but when this love shall stir up love to God, and bring a greater increase of love to God above a man's self, how will that work! I appeal to you, good souls, if Christ do but look toward you a little, how holy doth it make you! Much more, then, when the Holy Ghost is poured out upon you, and when you are baptized with the Holy Ghost as a Comforter.[100]

In sum, assurance reaps blessed fruits, such as, deepening communion with the triune God; quickening of spiritual understanding; greater tirelessness in Christian service; and "joy unspeakable and full of glory" (1 Peter 1:8). Such assurance, far from promoting presumption or indifference, is, as Packer said, "the strongest possible incentive against sin, for its possessor knows that by sinning he will jeopardize his assurance, prompting God to withdraw it, and there is nothing that he is more anxious to avoid than that."[101] Goodwin said that assurance "causeth the heart to be more thankful, and more fruitfully and cheerfully obedient; it perfects love, opens and gives vent to a new stream of godly sorrow, adds new motives, enlargeth and encourageth the heart in prayer, winds up all graces to a new and higher key and strain, causeth a spring tide of all."[102]

Obedience comes spontaneously and is like "fruit brought forth."[103] The believer becomes the willing servant of Exodus 21:1-6,[104] whose obedience is motivated by love from holy principles within the heart[105] rather than from command.[106]

Goodwin and Comrie

Goodwin and Comrie had much in common. Both said that true spiritual experience is Word-regulated and Trinitarian in framework. Authentic experience is the gift of the Father, flows from Christ, and is activated by His Spirit. In their respective doctrines of faith and assurance, Goodwin and Comrie differed little. Both accented the work of the Holy Spirit in acts of faith and degrees of assurance.[107]

---

[100]Ibid., p. 251.

[101]"The Witness of the Spirit: The Puritan Teaching," p. 19.

[102]*Works of Goodwin* 8:347.

[103]Ibid., 7:162, 170ff.   [104]Ibid., 5:145.

[105]Ibid., 7:139; cf. Kevan, *The Grace of Law,* for a summary of the Puritan view on "Love for the Law," pp. 238ff.

[106]*Works of Goodwin* 5:221.

[107]See pp. 222-23, 259-62 above.

Goodwin did include saving knowledge under saving assent, but for all practical purposes their concepts of faith are parallel.

Both Goodwin and Comrie taught that assurance was by nature the essence of faith, but in the believer's consciousness a part of the well-being of faith. *Practically* speaking, both divines reached this conclusion through considerations for the weak in faith. *Theologically*, both found support for this from Scripture, the Reformed confessions, and Reformed theologians. Goodwin offered more scriptural support for this than Comrie did, however. *Philosophically*, both offered grounds for their conclusion in scholastic thought — Comrie more so than Goodwin, though Goodwin is sometimes viewed as the most philosophical Puritan.[108] Generally speaking, Comrie developed more practical, philosophical distinctions, such as *habitus* and *actus*, *abstracto* and *concreto*. In essence, Goodwin adhered to both distinctions, though he prioritized the acts of faith more than Comrie. Hence:

$$\text{Comrie} = \frac{\text{habitus}}{\text{actus}} \qquad \text{Goodwin} = \frac{\text{actus}}{\text{habitus}}$$

These different emphases had consequences. For example, they led Comrie to stress the sovereign nature of the gift of assurance and Goodwin to accent the solemn duty to strive for assurance. Obviously, both believed in the sovereignty of God in assurance and in the duty to seek it. But Comrie never wrote as strongly as Goodwin did in the following statement:

> It is the duty of every one that doth believe to grow up to assurance, and it is his sin not to make out for it; it is his sin to sit down on this side of it. . . .
> *Obj.* But here will one thing be said, Are the meanest Christians obliged to this? and may the lowest Christians attain to this?
> *Ans.* Yes, all sorts may; for you see John here writeth his epistle to all sorts: 1 John ii. 14, 'I write unto you babes,' as well as unto you 'young men' and 'fathers,' 'because your sins are forgiven you, for his name's sake, and because ye have known the Father.' And, saith he, your sins being forgiven you, I write these things unto you, that you may grow up to the knowledge of this, and that you may know that you have eternal life; and though it be true, as I said, that the first act of faith which those that are newly converted do put forth cannot be assurance, yet it may be the very next act.[109]

---

[108]Whyte, *Thirteen Appreciations*, p. 166.
[109]*Works of Goodwin* 8:372-73.

Calling assurance "the very next act of faith after the first one," Goodwin certainly helped the believer expect that he too could attain it by the gracious influence of the Holy Spirit. This expectation is a predictable result of emphasizing the acts of faith.

Goodwin and Comrie vary slightly in their views on the Spirit's sealing. Like Goodwin, Comrie said the Spirit's seal is a special experience, but he also extended this to the syllogisms. Thus, whereas Goodwin believed that the syllogisms had to be Spirit-enlightened, while Spirit-sealing was reserved only for the rare form of intuitive assurance, Comrie said that the syllogisms are valid only when Spirit-enlightened *and Spirit-sealed*. Thus, the syllogisms as well are moved beyond the grasp of the typical believer. The effects this difference would have made in the pastoral ministry would appear to be substantial. If the typical child of God is taught that few attain assurance by syllogisms, that might discourage him from examining himself for the marks of grace that provide such assurance under the Spirit's enlightening. In effect, by making both the syllogisms and immediate assurance special acts of Spirit-sealing, Comrie taught that the two forms of assurance for all practical purposes are equal to each other. By combining these two forms of assurance into one level, Comrie implied that the believer simply has or does not have assurance. Goodwin, on the other hand, in teaching degrees of assurance, would be more inclined to sympathize with Samuel Petto's comments: "Christians think to have assurance all at once, upon a sudden, and are apt to be very much troubled if it commeth not in by the lumpe: whereas the will of God is, to let it in sometimes by little and little; and the soule may be a long time in attaining it."[110]

Owen would be even more sympathetic than Goodwin to the idea of assurance "little by little" rather than by the "lumpe." We might show the differences between Owen, Goodwin, and Comrie as follows:

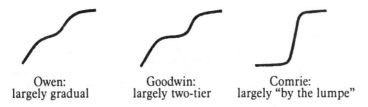

| Owen: | Goodwin: | Comrie: |
| largely gradual | largely two-tier | largely "by the lumpe" |

---

[110]*The Voyce of the Spirit. Or, an essay towards a discoverie of the witnessings of the Spirit by opening and answering these following weighty queries* (London: L. Chapman, 1654), p. 20.

In some ways, this chart is an exaggeration, for in essence what assurance of sense and adoption were to Comrie, intuitive assurance was to Goodwin, and the immediate witness of the Spirit was to Owen.

This distinction between Goodwin and Comrie has continued to the present day in churches that have remained loyal to English Puritanism and the Dutch Second Reformation. In general, English Puritan congregations continue to regard assurance by syllogism as normative, whereas many in those denominations influenced by Comrie in the Netherlands maintain that most assurance is less than normative.[111] That may be why Comrie focused on justification in the court of conscience[112] and schematized the steps of grace more than Goodwin.

In summary, Goodwin acted as bridge builder between Puritan brethren who were less conscious of the steps of grace than he and Dutch Second Reformation divines such as Comrie, whose order in the steps of grace allowed for less flexibility. Owen allowed more flexibility than Goodwin. Ultimately, however, all three were united in their goal of tracing the Holy Spirit's work in faith and assurance to the glory of God Triune, to the growth in grace of the true believer, and to unmask temporary, historical, or miraculous faith.

---

[111]This is particularly true of the "Gereformeerde Gemeenten in Nederland" and the "Gereformeerde Gemeenten," the latter of which was founded under the leadership of G. H. Kersten, whose theology was greatly influenced by Comrie.

[112]Unlike Owen, Goodwin did not use the courtroom-in-conscience scene to illustrate the experience of justification (see pp. 182-85 above). Note, too, that Comrie's insistence that justification in the court of conscience transpires for the *ungodly* sinner rather than for the *godly* who have moved toward assurance "little by little" coincides with the above chart. Not all the Second Reformation divines, however, held this view. W. à Brakel, who stressed the *actus* of faith rather than the *habitus*, allotted a greater role than Comrie to sanctification in assurance.

X. CONCLUSION

The word "faith" has been described as *the* Christian word. Among the terms that refer to the Christian movement, none occurs so frequently in the Bible as faith and its cognates. In the New Testament, the word "faith" (*pistis*) occurs 243 times; "believe" (*pisteuo*) also 243 times, and "faithful" (*pistos*) 67 times. Faith is used more than two times as frequently as charity and more than five times as frequently as hope. In the New Testament triad of faith, hope, and charity, faith outweighs hope and charity in constitutive importance, though not in excellence (1 Corinthians 13:13).

The doctrine of saving faith is important to Christianity for numerous reasons. Most important, faith is the heart of the believer's relationship to God and to life itself. We are saved and justified by faith alone. Paul summarized the comprehensive nature of faith in the words "bringing into captivity every thought to the obedience of Christ" (2 Corinthians 10:5b). Essentially, Paul was saying: The man of faith wrestles to bring his entire being under the lordship of Christ in order to live wholly to God. Faith submits all of life to all of Scripture; it aims for a God-centered world-life view.

Second, saving faith is essential to a genuine study of Christian theology. Theology itself revolves about faith. Even as a scientific undertaking, theology cannot be divorced from faith. Theology is "faith seeking understanding," Anselm said. Faith must enter the presuppositional area and prolegomena of theology; it must control hermeneutics and permeate the content of every theological field. This includes systematic theology in particular, for the task of systematic theology is to construct a coherent, scriptural explanation of the Christian faith by incorporating the data of exegetical, biblical, historical, and practical theology.

Third, saving faith is the root of every kind and degree of

personal assurance of salvation. Assurance that flows from each exercise of faith,[1] applied promises, inward evidences of grace, and witness of the Spirit, enables the believer to live increasingly in comfort and peace before God (*coram Deo*). Assurance is essential for living that overcomes the world and walks in the tender fear of God through Christ Jesus. Assurance of faith confesses with Paul in Scripture's richest chapter on assurance, "I am persuaded, that neither death, nor life, nor angels, nor principalities, nor powers, nor things present, nor things to come, nor height, nor depth, nor any other creature, shall be able to separate us from the love of God, which is in Christ Jesus our Lord" (Romans 8:38-39).

Reformation and post-Reformation divines were intimately acquainted with the richness of faith. Calvin and his followers were acutely aware of the effect their theology had on the concept of faith, especially in its soteriological dimensions. They had to wrestle with questions such as: Is saving faith able to carry out its multifaceted, Christ-centered mandate? If the wide calling of faith is rooted in our personal relationship with God, how solid is it? What is faith, and how is it related to assurance of salvation?

The relationship of faith and assurance became a focal point in Reformation and particularly in post-Reformation theology. The theologians of that time were aware that their explanation of that relationship required a delicate balance between objectivity and subjectivity, Scripture and experience, Word and Spirit.

They also recognized faith as an elusive term, which defies definition. They had to deal with questions such as: May faith be defined by its actions? Are the fruits of faith separate from faith? Does each activity of faith have a saving nature? May the activities of faith be broken down into categories? Is faith itself lost in such a system?

In addition, the matter of assurance prompted questions, such as: What is the relationship of faith and assurance? Is there assurance in faith itself? Is assurance part of the essence of faith, or a constituent element of faith? Is it possible to have faith without assurance? If so, does faith lose its vitality, and assurance its normalcy?

In dealing with these questions, Reformation and post-Reformation theologians struggled against the assertion of Roman Catholicism that no form of assurance was normal. They also

---

[1]"In every exercise of true faith, there is an assurance and perswasion of that which it beleeveth" (Thomas Wilson, *A Commentary on Romanes* [London: Isaac Iaggard, 1627], p. 131). Faith is self-evidencing (von Rohr, *The Covenant of Grace in Puritan Thought*, p. 167).

struggled because of their allegiance to Scripture. They wrestled with biblical data, exegesis, and hermeneutics, for Scripture presents a formidable tension between vital faith and some kind of assurance, along with the possibility of no assurance at all. On the one hand, Scripture describes faith as assurance of things hoped for, a conviction of things not seen (Hebrews 11:1). That assurance is a kind of constituent element of faith. And biblical philology, exegesis, and biblical theology support the intertwining of faith and assurance.

First, in biblical philology this intertwining is indicated by the Hebrew הֶאֱמִין and the Greek πιστεύω. Particularly πιστεύω, a key word in the New Testament, describes an aspect of assured trust in God through Christ. When used in its common Christ-centered context, the complexity of this idea is reflected in various constructions used with the verb: ἐν and ἐπί with the dative, signifying restful reliance on Jesus; εἰς with the accusative, conveying the movement of trust laying hold of the object of its confidence, *solus Christus*.

Second, Bible saints, such as David (Psalm 23) and Paul (2 Timothy 1:12), as well as biblical exegesis confirm that faith includes an element of assurance.[2] Consider Genesis 15:6, the first explicit reference to faith in Scripture: "[Abram] believed in the LORD, and he counted it to him for righteousness." The word for Abraham's faith is the common Old Testament designation, the Hiphil of אָמַן. The root has a variety of meanings, but in the context of Genesis 15 it conveys the idea of firm reliance upon and trust in the testimony of another. The construction with the preposition בְּ indicates that the object of Abraham's trust is the personal God. Geerhardus Vos said this construction must be literally translated, "he developed assurance in Jehovah."[3] That is to say, Abraham fixed himself by faith upon his covenant God with growing assurance.[4] That understanding is confirmed by Paul in Romans 4:5 where the strong fiducial πιστεύειν is present with the preposition ἐπί signifying a restful state of assurance in trusting God. Moreover, in Romans 4:16-22, Paul interprets Abraham's faith as assurance that God would accomplish His promise to him.

---

[2]Cf. Benjamin B. Warfield, *Biblical and Theological Studies*, ed. Samuel G. Craig (Philadelphia: Presbyterian and Reformed, 1968), pp. 428-44.

[3]*Biblical Theology* (reprint ed., Grand Rapids: Eerdmans, 1948), p. 84.

[4]"From Gen. 15 we learn that there was at one and the same time in Abraham a

Finally, biblical theology reinforced this relationship of faith and assurance through studying progressive history of redemptive revelation. Israel's confidence in God's presence and work in redemptive history is of an assuring nature. The Psalms revel in assuring faith, eliciting confidence in the mercy of a forgiving God, who does not destroy His people, even when they fail to trust His saving power. Through all the ups and downs of God's children in the Old Testament, faith relies upon the promises of the covenant God. The faith of Old Testament saints is commended for its assured trust (Hebrews 10:39-12:2). Continuity is avowed here, but also novelty; for faith, receiving God's new utterance in the words and deeds of Christ (Hebrews 1:1-2), becomes an assurance of present salvation. In the New Testament, assured faith is a privilege and a blessing. The Synoptic Gospels and Acts present faith as assuring trust in the Messiah who grants forgiveness of sins. The Gospel and Epistles of John point to the full communion with Christ that results from the fiducial nature of saving faith. The Pentecostal outpouring of the Spirit enriches the fulness of assurance. In the Pauline epistles, faith is assured hope based on divine promises that are completed in Christ. In Hebrews, faith is based upon the certainty of Christ's completed work which supersedes Old Testament sacrifices. James views faith as antithetical to doubt. Peter's epistles show faith as trustful hope which ushers in love and joy.

The very character of the New Covenant, based on Christ's death and resurrection and the Spirit's indwelling, indicates that assurance must be a constitutive element of saving faith. In sum, assurance, whatever form it takes in different stages of redemptive revelation, appears to coalesce with faith.[5] Moreover, the scriptural sanction for including saving faith with assurance as a constituent element is supported by such concepts as the fidelity of God, the truth of His promise, the centrality of Christ and His mediatorial work, the infallible testimony of the Holy Spirit, the radical nature of salvation, and the sovereignty of grace.

Nevertheless, certain portions of Scripture, especially some of

---

relatively mature faith, and an intense desire to have the insufficiency of his faith relieved by further assurance" (ibid., p. 83).

[5]Leander E. Keck, *The New Testament Experience of Faith* (St. Louis: Bethany Press, 1976). Cf. Letham, "Relationship between Saving Faith and Assurance," pp. 60ff; Dulles, *The Assurance of Things Hoped For*, pp. 7-19; Michael Eaton, *No Condemnation: A New Theology of Assurance* (Downers Grove, Ill.: InterVarsity Press, 1995).

the Psalms, indicate that believers occasionally lack assurance and feel the absence of divine favor. For example, David in Psalm 38, Asaph in Psalm 73, and Heman in Psalm 88 cry out in confusion, asking why God has withdrawn his favor. Psalm 88, in particular, expresses thoughts of bleak despondency over the lack of awareness of God's grace.

Moreover, the New Testament recognizes the possible lack of assurance in the Christian's life by repeated admonitions to seek assurance. Peter urges, "Give diligence to make your calling and election sure" (2 Peter 1:10). The First Epistle of John repeatedly refers to how believers may know that they know God (1:7, 2:3, 2:5, 2:23, 2:27, 3:14, 3:19, 4:13, 5:2, 5:13), and the writer of Hebrews exhorts to "draw near with a true heart in full assurance of faith" (10:22), implying that there were those who were experiencing something less than full assurance of faith.

Essentially at stake in the discussion of faith and assurance in Reformation and post-Reformation writing was the fleshing out of this scriptural tension in a pastoral context. In a meticulous addition to early Reformation doctrinal principles, post-Reformation divines affirmed that assurance was more complex than simply resting objectively on the promises of God in Christ. When properly set in the context of Scripture, Christ, and the Trinity, the inward evidences of grace and the witness of the Spirit have a valid place as secondary grounds in the believer's assurance.

The grounds of assurance acquired a particular intensity in English Puritanism and the Dutch Second Reformation as divines developed terminology and treatises on assurance. Their pastoral overtones of compassion for the weak in faith, pressing admonitions and invitations to grow in faith, and dissecting of temporary faith and other false forms of faith show how they relished communion with God in Christ. By elevating the importance of the secondary grounds of assurance to a "mainline" from the "sideline" they occupied in Calvin's thought, the post-Reformers only enlarged, for pastoral reasons, as Graafland asserts, the "pores" that Calvin had already opened in allowing "signs which are sure attestations" of faith.[6] Those who accuse the post-Reformers of morbid introspec-

---

[6]Graafland faults the Second Reformation divines for allowing the subjective line of assurance to "overrule" the objective, but recognizes that this accentuation of subjective assurance was an outgrowth of combatting various forms of pseudo-faith. He asserts that when subjective assurance is prominent as in the Second Reformation,

tion and anthropocentrism have simply missed the mark. The truth is, contemporary Christians have much to learn from the English Puritans and Second Reformation divines, who carefully examined personal, spiritual experience because they were eager to trace the hand of God Triune in their lives and then return all glory to the electing Father, redeeming Son, and applying Spirit.

Kendall's distancing of the post-Reformers from the Reformers shows an insensitivity to the unique, historical situation of first-generation Reformers who embraced the doctrines of grace with unparalleled zeal, and moved forward with special degrees of assurance. When subsequent generations emerged, that zeal for the truth cooled. As Richard Lovelace wrote:

> Second-generation Lutheran and Calvinist leaders found that their valid emphasis on justification was being used as a pretext for cheap grace. Many church people seem to have agreed with Heinrich Heppe: "Things are admirably arranged. God likes forgiving sins, and I like committing them."
>
> "This led to a second stage in the development of evangelical spirituality — the efforts of Calvinist Puritans and Lutheran Pietists [and Dutch Second Reformation divines] to "complete the Reformation" through "reforming our lives as well as our doctrines."[7]

Consequently, it became pastorally essential to define the difference between saving and common grace, saving and common convictions, saving and pseudo-faith. Post-Reformation pastors were faithful to their members as they labored to lead them into a personal, assuring union with Jesus Christ.

As an outgrowth of Calvin and the early Reformers' views on assurance, the post-Reformers further developed the doctrine of assurance — both pastorally and theologically — moving it from a Christological to a Trinitarian framework. The Reformers and post-Reformers may have different emphases, but they were one in this: *Assurance of salvation ought to be regarded as the possession of all*

---

assurance itself becomes problematical and is prone to be viewed as a scarce entity belonging to the quintessence rather than the essence of faith. The post-Reformers, Graafland concludes, "end where Calvin begins" ("Waarheid in het Binnenste," pp. 69ff.). Though Graafland is largely correct, he overstates his conclusions, since the post-Reformers still retained the priority of the promises of God. He neglects to point out that the post-Reformers made more use of the secondary grounds of assurance than Calvin in order to validate that the promises of God were intended particularly for the believer.

[7]"Evangelicalism: Recovering a Tradition of Spiritual Depth," *The Reformed Journal* 40, 7 (September 1990), p. 21.

Christians in principle, despite varying measures of consciousness.[8] The "despite" clause is essential, for passages such as Psalm 88 warn us not to deny our redemption if we lack assurance. This shows the pastoral sensitivity of Scripture in two respects: first, it confirms that what is normal should not be equated with what is necessary in the matter of assurance; second, the lack of assurance directs us to Scripture's stress on the ministry of the Word, the Spirit, and the sacraments in cultivating assuring faith within the covenantal community of the living church.

For the post-Reformers, assurance was a gift of God that involved the whole man, including his understanding and his will. Because the human will is so depraved, incapable of choosing or cleaving to God in its own strength, the post-Reformers felt a great need to develop a salient doctrine of assurance. They knew the deceitfulness of their own hearts and trembled to assume what God had not applied. On the other hand, they also detested unbelief. God was worthy of being trusted, they knew. So their goal, duty, and desire were faith and assurance in Him.[9]

In one sense, assurance was the most crucial issue of the post-Reformation. And the churches, for the most part, benefitted by it. The post-Reformation expositions of assurance contributed to the spiritual health of the congregations as long as they did not degenerate into unbiblical mysticism. As a rule, the divines exemplified a healthy, Pauline mysticism that was Word-regulated within a Christ-centered and Trinitarian matrix. Out of that grew their strong emphasis on experimental religion that was not intended to lead *from* but *to* Christ for increased faith and assurance. By sincerely believing that sound experimental religion was from Christ and by His Spirit, they aimed to rest that experience in the objective gospel.

The divines made no attempt to divorce subjective religion from the objective. That kind of religion, they would have said, may produce a full head while retaining an empty heart. That, they would not endorse. The post-Reformers aimed for whole-souled, intelligent piety. They wanted the kind of faith and assurance that feels the

---

[8]"Reformed theology is fond of insisting that, while full assurance is frequently experienced, it is never inevitable, never continuously sustained and certainly does not patently characterise every degree of Christian stature here below" (G. Thomson, "Assurance," *The Evangelical Quarterly* 14 [1942]:7).

[9]Hence Bunyan has Christian walking over a narrow precipice with the yawning cavern of presumption on one side and unbelief on the other (*The Complete Works of John Bunyan* 2:38).

power of God's grace and rests in its objective foundations with zealous adoration. Some of the post-Reformers should have tied their experiential emphasis more thoroughly to the Word and to Christ, but their teaching left little doubt that this was what they intended.

What the English Puritans and the Dutch Second Reformation divines believed on assurance far outweighed their differences. Both groups taught that full assurance of personal salvation constitutes the well-being or fruit of faith rather than the essence of faith. Both taught that assurance may not be divorced from a scriptural, Trinitarian, and Christological framework. Both taught that assurance comes from the Holy Spirit. The Spirit directs the believer to rest in the promises of God, enlightens him to conclude from the marks of grace that he is a child of God, and applies the Word as a direct testimony to his conscience that Christ is *his* Savior.

Some leaders in both groups may have inappropriately ranked the importance of those modes of assurance. This minority failed to recognize that various forms of assurance may be applied with various degrees of benefit. Some said the direct testimony of the Spirit is superior to assurance gleaned from reflecting by faith on inward evidences of grace. Others, recognizing that danger, combined these two forms of assurance. Nearly all agreed on the essence of assurance, saying the primary ground of assurance lies in the promises of God, though some in both groups chose to focus more on Spirit-enlightened, syllogistic reasoning.

The majority of divines in both groups recognized that the believer finds himself in constant flux in regard to his personal, experiential milieu. They taught that the Spirit knows best which kind of assurance to apply to the believer at any given time. Both groups acknowledged that assurance is covenantally based, sealed with the blood of Christ, and grounded ultimately in eternal election. Both affirmed that though assurance remains incomplete in this life, varies in degree, and is often assaulted by affliction and doubt, its riches must never be taken for granted. It is always the sovereign gift of the triune God. Nevertheless, it must be diligently sought through the means of grace. And it only becomes well-grounded when it evidences fruits and marks of grace, such as love to God and for His kingdom, filial obedience, godly repentance, hatred for sin, brotherly love, and humble adoration.[10]

---

[10]MacLeod, "Christian Assurance 2," *Banner of Truth*, no. 133 (November 1974):1-7.

The English Puritans and the Dutch Second Reformation divines do differ generally on some aspects of assurance. The following are the most significant:

As a whole, the English Puritans tended to emphasize the marks of grace more than the Dutch Second Reformation divines, who, in turn, stressed the steps of grace.[11] In this respect, it appears that the English had more impact on the Dutch than vice versa.[12] Jacobus Koelman, a notable Second Reformation divine and translator of numerous Puritan works, confessed that "books concerning the practice of godliness are rare; consequently, we are dependent upon England since the theologians there are very well exercised in this respect."[13]

The Dutch were more prone to schematize God's work of grace than the English, placing a higher premium on the Spirit's advanced steps of grace.[14] For example, the Dutch stressed the Spirit's immediate internal witness, and distanced that witness from syllogistic conclusions more than the English.[15] The Dutch also regarded the sealing of the Spirit as a special work above and beyond a normal experience of faith.[16] And they paid more attention to justification in the court of conscience as an advanced step in grace.

The greater emphasis the Dutch had on the advanced steps in grace and lesser emphasis on normal steps in grace, is one reason why the English Puritans made greater allowance for various degrees of assurance. The English had greater hope for assurance by means of the promises and syllogisms. No English Puritan taught, as Teellinck did, that scarce one in ten rises even to these forms of assurance.[17]

The Dutch emphases led to stressing assurance as a sovereign gift whereas the English emphasized assurance as a solemn duty.

[11]Cf. pp. 143-46, 237-41 above.

[12]E.g., William Ames, professor in theology at Franeker University (1622-33). According to Matthias Nethenus, Voetius's colleague at the University of Utrecht: "In England ... the study of practical theology has flourished marvelously; and in the Dutch churches and schools, from the time of Willem Teellinck and Ames it has ever more widely spread, even though all do not take to it with equal interest" (introduction to Ames, *Omnia Opera*, trans. and ed. by Douglas Horton, in *William Ames* [Harvard: Harvard Divinity School Library, 1965], p. 15). Cf. W. van 't Spijker, "Guilelmus Amesius (1576-1633)," in *De Nadere Reformatie en het Gereformeerd Piëtisme*, pp. 53-86, and Joel Beeke, "Meet the Puritans...In Print!," *Banner of Truth* 52 (1986):44-45.

[13]Cited by Graafland, "De Invloed van het Puritanisme op het Ontstaan van het Gereformeerd Pietisme in Nederland," *Documentatie blad Nadere Reformatie* 7 (1983):5. Cf. Sprunger, *Dutch Puritanism*, pp. 359-60; van der Haar, *Van Abbadie tot Young*; Schoneveld, *Intertraffic of the Mind*.

[14]Cf. pp. 182-85 above. [15]Cf. pp. 107-108, 233-34 above.
[16]Cf. p. 256 above. [17]Cf. pp. 105, 194-95, 265-68 above.

Hence the English often provided elaborate directions, even entire treatises, on how to obtain assurance and why the believer must strive for it.[18] Accordingly, the Puritan stress was on the act (*actus*) of faith; the Dutch, on the principle or habit (*habitus*) of faith. Many divines in both groups, however, worked for balance between the habit and acts of faith. They recognized that if the habit of faith was neglected, voluntarism might be encouraged; if the acts of faith were minimized, a lethargic brand of antinomianism, which viewed faith as something to *have* rather than to *exercise*, might result.

The English underscored the need for the fruits of assurance more than the Dutch.[19] The English emphasized the practical syllogism; the Dutch increasingly leaned toward the mystical syllogism.[20] Moreover, an underlying emphasis on the activity of faith influenced the English toward a greater evangelistic thrust[21] and greater use of sense perception[22] in describing assurance of faith.

The varying emphases of the English Puritans and Second Dutch Reformation divines should not be exaggerated. Both movements contained such varying emphases that whatever was true of their differences as groups, was not true of each individual. For example, the English and Dutch divines who stressed predestination and the monopleuric character of the covenant also tended to emphasize assurance apart from ourselves (*extra nos*) in the promises of God. Those who taught conditionality in the covenant, frequently emphasized assurance found within (*intra nos*) by means of the syllogisms and the direct testimony of the Spirit.[23] The different emphases of Puritans, such as Owen and Baxter, and Second Reformation divines, such as à Brakel and Comrie, show considerable differing emphases within a broad consensus.

Thomas Goodwin offered a mix of emphases of English Puritanism

---

[18]Cf. pp. 154-56, 191-99 above.   [19]Cf. pp. 266-67 above.
[20]Cf. pp. 131-42 above.   [21]Cf. p. 251n above.
[22]Cf. pp. 263-64 above.

[23]See Letham, "Saving Faith and Assurance in Reformed Theology," 1:362ff., who argues that this distinction is traceable to the sixteenth century as well. In the former group, Letham places Zwingli, Bucer, Martyr, Calvin, Bucanus, Polanus, Zanchius, Olevianus, Crocius, Dering, and Greenham; in the latter group, Bullinger, Capito, Oecolampadius, Musculus, Tyndale, Hooper, Knox, Ursinus, Junius, Gomarus, Fenner, and Rollock (see bibliography). Cf. Stephen Strehle, *Calvinism, Federalism, and Scholasticism: A Study of the Reformed Doctrine of Covenant* (New York: Peter Lang, 1988), pp. 137ff., 188ff., 386-92.

and the Dutch Second Reformation. He promoted both the marks and steps of grace. He schematized grace more than Owen but less than Comrie. He stressed the Spirit's internal witness but allowed a role of providing "comfortable believing" to the syllogisms. He affirmed expectation for assurance but stressed the rarity of full assurance. He accentuated assurance both as a solemn duty and a sovereign gift. He emphasized both the habit and the acts of faith.[24]

To conclude our study of assurance with a clinical analysis of the differences between post-Reformation divines would be insensitive to the subject as well as the concerns of the writers we have studied. The question of the relevance of the doctrine of assurance should also be addressed, however briefly. Today many, even in the Reformed tradition, suggest that this doctrine is no longer relevant since "nearly all Christians possess assurance."[25] But we are convinced that the doctrine of assurance is relevant precisely because we live in a day of minimal assurance. Sadly, the church, for the most part, is scarcely aware that it is crippled by a comparative absence of strong, full assurance.

Today many simply *believe* and seldom ask if their lives *reflect* true faith. What the post-Reformers called historical and temporary faith is sufficient for many; the question of vital, fruit-bearing faith is seldom addressed. Today's lack of certainty among many professing Christians may be a primary cause for the questioning of the witness, inspiration, and inerrancy of Scripture.

Scripture, the Reformers, and post-Reformers did not tire of saying that assurance is known by fruits such as: close fellowship with God, involving childlike obedience; a thirsting after God and exercises that extol Him; a longing to glorify Him by carrying out the Great Commission. Assurance, like salvation, has two sides. It is the summit of intimacy by which the believer both knows Christ and knows he is known of Him. Assurance is not a self-given but a Spirit-applied certainty that moves the believer Godward through Christ. Assurance is the opposite of self-satisfaction. Assurance is God-centered; it does not rely on personal righteousness or service for justification. Assurance

---

[24]E.g., Goodwin emphasized the Spirit's implanting of faith in *The Work of the Holy Spirit*, but stressed the acts of faith in *The Objects and Acts of Justifying Faith* (*Works of Thomas Goodwin*, vols. 6 and 8).

[25]The opinion of a *Reformed* professor of theology when this study was originally suggested!

always reveals vibrant concern for God's honor and mission.[26] Revival is prayerfully anticipated in subjection to an eschatalogical hope; assured believers view heaven as their home and long for the second advent of Christ and their translation to glory (2 Timothy 4:6-8).

Compared to the Reformers and post-Reformers, Christians today are seriously deficient in spiritual exercises. The desire to fellowship with God, the relish for God's glory and heaven, and intercession for revival appear to fall short of a former day. When the church's emphasis on earthly good overshadows her conviction that she is traveling through this world on her way to God and glory, assurance wanes.

The need for a biblically based doctrine of assurance is compounded by our culture's emphasis on feeling. How we feel often takes precedence over what we believe. That spirit has also infiltrated the church. Perhaps a reason for the significant rise and growth of the charismatic movement can be attributed to a formal, lifeless Christianity. This movement offers its adherants phenomena, feeling, and excitement to fill the void created by a lack of genuine assurance of faith which manifests itself in godly living. The divines we have studied offer what we most need today: right, rich doctrinal thinking coupled with and leading to sanctified, vibrant living.

This leads to three conclusions. First, this study has shown the critical importance of doctrinal assurance. Assurance is the center of doctrine put in use, as the Puritans would say.[27] Our studies have shown that assurance involves the work of the Spirit in relation to faith, repentance, justification, sanctification, conversion, adoption, sealing, perseverance, anointing, witnessing, obedience, sin, grace, atonement, and union with Christ. Assurance is inseparable from the marks and steps of grace. It touches on divine sovereignty and human responsibility; is intimately connected with Holy Scripture; and flows out of election, the promises of God, and the covenant of grace. It is fortified by preaching, the sacraments, and prayer. Assurance is broad in scope, profound in depth, and glorious in height. Many doctrines may escape a typical believer's notice

---

[26]"If [the Church] be a diffident missionary, her assurance is small and accordingly she does not infect her pagan environment with the heavenly leaven, she does not win souls for Christ" (Thomson, "Assurance," *Evangelical Quarterly* 14 [1942]:4).

[27]Cf. K. Clifford, "The Reconstruction of Puritan Casuistry" (Ph.D. dissertation, University of London, 1957).

without serious consequences, but assurance is not one of them. Scripture exhorts us: "Wherefore the rather, brethren, give diligence to make your calling and election sure: for if ye do these things, ye shall never fall: for so an entrance shall be ministered unto you abundantly into the everlasting kingdom of our Lord and Saviour Jesus Christ" (2 Peter 1:10-11).

Second, this study has shown the pastoral role of assurance. Each theologian or Reformed confession we considered showed the pastorally motivated desire for a balanced, scriptural presentation of assurance. "How do I know?" is what Perkins — as well as pastors today — hear frequently.

Two mistakes are frequently made in responding to this question. The first is to respond, "Have you believed in Christ?" This response refers to *salvation* but not to *assurance*. It confuses *faith in Christ* with *faith that I am in Christ*. Salvation and assurance are not identical.[28]

Others have a wrong perception of the object of faith. They think that faith means to believe with assurance in their divine sonship. This would mean that the object of faith would no longer be Jesus Christ and the promises of the gospel. Thus, they may have refuge-taking faith without peace because they deny personal grace until they have full assurance. One error leads to assuming more than has been experienced; the latter negates what has already been experienced.

The long-term welfare of a congregation is affected by how pastors present well-grounded assurance. What J.I. Packer stated about the Puritans is equally true of the Reformers and the Dutch Second Reformation divines: "It is evident that 'assurance' to the Puritans was something quite other than the 'assurance' commonly given to the convert of five minutes' standing in the enquiry room ('You believe that John 1:12 is true and you have "received him"? Then you are a son of God'). The Puritans would not have called mere formal assent to such an inference *assurance* at all."[29]

If assurance is *assumed*, pastors build congregations that won't appreciate the depths of Christian experience. If assurance is *compelled*, Calvinism could collapse into neonomianism. If assurance is *ignored*, churches may be reduced to legalistic morality that lacks

---

[28]As J. G. Vos notes: "A person may be really saved, and still not be sure, in his own mind, of his salvation. Such a person is safe, and his safety is sure, but he is not sure about his safety. His salvation is not in doubt, but he may be in doubt about his salvation" ("Assurance of Salvation: Its Possibility and True Basis," *Blue Banner Faith and Life* 13 [1958]:145).

[29]*A Quest for Godliness*, p. 182.

evangelistic zeal for God. But if assurance is *cultivated*, the faith of believers is brought to rest in a faithful God whose grace is mightier than their proneness to backslide (Malachi 3:6; Philippians 1:6).[30] Much wisdom and patience are needed pastorally to deal with lack of assurance due to guilt, ignorance, sin, calamity, uncertainty, temptation, inconsistency, laziness, fleshliness, and disobedience.[31] Pastors must address such hindrances to assurance as those Donald MacLeod suggested: looking on assurance with suspicion, failing to understand the doctrine of justification, erring views on conversion and the depth of conviction of sin, confusing *faith* with *strong faith*, lacking special gifts or vivid and immediate experiences.[32] They must recognize that assurance is complex because of the variegated character of Christian experience. Believers vary in personality, constitution, background, and outlook. Some are blessed with health and prosperity; others are assaulted with illness, loss, and personal tragedy. The child who comes to Christ and finds assurance is different from a profligate who has tasted the bitter fruits of a far country. Though the elements in conversion are the same — repentance before God and faith toward Jesus Christ — pastors err if they expect all to follow the same path in ascertaining their faith.

The implications of the relationship between faith and assurance are far-reaching. Today the church suffers from a crisis of confidence and authority, and therefore of assurance. A renewal of individual and collective assurance is much to be desired. If assurance was more widely experienced, the church would be renewed, and she would live "in the strength of the Lord God" (Psalm 71:16a) for Christ and the gospel. As Brooks said, "Assurance will strongly put men upon the winning of others. . . . A soul under assurance is unwilling to go to heaven without company."[33] Assurance makes a man work for God ten times more than before, Goodwin added.[34]

---

[30]Cf. Edwin H. Palmer, "The Significance of the Canons for Pastoral Work," in *Crises in the Reformed Churches: Essays in Commemoration of the Great Synod of Dort, 1618-1619* (Grand Rapids: Reformed Fellowship, 1968), pp. 141ff.

[31]Cf. Whitney, *How Can I be Sure I'm a Christian?*, pp. 21-25, 81-114; à Brakel, *The Christian's Reasonable Service* 2:391-414; John MacArthur, Jr., *A Believer's Assurance: A Practical Guide to Victory Over Doubt* (Panorama City, Calif.: Master's Communication, 1990), pp. 11-23; Ferguson, "The Assurance of Salvation," *Banner of Truth*, no. 186 (March 1979):7-9.

[32]"Christian Assurance 1," *Banner of Truth*, no. 132 (October 1974):16-25.

[33]*The Works of Thomas Brooks* 2:515-16.

[34]*The Works of Thomas Goodwin* 1:250.

Finally, the doctrine of assurance is personally important. The question "Is assurance of the essence of faith?" is not a mere abstract debate. The *personal* answer of Scripture, Calvin *and* the Calvinists is: organically, *yes*; in actual consciousness, *no*. What unites Scripture, Calvin, and Calvinism on this issue is the organic relationship of faith to assurance, for a Christian may have and grow in assurance, yet not always be aware of possessing it.[35]

In Scripture, the Reformers, and post-Reformation divines, faith operates according to the "already/not yet" dynamic of the New Testament. Even personal consciousness of justification does not mean sanctification is consciously assured. The image of God must be, but is not yet, wholly restored. The reign of Satan is broken, but his armies must yet be swept off the field. Assurance is real but beset by doubts which must yet be conquered. The Christian life includes ongoing tension between assurance and doubt, notwithstanding that faith's victory is sure.

Assurance is reflected in our walk of life. Daily we must learn the lessons taught by the Reformers, English Puritans, and Dutch Second Reformation divines. Our primary ground of assurance is the promises of God. These promises must be applied to our hearts and worked out in our lives, however. This often involves profound spiritual struggle. Bunyan spoke of pulling at one end of God's promise while the devil was pulling at the other end. He could not apply God's promises to himself, but the Holy Spirit confirmed them in him. When this happens, promises reap fruit in our lives and cause us to relish the Spirit's witness with our spirit that we are sons of God.

Assurance involves objective promises, subjective sanctification, and internal testimony. The objective Christ must be subjectively realized by the work of the Spirit. We cannot know with certainty that God's promises are intended for us without manifesting, as à Brakel noted, "the qualities of those to whom the promises have been made."[36] Assurance obliges us to live accordingly. We are called to live fruitful lives, expressing the assurance God is pleased to grant us, speaking well of our great assuring God, and serving by His grace as lights in the world.

---

[35]Some divines continued to maintain that faith should be defined in terms of full persuasion, even though it is mixed with doubt. William Gouge provided three reasons: (1) A definition should adhere to the essential nature of the thing defined and not according to its degree within a particular individual. (2) Doubting is a defect in faith and as such does not belong to its nature and essence. (3) A definition of faith in terms of full persuasion will urge believers to seek assurance (*The Works in Two Volumes*, pp. 116-17).

[36]*The Christian's Reasonable Service* 2:409-411.

Many evangelicals today would agree with C. I. Scofield that "assurance rests only upon the Scripture promises."[37] But this view tends to separate those promises from the resulting obedience to which Scripture calls believers. Consequently, Lewis Chafer could assert, "A carnal Christian is as perfectly saved as a spiritual Christian; for no experience, or merit, or service can form any part of the grounds of salvation."[38]

Separating the promises of God from the evidences of sanctification is the heart of evangelical debate over lordship salvation[39] and is reminiscent of antinomianism's distrust of inherent graces that strengthen assurance. "Inherent qualifications are doubtful evidences for heaven," wrote Tobias Crisp.[40] Anne Hutchinson was more decisive: "Sanctification can be no evidence of a man's good estate. . . . It is a soul-damning error to make sanctification an evidence of justification."[41] Despite varying emphases, Calvin, the Reformers, and post-Reformers would agree with Kevan in contrasting the antinomian denial and the Puritan affirmation of the evidencing of justification by sanctification. As Kevan wrote:

> Considerable sympathy can be extended to the Antinomian distrust of the evidence of good works, but although assurance may not be built on this ground alone, it is, nevertheless, necessary to insist that the evidence of good works shall at least be regarded as a *sine qua non*. . . . This is fundamentally all that the Puritans were concerned to maintain. The truth is that without good works there is no evidence of new life, but that with this external evidence there must be also the witnessing of the Spirit of God "with our spirit, that we are the children of God." Assurance is something deeper than the collecting of evidence, and this is the important spiritual reality to which the Antinomians direct attention.[42]

The message that emerges from our studies is this: Assurance is

---

[37]*Scofield Reference Bible* (New York, 1917), p. 1328.

[38]Lewis S. Chafer, *Major Bible Themes* (Grand Rapids: Eerdmans, 1966), p. 197.

[39]E.g., see Zane Hodges, *The Gospel Under Siege* (Dallas: Redencion Viva, 1981), and a response by John F. MacArthur, Jr., *The Gospel According to Jesus* (Grand Rapids: Zondervan, 1988), answered by Hodges in *A Biblical Reply to Lordship Salvation: Absolutely Free!* (Grand Rapids: Zondervan, 1989).

[40]*Christ Alone Exalted: in the Perfection and Encouragements of the Saints, Notwithstanding Sins and Trials. Being the Complete Works of Tobias Crisp, D. D.* (London: R. Nole for J. Murgatroyd, 1791), 2:444.

[41]A. H. Newman, "Antinomianism," in *Schaff-Herzog Encyclopedia* 1:201.

[42]*The Grace of Law*, p. 212. Cf., "No man can have assurance, that he is justified, unlesse he be in some measure sanctified. . . . Dost thou endeavour to keepe a good conscience

the cream of faith. It is inseparable from each exercise of faith. Assurance grows by faith in the promises of God, by inward evidences of grace, and by the witness of the Spirit. Each of these kinds of assurance should be diligently prayed for and pursued; none should be separated from the others for undue emphasis on one will lead to a distortion of others.[43] For each the believer is dependent ultimately upon the application of the Holy Spirit. Salvation and assurance are "of the Lord" (Jonah 2:9).

By grace, faith will bear the fruit of varying degrees of assurance. For Christ's sake, faith must triumph because it rests on the triune God and His Word. Christians ought not to despair when they do not feel its triumph, but turn ever more fully to God's promise in Christ, recognizing that their certainty, both objective and subjective, lies wholly in Christ. As B. B. Warfield wrote: "It is not faith that saves, but faith in Jesus Christ. . . . It is not, strictly speaking, even faith in Christ that saves, but Christ that saves through faith. The saving power resides exclusively, not in the act of faith or the attitude of faith or the nature of faith, but in the object of faith; and in this the whole biblical representation centres, so that we could not more radically misconceive [Scripture] than by transferring to faith even the smallest fraction of that saving energy which is attributed in the Scriptures solely to Christ Himself."[44]

Christ shall ultimately win the day in believers through the instrument of faith. Since He rules in them as Lord, Calvin affirmed, doubt can storm the fort, but it shall never gain the victory.[45] This is the essence of faith and assurance as well as of Scripture, Reformation and post-Reformation theology, and life itself. "For of him, and through him, and to him, are all things: to whom be glory for ever" (Romans 11:36).

---

and to walke uprightly before God; then it is certaine that thou art justified" (George Downame, *The Covenant of Grace*, p. 35); "You may know there is life by the beating of the pulses: a living faith will be active, and bewray itself in some gracious effects. . . . Obedience is an inseparable companion of justification" (*The Complete Works of Thomas Manton, D. D.* [reprint ed., Worthington, Penn: Maranatha Publications, 1980], 4:237ff.).

[43]Ernest Reisinger asserts that to hold to assurance by means of the first (i.e., the promises of God) without affirming the second (i.e., Christian character and conduct) and third (i.e., the Spirit's witness), is *antinomianism*. To hold exclusively to the second without the first and third is *legalism*; to maintain the third at the expense of the first two, is "either *hypocrisy* or the *deepest self-delusion or fantasy*" (*Today's Evangelism: Its Message and Methods* [Phillipsburg, N.J.: Craig Press, 1982], pp. 127ff.).

[44]*Biblical and Theological Studies*, p. 425.

[45]Inst. 3.2.39.

APPENDIX: THE DUTCH SECOND REFORMATION (*DE NADERE REFORMATIE*)

The Dutch Reformation may be divided into four periods: the Lutheran period (1517-26), the Sacramentarian period (1526-31), the Anabaptist period (1531-45),[1] and the most influential, the period of Calvinist infiltration.[2] The Calvinist penetration into the Netherlands (southern Netherlands, c. 1545; northern, c. 1560) was far more influential from the start than its number of adherents might suggest. But then Dutch Calvinism did not flower profusely until the seventeenth century, cultivated by the Synod of Dort (1618-19) and fortified by *De Nadere Reformatie*, a primarily seventeenth-and early eighteenth-century movement paralleling English Puritanism. The *Nadere Reformatie* dates from such early representatives as Jean Taffin (1528-1602)[3] and Willem Teellinck (1579-1629),[4] to its last brilliant contributors, Alexander Comrie (1706-74)[5] and Theodorus van der Groe (1705-84).[6]

[1]Anabaptists were martyred until the 1570s in the Netherlands, though the movement lost impetus by 1545.

[2]W. Robert Godfrey, "Calvin and Calvinism in the Netherlands," in *John Calvin: His Influence in the Western World*, ed. W. Stanford Reid, pp. 95-122; Walter Lagerwey, "The History of Calvinism in the Netherlands," in *The Rise and Development of Calvinism*, ed. John Bratt, pp. 63-102; Jerry D. van der Veen, "Adoption of Calvinism in the Reformed Church in the Netherlands" (B.S.T. thesis, Biblical Seminary in New York, 1951); J. P. Elliott, "Protestantization in the Northern Netherlands: A Case Study — The Classis of Dordrecht 1572-1640," 2 vols. (Ph.D. dissertation, Columbia University, 1990).

[3]S. van der Linde, "Jean Taffin: eerste pleiter voor 'Nadere Reformatie' in Nederland," *Theologia Reformata* 25 (1982):6-29; and, *Jean Taffin: Hofprediker en raadsheer van Willem van Oranje* (Amsterdam: Ton Bolland, 1982).

[4]See pp. 98-108 above.

[5]See chapter 8 above.

[6]In addition to sources previously cited relative to Teellinck, Comrie, Witsius, and Ames (see pp. 98-99n, 215n, 255n, 277n above), studies published on Dutch Second

Appendix

The Term *Nadere Reformatie*

The term *Nadere Reformatie* is a problem[7] because it allows for no standard English translation of "nadere." Literally, *Nadere Reformatie* means a nearer, more intimate, or more precise Reformation. Its

Reformation divines include (the authors' names are within parentheses, cf. bibliography): Bogerman (van Itterzon, Edema van der Tuuk); W. à Brakel (Los); Colonius (Hoek); Hommius (Wijminga); Hoornbeeck (Hofmeyr, Ypma); Koelman (Janse, Krull); van Lodenstein (Proost, Slagboom, Trimp); Lubbertus (van der Woude); Rivetus (Honders, van Opstal); Saldenus (van den End); Schortinghuis (Kromsigt, de Vrijer, Spronck); Sluiter (Blokland); Smytegelt (de Vrijer); Taffin (van der Linde); Trigland (ter Haar); Voetius (van Andel, Bouwman, Duker, Janse, McCahagan, Steenblok); Udemans (Fieret, Meertens, Vergunst); Voetius (van Oort); Walaeus (De Lind van Wijngaarden); Wittewrongel (Groenendijk).

For an introduction to leading Second Reformation divines, see B. Glasius, ed., *Godgeleerd Nederland: Biographisch Woordenboek van Nederlandsche Godgeleerden*, 3 vols. ('s-Hertogenbosch: Gebr. Muller, 1851-56); Sietse Douwes van Veen, *Voor tweehonderd jaren: Schetsen van het leven onzer Gereformeerde Vaderen*, 2nd ed. (Utrecht: Kemink & Zoon, 1905); J. P. de Bie and J. Loosjes, eds., *Biographisch Woordenboek der Protestantsche Godgeleerden in Nederland*, 5 vols. ('s-Gravenhage: Martinus Nijhoff, 1907-1943); *Christelijke Encyclopedie*, 6 vols., 2nd ed. (Kampen: J. H. Kok, 1959); K. Exalto, *Beleefd Geloof: Acht schetsen van gereformeerde theologen uit de 17e Eeuw* (Amsterdam: Ton Bolland, 1974), and *De Kracht der Religie: Tien schetsen van Gereformeerde 'Oude Schrijvers' uit de 17e en 18e Eeuw* (Urk: De Vuurtoren, 1976); H. Florijn, ed., *Hollandse Geloofshelden* (Utrecht: De Banier, 1981); W. van Gorsel, *De IJver voor Zijn Huis: De Nadere Reformatie en haar belangrijkste vertegenwoordigers*; C. J. Malan, *Die Nadere Reformasie* (Potchefstroom: Potchefstroomse Universiteit vir CHO, 1981); H. Florijn, *100 Portretten van Godgeleerden in Nederland uit de 16e, 17e, 18e Eeuw* (Utrecht: Den Hertog, 1982); *Biografisch Lexicon voor de Geschiedenis van het Nederlandse Protestantisme*, 3 vols.; W. van't Spijker, et al., *De Nadere Reformatie: Beschrijving van haar voornaamste vertegenwoordigers* ('s-Gravenhage: Boekencentrum, 1986); W. van't Spijker, ed., *De Nadere Reformatie en het Gereformeerd Piëtisme*; Joel R. Beeke, "Biographies of Dutch Second Reformation Divines," *Banner of Truth* 54, 2 (1988) through 56, 3 (1990); Fred A. van Lieburg, *Levens van vromen: Gereformeerde piëtisme in de achttiende eeuw* (Kampen: De Groot, 1991); Teunis Brienen, et al., *Figuren en thema's van de Nadere Reformatie*, 3 vols. (Kampen: De Groot, 1987-93). Stoeffler, *The Rise of Evangelical Pietism*, pp. 109-68, covers twelve Second Reformation divines in varying depth and quality; Graafland, *De Zekerheid van het Geloof*, pp. 138-244, concentrates on the doctrine of faith and assurance in fourteen Second Reformation theologians; De Boer, *De Verzegeling met de Heilige Geest volgens de opvatting van de Nadere Reformatie*, examines the soteriological thought of fourteen Second Reformation divines.

For bibliography of the Dutch Second Reformation, see P. L. Eggermont, "Bibliographie van het Nederlandse Piëtisme in de zeventiende en achttiende eeuw," *Documentatieblad 18e eeuw* 3 (1969):17-31; W. van Gent, *Bibliotheek van oude schrijvers* (Rotterdam: Lindebergs, 1979); J. van der Haar, *Schatkamer van de Gereformeerde Theologie in Nederland (c. 1600-c.1800): Bibliografisch Onderzoek* (Veenendaal: Antiquariaat Kool, 1987).

[7]The term was already used by Jean Taffin. Cf. L. F. Groenendijk, "De Oorsprong van de uitdrukking 'Nadere Reformatie,'" *Documentatieblad Nadere Reformatie* 9

[287]

emphasis is the working out of the Reformation more intensively in people's lives, in the church's worship, and in society.

Those who attempt to translate the term *Nadere Reformatie* inevitably color the translation with their own judgments of its significance. For example, the term has been translated as "Further Reformation," which isn't accurate because it implies that the first Reformation did not go far enough. The *Nadere Reformatie* divines did not intend that at all. Rather, they sought to *apply* Reformation truths to the soul's daily experience and to practical, daily living. To avoid that false implication, Cornelis Graafland suggests the terms *Continuing Reformation* or *Second Reformation*. The term *continuing* has disadvantages, however: it does not sufficiently distinguish the *Nadere Reformatie* from the Reformation proper, it is of recent usage in English,[8] and it sounds awkward.

I have chosen to use "Dutch Second Reformation" or "Second Reformation." While this translation misses the Dutch term's emphasis on continuity,[9] it has a long pedigree and appears to be gaining acceptance among scholars.[10] Moreover, "Second Reformation" was a term already used by some Dutch divines of that movement. For example, Jacobus Koelman (1632-1695), who had much contact with Scotland's Second Reformation, spoke of the Dutch movement as a "Second Reformation" and a "second purging."[11]

I prefer not to use "Dutch Precisianism," "Dutch Puritanism," or "Dutch Pietism," because of the following reasons. Dutch Precisianism is too pejorative. It makes the *Nadere Reformatie* sound too legalistic (*wettisch*). It is true that most Second Reformation divines promoted a negative ethic. Gisbertus Voetius, for example, forbade such practices as "visiting public houses, playing with dice, the

---

(1985):128-34; S. van der Linde, "Jean Taffin: eerste pleiter voor 'Nadere Reformatie' in Nederland," *Theologia Reformata* 25 (1982):7ff.; van't Spijker, *De Nadere Reformatie en het Gereformeerd Piëtisme*, pp. 5ff.

[8]Jonathan Neil Gerstner, *The Thousand Generation Covenant: Dutch Reformed Covenant Theology and Group Identity in Colonial South Africa, 1652-1814* (Leiden: E. J. Brill, 1991), pp. 75ff.

[9]Ibid., p. 75n.

[10]Cornelis Pronk, "The Dutch Puritans," *The Banner of Truth*, nos. 154-55 (July-August 1976):1-10; J. W. Hofmeyr, "The Doctrine of Calvin as Transmitted in the South African Context by Among Others the *Oude Schrijvers*," in *Calvinus Reformator: His contribution to Theology, Church and Society* (Potchefstroom: Potchefstroom University for Christian Higher Education, 1983), p. 260.

[11]*Christelijke Encyclopedie* 5:128.

wearing of luxurious clothes, dancing, drunkenness, revelry, smoking and the wearing of wigs." Nevertheless, such precisianism was not an end in itself. Rather, it was cultivated in the face of the "alleged worldliness then prevailing" and as a means of sustaining and developing individual faith and conduct against spiritual shallowness.[12]

Secondly, the *Nadere Reformatie* is in fact the Dutch counterpart to English Puritanism (and in some senses, to the Scottish Covenanters). The link between these movements is strong historically and theologically.[13] Keith Sprunger has shown that during the seventeenth century tens of thousands of Anglo-Scottish believers of Puritan persuasion lived in the Netherlands. At one point, those believers represented more than 40 congregations and 350 ministers. The Dutch government allowed them to organize churches and form an English classis within the Dutch Reformed Church. The Dutch churches even ordained ministers for the Scots. The presence of so many English and Scottish Puritans was bound to have some influence upon the Dutch churches. "Many Dutch Reformed ministers were impressed by the practical divinity of the English Puritans," Cornelis Pronk says. "They saw it as a healthy corrective to the dry intellectualistic sermonizing that was becoming the trend in their churches."[14] And Douglas MacMillan wrote:

> Both Puritans and Covenanters were to interact very intimately with religious life in the Netherlands. These great spiritual movements were concerned with Second Reformation issues and that concern was to shape the course of the 17th century in England and Scotland. Events there were, in turn, to reach deeply into the Netherlands, influencing its theology, deepening its spirituality, and linking it closely into the traumatic experiences of the British Church. We have to learn to look at the Second Reformation not as a small, localised, Scottish, or even British, phenomenon but as a movement of international significance.[15]

[12]Martin H. Prozesky, "The Emergence of Dutch Pietism," *Journal of Ecclesiastical History* 28 (1977):33.

[13]For connections between seventeenth-century English and Dutch Calvinism, see especially the writings of Keith Sprunger, *Dutch Puritanism; The Learned Doctor William Ames: Dutch Backgrounds of English and American Puritanism,* and *Trumpets From The Tower: English Puritan Printing in the Netherlands 1600-1640* (Leiden: E.J. Brill, 1994). Cf. MacMillan, "The Connection between 17th Century British and Dutch Calvinism," in *Not by Might nor by Power,* 1988 Westminster Conference papers, pp. 22-31.

[14]"The Dutch Puritans," *Banner of Truth,* nos. 154-55 (July-August, 1976):3.

[15]"The Connection between 17th Century British and Dutch Calvinism," in *Not by Might nor by Power,* p. 24. Willem Jan op't Hof also shows the influence of Dutch refugee

The divines of British Puritanism and the *Nadere Reformatie* held each other in high esteem. They enriched each other through personal contact and their writings, both their Latin treatises and the many books translated from English into Dutch.[16] More Reformed theological books were printed in the seventeenth century in the Netherlands than in all other countries combined.[17] These movements embraced similar ideals and bore similar roles: to foster God-glorifying experiential piety and ethical precision in individuals, churches, and nations.

Despite similar outlooks, these parallel movements developed historically and theologically distinctive identities. To call the *Nadere Reformatie* "Dutch Puritanism" obscures the endemic nature of the Dutch movement. Hendrikus Berkhof is too simplistic in saying that the Second Reformation resulted merely from "the practical piety of the English Calvinists blowing over to the Netherlands."[18] Though British Puritanism was a primary influence on the *Nadere Reformatie*, particularly in its stress on the need for a personal, domestic, and congregational life of experimental and practical godliness,[19] it was not an exclusive influence. Non-English factors also contributed.[20]

---

congregations in England, concluding that the Dutch congregations in England were the foundation of the Puritanization of spiritual life in the Netherlands (*Engelse pietistische geschriften in het Nederlands, 1598-1622*, p. 639).

[16]"From 1598 to 1622 a total of 114 editions were issued of a total of 60 translations. These 60 translations concern works by . . . twenty-two English authors. . . . Two authors are numerically preeminent among them: Cowper (18 editions of 10 translations) and Perkins (71 editions of 29 translations). Indeed, Perkins alone eclipses all the others taken together. . . . Auction catalogues show that Udemans possessed 20 Puritan books in Latin and 57 in English. Similarly, Voetius possessed 30 works in Latin and 270 in English. . . . A rough estimate for the period from 1623-1699 gives 260 new translations, 580 editions and 100 new translators. . . . The flow of translations continued unabated during the whole of the seventeenth century" (ibid., pp. 636-37, 640, 645).

[17]In the seventeenth century, more than two thousand Reformed, pietistic titles were printed in Dutch, of which more than one-third were translations from Anglo-Saxon Puritan works. See Fred A. van Lieburg, "From Pure Church to Pious Culture: The Further Reformation in the Seventeenth-Century Dutch Republic," in *Later Calvinism: International Perspectives*, ed. W. Fred Graham (Kirksville, Mo.: Sixteenth Century Journal Publishers, 1994), pp. 423-425; C. W. Schoneveld, *Intertraffic of the Mind* (Leiden: E. J. Brill, 1983); Keith Sprunger, *Dutch Puritanism*, p. 307, and *Trumpets from the Tower: English Puritan Printing in the Netherlands 1600-1640*.

[18]*Geschiedenis der Kerk* (Nijkerk: G. F. Callenbach, 1955), p. 228.

[19]Op't Hof, *Engelse piëtistische geschriften in het Nederlands, 1598-1622*, pp. 583-97, 627-35, 645-46; Cornelis Graafland, "De Invloed van het Puritanisme op het Ontstaan van het Gereformeerd Piëtisme in Nederland," *Documentatieblad Nadere Reformatie* 7, 1 (1983):1-19. Graafland details influences on preaching, the art of meditation, casuistry, covenanting, the administration of the Lord's Supper, and eschatology.

[20]Ibid., pp. 2, 15-16.

In some respects, the Dutch movement was more Puritan than English Puritanism itself. As Jonathan Gerstner says, "In England from an orthodox Reformed perspective, for all but a short period under Cromwell, there were always grossly unbiblical things to fight: the presence of bishops, superstitious rites in the Book of Common Prayer, vestments, etc. In the Netherlands none of these were present, and the task was all the more subtle. Defenders of the *status quo* were not so clearly unreformed as in England. In this context the true spirit of Puritanism came to the fore."[21]

Divines of the Dutch Second Reformation were, generally speaking, less interested in reforming the government and in the organization of the church (as long as the church was not controlled by the state) than were their English brethren. Their theological emphases also varied at times. I have shown that variations existed on the doctrine of assurance.[22] Then too, the Dutch were more inclined to emphasize theology as a science, whereas the English emphasized the practical aspects of theology.[23] Sprunger notes that William Ames found the Dutch too intellectual and not sufficiently practical, and therefore promoted Puritan piety in an effort to "make Dutchmen into Puritans."[24] These variations are not sufficiently respected when the Dutch movement is narrowly defined as Dutch Puritanism.[25]

Dutch Pietism might initially seem to be an acceptable translation of *Nadere Reformatie*. It has been widely used to show the movement's pietistic emphasis.[26] However, that term is also

[21]Gerstner, *Thousand Generation Covenant*, pp. 77-78.

[22]See pp. 276-78 above.

[23]Pronk, *The Banner of Truth*, nos. 154-55 (July-August, 1976):6. Gerstner wrote: "Dutch Reformed thought while retaining a strong emphasis on the pulpit, produced a remarkable number of theological works, the majority addressed to the average person. Catechism preaching was perhaps part of the reason, but it seems they possessed a greater tendency towards system building" (*Thousand Generation Covenant*, p. 78). Cf. Hugo Visscher, *Guilielmus Amesius, Zijn Leven en Werken* (Haarlem: J. M. Stap, 1894).

[24]*The Learned Doctor Ames: Dutch Backgrounds of English and American Puritanism*, 260. Cf. Hugo Visscher, *Guilielmus Ames, Zijn Leven en Werken* (Haarlem: J.M. Stap, 1894).

[25]This term has been used more accurately to depict English-speaking Puritan churches in the Netherlands (cf. Douglas Campbell, *The Puritan in Holland, England, and America*, 4th ed., 2 vols. [New York: Harper and Brothers, 1892]; Sprunger, *Dutch Puritanism*; T. Brienen, *De prediking van de Nadere Reformatie* [Amsterdam: Ton Bolland, 1974]). Van der Linde prefers "English Puritanism in the Netherlands" to "Dutch Puritanism," since the English Puritans in the Netherlands confined themselves largely to their own circles ("Jean Taffin: eerste pleiter voor 'Nadere Reformatie' in Nederland," *Theologia Reformata* 25 [1982]: 6ff.). Then too, the problem of using English Puritanism is compounded by the difficulty of defining Puritanism (cf. pp. 82-83n above).

[26]"The word 'Pietist' originally indicated 'an affected and indeed feigned kind of

problematic, for three reasons: First, it too strongly suggests an intimate German connection.[27] The *Nadere Reformatie* predates Spener's appeal for reform by nearly half a century and became a more extensive movement than German Pietism. Second, Pietism in German Lutheranism was more concerned with the believer's inner life than with transforming society, whereas most *Nadere Reformatie* divines were concerned with both.[28] And third, Pietism is usually regarded as a protest against Protestant scholastic theology and doctrinal precision, whereas many *Nadere Reformatie* divines helped formulate Reformed orthodoxy and analyze doctrine. As Gerstner writes, "Gisbertus Voetius is generally acknowledged as both the greatest Dutch Reformed scholastic theologian and one of the greatest representatives of the Continuing Reformation. Pietism as it would later develop would more and more show marked antipathy for all but the most simple doctrinal concepts."[29]

Confusing misconceptions arise when Pietism is used to describe the Second Reformation, for these terms represent distinct

righteousness.' So writes K. D. Schmidt, *Grundriss der Kirchengeschichte*, 5th ed., Göttingen 1967, p. 416. M. Schmidt reports that the term became established after J. Feller, Professor of Poetry at Leipzig, used it with favourable connotations in two popular verses in 1689. See M. Schmidt, 'Pietismus' in *Die Religion in geschichte und Gegenwart*, 3rd ed., Tubingen 1961, v. col. 374" (Prozesky, "The Emergence of Dutch Pietism," *Journal of Ecclesiastical History* 28 [1977]:29-37).

[27]Stoeffler (*The Rise of Evangelical Pietism*, pp. 1-23) and Tanis (*Dutch Calvinistic Pietism in the Middle Colonies: A Study in the Life and Theology of Theodorus Jacobus Frelinghuysen* [The Hague: Martinus Nijhoff, 1967] and "The Heidelberg Catechism in the Hands of the Calvinistic Pietists," *Reformed Review* 24 [1970-71]:154-61) follow German church historians in using "Dutch Pietism," notably Heppe (*Geschichte des Pietismus und der Mystik in der Reformierten Kirche, namentlich der Niederlande*) and Albrecht Ritschl (*Geschichte des Pietismus*, 3 vols. [Bonn: Marcus, 1880-86]).

For the influence of German Pietism on the Dutch Second Reformation, see Graafland, "De Gereformeerde Orthodoxie en het Piëtisme in Nederland," *Nederlands Theologisch Tijdschrift* 19 (1965):466-79; J. Steven O'Malley, *Pilgrimage of Faith: The Legacy of the Otterbeins* (Metuchen, N.J.: The Scarecrow Press, 1973); Stoeffler, *The Rise of Evangelical Pietism*; sources listed on pp. 4-5n above.

[28]S. van der Linde, *Vromen en Verlichten: Twee eeuwen Protestantse Geloofsbeleving 1650-1850* (Utrecht: Aartsbisschoppelijk Museum Utrecht, 1974), p. 2; Gerstner, *Thousand Generation Covenant*, p. 76.

[29]Ibid., p. 76. Graafland says Dutch Second Reformation divines were united in emphasizing the importance of doctrine. Many of them, including the Teellincks and the à Brakels, viewed themselves as being free from "scholasticizing" in formulating doctrine but were actually immersed in it. Flexibility and variety in terms of scholastic methodology were welcomed. No Second Reformation divine viewed Reformed scholasticism as cold and irrelevant, unlike German Pietists. Even Cocceius, known for his approach of biblical theology in a covenantal matrix, used a substantial amount of

movements that vary in several important areas.[30] German Pietism, English Puritanism, and the Dutch Second Reformation had much in common. Each was rooted deeply in the sixteenth-century Reformation and longed for more thorough reform; yet each movement showed a distinct historical, theological, and spiritual character. All three movements began within their respective churches, but, over time, developed into distinctive phenomena, partly formed by the reactions of authorities and the responses of different groups in society. Despite similar forms of religious experience and ethos, they developed into complex, religious and social movements that spanned all classes of society.[31]

The Essence of the Dutch Second Reformation

Several developments furthered the emergence of the Dutch Second Reformation. The push for a state church in the Netherlands was one factor. During the Reformation in the Netherlands, strenuous efforts were made to replace the Roman Catholic Church with the Reformed Church as the people's church (*volkskerk*). At that time, one-tenth of the Dutch people were members of the Reformed Church. By 1650 more than half of the Dutch people were members of the Reformed Church, which had preferred status (*bevoorrechte*) with the government.[32]

The church's growth, which was related more to the number of members (*lidmaten*) than the number of so-called lovers (*liefhebbers*) of Reformed religion, had dire consequences for spiritual life.

---

scholastic methodology (ibid., pp. 68-75). Muller's conclusions about Reformed scholasticism (see p. 2n above) hold true also for the Dutch Second Reformation divines. Cf. Charles McCoy, "The Covenant Theology of Johannes Cocceius" (Ph.D. dissertation, Yale, 1957); H. B. Visser, *De Geschiedenis van den Sabbatstrijd onder de Gereformeerden in de Zeventiende Eeuw* (Utrecht: Kemink en Zoon, 1939).

[30]Van der Linde, "Jean Taffin: eerste pleiter voor 'Nadere Reformatie' in Nederland," *Theologia Reformata* 25 (1982):7.

[31]W. van't Spijker, "De Nadere Reformatie," in *De Nadere Reformatie: Beschrijving van haar voornaamste vertegenwoordigers*, pp. 6-16; Mary Fulbrook, *Piety and Politics: Religion and the Rise of Absolutism in England* (Cambridge: University Press, 1983), p. 19.

[32]Stoeffler, *The Rise of Evangelical Pietism*, pp. 115-16; A. Th. van Deursen, "Dutch Reformed Parish Life in the Second Half of the Seventeenth Century," in *Bunyan in England and Abroad: Papers Delivered at the Vrije University Amersterdam, 1988* (Amsterdam: Vrije University Press, 1990), pp. 105-120. Cf. Wiebe Bergsma, "The Low Countries," in *The Reformation in National Context*, ed. Bob Scribner, Roy Porter, and Mikuláš Teich (Cambridge: University Press, 1994), pp. 74-75. For political,

Catechetical and moral standards for admission to membership declined. Young adults often joined the church out of custom, more for the sake of their parents than by conscious choice. Abraham Kuyper claimed that the additional population that flooded into the church destroyed its Reformed distinctiveness. "From that moment on it was impossible to maintain church discipline," Kuyper said.[33] Many Calvinist leaders abandoned their original model of the church with its pure communion table. People participated in the Lord's Supper to demonstrate social respectability within their local communities more than to confess personal, saving faith in Jesus Christ. The church, in effect, surrendered to the public and to the regents. The pure church became the people's church, just as the regents had desired.

People were also confused about the role of the church. Many thought that being anti-Roman Catholic meant being Reformed. Nominal church membership along with loose living became the norm. Spiritual and ethical sterility increased as material property grew. The United East-India Company, formed in 1602, and other Dutch companies ushered in unparalleled affluence. People increasingly lived for this life rather than for the world to come.

The relationship between church and state also shifted as the government became more involved in church matters and church discipline.[34] The state controlled the universities where Reformed ministers were being trained. And those universities were showing the increasing influence of Rationalism, particularly via the philosophies of Descartes and Spinoza.

These spiritual, social, and intellectual developments clashed with historic Dutch Calvinism, which emphasized sound doctrine and piety. The stipulations that the Synod of Dort had made about the supervision of pastors, professors, and theological writings were not being followed.

---

ecclesiastical, social, and theological developments in the historical context of the Dutch Second Reformation, see *Documentatieblad Nadere Reformatie* 19 (1995):123-70.

[33]*E Voto Dordraceno* (Amsterdam: Höveker & Wormser, 1905), 3:215. Cf. van Lieburg, "From Pure Church to Pious Culture," p. 412.

[34]Jacobus Koelman, for example, "opposed governmental interference in church life on several fronts. He rejected the government's right to call ministers and to select elders and deacons. He fought against its low view of Christian living and its lack of maintaining Christian discipline in conjunction with the administration of the sacraments. And he staunchly opposed the use of read forms and the observance of church feast days" (Joel R. Beeke, "Jacobus Koelman," *The Banner of Truth* 55 [1989]:27).

All of these developments, combined with the influence of English Puritanism, German Pietism, the Genevan reform,[35] and native Dutch influences (e.g., medieval mysticism,[36] the *Devotio Moderna*, and Anabaptism[37]— each of which emphasized sanctification), gave rise to the Dutch Second Reformation. Reflecting the concern of the Second Reformation, P. de Witte wrote, "Oh times, oh morals! What do parents do but bring up their children to become the prey of all kinds of seductive spirits, such as the papists, anabaptists, Arminians, and libertines? Yes, even to become the booty of the devil, to be the heirs of eternal damnation and the firewood of hell."[38]

The Dutch Second Reformation rose from the ashes of the burning expectations that had motivated the early Reformers. The Dutch Reformers had envisioned a theocratic society and church in which most of the people would be involved in personal and communal renewal. The Reformers frequently referred to the unbreakableness of a "threefold cord" consisting of God, the Netherlands, and the House of Orange. But the vision that the

---

[35]Genevan input came particularly through Jean Taffin, who studied under Calvin and Beza, and whose views are similar to those of the Teellincks, who in turn were primarily influenced by English Puritanism. Balke feels that op't Hof minimizes Taffin's influence in order to emphasize the role of the Teellincks in the Second Reformation (W. J. op't Hof, *De Bibliografie van Eewout Teellinck* [Kampen: De Groot Goudriaan, 1988]; W. J. op't Hof, C. A. de Niet, H. Uil, *Eewout Teellinck in handschriften* [Kampen: De Groot Goudriaan, 1989]). Cf. van der Linde, "Jean Taffin: eerste pleiter voor 'Nadere Reformatie' in Nederland," *Theologia Reformata* 25 (1982):6-29.

[36]Graafland, "De invloed van het Puritanisme op het ontstaan van het Gereformeerd Pietisme in Nederland," *Documentatieblad Nadere Reformatie* 7 (1983):11-12; op't Hof, *Engelse piëtistische geschriften in het Nederlands, 1598-1622*, pp. 599-600, 640.

[37]Stoeffler, *The Rise of Evangelical Pietism*, pp. 118ff. The *Devotio Moderna* was a devotional movement of the fifteenth and sixteenth centuries associated with the Brethren of the Common Life, their founder Gerard Groote, and their best-known writer, Thomas à Kempis (P. H. Davids, "Devotio Moderna," in *Evangelical Dictionary of Theology*, ed. Walter Elwell, p. 317). Cf. R. R. Post, *The Modern Devotion* (Leiden: E. J. Brill, 1968); T. P. van Zijl, *Gerard Groote, Ascetic and Reformer* (1340-1384) (Washington, D.C.: Catholic University of American Press, 1963); Albert Hyma, *The Brethren of the Common Life* (Grand Rapids: Eerdmans, 1950).

With regard to Anabaptism, op't Hof concludes that the Second Reformation "was one of the answers to the Anabaptist reproach that Reformed doctrine did not lead to sanctity of life" (*Engelse piëtistische geschriften in het Nederlands, 1598-1622*, pp. 640-41).

[38]Dedication of his *Catechesatie over den Heidelbergschen Catechismus*, cited in W. Verboom, *De Catechese van de Reformatie en de Nadere Reformatie* (Amsterdam: Buijten en Schipperheijn, 1986), p. 251.

Netherlands would become "the Israel of the West" in society and church proved unattainable.

Post-Reformed, orthodox Calvinist clergymen of pietistic stripe grieved over the failure of that dream. They faced the painful reality that most church members had not become more spiritual after the Reformation. Their followers, many of whom favored conventicles (*gezelschappen*)[39] more than formal worship, found that the church was no longer the communion of saints. At best it was a mixed multitude, and at worst, a Babylon or Egypt. Jodocus van Lodenstein's assessment of the Reformed Church in his day was typical of Second Reformation divines. He wrote, "Babylon of Babylons, a thousand times worse than that of the Papacy because of the light that she had but did not rightly use."[40] He went on to say that the church seemed more deformed than reformed. "There is no practicing of the truth, but a parroting of the words of the catechism is all that one finds among Reformed people," he said.[41]

Bernardus Smytegelt, another prominent Second Reformation divine, complained: "There are few converted preachers. Many of them are lazy idlers, vain fops. . . . Among external professors you will find much chaff and hardly a grain of wheat. There are heaps of external professors, and are they not indifferent and ungodly? What are they like in the families? Dear man! Do you not know how scarce pious parents are? How few use the Bible regularly in the home!

---

[39]In the Second Reformation a desire for intimate Christian fellowship led to the development of "gatherings of the godly" to explain the Scriptures and to share the experimental leadings of God with His people. These became called *gezelschappen* (literally, "fellowships") in the Netherlands. Fellowship, however, does not fully convey the meaning of *gezelschap*, which is usually translated as "conventicle," the term ascribed to parallel meetings in Scotland. (Similar meetings in English Puritanism were called "prophesyings" and in German Pietism, *collegiae pietatis*.) Conventicles were more successful in Scotland than in the Netherlands due to closer supervision by the presbyters. In the Netherlands *gezelschappen* were also spiritually beneficial to many and were supervised for a time but on occasion they turned into unsupervised, elitist groups that criticized sermons and promoted introspective spirituality. Cf. van't Spijker, "De Nadere Reformatie," in *De Nadere Reformatie: Beschrijving van haar voornaamste vertegenwoordigers*, p. 14; Fred A. van Lieburg, "Het gereformeerde conventikelwezen in de classis Dordrecht in de 17e en 18e eeuw," *Holland, regional-historisch tijdschrift* 23 (1991):2-21; Stoeffler, *The Rise of Evangelical Pietism*, p. 160; Osterhaven, "The Experiential Theology of Early Dutch Calvinism," *Reformed Review* 27 (1974):189.

[40]*J. van Lodensteyn's Negen Predicatien*, ed. Evarardus van der Hooght (Rotterdam: Gebr. Huge, n.d.), p. 197.

[41]Pieter Proost, *Jodocus van Lodenstein* (Amsterdam: J. Brandt en Zoon, 1880), pp. 133-34.

How few pray with each other, teach each other, and seek to lead each other toward heaven!"[42]

In opposition to increasing spiritual and moral laxity, an urgent call went out for personal, church,[43] and societal reform: *The scriptural appeal for sanctification must be zealously pursued; Reformation doctrine must be lived*, said Second Reformation divines. Worldly practices and luxuries must be rejected, so that the complete reformation of doctrine and life might be realized in the Netherlands. Many Second Reformation preachers maintained the ideological perspective that regarded the Netherlands as the New Israel led out of the Spanish house of bondage by God Himself.

S. van der Linde, a leading scholar on the Dutch Second Reformation, said that the movement must not be equated with "non-dogmatical" (*ondogmatisch*) Christendom; rather, its goal was to wed doctrine to the whole of daily life.[44] Van der Linde said, "The protest of the Second Reformation is not primarily against dogmatism as engendering a quenching of the Spirit, but much more against a certain *vitalism* as well as *secularism* whereby one observes the Spirit as being grieved."[45] In summary, "The Second Reformation sides entirely with the Reformation and levels criticism not so much against the *reformata* (the church which is reformed), but rather against the *reformanda* (the church which needs to be reformed)."[46]

Though the Second Reformation is preeminently concerned with spiritual life and experience, that concern is expressed in a variety of ways: "In Voetius we have the church-organizer, in Ames a very original theologian, in Teellinck and à Brakel, divines of practical religion, and in Lodensteyn and Saldenus, the men of 'mysticism,' cross-bearing, and meditation upon the life to come," wrote van der Linde.[47]

Despite those differing emphases, van der Linde concluded there

---

[42]*Des Christens Eenige Troost in Leven en Sterven, of Verklaringe over den Heidelbergschen Catechismus in LII Predicatien; Benevens V Belydenis-Predicatien* (Middelburg: Ottho en Pieter van Thol, Den Haag, en A. L. en M. H. Callenfels, 1747), p. 336.

[43]For the ecclesiology of the Second Reformation, see van der Linde, *Opgang en voortgang der reformatie*, pp. 189-200.

[44]"De Godservaring bij W. Teellinck, D. G. à Brakel en A. Comrie," *Theologia Reformata* 16 (1973):205.

[45]"Het Werk van de Heilige Geest in de Gemeente: Een appreciatie van de Nadere Reformatie," *Nederlands Theologisch Tijdschrift* 10 (1956):3.

[46]"De betekenis van de Nadere Reformatie voor Kerk en Theologie," *Kerk en Theologie* 5 (1954):216.

[47]Ibid., p. 218.

is an underlying element of precision in the Second Reformation that is inseparable from a fervent desire to counteract impiety with a piety that "consciously consecrates all of life to God."[48]

Several attempts have been made to define the core of the Dutch Second Reformation as a logical development from and application of the Reformation proper.[49] Witsius emphasized that the motto, "the Reformed church needs to be ever reforming" (*ecclesia reformata, semper reformanda*) applies only to the church's life and not to doctrine since Reformation doctrine was soundly established. Second Reformation preachers felt that the body of the church had been renewed in the "first" Reformation, but this renewal had yet to be carried by the Spirit into head and heart, hands and feet in a vital, practical way. Most of these ministers were convinced they were upholding Reformed orthodoxy, though some pointed out defects in the Reformation era. For example, Teellinck chided the Reformers for being more concerned with the reformation of doctrine than of life, with justification than sanctification.[50]

Heppe defined the Second Reformation as "a striving for the completion of the church reformation of the sixteenth century (as being a mere reform of doctrine) by way of a revival of piety or by a reformation of life."[51] J. W. Hofmeyr stated, "Although this movement also had other spiritual fathers, it can be contended that the central thrust of the Second Reformation (which involves a personal spiritual piety, an articulated ecclesiology and a theocratic outlook on society) is broadly derived from Calvin. It should therefore be regarded not as a correction but as a development of the Reformation."[52]

And van Genderen concluded: "By this term, *Nadere Reformatie*, we mean a movement in the 17th century which was a reaction

---

[48]*Het Gereformeerde Protestantisme* (Nijkerk: G. F. Callenbach, 1957), p. 9.

[49]Gerstner, *Thousand Generation Covenant*, pp. 75-76; F. G. M. Broeyer, "Het begrip Nadere Reformatie," *Documentatieblad Nadere Reformatie* 12 (1988):51-57; Cornelis Graafland, "De verhouding Reformatie en Nadere Reformatie een voortgaand onderzoek," *Documentatieblad Nadere Reformatie* 17 (1993):94-111.

[50]Cornelis Graafland, "Kernen en contouren van de Nadere Reformatie," in *De Nadere Reformatie: Beschrijving van haar voornaamste vertegenwoordigers*, pp. 351-52. Cf. W. J. op't Hof, "Gisbertus Voetius' evaluatie van de Reformatie," *Theologia Reformata* 32 (1989):211-42.

[51]*Geschichte des Pietismus und der Mystik in der Reformierten Kirche, namentlich der Niederlande*, p. 6.

[52]"The Doctrine of Calvin as Transmitted in the South African Context by Among Others the *Oude Schrijvers*," in *Calvinus Reformator: His contribution to Theology, Church and Society*, p. 260.

against dead orthodoxy and secularisation of Christianity in the Church of the Reformation and which insisted on the practise of faith. . . . This movement is not meant as a correction of the Reformation but as the consequence of it."[53] Graafland referred to the Dutch Second Reformation as a movement "which turned against the generally poor conditions prevailing in the Reformed church. . . to achieve a radical and complete sanctification of all facets of life [through a] deepening and broadening of the sixteenth-century Reformation."[54] P. B. van der Watt's definition of the Second Reformation is paraphrased by Hofmeyr as follows:

> [The Second Reformation] revolted against the unspiritual state of the nation, ministers, and congregations. They plead also for a personal commitment to Christ. The experienced and tested religion is to them of central importance. Although nothing is done to undermine the church, the office, the sacrament, and the covenant, they regard rebirth as the priority. They also assume a reasonably strong Puritan point of view. They plead for the observance of the Sabbath and the carrying out of the demands of the Lord. The church must be pure and should be cleansed of all that is unholy. Finally, they had a high regard for the Scriptures and for the Heidelberg Catechism.[55]

Finally, scholars responsible for the periodical *Documentatieblad Nadere Reformatie* offer two, well-stated definitions of the Dutch Second Reformation.[56] The first definition, formulated in 1983, is the following:

> This movement within the Nederduits Gereformeerde Kerk, (Dutch Reformed Church), while opposing generally prevailing abuses and misconceptions and pursuing the broadening and progressive advancement of the sixteenth-century Reformation, urges and strives with prophetic zeal for both the inner experience

---

[53]*Herman Witsius: Bijdrage tot de Kennis der Gereformeerde Theologie*, p. 264; see pp. 220-25 for an exposition of this summary.

[54]"De Nadere Reformatie en haar culturele context," in *Met het woord in de Tijd*, ed. L. Westland ('s-Gravenhage: Boekencentrum, 1985), pp. 117-38.

[55]*Die Nederduitse Gereformeerde Kerk, 1652-1824* (Pretoria: N. G. Kerkboekhandel, 1976), 1:83, cited in "The Doctrine of Calvin as Transmitted in the South African Context by Among Others the *Oude Schrijvers*," in *Calvinus Reformator: His contribution to Theology, Church and Society*, p. 262.

[56]Those scholars now have an officially organized society in the Netherlands, *Stichting Studie der Nadere Reformatie* with branches in the United States and South Africa. The goal of the SSNR is to promote in-depth study of the Dutch Second Reformation.

of Reformed doctrine and personal sanctification, as well as the radical and total sanctification of all spheres of life.

The second definition, formulated in 1995, is more refined:

The Dutch Second Reformation is that movement within the Neder-duits Gereformeerde Kerk during the seventeenth and eighteenth centuries, which, as a reaction to the declension or absence of a living faith, made both the personal experience of faith and godliness matters of central importance. From that perspective the movement formulated substantial and procedural reformation initiatives, submitting them to the proper ecclesiastical, political, and social agencies, and/or in conformity therewith, pursued in both word and deed a further reformation of the church, society, and state.[57]

These definitions of the Dutch Second Reformation are necessarily somewhat simplistic. As Graafland points out, the Second Reformation had no organizational structure beyond a strong feeling of spiritual kinship among its divines. At times this led to small organizations, such as the "Utrecht Circle" under the leadership of Voetius, or to programs for action, such as those promoted by the leadership of Willem Teellinck and Jacobus Koelman. For the most part, however, each divine of the Second Reformation stressed the necessity of reform to his own parishioners. That call to reform naturally varied according to locality and generation.[58]

Due to this lack of organization and an increasing emphasis on the experiential life of the soul, the Second Reformation's initial call to action in every sphere of life diminished rapidly.[59] For example, in its earlier, so-called *classical* period, the Second Reformation strongly opposed a state-dominated church and worked strenuously for the church's independence. Opposition from government and citizens, however, made it difficult to retain this position.

---

[57]*Documentatieblad Nadere Reformatie* 7 (1983):109; 19 (1995):108, translated by Bartel Elshout in his *The Pastoral and Practical Theology of Wilhelmus à Brakel* (Grand Rapids: Reformation Heritage Books, 1997), 9.

[58]Graafland, "Kernen en contouren van de Nadere Reformatie," in *De Nadere Reformatie: Beschrijving van haar voornaamste vertegenwoordigers*, p. 350. Cf. Fred A. Lieburg, *De Nadere Reformatie in Utrecht ten tijde van Voetius* (Rotterdam: Lindenberg, 1989); Joel R. Beeke, "Gisbertus Voetius: Toward a Reformed Marriage of Knowledge and Piety," in *Protestant Scholasticism: Essays in Reassessment*, ed. Carl Trueman and R. Scott Clark (Carlisle: Paternoster, 1998); C. J. Meeuse, "De visie van Koelman op de puriteinen," pp. 44-61.

[59]Balke is of the opinion that this spirit of religious-social activism only applies to the prologue of the Second Reformation. For the Second Reformation on missions, see van der Linde, "De Nadere Reformatie en de zending," *Theologia Reformata* 10 (1967):5-16.

Anabaptist tendencies towards isolation increased with time. Various sub-movements, such as the Labadists, tended to withdraw from civil and church affairs, and became separatistic but continued to bear substantial influence on the larger movement.[60] Though few Second Reformation divines condoned separatism,[61] numerous conventicles were formed to nourish spiritual life. In time, the Second Reformation became reminiscent of the *Devotio Moderna* in its emphasis on separation from the unredeemed world. This is indicated in a comparison of Willem Teellinck and Wilhelmus Schortinghuis (1700-1750; renowned for his *Het Innige Christendom* [Inward Christendom]). As Graafland wrote: "For Teellinck the experience of the heart remained central, but then as a center which penetrated a wide area, including not only the family and the congregation, but also the entire church and nation, politics inclusive. For Schortinghuis subjective experience is the fort to which the believer withdraws himself from the world and even from the congregation around him."[62]

These differences must not be exaggerated, however, for Teellinck also showed some indications of internal withdrawal, as did other early Second Reformation divines such as Koelman and van Lodenstein.[63] Van der Groe, however, who is often considered the last representative of the movement, strongly emphasized church and social life as a whole.[64] Van der Linde wrote: "Most of those who can be considered representative of the Second Reformation, being promoters of a theocratic structure as far as the

[60]The Labadists were followers of Jean de Labadie (1610-1674). Labadie founded a Dutch quietistic and separatistic sect in an attempt to establish a congregation of the truly regenerate. Cf. Heppe, *Geschichte des Pietismus und der Mystik in der Reformierten Kirche, namentlich der Niederlande*, pp. 240-374; Otto Ritschl, *Dogmengeschichte des Protestantismus* (Leipzig: Hinrichs, 1908), 1:194-268; Goeters, *Die Vorbereitung des Pietismus in der reformierten Kirche der Niederlande*, pp. 139-286; Stoeffler, *The Rise of Evangelical Pietism*, pp. 162-69; C. Graafland, "De Nadere Reformatie en het Labadisme," in *De Nadere Reformatie en het Gereformeerd Piëtisme*, pp. 275-346; T. J. Saxby, *The Quest for the New Jerusalem: Jean de Labadie and the Labadists, 1610-1744* (Dordrecht: Nijhoff, 1987).

[61]W. à Brakel issued strong warnings against separatistic pietists and their denigration of the church (*The Christian's Reasonable Service*, vol. 2, chap. 43). The Second Reformation divines were church loyalists, not separatists, who sought to bring the apostate church back to God.

[62]Graafland, "Kernen en contouren van de Nadere Reformatie," p. 350.

[63]Stoeffler, *The Rise of Evangelical Pietism*, p. 144.

[64]Graafland, "Kernen en contouren van de Nadere Reformatie," pp. 350-51.

relationship between church and state are concerned, are open for that which is not so purely spiritual, such as the political state."[65] The Dutch Second Reformation focused on a number of issues. In summarizing the movement, Graafland included such themes as election, regeneration, sanctification, the family and the congregation, the church, creation and natural theology, eschatology, and theocracy.[66] Through its promotion of piety and a God-centered life nourished by family worship, the parish and the church, the Second Reformation stressed the need for moral and spiritual discipline in all spheres of life. Second Reformation sermons addressed all of these active themes, but also stressed the fall of Adam, man's inability to do good, the sovereignty of divine predestination and grace, the necessity of conviction of sin, the experience of conversion, and the simplicity of true worship.[67] Case Vogelaar's summary of the preaching of Bernardus Smytegelt is typical particularly of the later period of the Second Reformation: "In [Smytegelt's] sermons much emphasis was laid on the practice of godliness, on the holy duties of Christians, on the life of God's people and frames of their hearts, as well as their experiences of light and darkness, the leading and operation of the Holy Spirit, and giving instructions and directions to the godly."[68]

Like English Puritanism, the preaching of the Second Reformation emphasized experiential theology, featuring a well wrought-out theology of Christian experience. M. Eugene Osterhaven defines that theology as "that broad stream of Reformed teaching which, accepting

---

[65]"De Godservaring bij W. Teellinck, D. G. à Brakel en A. Comrie," *Theologia Reformata* 16 (1973):198.

[66]Graafland, "Kernen en contouren van de Nadere Reformatie," pp. 354-65. Cf. O.J. de Jong, et al., *Het eigene van de Nederlandse Nadere Reformatie* (Houten: Den Hertog, 1992); Teunis Brienen, et al., *Theologische aspecten van de Nadere Reformatie* (Zoetermeer: Boekencentrum, 1993), and A. De Reuver's review, "Wat is het eigene van de Nadere Reformatie?" *Documentatieblad Nadere Reformatie* 18 (1994):145-54.

[67]The emphasis on personal experience frequently led to a decrease in communicant members, especially in the later part of the Second Reformation. Willem Balke has noted: "The experiential theology of Schortinghuis caused a great decrease in Communion attendance. At the beginning of the eighteenth century, 187 came to the Lord's table in Manslagt, in Groothusen 171, in Pilsum 277. At the end of that century, the number of communicants were ten in Manslagt, seven in Groothusen, and ten in Pilsum" ("Het Pietisme in Oostfriesland," *Theologia Reformata* 21 [1978]:324). Cf. Arie Blok, "The Heidelberg Catechism and the Dutch *Nadere Reformatie*," pp. 47ff.

[68]"Bernardus Smytegelt: Spiritual Advisor of God's Children," *The Banner of Truth* 53 (1987):210. Smytegelt listed 296 marks of the godly life in preaching 145 sermons on Matthew 12:20-21 (*Het Gekrookte Riet*, 2 vols. ['s-Gravenhage: Ottho en Pieter van Thol, 1744]).

the creeds of the church, emphasized the new birth, the conversion, and the sanctification of the believer so that he might acquire an experiential or personal knowledge of Christ's saving grace."[69] Religion, orthodox doctrine, and theological propositions aren't enough; feeling, experience, spiritual warfare, and prayer are also essential for faith and practice.[70] The head knowledge of doctrine, albeit necessary, must be accompanied by the heart knowledge of scriptural experience.[71] For Second Reformation adherents, as well as for Puritans, "formal Christianity, by which they meant a Christianity that exhausted itself in externals, was only slightly better than none at all. For that reason they, like the mystics before them, emphasized the importance of the inward response to God."[72] Struggles of faith thus were primary.[73]

With regard to assurance of faith, the Second Reformation not only emphasized the promises of God and the witness of the Spirit, but also increasingly accentuated the syllogisms, making a transition from the practical syllogism in the classical period to the mystical syllogism in the later period.[74] Graafland and van der Linde are sharply critical of that transition, but they failed to note that the mystical syllogism is also inseparable from the enlightening of the Spirit. Van der Linde concluded: "We are without expectation as far as the mystical syllogism is concerned. If this is not conjoined to the external practice of faith, there will be nothing to hold on to for the man who is genuinely in need.... His only certainty is definitely not a syllogism, for it is not logic which reigns in the grace of God, but only the witness of the Holy Spirit in and through the gospel."[75]

Assessment in Secondary Sources

The Dutch Second Reformation has been difficult to understand, partly because of how it has been evaluated by scholars through the

---

[69]"The Experiential Theology of Early Dutch Calvinism," *Reformed Review* 27 (1974):180.

[70]Ibid., pp. 183-84.

[71]Ibid.

[72]Stoeffler, *The Rise of Evangelical Pietism*, p. 14.

[73]Van der Linde, "De betekenis van de Nadere Reformatie voor Kerk en Theologie," in *Opgang en voortgang der reformatie*, p. 146.

[74]Graafland, "Van *syllogismus practicus* naar *syllogismus mysticus*," in *Wegen en Gestalten in het Gereformeerd Protestantisme*, pp. 105-122.

[75]"De Godservaring bij W. Teellinck, D. G. à Brakel en A. Comrie," *Theologia Reformata* 16 (1973):202-203. Cf. van der Linde, *Opgang en voortgang der reformatie*, p. 146.

years. For example, the nineteenth-century theologians at Groningen were the first to study the Second Reformation seriously as a distinct historical movement. Willem van't Spijker shows how those divines, such as P. Hofstede de Groot, differed little from the view of Ypeij and Dermout in their *Geschiedenis der Nederlandsche Hervormde Kerk* (History of the Reformed Church of the Netherlands). Neither Ypeij and Dermout nor the Groningen professors researched the movement from its primary sources, however, but measured the movement by their own ideals. In particular, the Groningen theologians viewed divines such as Willem Teellinck and Jodocus van Lodenstein as their mentors.[76]

Later in the nineteenth century (1879), Heinrich Heppe published *Geschichte des Pietismus und der Mystik in der Reformierten Kirche, namentlich der Niederlande* (The History of Pietism and Mysticism in the Reformed Church, particularly in the Netherlands). The following decade, Albrecht Ritschl's three-volume history of pietism was published (*Geschichte des Pietismus,* 1880-86). Those works helped to explain the primary issues involved in the Second Reformation and are still being discussed by scholars of the movement today.

Heppe said that the roots of pietism are found in Puritanism. He believed that the "second reformation" moved from English Puritanism to the Dutch Second Reformation to German Pietism.

Ritschl said pietism was more like other reform movements present in the Western church since the Middle Ages. Concerning the Dutch Second Reformation, he pointed particularly to Franciscan observances, the mystical theology of Bernard de Clairveaux, and the Anabaptists.[77]

Van't Spijker views the 1911 work of W. Goeters (*Die Vorbereitung des Pietismus in der reformierten Kirche der Niederlande bis zur labadistischen Krisis 1670;* The Groundwork for Pietism in the Netherlands until the Labadistic Crisis in 1670) as a significant step forward in understanding the Dutch Second Reformation. Goeters emphasized the need to study various divines of the movement. He detected several streams of thought in the Second Reformation, which taught him to avoid simplistic assessments of their origins. In addition to theological and practical issues that shaped the movement, Goeters found social and historical roots that paved the

---

[76]"Bronnen van de Nadere Reformatie," in *De Nadere Reformatie en het Gereformeerd Piëtisme,* p. 6.
[77]Ibid., p. 7.

Appendix

way for the movement. He also highlighted important themes of the Second Reformation, such as striving for an ideal church. He also defined "the essence of this movement to be a striving of the visible church to approximate her essence (which is found in the invisible church) as much as possible."[78] Much negative reaction against the Second Reformation can be traced to Abraham Kuyper. Early in his ministry, Kuyper was profoundly influenced by a simple, God-fearing woman, Pietje Baltus, who emphasized the necessity of experimental conversion. Subsequently, however, Kuyper feared that the Christians among whom he labored had become too pietistic because of their constant diet of reading Second Reformation authors, fondly called the "old writers" (*oude schrijvers*). At times Kuyper referred to pietists in the Dutch church as "Methodists,"[79] though he retained a strong element of piety as well as respect for the Second Reformation divines in his own devotional writings.[80]

Kuyper's attempts to teach people how to apply Christianity to all spheres of life led to a revival of Calvinism in the Netherlands. His followers, however, frequently called neo-Calvinists, went beyond Kuyper by rejecting nearly all semblances of piety and by externalizing the gospel in a flurry of kingdom activity. Still today, as Pronk notes, "The neo-Calvinists in the Netherlands on the whole are quite antagonistic toward the Second Reformation. They see it as an other-worldly, anti-cultural and scholastic movement which has done the church more harm than good."[81]

Others also reacted negatively to the Second Reformation. Otto Ritschl viewed the Second Reformation as a falsification of the Reformation.[82] Theodorus L. Haitjema regarded it as degeneration from the Reformation.[83] Aart A. van Schelven said it was overly baptistic, spiritualistic, and influenced by Semi-Pelagianism.[84] E. D. Kraan considered the Second Reformation too steeped in

---

[78]Ibid., pp. 7-9. Cf. W. J. op't Hof, "Studie der Nadere Reformatie: verleden en toekomst," *Documentatieblad Nadere Reformatie* 18 (1994):1-50.

[79]*The Work of the Holy Spirit*, pp. xii, 300.

[80]See *Het Calvinisme* (Amsterdam: Höveker & Wormser, 1898); William Young, "Historic Calvinism and Neo-Calvinism," *Westminster Theological Journal* 36 (1973):48ff.

[81]Pronk, *The Banner of Truth*, nos. 154-55 (July-August 1976):7-10.

[82]*Dogmengeschichte des Protestantismus* 1:180.

[83]*Cultuurgeschiedenis van het Christendom* 3:337; cf. his *Prediking des Woords en bevinding* (Wageningen: H. Veenman & Zonen, 1950).

[84]"Het Zeeuwsche Mysticisme," *Gereformeerd Theologisch Tijdschrift* 17 (1916):141-62.

subjectivism,[85] while Rudolf Boon stated that it "inclines to Anabaptism."[86] Teunis Brienen said Second Reformation preaching spoke too much to various "soul conditions" among the hearers.[87] Some scholars have been more supportive of the Second Reformation. Hans Emil Weber,[88] Arie Vergunst,[89] James Tanis,[90] J. H. R. Verboom,[91] Jonathan Gerstner,[92] Willem Jan op't Hof[93] and others view the Second Reformation as a profitable outgrowth of Calvinism. And Stoeffler's assessment is a helpful corrective. He writes that the Second Reformation was a "thoroughly responsible, evangelical movement. On the personal level it emphasized love for God and man and a type of daily conduct based on what it regarded as the New Testament ethic. Like the rise of any reform movement which tends to challenge the established order of things, [the Second Reformation] caused some strains and difficulties. At the end, . . . however, the Reformed churches were the better for having made the necessary adjustments."[94]

Other writers view the movement with mixed feelings. This is particularly true of several Reformed scholars in the Netherlands, who have done pioneer work on the Second Reformation. Those include J. G. Woelderink, Arnold A. van Ruler, S. van der Linde, Cornelis Graafland, Willem Balke,[95] K. Exalto, W. van't Spijker, J. van Genderen, and Fred A. van Lieburg.[96]

[85]"De Heilige Geest en het na-reformatorische subjectivisme," in *De Heilige Geest*, ed. J. H. Bavinck, et al. (Kampen: Kok, 1949), pp. 228-63.

[86]*Het probleem der christelijke gemeenschap: Oorsprong en ontwikkeling der congregationalistisch geordende kerken in Massachusetts* (Amsterdam: Stichting Universitaire Uitgaven, 1951), p. 164.

[87]*De Prediking van de Nadere Reformatie* (Amsterdam: Ton Bolland, 1974). Brienen's study, which exaggerates the weaknesses of Second Reformation preaching, asserts that Second Reformation preaching no longer appeals to God's promises or takes His covenant seriously; rather, the stress is on individuals by dividing listeners into various classifications.

[88]*Reformation, Orthodoxie und Rationalismus: Beiträge zur Förderung christlicher Theologie*, 2 vols. (Gütersloh: C. Bertelsmann, 1937-51).

[89]Vergunst, *Neem de wacht des Heeren waar* (Utrecht: Den Hertog, 1983), pp. 232-36.

[90]*Dutch Calvinistic Pietism in the Middle Colonies*, pp. 4ff.

[91]*Dr. Alexander Comrie, predikant van Woubrugge*, pp. 185ff.

[92]*Thousand Generation Covenant*, pp. 68-79.

[93]*Engelse piëtistische geschriften in het Nederlands, 1598-1622*, stellingen no. 6.

[94]*The Rise of Evangelical Pietism*, pp. 178-79.

[95]Balke feels that the Second Reformation's theology was more irenic prior to the Synod of Dort (1618-1619), but that it became too rigid in "post-Dort" years (cf. "Calvijn en Luther," in *Luther en het Gereformeerd Protestantisme* ['s-Gravenhage: Boekencentrum, 1983]).

[96]Cf. bibliography.

Generally speaking, these scholars appreciate the classical expression of the Second Reformation, though they feel that it was not as theologically rich as the Reformation. S. van der Linde and Cornelis Graafland teach that the early expression of the Second Reformation deteriorated through excessive introspection, which was why the movement failed in the late seventeenth and early eighteenth centuries.[97] Similarly, Hofmeyr asserts that "the classical phase of the Second Reformation shows definite links with Calvin, while the distance between Calvin and the stricter pietism of the later phase of the Second Reformation is much greater."[98]

Prozesky concludes that "the movement as a whole underwent gradual change with its early precisianism losing ground to devotional and on occasion mystical pursuits, besides also evolving or adapting its own typical institutions, such as conventicles, edificatory sermons and pietistic literature."[99] Osterhaven describes two trends in the Second Reformation: "The one stream emphasized mysticism, inwardness, felicity, prayer, spiritual elation, and joy in the Lord. The other stream was activistic and laid stress on doing the will of the Lord. Whatever the emphasis," Osterhaven wrote, "all pietists believed heartily in experiential theology and were known as *de ernstige*, the earnest, zealous Christians of their place and time. In its better representatives, like Wilhelmus à Brakel, the experiential theology sought a healthy balance between mysticism and precisionism."[100] Van Ruler calls the movement as a whole a "legitimate experiment."[101]

The wide range of these opinions calls for further study of the Dutch Second Reformation. It also begs for more careful study of the movement within its spiritual, theological, and political milieu. Too often the Second Reformation is judged by the Reformation

[97]Van der Linde, *Vromen en Verlichten*, p. 2; cf. Graafland, "Het eigene van het Gereformeerd Pietisme in de 18e eeuw in onderscheid van de 17e eeuw," *Documentatieblad Nadere Reformatie* 11 (1987):37-53.

[98]"The Doctrine of Calvin as Transmitted in the South African Context by Among Others the *Oude Schrijvers*," in *Calvinus Reformator: His contribution to Theology, Church and Society*, p. 260.

[99]Martin H. Prozesky, "The Emergence of Dutch Pietism," *Journal of Ecclesiastical History* 28 (1977):37.

[100]"The Experiential Theology of Early Dutch Calvinism," *Reformed Review* 27 (1974):182.

[101]"Licht- en schaduwzijden in de bevindelijkheid," in *Theologisch Werk* (Nijkerk: G. F. Callenbach, 1971), 3:43-60.

proper, the latter being regarded as normative. Calvin is presented by A. Ritschl and others as the ideal, and all who differ from him, even in areas where his thinking is largely embryonic, such as covenant theology,[102] are considered wanting. Quite unfairly, scholars then conclude that the Second Reformation is not a "further reformation" (*nadere reformatie*), but a "further deformation" (*verdere deformatie*).[103]

We believe that a more careful, objective study of the Second Reformation will show that the Dutch divines as a whole did not misread Calvin and the Reformers but simply applied the teaching of the early Reformers to their own day.

Additional work also needs to be done on how Philipp Jakob Spener, August Hermann Francke, Friedrich Adolph Lampe, Gerhard Tersteegen, and other German Pietists influenced the Dutch Second Reformation. Profiles should be written on several Second Reformation divines who have not yet been thoroughly studied.[104] Caricatures of the movement and the influence of Reformed scholastic orthodoxy must be debunked. And more primary and secondary sources must be published in English on the Dutch Second Reformation.[105]

The Dutch Second Reformation divines deserve to be treated with the same scholarly care that is devoted to their Puritan counterparts. Such treatment will show the long-term influence of the Second Reformation. As Stoeffler wrote:

> While the [Second Reformation] dream of reforming the Reformed never succeeded it could hardly be doubted that the perfectionistic ideals of this reform party brought about significant

---

[102]Cf. Peter Lillback, "The Binding of God: Calvin's Role in the Development of Covenant Theology" (Ph. D. dissertation, Westminster Theological Seminary, 1985).

[103]Graafland, "Kernen en contouren van de Nadere Reformatie," in *De Nadere Reformatie: Beschrijving van haar voornaamste vertegenwoordigers*, pp. 352, 366.

[104]E.g., Theodorus G. à Brakel, Theodorus van der Groe, Adrianus Hasius, Abraham Hellenbroek, Nicolaas Holtius, David Knibbe, Johannes à Marck, Petrus van Mastricht, Gregorius Mees, Franciscus Ridderus, and Rippertus Sixtus.

[105]Happily, some Dutch Second Reformation divines are finally being translated into English, including Wilhelmus à Brakel's classic, *The Christian's Reasonable Service*, 4 vols., Alexander Comrie's *ABC of Faith*, and Petrus Dathenus's *The Pearl of Christian Comfort* (Grand Rapids: Reformation Heritage Books, 1997). Two organizations and one book publisher that have sprung up in the 1990s — the Dutch Reformed Translation Society, the North American branch of *Stichting Studie der Nadere Reformatie*, and Reformation Heritage Books — are working to enlarge the number of such translations. Work is presently being done on translating into English writings of Jacobus Koelman, Lambertus Myseras, Bernardus Smytegelt, Willem Teellinck, and Gisbertus Voetius.

changes in the life of the Church. It was responsible for an emphasis upon effective, religiously significant preaching such as is seldom found in territorial churches, together with a similar emphasis upon pastoral work. . . . Many of the classes and synods began to stress catechization to a degree unknown since the early days of the Genevan reformation. Church discipline, which had been exercised almost solely with regard to faith and order, was oriented to include the daily conduct of church members. A devotional literature was created such as continental Protestantism had never known because its need had not been recognized.[106]

The influence of Second Reformation devotional writings and sermons has remained for later generations, all the way to contemporary Dutch pietistic groups in the Netherlands, North America, and South Africa.[107] Today such writings are being reprinted as rapidly as Puritan books are in the English-speaking world.[108] Such literature is a tangible point of reference for those identifying with the distinctive religious convictions in the experimental Reformed tradition.

[106]*The Rise of Evangelical Pietism*, pp. 178-79. Cf. Joel R. Beeke, "Insights for the Church from the Dutch Second Reformation," *Calvin Theological Journal* 28, 2 (1993):420-24.

[107]Hofmeyr, "The Doctrine of Calvin as Transmitted in the South African Context by Among Others the *Oude Schrijvers*," in *Calvinus Reformator: His contribution to Theology, Church and Society*, pp. 261-62; cf. Gerstner, *Thousand Generation Covenant*.

[108]For an annotated bibliography of the revival in Puritan literature which began in the 1950s, see Joel R. Beeke, "Meet the Puritans...In Print!," *Banner of Truth* 52 (1986):44-45, 102-103, 156-57, 240-41, 292-93; 53 (1987):154-55, 184-85, and "Reading the Best in Puritan Literature: A Modern Bibliography," *Reformation and Revival* 5, 2 (1996):117-158. The former series of articles covers Puritan reprints from 1957-1985; the latter article, from 1986-1995.

BIBLIOGRAPHY

Primary Sources

Adams, Thomas. *Heaven Made Sure; or, The Certainty of Salvation.* London, 1614.

_____. *The Works of Thomas Adams: being the Sum of His Sermons, Meditations, and other Divine and Moral Discourses.* 3 vols. London: Printed by T. Harper for J. Grismand, 1629; reprint ed., with memoir by Joseph Angus, ed. T. Smith. Eureka, Calif.: Tanski Publications, 1998.

Alleine, Joseph. *Divers Practical Cases of Conscience Satisfactorily Resolved.* London: Printed for Nevil Simmons, 1672.

Alleine, Richard. *Instructions about Heart-work. What is to be done on Gods part, and Ours, for the Cure and Keeping of the Heart that we may live in the Exercise and Growth of Grace here, and have a comfortable Assurance of Glory to Eternity.* London: Printed for J. Greenwood, 1681.

Ambrose, Isaac. *The Compleat Works of that Eminent Minister of God's Word, Mr. Isaac Ambrose.* London: Printed for R. Chiswel, B. Tooke, and T. Sawbridge, 1689.

Ames, William. *Conscience with the Power and Cases Thereof.* London: Printed by E. G. for Iohn Rothwell, 1643.

_____. *The Marrow of Theology.* Trans. from the 3rd Latin edition, 1629, ed. John D. Eusden. Boston: Pilgrim Press, 1968.

_____. *The Svbstance of Christian Religion: Or, a plain and easie Draught of the Christian Catechisme, in LII Lectures.* London: Printed by T. Mabb for T. Davies, 1659.

Aquinas, Thomas. *Summa theologiae.* Blackfriars Latin text and English translation. 60 vols. New York: McGraw-Hill, 1963-76.

Arminius, Jacobus. *The Works of James Arminius.* Trans. James Nichols and W. R. Bagnall. 3 vols. London: Printed for Longman, Hurst, Rees, Orme, Brown and Green, 1825-28; reprint ed., Grand Rapids: Baker, 1956.

The Articles of the Synod of Dort, and its Rejection of Errors: with the History of Events which made way for that Synod. Trans. with notes by Thomas Scott. Uttica: William Williams, 1831.

Augustine, Aurelius. *A Select Library of the Nicene and Post-Nicene Fathers of the Christian Church.* First Series. Vols. 1-8. Ed. Philip Schaff. New York: Christian Literature Co., 1886-90; reprint ed., Grand Rapids: Eerdmans, 1974.

Baillie, Robert. *The Letters and Journals of Robert Baillie.* 3 vols. Ed. David Laing. Edinburgh: Robert Ogle, 1841-42.

Ball, John. *A Treatise of Faith. Divided into two Parts: The first showing the Nature, the second, the Life of Faith. Both tending to direct the weak Christian how he may possesse the whole Word of God as his owne, overcome temptations, better his obedience, and live comfortably in all estates.* 3rd ed. London: Printed for Edward Brewster, 1657.

Ball, Thomas. *The Life of the Renouned Doctor Preston writ by his pupil master Thomas Ball, D.D.* Ed. E. W. Harcourt. Oxford: Parker and Co., 1885.

Bates, William. *The Whole Works of the Rev. W. Bates, D.D.* 4 vols. Reprint ed., Harrisonburg, Va.: Sprinkle Publications, 1989-91.

Baxter, Richard. *A Christian Directory: or, A Summ of Practical Theologie, and Cases of Conscience.* London: Printed by Robert White for Nevil Simmons, 1673.

_____. *The Life of Faith, as it is the Evidence of Things Unseen.* London: Printed by R. W. and A. M. for Francis Tyton and Jane Underhill, 1660.

_____. *The Practical Works of Richard Baxter.* Introduction and life by William Orme. 23 vols. London: James Duncan, 1830; reprint ed. in 4 vols., London: George Virtue, 1857 and Morgan, Pa.: Soli Deo Gloria Publications, 1990-91.

Bayley, Lewis. *The Practise of Pietie.* London: John Hodgetts, 1620; reprint ed., with intro. by Joel R. Beeke, Morgan, Pa.: Soli Deo Gloria Publications, 1995.

Baynes, Paul. *Briefe Directions unto a Godly Life: wherein every Christian is furnished with most Necessary Helps for the Furthering of him in a godly Course here upon Earth, so that He may Attaine Eternall Happiness in Heaven.* London: Printed by A. Griffins for J. Norton, 1637.

_____. *An Entire Commentary vpon the Whole Epistle of the Apostle Paul to the Ephesians.* London: Printed by M. F. for R. Milbourne and I. Bartlet, 1643. Reprint ed., *Exposition of Ephesians, chapter 2:11-6:18.* N.p.: Sovereign Grace Publishers, 1959.

_____. *The Trial of a Christians Estate: Or A Discoverie of the Cavses, degrees, signes and differences of the Apostasie both of true Christians and false.* London: F. Kyngston for N. Newberry, 1618.

Beardslee, John W. III, ed. and trans. *Reformed Dogmatics: J. Wollebius, G. Voetius, F. Turretin. A Library of Protestant Thought.* New York: Oxford University Press, 1965; reprint ed., Grand Rapids: Baker, 1977.

Beza, Theodore. *Confessio Christianae fidei, et eiusdem collation cum Papisticis haeresibus.* Genevae: apud Eustathium Vignon, 1587. [*A briefe and pithie Summe of Christian faith made in forme of a Confession, with a confutation of al such superstitious errors, as are contrarie thervnto.* Trans. out of French by R(obert) F(yll). London: Roger Ward, 1639. Also *The Christian Faith.* Trans. James Clark. Lewes, East Sussex: Focus Christian Ministries Trust, 1992.]

_____. *Correspondance.* Collected by H. Aubert. Ed. F. Aubert; H. Meylan; A. Dufour; and A. Tripet. 20 vols. Geneva: Droz, 1960-.

_____. *An evident Display of Popish Practices or Patched Pelagianisme, where in is mightelie cleared the soveraigne truth of Gods eternall Predestination.* London: Ralph Newberie, 1578.

_____. *Maister Beza's Household Prayers for the Consolation and Perfection of a Christian Life.* London: Nicholas Okes, 1607.

_____. *Jesu Christi domini nostri Novum Testamentum, sive novum foedus; cuius graeco contextui respondent interpretationes duae Theodori Bezae.* Accessit etiam Joachimi Camerarii in Novum foedus commentarius. Cantabrigiae: Roger Daniel, 1642.

_____. *De praedestinationis doctrina et vero usu tractatio absolutissima. Excerpta Th. Bezae praelectionibus in nonum epistolae ad Romanos caput.* Genevae: apvd Evstathivm Vignon, 1582.

_____. *Questionum & responsionum christianarum libellus.* Londini: apud Henricum Bynneman, 1571. [*A booke of Christian Questions and answers. Wherein are set foorth the cheef points of the Christian religion.* Trans. Arthur Golding. London: William Horn, for Abraham Veale, 1574. Also, *A Little Book of Christian Questions and Responses.* Trans. Kirk Summers. Alllison Park, Pa.: Pickwick Publications, 1986.]

_____. *De remediis adversus praecipuous insultus Satanae, tractatio. In Panoplia Christiana seu adversus varias tentationes et afflictiones, quibus pii in mundo exercuntur, munimenta et remedia. Ex doctissimorum theologorum Scriptis.* Genevae: apud Eustathium Vignon, 1588.

_____. *Summa Totius Christianismi, Sive Descriptio et Distributio Causarum Salutis Electorum, et Exitii Reproborum, ex Sacris Literis Collecta.* Genevae: apud Eustathium Vignon, 1565. [*A Briefe Declaration of the chiefe points of the Christian religion, Set Forth in a Table.* Trans. William Whittingham. London: Imprinted by Dauid Moptid and Iohn Mather, 1575. This work became better known in the subsequent translation of John Stockwood, *The Treasure of Trueth, Touching the grounde works of man his salvation, and Chiefest Points of Christian Religion: with a brief Sum of the Comfortable Doctrine of God His Providence, Comprised in 38 Short Aphorisms.* London: for Thomas Woodcocke, 1576.]

_____. *Theses theologicae in schola Genevensi: ab aliquot Sacrarum literaru[m] studioris sub D.D. Th. Beza & Anton. Fayo S. S. Theologiae professoribus propositae & disputatae. In quibus methodica locorum communium S. S. Theologiae epitome continentur.* Altera edition emendatior & auctior priore. Genevae: apud haeredes Eustathii Vignon, 1591. [*Propositions and Principles of Divinitie Propounded and Disputed in the University of Geneva under M. Theod. Beza and M. Anthonie Faius.* Edinburgh: Printed by Robert Waldegraue, 1591.]

_____. *Theodori Bezae Vezelii Volumen primum (-tertium) Tractationum Theologicarum, in Quibus Pleraque Christiana Religionis Dogmata Adversus Maeresos Nostris Temporibus Renevatas Solide ex Berbo Dei Defenduntur.* 2nd ed. Genevae: apud Eustathium Vignon, 1582.

Binning, Hugh. *The Works of the Rev. Hugh Binning, M.A.* Ed. M. Leishman, D.D. 3rd ed. London: A. Fullarton and Co., 1851; reprint ed., Ligonier, Pa.: Soli Deo Gloria Publications, 1992.

Blake, Thomas. *Vindiciae Foederis, or a Treatise of the Covenant of God entered with man-kinde, in the several Kindes and Degrees of it, in which the agreement and respective differences of the Covenant of works and the Covenant of grace, of the old and New Covenant are discust.* London: Printed for A. Roper, 1653.

Bolton, Robert. *A Discourse About the State of True Happiness.* London: Printed by Felix Kyngston for Thomas Weaver, 1631.

_____. *Instructions for a Right Comforting of Afflicted Consciences, with speciall*

Antidotes against some grievous temptations. London: Printed by Felix Kyngston for Thomas Weaver, 1631; reprint ed., Morgan, Pa.: Soli Deo Gloria Publications, 1991.

_____. *The Saints Selfe-enriching Examination. Or a Treatise concerning the Sacrament of the Lord's Supper, which, as a Glasse or Touch-stone, clearly discovers the triall and truth of grace; requisite to be looked into daily; chiefly before we come to the Lord's Table.* London: Printed by Anne Griffin for Rapha Harford, 1634.

_____. *Some General Directions for a Comfortable Walking with God.* London: Printed by Felix Kyngston for Edmund Weaver, 1625; reprint ed., Morgan, Pa.: Soli Deo Gloria Publications, 1995.

_____. *The Workes of the Reverend, truly Pious, and Iudiciously learned Robert Bolton, as they were finished by Himselfe in his Life Time.* 4 vols. London: Printed by George Miller, 1641.

Bolton, Samuel. *The True Bovnds of Christian Freedome.* London: Printed for Philemon Stephens by J. L., 1645; reprint ed., London: Banner of Truth Trust, 1964.

Boston, Thomas. *The Complete Works of the Late Rev. Thomas Boston, Ettrick.* 12 vols. Ed. Samuel M'Millan. London: William Tegg & Co., 1855; reprint ed., Wheaton, Ill.: Richard Owen Roberts Publishers, 1980.

Bradford, John. *The Writings of John Bradford, M.A., Fellow of Pembroke Hall, Cambridge, and Prebendary of St. Paul's, Martyr, 1555.* 2 vols. Ed. Aubrey Townsend. Cambridge: University Press, 1848-53.

Bradshaw, William. *English Puritanisme. Containeing: the maine Opinions of the Rigidest Sort of those that are called Puritanes in the realme of England.* Amsterdam: n.p., 1605.

Bradwardine, Thomas. *De causa Dei contra pelagium, et de virtute causarum, ad suos Mertonenses, libri tres.* Opera et Studio Henrici Savilii. Ex scriptis codicibus nunc primum editi. Londini: ex officina Nortoniana apud Joannem Billium, 1618; reprint ed., Frankfurt am Main: Minerva, 1964.

Brahé, Jan Jacob. *Aanmerkingen over de Vijf Walchersche Artikelen.* Amsterdam: Yntema en Ticboel, 1782; reprint ed., Rotterdam: De Banier, 1937.

_____. *Godgeleerde Stellingen over de Leer der Regtvaardigmaking des Zondaars voor God.* Reprint ed., Amsterdam: N. Byl, 1883.

Brakel, Theodorus à. *De trappen Des Geestelijken Levens.* 8th edition. Amsterdam: Abraham Cornelis, 1670.

Brakel, Wilhelmus à. *The Christian's Reasonable Service.* Trans. Bartel Elshout. 4 vols. Morgan, Pa.: Soli Deo Gloria Publications, 1992-95.

_____. *De Waare christen of opregte gelovige hebbende deel aan God in Christus.* Amsterdam: N. Byl, 1712; reprint ed., Leiden: J. J. Groen & Zoon, 1852.

Breward, Ian, ed. *The Work of William Perkins.* The Courtenay Library of Christian Classics, no. 3. Abingdon: Sutton Courtenay Press, 1970.

Bridge, William. *The Works of William Bridge, sometime fellow of Emmanuel College in Cambridge; now preacher of the Word of God at Yarmouth.* 3 vols. London:

for P. Cole, 1649; reprint ed. in 5 vols., Morgan, Pa.: Soli Deo Gloria Publications, 1989.

_____. *The Wovnded Conscience Cvred, the VVeak One Strengthened, and the Doubting Satisfied.* London: for Benjamin Allen, 1642.

Brooks, Thomas. *Heaven on Earth. Or a Serious Discourse touching a well-grounded Assurance of Men's Everlasting Happiness and Blessedness. Discovering the Nature of Assurance, the possibility of Attaining it, the Causes, Springs, and Degrees of it; with the Resolution of severall weighty Questions.* The Second Edition Corrected and Enlarged. London: Printed by M. S. for John Hancock, 1657; reprint ed., London: Banner of Truth Trust, 1961.

_____. *The Works of Thomas Brooks.* 6 vols. Ed. A. Grosart. London: James Nichol, 1861-66; reprint ed., Edinburgh: Banner of Truth Trust, 1980.

Brown, John (of Haddington). *A Compendious View of Natural and Revealed Religion.* 2nd ed. Edinburgh: Murray & Cochrane, 1796.

Brown, John (of Wamphray). *The Life of Justification Opened. Or, a treatise grounded upon Gal. 2. II. Wherein the orthodox doctrine of Justification by faith, & Imputation of Christ's Righteousness, is clearly expounded.* Utrecht: n.p., 1695.

Brown, John (of Whitburn). *Gospel Truth Accurately Stated and Illustrated.* Glasgow: Blackie Fullarton & Co., 1831.

Bucer, Martin. *The Commonplaces of Martin Bucer.* Trans. and ed. D. F. Wright. The Courtenay Library of Reformation Classics, no. 4. Appleford: The Sutton Courtenay Press, 1972.

_____. *Melanchthon and Bucer.* Ed. Wilhelm Pauck. Library of Christian Classics, no. 19. Philadelphia: Westminster Press, 1969.

Bulkeley, Peter. *The Gospel-Covenant; or the Covenant of Grace Opened.* 2nd ed. London: Matthew Simmons, 1651.

Bullinger, Henrich. *Commonplaces of the Christian Religion compendiously written.* Trans. John Stockwood. London: George Byshop, 1572.

_____. *Confessio Helvetica posterior, A. D. 1566. [The Second Helvetic Confession.] The Creeds of Christendom,* III, 233-306. Ed. Philip Schaff. New York: Harper & Brothers, Publishers, 1878.

_____. *The Decades of Henry Bullinger.* 5 vols. in 4. Trans. H. I. Ed. Thomas Harding. Cambridge: University Press, 1849-51.

_____. *De gratia Dei iustificante nos propter Christum, per solam fidem absque operibus bonis, fide interim exuberante in opera bona, Libri IIII. ad Sereniss.* Tiguri: ex occicina Froschoviana, 1554.

_____. *A hundred sermons upon the Apocalipse of Iesu Christ, reveilled by the angell of the Lord: but seene or received and written by the holy apostle and evangelist S. Iohn.* London: Iohn Daye, 1561.

Bunyan, John. *The Complete Works of John Bunyan.* 4 vols. in 3. Reprint ed., Marshallton, Del.: National Foundation for Christian Education, 1968.

Burgess, Anthony. *Spiritual Refining: or a Treatise of Grace and Assurance. Wherein are handled, the doctrine of assurance. The use of signs in self-examination. How true graces may be distinguished from counterfeit. Several true signs of grace, and many false ones. The nature of grace under divers Scripture notions or titles, as regeneration, the new-creature, the heart of flesh, vocation, sanctification, &c.* London: A. Miller for Thomas Vnderhil, 1652; reprint ed., Ames, Ia.: International Outreach, 1990.

_____. *The True Doctrine of Iustification Asserted and Vindicated,* London: Robert White for Thomas Vnderhil, 1648.

_____. *Vindiciae Legis: or, A Vindication of the Moral Law, and the Covenants.* 2nd edition. London: James Young, for Thomas Vnderhil, 1647.

Burgess, Cornelius. *A Chain of Graces drawn out at length for a Reformation of Manners. Or, A brief Treatise of Virtue, Knowledge, Temperance, Patience, Godliness, Brotherly kindness, and Charity, so far as they are urged by the Apostle, in 2 Pet. i. 5,6,7.* London, 1622.

_____. *Vindiciae Foederis, or a Treatise of the Covenant of God entered with man-kinde, in the several Kindes and Degrees of it.* London: A. Roper, 1653.

Burroughs, Jeremiàh. *An Exposition of the Prophecy of Hosea.* Reprint ed., Morgan, Pa.: Soli Deo Gloria Publications, 1988.

_____. *The Saints' Happiness, Together with the Several Steps Leading Thereunto. Delivered in Divers Lectures on the Beatitudes.* London: M.S. for Nathaniel Brook and Thomas Parkhurst, 1660; reprint ed., Morgan, Pa.: Soli Deo Gloria Publications, 1988.

Byfield, Nicholas. *The signes, or an Essay concerning the Assurance of Gods Love and Mans salvation; gathered out of the Holy Scriptures.* London: Printed by A. M. for Philemon Stephens, and Christopher Meredith, 1637.

_____. *The Spiritual Tovchstone: or, the signes of a godly man: drawn in so plaine and profitable a maner, as all sorts of Christians may trie themselves thereby. Together with Directions, how the weake Christian, by the vse of these Signes may establish his assurance.* London: Printed by R. Field for Ionas Man, 1619.

Byfield, Richard. *The Light of Faith, and the Way of Holiness; shewing how and what to believe in all estates and conditions.* London: Printed by T.H. for Ph. Stephens and Ch. Meredith, 1630.

Calamy, Edmund. *The Nonconformist's Memorial.* Ed. Samuel Palmer. 2 vols. London: Printed for W. Harris, 1775.

Calvin, John. *Commentaries of Calvin.* 46 vols. Various translators. Edinburgh: Calvin Translation Society, 1843-55; reprint ed. in 22 vols., Grand Rapids: Baker, 1979.

_____. *Concerning the Eternal Predestination of God.* Trans. J. K. S. Reid. London: James Clarke, 1961.

_____. *Institutes of the Christian Religion.* Ed. John T. McNeill. Trans. Ford Lewis Battles. 2 vols. Library of Christian Classics, no. 20-21. Philadelphia: Westminster Press, 1960.

_____. *Joannis Calvini Opera Selecta.* Ed. Peter Barth and Wilhelm Niesel. Munich, 1926-52.

_____. *Letters of John Calvin.* Ed. Jules Bonnet; trans. David Constable and Marcus Robert Gilchrist. 4 vols. Reprint ed., New York, 1972.

_____. *New Testament Commentaries*. Ed. David W. Torrance and Thomas F. Torrance. 12 vols. Grand Rapids: Eerdmans, 1960-72.

_____. *Opera quae supersunt omnia*. Ed. Guilielmus Baum, Eduardus Cunitz, and Eduardus Reuss. 59 vols. *Corpus Reformatorum: Volumen XXIX-LXXXVII*. Brunsvigae: C. A. Schwetschke et filium, 1863-1900.

_____. *Sermons from Job*. Trans. Harold Dekker. Grand Rapids: Eerdmans, 1952.

_____. *Sermons of M. John Calvin, on the Epistles of S. Paule to Timothie and Titus*. Trans. L. T. London: Imprinted for G. Bishop and T. Woodcoke, 1579; reprint ed., Edinburgh: Banner of Truth Trust, 1983.

_____. *Sermons of Master John Calvin upon the Fifthe Book of Moses called Deuteronomie*. Trans. Arthur Golding. London, 1583; reprint ed., Edinburgh: Banner of Truth Trust, 1987.

_____. *Sermons on the Epistle to the Ephesians*. Trans. Arthur Golding. London, 1577; reprint ed., Edinburgh: Banner of Truth Trust, 1973.

_____. *Sermons on Isaiah's Prophecy of the Death and Passion of Jesus Christ*. Trans. T. H. L. Parker. London: James Clarke, 1956.

_____. *Sermons on the Ten Commandments*. Ed. and trans. Benjamin W. Farley. Grand Rapids: Baker, 1980.

_____. *Sermons on the Saving Work of Christ*. Trans. Leroy Nixon. Grand Rapids: Eerdmans, 1950.

_____. *Tracts and Treatises*. Trans. Henry Beveridge. 3 vols. Grand Rapids: Eerdmans, 1958.

Caryl, Joseph. *An Exposition with Practicall Observations of the Book of Job*. 12 vols. London: M. Simmons, 1647-66.

Cawdrey, Daniel. *Selfe-examination required in everyone, for the worthy receiving of the Lord's Supper*. 2nd ed. London: T. Walkley, 1648.

Charnock, Stephen. *The Works of Stephen Charnock*. 2 vols. London: Printed for Ben. Griffen and Thomas Cockeril, 1684. Reprint ed., ed. T. Smith, intro. by James M'Cosh. 5 vols. Edinburgh: James Nichol, 1864-66.

Chauncy, Isaac. *Neonomianism Unmask'd: or, The Ancient Gospel Pleaded, against the other, called, the new law*. London: H. Barnard, 1693.

Clagett, William. *A Discourse Concerning the Operations of the Holy Spirit; with a Confutation of Some Part of Dr. Owen's Book Upon that Subject*. London: Printed for Henry Brome, 1680.

Cocceius, Johannes. *Opera Omnia Theologica, Exegetica, Didactica, Polemica, Philologica*. 3rd ed. 10 vols. Amstelodami: P. & J. Blaer, 1701.

Cole, Nathanael. *The Godly Mans Assurance; or a Christians certaine Resolution of his Owne Salvation. Wherein are set down the Infallible Marks of God's children*. London: T. S[nodham] for Richard Woodroffe, 1615.

Cole, Thomas. *A Discourse of Regeneration, Faith, and Repentance*. London: for Thomas Cockerill, 1689.

Comrie, Alexander. *Aanspraak aan Do. Antonius van der Os*. Amsterdam: N. Byl, 1753.

_____. *Het A.B.C. dess Geloofs*. Sneek: F. Holtkamp, 1860. [*The ABC of Faith*. Trans. J. Marcus Banfield. Ossett, W. Yorks: Zoar Publications, 1978.]

_____. *Baniere van wegen de Waarheid Opgeregt tegen den Heer Joan van den Honert*. Amsterdam: N. Byl, 1753.

_____. *Een beknopte Verhandeling van het Verbond der Werken*. Ed. G. H. Kersten. Rotterdam: De Banier, 1932.

_____. *Berigt nopens de waarschuwinge van de Heer J. J. Schultens*. Amsterdam: N. Byl, 1755.

_____. *Brief over de Rechtvaardigmakinge des Zondaars door de onmiddelyke Toereekening der Borggerechtigheit van Christus*. Amsterdam: N. Byl, 1761; reprint ed., Minnertsga: J. Bloemsma, 1832.

_____. *Missive van den Wel Eerw: zeer Geleerden Heere Alexander Comrie, wegens de Regtvaardigmakinge des Zondaars en die toeeigeninge van deze weldaad van Gods Vrye Genade aan hem door het ingewrocht gelove*. Amsterdam: N. Byl, 1757; reprint ed., Bolsward: H. Bokma, 1851.

_____. *Stellige en Praktikale Verklaaringe van den Heidelbergschen Catechismus volgens de leer en gronden der Hervorming, waarin de waarheden van onzen Godsdienst op een klare en bevindelijke wijze voorgesteld en betoogd worden, de natuurlingen ontdekt, de zoekenden bestuurd, de zwakken vertroost en de sterken tot hun plicht, volgens een Evangelische leiding, opgewekt worden*. Amsterdam: N. Byl, 1753; reprint ed., Barneveld: G. J. van Horssen, 1976.

_____. *Twee Pastorale brieven van Alexander Comrie*. Veenendaal: Kool, 1985.

_____. *Verhandeling van eenige Eigenschappen des Zaligmakenden Geloofs, zijnde een' verklaring en toepassing van verscheidene uitgekipte teksten des O. en N. Testaments*. Leiden: Johannes Hasebroek, 1744; reprint ed., Amsterdam: F. G. L. Holst, n.d.

_____. *Verzameling van Leerredenen*. Leiden: Johannes Hasebroek, 1749.

_____, and Holtius, Nicolaus. *Examen van het Ontwerp van Tolerantie. Tien samenspraken in 9 stukjes*. Amsterdam: N. Byl, 1753-59.

The Confession of Faith; The Larger and Shorter Catechisms, with the Scripture Proofs at Large together with The Sum of Saving Knowledge. Issued by Pubs. Com. of Free Presbyterian Church of Scotland. Inverness: Eccleslitho, 1970.

Cotton, John. *Gospel Conversion: Discovering, 1. Whether any gracious conditions, or qualifications, are wrought in the soule before faith in Christ. 2. How the assurance of a mans salvation is to be evidenced. 3. The manner of the soules closing with Christ*. London: Printed by J. Dawson for Francis Cornwell, 1646.

_____. *The Way of Faith*. A Library of American Puritan Writings, the Seventeenth Century, no. 13. Series editor: Sacvan Bercovitch. New York: AMS Press, 1983.

Crisp, Tobias. *Christ Alone Exalted; in the Perfection and Encouragements of the Saints, Notwithstanding Sins and Trials. Being the Complete Works of Tobias Crisp, D.D.* 2 vols. 4th ed. Memoir and notes by John Gill. London: Printed by R. Noble for J. Murgatroyd, 1791.

Culverwell, Ezekiel. *A Treatise of Faith: Wherein is Declared How a Man May Live by Faith, and Find Relief in all His Necessities. Applied Especially unto the Use of the Weakest Christians.* London: Printed by I. D. for Hen: Overton, 1633.

_____. *A Briefe Answere to Certaine Objections against the Treatise of Faith.* London: Printed by I. D. for Hen: Overton, 1633.

Culverwell, Nathaniel. *The White Stone: or a Learned and Choice Treatise of Assurance. Very usefull for all, but especially Weak Believers.* London: J. Rothwell, 1654.

De Moor, Bernadinus. *De Rechtvaardigmaking van eeuwigheid.* Leiden: Johannes Hasebroek, 1762; reprint ed., Kampen: Kok, 1905.

Dent, Arthur. *The Plain Man's Pathway to Heaven: Wherein Every Man May Clearly See, Whether He shall be Saved or Damned.* London: for Robert Dexter by McKerrow, 1601; reprint ed., Morgan, Pa.: Soli Deo Gloria Publications, 1994.

Dering, Edward. *M. Derings Workes.* London: I. R., 1597; reprint ed., New York: Da Capo Press, 1972.

Dickson, David. *Therapeutica Sacra; showing briefly the method of Healing the Diseases of the Conscience, concerning Regeneration.* Edinburgh: Evan Taylor, 1664.

Diodati, Giovanni. *Pious and Learned Annotations upon the Holy Bible.* 2nd ed. London: Printed by Miles Flesher, for Nicholus Fussell, 1648.

Dixon, Robert. *The Doctrine of Faith, Justification, and Assurance.* London: William Godbid, 1668.

Documenta Reformatia: Teksten uit de Geschiedenis van Kerk en Theologie in de Nederlanden sedert de Hervorming. 2 vols. Ed. J. N. Bakhuizen van den Brink, et al. Kampen: Kok, 1960-62.

Doolittle, Thomas. *A Treatise concerning the Lords Supper; with three Dialogues for the most Useful Information of the Weak, in the Nature and Use of this Sacrament.* 20th ed. Boston: B. Green for Benjamin Eliot, 1708; reprint ed., Morgan, Pa.: Soli Deo Gloria Publications, 1998.

Downame, George. *The Covenant of Grace, or an Exposition Vpon Lvke I.73.74.75.* Dublin: Society of Stationers, 1631.

_____. *A Treatise of the Certainty of Perseverance.* Dublin: Society of Stationers, 1634.

_____. *A Treatise of Iustification.* London: Felix Kyngston for Nicolaus Bourne, 1633.

Downame, John. *The Christian Warfare aginst the Deuill, World, and Flesh.* London: William Stansby, for Philemon Stephens and Christopher Meredith, 1634.

_____. *A Guide to Godlynesse, or a treatise of a Christian Life. Shewing the duties, helpes, & Impediments.* London: Felix Kyngston, for Ed. Weuer & W. Bladen, 1622.

_____. *The Summe of Sacred Diuinitie. First Briefly and Methodically Propounded; And then More Largly & Cleerely handled and explaned.* London: William Stansby for W. Barrett, 1630.

_____. *A treatise of secvritie: diuided into two bookes. The former, intreating of carnall secvritie and hardnes of heart. The latter, intreating of spiritvall and*

Christian secvritie; wherein is shewed what it is, the causes and effects of it, and the meanes whereby it may be obtayned and preserued. London: William Stansby, 1622.

————. *A Treatise of the True Nature and Definition of Justifying Faith.* Oxford: Printed by I. Lichfield for E. Forrest, 1635.

Draxe, Thomas. *The Churches Securitie. Together with the antidote or preservative of ever waking faith.* London: Printed by George Eld for John Wright, 1608.

Driessen, Anthonias. *Het zaligmakend geloof verdedigd tegen de verbastering van het gereformeerd geloof.* Groningen, 1722.

Du Moulin, Pierre. *The Anatomy of Arminianisme: or the Opening of the Controversies lately handled in the Low Countries, concerning the Doctrine of Predestination, of the Death of Christ, of the Nature of Grace.* London: T. S., 1620.

Durham, James. *Heaven upon Earth, In the serene Tranquillity, and calm Composure; in the sweet Peace and solid Joy, of a good Conscience; sprinkled with the Blood of Jesus; and exercised always to be void of offence toward God and toward Men.* Edinburgh: Printed by the Heir of Andrew Anderson, 1685.

Dwight, Timothy. *Theology; Explained and Defended, in a Series of Sermons.* 5 vols. Middleton, Conn.: Printed by Clark and Lyman for Timothy Dwight, 1818-19.

Dyke, Daniel. *The Mystery of Selfe-deceiving. Or, a discourse and discovery of the Deceitfulness of mans Heart.* London: Printed by Edvvard Griffin, for Ralph Mab, 1614.

Eaton, John. *The Discovery of the most dangerous Dead Faith and Abrahams Steps of Faith.* London: J. Hart for J. Lewis, 1745.

————. *The Honey-combe of Free Justification by Christ Alone.* London: Printed by R. B. at the charge of R. Lancaster, 1642.

Edwards, Jonathan. *Works of Jonathan Edwards.* Ed. Edward Hickman, with a memoir by Soreno E. Dwight. 2 vols. London, 1834; reprint ed., Edinburgh: Banner of Truth Trust, 1974.

Elton, Edward. *Three Excellent and Pious Treatises, viz. 1. The Complaint of a Sanctifyed Sinner. 2. The Triumph of a true Christian. 3. The Great Mystery of Godlinesse Opened.* London: Printed by J. L. for Christopher Meredith, 1653.

The English Revolution: Fast Sermons to Parliament, 1640-1653. 34 vols. London: Cornmarket Press, 1970-71.

Erskine, Ebenezer. *The Whole Works of Ebenezer Erskine.* 3 vols. London: W. Baynes, 1810.

————, and Fisher, James. *The Westminster's Shorter Catechism Explained.* 14th ed. Edinburgh: D. Schaw, 1800; reprint ed., Lewes, East Sussex: Berith Publications, 1998.

Erskine, Ralph. *The Sermons and Practical Works of Ralph Erskine.* 7 vols. Aberdeen: George and Robert King, n.d.

Fenner, Dudley. *Certain Godly and Learned Treatises.* Edinburgh: Robert Waldegrave, 1592.

_____. *The Sacred Doctrine of Divinity, Gathered Out of the Worde of God.* N.p., 1599.

Firmin, Giles. *The real Christian, or A treatise of effectual calling.* London: D. Newman, 1670; reprint ed., Boston: Printed by Rogers & Fowle, for J. Edwards, and J. Blanchard, 1742.

F[isher], E[dward]. *The Marrow of Modern Divinity. Touching both the Covenant of Works and the Covenant of Grace: with their use and end.* 5th ed. London: Printed by R. Ibbitson for G. Calvert, 1647. [Edition with notes by Thomas Boston. London: T. Tegg, 1837.]

Flavel, John. *The Works of John Flavel.* 6 vols. London: W. Baynes and Son, 1820; reprint ed., London: Banner of Truth Trust, 1968.

Forbes, John. *A Letter for resolving this Question: How a Christian man may discerne the testimonie of Gods spirit, from the testimonie of his owne spirit, in witnessing his Adoption.* Middelburg: Richard Schilders, 1616.

_____. *A Treatise Tending to Cleare the Doctrine of Justification.* Middelburg: Richard Schilders, 1616.

Ford, Simon. *The spirit of bondage and adoption: largely and practically handled, with reference to the way and manner of working both those effects; and the proper cases of conscience belonging to them both.* London: Printed by T. Maxey for Sa. Gellibrand, 1655.

Foxe, John. *Acts and Monuments of the Christian Martyrs, and Matters Ecclesiasticall passed in the Church of Christ, from the Primitive beginning to these our daies.* 4 vols. London: Printed for the Company of Stationers, 1641.

Fraser, James. *A Treatise concerning Justifying and Saving Faith.* Edinburgh: John Mosman and Company, 1722.

Frere, Walter H., and Douglas, Charles E., eds. *Puritan Manifestoes.* London: Society for Promoting Christian Knowledge, 1954.

Fuller, Thomas. *Abel Redevivus; or, The Dead Yet Speaking. The Lives and Deaths of Modern Divines.* 2 vols. London: William Tegg, 1867.

_____. *The Worthies of England.* Ed. John Freeman. London: George Allen & Unwin, n.d.

Gataker, Thomas. *The Works of Thomas Gataker.* London: Jacob Benjamin, 1659.

Gib, Adam. *The Present Truth: A Display of the Secession Testimony.* 2 vols. Edinburgh: R. Fleming and A. Neill, 1774.

Gill, John. *A Body of Doctrinal and Practical Divinity; or a System of Practical Truths Deduced from the Sacred Scriptures.* London: Button and Son, and Whittingham and Arliss, 1815; reprint ed., Grand Rapids: Sovereign Grace Publishers, 1971.

Gillespie, George. "Notes of Debates and Proceedings of the Assembly of Divines and Other Commissioners at Westminster, February 1644 to January 1645." *The Presbyterian Armory,* vol. 2. Edinburgh: Robert Ogle, Oliver and Boyd, 1846.

_____. *A Treatise of Miscellany Questions.* Edinburgh: Gedeon Lithgovv, for George Svvintuun, 1649.

_____. *The Works of George Gillespie*. 2 vols. Reprint ed., Edmonton: Still Waters Revival Books, 1992.

Glay, Jacob. *Het fondament van het waarachtige Christendom, ofte de vrye rechtveerdigmakinge in de Vierschare Gods*. Middelburg, 1728.

Gomarus, Franciscus. *Over het rechtvaardigmakend geloof*. Leiden: N. Byl, 1723.

Goodwin, Thomas. *A Child of Light Walking in Darkness: or A Treatise Shewing the Causes, by which, the Cases, wherein, and the Ends, for which God Leaves His Children to Distresses of Conscience. Together with Directions How to Walk, so as to Come Forth of Such Condition*. London: Printed by F. G. for R. Dawlman, 1659.

_____. *The Object and Acts of Justifying Faith*. Reprint ed., Marshallton, Del.: The National Foundation for Christian Education, 1959.

_____. *The Tryall of a Christian's Growth. in Mortification, or Purging Out Corruption*. London: Printed for R. Dawlman, 1643.

_____. *The Works of Thomas Goodwin, D.D.* 12 vols. Ed. John C. Miller. Edinburgh: James Nichol, 1861-67; reprint ed., Eureka, Calif.: Tanski Publications, 1996.

Goodwin, T.; Nye, P.; Simpson, S.; Burroughes, J.; Bridge, W. *An Apologeticall Narration of Some Ministers Formerly Exiles in the Netherlands: Now Members of the Assembly of Divines, Humbly Submitted to the Honourable House of Parliament*. London, 1643.

Gouge, William. *The Works in Two Volumes: the First, Domesticall Duties. The Second, The Whole Armour of God*. London: John Beale, 1627.

Gray, Andrew. *The Mystery of Faith Opened Up: Or, some Sermons Concerning Faith*. Edinburgh: Printed by the Heirs and Successors of Andrew Anderson, 1697.

_____. *The Works of the Reverend and Pious Andrew Gray*. Glasgow: D. M'Kenzie, 1813; reprint ed., Morgan, Pa.: Soli Deo Gloria Publications, 1992.

Green, James Benjamin. *A Harmony of the Westminster Presbyterian Standards*. New York: Wm. Collins and World, 1976.

Greenham, Richard. *The Works of the Reverend and faithfull servant of Iesus Christ M. Richard Greenham*. London: imprinted by Felix Kingston for Robert Dexter, 1599; reprint ed., New York: De Capo Press, 1973.

Greenhill, William. *An Exposition of the prophet Ezekiel*. 2nd ed. London: Samuel Holdsworth, 1837; reprint ed., Edinburgh: Banner of Truth Trust, 1994.

_____. *The Sound-hearted Christian*. London: N. Crouch, 1670.

Grew, Obadiah. *A Sinner's Justification, or the Lord Jesvs Christ the Lord our righteousnesse*. London: Printed for Nevil Simmons, 1670.

Groenewegen, Jacob. *Eenige Brieven tot wederlegging van het systema of Dr. Alexander Comrie*. 's-Gravenhage, 1755.

Gurnall, William. *The Christian in Compleat Armour; A Treatise of the Saints' War against the Devil*. 3 vols. London: Printed for Ralph Smith, 1655-62; reprint ed. in one volume with biographical introduction by J. C. Ryle. Edinburgh: Banner of Truth Trust, 1974.

Guthrie, William. *The Christian's Great Interest.* 3rd ed. Boston: T. Green for Nicholas Boone, 1701; reprint ed., Edinburgh: Banner of Truth Trust, 1982.

Hadow, James. *The Antinomianism of the Marrow of Modern Divinity Detected.* Edinburgh: John Mosman & Co., 1721.

Hales, John. *Letters from the Synod of Dort to Sir Dudley Carlton, the English embassador at the Hague.* Glasgow: Robert and Andrew Foulis, 1765.

_____. *The Workes of the ever memorable Mr. John Hales of Eaton. Now first collected together.* 3 vols. Glasgow: R. and A. Foulis, 1765.

Hall, Joseph. *The Works of the Right Reverend Joseph Hall.* Ed. Philip Wynter. 10 vols. Oxford: University Press, 1863.

Halyburton, Thomas. *The Works of Thomas Halyburton.* Ed. Robert Burns. Glasgow: Blackie & Son, 1837.

Harris, Robert. *The VVay to Trve Happinesse. Deliuered in xxiv. sermons vpon the beatitvdes.* 2 vols. London: I. Bartlett, 1632; reprint ed., Morgan, Pa.: Soli Deo Gloria Publications, 1998.

Harsnet, Adam. *A Touchstone of Grace, Discouering the differences betweene true and counterfeit Grace: Laying downe infallible Evidences and markes of true Grace.* London: Printed by A. G. for P. Stephens and C. Meredith, 1635.

Hellenbroek, Abraham. *Wilhelmus à Brakel.* Leiden: Rouklagte, 1724.

_____. *A Specimen of Divine Truths.* Trans. Joel R. Beeke. Grand Rapids: Reformation Heritage Books, 1998.

Helwys, Thomas. *A Declaration of the Faith of English People Remaining at Amsterdam in Holland.* N.p., 1611.

Heppe, Heinrich. *Reformed Dogmatics.* Trans. G. T. Thomson. London: George Allen and Unwin, 1950.

Hieron, Samuel. *The Spirituall Sonne-ship.* London: William Hall for Samuel Macham, 1611.

Hildersam, Arthur. *CLII Lectures Upon Psalm LI.* London: George Miller for Edward Brewster, 1635.

_____. *The Doctrine of Communicating Worthily in the Lords Svpper.* London: Iohn Hauiland, 1630.

Hindson, Edward, ed. *Introduction to Puritan Theology: A Reader.* Foreword by J. I. Packer. Grand Rapids: Baker, 1976.

Hog, James. *The Controversy concerning the Marrow of Modern Divinity, dialogues I and II.* 2 vols. Edinburgh: for John Macky, 1721-22.

_____. *Remarks concerning the Rooting, Growth, and Ripeness of a Work of Grace in the Soul.* Edinburgh: the Heirs and Successors of Andrew Anderson, 1715.

Hollingworth, Richard. *The Holy Ghost on the Bench, other spirits at the bar; or the judgment of the Holy Spirit of God upon the spirits of the times.* London: Printed by J. M. for Luke Fawn, 1656.

Holtius, Nicolaus. *Bedenkingen over de Regtvaerdigmakinge.* Amsterdam: N. Byl, 1756.

_____. *Brief aan deszelfs broeder Jan Jacob Maurits Brahé*. Amsterdam: N. Byl, 1760.

_____. *Twee verhandelingen over Geloof*. Leiden: Johannes Hasebroek, 1759.

_____. *De zondaar gerechtvaardigd om niet*. Leiden: Johannes Hasebroek, 1757.

Hommius, Festus. *Oordeel des Synod: Nationalis Der Gereformeerde Kercken van de Vereenichde Nederlanden*. Dordrecht: n.p., 1619.

Hooker, Richard. *A Learned and Comfortable Sermon [on Habakkuk 1:4] of the certaintie and perpetuitie of faith in the Elect*. Oxford: n.p., 1612.

Hooker, Thomas. *The Application of Redemption by the Effectual Work of the Word and Spirit of Christ, for the Bringing Home of Lost Sinners to God*. London: Printed by Peter Cole, 1657-59; reprint ed., New York: Arno Press, 1972.

_____. *The Christian's two Chiefe Lessons, viz. Selfe-deniall, and Selfe-tryall. As also the Privilege of Adoption and Triall thereof*. London: T. B. for P. Stephens and C. Meredith, 1640; reprint ed., Ames, Ia.: International Outreach, 1997.

_____. *The Covenant of Grace Opened: Wherein These Particulars are Handled: viz. 1. What the Covenant of Grace Is, 2. What the Seales of the Covenant Are, 3. Who are the Parties and Subjects Fit to Receive These Seals. From All which Particulars Infants Baptisme Is Fully Proved and Vindicated*. London: G. Dawson, 1649.

_____. *The Poore Doubting Christian Drawne to Christ. Wherein the main Letts and Hindrances which Keepe Men from Comming to Christ are Discovered. With Speciall Helps to Recover God's Favour*. London: for R. Dawlman and L. F., 1635; reprint ed., Worthington, Pa.: Maranatha Publications, [1977].

_____. *The Soules Exaltation. A Treatise containing The soules Vnion with Christ, on 1 Cor. 6:17. The Soules Benefit from vnion with Christ, on 1 Cor. 1:30. The soules Justification, on 2 Cor. 5:21*. London: Iohn Haviland, for Andrew Crooke, 1638.

_____. *The Soules Preparation for Christ; or, a Treatise of Contrition: Wherein is Discovered How God Breaks the Heart and Wounds the Soule, in the Conversion of a Sinner to Himself*. London: for R. Davvlman, 1632; reprint ed., Ames, Ia.: International Outreach, 1994.

_____. *The Works of Rev. Thomas Hooker*. 4 vols. London: n.p., 1637-45.

Hooper, John. *The Early Writings of John Hooper, D.D. Lord Bishop of Gloucester and Worcester, Martyr, 1555*. Ed. for the Parker Society by Samuel Carr, M.A. Cambridge: Cambridge University Press, 1843.

_____. *Later Writings of Bishop Hooper, together with his letters and other pieces*. Ed. for the Parker Society by Charles Nevinson, M.A. Cambridge: Cambridge University Press, 1852.

Hoornbeeck, Johannes. *Theologia Practica*. 2 vols. Ultrajecti: Waesberge, 1658.

Hopkins, Ezekiel. *The Whole Works of Ezekiel Hopkins*. Edinburgh: A. C. Black, 1841; reprint ed., Morgan, Pa.: Soli Deo Gloria Publications, 1997.

Howe, John. *The Whole Works of John Howe*. 8 vols. Ed. John Hunt. London: F. Westley, 1822; reprint ed. in 3 vols., Ligonier, Pa.: Soli Deo Gloria Publications, 1990.

Immens, Petrus. *The Pious Communicant Encouraged.* Trans. John Bassett. 2 vols. New York: Isaac Collins, 1801.

Knappen, Marshall M., ed. *Two Elizabethan Puritan Diaries.* Chicago: American Society of Church History, 1933.

Knox, John. *The Works of John Knox.* Ed. David Laing. 6 vols. Edinburgh: Wodrow Society (vols. 1-3), 1846-54; Johnstone and Hunter (vol. 4), 1855; Bannatyne Club (vols. 5-6), 1856-64.

Koelman, Jacobus. *De Natuur en Gronden des Geloofs. By wege van een Brief ingeregt ter Vaststelling van de Staat dergenen die Christ in Geloof Omhelsen.* 2nd ed. 's-Gravenhage: Gerardus Winterswyk, 1724.

Lampe, Friedrich Adolph. *De verborgentheit van het Genaade-Verbondt.* Amsterdam: Hendrik Vievoet, 1743.

_____. *De Gestalte der Bruyd Christi voor haaren uitgang uyt Babel.* Trans. J. Le Long. Amsterdam: Antony Schoonenburg, 1719.

_____. *Milch der Wahrheit volgens Anleitung des Heidelberger Katechismus.* 's-Gravenhage: Gerardus Winterswyk, 1750.

_____. *Vier academische verhandelingen over het zaligmakend geloof.* Amsterdam: Hendrik Vieroot, 1723.

_____. *Viertien Betrachtingen over de Voorbooden der Eeuwigheid.* Amsterdam: Hendrik Vieroot, 1736.

Lawrence, Matthew. *The Use and Practice of Faith: or, Faiths Vniversal Vsefulness, and Quickning Influence into every Kinde and Degree of the Christian Life.* London: A. Maxey for Willian, 1657.

Leigh, Edward. *A Systeme or Body of Divinity.* 2nd ed. London: Printed by A. M. for William Lee, 1662.

Leydekker, Melchoir. *De Verborgentheid des Geloofs eenmaal den Heiligen Overgelevert.* Amsterdam: Schouten, 1729.

Lightfoot, John. "The Journal of the Proceedings of the Assembly of Divines from January 1, 1643, to December 31, 1644; and the Letters to and from Dr. Lightfoot," *The Whole Works of the Rev. John Lightfoot,* vol. 13. Ed. John Rogers Pitman. London: J.F. Dove, 1844.

Linacre, Robert. *A Comfortable Treatise for the reliefe of such as are Afflicted in Conscience.* London: H. L. for William Leake, 1610.

Love, Christopher. *Grace: The Truth and Growth and Different Degrees thereof.* London: T. R. and E. M. for John Rothwell, 1652; reprint ed., Morgan, Pa.: Soli Deo Gloria Publications, 1997.

_____. *A treatise of effectual calling and election. In xvi sermons, on 2 Pet. 1:10. Wherein a Christian may discern, whether yet he be effectually called and elected. And what course he ought to take that he may attain the assurance thereof.* London: Printed for John Rothwell, 1655; reprint ed., Morgan, Pa.: Soli Deo Gloria Publications, 1998.

_____. *The Works of that Faithful Servant of Jesus Christ, Mr. Christopher Love.* 3 vols. Dalry: J. Gemmill, 1805; reprint ed., *The Works of Christopher Love,* Vol. 1 only. Morgan, Pa.: Soli Deo Gloria Publications, 1995.

Luther, Martin. *D. Martin Luthers Werke*. Kritische Gesamtausgabe. 109 volumes. Ed. J. C. F. Knaake, et al. Weimar: Herman Bohlaus, 1883-.

————. *Lectures on Romans*. Ed. Wilhelm Pauck. Library of Christian Classics, no. 15. Philadelphia: Westminster Press, 1961.

————. *Luther's Works*. Ed. J. Pelikan, et al. 55 vols. St. Louis: Concordia Publishing House (vols. 1-30); Philadelphia: Fortress Press (vols. 31-55), 1955-79.

————. *Works*. 6 vols. Philadelphia: Muhlenberg Press, 1930-1943.

Maccovius, Johannes. *Loci communes theologici*. Editio postrema. Opera & Studio Nicolai Arnoldi. Amstelodami: apud Ludovicum & Danielem Elzevirios, 1658.

M'Millan, Samuel. *The Beauties of the Rev. Ralph Erskine being a Selection of the most striking Illustrations of Gospel Doctrine Contained in his Whole Works*. 4th ed. 2 vols. Glasgow: Archibald Fullarton, 1836.

Manton, Thomas. *The Complete Works of Thomas Manton, D.D.* With memoir of the author by William Harris. Ed. T. Smith. 22 vols. London: J. Nisbet, 1870-75; reprint ed., Worthington, Pa.: Maranatha Publications, [1980].

Marck, Johannes à. *Het Merch der Christene Got-geleertheit; Behelsende te Gelyk Eene Korte Leeringe der Waarheden*. Rotterdam: Nicolaas en Paulus Topijn, 1730.

Marshall, Walter. *The Gospel Mystery of Sanctification Open'd in Sundry Practical Directions*. 2nd ed. London: for J. L., J. N., and B. S. and N. Cliff and D. Jackson, 1714; reprint ed., Grand Rapids: Zondervan, 1956.

Martyr, Peter. *The Common Places of the Most Famous and Renowned Divine Doctor Peter Martyr*. Trans. A. Martin. London: Printed for Henrie Denham, Thomas Chard, William Broome, Andrew Maunsell, 1583.

————. *Most Learned and Fruitful Commentaries of D. Peter Martyr upon the Epistle of S. Paul to the Romans*. London: John Daye, 1568.

Matthews, A. G., ed. *The Savoy Declaration of Faith and Order*. London: Independent Press, 1959.

Maxey, Anthony. *The Goulden Chaine of Mans Saluation*. London: F. K. for Clement Knight, 1610.

Mead, Matthew. *The Almost Christian Discovered; Or the False Professor Tried and Cast*. London: T. Parkhurst, 1662; reprint ed., Morgan, Pa.: Soli Deo Gloria Publications, 1988.

Melanchthon, Philip. *Melanchthon on Christian Doctrine: Loci Communes 1555*. Trans. and ed. Clyde L. Manschreck. Intro. Hans Engelland. Oxford: University Press, 1965; reprint ed., Grand Rapids: Baker, 1982.

————. *Philippi Melancthonis opera quae supersunt omnia*. Corpus Reformatorum, volumes 1-28. Ed. C. G. Bretschneider and H. E. Bindseil. Brunsvigae: C. A. Schwetschke et filium, 1834-60.

Merrill, Thomas F., ed. and intro. *William Perkins, 1558-1602. English Puritanist. His Pioneer Works on Casuistry: "A Discourse of Conscience" and "The Whole Treatise of Cases of Conscience."* Nieuwkoop: B. DeGraaf, 1966.

Middleton, Erasmus. *Biographia Evangelica: Or, An Historical Account of the Lives and Deaths Of the most eminent and evangelical Authors or Preachers, Both*

British and Foreign, in the several Denominations of Protestants. London: R. Denham for the Author, 1779-86.

Mitchell, Alexander F. *Catechisms of the Second Reformation.* London: James Nisbet & Co., 1886.

_____, and Struthers, John, eds. *Minutes of the Sessions of the Westminster Divines.* Edinburgh: William Blackwood and Sons, 1874.

Mosse, Miles. *Ivstifying and Saving Faith Distingvished from the faith of the Deuils.* Cambridge: Cantrell Legse, 1614.

Musculus, Wolfgang. *Commonplaces of Christian religion, Gathered by Wolfgang Musculus, for the Use of Such as Desire the Knowledge of Godly Truth.* Trans. Iohn Man. London: Henry Bynneman, 1578.

Myseras, Lambertus. *Der Vromen Ondervinding op den Weg Naar den Hemel, Voorgesteld in Vragen en Antwoorden.* Reprint ed., 's-Gravenhage: C. de Bruin, n.d.

Neal, Daniel. *History of the Puritans, or Protestant Non-Conformists from the Reformation to the Toleration Act of King William and Queen Mary.* 4 vols. Dublin: Printed for Brice Edmond, 1755; reprint ed. in 3 vols., Minneapolis: Klock & Klock Christian Publishers, 1979.

Newton, John. *The Works of the Rev. John Newton.* With memoir of his life by Richard Cecil. 3rd ed. 6 vols. London: Hamilton, Adams & Co., 1820; reprint ed., Edinburgh: Banner of Truth Trust, 1985.

Nicols, Thomas. *An Abridgement of the Whole Body of Divinity Extracted from the learned works of that ever-famous, and revered Divine — Mr. Wm. Perkins.* London: W. B., 1684.

Olevianus, Caspar. *An Exposition of the Symbole of the Apostles, or rather of the Articles of Faith. In which the chief points of the everlasting and free covenant between God and the faithful is briefly and plainly handled.* Trans. John Field. London: H. Middleton, 1581.

Owen, John. *Biblical Theology.* Trans. Stephen Westcott. Morgan, Pa.: Soli Deo Gloria Publications, 1996.

_____. *An Exposition of the Epistle to the Hebrews.* Ed. William H. Goold. 7 vols. London: Johnstone & Hunter, 1855; reprint ed., Grand Rapids: Baker, 1980.

_____. *The Works of John Owen.* Ed. William H. Goold. 24 vols. London: Johnstone & Hunter, 1850-53; reprint ed. of 16 vols., which lacks exposition of Hebrews. Edinburgh: Banner of Truth Trust, 1976.

Pareus, David. *Operum theologicorum exegeticorum.* Francofurti: apud Viduam Ionae Rosae, 1647.

Pearse, Edward. *The Best Match, or, The Soul's Espousal to Christ.* Reprint ed., Morgan, Pa.: Soli Deo Gloria Publications, 1994.

Perkins, William. *The Workes of that Famovs and VVorthy Minister of Christ in the Vniuersitie of Cambridge, Mr. William Perkins.* 3 vols. London: John Legatt, 1612-13.

Petto, Samuel. *The Voyce of the Spirit. Or, an essay towards a discoverie of the witnessings of the Spirit.* London: L. Chapman, 1654.

Pictet, Benedict. *Christian Theology.* Trans. Frederick Reyroux. Philadelphia: Presbyterian Board of Publications, n.d.

Piscator, Johannes. *A Learned and Profitable Treatise of Mans Iustification.* London: Thomas Creede for Robert Dexter, 1599.

Polhill, Edward. *Precious Faith.* London: Thomas Cockerill, 1675.

Preston, John. *The Breast-Plate of Faith and Love.* 5th ed. London: Imprinted by W. I. for Nicholas Bourne, 1632; reprint ed., Edinburgh: Banner of Truth Trust, 1979.

_____. *The Golden Sceptor Held Forth to the Humble.* Reprint ed., Ligonier, Pa.: Soli Deo Gloria Publications, 1990.

_____. *The New Covenant, or the Saints Portion: A Treatise Unfolding the all-sufficiencie of God, Man's uprightness, and the Covenant of Grace.* 10th edition. London: Imprinted by I. D. for Nicholas Bourne, 1639.

_____. *The Saints Qualification; or, A Treatise of Humiliation and Sanctification.* 3rd ed. London: R. B. for Nicholas Bourne, 1637.

_____. *A Treatise of Effectvall Faith. Deliuered in sixe Sermons vpon I Thes. 1:3.* London: for Nicholas Bourne, 1631.

Puritan Sermons 1659-1689: Being the Morning Exercises at Cripplegate, St. Giles in the Fields, and in Southwark by Seventy-five Ministers of the Gospel in or near London. With notes and translations by James Nichols. 6 vols. London, 1674; reprint ed., Wheaton, Ill.: Richard Owen Roberts Publishers, 1981.

Purnell, Robert. *The Way Step by Step to Sound and Saving Conversion, with a clear discovery of the two states, viz: nature and grace: and how to know in which state one is, and the way to come out of the one to the other.* London: T. Childe and L. Parry for Edw. Thomas, 1659.

Ramus, Peter. *The Art of Logick (Gathered Out of Aristotle and Set in Due Forms) According to his instructions.* Trans. Antony Wooten. London: I. D. for Nicholas Bourne, 1626.

Reynolds, Edward. *Three Treatises of The Vanity of the Creature. The Sinfulnesse of Sinne. The Life of Christ.* London: R. B. for Rob. Boftocke and George Badger, 1642.

_____. *The Whole Works of the Right Rev. Edward Reynolds, D.D.* 6 vols. Morgan, Pa.: Soli Deo Gloria Publications, 1992-.

Roberts, Francis. *Believers Evidences for Eternall Life.* London: T. R., 1649.

Robinson, John. *The Works of John Robinson, Pastor of the Pilgrim Fathers.* Ed. Robert Ashton. 3 vols. London: John Snow, 1851.

Rogers, John. *The Doctrine of Faith: wherein are particularly handled twelve Principall Points, which explaine the Nature and Vse of it.* London: for N. Newbery and H. Overton, 1629.

Rogers, Richard. *Certain Sermons Preached and Penned by Richard Rogers, Preacher of Weathersfield in Essex, Directly Tending to These Three Ends. First, to Bring Any Bad Person (That Has Not Committed the Sin that is Unpardonable) to True Conversion. Secondly, to Stablish and Settle All Such as Are Converted, in Faith and Repentance. Thirdly, to Lead Them Forward (That Are so Settled) in the Christian Life, to Bring Forth the Fruit of Both*. London: Felix Kyngston for Thomas Man, 1612.

_____. *Seven Treatises Containing Such Direction as Is Gathered out of the Holy Scriptures, Leading and Guiding to True Happiness, Both in This Life, and in the Life to Come: and May Be Called the Practise of Christianity*. London: Felix Kyngston for Thomas Man, 1610.

Rogers, Timothy. *The Righteous Mans Evidences for Heaven: Or, a Treatise Shewing how Every One, While He Lives Here, may Certainly Know what shall become of Him after His Departure out of This Life*. 12th ed. London: R. Young for E. Brewster, 1637.

Rollock, Robert. *Select Works of Robert Rollock*. Edinburgh: The Wodrow Society, 1849.

_____. *A Treatise of Gods Effectual Calling*. Trans. Henry Holland. Preface by Theodore Beza. London: Felix Kyngston, 1603.

Romaine, William. *The Life, Walk and Triumph of Faith*. With an Account of His Life and Work by Peter Toon. London: William Baynes & Son, 1824; reprint ed., London: James Clarke & Co., 1970.

_____. *The Whole Works of the late Reverend William Romaine*. London: Printed for Thomas Tegg and Son, 1837.

Rous, Francis. *The Heavenly Academy, i.e.: or, The Highest School vvhere alone is that Highest Teaching, the Teaching of the Heart*. London: by R. Young for J. Dartlet, 1638.

_____. *The Mysticall Marriage; or, Experimental Discoveries of the Heavenly Marriage betweene a Soul and her Saviour*. London: William Iones, 1631.

Rutherford, Samuel. *Christ Dying and Drawing Sinners to Himselfe*. London: Printed by J. D. for Andrew Cooke, 1647.

_____. *Fourteen Communion Sermons*. Glasgow: Charles Glass and Co., 1877; reprint ed., Edinburgh: James A. Dickson, 1986.

_____. *The Covenant of Life Opened, or a Treatise of the Covenant of Grace*. Edinburgh: Printed by Andro Anderson for Robert Broun, 1655.

_____. *Influences of the Life of Grace*. London: T.C. for Andrew Crook, 1659.

_____. *Letters of the Rev. Samuel Rutherford*. New York: Robert Carter & Brothers, 1881.

_____. *The Trial and Triumph of Faith*. Edinburgh: Printed for the Assembly's Committee of the Free Church of Scotland by William Collins and Co., 1845.

Schaff, Philip. *The Creeds of Christendom, with a History and Critical Notes*. 3 vols. New York: Harper and Brothers Publishers, 1877-78.

Schortinghuis, Wilhelmus. *Het Innige Christendom tot Overtuiginge van Onbegenadigde, Bestieringe en Opwekkinge van Begenadigde Zielen*. Reprint ed., Nieuw-Beijerland: J. P. van den Tol, 1929.

Scudder, Henry. *The Christian's Daily Walk, in holy Security and Peace*. Reprint ed., Harrisburg, Va.: Sprinkle Publications, 1984.

Sedgwick, Obadiah. *The Dovbting Beleever: or, A Treatise Containing 1. The Nature*

2. *The Kinds* 3. *The Springs* 4. *The Remedies of Dovbtings, incident to weak Beleevers.* London: Printed by M. F. for Thomas Nicols, 1641; reprint ed., Morgan, Pa.: Soli Deo Gloria Publications, 1993.

_____. *The Humbled Sinner Resolved what He should do to be Saved; Or, Faith in the Lord Jesus Christ the only way of salvation for sensible sinners. Discovering the quality, object, acts, seat, subject, inseparable concomitants and degrees of Justifying Faith.* London: T. R. & E. M. for A. Byfield, 1656.

Shaw, Samuel. *Communion with God.* Glasgow: Printed by R. Urio, 1749; reprint ed., Glasgow: for William Collins, 1829.

Shepard, Thomas. *The Complete Works of Thomas Shepard.* 3 vols. Ed. John A. Albro. Boston: Doctrinal Tract & Book Society, 1853; reprint ed., Ligonier, Pa.: Soli Deo Gloria Publications, 1991-92.

Sibbes, Richard. *The Complete Works of Richard Sibbes.* Ed. with memoir by Alexander Ballach Grosart. 7 vols. Edinburgh: James Nichol, 1862; reprint ed., Edinburgh: Banner of Truth Trust, 1973-82.

Smith, Henry. *The Works of Henry Smith.* Ed. Thomas Smith. 2 vols. Edinburgh: James Nichol, 1866-67.

Smytegelt, Bernardus. *Des Christens Eenige Troost in Leven en Sterven, of Verklaringe over den Heidelbergschen Catechismus in LII Predicatien; Benevens V Belydenis-Predicatien.* Middelburg: Ottho en Pieter van Thol, Den Haag, en A. L. en M. H. Callenfels, 1747.

_____. *Het Gekrookte Riet, of Hondert-vyf-en-veertig Predicatien over Mattheus XII:20-21.* 2 vols. Middelburg: Ottho en Pieter van Thol; A. L. en M. H. Callenfels, 1744.

_____. *Keurstoffen of verzameling van vijftig uitmuntende Predikatien, waaronder eenige over zeer gewigtige Praktikale Stoffen.* Amsterdam, 1764; reprint ed., Ter Aa: Gebr. Den Hertog, 1914.

_____. *Maandagse Catechisatien Naar Aanleiding der Heidelbergse Catechismus: Zijnde een Huis en Handboek tot Onderwijzing in de Gereformeerde Leer. Voorgesteld in Vragen en Antwoorden.* Utrecht: W. M. den Hertog, 1837.

_____. *De Weg der Heiligmaking, voorgesteld in negen predikatien over Mattheus V:4, 7.* Reprint ed., Zerikzee: P. de Looze, 1857.

Spanheim, Frederick, Jr. *Opera omnia.* 3 vols. Leiden: Boutestein & Luchtmans, 1701-1703.

Sparke, Thomas. *A Short Treatise, very comfortable to all those Christians that be troubled and disquieted in theyr Consciences with the sight of their own Infirmities; Wherein is shewed how such may in their own Selves finde whereby to Assure them of their Free Election, Effectual Vocation, and Justification.* London: Ralph Newbery, 1580.

Spranckhuysen, Dionisius. *Een korte voorstellinge van de natuur v. h. waare Zaligmakende Geloove.* Dordrecht, 1736.

Spurstowe, William. *The Wells of Salvation Opened: or A Treatise discovering the nature, preciousness, and usefulness, of the Gospel Promises, and Rules for the Right Application of them.* London: T. R. & E. M. for Ralph Smith, 1655.

Stoddard, Solomon. *A Guide to Christ, or the Way of Directing Souls that are under the work of Conversion*. London: J. Allen for N. Boone, 1714; reprint ed., Ligonier, Pa.: Soli Deo Gloria Publications, 1993.

_____. *The Tryal of Assurance, Set forth in a Sermon*. Boston: Printed by B. Green and J. Allen, 1698.

Symonds, Joseph. *The Case and Cvre of a Deserted Soul or a Treatise Concerning the Nature, Kinds, Degrees, Symptoms, Causes, Cure of and Mistakes about Spirituall Desertions*. London: T. Badger, for Luke Fawne, 1641; reprint ed., Ligonier, Pa.: Soli Deo Gloria Publications, 1996.

Synopsis of overzicht van de Zuiverste Theologie samengevat in twee en vijftig verhandelingen. Trans. Dirk van Dijk. 2 vols. Enschede: J. Boersma, 1964-66.

Taffin, Jean. *The Amendment of Life, Comprised in Fower Books*. London: G. Bishop, 1595.

_____. *Of the Marks of the Children of God, and of Their Comforts in Afflictions*. Trans. Anne Prowse for Thomas Man. London: Thomas Orwin, 1590.

Tappert, Theodore, ed. *The Book of Concord: The Confessions of the Evangelical Lutheran Church*. Philadelphia: Fortress Press, 1959.

Taylor, Thomas. *The Progress of Saints to Fvll Holinesse*. London: W. I. for Iohn Bartlet, 1630.

_____. *The Works of that faithful servant of Jesus Christ, Dr. Thom. Taylor*. London: T. R. & E. M. for John Bartlet the elder and John Bartlet the younger, 1653.

Teellinck, Willem. *Alle de wercken van Mr. Willem Teellinck*. 3 vols. Utrecht: Johannes van Someren, 1659-64.

_____. *The Ballance of the Sanctuarie*. Trans. C. Harmar. Ed. T. Gataker. London: I. D. for William Sheffard, 1621.

_____. *The Christian Conflict and Conquest*. London: John Pawlar for I. Bellamie, 1622.

_____. *Het Nieuwe Jeruzalem vertoond in eene samenspraak, tusschen Christus en Maria, zittende aan Zijne voeten*. Utrecht: Johannes van Someren, 1652; reprint ed., Middelburg: F. P. D'Huij, 1884.

_____. *Pauls Complaint against his Naturall Corruption: With the Means how to bee Delivered from the power of the same*. London: John Dawson: for I. Bellamie, 1621.

_____. *The Resting Place of the Minde, That is, a Propounding of the Wonderfull Providence of God, whereupon a Christian man ought to Rest and Repose Himselfe when Outward Means Fail Them*. Ed. T. Gataker. London: Iohn Haviland for Edward Brewster, 1622.

_____. *De Toets-steen des geloofs, waerin de gelegentheyt des waren Saligmakende geloofs nader ontdekt wordt, zoodat een yder sich selven daer aen kan Toetsen, of hij oock het ware salighmakende geloove heeft*. Utrecht: Johannes van Someren, 1662.

Toon, Peter, ed. *The Correspondence of John Owen, 1616-1683*. London: James Clarke & Co., 1970.

Toplady, Augustus. *The Works of Augustus Toplady*. 6 vols. London: Printed for

William Baynes and Son, and H. S. Baynes, by W. Gracie, 1825; reprint ed. in 1 vol., Harrisonburg, Va.: Sprinkle Publications, 1987.

Traill, Robert. *The Works of the late Reverend Robert Traill, A.M.* 4 vols. Edinburgh: Printed by Geo. Caw for J. Ogle, M. Ogle, and J. Steven & Co., R. Ogle, and T. Hamilton, and T. Johnston, 1810; reprint ed., 4 vols. in 2, Edinburgh: Banner of Truth Trust, 1975.

Turretin, Francis. *Institutes of Elenctic Theology.* Trans. George Musgrave Giger. Ed. James T. Dennison, Jr. 3 vols. Phillipsburg, N.J.: P & R Publishing, 1992-97.

Twisse, William. *A briefe Catecheticall Exposition of Christian Doctrine.* London: G. M. for Robert Bird, 1632.

_____. *The Doctrine of the Synod of Dort and Arles, reduced to the practise.* Amsterdam: G. Thorp, 1631.

_____. *The Doubting Conscience Resolved.* London: n.p., 1652.

_____. *The Riches of Gods Love Unto the Vessells of Mercy, Consistent with His Absolute Hatred or Reprobation of the Vessells of Wrath.* Oxford: Leonard Lichfield and H. Hall for Tho. Robinson, 1653.

_____. *A Treatise of Mr. Cottons, Clearing certaine Doubts Concerning Predestination. Together with an Examination Thereof.* London: Printed by J. D. for Andrew Crook, 1646.

_____. *Vindiciae gratiae, potestatis, ac providentia Dei, hoc est, ad Examen Libelli Perkinsiani de Praedestinationis Modo et Ordine, institum a Jacobo Arminio, responsio scholastica, tribus libris absoluta.* Amstelodami: apud Joannem Janssonium, 1632.

Udemans, Godefridus Cornelisz. *Christelycke bedenckingen, die een geloovige ziele dagelycx behoort te betrachten, gestelt op elcke dagh van de week. Noch is hier bygevoeght De Leeder van Iacob, dat is: Korte ende Naeckte Afbeeldinghe van den rechten wegh, na den Hemel, in sekere trappen onderscheyden.* Dordrecht: Voor F. Boels, 1603.

_____. *Practycke, dat is wercklycke oeffeninge van de Christelijcke hooft-deuchden, gheloove, hope ende liefde.* Dordrecht: Fransoys Boels, 1632.

Ursinus, Zacharias. *A Collection of Certaine Learned and Excellent Discourses: Treating and Discussing Diverse Hard and Difficult Points of Christian Religion.* Collected and published in Latin by D. David Pareus. London: H. L. for Iohn Royston, 1613.

_____. *Opera theologica.* Tomi tres. Ed. Quirini Reuteri. Heidelbergae: Impensis Iona Rosae, 1612.

_____. *The Commentary of Dr. Zacharias Ursinus on the Heidelberg Catechism.* Trans. G. W. Willard. 2nd ed. Columbus: Scott and Bascom, 1852.

Ussher, James. *A Body of Divinitie: Or the Sum and Substance of Christian Religion.* London: Tho. Bovvnes and Geo. Badger, 1645; reprint ed., London: R. B. Seeley and W. Burnside, 1841.

Van der Groe, Theodore. *De Bekeering. Verzameling van zeventien op elkander volgende leerredenen.* 2nd ed. Reprint ed., Amsterdam, 1854.

_____. *Beschryvinge van het oprecht en zielzaligend geloove*. Rotterdam: E. van Praag, 1812.

_____. *Des Christens Eenige Troost in Leven en Sterven, of Verklaring over den Heidelbergschen Catechismus*. 3 vols. Rotterdam: J. van der Vliet, 1838-39; reprint ed., Rotterdam: Gebr. Huge, 1890.

_____. *De Gereformeerde Grondleer van de Genadige Rechtvaardigmaking door het Geloof*. Reprint ed., Veenendaal: G. Kool, 1978.

_____. "Over the noodige voorbereidselen, wezenlyke eigenschappen en onafscheidelijke gevolgen van het ware zaligmakende geloof." Forward to *De trapsgewijze overwinning*, by Ralph Erskine. Nijkerk: I. J. Malga, 1862; reprint ed., Utrecht: Den Hertog's Uitgeverij, [1985].

_____. *Toetssteen der ware en valsche Genade*. 2 vols. in 1. Nijkerk: Malga, 1866.

_____. *Het Zaligmakende Geloof*. Amsterdam: H. Hoveker, 1838.

Van der Kemp, Johannes. *The Christian Entirely the Property of Christ, in Life and Death: Exhibited in Fifty-three Sermons on the Heidelbergh Catechism*. 2 vols. Trans. John M. Van Harlingen. New Brunswick, N.J.: A. Blauwelt, 1810; reprint ed., Grand Rapids: Reformation Heritage Books, 1997.

_____. *Drie Bevindelijke Brieven over de Rechtvaardigmaking*. Nieuw-Beijerland: J. P. v.d. Tol, n.d.; reprint ed., ed. C.R. van den Berg. Kampen: De Groot, 1991.

Van Groenewoud, L. *Een nauwkeurige behandeling van het zaligmaakende geloov*. Leiden, 1726.

Van Lodenstein, Jodocus. *Beschouwinge van Zion*. Amsterdam: J. van Hardenburg, 1718.

_____. *De Heerlykheyd Van een Waar Christelijk Leven. Uytblinkende in een Godsaligen Wandel, volgens het Geestelijk Licht des Evangeliums, te sien in Jezus heerlyk Voorbeeld, nedrige Geboorte en Armoede, om ons to Wederbaren, en Rijk in God te maken*. Amsterdam: Jacobus van Hardenburg, 1711.

_____. *Het Vervolg van den Geestelyken Opwekker, Voorgestelt in Negen Predicatien*. Amsterdam: Jacobus van Hardenburg, 1707.

Van Mastricht, Petrus. *Beschouwende en praktikale Godgeleerdheit*. 4 vols. Rotterdam: Van Pelt, 1749.

Van Thuynen, Theodore. *Korte uitlegginge van het gereformeerde geloof*. 2nd ed. Leeuwarden, 1722.

Vermeer, Justus. *De Leere der Waarheid*. 2 vols. Utrecht: Nicolaas van Vucht, 1749-50.

Verschuir, Johan. *Waarheit in het Binneste, of, Bevindelyke Godtgeleertheit, hoe de Waarheden Christi in syn koningkryk van desselfs onderdanen beschouwelyk en bevindelyk moeten gekent worden tot Saligheit*. 2nd ed. Groningen: Pieter Bandsma, 1738.

Vines, Richard. *Gods Drawing, and Mans Coming to Christ. With the difference between a true inward Christian, and the outward formalist*. London: for Abel Roper, 1662.

Voetius, Gisbertus. *Catechisatie over den Heidelbergschen Catechismus*. Ed. A. Kuyper. 2 vols. Rotterdam: Gebroeders Huge, 1891.

_____. *Disputationes theologicae*. 5 vols. Ultrajecti: apud Joannem à Waesberge, Anonium Smytegelt, 1648-69.

_____. *Geestelijke Verlatingen*. Voortgezet door Johannes Hoornbeeck. Utrecht: Lambert Roeck, 1646; reprint ed., n.p.: Het Traktaat-genootschap "Filippus," 1898.

_____. *Proeve van de Kracht der Godzaligheydt*. Utrecht: Simon de Vries, 1656.

_____. *Selectarum disputationum fasciculus*. Recognovit et praefatus est Abraham Kuyper. Bibliotheca Reformata, Volumen Quartum. Amstelodami: Joannem Adamum Wormser, 1887.

_____. *Te asketika sive Exercitia Pietatis*. Gorinchen: Vink, 1654.

Walker, Williston, ed. *The Creeds and Platforms of Congregationalism*. New York: Charles Scribner's Sons, 1893.

Watson, Thomas. *The Select Works of the Rev. Thomas Watson, Comprising His Celebrated Body of Divinity, in a series of Lectures on the Shorter Catechism, and Various Sermons and Treatises*. New York: Robert Carter & Brothers, 1856.

Wesley, John. *The Works of the Reverend John Wesley*. Ed. Thomas Jackson. 3rd ed. 14 vols. London: Wesleyan Conference Office, 1872; reprint ed., Grand Rapids: Baker, 1983.

Whitaker, Jeremiah. *The Christians Great Design on Earth, is, to attain Assurance for Heaven: or, how in this life hee may lay hold on Eternall Life*. London: G. Miller for John Bellamie, 1645.

Whitefield, George. *The Works of George Whitefield*. 6 vols. London: Printed for Edward and Charles Dilly, 1771.

Wilcox, Thomas. *A Discourse Touching the Doctrine of Doubting*. Cambridge: I. Legat for the Vniuersitie of Cambridge, 1598.

_____. *The Works of Thomas Wilcox*. London: Iohn Haviland, 1624.

Willard, Samuel. *A Compleat Body of Divinity in Two Hundred and Fifty Expository Lectures on the Assembly's Shorter Catechism*. Boston: B. Green and S. Kneeland for B. Eliot and D. Henchman, 1726.

Williams, George, et al., eds. *Thomas Hooker: Writings in England and Holland, 1626-1633*. Harvard Theological Studies, no. 28. Cambridge: University Press, 1975.

Willison, John. *The Whole Practical Works of John Willison*. Aberdeen: D. Chalmers and Co., 1817.

Wilson, Thomas. *A Dialogve About Ivstification by Faith*. London: W. Hall for N. Butter, 1610.

Witsius, Herman. *The Oeconomy of the Covenants between God and Man. Comprehending A Complete Body of Divinity*. Trans. William Crookshank, with life of author prefixed. 3 vols. London: Printed for Edward Dilly, 1763; reprint ed. in 2 vols., Escondido, Calif.: The den Dulk Christian Foundation, 1991.

_____. *Sacred Dissertations on the Apostles' Creed*. Trans. with notes by Donald

Fraser. 2 vols. Glasgow: Khull, Blackie & Co., et al., 1823; reprint ed., Escondido, Calif.: The den Dulk Christian Foundation, 1993.

_____. *Sacred Dissertations on the Lord's Prayer.* Trans. with notes by William Pringle. Edinburgh: T. Clark, 1839; reprint ed., Escondido, Calif.: The den Dulk Christian Foundation, 1994.

_____. *A Treatise on Christian Faith.* Extracted and trans. R. Madan. London: E. Dilly and T. Fuller, 1761.

Woodbridge, Benjamin. *The Method of Grace in the Justification of Sinners.* London: T. R. and E. M. for E. Paxton, 1656.

Yarrow, Robert. *Soveraigne Comforts for a Troubled Conscience wherein the Subtilties of Satan are Discovered.* London: G. M. for P. Stephens and C. Meredith, 1634.

Zanchius, Hieronymus. *The Doctrine of Absolute Predestination Stated and Asserted.* Trans. A. Toplady. Wilmington: Adams's Press, 1793; reprint ed., Grand Rapids: Sovereign Grace Publishers, 1971.

_____. *An Excellent and Learned Treatise of the spiritual marriage betvveene Christ and the Church, and every faithfull man.* London: Iohn Legate for the Vniversitie of Cambridge, 1592.

_____. *H. Zanchivs: His Confession of Christian Religion: Which Now at length being 70 years of Age, He Caused to be Published in the Name of Himself and His Family.* Cambridge: Iohn Legat, 1599.

_____. *Speculum Christianum or A Christian Survey for the Conscience.* Trans. H. N. London: George Eld, 1614.

_____. *Clariss. Viri D. Hier Zanchii Omnium operum theologicorum.* Tomi octo. Genevae: sumptibus Samuelis Crispini, 1619.

Zwingli, Huldreich. *Huldreich Zwinglis sämtliche Werke.* Ed. Emil Egli, George Finsler, et al. Vols. LXXXVIII-CI of the Corpus Reformatorum. 14 vols. Berlin: C. A. Schwetschke und Sohn (vol. I); Leipzig: M. Heinsius Nachfolger (vol.II-V, VII-XI); Zurich: Verlag Berichthaus (vols. VI/1, VI/2, XII-XIV), 1905-1968.

_____. *The Latin Works and the Correspondence of Huldreich Zwingli.* Ed. Samuel Macaulay Jackson, et al. 3 vols. Philadelphia: Heidelberg Press, 1912-29.

_____. *Opera.* Ed. M. Chuler and J. Schulthess. 3 vols. Zurich: F. Schulthessium, 1829-42.

_____. *Zwingli and Bullinger: Selected Translations,* with introductions and notes by G. W. Bromiley. Philadelphia: Westminster Press, 1953.

Secondary Sources

Adams, Marilyn M. "Intuitive Cognition, Certainty, and Skepticism in William Ockham." *Traditio* 26 (1970):389-98.

Addison, William. *The Life and Writings of Thomas Boston of Ettrick.* Edinburgh: Oliver and Boyd, 1936.

Affleck, Bert, Jr. "The Theology of Richard Sibbes, 1577-1635." Ph.D. dissertation, Drew University, 1968.

Aldrich, Willard M. "Assurance." *Bibliotheca Sacra* 114 (1957):308-315.

Alexander, Archibald. *Thoughts on Religious Experience.* 3rd ed. Philadelphia: Presbyterian Board of Publications, 1844; reprint ed., London: Banner of Truth Trust, 1967.

Alexander, G. M. *Changes for the Better.* 2 vols. Ossett, W. Yorks: Zoar Publications, 1978.

Alexander, James W. *Consolation in Discourses on Select Topics, Addressed to the Suffering People of God.* New York: Charles Scribner, 1852; reprint ed., Ligonier, Pa.: Soli Deo Gloria Publications, 1992.

Althaus, Paul. *The Theology of Martin Luther.* Trans. Robert Schultz. Philadelphia: Fortress Press, 1966.

Armstrong, Brian G. *Calvinism and the Amyraut Heresy: Protestant Scholasticism and Humanism in Seventeenth-Century France.* Madison: University of Wisconsin Press, 1969.

Bainton, Roland H. *Here I Stand: A Life of Martin Luther.* Nashville: Abingdon, 1950.

_____, and Gritsch, Eric W. *Bibliography of the Continental Reformation.* 2nd ed. Hamden, Conn.: Archon Books, 1972.

Baird, Henry M. *Theodore Beza: the Counsellor of the French Reformation, 1519-1605.* New York: G. P. Putnam's Sons, 1899.

Baker, J. Wayne. *Heinrich Bullinger and the Covenant: The Other Reformed Tradition.* Athens: Ohio University Press, 1980.

Balke, Willem. "Het Pietisme in Oostfriesland." *Theologia Reformata* 21 (1978): 308-327.

_____. "The Word of God and *Experientia* according to Calvin." In *Calvinus Ecclesiae Doctor*, pp. 19-31. Ed. W. H. Neuser. Kampen: Kok, 1978.

Balke, W., et al. *Luther en het Gereformeerd Protestantisme.* 's-Gravenhage: Boekencentrum, 1983.

Balke, W., and van't Spijker, W., eds. *Reformed Protestantism: sources of the 16th and 17th centuries on microfiche.* Zug, Switzerland: Inter Documentation Co., 1983.

Balke, W., van't Spijker, W., Tukker, C. A., and Witteveen, K. M. *Zwingli in vierderlei perspectief.* Utrecht: De Banier, 1984.

Balserak, Jon. "Toward an Understanding of Calvin's View of Faith: The Two-Fold Presentation of the Believer's Reception of the Word." Th.M. thesis, Reformed Theological Seminary, 1996.

Bangs, Carl. *Arminius: A Study in the Dutch Reformation.* Nashville: Abingdon Press, 1971.

Barth, Karl. *Church Dogmatics.* Ed. Geoffrey W. Bromiley and Thomas F. Torrance. 13 vols. Edinburgh: T. & T. Clark, 1936-69.

Bass, William Ward. "Platonic Influences on Seventeenth Century English Puritan Theology as expressed in the thinking of John Owen, Richard Baxter, and John Howe." Ph.D. dissertation, University of Southern California, 1958.

Battis, John Emery. "Troublers in Israel: The Antinomian Controversy in the Massachusetts Bay Colony, 1636-1638." Ph.D. dissertation, Columbia University, 1958.

Battles, Ford Lewis. *The Piety of John Calvin. An Anthology Illustrative of the Spirituality of the Reformer of Geneva.* Grand Rapids: Baker, 1978.

Baum, Johann Wilhelm. *Theodor Beza.* 2 vols. Leipzig: Weidmann'sche Buchhandlung, 1843-51.

Bavinck, Herman. *The Certainty of Faith.* Trans. Harry Nederlanden. St. Catharines, Ont.: Paideia Press, 1980.

_____. *The Doctrine of God.* Trans. and ed. William Hendriksen. Grand Rapids: Eerdmans, 1951.

_____. *Gereformeerde Dogmatiek.* 4th ed. 4 vols. Kampen: Kok, 1928-30.

_____. *Johannes Calvijn.* Kampen: Kok, 1909.

_____. *Our Reasonable Faith.* Trans. Henry Zylstra. Grand Rapids: Baker, 1956.

Beardslee, John Walter, III. "Theological Development at Geneva under Francis and Jean-Alphonse Turretin, 1648-1737." Ph.D. dissertation, Yale University, 1956.

Beaton, D. "'The Marrow of Modern Divinity' and the Marrow Controversy." *Princeton Theological Review* 4, 3 (1906):86-97.

Beeke, Joel R. "Anthony Burgess on Assurance." In *The Answer of a Good Conscience.* Westminster Conference, 1997, pp. 27-52. London: Westminster Conference, 1998.

_____. *Assurance of Faith: Calvin, English Puritanism, and the Dutch Second Reformation.* American University Studies, Series VII, Theology and Religion, vol. 89. New York: Peter Lang, 1991.

_____. *Backsliding: Disease and Cure.* Grand Rapids: Eerdmans, 1982.

_____. "Biographies of Dutch Second Reformation Divines." *Banner of Truth* 54-56 (1988-90): "Willem Teellinck" 54 (2):55; "Godefriedus Udemans" 54 (3):82; "Gisbertus Voetius" 54 (5):139; "Johannes Bogerman" 54 (6):167; "Jean Taffin" 54 (7):195; "Abraham Hellenbroek" 54 (8):223; "Petrus Dathenus" 54 (9):251; "Theodorus à Brakel" 54 (10):279; "Wilhelmus à Brakel" 54 (11):307; "Johannes Beukelman" 54 (12):334; "Jacobus Koelman" 55 (1):27; "Johannes Polyander" 55 (2):55; "Theodorus van der Groe" 55 (3):83; "Johannes Fontanus" 55 (4):111; "Alexander Comrie" 55 (5):139; "Herman Witsius" 55 (6):167; "Franciscus Junius" 55 (7):195; "Sibrandus Lubbertus" 55 (8):223; "Johannes Maccovius" 55 (9):251; "Antonius Walaeus" 55 (10):279; "Samuel Maresius" 55 (11):307; "Johannes Hoornbeeck" 55 (12):335; "Petrus Wittewrongel" 56 (1):27; "Festus Hommius" 56 (2):55; "Florentius Costerus" 56 (3):83.

_____. "Cultivating Holiness." *Reformation and Revival* 4, 2 (1995):81-112.

_____. "Did Beza's Supralapsarianism Spoil Calvin's Theology?" *Reformed Theological Journal* 13 (1997):58-69.

_____. "Does Assurance Belong to the Essence of Faith? Calvin *and* the Calvinists." *The Master's Seminary Journal* 5, 1 (1994):43-71.

_____. "Faith & Assurance in the Heidelberg Catechism and its Primary

Composers: A Fresh Look at the Kendall Thesis." *Calvin Theological Journal* 27, 1 (1992):39-67.

_____. "Gisbertus Voetius: Toward a Reformed Marriage of Knowledge and Piety." In *Protestant Scholasticism: Essays in Reassessment.* Eds. Carl Trueman and R. Scott Clark. Carlisle: Paternoster, 1998.

_____. "Heidelberg Catechism Sermons." 5 vols. Grand Rapids: Reformation Heritage Books, 1998.

_____. *Holiness: God's Call to Sanctification.* Edinburgh: Banner of Truth Trust, 1994.

_____. "Insights for the Church from the Dutch Second Reformation." *Calvin Theological Journal* 28, 2 (1993):420-24.

_____. "Introduction." In *The Works of Thomas Goodwin,* Vol. 1, pp. 1-23. Eureka, Calif.: Tanski Publications, 1996.

_____. *Jehovah Shepherding His Sheep.* Grand Rapids: Eerdmans, 1982.

_____. "Justification *by* Faith Alone: The Relation of Faith to Justification." In *Justification by Faith Alone,* pp. 53-105. Ed. Don Kistler. Morgan, Pa.: Soli Deo Gloria Publications, 1995.

_____. *Justification by Faith: Selected Bibliography.* Grand Rapids: Reformation Heritage Books, 1995.

_____. "Meet the Puritans...In Print!" *Banner of Truth* 52 (1986):44-45, 102-103, 156-157, 240-241, 292-293; 53 (1987):154-55, 184-85.

_____. "The Order of the Divine Decrees at the Genevan Academy: From Bezan Supralapsarianism to Turretinian Infralapsarianism." In *The Identity of Geneva: The Christian Commonwealth, 1564-1864,* pp. 57-75. Ed. John B. Roney and Martin I. Klauber. Westport, Conn.: Greenwood Press, 1997.

_____. "Personal Assurance of Faith: The Puritans & Chapter 18.2 of the Westminster Confession." *Westminster Theological Journal* 55, 1 (1993):1-33.

_____. "Reading the Best in Puritan Literature: A Modern Bibliography." *Reformation and Revival* 5, 2 (1996):117-58.

_____. *A Tocha dos Puritanos: Evangelização Bíblica.* São Paulo: Evangélicas Selecionadas, 1996.

_____. *Truth that Frees: A Workbook on Reformed Doctrine for Young Adults.* Grand Rapids: Reformation Heritage Books, 1998.

_____. "Understanding Assurance." *Banner of Truth,* no. 392 (1995):16-21; no. 394 (1995):9-17.

_____. "William Cunningham." In *Historians of the Christian Tradition: Their Methodology and Influence on Western Thought,* pp. 209-26. Ed. Michael Bauman and Martin I. Klauber. Nashville: Broadman & Holman, 1995.

_____, ed. *Experiential Grace in Dutch Biography.* Grand Rapids: Eerdmans, 1985.

_____, and Clark, R. Scott. "Ursinus, Oxford and the Westminster Divines." In *The Westminster Confession into the 21ˢᵗ Century: Essays in Remembrance of the 350ᵗʰ Anniversary of the Publication of the Westminster Confession of Faith.*

Eds. Ligon Duncan and Duncan Rankin. Jackson: Reformed Academic Press, 1999.

_____, and Ferguson, Sinclair. *Reformed Confessions Harmonized.* Grand Rapids: Baker, 1999.

_____, and Greendyk, James D. *Knowing and Living the Christian Life.* Grand Rapids: Reformation Heritage Books, 1997.

_____, and Lanning, Ray B. "Glad Obedience: The Third Use of the Law." In *Trust and Obey,* pp. 154-200. Ed. Don Kistler. Morgan, Pa.: Soli Deo Gloria Publications, 1996.

_____, and Lanning, Ray B. "The Transforming Power of Scripture." In *Sola Scriptura!,* pp. 221-76. Ed. Don Kistler. Morgan, Pa.: Soli Deo Gloria Publishers, 1995.

_____, and Pronk, Cornelis. "Theodore Jacobus Frelinghuysen (1691-1747): Precursor of the Great Awakening." *Banner of Truth,* no. 407 (Aug-Sept 1997):38-59.

Bell, M. Charles. *Calvin and Scottish Theology: The Doctrine of Assurance.* Edinburgh: The Handsel Press, 1985.

Benner, Forest T. "The Immediate Antecedents of the Wesleyan Doctrine of the Witness of the Spirit." Ph.D. dissertation, Temple University, 1966.

Berkhof, Hendrikus. "The Act of Faith in the Reformed Tradition." In *Faith: Its Nature and Meaning,* pp. 99-115. Ed. Paul Surlis. Dublin: Gill and MacMillan, 1972.

_____. *An Introduction to the Study of Faith.* Trans. Sierd Woudstra. Grand Rapids: Eerdmans, 1979.

Berkhof, Louis. *The Assurance of Faith.* Grand Rapids: Smitter Book Co., 1928.

_____. *Systematic Theology.* 4th ed. Reprint ed., London: Banner of Truth Trust, 1977.

Berkouwer, Gerrit C. *Divine Election.* Trans. Hugo Bekker. Grand Rapids: Eerdmans, 1960.

_____. *Faith and Justification.* Trans. Lewis B. Smedes. Grand Rapids: Eerdmans, 1954.

_____. *Faith and Perseverance.* Trans. Robert D. Knudsen. Grand Rapids: Eerdmans, 1958.

_____. *Sin.* Trans. Philip Holtrop. Grand Rapids: Eerdmans, 1971.

Beveridge, W. *Makers of the Scottish Church.* Edinburgh: T. & T. Clark, 1908.

Bierma, Lyle D. *German Calvinism in the Confessional Age: The Covenant Theology of Caspar Olevianus.* Grand Rapids: Baker, 1996.

Birkner, Gerd. *Heilsgewissheit und Literatur: Metapher, Allegorie und Auto-biographie im Puritanismus.* München: Willem Fink, 1972.

Bizer, Ernst. "Reformed Orthodoxy and Cartesianism." Trans. C. MacCormick. *Journal for Theology and the Church* 2 (1965):20-82.

Blanke, Fritz. *Der junge Bullinger 1504-1531.* Zurich: Zwingli Verlag, 1942.

Blench, J. W. *Preaching in England in the Late Fifteenth and Sixteenth Century.* Oxford: Basil Blackwell, 1964.

Blokland, C. *Willem Sluiter, 1627-1673.* Neerlandica Traiectina, no. 16. Assen, 1965.

Bogue, Carl W. *Jonathan Edwards and the Covenant of Grace.* Cherry Hill, N.J.: Mack Publishing Co., 1975.

Bouwman, H. *Willem Teellinck en de praktijk der godzaligheid.* Kampen: Kok, 1928.

Bouwmeester, G. *Caspar Olevianus en Zijn Reformatorische Arbeid.* 's-Gravenhage: Willem de Zwijgerstichting, 1954.

Bouwsma, William. *John Calvin. A Sixteenth-Century Portrait.* New York: Oxford University Press, 1988.

Bowman, H. O. "William Guthrie, 1620-1665." Ph.D. dissertation, Edinburgh, 1953.

Boyle, Robert Martin. "The Doctrine of the Witness of the Holy Spirit in John Calvin's Theology Considered against an Historical Background." M.A. thesis, Abilene Christian College, 1967.

Bozeman, Theodore Dwight. *To Live Ancient Lives: The Primitivist Dimension in Puritanism.* Chapel Hill: University of North Carolina, 1988.

Brandt, Geeraerdt. *The History of the Reformation and Other Ecclesiastical Transactions in and about the Low-Countries, from the Beginning of the Eighth Century, down to the Famous Synod of Dort.* 4 vols. London: T. Wood, 1720-23.

Bratt, John H., ed. *The Rise and Development of Calvinism.* Grand Rapids: Eerdmans, 1959.

Brauer, Jerald C. "Reflections on the Nature of English Puritanism." *Church History* 23 (1954):98-109.

Bray, John S. *Theodore Beza's Doctrine of Predestination.* Nieuwkoop: B. DeGraaf, 1975.

_____. "The Value of Works in the Theology of Calvin and Beza." *Sixteenth Century Journal* 4 (1973):77-86.

Brecht, Martin. *Martin Luther. His Road to Reformation, 1483-1521.* Trans. James L. Schaaf. Philadelphia: Fortress Press, 1981.

Breward, Ian. "The Life and Theology of William Perkins." Ph.D. dissertation, University of Manchester, 1963.

_____. "The Significance of William Perkins." *Journal of Religious History* 4 (1966):113-28.

_____. "William Perkins and the Origins of Puritan Casuistry." In *Faith and a Good Conscience,* pp. 5-17. Puritan and Reformed Studies Conference, 1962. London: A. G. Hasler, 1963.

_____. "William Perkins and the Origins of Reformed Casuistry." *The Evangelist Quarterly* 40 (1968):3-20.

Brienen, Teunis. *De prediking van de Nadere Reformatie.* Amsterdam: Ton Bolland, 1974.

_____. "De 22 regels van Willem Teellinck over het maken van preken." *Documentatieblad Nadere Reformatie* 6 (1982): 16-22.

_____, et al. *Figuren en thema's van de Nadere Reformatie.* 3 vols. Kampen: De Groot, 1987-93.

_____, et al. *Theologische aspecten van de Nadere Reformatie*. Zoetermeer: Boekencentrum, 1993.

_____, Exalto, K., van Genderen, J., Graafland, C., and van't Spijker, W. *De Nadere Reformatie. Beschrijving van haar voornaamste vertegenwoordigers*. 's-Gravenhage: Boekencentrum, 1986.

Broes, Wilhelm. *De Engelsche Hervormde Kerk, benevens haren invloed op onze Nederlandsche, van den tijd der Hervorming*. 2 vols. Delft: Allart, 1825.

Broeyer, F. G. M. "Het begrip Nadere Reformatie." *Documentatieblad Nadere Reformatie* 12 (1988):51-57.

Bromiley, Geoffrey W. *Historical Theology: An Introduction*. Grand Rapids: Eerdmans, 1978.

Bronkema, Ralph. *The Essence of Puritanism*. Goes, Netherlands: Oosterbaan and LeCointre, 1929.

Brook, Benjamin. *The Lives of the Puritans*. 3 vols. London: Printed for J. Black, 1813; reprint ed. with intro. by Joel R. Beeke, Pittsburgh: Soli Deo Gloria Publications, 1994.

Brown, George, Jr. "Pietism and the Reformed Tradition." *Reformed Review* 23 (1970):143-53.

Brown, John. *The English Puritans*. London: Cambridge University Press, 1912.

_____. *Puritan Preaching in England*. New York: Charles Scribner's Sons, 1900.

Brown, Paul Edward. "The Principle of the Covenant in the Theology of Thomas Goodwin." Ph.D. dissertation, Drew University, 1950.

Brown, Robert. *Doctrinal and Experimental Theology*. London: William Wileman, 1899.

Brown, William Adams. *Pathways to Certainty*. New York: Charles Scribner's Sons, 1930.

Browning, W. H. *An Examination of the Doctrine of the Unconditional Final Perseverance of the Saints as Taught by Calvinists*. Ed. Thomas V. Summers. Nashville: Southern Methodist Publishing House, 1860.

Bruggink, Donald J. "The Theology of Thomas Boston, 1676-1732." Ph.D. dissertation, Edinburgh, 1956.

Buchanan, James. *The Doctrine of Justification: An Outline of Its History in the Church and of Its Exposition from Scripture*. Edinburgh: T. & T. Clark, 1867; reprint ed., Grand Rapids: Baker, 1977.

Burgess, Walter H. *John Robinson, Pastor of the Pilgrim Fathers: A Study of His Life and Times*. London: Williams and Norgate, 1920.

Byington, Ezra Hoyt. *The Puritan in England and New England*. Boston: Little, Brown and Co., 1900.

Calderwood, David. *The History of the Kirk of Scotland*. 8 vols. Edinburgh: Wodrow Society, 1842-43.

Caldwell, Patricia. *The Puritan conversion narrative*. New York: Cambridge University Press, 1985.

Calvinus Reformator: His Contribution to Theology, Church and Society.

Potchefstroom, Republic of South Africa: Potchefstroom University for Christian Higher Education, 1982.

Campbell, Douglas. *The Puritan in Holland, England, and America.* 4th ed. 2 vols. New York: Harper and Brothers, 1892.

Cannon, William Ragsdale. *The Theology of John Wesley with Special Reference to the Doctrine of Justification.* New York: Abingdon-Cokesbury Press, 1946.

Carden, Allen. *Puritan Christianity in America: Religion and Life in Seventeenth-Century Massachusetts.* Grand Rapids: Baker, 1990.

Carruthers, S. W. *The Everyday Work of the Westminster Assembly.* Philadelphia: Presbyterian Historical Society, 1943.

_____. *The Westminster Confession of Faith.* Manchester: R. Aikman & Son, 1937.

Carter, Alice. *The English Reformed Church in Amsterdam in the Seventeenth Century.* Amsterdam: Scheltema & Holkema, 1964.

Carter, R. B. "The Presbyterian-Independent Controversy with Special Reference to Dr. Thomas Goodwin and the Years 1640 to 1660." Ph.D. dissertation, Edinburgh, 1961.

Chalker, William H. "Calvin and Some Seventeenth Century English Calvinists." Ph.D. dissertation, Duke University, 1961.

Chan, Simon K.H. "The Puritan Meditative Tradition, 1559-1691: A Study of Ascetical Piety." Ph.D. dissertation, Cambridge University, 1986.

Cherry, Conrad. "The Puritan Notion of the Covenant in Jonathan Edwards' Doctrine of Faith." *Church History* 34 (1965):328-41.

_____. *The Theology of Jonathan Edwards: A Reappraisal.* Garden City, N.Y.: Doubleday and Co., 1966; reprint ed., Gloucester, Mass.: Peter Smith, 1974.

Christelijke Encyclopedie. 6 vols. 2nd ed, revised. Kampen: Kok, 1959.

Citron, Bernhard. *New Birth: A Study of the Evangelical Doctrine of Conversion in the Protestant Fathers.* Edinburgh: University Press, Clarke, Irwin, 1951.

Clifford, K. "The Reconstruction of Puritan Casuistry." Ph.D. dissertation, University of London, 1957.

Cockerton, J. C. P. *To Be Sure. Christian Assurance — Presumption or Privilege.* London: Hodder and Stoughton, 1967.

Cohen, Charles Lloyd. *God's Caress: the Psychology of Puritan Religious Experience.* New York: Oxford University Press, 1986.

Collinson, Patrick. *The Elizabethan Puritan Movement.* Berkeley: University of California Press, 1967.

_____. *A Mirror of Elizabethan Puritanism: The Life and Letters of 'Godly Master Dering.'* London: Dr. William's Trust, 1964.

Colquhoun, John. *A Treatise on Spiritual Comfort.* Edinburgh: for J. Ogle, 1814; reprint ed., Morgan, Pa: Soli Deo Gloria Publications, 1998.

_____. *View of Saving Faith from the Sacred Records.* Edinburgh: Thomsons, 1824.

Come, Donald R. "John Cotton: Guide of the Chosen People." Ph.D. dissertation, University of Illinois, 1956.

Conditt, Marion W. *More Acceptable than Sacrifice: Ethics and Election as Obedience to God's Will in the Theology of Calvin*. Basel: Friedrich Reinhardt Kommissionsverlag, 1973.

Cook, Paul. "Thomas Goodwin — Mystic?" In *Diversities of Gifts*, pp. 45-56. Westminster Conference, 1980. London: The Westminster Conference, 1981.

Cottrell, Jack Warren. "Covenant and Baptism in the Theology of H. Zwingli." Th.D. dissertation, Princeton Theological Seminary, 1971.

Courvoisier, Jacques. *Zwingli: A Reformed Theologian*. Richmond: John Knox Press, 1963.

Couvee, H. J. *Calvijn en Calvinisme: Een studie over Calvijn en ons geestelijk en kerkelijk leven*. Utrecht: Kemink en Zoon, 1936.

Cowper, Macknight Crawford. "Calvin's Doctrine of Predestination and its Ethical Consequences." Ph.D. dissertation, Union Theological Seminary, 1942.

Cragg, C. R. *Puritanism in the Period of the Great Persecution, 1660-1688*. London: Cambridge University Press, 1957.

Cramer, J. A. *De Theologische Faculteit te Utrecht ten tijde van Voetius*. Utrecht: Kemink en Zoon, 1932.

Cremeans, Charles D. *The Reception of Calvinistic Thought in England*. Urbana: University of Illinois Press, 1958.

Crompton, Gordon Douglas. "The Life and Theology of Thomas Goodwin." Th.M. thesis, Greenville Presbyterian Theological Seminary, 1997.

Cross, Wilfred Oakland. "The Role and Status of the Unregenerate in the Massachusetts Bay Colony, 1629-1729." Ph.D. dissertation, Columbia University, 1957.

Cubine, M. V. *Calvin's Doctrine of the Work of the Holy Spirit*. Ann Arbor: University Microfilms, 1955.

Cunningham, William. *Historical Theology: A Review of the Principal Doctrinal Discussions in the Christian Church Since the Apostolic Age*. 2 vols. Edinburgh: Clark, 1863; reprint ed., London: Banner of Truth Trust, 1960.

_____. *The Reformers and the Theology of the Reformation*. Edinburgh: Clark, 1862; reprint ed., London: Banner of Truth Trust, 1967.

Curtis, Mark H. *Oxford and Cambridge in Transition 1558-1642*. Oxford: Clarendon Press, 1959.

Cushman, Robert E. "Faith and Reason in the Thought of St. Augustine." *Church History* 19 (1950):271-94.

Dabney, Robert L. *Discussions: Evangelical and Theological*. 2 vols. Richmond: Presbyterian Committee of Publication, 1890-97; reprint ed., London: Banner of Truth Trust, 1967.

_____. *Lectures in Systematic Theology*. Richmond: Shepperson & Graves, 1871; reprint ed., Grand Rapids: Zondervan, 1972.

Dallimore, Arnold. *George Whitefield*. 2 vols. London: Banner of Truth Trust, 1970-80.

Daniel, Curt. "Hyper-Calvinism and John Gill." Ph.D. dissertation, Edinburgh, 1983.

Dankbaar, W. F. *Hoogtepunten uit het Nederlandsche Calvinisme in de zestiende eeuw.* Haarlem: Tjeenk Willink, 1946.

Dantine, Johannes. "Das christologische Problem in Rahmen der Prädestinationslehre von Theodor Beza." *Zeitschrift für Kirchengeschichte* 86 (1966):81-96.

_____. "Die prädestinationslehre bei Calvin und Beza." Ph.D. dissertation, Göttingen University, 1965.

Dantine, Wilhelm. *Justification of the Ungodly.* Trans. Eric W. Gritsch and Ruth C. Gritsch. St. Louis: Concordia Publishing House, 1968.

D'Assonville, V. E. *John Knox and the Institutes of Calvin.* Durban: Drakensberg Press, 1969.

D'Aubigne, J. H. Merle. *History of the Reformation in Europe in the Time of Calvin.* 8 vols. London: Longmans, Green, and Co., 1863-78.

Davies, Godfrey. "Arminian versus Puritan in England, 1620-1640." *Huntington Library Bulletin* 5 (1934):157-79.

Davies, Horton. *The Worship of the English Puritans.* London: Dacre Press, 1948.

_____. *Worship and Theology in England: From Andrewes to Baxter and Fox, 1603-1690.* Princeton: Princeton University Press, 1975.

_____. *Worship and Theology in England: From Cranmer to Hooker, 1543-1603.* Princeton: Princeton University Press, 1970.

Davis, J. C. W. "John Owen, D.D.: Puritan Preacher and Ecclesiastical Statesman." M.A. thesis, Liverpool University, 1962.

De Bie, H. J. "De Dubbele Predestinatie en de Prediking." *Theologia Reformata* 18 (1975):297-316.

De Bie, J. P., and Loosjes, J., eds. *Biographisch Woordenboek der Protestantsche Godgeleerden in Nederland.* 5 vols. 's-Gravenhage: Martinus Nijhoff, 1907-43.

De Boer, Johannes. *De Verzegeling met de Heilige Geest volgens de opvatting van de Nadere Reformatie.* Rotterdam: Bronder, 1968.

Dee, S. P. *Het geloofsberijp van Calvijn.* Kampen: Kok, 1918.

De Graaf, S. G. *Het Ware Geloof.* Kampen: Kok, 1954.

De Greef, Wulfert. *The Writings of John Calvin.* Trans. Lyle D. Bierma. Grand Rapids: Baker, 1993.

De Jong, O. J., et al. *Het eigene van de Nederlandse Nadere Reformatie.* Houten: Den Hertog, 1992.

De Jong, Peter Y. *The Covenant Idea in New England Theology, 1620-1847.* Grand Rapids: Eerdmans, 1945.

_____, ed. *Crises in the Reformed Churches: Essays in Commemoration of the Great Synod of Dort, 1618-1619.* Grand Rapids: Reformed Fellowship, 1968.

De Jonge, Christiaan. "Franciscus Junius (1545-1602) en de Engelse Separatisten te Amsterdam." *Nederlands Archief voor Kerkgeschiedenis* 59 (1978):132-59.

_____. *De Irenische Ecclesiologie van Franciscus Junius, 1545-1602.* Leiden: Nieuwkoop, 1980.

De Koster, Lester. "Living Themes in the Thought of John Calvin: A Bibliographical Study." Ph.D. dissertation, University of Michigan, 1964.

De Lind van Wijngaarden, J. D. *Antonius Walaeus.* Leiden, 1891.

De Marest, David D. *History and Characteristics of the Reformed Protestant Dutch Church.* 2nd edition. New York: Board of Publication of the Reformed Protestant Dutch Church, 1856.

Den Boer, C. *Om 't eeuwig welbehagen (Verhandelingen over de Dordtse Leerregels).* Utrecht: De Banier, 1983.

Denholm, Andrew T. "Thomas Hooker: Puritan Preacher, 1586-1647." Ph.D. dissertation, Hartford Seminary Foundation, 1961.

Dentz, Fred. Oudschans. *History of the English Church at the Hague, 1586-1929.* Delft: W. D. Meinema, 1929.

De Pater, Jan Cornelius Hendrik. *Guido de Brès en de Gereformeerde Geloofsbelijdenis.* 's-Gravenhage: Willem de Zwijger-Stichting, 1950.

De Reuver, A. "Een mystieke ader in de Nadere Reformatie." *Documentatieblad Nadere Reformatie* 21 (1997):1-54.

_____."Wat is het eigene van de Nadere Reformatie?" *Documentatieblad Nadere Reformatie* 18 (1994):145-54.

Dever, Mark. "Richard Sibbes and the 'Truly Evangelical Church of England': A Study in Reformed Divinity and Early Stuart Conformity." Ph.D. dissertation, Cambridge University, 1992.

De Vrijer, Marinus Johannes Antonie. *Ds. Bernardus Smytegelt en zijn "gekrookte riet."* Amsterdam: H. J. Spruyt, 1947.

_____. *Schortinghuis en zijn analogieën.* Amsterdam: H. J. Spruyt, 1942.

De War, M. W. "How Far is the Westminster Assembly an Expression of Seventeenth-Century Anglican Theology?" Ph.D. dissertation, Queen's University (Belfast), 1960.

De Witt, John Richard. *Jus Divinum: The Westminster Assembly and the Divine Right of Church Government.* Kampen: Kok, 1969.

De Zeeuw, J. Gzn. *Guido de Brès, opsteller van de Nederlandse Geloofsbelijdenis.* 's-Gravenhage, 1963.

Dickens, A. G. *The English Reformation.* London: B. T. Batsford, 1964.

Donnelly, John Patrick. *Calvinism and Scholasticism in Vermigli's Doctrine of Man and Grace.* Studies in Medieval and Reformation Thought, no. 18. Leiden: E. J. Brill, 1976.

Dorer, Robert F. "John Calvin's Doctrine of Justification by Faith." B.D. thesis, New Brunswick Seminary, 1955.

Dorioni, Daniel M. "The Godly Household in Puritan Theology, 1560-1640." Ph.D. dissertation, Westminster Theological Seminary, 1986.

Doumergue, Emile. *Jean Calvin: Les hommes et les choses de son temps.* 7 vols. Vols. 1-5, Lausanne: Georges Bridel & Cie., 1899-1917; vols. 6-7, Neuilly sur Seine, editions de "La Cause," 1927-29.

Dowey, Edward. *The Knowledge of God in Calvin's Theology.* New York: Columbia University Press, 1965; reprint ed., Grand Rapids: Eerdmans, 1994.

Doyle, I. B. "John Brown of Wamphray: a study in his life, work, and thought." Ph.D. dissertation, Edinburgh, 1956.

Duffield, G. E., ed. *John Calvin.* Courtenay Studies in Reformation Theology, no. 1. Appleford: Sutton Courtenay Press, 1966.

Duke, Alastair. *Reformation and Revolt in the Low Countries.* London: Hambledon, 1990.

Duker, Arnoldus Cornelius. *Gisbertus Voetius.* 4 vols. Leiden: E. J. Brill, 1897-1914; reprint ed., Leiden: J. J. Groen en Zoon, 1989.

Dulles, Avery. *The Assurance of Things Hoped For: A Theology of Christian Faith.* New York: Oxford University Press, 1994.

Duurschmidt, Kurt. "Some Aspects of Justification and Sanctification as seen in the Writings of some of the Magisterial and Radical Reformers." Ph.D. dissertation, Syracuse University, 1971.

Eaton, Michael A. *Baptism with the Spirit. The Teaching of Dr. Martyn Lloyd-Jones.* Leicester: Inter-Varsity Press, 1989.

_____. *No Condemnation: A New Theology of Assurance.* Downers Grove, Ill.: InterVarsity Press, 1995.

Ebeling, Gerhard. *Luther: An Introduction to His Thought.* Trans. R. A. Wilson. Philadelphia: Fortress Press, 1970.

Ebner, Dean. *Autobiography in Seventeenth-Century England: Theology and the Self.* The Hague: Mouton, 1971.

Eekhof, A. *De Theologische Faculteit te Leiden in de 17de Eeuw.* Utrecht: G. J. A. Ruys, 1921.

_____. "Religious Thought and Life in Holland." In *Lectures on Holland for American Students*, pp. 48-66. Leiden: A. W. Sijthoff, 1924.

Eells, H. *Martin Bucer.* New Haven: Yale University Press, 1931.

Eggermont, P. L. "Bibliografie van het Nederlandse Piëtisme in de zeventiende en achttiende eeuw." *Documentatieblad Werkgroep 18e eeuw* 3 (1969):17-31.

Ehalt, David R. "The Development of Early Congregational Theory of the Church with Special Reference to the Five 'Dissenting Brethren' at the Westminster Assembly." Ph.D. dissertation, Claremont, 1969.

Elert, Werner. *The Structure of Lutheranism.* Trans. Walter A. Hansen. Vol. 1. St. Louis: Concordia, 1962.

Elliott, J. P. "Protestantization in the Northern Netherlands: A Case Study — The Classis of Dordrecht 1572-1640." 2 vols. Ph.D. dissertation, Columbia University, 1990.

Elwell, Walter A., ed. *Evangelical Dictionary of Theology.* Grand Rapids: Baker, 1984.

Emerson, Everett H. "Calvin and Covenant Theology." *Church History* 25 (1956):136-44.

_____. *English Puritanism from John Hooper to John Milton.* Durham, N.C.: Duke University Press, 1968.

_____. *Puritanism in America.* Boston: Twayne Publishers, 1977.

_____. "Thomas Hooker." *Anglican Reformed Review* 49 (1967):190-203.

_____. "Thomas Hooker and the Reformed Theology: The Relation of Hooker's Conversion Preaching to its Background." Ph.D. dissertation, Louisiana State University, 1955.

Emmett, Peter Alan. "Calvin's Doctrine of Sanctity." M.Div. thesis, Asbury Theological Seminary, 1970.

Engelberts, Willem Jodocus Matthias. *Willem Teellinck.* Amsterdam: Scheffer & Co., 1898.

Entwistle, F. R. "Some Aspects of John Owen's Doctrine of the Person and Work of Christ." In *Faith and a Good Conscience,* pp. 47-63. Puritan and Reformed Studies Conference, 1962. London: n.p., 1963.

Everson, Don Marvin. "The Puritan Theology of John Owen." Th.D. dissertation, Southern Baptist Theological Seminary, 1959.

Exalto, K. *Beleefd geloof: Acht schetsen van gereformeerde theologen uit de 17e Eeuw.* Amsterdam: Ton Bolland, 1974.

_____. *De Kracht der Religie: Tien schetsen van Gereformeerde 'Oude Schrijvers' uit de 17e en 18e Eeuw.* Urk: De Vuurtoren, 1976.

_____. *De Zekerheid des Geloofs bij Calvijn.* Apeldoorn: Willem de Zwijger-stichting, 1978.

Farrell, Frank E. "Richard Sibbes: A Study in Early Seventeenth Century English Puritanism." Ph.D. dissertation, Edinburgh, 1955.

Fast, Heinold. *Heinrich Bullinger und die Täufer: Ein beitrag zur historiographie und theologie im 16. jahrhundert.* Schriftenreihe des Mennonitischen Geschichtsverein, no. 7. Weierhof, 1959.

Ferguson, Sinclair. "Assurance of Salvation." *Banner of Truth,* no. 186 (March 1979):1-9.

_____. "Doctrine of the Christian Life in the Teaching of Dr John Owen (1616-83)." Ph.D. dissertation, University of Aberdeen, 1979.

_____. *John Owen on the Christian Life.* Edinburgh: Banner of Truth Trust, 1987.

_____. "John Owen on Conversion." *Banner of Truth,* no. 134 (November 1974):20-25.

_____. *Know Your Christian Life.* Grand Rapids: Zondervan, 1982.

_____. *Taking the Christian Life Seriously.* Grand Rapids: Zondervan, 1982.

_____. "The Westminster Conference, 1976." *Banner of Truth,* no. 168 (September 1977):15-22.

Fienberg, Stanley P. "Thomas Goodwin, Puritan Pastor and Independent Divine." Ph.D. dissertation, University of Chicago, 1974.

Fieret, W. *Udemans: Facetten uit zijn leven en werk.* Houten, 1985.

Fix, Andrew C. *Prophecy and Reason: The Dutch Collegiants in the Early Enlightenment.* Princeton: University Press, 1991.

Flato, L. "How does Sinful Man come to a Knowledge of God? A Comparison of Luther and Calvin." Master's thesis, Wycliffe College, 1957.

Florijn, H., ed. *Hollandse Geloofshelden.* Utrecht: De Banier, 1981.

Foster, Herbert Darling. "Liberal Calvinism: the Remonstrants at the Synod of Dort in 1618." *Harvard Theological Review* 16 (1973):1-37.

Foxgrover, David. "John Calvin's Understanding of Conscience." Ph.D. dissertation, Claremont, 1978.

_____. "Self-Examination in John Calvin and William Ames." In *Later Calvinism: International Perspectives*, pp. 451-70. Ed. W. Fred Graham. Kirksville, Mo.: Sixteenth Century Journal Publishers, 1994.

_____. "'Temporary Faith' and the Certainty of Salvation." *Calvin Theological Journal* 15 (1980):220-32.

Fraser, Donald. *Life and Diary of Ebenezer Erskine*. Edinburgh: William Oliphant and Son, 1831.

_____. *Life and Diary of Ralph Erskine*. Edinburgh: William Oliphant and Son, 1834.

Freer, Brian. "Thomas Goodwin, the Peaceable Puritan." In *Diversities of Gifts*, pp. 7-20. Westminster Conference, 1980. London: Westminster Conference, 1981.

Fulcher, John Rodney. "Puritan Piety in Early New England: A Study in Spiritual Regeneration from the Antinomian Controversy to the Cambridge Synod of 1648 in the Massachusetts Bay Colony." Ph.D. dissertation, Princeton University, 1963.

Fulbrook, Mary. *Piety and Politics: Religion and the Rise of Absolutism in England, Württemberg and Prussia*. Cambridge: Cambridge University Press, 1983.

Gäbler, Ulrich. *Huldrych Zwingli. His Life and Works*. Trans. Ruth C. L. Gritsch. Philadelphia: Fortress Press, 1986.

Ganoczy, A. *The Young Calvin*. Trans. David Foxgrover and Wade Provo. Philadelphia: Westminster Press, 1987.

Gardiner, Samuel Rawson. *History of England from the Accession of James I. to the Outbreak of the Civil War 1603-1642*. 10 vols. New York: Longmans, Green, and Co., 1896-1901.

Garrett, Christina H. *The Marian Exiles: A Study in the Origins of Elizabethan Puritanism*. Cambridge: Cambridge University Press, 1938.

Geesink, W. *Calvinisten in Holland*. Amsterdam, 1887; reprint ed., Genevae: Slatkine Reprints, 1970.

George, A. C. "Martin Luther's Doctrine of Sanctification with Special Reference to the Formula '*Simul Iustus Et Peccator*': A Study in Luther's Lectures on Romans and Galatians." Th.D. dissertation, Westminster Theological Seminary, 1982.

George, Charles H. "Puritanism as History and Historiography." *Past and Present* 41 (1968):77-104.

George, Charles H. and Katherine. *The Protestant Mind of the English Reformation, 1570-1640*. Princeton: Princeton University Press, 1961.

George, Thomas. *The Theology of the Reformers*. Nashville: Broadman Press, 1988.

Gerrish, Brian A. "Atonement and Saving Faith." *Theology Today* 17(1960):181-91.

_____. *Grace and Reason: A Study in the Theology of Luther*. Oxford: Clarendon Press, 1962.

Gerstner, John H. *The Rational Biblical Theology of Jonathan Edwards*, 3 Vols. Powhatan, Va.: Berea Publications, 1991-93.

_____. *Steps to Salvation: The Evangelistic Message of Jonathan Edwards.* Philadelphia: Westminster Press, 1960; reprint ed., *Jonathan Edwards, Evangelist.* Morgan, Pa.: Soli Deo Gloria Publications, 1995.

_____, and Gerstner, Jonathan Neil. "Edwardsean Preparation for Salvation." *Westminster Theological Journal* 42 (1979):5-71.

Gerstner, Jonathan N. *The Thousand Generation Covenant: Dutch Reformed Covenant Theology and Group Identity in Colonial South Africa.* Leiden: E. J. Brill, 1991.

Geyl, Pieter. *The Netherlands in the Seventeenth Century.* 2 vols. London: Benn, 1961-64.

Glasius, B. *Geschiedenis der Nationale Synode in 1618 en 1619 gehouden te Dordrecht.* 2 vols. Leiden: E. J. Brill, 1860-61.

_____, ed. *Godgeleerd Nederland: Biographisch Woordenboek van Nederlandsche Godgeleerden.* 3 vols. 's-Hertogenbosch: Gebr. Muller, 1851-56.

Godfrey, W. Robert. "The Dutch Reformed Response." In *Discord, Dialogue and Concord*, pp. 166-77. Ed. Lewis W. Spitz and Wenzel Lohff. Philadelphia: Fortress Press, 1977.

_____. "Tensions within International Calvinism: The Debate on the Atonement at the Synod of Dordt, 1618-1619." Ph.D. dissertation, Stanford University, 1974.

Goeters, W. *Die Vorbereitung des Pietismus in der reformierten Kirche der Niederlande.* Leipzig: J. C. Hinrichs'sche Buchhandlung, 1911; reprint ed., Amsterdam: Ton Bolland, 1974.

Gohler, Alred. *Calvins Lehre von der Heiligung.* Munich: Kaiser, 1934.

Golverdingen, M. *Avonden met Teellinck: Actuele thema's uit zijn werk.* Houten: Den Hertog, 1993.

Good, James I. *Famous Reformers of the Reformed and Presbyterian Churches.* Philadelphia: The Heidelberg Press, 1916.

_____. *History of the Reformed Church of Germany, 1620-1890.* Reading, Pa.: Daniel Miller, Publisher, 1894.

_____. *The Reformed Reformation.* Philadelphia: The Heidelberg Press, 1916.

Gooszen, Maurits Albrecht. *Heinrich Bullinger en de strijd over de Praedestinatie.* Rotterdam: D. J. P. Storm Lotz (H. van Tricht), 1909.

Gordh, G. "Calvin's Conception of Faith." *Review and Expositor* 51 (1954):207-15.

Gore, Ralph J. "The Lutheran Ordo Salutis with Special Reference to Justification and Sanctification: A Reformed Analysis." Master's thesis, Faith Theological Seminary, 1983.

Gossett, Earl Fowler, Jr. "The Doctrine of Justification in the Theology of John Calvin, Albrecht Ritschl, and Reinhold Niebuhr." Ph.D. dissertation, Vanderbilt University, 1961.

Graafland, Cornelis. *Van Calvijn tot Barth: Oorsprong en ontwikkeling van de leer der verkiezing in het Gereformeerd Protestantisme.* 's-Gravenhage: Boeken-centrum, 1987.

_____. "Het eigene van het Gereformeerd Piëtisme in de 18e eeuw in onderscheid van de 17e eeuw." *Documentatieblad Nadere Reformatie* 11 (1987):37-53.

_____. "De gereformeerde Orthodoxie en het Piëtisme in Nederland." *Nederlands Theologisch Tijdschrift* 19 (1965):466-79.

_____. "Gereformeerde Scholastiek V. De invloed van de scholastiek op de Gereformeerde Orthodoxie." *Theologia Reformata* 30 (1987):4-25.

_____. "Gereformeerde Scholastiek VI. De invloed van de scholastiek op de Nadere Reformatie." *Theologia Reformata* 30 (1987):109-131, 313-40.

_____. "De invloed van het Puritanisme op het ontstaan van het Gerefor-meerd Piëtisme in Nederland." *Documentatieblad Nadere Reformatie* 7 (1983):1-24.

_____. "Kernen en contouren van de Nadere Reformatie." In *De Nadere Reformatie: Beschrijving van haar voornaamste vertegenwoordigers,* pp. 349-67. Ed. W. van't Spijker, et al. 's-Gravenhage: Boekencentrum, 1986.

_____. "De Nadere Reformatie en haar culturele context." In *Met het Woord in de Tijd,* pp. 117-38. Ed. L. Westland. 's-Gravenhage: Boekencentrum, 1985.

_____. "Nadere Reformatie. G. Voetius, W. à Brakel, J. Verschuir." In *Bij brood en beker. Leer en gebruik van het heilig avondmaal in het Nieuwe Testament en in de geschiedenis van de westerse kerk,* pp. 248-278. Ed. W. van't Spijker, et al. Kampen: De Groot, 1980.

_____. "Van syllogismus practicus naar syllogismus mysticus." In *Wegen en Gestalten in het Gereformeerd Protestantisme,* pp. 105-122. Ed. W. Balke, C. Graafland, and H. Harkema. Amsterdam: Ton Bolland, 1976.

_____. "De verhouding Reformatie en Nadere Reformatie een voortgaand onderzoek." *Documentatieblad Nadere Reformatie* 17 (1993):94-111.

_____. "'Waarheid in het Binnenste': Geloofszekerheid bij Calvijn en de Nadere Reformatie." In *Een Vaste Burcht,* pp. 53-81. Ed. K. Exalto. Kampen: Kok, 1989.

_____. *De zekerheid van het geloof: Een onderzoek naar de geloof- beschouwing van enige vertegenwoordigers van reformatie en nadere reformatie.* Wageningen: H. Veenman & Zonen, 1961.

_____; op't Hof, W. J.; van Lieburg, F. A. "Nadere Reformatie: opnieuw een poging tot begripsbepaling." *Documentatieblad Nadere Reformatie* 19 (1995):107-184.

Graham, W. Fred, ed. *Later Calvinism: International Perspectives.* Kirksville, Mo.: Sixteenth Century Journal Publishers, 1994.

Gravemeijer, Henricus E. *Leesboek over de Gereformeerde Geloofsleer.* 3 vols. Utrecht: H. Ten Hove, n.d.

Graves, Frank Pierrepont. *Peter Ramus and the Educational Reformation of the Sixteenth Century.* New York: The MacMillan Company, 1912.

Greaves, Richard. *John Bunyan.* Grand Rapids: Eerdmans, 1969.

_____. "John Bunyan and Covenant Thought in the Seventeenth Century." *Church History* 36 (1967):151-69.

_____. "The Origins and Early Development of English Covenant Thought." *The Historian* 31 (November 1968):21-35.

_____. *Theology and Revolution in the Scottish Reformation: Studies in the Thought of John Knox.* Grand Rapids: Christian University Press, 1980.

Greve, Lionel. "Freedom and Discipline in the Theology of John Calvin, William Perkins, and John Wesley: An Examination of the Origin and Nature of Pietism." Ph.D. dissertation, The Hartford Seminary Foundation, 1976.

Grimes, C. H. D. *The Early Story of the English Church at Utrecht.* Chambery: Imprimeries Reunies, 1930.

Groenendijk, L. F. *De Nadere Reformatie van het Gezin: De visie van Petrus Wittewrongel op de christelijke huishouding.* Dordrecht: J. P. van den Tol, 1984.

_____. "Jacobus Koelman's actieplan voor de nadere reformatie." *Documentatieblad Nadere Reformatie* 2 (1978):121-126.

_____. "De Oorsprong van de uitdrukking 'Nadere Reformatie.'" *Documentatieblad Nadere Reformatie* 9 (1985):128-34.

_____. "Willem Teellinck over de gezinsreformatie." *Documentatieblad Nadere Reformatie* 7 (1984):41-51.

Gründler, Otto. "Thomism and Calvinism in the Theology of Girolamo Zanchi (1516-1590)." Th.D. dissertation, Princeton Theological Seminary, 1961.

Gulley, Frank. "The Influence of Heinrich Bullinger and the Tigurine Tradition upon the English Church in the Sixteenth Century." Ph.D. dissertation, Vanderbilt, 1961.

Gustafsson, Berndt. *The Five Dissenting Brethren: A Study of the Dutch Background of Their Independentism.* London: C. W. K. Gloerup, 1955.

Hagans, J. M. "*The Marrow of Modern Divinity* and the Controversy concerning it in Scotland." B.D. thesis, Trinity College, Dublin, 1966.

Haitjema, Theodorus Lambertus. *Prediking des Woords en bevinding.* Wageningen: H. Veenman & Zonen, 1950.

Haley, K. H. P. *The Dutch in the Seventeenth Century.* Norwich, England: Jarrold and Sons Ltd., 1972.

Hall, Basil. "Calvin against the Calvinists." In *John Calvin*, pp. 19-37. Ed. G. E. Duffield. Courtenay Studies in Reformation Theology, no. 1. Appleford: Sutton Courtenay Press, 1966.

_____. "Puritanism: The Problem of Definition." In *Studies in Church History*, vol. 2, pp. 283-96. Ed. G. J. Cumming. London: Nelson, 1965.

Hall, C. A. *With the Spirit's Sword: The Drama of Spiritual Warfare in the Theology of John Calvin.* Richmond: John Knox Press, 1970.

Hall, David. *The Faithful Shepherd: A History of the New England Ministry in the Seventeenth Century.* Chapel Hill: University of North Carolina Press, 1972.

Hall, Edwin. *The Puritans and Their Principles.* New York: Baker and Scribner, 1847.

Haller, William. *Liberty and Reformation in the Puritan Revolution.* New York: Columbia University Press, 1955.

_____. *The Rise of Puritanism.* New York: Columbia University Press, 1938.

Hamming, R. "Willem Teellinck." *Gereformeerd Theologisch Tijdschrift* 27 (1926-27):97-115.

Hanko, H. "Predestination in Calvin, Beza, and Later Reformed Theology." *Protestant Reformed Theological Journal* 10, 2 (1977):1-24.

Hambrick-Stowe, Charles E. *The Practice of Piety. Puritan Devotional Disciplines in Seventeenth-Century New England.* Williamsburg, Va.: University of North Carolina Press, 1982.

Hansen, Maurice G. *The Reformed Church in the Netherlands.* New York: Board of Publication of the Reformed Church in America, 1884.

Harbaugh, Henry. *The Fathers of the German Reformed Church in Europe and America.* 2 vols. Lancaster: Sprenger and Westhaeffer, 1857.

Hargrave, O. T. "The Doctrine of Predestination in the English Reformation." Ph.D. dissertation, Vanderbilt University, 1966.

Harinck, C. "Geloof en zekerheid bij Calvijn." *De Saambinder* 68 (1990) no. 38:5-7; no. 39:5-7; no. 40:3-4; no. 41:4-5.

_____. *De Schotse Verbondsleer: Van Robert Rollock tot Thomas Boston.* Utrecht: De Banier, 1986.

Harnack, Adolph. *History of Dogma.* Trans. N. Buchanan, et al. 7 vols. Boston: Roberts Brothers, 1897.

Haroutunian, Joseph. *Piety versus Moralism.* American Religious Series, no. 4. New York: Henry Holt and Co., 1932.

Harper, George. "Calvin and English Calvinism to 1649: A Review Article." *Calvin Theological Journal* 20 (1985):255-62.

Harrison, A. W. *The Beginnings of Arminianism to the Synod of Dort.* London: University of London, 1926.

Hasler, R. A. "Thomas Shepard: Pastor-Evangelist (1605-1649): A Study in New England Ministry." Ph.D. dissertation, Hartford Seminary Foundation, 1964.

Hastie, William. *The Theology of the Reformed Church.* Edinburgh: T. & T. Clark, 1904.

Hauck, Wilhelm A. *Die Erwählten: Prädestination und Heilsgewissheit bei Calvin.* Gütersloh: C. Bertelsmann, 1950.

Hawkes, Richard Mitchell. "The Logic of Assurance in English Puritan Theology." *Westminster Theological Journal* 52 (1990): 247-61.

_____. "The Logic of Grace in John Owen, D.D.: An Analysis, Exposition, and Defense of John Owen's Puritan Theology of Grace." Ph.D. dissertation, Westminster Theological Seminary, 1987.

Hazen, Harry Booth. "Calvin's Doctrine of Faith." Ph.D. dissertation, University of Chicago, 1903.

Helm, Paul. *Calvin and the Calvinists.* Edinburgh: Banner of Truth Trust, 1982.

_____. "Calvin, English Calvinism and the Logic of Doctrinal Development." *Scottish Journal of Theology* 34 (1981):179-85.

Henderson, G. D. *Religious Life in Seventeenth-Century Scotland.* Cambridge: Cambridge University Press, 1937.

Henson, H. Hensley. *Studies in English Religion in the Seventeenth Century.* New York: E. P. Dutton, 1903.

Heppe, Heinrich. *Dogmatik des deutschen Protestantismus im sechzehnten Jahrhundert.* 3 vols. Gotha: Friedrich A. Perthes, 1857.

_____. *Geschichte des Pietismus und der Mystik in der Reformierten Kirche, namentlich der Niederlande.* Leiden: E. J. Brill, 1879.

_____. *Theodor Beza: Leben und ausgewählte Schriften.* Elberfeld: R. L. Friedrichs, 1861.

Hesselink, I. John. *Calvin's Concept of the Law.* Allison Park, Pa.: Pickwick Publications, 1992.

_____. *Calvin's First Catechism: A Commentary.* Louisville: Westminster John Knox, 1997.

Hetherington, W. M. *History of the Westminster Assembly of Divines.* New York: Robert Carter & Brothers, 1859.

Hicks, John M. "The Theology of Grace in the Thought of Jacobus Arminius and Philip van Limborch: A Study in the Development of Seventeenth-Century Dutch Arminianism." Ph.D. dissertation, Westminster Theological Seminary, 1985.

Hill, Christopher. *Puritanism and Revolution: Studies in Interpretation of the English Revolution of the 17th Century.* New York: Schocken Books, 1964.

_____. *Society and Puritanism in Pre-Revolutionary England.* 2nd ed. New York: Schocken Books, 1967.

Hillman, Robert John. "Grace in the Preaching of Calvin & Wesley: A Comparative Study." Ph.D. dissertation, Fuller Seminary, 1978.

A History of the Westminster Assembly of Divines. Embracing an Account of Its Principal Transactions, and Biographical Sketches of Its Most Conspicuous Members. Philadelphia: Presbyterian Board of Publications, 1841.

Hodge, A. A. *The Confession of Faith.* Philadelphia: Presbyterian Board of Publication, 1869; reprint ed., London: Banner of Truth Trust, 1961.

_____. *Outlines of Theology: Rewritten and Enlarged.* Chicago: Bible Institute Colportage Ass'n, 1878; reprint ed., Edinburgh: Banner of Truth Trust, 1991.

Hodge, Charles. *Exposition of 1 and 2 Corinthians.* Reprint ed., Wilmington, Del.: Sovereign Grace Publishers, 1972.

_____. *Systematic Theology.* 3 vols. New York: Scribner, Armstrong, & Co., 1877.

Hoek, J. *Daniel Colonius (1566-1635): Theoloog tussen Reformatie en Orthodoxie.* Huizen: J. Bout en Zonen, 1981.

Hoekema, Anthony A. "The Covenant of Grace in Calvin's Teaching." *Calvin Theological Journal* 2 (1967):133-61.

Hoeksema, Herman. *Reformed Dogmatics.* Grand Rapids: Reformed Free Publishing Association, 1973.

Hoeksema, Homer. *The Voice of our Fathers: An Exposition of the Canons of Dordrecht*. Grand Rapids: Reformed Free Publishing Association, 1980.

Hofmeyr, Johannes Wynand. *Johannes Hoornbeeck as polemikus*. Kampen: Kok, 1975.

Holifield, E. Brooks. *The Covenant Sealed: The Development of Puritan Sacramental Theology in Old and New England, 1570-1720*. New Haven: Yale University Press, 1974.

Holley, Larry Jackson. "The Divines of the Westminster Assembly: A Study of Puritanism and Parliament." Ph.D. dissertation, Yale University, 1979.

Honders, Huibert Jacob. *Andreas Rivetus als invloedrijk Gereformeerd theoloog in Holland's bloeitijd*. 's-Gravenhage: Martinus Nijhoff, 1930.

Honig, Anthonie Gerrit. *Alexander Comrie*. Utrecht: H. Honig, 1892.

Hopf, Constantin. *Martin Bucer and the English Reformation*. New York: Macmillan, 1947.

Horst, Irvin Buckwaiter. *The Dutch Dissenters: A Critical Companion to their History and Ideas*. Leiden: E. J. Brill, 1986.

Horton, Douglas, trans. and ed. *William Ames*. Cambridge: Harvard Divinity School Library, 1965.

Horton, Michael. "Christ Set Forth: Thomas Goodwin and the Puritan Doctrine of Assurance, 1600-80." Ph.D. dissertation, Wycliffe Hall, Oxford and Coventry University, 1996.

Huelin, Gordon. "Peter Martyr and the English Reformation." Ph.D. dissertation, University of London, 1955.

Hughes, Philip. *Theology of the English Reformers*. Grand Rapids: Eerdmans, 1965; reprint ed., Grand Rapids: Baker, 1980.

Hulse, Errol. *The Believer's Experience*. Haywards Heath, Sussex: Carey Publications, 1977.

Humphrey, Richard Alan. "The Concept of Conversion in the Theology of Thomas Shepard (1605-1649)." Ph.D. dissertation, Drew University, 1967.

Ives, Robert B. "The Theology of Wolfgang Musculus, 1497-1563." Ph.D. dissertation, Manchester University, 1965.

Jacob, Günter. *Der Gewissensbegriff in der Theologie Luthers*. Tubingen: J. C. B. Mohr, 1929.

Jacobs, Paul. *Prädestination und verantwortlichkeit bei Calvin*. Neukirchen: Erziehungsvereins, 1937.

Jager, H. J. *Rechtvaardiging en zekerheid des geloofs*. Utrecht: Kemink & Zoon, 1939.

Janse, L. *Gisbertus Voetius, 1589-1676*. Utrecht: De Banier, 1971.

_____. *Jacobus Koelman, 1632-1695*. Utrecht: De Banier, n.d.

Johnson, E. W. *Questions Concerning Christian Assurance*. Pine Bluff, Ark.: Sovereign Grace Publishers, 1990.

Jones, J. M. "The Problem of Faith and Reason in the Thought of John Calvin." Ph.D. dissertation, Duke University, 1942.

Jones, James William, III. "The Beginnings of American Theology: John Cotton, Thomas Hooker, Thomas Shepard and Peter Bulkeley." Ph.D. dissertation, Brown University, 1970.

Kaajan, H. *De Groote Synode van Dordrecht in 1618-1619*. Amsterdam: N. V. de Standaard, 1918.

Kantzer, Kenneth S. "Calvin's Theory of the Knowledge of God and the Word of God." Ph.D. dissertation, Harvard University, 1950.

Karlberg, Mark Walter. "The Mosaic Covenant and the Concept of Works in Reformed Hermeneutics: A Historical-Critical Analysis with Particular Attention to Early Covenant Eschatology." Th.D. dissertation, Westminster Theological Seminary, 1980.

Kaufmann, U. F. *The Pilgrim's Progress and Traditions in Puritan Meditation*. New Haven: Yale University Press, 1966.

Keddie, Gordon J. "'Unfallible Certenty of the Pardon of Sinne and Life Everlasting': the Doctrine of Assurance in the Theology of William Perkins." *Evangelical Quarterly* 48 (1976):230-44.

Keep, David J. "Heinrich Bullinger, 1504-1575: A Sketch of His Life and Work, with Special Reference to Recent Literature." *London Quarterly and Holborn Review* 191 (1966):135-46.

_____. "Henry Bullinger and the Elizabethan Church." Ph.D. dissertation, Sheffield, 1970.

Kempff, D. *A Bibliography of Calviniana*, 1959-1974. Potchefstroom: I.A.C., 1975.

Kendall, Robert T. *Calvin and English Calvinism to 1649*. New York: Oxford University Press, 1979.

_____. "Living the Christian Life in the Teaching of William Perkins and His Followers." In *Living the Christian Life*, pp. 45-60. Westminster Conference, 1973. London: Westminster Conference, 1974.

_____. "The Puritan Modification of Calvin's Theology." In *John Calvin: His Influence in the Western World*, pp. 199-214. Ed. W. Stanford Reid. Grand Rapids: Zondervan, 1982.

Kersten, Gerrit H. *Reformed Dogmatics: A Systematic Treatment of Reformed Doctrine, Explained for the Congregations*. 2 vols. Trans. Joel R. Beeke and Jan C. Weststrate. Grand Rapids: Eerdmans, 1980-83.

Kevan, Ernest F. *The Grace of Law: A Study in Puritan Theology*. London: Carey Kingsgate Press, 1964; reprint ed., Grand Rapids: Baker, 1976.

Kickel, Walter. *Vernunft und offenbarung bei Theodor Beza*. Beiträge zur geschichte und lehre der Reformierten Kirche, no. 25. Neukirchen- Vluyn: Neukirchener Verlag des Erziehungsvereins, 1967.

Kim, Seung Lak. "John Wesley's Doctrine of the Witness of the Spirit or the Assurance of Salvation." Ph.D. dissertation, Southern Baptist Theological Seminary, 1932.

Kirby, Reginald. *The Threefold Bond*. London: Marshall, Morgan, and Scott, n.d.

Kittelson, James M. *Luther the Reformer. The Story of the Man and His Career*. Minneapolis: Augsburg Publishing House, 1986.

Klooster, Fred. "Assurance." In *The Encyclopedia of Christianity*. Vol. 1, pp. 444-48. Ed. Edwin Palmer. Wilmington, Del.: National Foundation for Christian Education, 1964.

_____. *Calvin's Doctrine of Predestination*. Grand Rapids: Calvin Theological Seminary, 1961; reprint ed., Grand Rapids: Baker, 1977.

Klunder, Jack D. "The Application of Holy Things: A Study of the Covenant Preaching in the Eighteenth Century Dutch Colonial Church." Ph.D. dissertation, Westminster Theological Seminary, 1984.

Knappen, M. M. "Richard Greenham and the Practical Puritans under Elizabeth." Ph.D. dissertation, Cornell University, 1927.

_____. *Tudor Puritanism: A Chapter in the History of Idealism*. Chicago: University of Chicago Press, 1939.

Knoepp, Walther T. "Jonathan Edwards: The Way of Sanctification." Ph.D. dissertation, Hartford Seminary Foundation, 1937.

Knox, David Broughton. *The Doctrine of Faith in the Reign of Henry VIII*. London: James Clarke & Co., 1961.

_____. "The Doctrine of Justification by Faith in the English Reformers." Ph.D. dissertation, Oxford University, 1972.

Knox, S. J. *Walter Travers: Paragon of Elizabethan Puritanism*. London: Methuen, 1962.

Knuttel, Willem Pieter Cornelis. *Balthasar Bekker: De Bestrijder van het Bijgeloof*. 's-Gravenhage: Martinus Nijhoff, 1906.

Koeman, P. "Van Lodenstein en Calvijn over de heiliging." *Theologia Reformata* 20 (1977):281-306.

Kraan, E. D. "De Heilige Geest en het na-reformatorische subjectivisme." In *De Heilige Geest*, pp. 228-63. Ed. J. H. Bavinck, et al. Kampen: Kok, 1949.

Kromsigt, Johannes Christiaan. *Wilhelmus Schortinghuis. Eene bladzijde uit de geschiedenis van het Pietisme in de Gereformeerde Kerk van Nederland*. Groningen: J. B. Wolters, 1904.

Kruger, J. C. *Die verhouding van uitverkiesing tot bekering met spesiale verwysing na die Dordtse Leerreels*. Pretoria: Kerkboekhandel, 1974.

Krull, F. A. *Jacobus Koelman: Een kerkhistorische Studie*. Reprint ed., Amsterdam: Ton Bolland, 1972.

Krusche, Werner. *Das Wirken des Heiligen Geistes nach Calvin*. Göttingen: Vandenhoeck & Ruprecht, 1957.

Kuizinga, Henry Bernard. "The Idea of Grace in John Calvin." Ph.D. dissertation, Yale University, 1952.

Kurz, Alfred. *Die heilsgewissheit bei Luther*. Gütersloh: C. Bertelsmann, 1933.

Kuiper, J. *Geschiedenis van het Godsdienstig en Kerkelijk Leven van het Nederlandsche Volk*. Nijkerk: G. F. Callenbach, 1903.

Kuyper, Abraham. "Alexander Comrie: His Life and Work in Holland." *Catholic Presbyterian* 7 (1882):20-29, 192-201, 278-84.

_____. *Dictaten Dogmatiek*. 5 vols. Kampen: Kok, n.d.

_____. *E Voto Dordraceno*. 4 vols. Amsterdam: Höveker & Wormser, 1905.

_____. *The Work of the Holy Spirit*. Trans. Henri de Vries. New York: Funk and Wagnalls, 1900.

Kuyper, Herman Huber. *Calvijn en Nederland*. Utrecht: G. J. A. Ruys, 1909.

_____. *De Post-Acts of Nahandelingen van de Nationale Synode van Dordrecht in 1618 en 1619 Gehouden*. Amsterdam: Hoveker & Wormser, [1899].

Lachman, David. *The Marrow Controversy, 1718-1723: An Historical and Theological Analysis*. Rutherford Studies Series One: Historical Theology. Edinburgh: Rutherford House, 1988.

_____. "The Marrow Controversy: An Historical Survey with special reference to the Free Offer of the Gospel, the Extent of the Atonement, and Assurance and Saving Faith." Th.M. thesis, Westminster Theological Seminary, 1973.

Lake, Peter. *Moderate Puritans and the Elizabethan Church*. New York: Cambridge University Press, 1982.

Laman, H. W. *Geloofsbezwaren opgelost door Wilhelmus à Brakel*. Kampen: Kok, 1929.

Lamont, William. "Puritanism as History and Historiography: Some Further Thoughts." *Past and Present* 42 (1969):133-46.

Lampe, G. W. H. *The Seal of the Spirit*. London: Longmans, 1951.

Lane, A. N. S. "Calvin's Doctrine of Assurance." *Vox Evangelica* 11 (1979):32-54.

Lang, August. *Puritanismus und Piëtismus: Studies zu ihrer Entwicklung von M. Butzer bis zum methodismus*. Ansbach: Brugel, 1941.

Laurence, David Ernst. "Religious Experience in the Biblical World of Jonathan Edwards: A Study in Eighteenth Century Supernaturalism." Ph.D. dissertation, Yale University, 1976.

Leff, Gordon A. *Bradwardine and the Pelagians*. Cambridge: University Press, 1957.

_____. *Gregory of Rimini: Tradition and Innovation in Fourteenth Century Theology*. New York: Barnes and Noble, 1971.

_____. *Medieval Thought, St. Augustine to Ockham*. Reprint ed., Atlantic Highlands, N.J.: Humanities Press, 1980.

Leith, John H. *Assembly at Westminster: Reformed Theology in the Making*. Richmond: John Knox Press, 1973.

_____. *John Calvin's Doctrine of the Christian Life*. Louisville: Westminster Press, 1989.

Letham, Robert. "Faith and Assurance in Early Calvinism: A Model of Continuity and Diversity." In *Later Calvinism: International Perspectives*, pp.355-85. Ed. W. Fred Graham. Kirksville, Mo.: Sixteenth Century Journal Publishers, 1994.

_____. "The Relationship between Saving Faith and Assurance of Salvation." Th.M. thesis, Westminster Theological Seminary, 1976.

_____. "Saving Faith and Assurance in Reformed Theology: Zwingli to the Synod of Dort." 2 vols. Ph.D. dissertation, University of Aberdeen, 1979.

Leurdijk, G. "Alexander Comrie: Een vaderlijke vriend." *De Saambinder* 61 (1983):3-4 (February 3), and 2-3 (February 10).

_____. "Het begin van de Nadere Reformatie in Holland." *Documentatieblad Nadere Reformatie* 11 (1987):1-5.

Levy, Babette May. *Preaching in the First Century of New England History.* Hartford, Conn.: American Society of Church History, 1945.

Lewis, Peter. *The Genius of Puritanism.* Haywards Heath, Sussex: Carey Publications, 1975.

Lillback, Peter. "The Binding of God: Calvin's Role in the Development of Covenant Theology." Ph.D. dissertation, Westminster Theological Seminary, 1985.

Lindberg, Richard L. "The Westminster and Second London Baptist Confessions of Faith: A Historical-Theological Comparison." Th.M. thesis, Westminster Theological Seminary, 1980.

Lindeboom, Johannes. *Austin Friars: History of the Dutch Reformed Church in London, 1550-1950.* Trans. D. DeIongh. The Hague: Nijhoff, 1950.

Linder, Robert D. "Pierre Viret and the Sixteenth-Century English Protestants." *Archiv für Reformationsgeschichte* 58 (1967):149-70.

Lindstrom, Harald. *Wesley and Sanctification.* London: Epworth Press, 1950.

Littell, Franklin H., ed. *Reformation Studies.* Richmond: John Knox Press, 1962.

Lloyd-Jones, D. M. *The Puritans: Their Origins and Successors. Addresses delivered at the Puritan and Westminster Conferences 1959-1978.* Edinburgh: The Banner of Truth Trust, 1987.

_____. *Romans, An Exposition of Chapter 5: Assurance.* Grand Rapids: Zondervan, 1977.

Locher, Gottfried W. "The Change in the Understanding of Zwingli in Recent Research." *Church History* 34 (1965):3-24.

_____. "Die prädestinationslehre Huldrych Zwinglis." *Theologische Zeitschrift* 13 (1956):526-49.

_____. "The Shape of Zwingli's Theology: A Comparison with Luther and Calvin." *Pittsburgh Perspective* 8 (1967):5-26.

_____. *Die theologie H. Zwinglis im lichte seines Christologie.* Studien zur dogmengeschichte und systematischen theologie, no. 1. Zürich: Zwingli-Verlag, 1952.

_____. "Zwinglis einfluss in England und Schottland. Daten und probleme." *Zwingliana* 24 (1975):165-209.

_____. *Zwingli's Thought: New Perspectives.* Leiden: E. J. Brill, 1981.

Logan, Samuel T., Jr. "The Doctrine of Justification in the Theology of Jonathan Edwards." *Westminster Theological Journal* 46 (1984):26-52.

Lohse, Bernard. *Martin Luther: An Introduction to his Life and Work.* Trans. Robert C. Schutz. Philadelphia: Fortress Press, 1986.

Los, Frans Johannes. *Wilhelmus à Brakel.* Leiden: G. Los, 1892.

Lovelace, Richard. *The American Pietism of Cotton Mather.* Grand Rapids: Eerdmans, 1979.

_____. "Evangelicalism: Recovering a Tradition of Spiritual Depth." *Reformed Journal* 40, 7 (September 1990):20-25.

Lowrie, Ernest B. *The Shape of the Puritan Mind: The Thought of Samuel Willard.* New Haven: Yale University Press, 1974.

Lyon, Olof Halvard. "The Element of Subjectivity in Calvin." Th.M. thesis, Columbia Theological Seminary, 1968.

MacArthur, John, Jr. *A Believer's Assurance: A Practical Guide to Victory Over Doubt.* Panorama City, Calif.: The Master's Communication, 1990.

Macauley, George. *Puritan Theology.* 2 vols. London: James Nisbet, 1872.

McCahagan, Thomas Arthur. "Cartesianism in the Netherlands, 1639-1676: The New Science and the Calvinist Counter-Reformation." Ph.D. dissertation, University of Pennsylvania, 1976.

McClelland, J. C. *The Visible Words of God: An Exposition of the Sacramental Theology of Peter Martyr Vermigli, A.D. 1500-1562.* Edinburgh: Oliver & Boyd, 1957.

M'Clintock, John, and Strong, James. *Cyclopaedia of Biblical, Theological, and Ecclesiastical Literature.* 12 vols. New York: Harper and Brothers, 1894-95.

McCoy, Charles. "The Covenant Theology of Johannes Cocceius." Ph.D. dissertation, Yale University, 1957.

McCoy, Charles S., and Baker, J. Wayne. *Fountainhead of Federalism: Heinrich Bullinger and the Covenantal Tradition.* Louisville: Westminster/John Knox, 1992.

MacEwen, A. R. *The Erskines.* Edinburgh: Oliphant Anderson & Ferrier, 1900.

McEwen, James S. *The Faith of John Knox.* London: Lutterworth Press, 1960.

McGee, James Sears. "Conversion and the Imitation of Christ in Anglican and Puritan Writing." *Journal of British Studies* 16 (1976):21-39.

_____. *The Godly Man in Stuart England: Anglicans, Puritans, and the Two Tables, 1620-1670.* New Haven: Yale University Press, 1976.

McGiffert, Arthur. *A History of Christian Thought.* New York: Scribner's, 1954.

McGrath, Alister. *Iustitia Dei: A History of the Doctrine of Justification.* 2 vols. Cambridge: Cambridge University Press, 1986.

_____. *A Life of John Calvin: A Study in the Shaping of Western Culture.* Oxford: Basil Blackwell, 1990.

_____. *Luther's Theology of the Cross: Martin Luther's Theological Breakthrough.* New York: Basil Blackwell, 1985.

McIntyre, D. M. "First Strictures on 'The Marrow of Modern Divinity.'" *Evangelical Quarterly* 10 (1938):61-70.

McKee, William Wakefield. "The Idea of Covenant in Early English Puritanism (1580-1643)." Ph.D. dissertation, Yale University, 1948.

McKenzie, P. R. "The Invisibility of the Church for Luther and Calvin." Ph.D. dissertation, Edinburgh, 1953.

McKerrow, John. *History of the Secession Church.* Edinburgh: A. Fullarton, 1845.

McKim, Donald Keith. *Ramism in William Perkins' Theology.* American

University Studies, Series VII, Theology and Religion, no. 15. New York: Peter Lang, 1987.

_____. "William Perkins and the Theology of the Covenant." In *Studies of the Church in History*, pp. 85-101. Ed. Horton M. Davies. Allison Park, Pa.: Pickwith Publications, 1983.

Mackintosh, H. R. *The Christian Experience of Forgiveness*. New York: Harper and Brothers, 1927.

MacLear, James F. "'The Heart of New England Rent': the Mystical Element in Early Puritan History." *Mississippi Valley Historical Review* 42 (March 1956):621-52.

_____. "The Puritan Party, 1603-1643: A Study in a Lost Reformation." Ph.D. dissertation, University of Chicago, 1947.

M'Leod, Alexander. *The Life and Power of True Godliness*. New York: Eastburn, 1816.

Macleod, Donald. "Christian Assurance." *Banner of Truth* no. 133 (Oct. 1974):16-25; no. 134 (Nov. 1974):1-7.

Macleod, John. *Scottish Theology: In Relation to Church History Since the Reformation*. Reprint ed., London: Banner of Truth Trust, 1974.

MacMillan, Douglas. "The Connection between 17th Century British and Dutch Calvinism." In *Not by Might nor by Power*, pp. 22-31. Westminster Conference, 1988. Colchester: Christian Design & Print, 1989.

McNally, Alexander. "Some Aspects of Thomas Goodwin's Doctrine of Assurance." Th.M. thesis, Westminster Theological Seminary, 1972.

McNeill, John T. *The History and Character of Calvinism*. New York: Oxford University Press, 1973.

Macphail, Andrew. *Essays in Puritanism*. London: T. Fisher Unwin, 1905.

McPhee, Ian. "Conserver or Transformer of Calvin's Theology? A Study of the Origins and Development of Theodore Beza's Thought, 1550-1570." Ph.D. dissertation, University of Cambridge, 1979.

Malan, C. J. *Die Nadere Reformasie*. Potchefstroom, Republic of South Africa: Potchefstroomse Universiteit vir CHO, 1981.

Manschreck, Clyde. *Melanchthon, the Quiet Reformer*. New York: Abingdon Press, 1958.

Markham, C. C. "William Perkins' Understanding of the Function of Conscience." Ph.D. dissertation, Vanderbilt University, 1967.

Marsden, George M. "Perry Miller's Rehabilitation of the Puritans, A Critique." *Church History* 39 (1970):91-105.

Marsden, J. P. *The History of the Early Puritans*. 2nd ed. London: Hamilton, Adams, & Co., 1853.

_____. *The History of the Later Puritans*. 3rd ed. London: Hamilton, Adams, & Co., 1872.

Marshall, John E. "'Rabbi' Duncan and the Problem of Assurance." *Banner of Truth*, no. 201 (June 1980):16-27; no. 202 (July 1980):24-31.

Martin, Hugh. *Puritanism and Richard Baxter*. London: SCM Press, 1954.

Maruyama, Tadataka. *The Ecclesiology of Theodore Beza.* Genève: Librairie Droz, 1978.

Mechie, Stewart. "The Marrow Controversy Reviewed." *Evangelical Quarterly* 22 (1950):20-31.

Meertens, P. J. "Godefrides Cornelisz Udemans." *Nederlandsch Archief voor Kerkgeschiedenis* 28 (1936):65-106.

Meeuse, C. J. "De visie van Koelman op de puriteinen." *Documentatieblad Nadere Reformatie* 20 (1996):44-61.

Meijerink, H. J. *Reformatie en Mystiek.* Goes: Oosterbaan and Le Cointe, 1956.

Middlekauff, Robert. *The Mathers: Three Generations of Puritan Intellectuals 1596-1728.* New York: Oxford University Press, 1971.

Middleton, Erasmus. *Biographia Evanglica.* 4 vols. London: Baynes, 1810.

Miller, Basil W. "John Wesley's Doctrine of the Witness of the Spirit." B.S.T. thesis, Biblical Seminary, 1951.

Miller, Glenn. "The Rise of Evangelical Calvinism: A Study in Jonathan Edwards and the Puritan Tradition." Th.D. dissertation, Union Theological Seminary, 1971.

Miller, Perry. *Errand into the Wilderness.* Cambridge: Belknap Press, 1956.

_____. *Jonathan Edwards.* New York: William Sloane, 1949; reprint ed., Westport, Conn.: Greenwood Press, 1973.

_____. *The New England Mind: From Colony to Province.* Cambridge: Harvard University Press, 1953; reprint ed., Boston: Beacon Press, 1961.

_____. *The New England Mind: The Seventeenth Century.* Cambridge: Harvard University Press, 1939; reprint ed., Boston: Beacon Press, 1961.

_____. *Orthodoxy in Massachusetts.* Cambridge: Harvard University Press, 1933; reprint ed., Gloucester, Mass.: Peter Smith, 1965.

_____. "'Preparation for Salvation' in Seventeenth-Century New England." *Journal of the History of Ideas* 4 (1943):253-86.

Mitchell, Alexander F. *The Westminster Assembly, Its History and Standards.* Philadelphia: Presbyterian Board of Publications, 1884.

Moffatt, Charles L., Jr. "James Hog of Carnock (1658-1734), Leader of the Evangelical Party in Early Eighteenth Century Scotland." Ph.D. dissertation, University of Edinburgh, 1960.

Molhuysen, Philip Christiaan, ed. *Nieuw Nederlandsch Biografisch Woordenboek.* 10 vols. Leiden: A. W. Sijthoff, 1911-37.

Mohr, James D. "Heinrich Bullinger's Opinions concerning Martin Luther." Ph.D. dissertation, Kent State, 1972.

Moller, Jens G. "The Beginnings of Puritan Covenant Theology." *The Journal of Ecclesiastical History* 14 (1963):46-67.

Moltmann, Jürgen. *Prädestination und Perseveranz: Geschichte und Bedeutung der reformierten Lehre "de perseverantia sanctorum."* Neukirchen: Neukirchner Verlag, 1961.

Monk, Robert C. *John Wesley: His Puritan Heritage.* Nashville: Abingdon Press, 1966.

Montgomery, Michael S. *American Puritan Studies: An Annotated Bibliography of Dissertations, 1882-1981.* Bibliographies and Indexes in American History, no. 1. Westport, Conn.: Greenwood Press, 1984.

Morgan, Edmund. *Visible Saints.* New York: New York University Press, 1963.

Morgan, Irvonwy. *The Godly Preachers of the Elizabethan Church.* London: Epworth Press, 1965.

————. *Puritan Spirituality: Illustrated from the Life and Times of the Rev. Dr. John Preston.* London: Epworth Press, 1973.

Morris, Edward D. *Theology of the Westminster Symbols.* Columbus, Ohio: Champlin Press, 1900.

Mosse, George L. "Puritan Political Thought and the 'Cases of Conscience.'" *Church History* 23 (1954):109-118.

Motley, John Lothrop. *The Rise of the Dutch Republic.* 3 vols. New York: Harper & Brothers, 1899.

Muller, Richard A. *Christ and the Decrees: Christology and Predestination in Reformed Theology from Calvin to Perkins.* Grand Rapids: Baker, 1988.

————. "Covenant and Conscience in English Reformed Theology." *Westminster Theological Journal* 42 (1980):308-34.

————. "Perkins' *A Golden Chaine*: Predestinarian System or Schematized Ordo Salutis?" *Sixteenth Century Journal* 9, 1 (1978):69-81.

————. *Post-Reformation Reformed Dogmatics.* 2 vols. Grand Rapids: Baker, 1987-91.

————. "Predestination and Christology in Sixteenth Century Reformed Theology." Ph.D. dissertation, Duke University, 1976.

Mullinger, James Bass. *The University of Cambridge.* 3 vols. Cambridge: Cambridge University Press, 1873-1911.

Munson, Charles R. "William Perkins, Theologian of Transition." Ph.D. dissertation, Case Western Reserve, 1971.

Murdock, Kenneth B. *Increase Mather: the Foremost American Puritan.* Cambridge: Harvard University Press, 1925.

Murray, Iain H. *D. Martyn Lloyd-Jones.* 2 vols. Edinburgh: Banner of Truth Trust, 1982-90.

————. "Martin Lloyd-Jones on the Baptism with the Holy Spirit." *Banner of Truth* no. 257 (February 1985):8-16.

————. *The Puritan Hope.* London: Banner of Truth Trust, 1971.

Murray, John. *Collected Writings.* 4 vols. Edinburgh: Banner of Truth Trust, 1978-83.

————. "Covenant Theology." *The Encyclopedia of Christianity,* vol. 3, pp. 199-216. Ed. Philip E. Hughes. Marshallton, Del.: National Foundation for Christian Education, 1972.

Nauta, D. *Het Calvinisme in Nederland.* Franeker: Wever, 1949.

————. *De Nederlandsche Gereformeerden en het Independentisme in de zeventiende eeuwe.* Amsterdam: H. J. Paris, 1935.

_____. *Samuel Maresius*. Amsterdam: H. J. Paris, 1935.

_____, ed. *Biografisch Lexicon voor de Geschiedenis van het Nederlands Protestantisme*. 3 vols. Kampen: Kok, 1978-88.

New, John F. *Anglican and Puritan: The Basis of Their Opposition, 1558-1640*. Stanford: Stanford University Press, 1964.

Niesel, Wilhelm. "*Syllogismus practicus?*" In *Aus Theologie und Geschichte der reformierten Kirche*, pp. 158-79. Neukirchen: K. Moers, 1933.

_____. *The Theology of Calvin*. Trans. Harold Knight. London: Butterworth Press, 1956; reprint ed., Grand Rapids: Baker, 1980.

Nijenhuis, W. *Ecclesia Reformata: Studies in the Reformation*. Leiden: E. J. Brill, 1972.

Nobbs, Douglas. *Theocracy and Toleration: A Study in the Disputes in Dutch Calvinism from 1600-1650*. Cambridge: University Press, 1938.

Noll, Mark. "John Wesley and the Doctrine of Assurance." *Bibliotheca Sacra* 132 (April 1975):161-77.

Nuttall, Geoffrey F. "English Dissenters in the Netherlands, 1640-1689." *Nederlands Archief voor Kerkgeschedenis* 59 (1978):37-54.

_____. *The Holy Spirit in Puritan Faith and Experience*. Oxford: Basil Blackwell, 1946; reprint ed., Chicago: University of Chicago Press, 1992.

Oberman, Heiko Augustinus. "Archbishop Thomas Bradwardine: A Fourteenth Century Augustinian." Th.D. dissertation, Utrecht University, 1957.

_____. *Forerunners of the Reformation: The Shape of Late Medieval Thought Illustrated by Key Documents*. New York: Holt, Rinehart and Winston, 1966; reprint ed., Philadelphia: Fortress Press, 1981.

_____. *The Harvest of Medieval Theology: Gabriel Biel and Late Medieval Nominalism*. Revised edition. Grand Rapids: Eerdmans, 1967.

_____. "'Iustitia Christi' and 'Iustitia Dei'; Luther and the Scholastic Doctrines of Justification." *Harvard Theological Review* 59 (1966):1-26.

_____. *Luther: Man Between God and the Devil*. New Haven: Yale University Press, 1989.

Oki, Hideo. "Ethics in Seventeenth Century English Puritanism." Ph.D. dissertation, Union Theological Seminary, 1960.

O'Malley, J. Steven. *Pilgrimage of Faith: The Legacy of the Otterbeins*. ATLA Monograph Series, No. 4. Metuchen, N.J.: Scarecrow Press, 1973.

Ong, Walter J. *Ramus, Method, and the Decay of Dialogue: From the Art of Discourse to the Art of Reason*. Cambridge: Harvard University Press, 1958.

Oorthuys, G. "De beteekenis van het nieuwe leven voor de zekerheid des geloofs, volgens Calvijns Institutie." *Onder Eigen Vaandel* 13 (1938):246-69.

Op't Hof, Willem Jan. *Bibliografische lijst van de geschriften van Willem Teellinck*. Rotterdam: Lindenberg, 1993.

_____. *Engelse piëtistische geschriften in het Nederlands, 1598-1622*. Rotterdam: Lindenberg, 1987.

_____. "Gisbertus Voetius' evaluatie van de Reformatie." *Theologia Reformata* 32 (1989):211-42.

_____. "Johannes Polyander en Willem Teellinck." *Documentatieblad Nadere Reformatie* 7 (1983):126-143.

_____. "De Nederlandse vertalers van William Perkins' geschriften voor 1650." *Documentatieblad Nadere Reformatie* 8 (1984):56-60.

_____. "Studie der Nadere Reformatie: verleden en toekomst." *Documentatieblad Nadere Reformatie* 18 (1994):1-50.

_____. "De visie op de Reformatie in de Nadere Reformatie tijdens het eerste kwart van de zeventiende eeuw." *Documentatieblad Nadere Reformatie* 6 (1982):89-108.

_____. *Voorbereiding en bestrijding: De oudste gereformeerde piëtistische voorbereidingspreken tot het Avondmaal en de eerste bestrijding van de Nadere Reformatie in druk.* Kampen: DeGroot, 1987.

_____. "Willem Teellinck in het licht zijner geschriften." *Documentatieblad Nadere Reformatie* 1 (1977):3-14, 33-41, 69-76, 105-114; 2 (1978):1-12, 33-62, 65-88, 97-105; 3 (1979):33-40, 97-100; 4 (1980):1-9, 33-38, 97-103; 5 (1981):1-5, 34, 70-82, 107-108; 6 (1982):1-4, 37-45; 7 (1983):25-30, 37-42, 117-125; 8 (1984):9-17, 37-40, 73-80, 109-113; 9 (1985):37-42, 73-77, 109-118; 10 (1986):31-36, 64-66, 73-76; 11 (1987):62-67; 12 (1988):109-115; 13 (1989):2-24, 135-144; 14 (1990):57-65, 117-127; 15 (1991):44-52, 132-136; 16 (1992):28-34, 93-96; 17 (1993):47-54; 18 (1994):93-98; 20 (1996):90-98; 21 (1997):81-98.

Orme, William. *Life of the Rev. John Owen, D.D.* Reprint ed., Choteau, Mont.: Gospel Mission Press, 1981.

Osterhaven, M. Eugene. "The Experiential Theology of the Early Dutch Calvinism." *Reformed Review* 27 (1973-74):180-89.

Owen, T. E. *Methodism Unmasked; or, The Progress of Puritanism from the Sixteenth to the Nineteenth Century.* London: Printed for J. Hatchard, 1802.

Ozment, Steven. *The Age of Reform 1250-1550: An Intellectual and Religious History of Late Medieval and Reformation Europe.* New Haven: Yale University Press, 1980.

_____, ed. *Reformation Europe: A Guide to Research.* St. Louis: Center for Reformed Research, 1982.

Packer, J. I. "John Owen on Communication from God." In *One Stedfast High Intent*, pp. 17-30. Puritan and Reformed Studies Conference, 1966. London: n.p., 1967.

_____. "The Puritan Idea of Communion with God." In *Press Toward the Mark*, pp. 16-28. Puritan and Reformed Studies Conference, 1961. London: n.p., 1962.

_____. *A Quest for Godliness: The Puritan Vision of the Christian Life.* Wheaton, Ill.: Crossway Books, 1990.

_____. "The Redemption and Restoration of Man in the Thought of Richard Baxter." D.Phil. dissertation, Oxford, 1954.

_____. "The Witness of the Spirit: The Puritan Teaching." In *The Wisdom of our Fathers*, pp. 14-25. Puritan Conference, 1956. London: n.p., 1957.

Palmer, B. M. *The Threefold Fellowship and the Threefold Assurance: An Essay in two Parts.* Richmond, Va.: Presbyterian Committee of Publication, 1902; reprint ed., Harrisonburg, Va.: Sprinkle Publications, 1980.

Parker, T. H. L. *The Doctrine of the Knowledge of God: A Study in the Theology of John Calvin.* Edinburgh: Oliver and Boyd, 1952.

Parratt, J. K. "The Witness of the Holy Spirit: Calvin, the Puritans and St. Paul." *Evangelical Quarterly* 41 (1969):161-68.

Partee, Charles. *Calvin and Classical Philosophy.* Studies in the History of Christian Thought, no. 14. Leiden: E. J. Brill, 1977.

_____. "Calvin and Experience." *Scottish Journal of Theology* 26 (1973):169-81.

Paul, Robert. *The Assembly of the Lord: Politics and Religion in the Westminster Assembly and the Grand Debate.* Edinburgh: T. & T. Clark, 1985.

Pelkonen, J. P. "The Teaching of John Calvin on the Nature and Function of the Conscience." *Lutheran Quarterly* 21 (1969):24-88.

Pellman, Hubert. "Thomas Hooker: A Study in Puritan Ideals." Ph.D. dissertation, University of Pennsylvania, 1958.

Pestalozzi, Carl. *Heinrich Bullinger: Leben und ausgewählte Schriften. Nach handschriftlichen und gleichzeitigen Quellen.* Leben und ausgewählte Schriften der Vater und Begründer der reformirten Kirche, no. 5. Elberfeld: R. I. Friderichs, 1858.

Pettit, Norman. *The Heart Prepared: Grace and Conversion in Puritan Spiritual Life.* New Haven: Yale University Press, 1966.

_____. "Hooker's Doctrine of Assurance: A Critical Phase in New England Spiritual Thought." *New England Quarterly* 47 (1974):518-534.

Pfürtner, Stephan H. *Luther and Aquinas, a Conversation: Our Salvation, Its Certainty and Peril.* Trans. Edward Quinn. London: Darton, Longman, & Todd, 1964.

Phillips, James M. "Between Conscience and the Law: The Ethics of Richard Baxter (1615-1691)." Ph.D. dissertation, Princeton University, 1959.

Pipa, Joseph A., Jr. "William Perkins and the Development of Puritan Preaching." Ph.D. dissertation, Westminster Theological Seminary, 1985.

Platt, John. *Reformed Thought and Scholasticism: The Arguments for the Existence of God in Dutch Theology, 1575-1650.* Studies in the History of Christian Thought, no. 29. Ed. Heiko A. Oberman. Leiden: E. J. Brill, 1982.

Plooij, D. *The Pilgrim Fathers from a Dutch Point of View.* New York: New York University Press, 1932.

Pollard, Alfred William, and Redgrave, G. R., eds. *A Short-Title Catalogue of Books Printed in England, Scotland, and Ireland, 1475-1640.* London: The Biblio-Society, 1946.

Polman, A. D. R. *De praedestinatieleer van Augustinus, Thomas van Aquino en Calvijn: Een dogmahistorische studie.* Franeker: T. Wever, 1936.

Pont, A. D. "Die sekerheid van die geloof bij Calvijn en sommige van sij navalogers." *Hervormde Teologicse Studies* 44 (1988):404-419.

Poole, Harry A. "The Unsettled Mr. Cotton." Ph.D. dissertation, University of Illinois, 1956.

Porter, H. C. *Puritanism in Tudor England*. New York: The MacMillan Co., 1970.

_____. *Reformation and Reaction in Tudor Cambridge*. London: Cambridge University Press, 1958.

Post, Regnerus Richardus. *The Modern Devotion: Confrontation with Reformation and Humanism*. Leiden: E. J. Brill, 1968.

Potter, George Richard. *Zwingli*. Cambridge: Cambridge University Press, 1976.

Pratt, Melvyn E. "Zwinglianism in England during the Reign of Elizabeth." Ph.D. dissertation, Stanford University, 1953.

Prestwich, Menna, ed. *International Calvinism, 1541-1715*. Oxford: Clarendon Press, 1985.

Preus, Robert D. *The Theology of Post-Reformation Lutheranism: A Study of Theological Prolegomena*. 2 vols. St. Louis: Concordia, 1970-72.

Priebe, Victor L. "The Covenant Theology of William Perkins." Ph.D. dissertation, Drew University, 1967.

Pronk, Cornelis. "Assurance of Faith." *Messenger* 24 (March 1977):9-10, (April 1977):5-6, (May 1977):5-7.

_____. "The Dutch Puritans." *The Banner of Truth* nos. 154-55 (July-August 1976):1-10.

Proost, Pieter. *Jodocus van Lodenstein*. Amsterdam: J. Brandt en Zoon, 1880.

Prozesky, Martin H. "The Emergence of Dutch Pietism." *The Journal of Ecclesiastical History* 28 (1977):29-37.

Pytches, P. N. L. "A Critical Exposition of the Teaching of John Owen on the work of the Holy Spirit in the Individual." M.Litt. thesis, Bristol, 1967.

Raitt, Jill. *The Eucharistic Theology of Theodore Beza: Development of the Reformed Doctrine*. American Academy of Studies in Religion, no. 4. Chambersburg, Pa.: American Academy of Religion, 1972.

_____, ed. *Shapers of Religious Traditions in Germany, Switzerland, and Poland, 1560-1600*. New Haven: Yale University Press, 1981.

Ramm, Bernard. *The Witness of the Holy Spirit*. Grand Rapids: Eerdmans, 1959.

Reid, James. *Memoirs of the Lives and Writings of those Eminent Divines who convened in the famous Assembly at Westminster in the Seventeenth Century*. 2 vols. Paisley: Stephen and Andrew Young, 1811; reprint ed., 2 vols. in 1, Edinburgh: Banner of Truth Trust, 1982.

Reid, W. Stanford. *Trumpeter of God: A Biography of John Knox*. New York: Charles Scribner's Sons, 1974.

_____, ed. *John Calvin: His Influence in the Western World*. Grand Rapids: Zondervan, 1982.

Reisinger, Ernest C. *Today's Evangelism: Its Message and Methods*. Phillipsburg, N.J.: Craig Press, 1982.

Reitsma, J., and Lindeboom, J. *Geschiedenis van de Hervorming en de Hervormde Kerk der Nederlanden*. 5th ed. 's-Gravenhage: Martinus Nijhoff, 1949.

Rhoades, Donald Hosea. "Jonathan Edwards: Experimental Theologian." Ph.D. dissertation, Yale University, 1945.

Richard, Lucien Joseph. *The Spirituality of John Calvin*. Atlanta: John Knox Press, 1974.

Ridgley, Thomas. *A Body of Divinity wherein the Doctrines of the Christian Religion are explained and defended. Being the substance of Several Lectures on the Assembly's Larger Catechism*. With notes by James P. Wilson. 4 vols. Philadelphia: William W. Woodward, 1815; reprint ed., 4 vols. in 2, Edmonton: Still Waters Revival, 1993.

Rilliet, Jean Horace. *Zwingli: The Third Man of the Reformation*. Trans. Harold Knight. London: Lutterworth Press, 1964.

Ritschl, Albrecht B. *A Critical History of the Chrisitan Doctrine of Justification and Reconciliation*. Trans. John S. Black. Edinburgh: Edmonston and Douglas, 1872.

_____. *Geschichte des Pietismus*. 3 vols. Bonn: Marcus, 1880-86.

Ritschl, Otto. *Dogmengeschichte des Protestantismus*. 4 vols. Leipzig: Hinrichs, 1908-1912.

Robins, Henry Burke. *The Basis of Assurance in Recent Protestant Theologies*. Kansas City: Charles E. Brown, 1912.

Robinson, H. Wheeler. *The Christian Experience of the Holy Spirit*. London: Nisbet and Co., 1928.

Robinson, Lewis Milton. "A History of the Half-Way Covenant." Ph.D. dissertation, University of Illinois, 1963.

Rogers, Jack B. *Scripture in the Westminster Confession*. Grand Rapids: Eerdmans, 1967.

Rogers, Jack B., and McKim, Donald K. *The Authority and Interpretation of the Bible: An Historical Approach*. San Francisco: Harper and Row, 1979.

Rogness, Michael. *Philip Melanchthon: Reformer Without Honor*. Minneapolis: Augsburg Publishing House, 1969.

Rolston, Holmes, III. *John Calvin versus the Westminster Confession*. Richmond: John Knox Press, 1972.

Routley, Eric. *The Gift of Conversion*. Philadelphia: Muhlenberg Press, 1955.

Rupp, Gordon. "Patterns of Salvation in the First Age of the Reformation." *Archiv für Reformationsgeschichte* 57 (1966):52-66.

_____. *The Righteousness of God: Luther Studies*. London: Hodder and Stoughton, 1953.

Russell, Conrad. *The Crisis of Parliaments: English History, 1509-1660*. Oxford: Oxford University Press, 1990.

Rutgers, F. L. *Calvijns Invloed op de Reformatie in de Nederland*. Leiden: E. J. Brill, 1899.

Rutman, Darret B. *American Puritanism: Faith and Practice*. Philadelphia: J. P. Lippincott, 1970.

Ryle, J. C. *Assurance*. Reprint ed., Houston: Christian Focus Publishers, 1989.

Sceats, David. *The Experience of Grace: Aspects of the Faith and Spirituality of the Puritans*. Cambridge: Grove, 1997.

Schaefer, Paul R. "Richard Sibbes and the Union of the Heart with Christ:

Lessons on Godliness." In *The Compromised Church: The Present Evangelical Crisis*, pp. 215-40. Ed. John H. Armstrong. Wheaton, Ill.: Crossway, 1998.

_____. "The Spiritual Brotherhood on the Habits of the Heart: Cambridge Protestants and the Doctrine of Sanctification from William Perkins to Thomas Shepard." D.Phil. dissertation, Oxford University, 1994.

Schaff, Philip. *History of the Christian Church*. 8 vols. New York: Charles Scribner's Sons, 1910; reprint ed., Grand Rapids: Eerdmans, 1985.

Schilder, Klaas. *Heidelbergse Catechismus*. 4 vols., covering Lord's Days 1-10. Kampen: Kok, 1938-42.

Schlosser, Friedrich C. *Leben des Theodor de Beza und des Peter Martyr Vermigli*. Heidelberg: Mohr und Zimmer, 1809.

Schmid, Heinrich. *Die Geschichte des Piëtismus*. Nördlingen: C. H. Beck, 1863.

Schmidt, Albert-Marie. *John Calvin and the Calvinistic Tradition*. Trans. Ronald Wallace. New York: Harper and Brothers, 1960.

Schneider, Herbert Wallace. *The Puritan Mind*. London: Constable and Co., 1931.

Schoneveld, Cornelis W. *Intertraffic of the Mind: Studies in Seventeenth Century Anglo-Dutch Translation*. Leiden: E. J. Brill, 1983.

Schrog, Felix James. *Pietism in Colonial America*. Chicago: The University of Chicago, 1948.

_____. "Theodorus Jacobus Frelinghuysen, the Father of American Pietism." *Church History* 14 (1945):201-216.

Schuldiner, Michael. *Gifts and Works: The Post-Conversion Paradigm and Spiritual Controversy in Seventeenth-Century Massachusetts*. Macon, Ga.: Mercer University Press, 1991.

Schutzeichel, H. *Katholische Beiträge zur Calvinforschung*. Trier: Paulinus Verlag, 1988.

Schweizer, Alexander. *Die protestantischen Centraldogmen in ihrer Entwicklung innerhalb der reformirten Kirche*. 2 vols. Zürich: Orell, Fussli und cie., 1854-56.

Sebestyén, Paul. "The Object of Faith in the Theology of Calvin." Ph.D. dissertation, University of Chicago, 1963.

Seeberg, Reinhold. *Text-book of the History of Doctrines*. Trans. Charles Hay. Grand Rapids: Baker, 1966.

Sepp, Christiaan. *Het Godgeleerd Onderwijs in Nederland, gedurende de 16e en 17e eeuw*. 2 vols. Leiden: De Breuk en Smits, 1873-74.

Shaw, Mark. "Drama in the Meeting House: The Concept of Conversion in the Theology of William Perkins." *Westminster Theological Journal* 45 (1983):41-72.

_____. "The Marrow of Practical Divinity: A Study in the Theology of William Perkins." Th.D. dissertation, Westminster Theological Seminary, 1981.

Shedd, W. G. T. *Dogmatic Theology*. 3 vols. Reprint ed., Grand Rapids: Zondervan, 1971.

Shelly, Harold Patton. "Richard Sibbes: Early Stuart Preacher of Piety." Ph.D. dissertation, Temple University, 1972.

Shepherd, Norman. "Zanchius on Saving Faith." *Westminster Theological Journal* 36 (1973):31-47.

Shepherd, Victor A. *The Nature and Function of Saving Faith in the Theology of John Calvin.* Macon, Ga.: Mercer University Press, 1983.

Shields, James Leroy. "The Doctrine of Regeneration in English Puritan Theology, 1604-1689." Ph.D. dissertation, Southwestern Baptist Theological Seminary, 1965.

Short, K. R. M. "The Educational Foundations of Elizabethan Puritanism: with Special Reference to Richard Greenham (1535?-1594)." Ed.D. dissertation, University of Rochester, 1970.

Shuffleton, Frank. *Thomas Hooker, 1587-1647.* Princeton: Princeton University Press, 1977.

Siktberg, William R. "The Mystical Element in the Theology of John Calvin." S.T.M. thesis, Union Theological Seminary, 1951.

Sinnema, Donald W. "The Issue of Reprobation at the Synod of Dort (1618-19) in Light of the History of this Doctrine." Ph.D. dissertation, University of St. Michael's College, 1985.

Simpson, Alan. *Puritanism in Old and New England.* Chicago: University of Chicago Press, 1955.

Sisson, Rosemary A. "William Perkins." M.Litt. dissertation, Cambridge, 1952.

Slagboom, D. *Jodocus van Lodensteyn.* Utrecht, 1966.

Smeaton, George. *Work of the Holy Spirit.* Reprint ed., Edinburgh: Banner of Truth Trust, 1974.

Smid, T. D. "Beza en Nederland." *Nederlands archief voor Kerkgeschiedenis* 46 (1963-64):169-91.

Smithen, Frederick J. *Continental Protestantism and the English Reformation.* London: J. Clarke & Co., 1927.

Snijders, Gerrit. *Friedrich Adolph Lampe.* Harderwijk: Flevo v.h. Gebr. Mooij, 1954.

Sommerville, C. J. "Conversion, Sacrament and Assurance in the Puritan Covenant of Grace to 1650." M.A. thesis, University of Kansas, 1963.

_____. "Conversion *versus* the Early Puritan Covenant of Grace." *Journal of Presbyterian History* 44 (1966):178-97.

Spear, Wayne. "Covenantal Uniformity in Religion: The Influence of the Scottish Commissioners Upon the Ecclesiology of the Westminster Assembly." Ph.D. dissertation, University of Pittsburgh, 1976.

Spronck, H. H. *Wilhelmus Schortinghuis: Eene Bladzijde uit de Geschiedenis van het Piëtisme in de Gereformeerde Kerk van Nederland.* Groningen: Wolters, 1904.

Sprunger, Keith. "Ames, Ramus, and the Method of Puritan Theology." *Harvard Theological Review* 59 (1966):133-51.

_____. *Dutch Puritanism. A History of English and Scottish Churches of the*

Netherlands in the Sixteenth and Seventeenth Centuries. Studies in the History of Christian Thought, no. 31. Leiden: E. J. Brill, 1982.

_____. *The Learned Doctor William Ames: Dutch Backgrounds of English and American Puritanism.* Chicago: University of Illinois Press, 1972.

_____. *Trumpets from the Tower: English Puritan Printing in the Netherlands 1600-1640.* Leiden: E. J. Brill, 1994.

Stadtland, Tjarko. *Rechtfertigung und Heiligung bei Calvin.* Beiträge zur Geschichte und Lehre der Reformierten Kirche, no. 32. Neukirchen-Vleyn: Neukirchener Verlag, 1972.

Staedtke, Joachim. *Die theologie des jungen Bullingers.* Studien zur dogmengeschichte und systematischen theologie, no. 16. Zurich: EVZ-Verlag, 1962.

Stakemeier, Adolf. *Das Konzil von Trent über die Heilsgewissheit.* Heidelberg: F. H. Kerle, 1947.

Stam, David Harry. "England's Calvin: A Study of the Publication of John Calvin's Works in Tudor England." Ph.D. dissertation, Northwestern University, 1978.

Stearns, Raymond P. *Congregationalism in the Dutch Netherlands.* Chicago: The American Society of Church History, 1940.

Steenblok, C. *Voetius en de Sabbat.* Gouda: Gereformeerde Pers, 1975.

_____. *Gisbertus Voetius: zijn leven en werken.* 2nd ed. Gouda: Gereformeerde Pers, 1976.

Steinmetz, David C. *Misericordia Dei: The Theology of Johannes von Staupitz in its Late Medieval Setting.* Leiden: E. J. Brill, 1968.

_____. *Reformers in the Wings.* Philadelphia: Fortress Press, 1971; reprint ed., Grand Rapids: Baker, 1981.

Stephen, Sir Leslie, and Lee, Sir Sidney, eds. *The Dictionary of National Biography.* 22 vols. London: Oxford University Press, 1949-50.

Stephens, W. P. *The Holy Spirit in the Theology of Martin Bucer.* Cambridge: Cambridge University Press, 1970.

_____. *The Theology of Huldrych Zwingli.* New York: Oxford University Press, 1986.

Steven, William. *The History of the Scottish Church, Rotterdam.* Edinburgh: Wangh & Innes, 1883.

Stoeffler, F. Ernest. *German Pietism During the Eighteenth Century.* Studies in the History of Religions, no. 24. Leiden: E. J. Brill, 1973.

_____. *The Rise of Evangelical Pietism.* Studies in the History of Religions, no. 9. Leiden: E. J. Brill, 1971.

_____. "The Wesleyan Concept of Religious Certainty — Its Pre-History and Significance." *The London Quarterly and Holborn Review* 189 (April 1965):128-39.

Stoever, William K. B. *'A Faire and Easie Way to Heaven': Covenant Theology and Antinomianism in Early Massachusetts.* Middletown: Wesleyan University Press, 1978.

Stout, Harry S. *The New England Soul: Preaching and Religious Culture in Colonial New England.* New York: Oxford, 1986.

Stoute, Douglas Andrew. "The Origins and Early Development of the Reformed Idea of the Covenant." Ph.D. dissertation, Cambridge, 1979.

Stover, Dale Arden. "The Pneumatology of John Owen: A Study of the Role of the Holy Spirit in Relation to the Shape of a Theology." Ph.D. dissertation, McGill University, 1967.

Strehle, Stephen. *Calvinism, Federalism, and Scholasticism: A Study of the Reformed Doctrine of Covenant.* Basler und Berner Studien zur historischen und systematischen Theologie, Band 58. New York: Peter Lang, 1988.

Strickland, D. R. "Union with Christ in the Theology of Samuel Rutherford: an examination of his doctrine of the Holy Spirit." Ph.D. dissertation, Edinburgh, 1972.

Strong, Augustus. *Systematic Theology: A Compendium, Designed for the Use of Theological Students.* Westwood: Fleming H. Revell Co., 1963.

Stuart, Robert Orkney. "The Breaking of the Elizabethan Settlement of Religion: Puritan Spiritual Experience and the Theological Division of the English Church." Ph.D. dissertation, Yale University, 1976.

Stuermann, W. E. "A Critical Study of Calvin's Concept of Faith." Ph.D. dissertation, University of Tulsa, 1952.

Sturm, Edmann K. *Der junge Zacharias Ursin.* Neukirchen: Neukirchener Verlag, 1972.

Sudhoff, Karl. *C. Olevianus und Z. Ursinus: Leben und ausgewählte Schriften.* Elberfeld: R. L. Friderichs, 1857.

Sundquist, Ralph Roger. "The Third Use of the Law in the Thought of John Calvin: An Interpretation and Evaluation." Ph.D. dissertation, Union Theological Seminary, 1970.

Tanis, James. *Dutch Calvinistic Pietism in the Middle Colonies: A Study in the Life and Theology of Theodorus Jacobus Frelinghuysen.* The Hague: Martinus Nijhoff, 1967.

_____. "The Heidelberg Catechism in the Hands of the Calvinistic Pietists." *Reformed Review* 24 (1970-71):154-61.

_____. "Reformed Pietism and Protestant Missions." *Harvard Theological Review* 67 (1974):65-80.

Ter Haar, Hendrik Willem. *Jacobus Trigland.* 's-Gravenhage: Martinus Nijhoff, 1891.

Thelemann, Carl Otto. *Friedrich Adolf Lampe: sein Leben seine Theologie.* Bielefeld: Belhagen & Klasing, 1868.

Thomas, Geoffrey. "Alexander Comrie: Contender for the Faith." *Banner of Truth* 65 (February 1969):4-8; 66 (March 1969):29-35.

Thomson, G. T. "Assurance." *Evangelical Quarterly* 14 (1942):2-8.

Tigchelaar, J. J. "De functie van de praedestinatie in de theologie van Calvijn en Brakel." *Theologie Reformata* 1 (1958):171-88.

Tillich, Paul. *Dynamics of Faith.* New York: Harper Torchbooks, 1957.

_____. *A History of Christian Thought.* Ed. Carl E. Braaten. New York: Simon & Schuster, 1968.

Tipson, Lynn Baird, Jr. "The Development of a Puritan Understanding of Conversion." Ph.D. dissertation, Yale University, 1972.

_____. "Invisible Saints: The 'Judgment of Charity' in the Early New England Churches." *Church History* 44 (1975):460-71.

Toft, Daniel John. "Zacharias Ursinus: A Study in the Development of Calvinism." Master's thesis, University of Wisconsin, 1962.

Toon, Peter. *The Emergence of Hyper-Calvinism in English Nonconformity, 1689-1765.* London: The Olive Tree, 1967.

_____. *God's Statesman: The Life and Work of John Owen.* Exeter: Paternoster, 1971.

_____. *Puritans and Calvinism.* Swengel, Pa.: Reiner, 1973.

Torrance, James B. "Covenant or Contract? A Study of the Theological Background of Worship in Seventeenth-Century Scotland." *Scottish Journal of Theology* 23 (1970):51-76.

Torrance, Iain R. "Patrick Hamilton and John Knox: A Study in the Doctrine of Justification by Faith." *Archiv für Reformationsgeschichte* 65 (1974):171-85.

Torrance, Thomas F. *The Hermeneutics of John Calvin.* Edinburgh: Scottish Academic Press, 1988.

_____. *The School of Faith: The Catechisms of the Reformed Church.* London: James Clarke & Co., 1959.

Townsend, James Arthur. "Feelings related to Assurance in Charles Wesley's Hymns." Ph.D. dissertation, Fuller Theological Seminary, 1979.

Trimp, J. C. *Jodocus van Lodensteyn, Predikant en dichter.* Kampen: Kok, 1987.

Trinterud, Leonard J. *The Forming of an American Tradition: A Reexamination of Colonial Presbyterianism.* Philadelphia: Westminster Press, 1949.

_____. "The Origins of Puritanism." *Church History* 20 (1951):37-57.

_____, ed. *Elizabethan Puritanism.* New York: Oxford University Press, 1971.

Tufft, J. R. "William Perkins, 1558-1602." Ph.D. dissertation, Edinburgh, 1952.

Tyacke, Nicholas. *Anti-Calvinists: The Rise of English Arminianism c. 1589-1640.* Oxford: Clarendon Press, 1987.

Van Baarsel, J. J. *William Perkins. Eene bijdrage tot de kennis der religieuse ontwikkeling in Engeland, ten tijde van Koningin Elisabeth.* Amsterdam: Ton Bolland, 1975.

Van Buren, Paul. *Christ in our Place: The Substitutionary Character of Calvin's Doctrine of Reconciliation.* Edinburgh: Oliver and Boyd, 1957.

Van den End, G. "Guiljelmus Saldenus." *Theologia Reformata* 12 (1969):77-90.

Van der Aa, Abraham Jacob, ed. *Biographisch Woordenboek der Nederlanden.* 21 vols. in 27. Haarlem: J. J. van Brederode, 1852-78.

Van der Haar, J. *From Abbadie to Young. A Bibliography of English, mostly Puritan Works, Translated i/t Dutch Language.* 2 vols. in 1. Veenendaal: Kool, 1980.

_____. "Nederlandse theologen onder Engelse puriteinen." *Documentatie-blad Nadere Reformatie* 10 (1986):105-108.

_____. "Puriteinse invloed uit Engeland." *Documentatieblad Nadere Reformatie* 2 (1978):117-120.

_____. *Schatkamer van de Gereformeerde Theologie in Nederland (c. 1600-1800): Bibliografisch Onderzoek.* Veenendaal: Antiquariaat Kool, 1987.

Van der Linde, S. "De betekenis van de Nadere Reformatie voor Kerk en Theologie." *Kerk en Theologie* 5 (1954):215-25.

_____. "Calvijn, Calvinisme en Nadere Reformatie." *Documentatieblad Nadere Reformatie* 6 (1982):73-88.

_____. *Het gereformeerde protestantisme.* Nijkerk: G. F. Callenbach, 1957.

_____. "De Godservaring bij W. Teellinck, D. G. à Brakel en A. Comrie." *Theologia Reformata* 16 (1973):193-205.

_____. "De Heilige Geest in Reformatie en Nadere Reformatie." In *Leven door de Heilige Geest*, pp. 49-81. Ed. A. Noordegraaf. Amersfoort, n.d.

_____. "Jean Taffin: eerste pleiter voor 'Nadere Reformatie' in Nederland." *Theologia Reformata* 25 (1982):6-29.

_____. *Jean Taffin. Hofprediker en raadsheer van Willem van Oranje.* Amsterdam: Ton Bolland, 1982.

_____. "Mystiek en bevinding in het Gereformeerde Protestantisme." In *Mystiek en bevinding*, pp. 45-61. Ed. G. Quispel, et al. Kampen: Kok, 1976.

_____. "'De Nadere Reformatie,' een nieuwe start." *Theologia Reformata* 29 (1986):188-197.

_____. *Opgang en voortgang der reformatie.* Amsterdam: Ton Bolland, 1976.

_____. "De prediking van de Nadere Reformatie." *Theologia Reformata* 19 (1976):6-21.

_____. *Vromen en Verlichten: Twee eeuwen Protestantse Geloofsbeleving 1650-1850.* Utrecht: Aartsbisschoppelijk Museum Utrecht, 1974.

_____. "Het werk van de Heilige Geest in de gemeente: Een appreciatie van de Nadere Reformatie." *Nederlands Theologisch Tijdschrift* 10 (1956):1-13.

Van der Tuuk Edema, H. *Johannes Bogerman.* Groningen: J. B. Walters, 1868.

Van der Veen, Jerry D. "Adoption of Calvinism in the Reformed Church in the Netherlands." B.S.T. thesis, Biblical Seminary in New York, 1951.

Van der Woude, Cornelius. *Sibrandus Lubbertus, Leven en werken.* Kampen: Kok, 1963.

Van Deursen, A. Th. "Dutch Reformed Parish Life in the Second Half of the Seventeenth Century." In *Bunyan in England and Abroad: Papers Delivered at the Vrije University Amsterdam, 1988,* pp. 105-20. Amsterdam: Vrije University Press, 1990.

Van Dorsten, J., ed. *Ten Studies in Anglo-Dutch Relations.* London: University Press for Sir Thomas Brown Institute, 1974.

Van Genderen, J. *Geloofskennis en geloofsverwachting.* Kampen: Kok, 1982.

_____. *Herman Witsius: Bijdrage tot de Kennis der Gereformeerde Theologie.* 's-Gravenhage: Guido de Brès, 1953.

_____. *Het practisch syllogisme: De sluitrede des geloofs.* Alphen a/d Rijn: Buijs, 1954.

_____. *Rechtvaardiging en Heiliging in de Theologie van deze tijd.* Amsterdam: Guijten en Schipperheijn, 1966.

Van Gent, W. *Bibliotheek van oude schrijvers.* Rotterdam: Lindenberg, 1979.

Van Gorsel, W. *De IJver voor Zijn Huis: De Nadere Reformatie en haar belangrijkste vertegenwoordigers.* Groede: Pieters, 1981.

Van Itterzon, G. P. *Franciscus Gomarus.* 's-Gravenhage: Martinus Nijhoff, 1930.

_____. *Het Gereformeerd Leerboek der 17de Eeuw: "Synopsis Purioris Theologiae."* 's-Gravenhage: Martinus Nijhoff, 1931.

_____. *Johannes Bogerman.* Amsterdam: Ton Bolland, 1980.

Van Langeraad, L. A. *Guido de Bray: Zijn leven en werken. Bijdrage tot de geschiedenis van het Zuid-Nederlandsche Protestantisme.* Zierikzee: S. Ochtman, 1884.

Van Leeuwen, Henry G. *The Problem of Certainty in English Thought.* 2nd ed. The Hague: Matinus Nijhoff, 1970.

Van Lieburg, Fred A. "From Pure Church to Pious Culture: The Further Reformation in the Seventeenth-Century Dutch Republic." In *Later Calvinism: International Perspectives*, pp. 409-30. Ed. W. Fred Graham. Kirksville, Mo.: Sixteenth Century Journal Publishers, 1994.

_____. "Het gereformeerde conventikelwezen in de classis Dordrecht in de 17e en 18e eeuw." *Holland, regional-historisch tijdschrift* 23 (1991):2-21.

_____. *Levens van vromen: Gereformeerde piëtisme in de achttiende eeuw.* Kampen: DeGroot, 1991.

_____. *De Nadere Reformatie in Utrecht ten tijde van Voetius: Sporen in de gereformeerde kerkeraadsacta.* Rotterdam: Lindenberg, 1989.

Van Oort, J., et al. *De onbekende Voetius.* Kampen: Kok, 1989.

Van Ruler, Arnold Albert. "De bevinding en die prediking." In *Theologisch Werk*, vol. 3, pp. 61-81. Nijkerk: G. F. Callenbach, 1971.

_____. "De bevinding. Proeve van een theologische benadering." In *Theologisch Werk*, vol. 3, pp. 43-60. Nijkerk: G. F. Callenbach, 1971.

_____. "Licht- en schaduwzijden in de bevindelijkheid." In *Theologisch Werk*, vol. 3, pp. 82-97. Nijkerk: G. F. Callenbach, 1971.

_____. "Stadia in het innerlijk leven." In *Theologisch Werk*, vol. 4, pp. 54-71. Nijkerk: G. F. Callenbach, 1972.

_____. "Ultra-Gereformeerd en vrijzinnig." In *Theologisch Werk*, vol. 3, pp. 98-163. Nijkerk: G. F. Callenbach, 1971.

Van Schelven, Aart Arnout. *De Bewerking van eene Piëtistisch-getinte Gemeente.* Goes, 1914.

_____. *Het Calvinisme gedurende zijn bloeitijd.* 3 vols. Amsterdam: W. Ten Have, 1943-65.

_____. *Marnix van Sint Aldegonde*. Utrecht: N. V. A. Oosthoek, 1939.

_____. "Het Zeeuwsche Mysticisme." *Gereformeerd Theologisch Tijdschrift* 17 (1916): 141-62.

Van't Hooft, Antonius Johannes. *De Theologie van Heinrich Bullinger in betrekking tot de Nederlandsche Reformatie*. Amsterdam: I. de Hoogh, 1888.

Van't Spijker, W. "Experientia in reformatorisch licht." *Theologia Reformata* 19 (1976):236-55.

_____. "'Extra Nos' and 'In Nobis' by Calvin in a Pneumatological Light." In *Calvin and the Holy Spirit*, pp. 39-73. Ed. Peter de Klerk. Grand Rapids: Calvin Studies Society, 1989.

_____. *Luther: Belofte en ervaring*. Goes: Oosterbaan & Le Cointre, 1983.

_____. *Luther en Calvijn*. Kampen: Kok, 1985.

_____. "Teellinck's opvatting van de menselijke wil." *Theologia Reformata* 7 (1964):125-42.

_____, ed. *De Nadere Reformatie. Beschrijving van haar voornaamste vertegenwoordigers*. 's-Gravenhage: Boekencentrum, 1986.

_____, ed. *De Nadere Reformatie en het Gereformeerd Piëtisme*. 's-Gravenhage: Boekencentrum, 1989.

Van Veen, Sietse Douwes. *Voor tweehonderd jaren. Schetsen van het leven onzer Gereformeerde Vaderen*. 2nd ed. Utrecht: Kemink & Zoon, 1905.

Van Woerden, P. *De Predestinatie en het Evangelie; en Het Geloof en de Rechtvaardigmaking*. Dordrecht: J. P. van den Tol, [1953].

Van Zijl, T. P. *Gerard Groote, Ascetic and Reformer (1340-1384)*. Studies in Medieval History, no. 18. Washington, D.C.: The Catholic University of American Press, 1963.

Vekeman, H. W. J. *Panorama van de Spiritualiteit in en om de Reformatie in de Nederlanden 1530-1800*. Nijmegen, 1982.

Venema, Cornelis Paul. "The Twofold Nature of the Gospel in Calvin's Theology: The *Duplex Gratia Dei* and the Interpretation of Calvin's Theology." Ph.D. dissertation, Princeton Theological Seminary, 1985.

Veninga, James Frank. "Covenant Theology and Ethics in the Thought of John Calvin and John Preston." Ph.D. dissertation, Rice University, 1974.

Verboom, J. H. R. *Dr. Alexander Comrie, predikant van Woubrugge*. Utrecht: De Banier, 1964.

Verboom, W. *De Catechese van de Reformatie en de Nadere Reformatie*. Amsterdam: Buijten en Schipperheijn, 1986.

Vergunst, A. "Dr. Alexander Comrie." *De Saambinder* 51 (1973): no. 25, p. 2; no. 27, p. 2; no. 29, p. 1; no. 31, p. 3; no. 32, p. 2.

_____. "Comrie on Faith." *Insight Into* (June 1983):3-7.

_____. *Neem de wacht des Heeren waar*. Utrecht: Den Hertog, 1983.

Verschoor, J. W. "Het geloof bij Brakel en Comrie." *Onder Eigen Vaandel* 3 (1928):272-94.

Visscher, Hugo. *Guilielmus Amesius, Zijn Leven en Werken*. Haarlem: J. M. Stap, 1894.

Vogelaar, Case. "Abraham Hellenbroek." *The Banner of Truth* 53 (1987): 126-27.

_____. "Bernardus Smytegelt." *The Banner of Truth* 53 (1987): 210-11.

_____. "'Father' Brakel." *The Banner of Truth* 53 (1987):66-67.

_____. "Gisbertus Voetius." *The Banner of Truth* 52 (1986):262-63; 55 (1989):182-83.

_____. "Johannes Beukelman." *The Banner of Truth* 53 (1987):264-65.

_____. "Pioneers of the Second Reformation." *The Banner of Truth* 52 (1986):150-51.

_____. "The Second or 'Further' Reformation." *The Banner of Truth* 52 (1986):40-41.

Von Campen, M. *Leven uit Gods Beloften: Een Central Thema bij Johannes Calvijn*. Kampen: Kok, 1988.

Von Rohr, John. "Covenant and Assurance in Early English Puritanism." *Church History* 34 (1965):195-203.

_____. *The Covenant of Grace in Puritan Thought*. Atlanta: Scholars Press, 1986.

Von Schulthess-Rechberg, Gustav. *Heinrich Bullinger, der Nachfolger Zwinglis*. Schriften des Vereins für Reformationsgeschichte, no. 22. Halle: Max Niemeyer, 1904.

Vorster, D. A. *Protestantse Nederlandse Mystiek*. Amsterdam: Meulenhoff, 1948.

Vos, Geerhardus. *Biblical Theology*. Reprint ed., Grand Rapids: Eerdmans, 1948.

Vos, J. G. "Assurance of Salvation: Its Possibility and True Basis." *Blue Banner Faith and Life* 13 (1958):145-47.

Vose, Godfrey Noel. "Profile of a Puritan: John Owen (1616-1683)." Ph.D. dissertation, State University of Iowa, 1963.

Wakefield, Gordon S. *Puritan Devotion: Its Place in the Development of Christian Piety*. London: Epworth Press, 1957.

Walker, James. *Theology and Theologians of Scotland*. Edinburgh: T. & T. Clark, 1888.

Wallace, Dewey D., Jr. "The Life and Thought of John Owen to 1660: A Study of the Significance of Calvinist Theology in English Puritanism." Ph.D. dissertation, Princeton University, 1965.

_____. *Puritans and Predestination: Grace in English Protestant Theology, 1515-1695*. Chapel Hill: University of North Carolina Press, 1982.

_____, ed. *The Spirituality of the Later English Puritans*. Macon, Ga.: Mercer University Press, 1987.

Wallace, Ronald S. *Calvin, Geneva and the Reformation*. Grand Rapids: Baker, 1988.

_____. *Calvin's Doctrine of the Christian Life*. Edinburgh: Oliver and Boyd, 1959.

_____. *Calvin's Doctrine of Word and Sacrament*. Edinburgh: Oliver and Boyd, 1953.

Wallmann, Johannes. *Philipp Jakob Spener und die Anfänge des Piëtismus*. Tübingen: Mohr Siebeck, 1970.

Walser, Peter. *Die Prädestination bei Heinrich Bullinger im Zusammenhang mit seiner Gotteslehre*. Studien zur Dogmengeschichte und systematischen Theologie, no. 11. Zürich: Zwingli Verlag, 1957.

Walters, Gwyn. "The Doctrine of the Spirit in John Calvin." Ph.D. dissertation, Edinburgh University, 1949.

Walvoord, John F. "The Doctrine of Assurance in Contemporary Theology." *Bibliotheca Sacra* 116 (1959):195-204.

Warfield, Benjamin B. *Calvin and Augustine*. Ed. Samuel G. Craig. Philadelphia: Presbyterian and Reformed, 1956.

_____. "A Review of 'De Zekerheid des Geloofs.'" *Selected Shorter Writings of Benjamin B. Warfield*, vol. 2, pp. 106-123. Ed. John E. Meeter. Nutley, N.J.: Presbyterian and Reformed, 1973.

_____. *The Westminster Assembly and Its Work*. Cherry Hill: Mack Publishing, 1972.

Watkins, Owen C. *The Puritan Experience*. London: Routledge and Kegan Paul, 1972.

Watson, Philip S. *Let God be God: An Interpretation of the Theology of Martin Luther*. Philadelphia: Fortress Press, 1966.

_____. "Luther and Sanctification." *Concordia* 30 (1959):243-59.

Watts, Michael. *The Dissenters: From the Reformation to the French Revolution*. Oxford: Oxford University Press, 1992.

Weber, Hans Emil. *Reformation, Orthodoxie und Rationalismus: Beiträge zur Förderung christlicher Theologie*. 2 vols. Gütersloh: C. Bertelsmann, 1937-51.

Weeks, John. "A Comparison of Calvin and Edwards on the Doctrine of Election." Ph.D. dissertation, University of Chicago, 1963.

Weir, D. A. *The Origins of the Federal Theology in Sixteenth-Century Reformation Thought*. Oxford: Clarendon Press, 1990.

Weisiger, Cary Nelson III. "The Doctrine of the Holy Spirit in the Preaching of Richard Sibbes." Ph.D. dissertation, Fuller Theological Seminary, 1984.

Welles, Judith B. "John Cotton, 1584-1652: Churchman and Theologian." Ph.D. dissertation, Edinburgh University, 1948.

Wells, David F. "*Decretum dei speciale:* An Analysis of the Content and Significance of Calvin's Doctrine of Soteriological Predestination." Th.M. thesis, Trinity Evangelical Divinity School, 1967.

Wendel, François. *Calvin: The Origins and Development of His Religious Thought*. Trans. Philip Mairet. New York: Harper and Row, 1963; reprint ed., Grand Rapids: Baker, 1997.

West, W. M. S. "John Hooper and the Origins of Puritanism." *The Baptist Quarterly* 15 (1954):346-68.

_____. "A Study of John Hooper: With Special Reference to his Contact with Henry Bullinger." Ph.D. dissertation, Universität Zurich, 1953.

White, Peter. *Predestination, Policy and Polemic: Conflict and Consensus in the English Church from the Reformation to the Civil War.* Cambridge: Cambridge University Press, 1992.

Whitney, Donald S. *How Can I Be Sure I'm a Christian? What the Bible Says About Assurance of Salvation.* Colorado Springs: NavPress, 1994.

Whyte, Alexander. *The Spiritual Life: The Teaching of Thomas Goodwin.* Edinburgh: Oliphant, Anderson & Ferrier, n.d.

_____. *Thirteen Appreciations.* Edinburgh: Oliphant, Anderson & Ferrier, 1913.

_____. *Thomas Shepard, Pilgrim Father and Founder of Harvard: His Spiritual Experience and Experiential Preaching.* London: Oliphant, Anderson & Ferrier, 1909.

Wijminga, Pieter Janszoon. *Festus Hommius.* Leiden: D. Donner, 1899.

Wilcox, William. "New England Covenant Theology: Its English Precursors and Early American Exponents." Ph.D. dissertation, Duke University, 1959.

Wiley, David N. "Calvin's Doctrine of Predestination: His Principal Soteriological and Polemical Doctrine." Ph.D. dissertation, Duke University, 1971.

Williams, George H. *The Radical Reformation.* 3rd ed. Kirksville, Mo.: Sixteenth Century Journal Publishers, 1992.

Williams, John Bickerton. *Letters on Puritanism and Nonconformity.* 2 vols. London: Jackson and Walford, 1843-46.

Willis, E. David. "The Influence of Laelius Socinus on Calvin's Doctrines of the Merits of Christ and the Assurance of Faith." In *Italian Reformation Studies in Honor of Laelius Socinus*, vol. 4, pp. 233-41. Ed. John A. Tedeschi, Florence: Felice Le Monnier, 1965.

Wing, Donald Goddard, ed. *Short-Title Catalog of Books Printed in England, Scotland, Ireland, Wales and British America and of English Books Printed in Other Countries, 1641-1700.* 3 vols. New York: Columbia University Press, 1945-51.

Wisse, G. *De rechte Godsvrucht.* Kampen: De Groot, 1994.

_____. *Uit het Zieleleven over Geloofs-verzekerdheid.* Kampen: Kok, 1920.

Woelderink, J. G. "Geloof en bevinding." *Onder Eigen Vaandel* 3 (1928):11-29.

_____. *De Rechtvaardiging Uit het Geloof Alleen.* Aalten: De Graafschap, 1941.

_____. *Van de Heilige Geest en van Zijn Werk.* 's-Gravenhage: Guido de Brès, n.d.

Wood, Thomas. *English Casuistical Divinity During the Seventeenth Century.* London: Society for the Promotion of Christian Knowledge, 1952.

Woolsey, Andrew. "Unity and Continuity in Covenantal Thought: A Study in Reformed Tradition to the Westminster Assembly." Ph.D. dissertation, University of Glasgow, 1988.

Wright, Louis B. "William Perkins: Elizabethan Apostle of Practical Divinity." *The Huntington Library Quarterly* 3 (1940):171-96.

Yates, Arthur. *The Doctrine of Assurance: With Special Reference to John Wesley.* London: Epworth Press, 1952.

Young, William. "Calvin and Westminster." *The Bulwark* 2 (May-June, 1980):15-18.

————. "Historic Calvinism and Neo-Calvinism." *Westminster Theological Journal* 36 (1973-74): 48-64, 156-73.

Zachman, Randall. *The Assurance of Faith: Conscience in the Theology of Martin Luther and John Calvin.* Minneapolis: Fortress Press, 1993.

Zens, Jon. "The Doctrine of Assurance: A History and an Application." *Baptist Reformation Review* 5 (Summer 1976):34-64.

Zerwas, Jack Lavere. "The Holy Spirit in Calvin." Th.D. dissertation, Union Theological Seminary, 1947.

Ziff, Larzer. *The Career of John Cotton, Puritanism and the American Experience.* Princeton: Princeton University Press, 1962.

————. *Puritanism in America: New Culture in a New World.* New York: Viking, 1973.

INDEX OF NAMES AND SUBJECTS

grace, 130-142; testimony of the Spirit, 142-147; pursuing both primary and secondary grounds of assurance, 146-147; organic relation of faith to assurance, 147-150; time element in faith's maturation, 150-152; means of assurance, 152-154; duty of seeking assurance, 154-155; fruit of assurance, 155-156; causes of lost or shaken assurance, 156-162; assurance revived, 162-164
Westminster divines. *See* Westminster Confession of Faith and individual divines.
Westminster standards. *See* Westminster Confession of Faith; Larger Catechism; Shorter Catechism.
Whitaker, Jeremiah, 113
Whitefield, George, 246n
Whitney, Donald, 6
Whyte, Alexander, 246n
Will, Divine, 95

Will, Human, 3, 25, 39n, 75, 86-87, 95, 100, 158, 225-227, 229, 275
Williams, Daniel, 224
Willis-Watkins, David, 58
Withdrawing of God, 159-162, 193
Witness of the Spirit. *See* Testimony of the Spirit.
Witsius, Herman, 227, 255n, 298
Woelderink, J. G., 241, 306
Word of God, 25-26, 37, 46, 59, 63, 71-72, 74, 107, 126-130, 137, 146, 152, 197, 205, 222-223, 228-229, 270-273, 275-276
Wrath of God, 48

Young, William, 225
Ypeij, 304

Zanchius, Hieronymus, 84, 87
Zeal, 299-300
Zens, Jon, 138
Zwingli, Huldrych, 27-31

INDEX OF BIBLICAL REFERENCES

Old Testament

New Testament